Teradata University Network

Both PVFC databases are pre-loaded into an SQL-compliant database at the Teradata University Network. Additional production-sized sample databases are also pre-loaded. Teradata SQL Assistant allows students to run SQL commands from a Web browser from any PC. Students can create their own databases and manage usage rights for team projects. On-line SQL exams can be administered, too.

Faculty: Register at **www.teradatauniversitynetwork.com**, and then access Teradata Database under the Apply & Do menu and follow the instructions to create a course environment for your students with one or more of our textbook databases. You may also use this site to upload additional databases for your students to access. Information is available on the Teradata Database page for all the features available under Teradata SQL Assistant.

Students: Point your browser to **www.teradatauniversitynetwork.com**. The general password for student access to the Teradata University Network must be obtained from your referring professor. Access the Teradata Database under the Apply & Do link, and obtain an SQL Assistant Account for the course environment your instructor has created. Your instructor may assign a special password for this environment.

Students and faculty can conduct a trial of Teradata SQL Assistant Web Edition by clicking on Teradata SQL Assistant Trial in the Access Content category of Quick Links. This trial and associated video and documentation can work effectively with Chapter 1 of this text.

Instructors: Additional materials for faculty are available on the **Instructor Resource Center** for this book.

Instructors can register for access to faculty-only material at **www.pearsonhighered.com/irc**. Once you register, you will not have additional forms to fill out, or multiple usernames and passwords to remember in order to access new titles and/or editions. As a registered faculty member, you can login directly to download resource files.

Need help? Our dedicated Technical Support team is ready to assist instructors with questions about the media supplements that accompany this text. Visit: **http://247pearsoned.custhelp.com** for answers to frequently asked questions and toll-free user support phone numbers.

ESSENTIALS OF DATABASE MANAGEMENT

Jeffrey A. Hoffer
University of Dayton

Heikki Topi
Bentley University

V. Ramesh
Indiana University

PEARSON

Boston   Columbus   Indianapolis   New York   San Francisco   Upper Saddle River
Amsterdam   Cape Town   Dubai   London   Madrid   Milan   Munich   Paris   Montréal   Toronto
Delhi   Mexico City   São Paulo   Sydney   Hong Kong   Seoul   Singapore   Taipei   Tokyo

Editor in Chief: Stephanie Wall	**Cover Designer:** Suzanne Duda
Executive Editor: Bob Horan	**Cover Art:** ©kras99/Fotolia
Editorial Project Manager: Kelly Loftus	**Media Project Manager, Editorial:** Alana Coles
Editorial Assistant: Kaylee Rotella	**Media Project Manager, Production:** Lisa Rinaldi
Director of Marketing: Maggie Moylan	**Composition/Full-Service Project**
Executive Marketing Manager: Anne Fahlgren	**Management:** PreMediaGlobal
Marketing Assistant: Gianna Sandri	**Printer/Binder:** Edwards Brothers Malloy
Senior Managing Editor: Judy Leale	**Cover Printer:** Lehigh-Phoenix Color/
Production Project Manager: Jane Bonnell	Hagerstown
Operations Specialist: Michelle Klein	**Text Font:** 10/12 PalatinoLTStd Roman
Creative Director: Jayne Conte	**Video Icon:** Do Ra/Fotolia

Credits and acknowledgments borrowed from other sources and reproduced, with permission, in this textbook appear on the appropriate page within text.

Microsoft and/or its respective suppliers make no representations about the suitability of the information contained in the documents and related graphics published as part of the services for any purpose. All such documents and related graphics are provided "as is" without warranty of any kind. Microsoft and/or its respective suppliers hereby disclaim all warranties and conditions with regard to this information, including all warranties and conditions of merchantability, whether express, implied or statutory, fitness for a particular purpose, title and non-infringement. In no event shall Microsoft and/or its respective suppliers be liable for any special, indirect or consequential damages or any damages whatsoever resulting from loss of use, data or profits, whether in an action of contract, negligence or other tortious action, arising out of or in connection with the use or performance of information available from the services.

The documents and related graphics contained herein could include technical inaccuracies or typographical errors. Changes are periodically added to the information herein. Microsoft and/or its respective suppliers may make improvements and/or changes in the product(s) and/or the program(s) described herein at any time. Partial screen shots may be viewed in full within the software version specified.

Microsoft® Windows®, and Microsoft Office® are registered trademarks of the Microsoft Corporation in the U.S.A. and other countries. This book is not sponsored or endorsed by or affiliated with the Microsoft Corporation.

MySQL®, the MySQL GUI Tools® (MySQL Query Browser® and MySQL Administrator®), the MySQL Command Line Client®, the MySQL Workbench®, and the MySQL Connector/ODBC® are registered trademarks of Sun Microsystems, Inc./Oracle Corporation. Screenshots and icons reprinted with permission of Oracle Corporation. This book is not sponsored or endorsed by or affiliated with Oracle Corporation. Oracle and Java are registered trademarks of Oracle and/or its affiliates. Other names may be trademarks of their respective owners.

Library of Congress Cataloging-in-Publication Data

Hoffer, Jeffrey A.
  Essentials of database management / Jeffrey A. Hoffer, University of Dayton, Heikki Topi, Bentley University, V. Ramesh, Indiana University.
    pages cm
  ISBN-13: 978-0-13-340568-2
  ISBN-10: 0-13-340568-0
  1. Database management.   I. Topi, Heikki.   II. Ramesh, V. (Venkataraman)   III. Title.
  QA76.9.D3H598 2014
  005.74—dc23

                                                                            2013007593

10 9 8 7 6 5 4 3 2 1

ISBN 10: 0-13-340568-0
ISBN 13: 978-0-13-340568-2

BRIEF CONTENTS

CONTENTS

PINE VALLEY FURNITURE

PINE VALLEY FURNITURE

PREFACE

It is our great pleasure to introduce this new text in database management. This book offers its users conceptually and technically solid content that focuses on the core issues covered in most introductory data and database management courses. We pay particular attention to providing in-depth coverage of the database development life cycle that extends from conceptual data modeling using (enhanced) entity-relationship modeling through relational modeling at the logical level to database implementation and use with Structured Query Language (SQL). Within this core area, we provide in-depth coverage that is based on the latest pedagogical and technical developments in data management.

This new text, *Essentials of Database Management,* builds on the strong foundation of *Modern Database Management* (*MDM,* currently in its 11th edition) and is designed for use in introductory courses in database management that do not require the full depth and breadth of advanced topics offered by *MDM.* This goal has been achieved without sacrificing quality or rigor of coverage. Several external factors have contributed to the need for a more succinct book: Particularly in business schools, information systems programs have less real estate in the curriculum, which means that all individual topic areas, including database management, have had to let some of their content go. The percentage of non-majors in the introductory database courses has also grown, and for the non-majors the most advanced technical knowledge in areas outside the core might not be in the center of their interests. Many integrated curricula have database modules significantly shorter than a full semester; this book fits well the needs of these course units, too.

In the marketplace of concise database textbooks, this new text offers the following advantages:

- It is built on the strong foundation and extensive development process of a leading textbook (*Modern Database Management*), ensuring state-of-the-art coverage of the core database management topics.
- It strives to maintain conceptual rigor in all of its coverage.
- It provides a sharp focus on the integrated database development cycle.
- It features tools and technologies targeted for professional designers and developers (instead of focusing on the end user).
- It offers a large number of field-tested review and practice materials at various levels of difficulty.
- It is informed by many years of teaching experience at a variety of universities and involvement in leading industry and curriculum groups by the authors.

The courses that can benefit from this book are typically required as part of information systems or information technology curricula in business schools, schools of information, computer technology programs, and applied computer science departments. The Association for Information Systems (AIS), the Association for Computing Machinery (ACM), and the International Federation of Information Processing Societies (IFIPS) curriculum guidelines all outline this type of database management course. For example, the coverage of *Essentials of Database Management* is sufficient for a great majority of the core database requirements suggested in IS 2010[1], the latest information systems undergraduate model curriculum. In addition to the majors in four-year undergraduate programs, this text can serve a number of additional audiences from information and computer technology programs at community colleges to data management modules in foundation courses in graduate programs. As discussed above, it will also serve well those non-IS majors whose interests are related to the broader area of information utilization. For example, this text would form an excellent foundation for a data management course targeted to business analytics students at either undergraduate or graduate level.

---

[1]Topi, Heikki; Valacich, Joseph S.; Wright, Ryan T.; Kaiser, Kate; Nunamaker, Jr., Jay F.; Sipior, Janice C.; and de Vreede, Gert Jan (2010) "IS 2010: Curriculum Guidelines for Undergraduate Degree Programs in Information Systems," Communications of the Association for Information Systems: Vol. 26, Article 18.

THE KEY STRENGTHS OF *ESSENTIALS OF DATABASE MANAGEMENT*

- One of our goals is to lead other books in coverage of the latest principles, concepts, and technologies. Our experience and expertise from *Modern Database Management* gives this text a strong foundation starting with this first edition. We believe in the value of systematic, thorough, and detailed coverage of the key topics, and this book implements this principle fully. The core database development cycle content is offered with a foundational description of the database environment and a number of contextual topics that are essential for the management of organizational data, such as database development for Internet-based applications, modern data warehousing concepts, and new infrastructure technologies (such as cloud computing).

- This text focuses on what leading practitioners say is most important for database developers and savvy database users. We work with many practitioners, including the professionals of the Data Management Association (DAMA) and The Data Warehousing Institute (TDWI), leading consultants, technology leaders, and authors of articles in the most widely read professional publications. We draw on these experts to ensure that what the book includes is important and covers not only important entry-level knowledge and skills, but also those fundamentals and mindsets that lead to long-term career success.

- We present the material in a way that students find highly accessible and effective from the perspective of supporting their learning. The content, review questions, and problems and exercises in this book benefit directly from *MDM*'s continuous market feedback for 30 years. Overall, the pedagogy of the book is sound. We use many illustrations that help to make important concepts and techniques clear. We use the most modern notations. The organization of the book is flexible, so you can use chapters in whatever sequence makes sense for your students. We supplement the book with data sets to facilitate hands-on, practical learning, and with new media resources to make some of the more challenging topics more engaging.

- You may have particular interest in introducing SQL early in your course. Our text can accommodate this. First, we cover SQL in depth, devoting two full chapters to this core technology of the database field. Second, we include many SQL examples in early chapters. Third, many instructors have successfully used the two SQL chapters early in their course. Although logically appearing in the life cycle of systems development as Chapters 6 and 7, part of the implementation section of the text, many instructors have used these chapters immediately after Chapter 1 or in parallel with other early chapters. Finally, we use SQL throughout the book, for example, to illustrate Web application connections to relational databases in Chapter 8 and online analytical processing in Chapter 9.

- We have the latest in supplements and Web site support for the text. See the supplement package for details on all the resources available to you and your students.

- This text is written to be part of a modern information systems curriculum with a strong business systems development focus. Topics are included and addressed so as to reinforce principles from other typical courses, such as systems analysis and design, networking, Web site design and development, MIS principles, and computer programming. Emphasis is on the development of the database component of modern information systems and on the management of the data resource. Thus, the text is practical, supports projects and other hands-on class activities, and encourages linking database concepts to concepts being learned throughout the curriculum the student is taking. Two of the authors of this text have served in leadership roles in the development of global information systems model curricula at both undergraduate and graduate levels, and they have been able to incorporate this broad curriculum understanding in this textbook.

SPECIFIC DIFFERENCES BETWEEN THIS BOOK AND *MODERN DATABASE MANAGEMENT*

The most important difference between this book and *Modern Database Management* by the same authors is that the advanced material covered in Chapters 10–14 and Appendices A through C of *MDM* is mostly outside the scope of this text. Some key elements of Data Quality and Integration (Chapter 10 of *MDM*) and Data and Database Administration (Chapter 11 of *MDM*) are, however, introduced within Chapters 1–9 of this book. The material on Distributed Databases (Chapter 12 of *MDM*), Object-Oriented Data Modeling (Chapter 13 of *MDM*) and Using Relational Databases to Provide Object Persistence (Chapter 14 of *MDM*) is not included at all in this text. In addition, the coverage in Chapters 1–9 has been streamlined to fit better the needs of the target audience of this book, including the following changes:

- Shortening the coverage of
  - Business rules
  - Modeling time-dependent data
  - Real-time data warehousing
  - Slowly changing dimensions
  - SQL online analytical processing (OLAP) querying
- Removing the coverage of
  - Entity clustering
  - Normal forms beyond the 3rd normal form
  - Enterprise key
  - Data volume and usage analysis
  - Partitioning
  - Clustering files
  - Certain specialized SQL commands
  - Certain specialized material on views
  - Specialized coverage on certain database management systems
  - PHP
  - Factless fact tables

Our strong intent is to continue to develop both *Modern Database Management* and this text in parallel, as texts that are closely connected but that have clearly different identities and target audiences.

SUMMARY OF THE CHAPTERS

The following sections present a chapter-by-chapter description of the chapters of the book. Each chapter description presents a statement of the purpose of that chapter and a brief summary of its core content.

PART I: THE CONTEXT OF DATABASE MANAGEMENT

Chapter 1: The Database Environment and Development Process

This chapter discusses the role of databases in organizations and previews the major topics in the remainder of the text. After offering a brief introduction to the basic terminology associated with storing and retrieving data, the chapter presents a well-organized comparison of traditional file-processing systems and modern database technology. The chapter then introduces the core components of a database environment and the range of database applications that are currently in use within organizations—personal, two-tier, multi-tier, and enterprise applications. The explanation of enterprise databases includes databases that are part of enterprise resource planning systems and data warehouses. A brief history of the evolution of database technology, from pre-database files to modern object-relational technologies, is also presented. The chapter then goes on to explain the process of database development in the context of structured life cycle, prototyping, and agile methodologies. The presentation remains consistent with the companion systems analysis texts by Hoffer, George, and Valacich. The chapter also discusses important issues in database development and frameworks for understanding database architectures and technologies (including the three-schema architecture). Reviewers frequently note the compatibility of this chapter with what students learn in systems analysis and design classes.

PART II: DATABASE ANALYSIS

Chapter 2: Modeling Data in the Organization

This chapter presents a thorough introduction to conceptual data modeling with the entity-relationship (E-R) model. The chapter title emphasizes the reason for the entity-relationship model: to unambiguously document the rules of the business that influence database design. Specific subsections explain in detail how to name and define elements of a data model, which are essential in developing an unambiguous E-R diagram. The chapter proceeds from simple to more complex examples, and it concludes with a comprehensive E-R diagram for the Pine Valley Furniture Company.

Chapter 3: The Enhanced E-R Model

This chapter presents a discussion of several advanced E-R data model constructs. The chapter particularly focuses on providing a thorough coverage of supertype/subtype relationships and includes a comprehensive example of an extended E-R data model for the Pine Valley Furniture Company.

PART III: DATABASE DESIGN

Chapter 4: Logical Database Design and the Relational Model

This chapter describes the process of converting a conceptual data model to a relational data model, as well as discusses how to merge new relations into an existing normalized database. It provides a conceptually sound and practically relevant introduction to normalization, emphasizing the importance of the use of functional dependencies and determinants as the basis for normalization. The chapter also features a discussion of the characteristics of foreign keys. The chapter emphasizes the basic concepts of the relational data model and the role of the database designer in the logical design process.

Chapter 5: Physical Database Design and Performance

This chapter describes the steps that are essential in achieving an efficient database design, with a strong focus on those aspects of database design and implementation that are typically within the control of a database professional in a modern database environment. The chapter has an emphasis on ways to improve database performance, with references to specific techniques available in Oracle and other database management systems (DBMSs) to improve database processing performance. The discussion of indexes includes descriptions of the types of indexes that are widely available in database technologies as techniques to improve query processing speed.

PART IV: IMPLEMENTATION

Chapter 6: Introduction to SQL

This chapter presents a thorough introduction to the SQL used by most DBMSs (SQL:1999) and introduces the changes that are included in the latest proposed standard (SQL:2008). The coverage of SQL is extensive and divided between this and the next chapter. This chapter includes examples of SQL code, using mostly SQL:1999 and SQL:2008 syntax, as well as some Oracle 11g and Microsoft SQL Server syntax. Some unique features of MySQL are mentioned. Dynamic views are also covered. Chapter 6 explains the SQL commands needed to create and maintain a database and to program single-table queries. Coverage of dual-table, IS NULL/IS NOT NULL, more built-in functions, derived tables, and rules for aggregate functions and the GROUP BY clause is included. The chapter also uses the Pine Valley Furniture Company case to illustrate a wide variety of practical queries and query results.

Chapter 7: Advanced SQL

This chapter continues the description of SQL, with a careful explanation of multiple-table queries, transaction integrity, data dictionaries, triggers and stored procedures (including a clear explanation of the differences between these two), and embedded SQL in other programming language programs. The OUTER JOIN command is also covered. Standard SQL is also used in Chapter 7. This chapter illustrates how to store the results of a query in a derived table and the CAST command to convert data between different data types. A section on self-joins is included, as is an explanation of when to use EXISTS (NOT EXISTS) versus IN (NOT IN). The chapter also covers subqueries and correlated subqueries, two of the most complex and powerful constructs in SQL.

Chapter 8: Database Application Development

This chapter provides a modern discussion of the concepts of client/server architecture and applications, middleware, and database access in contemporary database environments. Technologies that are commonly used to create two- and three-tier applications are presented. The chapter includes sample application programs that demonstrate how to access databases from popular programming languages such as Java, VB.NET, ASP. NET, and JSP. The chapter also presents expanded coverage of the role of Extensible Markup Language (XML) and related technologies in data storage and retrieval. Topics covered include basics of XML schemas, XQuery, and XSLT. The chapter concludes with an overview of Web services, associated standards and technologies, and their role in seamless, secure movement of data in Web-based applications. A brief introduction to service-oriented architecture (SOA) is also presented.

Chapter 9: Data Warehousing

This chapter describes the basic concepts of data warehousing, the reasons data warehousing is regarded as critical to competitive advantage in many organizations, and the database design activities and structures unique to data warehousing. The chapter also reviews best practices for determining requirements for a dimensional model and introduces the emerging column databases technology, which has been developed especially for data warehousing applications. The chapter includes material on important new approaches to and technologies supporting data management that are currently generating a high level of interest, including the big data concept and associated tools and techniques. Exercises provide hands-on practice with a data mart, using SQL and a BI tool called MicroStrategy that is available on Teradata University Network. Additional topics include alternative data warehouse architectures and the dimensional data model (or star schema) for data warehouses. A deep explanation of how to handle slowly changing dimensional data is provided. Operational data store; independent, dependent, and logical data marts; and various forms of online analytical processing (OLAP) are defined. User interfaces, including OLAP, data visualization, business performance management and dashboards, and data mining are also described. Brief coverage of data quality and governance is also included in this chapter.

PEDAGOGY

This text includes a broad range of teaching resources to support a variety of pedagogical approaches. The chapters are sufficiently independent so that they can be used in a variety of sequences, depending on the instructor's preference. As discussed earlier, some instructors might prefer to introduce SQL and hands-on database work earlier in the course than the chapter sequence suggests; others might decide to wait to cover physical database design and database implementation at the end of the course.

The chapters include several standard features that support the teaching and learning processes in a consistent way:

1. Learning objectives appear at the beginning of each chapter, as a preview of the major concepts and skills students will learn from that chapter. The learning objectives also provide a great study review aid for students as they prepare for assignments and examinations.
2. Chapter introductions and summaries both encapsulate the main concepts of each chapter and link material to related chapters, providing students with a comprehensive conceptual framework for the course.
3. Each chapter includes a review section, which features Key Terms, Review Questions, and Problems and Exercises. These elements will be discussed in more detail below.
4. A running glossary defines key terms in the page margins as they are discussed in the text. These terms are also defined at the end of the text, in the Glossary of Terms. Also included is the end-of-book Glossary of Acronyms for abbreviations commonly used in database management.

The end-of-chapter materials include the following elements:

A. *Key Terms* A key terms list provides an easy reference to the students with which they can test their grasp of important concepts, basic facts, and significant issues.
B. *Review Questions* Each chapter includes a rich variety of review questions that cover the key content of the chapter and provide the students with a comprehensive tool for ensuring that they have mastered the conceptual content of the chapter.
C. *Problems and Exercises* All chapters include a comprehensive set of Problems and Exercises that are presented in the increasing order of difficulty, making it easier for instructors and students to find the appropriate material. The Problems and Exercises focus on systematic development of the skills featured in each chapter. In several chapters, the data sets provided for the text are used extensively.
D. *Web Resources* Each chapter contains a list of updated and validated URLs for Web sites that contain information that supplements the chapter. These Web sites cover online publication archives, vendors, electronic publications, industry standards organizations, and many other sources. These sites allow students and instructors to find updated product information, innovations that have appeared since the printing of the book, background information to explore topics in greater depth, and resources for writing research papers.

We encourage instructors to customize their use of this book to meet the needs of both their curriculum and student career paths. The modular nature of the text, its broad coverage, extensive illustrations, and its inclusion of advanced topics and emerging issues make customization easy. The many references to current publications and Web sites can help instructors develop supplemental reading lists or expand classroom discussion beyond material presented in the text.

SUPPLEMENTS: WWW.PEARSONHIGHERED.COM/HOFFER

A comprehensive and flexible technology support package is available to enhance the teaching and learning experience. All instructor and student supplements are available on the text Web site: *www.pearsonhighered.com/hoffer*.

For Students
The following online resources are available to students:

- The *Web Resources* module includes the Web links referenced at the end of each chapter in the text to help students further explore database management topics on the Web.
- A full *glossary* is available, along with a glossary of acronyms.

- *Links to sites where students can use our data sets* are provided. Although our data sets are provided in formats that are easily loaded on computers at your university or on student PCs, some instructors will not want the responsibility of supporting local data sets. The application service providers with whom we have developed arrangements (e.g., ***www.teradatauniversitynetwork.com***) provide thin-client interfaces to SQL coding environments. See the text's Web site and the inside front cover for more details.
- *Accompanying databases* are also provided. Two versions of the Pine Valley Furniture Company case have been created and populated. One version is scoped to match the textbook examples. A second version is fleshed out with more data and tables, as well as sample forms, reports, and modules coded in Visual Basic. This version is not complete, however, so that students can create missing tables and additional forms, reports, and modules. Databases are provided in several formats (ASCII tables, Oracle script, and Microsoft Access), but formats vary for the two versions. Some documentation of the databases is also provided. Both versions of the PVFC database are also provided on Teradata University Network.
- *Several custom-developed short videos that address key concepts and skills from different sections of the book* help students learn material that may be more difficult to understand. The videos integrate exercises and mini lectures.

For Instructors

The following online resources are available to instructors:

- The *Instructor's Resource Manual* provides chapter-by-chapter instructor objectives, classroom ideas, and answers to Review Questions and Problems and Exercises.
- The *Test Bank* and *TestGen* include a comprehensive set of test questions in multiple-choice, true/false, and short-answer format, ranked according to level of difficulty and referenced with page numbers and topic headings from the text. The Test Bank is available in Microsoft Word and as the Computerized TestGen. TestGen is PC/Mac compatible and preloaded with all of the test bank questions. You can manually or randomly view test questions and drag and drop to create a test. You can also add or modify test bank questions as needed.
- *PowerPoint Presentation slides* feature lecture notes that highlight key terms and concepts. Instructors can customize the presentation by adding their own slides or editing existing ones.
- The *Image Library* is a collection of the text art organized by chapter. It includes all figures, tables, and screenshots and can be used to enhance class lectures and PowerPoint slides.

ACKNOWLEDGEMENTS

Every book project is a collaborative effort to which numerous people contribute in addition to the authors. We are deeply grateful to all those who supported and enabled the preparation of this first edition of *Essentials of Database Management*. We particularly appreciate Executive Editor Bob Horan's guidance and his willingness to work with us to develop the concept for this book. The resulting identity is different from both *MDM* and competing textbooks, and we believe the book will serve a broad range of users well. Equally important are the contributions of the faculty members around the world who have used *MDM* and provided us with highly valuable feedback that has enabled the continuous improvement of *MDM* and motivated the development of this book. We would like to give special thanks to those colleagues who supported the process of developing the core ideas underlying this text and gave direct and insightful feedback, including Hillol Bala, Indiana University; Sue Brown, University of Arizona; Monica Garfield, Bentley University; Vijay Khatri, Indiana University; Ryan Wright, University of Massachusetts, Amherst; and Jennifer Xu, Bentley University.

We also wish to thank our reviewers for their detailed suggestions and insights: Jason Chen, Gonzaga University; Jinzhu Gao, University of Minnesota, Morris;

Rick Gibson, American University; William Hochstettler, Franklin University; Barbara Klein, University of Michigan-Dearborn; Alan Labouseur, Marist College; Lara Preiser-Huoy, California State Polytechnic University, Pomona; and Uzma Raja, University of Alabama.

We are also grateful to the staff and associates of Pearson Education for their support and guidance throughout this project. In addition to Executive Editor Bob Horan, we would like to thank Senior Editorial Project Manager Kelly Loftus, who kept us on track and made sure everything was complete; Production Project Manager Jane Bonnell; Executive Marketing Manager Anne Fahlgren; and Editorial Assistant Kaylee Rotella. Our special thanks go to Katy Gabel at PreMediaGlobal, whose supervision of the production process was excellent.

Finally, we give immeasurable thanks to our spouses, who were willing to not only accept but also support the additional requirements of this new project. In particular, we continue to marvel at the commitment of Patty Hoffer, who has lived the lonely life of a textbook author's spouse through 11 editions of *MDM* over more than 30 years in addition to this new text. We also want to offer our sincere thanks to Anne-Louise Klaus for her strong support for Heikki's involvement in this project. Similarly, Gayathri Mani's continued support and understanding are very much appreciated. Much of the value of this text is due to their patience, encouragement, and love; we alone bear the responsibility for any errors or omissions.

Jeffrey A. Hoffer

Heikki Topi

V. Ramesh

PART I

The Context of Database Management

AN OVERVIEW OF PART ONE

In this chapter and opening part of the book, we set the context and provide basic database concepts and definitions used throughout the text. In this part, we portray database management as an exciting, challenging, and growing field that provides numerous career opportunities for information systems students. Databases continue to become a more common part of everyday living and a more central component of business operations. From the database that stores contact information in your personal digital assistant (PDA) or smartphone to the very large databases that support enterprise-wide information systems, databases have become the central points of data storage that were envisioned decades ago. Customer relationship management and Internet shopping are examples of two database-dependent activities that have developed in recent years. The development of data warehouses that provide managers the opportunity for deeper and broader historical analysis of data also continues to take on more importance.

We begin by providing basic definitions of *data*, *database*, *metadata*, *database management system*, *data warehouse*, and other terms associated with this environment. We compare databases with the older file management systems they replaced and describe several important advantages that are enabled by the carefully planned use of databases.

The chapter in this introductory part of the book also describes the general steps followed in the analysis, design, implementation, and administration of databases. Further, this chapter also illustrates how the database development process fits into the overall information systems development process. Database development for both structured life cycle and prototyping methodologies is explained. We introduce enterprise data modeling, which sets the range and general contents of organizational databases. This is often the first step in database development. We introduce the concept of schemas and the three-schema architecture, which is the dominant approach in modern database systems. We describe the major components of the database environment and the types of applications, as well as two-tier, multitier, and enterprise databases. Enterprise databases include those that are used to support enterprise resource planning systems and data warehouses. Finally, we describe the roles of the various people who are typically involved in a database development project. The Pine Valley Furniture Company case is introduced and used to illustrate many of the principles and concepts of database management. This case is used throughout the text as a continuing example of the use of database management systems.

Chapter 1

The Database Environment and Development Process

The Database Environment and Development Process

Visit www.pearsonhighered.com/hoffer to view the accompanying video for this chapter.

LEARNING OBJECTIVES

After studying this chapter, you should be able to:

- Concisely define each of the following key terms: **database, data, information, metadata, database application, data model, entity, relational database, database management system (DBMS), data independence, user view, database administration, data administration, constraint, computer-aided software engineering (CASE) tools, repository, enterprise data modeling, systems development life cycle (SDLC), conceptual schema, logical schema, physical schema, prototyping, agile software development, enterprise resource planning (ERP),** and **data warehouse.**
- Name several limitations of conventional file processing systems.
- Explain at least 10 advantages of the database approach, compared to traditional file processing.
- Identify several costs and risks of the database approach.
- List and briefly describe nine components of a typical database environment.
- Identify four categories of applications that use databases and their key characteristics.
- Describe the life cycle of a systems development project, with an emphasis on the purpose of database analysis, design, and implementation activities.
- Explain the prototyping and agile-development approaches to database and application development.
- Explain the roles of individuals who design, implement, use, and administer databases.
- Explain the differences among external, conceptual, and internal schemas and the reasons for the three-schema architecture for databases.

INTRODUCTION

Over the past two decades, there has been enormous growth in the number and importance of database applications. Databases are used to store, manipulate, and retrieve data in nearly every type of organization, including business, health care, education, government, and libraries. Database technology is routinely used by individuals on personal computers, by workgroups accessing databases on network servers, and by employees using enterprise-wide distributed applications.

Databases are also accessed by customers and other remote users through diverse technologies, such as automated teller machines, Web browsers, smartphones, and intelligent living and office environments. Most Web-based applications depend on a database foundation.

Following this period of rapid growth, will the demand for databases and database technology level off? Very likely not! In the highly competitive environment of today, there is every indication that database technology will assume even greater importance. Managers seek to use knowledge derived from databases for competitive advantage. For example, detailed sales databases can be mined to determine customer buying patterns as a basis for advertising and marketing campaigns. Organizations embed procedures called *alerts* in databases to warn of unusual conditions, such as impending stock shortages or opportunities to sell additional products, and to trigger appropriate actions.

Although the future of databases is assured, much work remains to be done. Many organizations have a proliferation of incompatible databases that were developed to meet immediate needs rather than based on a planned strategy or a well-managed evolution. Enormous amounts of data are trapped in older, "legacy" systems, and the data are often of poor quality. New skills are required to design and manage data warehouses and to integrate databases with Internet applications. There is a shortage of skills in areas such as database analysis, database design, data administration, and database administration. We address these and other important issues in this textbook to equip you for the jobs of the future.

A course in database management has emerged as one of the most important courses in the information systems curriculum today. Many schools have added an additional elective course in data warehousing or database administration to provide in-depth coverage of these important topics. As information systems professionals, you must be prepared to analyze database requirements and design and implement databases within the context of information systems development. You also must be prepared to consult with end users and show them how they can use databases (or data warehouses) to build decision support systems and executive information systems for competitive advantage. And the widespread use of databases attached to Web sites that return dynamic information to users of these sites requires that you understand not only how to link databases to the Web-based applications but also how to secure those databases so that their contents can be viewed, but not compromised, by outside users.

In this chapter, we introduce the basic concepts of databases and database management systems (DBMSs). We describe traditional file management systems and some of their shortcomings that led to the database approach. Next, we consider the benefits, costs, and risks of using the database approach. We review the range of technologies used to build, use, and manage databases; describe the types of applications that use databases—personal, two-tier, three-tier, and enterprise; and describe how databases have evolved over the past five decades.

Because a database is one part of an information system, this chapter also examines how the database development process fits into the overall information systems development process. The chapter emphasizes the need to coordinate database development with all the other activities in the development of a complete information system. It includes highlights from a hypothetical database development process at Pine Valley Furniture Company. Using this example, the chapter introduces tools for developing databases on personal computers and the process of extracting data from enterprise databases for use in stand-alone applications.

There are several reasons for discussing database development at this point. First, although you may have used the basic capabilities of a database management system, such as Microsoft Access, you may not yet have developed an understanding of how these databases were developed. Using simple examples, this chapter briefly illustrates what you will be able to do after you complete a database course using this text. Thus, this chapter helps you develop a vision and context for each topic developed in detail in subsequent chapters.

Second, many students learn best from a text full of concrete examples. Although all of the chapters in this text contain numerous examples, illustrations, and actual database designs and code, each chapter concentrates on a specific aspect of database management. We have designed this chapter to help you understand, with minimal technical details, how all of these individual aspects of database management are related and how database development tasks and skills relate to what you are learning in other information systems courses.

Finally, many instructors want you to begin the initial steps of a database development group or individual project early in your database course. This chapter gives you an idea of how to structure a database development project sufficient to begin a course exercise. Obviously, because this is only the first chapter, many of the examples and notations we will use will be much simpler than those required for your project, for other course assignments, or in a real organization.

One note of caution: You will not learn how to design or develop databases just from this chapter. Sorry! We have purposely kept the content of this chapter introductory and simplified. Many of the notations used in this chapter are not exactly like the ones you will learn in subsequent chapters. Our purpose in this chapter is to give you a general understanding of the key steps and types of skills, not to teach you specific techniques. You will, however, learn fundamental concepts and definitions and develop an intuition and motivation for the skills and knowledge presented in later chapters.

BASIC CONCEPTS AND DEFINITIONS

Database

An organized collection of logically related data.

We define a **database** as an organized collection of logically related data. Not many words in the definition, but have you looked at the size of this book? There is a lot to do to fulfill this definition.

A database may be of any size and complexity. For example, a salesperson may maintain a small database of customer contacts—consisting of a few megabytes of data—on her laptop computer. A large corporation may build a large database consisting of several terabytes of data (a *terabyte* is a trillion bytes) on a large mainframe computer that is used for decision support applications (Winter, 1997). Very large data warehouses contain more than a petabyte of data. (A *petabyte* is a quadrillion bytes.) (We assume throughout the text that all databases are computer based.)

Data

Historically, the term *data* referred to facts concerning objects and events that could be recorded and stored on computer media. For example, in a salesperson's database, the data would include facts such as customer name, address, and telephone number. This type of data is called *structured* data. The most important structured data types are numeric, character, and dates. Structured data are stored in tabular form (in tables, relations, arrays, spreadsheets, etc.) and are most commonly found in traditional databases and data warehouses.

The traditional definition of data now needs to be expanded to reflect a new reality: Databases today are used to store objects such as documents, e-mails, maps, photographic images, sound, and video segments in addition to structured data. For example, the salesperson's database might include a photo image of the customer contact. It might also include a sound recording or video clip about the most recent product. This type of data is referred to as *unstructured* data, or as multimedia data. Today structured and unstructured data are often combined in the same database to create a true multimedia environment. For example, an automobile repair shop can combine structured data (describing customers and automobiles) with multimedia data (photo images of the damaged autos and scanned images of insurance claim forms).

Data

Stored representations of objects and events that have meaning and importance in the user's environment.

An expanded definition of **data** that includes structured and unstructured types is "a stored representation of objects and events that have meaning and importance in the user's environment."

Data Versus Information

The terms *data* and *information* are closely related and in fact are often used interchangeably. However, it is useful to distinguish between data and information. We define **information** as data that have been processed in such a way that the knowledge of the person who uses the data is increased. For example, consider the following list of facts:

Baker, Kenneth D.	324917628
Doyle, Joan E.	476193248
Finkle, Clive R.	548429344
Lewis, John C.	551742186
McFerran, Debra R.	409723145

Information

Data that have been processed in such a way as to increase the knowledge of the person who uses the data.

These facts satisfy our definition of data, but most people would agree that the data are useless in their present form. Even if we guess that this is a list of people's names paired with their Social Security numbers, the data remain useless because we have no idea what the entries mean. Notice what happens when we place the same data in a context, as shown in Figure 1-1a.

By adding a few additional data items and providing some structure, we recognize a class roster for a particular course. This is useful information to some users, such as the course instructor and the registrar's office. Of course, as general awareness of the importance of strong data security has increased, few organizations still use Social Security numbers as identifiers. Instead, most organizations use an internally generated number for identification purposes.

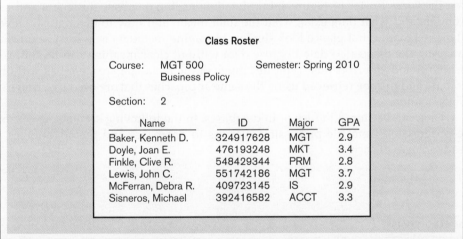

FIGURE 1-1 Converting data to information
(a) Data in context

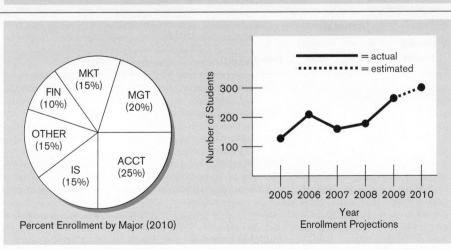

(b) Summarized data

Another way to convert data into information is to summarize them or otherwise process and present them for human interpretation. For example, Figure 1-1b shows summarized student enrollment data presented as graphical information. This information could be used as a basis for deciding whether to add new courses or to hire new faculty members.

In practice, according to our definitions, databases today may contain either data or information (or both). For example, a database may contain an image of the class roster document shown in Figure 1-1a. Also, data are often preprocessed and stored in summarized form in databases that are used for decision support. Throughout this text, we use the term *database* without distinguishing its contents as data or information.

Metadata

Metadata

Data that describe the properties or characteristics of end-user data and the context of those data.

As we have indicated, data become useful only when placed in some context. The primary mechanism for providing context for data is metadata. **Metadata** are data that describe the properties or characteristics of end-user data and the context of that data. Some of the properties that are typically described include data names, definitions, length (or size), and allowable values. Metadata describing data context include the source of the data, where the data are stored, ownership (or stewardship), and usage. Although it may seem circular, many people think of metadata as "data about data."

Some sample metadata for the Class Roster (Figure 1-1a) are listed in Table 1-1. For each data item that appears in the Class Roster, the metadata show the data item name, the data type, length, minimum and maximum allowable values (where appropriate), a brief description of each data item, and the source of the data (sometimes called the *system of record*). Notice the distinction between data and metadata. Metadata are once removed from data. That is, metadata describe the properties of data but are separate from that data. Thus, the metadata shown in Table 1-1 do not include any sample data from the Class Roster of Figure 1-1a. Metadata enable database designers and users to understand what data exist, what the data mean, and how to distinguish between data items that at first glance look similar. Managing metadata is at least as crucial as managing the associated data because data without clear meaning can be confusing, misinterpreted, or erroneous. Typically, much of the metadata are stored as part of the database and may be retrieved using the same approaches that are used to retrieve data or information.

Data can be stored in files or in databases. In the following sections, we examine the progression from file processing systems to databases and the advantages and disadvantages of each.

TABLE 1-1   Example Metadata for Class Roster

| Data Item | | | Metadata | | | |
Name	Type	Length	Min	Max	Description	Source
Course	Alphanumeric	30			Course ID and name	Academic Unit
Section	Integer	1	1	9	Section number	Registrar
Semester	Alphanumeric	10			Semester and year	Registrar
Name	Alphanumeric	30			Student name	Student IS
ID	Integer	9			Student ID (SSN)	Student IS
Major	Alphanumeric	4			Student major	Student IS
GPA	Decimal	3	0.0	4.0	Student grade point average	Academic Unit

TRADITIONAL FILE PROCESSING SYSTEMS

When computer-based data processing was first available, there were no databases. To be useful for business applications, computers had to store, manipulate, and retrieve large files of data. Computer file processing systems were developed for this purpose. Figure 1-2 shows an example of three computer applications based on the file processing approach used at Pine Valley Furniture Company. The systems shown are Order Filling, Invoicing, and Payroll. The figure also shows the major data files associated with each application.

A file is a collection of related records. Figure 1-2 shows, for example, that the Order Filling System has three files: Customer Master, Inventory Master, and Back Order. Notice that there is duplication of some of the files used by the three applications, which is typical of file processing systems.

As business applications became more complex, it became evident that traditional file processing systems had a number of shortcomings and limitations (described next). As a result, these systems have been replaced by database processing systems in most business applications today. Nevertheless, you should have at least some familiarity with the disadvantages of file processing systems since understanding the problems and limitations inherent in file processing systems can help you avoid the same problems when designing database systems.

Disadvantages of File Processing Systems

Several disadvantages associated with conventional file processing systems are listed in Table 1-2 and described briefly next.

PROGRAM-DATA DEPENDENCE   File descriptions are stored within each **database application** program that accesses a given file. For example, in the Invoicing System in Figure 1-2, Program A accesses the Inventory Pricing File and the Customer Master File. Because the program contains a detailed file description for these files, any change to a file structure requires changes to the file descriptions for all programs that access the file.

TABLE 1-2 Disadvantages of File Processing Systems
Program-data dependence
Duplication of data
Limited data sharing
Lengthy development times
Excessive program maintenance

Database application

An application program (or set of related programs) that is used to perform a series of database activities (create, read, update, and delete) on behalf of database users.

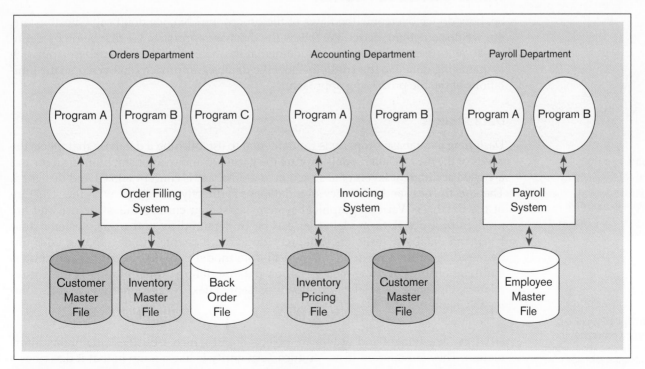

FIGURE 1-2   Old file processing systems at Pine Valley Furniture Company

DUPLICATION OF DATA   Because applications are often developed independently in file processing systems, unplanned duplicate data files are the rule rather than the exception. For example, in Figure 1-2, the Order Filling System contains an Inventory Master File, whereas the Invoicing System contains an Inventory Pricing File. These files contain data describing Pine Valley Furniture Company's products, such as product description, unit price, and quantity on hand. This duplication is wasteful because it requires additional storage space and increased effort to keep all files up to date.

LIMITED DATA SHARING   With the traditional file processing approach, each application has its own private files, and users have little opportunity to share data outside their own applications. Notice in Figure 1-2, for example, that users in the Accounting Department have access to the Invoicing System and its files, but they probably do not have access to the Order Filling System or to the Payroll System and their files.

LENGTHY DEVELOPMENT TIMES   With traditional file processing systems, each new application requires that the developer essentially start from scratch by designing new file formats and descriptions and then writing the file access logic for each new program. The lengthy development times required are inconsistent with today's fast-paced business environment, in which time to market (or time to production for an information system) is a key business success factor.

EXCESSIVE PROGRAM MAINTENANCE   The preceding factors all combined to create a heavy program maintenance load in organizations that relied on traditional file processing systems. In fact, as much as 80 percent of the total information system's development budget might be devoted to program maintenance in such organizations. This in turn means that resources (time, people, and money) are not being spent on developing new applications.

One way to overcome the limitations identified above is by using the database approach, which, as explained in the next section, is as much a way to manage organizational data as it is a set of technologies for defining, creating, maintaining, and using these data.

THE DATABASE APPROACH

So, how do we overcome the flaws of file processing? No, we don't call Ghostbusters, but we do something better: We follow the database approach. We first begin by defining some core concepts that are fundamental in understanding the database approach to managing data. We then describe how the database approach can overcome the limitations of the file processing approach.

Data Models

Designing a database properly is fundamental to establishing a database that meets the needs of the users. **Data models** capture the nature of and relationships among data and are used at different levels of abstraction as a database is conceptualized and designed. The effectiveness and efficiency of a database is directly associated with the structure of the database. Various graphical systems exist that convey this structure and are used to produce data models that can be understood by end users, systems analysts, and database designers. Chapters 2 and 3 are devoted to developing your understanding of data modeling. A typical data model is made up entities, attributes, and relationships and the most common data modeling representation is the entity-relationship model. A brief description is presented next. More details will be forthcoming in Chapters 2 and 3.

ENTITIES   Customers and orders are objects about which a business maintains information. They are referred to as "entities." An **entity** is like a noun in that it describes a person, a place, an object, an event, or a concept in the business environment for which

Data model

Graphical systems used to capture the nature and relationships among data.

Entity

A person, a place, an object, an event, or a concept in the user environment about which the organization wishes to maintain data.

information must be recorded and retained. CUSTOMER and ORDER are entities in Figure 1-3a. The data you are interested in capturing about the entity (e.g., Customer Name) is called an *attribute*. Data are recorded for many customers. Each customer's information is referred to as an *instance* of CUSTOMER.

RELATIONSHIPS A well-structured database establishes the *relationships* between entities that exist in organizational data so that desired information can be retrieved. Most relationships are one-to-many (*1:M*) or many-to-many (*M:N*). A customer can place (the Places relationship) more than one order with a company. However, each order is usually associated with (the Is Placed By relationship) a particular customer. Figure 1-3a shows the *1:M* relationship of customers who may place one or more orders; the *1:M* nature of the relationship is marked by the crow's foot attached to the rectangle (entity) labeled ORDER. This relationship appears to be the same in Figures 1-3a and 1-3b. However, the relationship between orders and products is *M:N*. An order may be

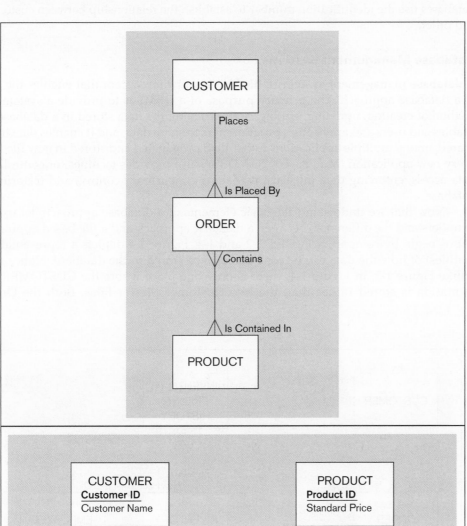

FIGURE 1-3 Comparison of enterprise and project-level data models
(a) Segment of an enterprise data model

(b) Segment of a project data model

for one or more products, and a product may be included on more than one order. It is worthwhile noting that Figure 1-3a is an enterprise-level model, where it is necessary to include only the higher-level relationships of customers, orders, and products. The project-level diagram shown in Figure 1-3b includes additional level of details, such as the further details of an order.

Relational Databases

Relational database

A database that represents data as a collection of tables in which all data relationships are represented by common values in related tables.

Relational databases establish the relationships between entities by means of common fields included in a file, called a relation. The relationship between a customer and the customer's order depicted in the data models in Figure 1-3 is established by including the customer number with the customer's order. Thus, a customer's identification number is included in the file (or relation) that holds customer information such as name, address, and so forth. Every time the customer places an order, the customer identification number is also included in the relation that holds order information. Relational databases use the identification number to establish the relationship between customer and order.

Database Management Systems

Database management system (DBMS)

A software system that is used to create, maintain, and provide controlled access to user databases.

A **database management system (DBMS)** is a software system that enables the use of a database approach. The primary purpose of a DBMS is to provide a systematic method of creating, updating, storing, and retrieving the data stored in a database. It enables end users and application programmers to share data, and it enables data to be shared among multiple applications rather than propagated and stored in new files for every new application (Mullins, 2002). A DBMS also provides facilities for controlling data access, enforcing data integrity, managing concurrency control, and restoring a database.

Now that we understand the basic elements of a database approach, let us try to understand the differences between a database approach and a file-based approach. Let us begin by comparing Figures 1-2 and 1-4. Figure 1-4 depicts a representation (entities) of how the data can be considered to be stored in the database. Notice that unlike Figure 1-2, in Figure 1-4, there is only one place where the CUSTOMER information is stored rather than the two Customer Master Files. Both the Order

FIGURE 1-4 Enterprise model for Figure 1-3 segments

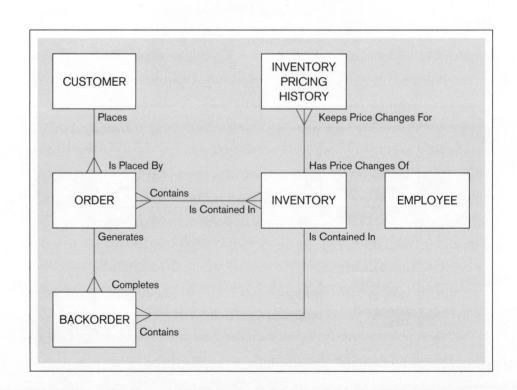

TABLE 1-3 Advantages of the Database Approach
Program-data independence
Planned data redundancy
Improved data consistency
Improved data sharing
Increased productivity of application development
Enforcement of standards
Improved data quality
Improved data accessibility and responsiveness
Reduced program maintenance
Improved decision support

Filling System and the Invoicing System will access the data contained in the single CUSTOMER entity. Further, what CUSTOMER information is stored, how it is stored and how it is accessed is likely not closely tied to either of the two systems. All of this enables us to achieve the advantages listed in the next section. Of course, it is important to note that a real-life database will likely include thousands of entities and relationships among them.

Advantages of the Database Approach

The primary advantages of a database approach, enabled by DBMSs, are summarized in Table 1-3 and described next.

PROGRAM-DATA INDEPENDENCE   The separation of data descriptions (metadata) from the application programs that use the data is called **data independence**. With the database approach, data descriptions are stored in a central location called the *repository*. This property of database systems allows an organization's data to change and evolve (within limits) without changing the application programs that process the data.

Data independence
The separation of data descriptions from the application programs that use the data.

PLANNED DATA REDUNDANCY   Good database design attempts to integrate previously separate (and redundant) data files into a single, logical structure. Ideally, each primary fact is recorded in only one place in the database. For example, facts about a product, such as the Pine Valley oak computer desk, its finish, price, and so forth, are recorded together in one place in the Product table, which contains data about each of Pine Valley's products. The database approach does not eliminate redundancy entirely, but it enables the designer to control the type and amount of redundancy. At other times, it may be desirable to include some limited redundancy to improve database performance, as we will see in later chapters.

IMPROVED DATA CONSISTENCY   By eliminating or controlling data redundancy, we greatly reduce the opportunities for inconsistency. For example, if a customer's address is stored only once, we cannot disagree about the customer's address. When the customer's address changes, recording the new address is greatly simplified because the address is stored in a single place. Finally, we avoid the wasted storage space that results from redundant data storage.

IMPROVED DATA SHARING   A database is designed as a shared corporate resource. Authorized internal and external users are granted permission to use the database, and each user (or group of users) is provided one or more user views into the database to

User view

A logical description of some portion of the database that is required by a user to perform some task.

facilitate this use. A **user view** is a logical description of some portion of the database that is required by a user to perform some task. A user view is often developed by identifying a form or report that the user needs on a regular basis. For example, an employee working in human resources will need access to confidential employee data; a customer needs access to the product catalog available on Pine Valley's Web site. The views for the human resources employee and the customer are drawn from completely different areas of one unified database.

INCREASED PRODUCTIVITY OF APPLICATION DEVELOPMENT A major advantage of the database approach is that it greatly reduces the cost and time for developing new business applications. There are three important reasons that database applications can often be developed much more rapidly than conventional file applications:

1. Assuming that the database and the related data capture and maintenance applications have already been designed and implemented, the application developer can concentrate on the specific functions required for the new application, without having to worry about file design or low-level implementation details.
2. The database management system provides a number of high-level productivity tools, such as forms and report generators, and high-level languages that automate some of the activities of database design and implementation. We describe many of these tools in subsequent chapters.
3. Significant improvement in application developer productivity, estimated to be as high as 60 percent (Long, 2005), is currently being realized through the use of Web services, based on the use of standard Internet protocols and a universally accepted data format (XML). Web services and XML are covered in Chapter 8.

Database administration

A technical function that is responsible for physical database design and for dealing with technical issues, such as security enforcement, database performance, and backup and recovery.

Data administration

A high-level function that is responsible for the overall management of data resources in an organization, including maintaining corporate-wide definitions and standards.

ENFORCEMENT OF STANDARDS When the database approach is implemented with full management support, the **database administration** function should be granted single-point authority and responsibility for establishing and enforcing data standards. These standards will include naming conventions, data quality standards, and uniform procedures for accessing, updating, and protecting data. The data repository provides database administrators with a powerful set of tools for developing and enforcing these standards. Unfortunately, the failure to implement a strong database administration function is perhaps the most common source of database failures in organizations. Equally important is **data administration**, a high-level function that is responsible for the overall management of data resources in an organization, including maintaining corporate-wide definitions and standards.

Constraint

A rule that cannot be violated by database users.

IMPROVED DATA QUALITY Concern with poor quality data is a common theme in strategic planning and database administration today. In fact, a recent report by The Data Warehousing Institute (TDWI) estimated that data quality problems currently cost U.S. businesses some $600 billion each year (**http://tdwi.org/research/2002/02/tdwis-data-quality-report.aspx?sc_lang=en**). The database approach provides a number of tools and processes to improve data quality. Two of the more important are the following:

1. Database designers can specify integrity constraints that are enforced by the DBMS. A **constraint** is a rule that cannot be violated by database users. We describe numerous types of constraints (also called "business rules") in Chapters 2 and 3. If a customer places an order, the constraint that ensures that the customer and the order remain associated is called a "relational integrity constraint," and it prevents an order from being entered without specifying who placed the order.
2. One of the objectives of a data warehouse environment is to clean up (or "scrub") operational data before they are placed in the data warehouse (Jordan, 1996). Do you ever receive multiple copies of a catalog? The company that sends you three copies of each of its mailings could recognize significant postage and printing savings if its data were scrubbed, and its understanding of its customers would also be enhanced if it could determine a more accurate count of existing customers. We describe data warehouses in Chapter 9.

IMPROVED DATA ACCESSIBILITY AND RESPONSIVENESS With a relational database, end users without programming experience can often retrieve and display data, even when they cross traditional departmental boundaries. For example, an employee can display information about computer desks at Pine Valley Furniture Company with the following query:

```
SELECT *
FROM Product_T
WHERE ProductDescription = "Computer Desk";
```

The language used in this query is called Structured Query Language, or SQL. (You will study this language in detail in Chapters 6 and 7.) Although the queries constructed can be *much* more complex, the basic structure of the query is easy for even novice, nonprogrammers to grasp. If they understand the structure and names of the data that fit within their view of the database, they soon gain the ability to retrieve answers to new questions without having to rely on a professional application developer. This can be dangerous; queries should be thoroughly tested to be sure they are returning accurate data before relying on their results, and novices may not understand that challenge.

REDUCED PROGRAM MAINTENANCE Stored data must be changed frequently for a variety of reasons: New data item types are added, data formats are changed, and so on. A celebrated example of this problem was the well-known "year 2000" problem, in which common two-digit year fields were extended to four digits to accommodate the rollover from the year 1999 to the year 2000.

In a file processing environment, the data descriptions and the logic for accessing data are built into individual application programs (this is the program-data dependence issue described earlier). As a result, changes to data formats and access methods inevitably result in the need to modify application programs. In a database environment, data are more independent of the application programs that use them. Within limits, we can change either the data or the application programs that use the data without necessitating a change in the other factor. As a result, program maintenance can be significantly reduced in a modern database environment.

IMPROVED DECISION SUPPORT Some databases are designed expressly for decision support applications. For example, some databases are designed to support customer relationship management, whereas others are designed to support financial analysis or supply chain management. You will study how databases are tailored for different decision support applications and analytical styles in Chapter 9.

Cautions About Database Benefits

The previous section identified 10 major potential benefits of the database approach. However, we must caution you that many organizations have been frustrated in attempting to realize some of these benefits. For example, the goal of data independence (and, therefore, reduced program maintenance) has proven elusive due to the limitations of older data models and database management software. Fortunately, the relational model and the newer object-oriented model provide a significantly better environment for achieving these benefits. Another reason for failure to achieve the intended benefits is poor organizational planning and database implementation; even the best data management software cannot overcome such deficiencies. For this reason, we stress database planning and design throughout this text.

Costs and Risks of the Database Approach

A database is not a silver bullet, and it does not have the magic power of Harry Potter. As with any other business decision, the database approach entails some additional costs and risks that must be recognized and managed when it is implemented (see Table 1-4).

TABLE 1-4 Costs and Risks of the Database Approach

New, specialized personnel

Installation and management cost and complexity

Conversion costs

Need for explicit backup and recovery

Organizational conflict

NEW, SPECIALIZED PERSONNEL   Frequently, organizations that adopt the database approach need to hire or train individuals to design and implement databases, provide database administration services, and manage a staff of new people. Further, because of the rapid changes in technology, these new people will have to be retrained or upgraded on a regular basis. This personnel increase may be more than offset by other productivity gains, but an organization should recognize the need for these specialized skills, which are required to obtain the most from the potential benefits.

INSTALLATION AND MANAGEMENT COST AND COMPLEXITY   A multiuser database management system is a large and complex suite of software that has a high initial cost, requires a staff of trained personnel to install and operate, and has substantial annual maintenance and support costs. Installing such a system may also require upgrades to the hardware and data communications systems in the organization. Substantial training is normally required on an ongoing basis to keep up with new releases and upgrades. Additional or more sophisticated and costly database software may be needed to provide security and to ensure proper concurrent updating of shared data.

CONVERSION COSTS   The term *legacy system* is widely used to refer to older applications in an organization that are based on file processing and/or older database technology. The cost of converting these older systems to modern database technology—measured in terms of dollars, time, and organizational commitment—may often seem prohibitive to an organization. The use of data warehouses is one strategy for continuing to use older systems while at the same time exploiting modern database technology and techniques (Ritter, 1999).

NEED FOR EXPLICIT BACKUP AND RECOVERY   A shared corporate database must be accurate and available at all times. This requires that comprehensive procedures be developed and used for providing backup copies of data and for restoring a database when damage occurs. These considerations have acquired increased urgency in today's security-conscious environment. A modern database management system normally automates many more of the backup and recovery tasks than a file system.

ORGANIZATIONAL CONFLICT   A shared database requires a consensus on data definitions and ownership, as well as responsibilities for accurate data maintenance. Experience has shown that conflicts on data definitions, data formats and coding, rights to update shared data, and associated issues are frequent and often difficult to resolve. Handling these issues requires organizational commitment to the database approach, organizationally astute database administrators, and a sound evolutionary approach to database development.

   If strong top management support of and commitment to the database approach are lacking, end-user development of stand-alone databases is likely to proliferate. These databases do not follow the general database approach that we have described, and they are unlikely to provide the benefits described earlier. In the extreme, they may lead to a pattern of inferior decision making that threatens the well-being or existence of an organization.

COMPONENTS OF THE DATABASE ENVIRONMENT

Now that you have seen the advantages and risks of using the database approach to managing data, let us examine the major components of a typical database environment and their relationships (see Figure 1-5). You have already been introduced to some (but not all) of these components in previous sections. Following is a brief description of the nine components shown in Figure 1-5:

Computer-aided software engineering (CASE) tools

Software tools that provide automated support for some portion of the systems development process.

1. *Computer-aided software engineering (CASE) tools*   **CASE tools** are automated tools used to design databases and application programs. These tools help with creation of data models and in some cases can also help automatically generate the "code" needed to create the database. We refer to the use of automated tools for database design and development throughout the text.

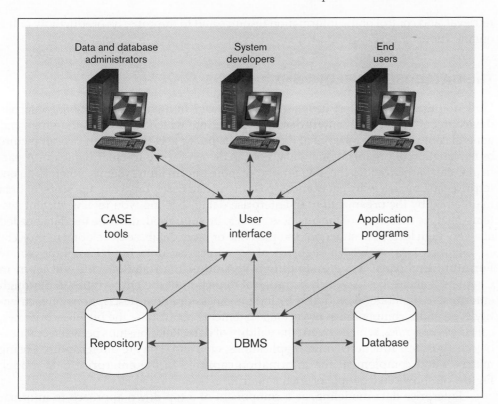

FIGURE 1-5 Components of the database environment

2. *Repository*   A **repository** is a centralized knowledge base for all data definitions, data relationships, screen and report formats, and other system components. A repository contains an extended set of metadata important for managing databases as well as other components of an information system.

3. *DBMS*   A DBMS is a software system that is used to create, maintain, and provide controlled access to user databases.

4. *Database*   A database is an organized collection of logically related data, usually designed to meet the information needs of multiple users in an organization. It is important to distinguish between the database and the repository. The repository contains definitions of data, whereas the database contains occurrences of data. We describe the activities of database design in Chapters 4 and 5 and of implementation in Chapters 6 through 9.

5. *Application programs*   Computer-based application programs are used to create and maintain the database and provide information to users. Key database-related application programming skills are described in Chapters 6 through 9.

6. *User interface*   The user interface includes languages, menus, and other facilities by which users interact with various system components, such as CASE tools, application programs, the DBMS, and the repository. User interfaces are illustrated throughout this text.

7. *Data and database administrators*   Data administrators are persons who are responsible for the overall management of data resources in an organization. Database administrators are responsible for physical database design and for managing technical issues in the database environment.

8. *System developers*   System developers are persons such as systems analysts and programmers who design new application programs. System developers often use CASE tools for system requirements analysis and program design.

9. *End users*   End users are persons throughout the organization who add, delete, and modify data in the database and who request or receive information from it. All user interactions with the database must be routed through the DBMS.

In summary, the database operational environment shown in Figure 1-5 is an integrated system of hardware, software, and people, designed to facilitate the storage,

Repository

A centralized knowledge base for all data definitions, data relationships, screen and report formats, and other system components.

retrieval, and control of the information resource and to improve the productivity of the organization.

THE DATABASE DEVELOPMENT PROCESS

Enterprise data modeling

The first step in database development, in which the scope and general contents of organizational databases are specified.

How do organizations start developing a database? In many organizations, database development begins with **enterprise data modeling**, which establishes the range and general contents of organizational databases. Its purpose is to create an overall picture or explanation of organizational data, not the design for a particular database. A particular database provides the data for one or more information systems, whereas an enterprise data model, which may encompass many databases, describes the scope of data maintained by the organization. In enterprise data modeling, you review current systems, analyze the nature of the business areas to be supported, describe the data needed at a very high level of abstraction, and plan one or more database development projects.

Figure 1-3a showed a segment of an enterprise data model for Pine Valley Furniture Company, using a simplified version of the notation you will learn in Chapters 2 and 3. Besides such a graphical depiction of the entity types, a thorough enterprise data model would also include business-oriented descriptions of each entity type and a compendium of various statements about how the business operates, called *business rules*, which govern the validity of data. Relationships between business objects (business functions, units, applications, etc.) and data are often captured using matrixes and complement the information captured in the enterprise data model. Figure 1-6 shows an example of such a matrix.

Enterprise data modeling, as a component of a top-down approach to information systems planning and development, represents one source of database projects. Such projects often develop new databases to meet strategic organizational goals, such as improved customer support, better production and inventory management, or more accurate sales forecasting. Many database projects arise, however, in a more bottom-up fashion. In this case, projects are requested by information systems users, who need certain information to do their jobs, or by other information systems professionals, who see a need to improve data management in the organization.

A typical bottom-up database development project usually focuses on the creation of one database. Some database projects concentrate only on defining, designing, and implementing a database as a foundation for subsequent information systems development. In most cases, however, a database and the associated information processing functions are developed together as part of a comprehensive information systems development project.

FIGURE 1-6 Example business function-to-data entity matrix

Business Functions \ Data Entity Types	Customer	Product	Raw Material	Order	Work Center	Work Order	Invoice	Equipment	Employee
Business Planning	X	X						X	X
Product Development		X	X		X			X	
Materials Management		X	X	X	X	X		X	
Order Fulfillment	X	X	X	X	X	X	X	X	X
Order Shipment	X	X		X	X		X		X
Sales Summarization	X	X		X			X		X
Production Operations		X	X	X	X	X		X	X
Finance and Accounting	X	X	X	X	X		X	X	X

X = data entity is used within business function

Systems Development Life Cycle

As you may know from other information systems courses you've taken, a traditional process for conducting an information systems development project is called the **systems development life cycle (SDLC)**. The SDLC is a complete set of steps that a team of information systems professionals, including database designers and programmers, follow in an organization to specify, develop, maintain, and replace information systems. Textbooks and organizations use many variations on the life cycle and may identify anywhere from 3 to 20 different phases.

The various steps in the SDLC and their associated purpose are depicted in Figure 1-7 (Hoffer et al., 2011). The process appears to be circular and is intended to convey the iterative nature of systems development projects. The steps may overlap in time, they may be conducted in parallel, and it is possible to backtrack to previous steps when prior decisions need to be reconsidered. Some believe that the most common path

Systems development life cycle (SDLC)

The traditional methodology used to develop, maintain, and replace information systems.

FIGURE 1-7 Database development activities during the systems development life cycle (SDLC)

through the development process is to cycle through the steps depicted in Figure 1-7, but at more detailed levels on each pass, as the requirements of the system become more concrete.

Figure 1-7 also provides an outline of the database development activities typically included in each phase of the SDLC. Note that there is not always a one-to-one correspondence between SDLC phases and database development steps. For example, conceptual data modeling occurs in both the Planning and the Analysis phases. We will briefly illustrate each of these database development steps for Pine Valley Furniture Company later in this chapter.

PLANNING—ENTERPRISE MODELING   The database development process begins with a review of the enterprise modeling components that were developed during the information systems planning process. During this step, analysts review current databases and information systems; analyze the nature of the business area that is the subject of the development project; and describe, in general terms, the data needed for each information system under consideration for development. They determine what data are already available in existing databases and what new data will need to be added to support the proposed new project. Only selected projects move into the next phase based on the projected value of each project to the organization.

PLANNING—CONCEPTUAL DATA MODELING   For an information systems project that is initiated, the overall data requirements of the proposed information system must be analyzed. This is done in two stages. First, during the Planning phase, the analyst develops a diagram similar to Figure 1-3a, as well as other documentation, to outline the scope of data involved in this particular development project without consideration of what databases already exist. Only high-level categories of data (entities) and major relationships are included at this point. This step in the SDLC is critical for improving the chances of a successful development process. The better the definition of the specific needs of the organization, the closer the conceptual model should come to meeting the needs of the organization, and the less recycling back through the SDLC should be needed.

ANALYSIS—CONCEPTUAL DATA MODELING   During the Analysis phase of the SDLC, the analyst produces a detailed data model that identifies all the organizational data that must be managed for this information system. Every data attribute is defined, all categories of data are listed, every business relationship between data entities is represented, and every rule that dictates the integrity of the data is specified. It is also during the Analysis phase that the conceptual data model is checked for consistency with other types of models developed to explain other dimensions of the target information system, such as processing steps, rules for handling data, and the timing of events. However, even this detailed conceptual data model is preliminary, because subsequent SDLC activities may find missing elements or errors when designing specific transactions, reports, displays, and inquiries. With experience, the database developer gains mental models of common business functions, such as sales or financial record keeping, but must always remain alert for the exceptions to common practices followed by an organization. The output of the conceptual modeling phase is a **conceptual schema**.

Conceptual schema

A detailed, technology-independent specification of the overall structure of organizational data.

DESIGN—LOGICAL DATABASE DESIGN   Logical database design approaches database development from two perspectives: First, the conceptual schema must be transformed into a logical schema, which describes the data in terms of the data management technology that will be used to implement the database. For example, if relational technology will be used, the conceptual data model is transformed and represented using elements of the relational model, which include tables, columns, rows, primary keys, foreign keys, and constraints. (You will learn how to conduct this important process in Chapter 4.) This representation is referred to as the **logical schema**.

Logical schema

The representation of a database for a particular data management technology.

Then, as each application in the information system is designed, including the program's input and output formats, the analyst performs a detailed review of the transactions, reports, displays, and inquiries supported by the database. During this so-called bottom-up analysis, the analyst verifies exactly what data are to be maintained in the database and the nature of those data as needed for each transaction, report, and so forth. It may be necessary to refine the conceptual data model as each report, business transaction, and other user view is analyzed. In this case, one must combine, or integrate, the original conceptual data model along with these individual user views into a comprehensive design during logical database design. It is also possible that additional information processing requirements will be identified during logical information systems design, in which case these new requirements must be integrated into the previously identified logical database design.

The final step in logical database design is to transform the combined and reconciled data specifications into basic, or atomic, elements following well-established rules for well-structured data specifications. For most databases today, these rules come from relational database theory and a process called *normalization*, which we will describe in detail in Chapter 4. The result is a complete picture of the database without any reference to a particular database management system for managing these data. With a final logical database design in place, the analyst begins to specify the logic of the particular computer programs and queries needed to maintain and report the database contents.

DESIGN—PHYSICAL DATABASE DESIGN AND DEFINITION   A **physical schema** is a set of specifications that describe how data from a logical schema are stored in a computer's secondary memory by a specific database management system. There is one physical schema for each logical schema. Physical database design requires knowledge of the specific DBMS that will be used to implement the database. In physical database design and definition, an analyst decides on the organization of physical records, the choice of file organizations, the use of indexes, and so on. To do this, a database designer needs to outline the programs to process transactions and to generate anticipated management information and decision-support reports. The goal is to design a database that will efficiently and securely handle all data processing against it. Thus, physical database design is done in close coordination with the design of all other aspects of the physical information system: programs, computer hardware, operating systems, and data communications networks.

Physical schema

Specifications for how data from a logical schema are stored in a computer's secondary memory by a database management system.

IMPLEMENTATION—DATABASE IMPLEMENTATION   In database implementation, a designer writes, tests, and installs the programs/scripts that access, create, or modify the database. The designer might do this using standard programming languages (e.g., Java, C#, or Visual Basic.NET) or in special database processing languages (e.g., SQL) or use special-purpose nonprocedural languages to produce stylized reports and displays, possibly including graphs. Also, during implementation, the designer will finalize all database documentation, train users, and put procedures into place for the ongoing support of the information system (and database) users. The last step is to load data from existing information sources (files and databases from legacy applications plus new data now needed). Loading is often done by first unloading data from existing files and databases into a neutral format (such as binary or text files) and then loading these data into the new database. Finally, the database and its associated applications are put into production for data maintenance and retrieval by the actual users. During production, the database should be periodically backed up and recovered in case of contamination or destruction.

MAINTENANCE—DATABASE MAINTENANCE   The database evolves during database maintenance. In this step, the designer adds, deletes, or changes characteristics of the structure of a database in order to meet changing business conditions, to correct errors in database design, or to improve the processing speed of database applications. The designer might also need to rebuild a database if it becomes contaminated or destroyed due to a program or computer system malfunction. This is typically the longest step of database development, because it lasts throughout the life of the database and its associated applications. Each time the database evolves, view it as an abbreviated database development process in which conceptual data modeling, logical and physical database design, and database implementation occur to deal with proposed changes.

Alternative Information Systems (IS) Development Approaches

The SDLC or slight variations on it are often used to guide the development of information systems and databases. The SDLC is a methodical, highly structured approach, which includes many checks and balances to ensure that each step produces accurate results and the new or replacement information system is consistent with existing systems with which it must communicate or for which there needs to be consistent data definitions. Whew! That's a lot of work! Consequently, the SDLC is often criticized for the length of time needed until a working system is produced, which occurs only at the end of the process. Instead, organizations increasingly use rapid application development (RAD) methods, which follow an iterative process of rapidly repeating analysis, design, and implementation steps until they converge on the system the user wants. These RAD methods work best when most of the necessary database structures already exist, and hence for systems that primarily retrieve data, rather than for those that populate and revise databases.

Prototyping

An iterative process of systems development in which requirements are converted to a working system that is continually revised through close work between analysts and users.

One of the most popular RAD methods is **prototyping**, which is an iterative process of systems development in which requirements are converted to a working system that is continually revised through close work between analysts and users. Figure 1-8 shows the prototyping process. This figure includes annotations to indicate roughly which database development activities occur in each prototyping phase. Typically, you make only a very cursory attempt at conceptual data modeling when the information system problem is identified. During the development of the initial prototype, you simultaneously design the displays and reports the user wants while understanding any new database requirements and defining a database to be used by the prototype. This is typically a new database, which is a copy of portions of existing databases, possibly with new content. If new content is required, it will usually come from external data sources, such as market research data, general economic indicators, or industry standards.

Database implementation and maintenance activities are repeated as new versions of the prototype are produced. Often security and integrity controls are minimal

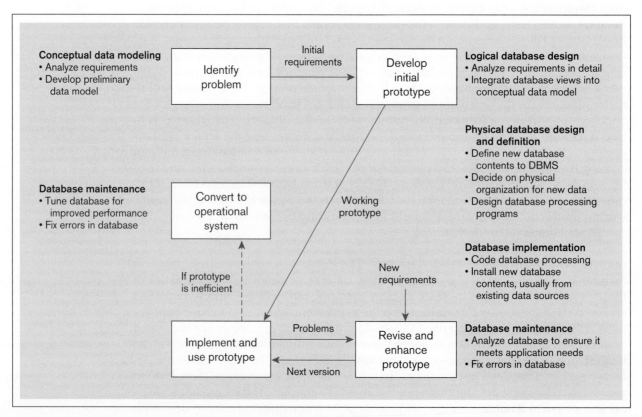

FIGURE 1-8 The prototyping methodology and database development process

because the emphasis is on getting working prototype versions ready as quickly as possible. Also, documentation tends to be delayed until the end of the project, and user training occurs from hands-on use. Finally, after an accepted prototype is created, the developer and the user decide whether the final prototype, and its database, can be put into production as is. If the system, including the database, is too inefficient, the system and database might need to be reprogrammed and reorganized to meet performance expectations. Inefficiencies, however, have to be weighed against violating the core principles behind sound database design.

With the increasing popularity of visual programming tools (such as Visual Basic, Java, or C#) that make it easy to modify the interface between user and system, prototyping is becoming the systems development methodology of choice to develop new applications internally. With prototyping, it is relatively easy to change the content and layout of user reports and displays.

The benefits from iterative approaches to systems development demonstrated by RAD and prototyping approaches have resulted in further efforts to create ever more responsive development approaches. In February 2001, a group of 17 individuals interested in supporting these approaches created "The Manifesto for Agile Software Development." For them, **agile software development** practices include valuing (**www .agilemanifesto.org**):

> *Individuals and interactions* over processes and tools
>
> *Working software* over comprehensive documentation
>
> *Customer collaboration* over contract negotiation, and
>
> *Responding to change* over following a plan

Emphasis on the importance of people, both software developers and customers, is evident in their phrasing. This is in response to the turbulent environment within which software development occurs, as compared to the more staid environment of most engineering development projects from which the earlier software development methodologies came. The importance of the practices established in the SDLC continues to be recognized and accepted by software developers including the creators of The Manifesto for Agile Software Development. However, it is impractical to allow these practices to stifle quick reactions to changes in the environment that change project requirements.

The use of agile or adaptive processes should be considered when a project involves unpredictable and/or changing requirements, responsible and collaborative developers, and involved customers who understand and can contribute to the process (Fowler, 2005). If you are interested in learning more about agile software development, investigate agile methodologies such as eXtreme Programming, Scrum, the DSDM Consortium, and feature-driven development.

Agile software development
An approach to database and software development that emphasizes "**individuals and interactions** over processes and tools, **working software** over comprehensive documentation, **customer collaboration** over contract negotiation, and **response to change** over following a plan."

Three-Schema Architecture for Database Development

The explanation earlier in this chapter of the database development process referred to several different, but related, models of databases developed on a systems development project. These data models and the primary phase of the SDLC in which they are developed are summarized here:

- Enterprise data model (during the Information Systems Planning phase)
- External schema or user view (during the Analysis and Logical Design phases)
- Conceptual schema (during the Analysis phase)
- Logical schema (during the Logical Design phase)
- Physical schema (during the Physical Design phase)

In 1978, an industry committee commonly known as ANSI/SPARC published an important document that described three-schema architecture—external, conceptual, and internal schemas—for describing the structure of data. Figure 1-9 shows the relationship between the various schemas developed during the SDLC and the ANSI three-schema architecture. It is important to keep in mind that all these schemas are just different ways of visualizing the structure of the same database by different stakeholders.

FIGURE 1-9 Three-schema
architecture

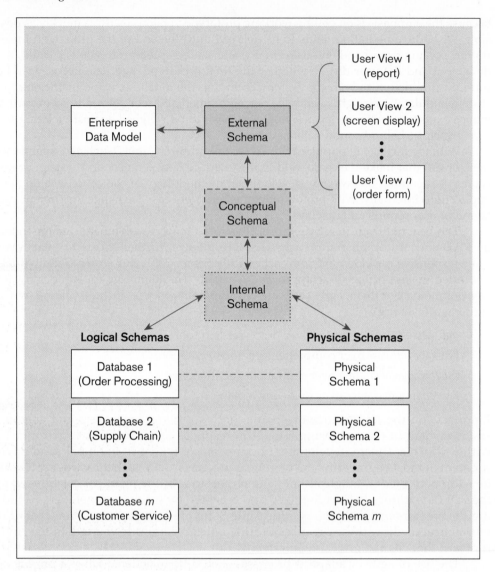

The three schemas as defined by ANSI (depicted down the center of Figure 1-9) are as follows:

1. *External schema* This is the view (or views) of managers and other employees who are the database users. As shown in Figure 1-9, the external schema can be represented as a combination of the enterprise data model (a top-down view) and a collection of detailed (or bottom-up) user views.
2. *Conceptual schema* This schema combines the different external views into a single, coherent, and comprehensive definition of the enterprise's data. The conceptual schema represents the view of the data architect or data administrator.
3. *Internal schema* As shown in Figure 1-9, an internal schema today really consists of two separate schemas: a logical schema and a physical schema. The logical schema is the representation of data for a type of data management technology (e.g., relational). The physical schema describes how data should be represented and stored in secondary storage using a particular DBMS (e.g., Oracle).

EVOLUTION OF DATABASE SYSTEMS

Database management systems were first introduced during the 1960s and have continued to evolve during subsequent decades. Figure 1-10a sketches this evolution by highlighting the database technology (or technologies) that were dominant during each decade. In most cases, the period of introduction was quite long, and the

FIGURE 1-10 **The range of database technologies: past and present**

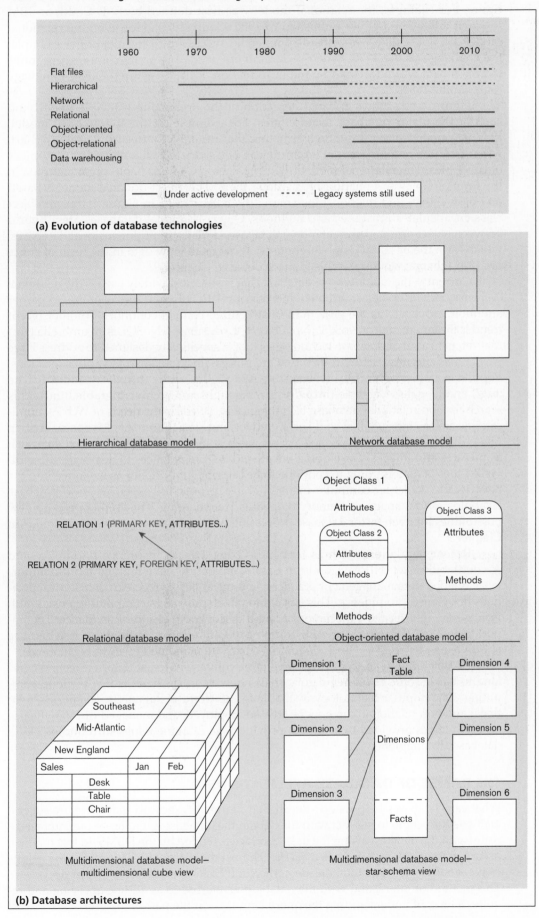

(a) Evolution of database technologies

Hierarchical database model

Network database model

RELATION 1 (PRIMARY KEY, ATTRIBUTES...)

RELATION 2 (PRIMARY KEY, FOREIGN KEY, ATTRIBUTES...)

Relational database model

Object Class 1
Attributes
Object Class 2
Attributes
Methods
Methods

Object Class 3
Attributes
Methods

Object-oriented database model

Southeast
Mid-Atlantic
New England
Sales   Jan   Feb
Desk
Table
Chair

Multidimensional database model—
multidimensional cube view

Dimension 1
Dimension 2
Dimension 3
Fact Table
Dimensions
Facts
Dimension 4
Dimension 5
Dimension 6

Multidimensional database model—
star-schema view

(b) Database architectures

technology was first introduced during the decade preceding the one shown in the figure. For example, the relational model was first defined by E. F. Codd, an IBM research fellow, in a paper published in 1970 (Codd, 1970). However, the relational model did not realize widespread commercial success until the 1980s. For example, the challenge of the 1970s when programmers needed to write complex programs to access data was addressed by the introduction of the Structured Query Language (SQL) in the 1980s.

Figure 1-10b shows a visual depiction of the organizing principle underlying each of the major database technologies. For example, in the hierarchical model, files are organized in a top-down structure that resembles a tree or genealogy chart, whereas in the network model, each file can be associated with an arbitrary number of other files. The relational model (the primary focus of this book) organizes data in the form of tables and relationships among them. The object-oriented model is based on object classes and relationships among them. As shown in Figure 1-10b, an object class encapsulates attributes and methods. Object-relational databases are a hybrid between object-oriented and relational databases. Finally, multidimensional databases, which form the basis for data warehouses, allow us to view data in the form of cubes or a star schema; we discuss this in more detail in Chapter 9.

Currently, the major type of database that is still most widely used is the relational database. However, object-oriented and object-relational databases continue to garner attention, especially as the growth in unstructured content continues. Another recent trend is the emergence of NoSQL (Not Only SQL) databases. NoSQL is an umbrella term that refers to a set of database technologies that is specifically designed to address large (structured and unstructured) data that are potentially stored across various locations. Popular examples of NoSQL databases are Apache Cassandra (**http://cassandra.apache .org/**) and Google's BigTable (**http://research.google.com/archive/bigtable.html**). This search for non-relational database technologies is fueled by the needs of Web 2.0 applications such as blogs, wikis, and social networking sites (Facebook, MySpace, Twitter, LinkedIn, etc.) and partially by how easy it has become to create unstructured data such as pictures and images. Developing effective database practices to deal with these diverse types of data is going to continue to be of prime importance as we move into the next decade. As larger computer memory chips become less expensive, new database technologies to manage in-memory databases are emerging. This trend opens up new possibilities for even faster database processing. We cover some of these new trends in Chapter 9.

Recent regulations such as Sarbanes-Oxley, Health Insurance Portability and Accountability Act (HIPAA), and the Basel Convention have highlighted the importance of good data management practices, and the ability to reconstruct historical positions has gained prominence. This has led to developments in computer forensics with increased emphasis and expectations around discovery of electronic evidence. The importance of good database administration capabilities also continues to rise because effective disaster recovery and adequate security are mandated by these regulations.

An emerging trend that is making it more convenient to use database technologies (and to tackle some of the regulatory challenges identified here) is that of cloud computing. One popular technology available in the cloud is databases. Databases, relational and non-relational, can now be created, deployed, and managed through the use of technologies provided by a service provider. We examine issues surrounding cloud databases in Chapter 8.

THE RANGE OF DATABASE APPLICATIONS

What can databases help us do? Recall that Figure 1-5 showed that there are several methods for people to interact with the data in the database: First, users can interact directly with the database using the user interface provided by the DBMS. In this manner, users can issue commands (called *queries*) against the database and examine the results or potentially even store them inside a Microsoft Excel spreadsheet or Word document. This method of interaction with the database is referred to as ad-hoc querying and requires a level of understanding of the query language on the part of the user.

Because most business users do not possess this level of knowledge, the second and the more common mechanism for accessing the database is using application programs. An application program consists of two key components. A graphical user interface accepts the users' request (e.g., to input, delete, or modify data) and/or provides a mechanism for displaying the data retrieved from the database. The business logic contains the programming logic necessary to act on the users' commands. The machine that runs the user interface (and sometimes the business logic) is referred to as the *client*. The machine that runs the DBMS and contains the database is referred to as the *database server*.

It is important to understand that the applications and the database need not reside on the same computer (and, in most cases, they don't). In order to better understand the range of database applications, we divide them into three categories based on the location of the client (application) and the database software itself: personal, two-tier, and multitier databases. We introduce each category with a typical example, followed by some issues that generally arise within that category of use.

Personal Databases

Personal databases are designed to support one user. Personal databases have long resided on personal computers (PCs), including laptops, and increasingly on smartphones and personal digital assistants (PDAs). The purpose of these databases is to provide the user with the ability to manage (store, update, delete, and retrieve) small amounts of data in an efficient manner. Simple database applications that store customer information and the details of contacts with each customer can be used from a PC and easily transferred from one device to the other for backup and work purposes. For example, consider a company that has a number of salespersons who call on actual or prospective customers. A database of customers and a pricing application can enable the salesperson to determine the best combination of quantity and type of items for the customer to order.

Personal databases are widely used because they can often improve personal productivity. However, they entail a risk: The data cannot easily be shared with other users. For example, suppose the sales manager wants a consolidated view of customer contacts. This cannot be quickly or easily provided from an individual salesperson's databases. This illustrates a common problem: If data are of interest to one person, they probably are or will soon become of interest to others as well. For this reason, personal databases should be limited to those rather special situations (e.g., in a very small organization) where the need to share the data among users of the personal database is unlikely to arise.

Two-Tier Client/Server Databases

As noted earlier, the utility of a personal (single-user) database is quite limited. Often, what starts off as a single-user database evolves into something that needs to be shared among several users. A workgroup is a relatively small team of people (typically fewer than 25 persons) who collaborate on the same project or application or on a group of similar projects or applications. These persons might be engaged (for example) with a construction project or with developing a new computer application and need to share data among the group.

The most common method of sharing data for this type of need is based on creating a two-tier client/server application as shown in Figure 1-11. Each member of the workgroup has a computer, and the computers are linked by means of a network (wired or wireless local area network [LAN]). In most cases, each computer has a copy of a specialized application (client) that provides the user interface as well as the business logic through which the data are manipulated. The database itself and the DBMS are stored on a central device called the database server, which is also connected to the network. Thus, each member of the workgroup has access to the shared data. Different group members (e.g., developer or project manager) may have different user views of this shared database. This arrangement overcomes the principal objection to PC databases, which is that the data are not easily shared. This arrangement, however, introduces many data management issues

FIGURE 1-11 Two-tier database
with local area network

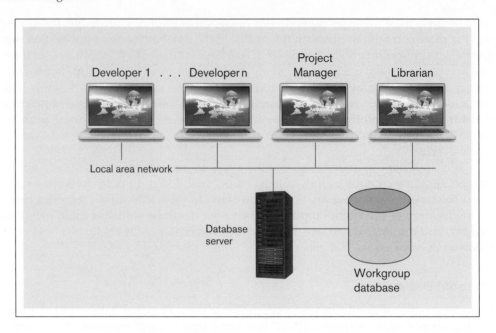

not present with personal (single-user) databases, such as data security and data integrity when multiple users attempt to change and update data at the same time.

Multitier Client/Server Databases

One of the drawbacks of the two-tier database architecture is that the amount of functionality that needs to be programmed into the application on the users' computer can be pretty significant because it needs to contain both the user interface logic as well as the business logic. This, of course, means that the client computers need to be powerful enough to handle the programmed application. Another drawback is that each time there is a change to either the business logic or user interface, each client computer that has the application needs to be updated.

To overcome these limitations, most modern applications that need to support a large number of users are built using the concept of multitiered architecture. In most organizations, these applications are intended to support a department (such as marketing or accounting) or a division (such as a line of business), which is generally larger than a workgroup (typically between 25 and 100 persons).

An example of a company that has several multitier applications is shown in Figure 1-12. In a three-tiered architecture, the user interface is accessible on the individual users' computers. This user interface may be either Web browser based or written using programming languages such as Visual Basic.NET, Visual C#, or Java. The application layer/Web server layer contains the business logic required to accomplish the business transactions requested by the users. This layer in turn talks to the database server. The most significant implication for database development from the use of multitier client/server architectures is the ease of separating the development of the database and the modules that maintain the data from the information systems modules that focus on business logic and/or presentation logic. In addition, this architecture allows us to improve performance and maintainability of the application and database. We will consider both two and multitier client/server architectures in more detail in Chapter 8.

Enterprise Applications

An enterprise (that's small "e," not capital "E," as in *Starship*) application/database is one whose scope is the entire organization or enterprise (or, at least, many different departments). Such databases are intended to support organization-wide operations and decision making. Note that an organization may have several enterprise databases, so such a database is not inclusive of all organizational data. A single operational enterprise

FIGURE 1-12 Three-tiered client/server database architecture

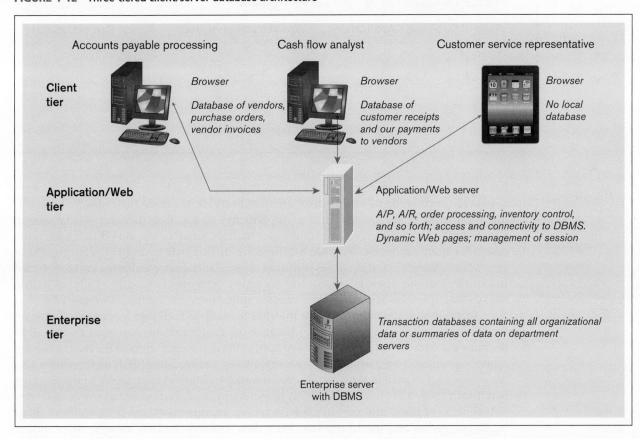

database is impractical for many medium to large organizations due to difficulties in performance for very large databases, diverse needs of different users, and the complexity of achieving a single definition of data (metadata) for all database users. An enterprise database does, however, support information needs from many departments and divisions. The evolution of enterprise databases has resulted in two major developments:

1. Enterprise resource planning (ERP) systems
2. Data warehousing implementations

Enterprise resource planning (ERP) systems have evolved from the material requirements planning (MRP) and manufacturing resource planning (MRP-II) systems of the 1970s and 1980s. These systems scheduled the raw materials, components, and subassembly requirements for manufacturing processes and also scheduled shop floor and product distribution activities. Next, extension to the remaining business functions resulted in enterprise-wide management systems, or ERP systems. All ERP systems are heavily dependent on databases to store the integrated data required by the ERP applications. In addition to ERP systems, several specialized applications, such as customer relationship management (CRM) systems and supply chain management (SCM) systems, also are dependent on data stored in databases.

Whereas ERP systems work with the current operational data of the enterprise, **data warehouses** collect content from the various operational databases, including personal, workgroup, department, and ERP databases. Data warehouses provide users with the opportunity to work with historical data to identify patterns and trends and answers to strategic business questions. We describe data warehouses in detail in Chapter 9.

Finally, one change that has dramatically affected the database environment is the ascendance of the Internet, and the subsequent development of applications that are used by the masses. Acceptance of the Internet by businesses has resulted in important changes in long-established business models. Even extremely successful companies

Enterprise resource planning (ERP)

A business management system that integrates all functions of the enterprise, such as manufacturing, sales, finance, marketing, inventory, accounting, and human resources. ERP systems are software applications that provide the data necessary for the enterprise to examine and manage its activities.

Data warehouse

An integrated decision support database whose content is derived from the various operational databases.

TABLE 1-5   Summary of Database Applications

Type of Database / Application	Typical Number of Users	Typical Size of Database
Personal	1	Megabytes
Two-tier	5–100	Megabytes–gigabytes
Three-tier	100–1000	Gigabytes
Enterprise resource planning	>100	Gigabytes–terabytes
Data warehousing	>100	Terabytes–petabytes

have been shaken by competition from new businesses that have employed the Internet to provide improved customer information and service, to eliminate traditional marketing and distribution channels, and to implement employee relationship management. For example, customers configure and order their personal computers directly from the computer manufacturers. Bids are accepted for airline tickets and collectables within seconds of submission, sometimes resulting in substantial savings for the end consumer. Information about open positions and company activities is readily available within many companies. Each of these Web-based applications use databases extensively.

In the previous examples, the Internet is used to facilitate interaction between the business and the customer (B2C) because the customers are necessarily external to the business. However, for other types of applications, the customers of the businesses are other businesses. Those interactions are commonly referred to as B2B relationships and are enabled by extranets. An *extranet* uses Internet technology, but access to the extranet is not universal, as is the case with an Internet application. Rather, access is restricted to business suppliers and customers with whom an agreement has been reached about legitimate access and use of one another's data and information. Finally, an *intranet* is used by employees of the firm to access applications and databases within the company.

Allowing such access to a business's database raises data security and integrity issues that are new to the management of information systems, whereby data have traditionally been closely guarded and secured within each company. These issues become even more complex as companies take advantage of the cloud. Now data are stored on servers that are not within the control of the company that is generating the data. We cover these issues in more detail in Chapter 8.

Table 1-5 presents a brief summary of the types of databases outlined in this section.

DEVELOPING A DATABASE APPLICATION FOR PINE VALLEY FURNITURE COMPANY

Pine Valley Furniture Company was introduced earlier in this chapter. By the late 1990s, competition in furniture manufacturing had intensified, and competitors seemed to respond more rapidly than Pine Valley Furniture to new business opportunities. While there were many reasons for this trend, managers believed that the computer information systems they had been using (based on traditional file processing) had become outdated. After attending an executive development session led by Fred McFadden and Jeff Hoffer (we wish!), the company started a development effort that eventually led to adopting a database approach for the company. Data previously stored in separate files have been integrated into a single database structure. Also, the metadata that describe these data reside in the same structure. The DBMS provides the interface between the various database applications for organizational users and the database (or databases). The DBMS allows users to share the data and to query, access, and update the stored data.

To facilitate the sharing of data and information, Pine Valley Furniture Company uses a local area network (LAN) that links employee workstations in the various departments to a database server, as shown in Figure 1-13. During the early 2000s, the company mounted a two-phase effort to introduce Internet technology. First, to improve intracompany communication and decision making, an intranet was installed

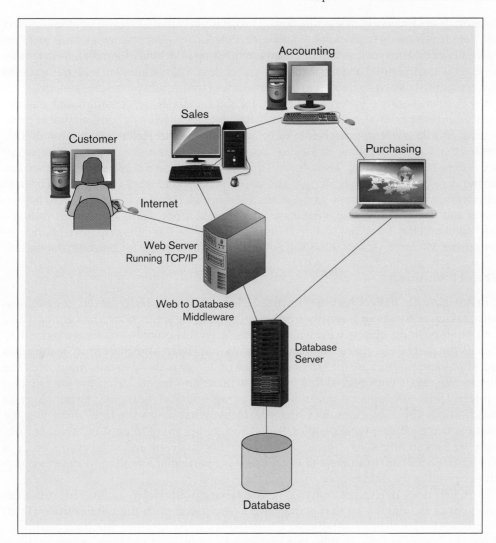

FIGURE 1-13   Computer System for Pine Valley Furniture Company

that allowed employees fast Web-based access to company information, including phone directories, furniture design specifications, e-mail, and so forth. In addition, Pine Valley Furniture Company also added a Web interface to some of its business applications, such as order entry, so that more internal business activities that require access to data in the database server could also be conducted by employees through its intranet. However, most applications that use the database server still do not have a Web interface and require that the application itself be stored on employees' workstations.

Database Evolution at Pine Valley Furniture Company

A trait of a good database is that it does and can evolve! Helen Jarvis, product manager for home office furniture at Pine Valley Furniture Company, knows that competition has become fierce in this growing product line. Thus, it is increasingly important to Pine Valley Furniture that Helen be able to analyze sales of her products more thoroughly. Often these analyses are ad hoc, driven by rapidly changing and unanticipated business conditions, comments from furniture store managers, trade industry gossip, or personal experience. Helen has requested that she be given direct access to sales data with an easy-to-use interface so that she can search for answers to the various marketing questions she will generate.

Chris Martin is a systems analyst in Pine Valley Furniture's information systems development area. Chris has worked at Pine Valley Furniture for five years and has experience with information systems from several business areas within Pine Valley.

Because Pine Valley Furniture has been careful in the development of its systems, especially since adopting the database approach, the company already has databases that support its operational business functions. Thus, it is likely that Chris will be able to extract the data Helen needs from existing databases. Pine Valley's information systems architecture calls for systems such as the one Helen is requesting to be built as stand-alone databases so that the unstructured and unpredictable use of data will not interfere with the access to the operational databases needed to support efficient transaction processing systems.

Further, because Helen's needs are for data analysis, not creation and maintenance, and are personal, not institutional, Chris decides to follow a combination of proto typing and life-cycle approaches in developing the system Helen has requested. This means that Chris will follow all the life-cycle steps but focus his energy on the steps that are integral to prototyping. Thus, he will quickly address project planning and then use an iterative cycle of analysis, design, and implementation to work closely with Helen to develop a working prototype of the system she needs. Because the system will be personal and likely will require a database with limited scope, Chris hopes the prototype will end up being the actual system Helen will use. Chris has chosen to develop the system using Microsoft Access, Pine Valley's preferred technology for personal databases.

Project Planning

Chris begins the project by interviewing Helen. Chris asks Helen about her business area, taking notes about business area objectives, business functions, data entity types, and other business objects with which she deals. At this point, Chris listens more than he talks so that he can concentrate on understanding Helen's business area; he interjects questions and makes sure that Helen does not try to jump ahead to talk about what she thinks she needs with regard to computer screens and reports from the information system. Chris asks general questions, using business and marketing terminology as much as possible. For example, Chris asks Helen what issues she faces managing the home office products; what people, places, and things are of interest to her in her job; how far back in time she needs data to go to do her analyses; and what events occur in the business that are of interest to her. Chris pays particular attention to Helen's objectives as well as the data entities that she is interested in.

Chris does two quick analyses before talking with Helen again. First, he identifies all of the databases that contain data associated with the data entities Helen mentioned. From these databases, Chris makes a list of all of the data attributes from these data entities that he thinks might be of interest to Helen in her analyses of the home office furniture market. Chris's previous involvement in projects that developed Pine Valley's standard sales tracking and forecasting system and cost accounting system helps him speculate on the kinds of data Helen might want. For example, the objective to exceed sales goals for each product finish category of office furniture suggests that Helen wants product annual sales goals in her system; also, the objective of achieving at least an 8 percent annual sales growth means that the prior year's orders for each product need to be included. He also concludes that Helen's database must include all products, not just those in the office furniture line, because she wants to compare her line to others. However, he is able to eliminate many of the data attributes kept on each data entity. For example, Helen does not appear to need various customer data such as address, phone number, contact person, store size, and salesperson. Chris does, though, include a few additional attributes, customer type and zip code, which he believes might be important in a sales forecasting system.

Second, from this list, Chris draws a conceptual data model (Figure 1-14) that represents the data entities as well as the major relationships among these data entities. The data model is represented using a notation called the Entity-Relationship (E-R) model. You will learn more about this notation in Chapters 2 and 3.

Analyzing Database Requirements

Prior to their next meeting, Chris sends Helen a rough project schedule outlining the steps he plans to follow and the estimated length of time each step will take. Because prototyping is a user-driven process, in which the user says when to stop iterating on

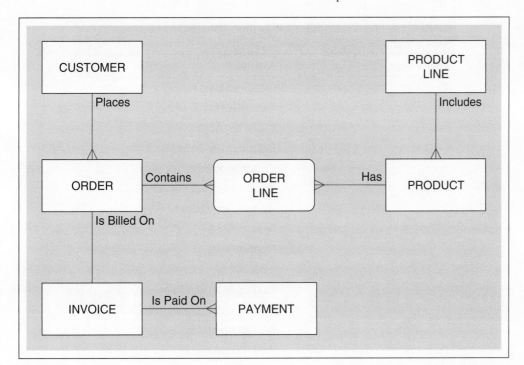

FIGURE 1-14 Preliminary data model for Home Office product line marketing support system

the new prototype versions, Chris can provide only rough estimates of the duration of certain project steps.

Chris does more of the talking at this second meeting, but he pays close attention to Helen's reactions to his initial ideas for the database application. He methodically walks through each data entity in Figure 1-14, explaining what it means and what business policies and procedures are represented by each line between entities.

A few of the rules he summarizes are listed here:

1. Each CUSTOMER *Places* any number of ORDERs. Conversely, each ORDER *Is Placed By* exactly one CUSTOMER.
2. Each ORDER *Contains* any number of ORDER LINEs. Conversely, each ORDER LINE *Is Contained In* exactly one ORDER.
3. Each PRODUCT *Has* any number of ORDER LINEs. Conversely, each ORDER LINE *Is For* exactly one PRODUCT.
4. Each ORDER *Is Billed On* one INVOICE and each INVOICE *Is a Bill for* exactly one ORDER.

Places, *Contains*, and *Has* are called one-to-many relationships because, for example, one customer places potentially many orders and one order is placed by exactly one customer.

In addition to the relationships, Chris also presents Helen with some detail on the data attributes for each entity. For example, Order Number uniquely identifies each order. Other data about an order Chris thinks Helen might want to know include the date when the order was placed and the date when the order was filled. (This would be the latest shipment date for the products on the order.) Chris also explains that the Payment Date attribute represents the most recent date when the customer made any payments, in full or partial, for the order.

As she reacts to the data model, Chris asks her how she intends to use the data she wants. Chris does not try to be thorough at this point because he knows that Helen has not worked with an information set like the one being developed; thus, she may not yet be positive about what data she wants or what she wants to do with it. Rather, Chris's objective is to understand a few ways in which Helen intends to use the data so he can develop an initial prototype, including the database and several computer displays or reports. The final list of attributes that Helen and Chris agree upon appears in Table 1-6.

TABLE 1-6	Data Attributes for Entities (Pine Valley Furniture Company)
Entity Type	**Attribute**
Customer	Customer Identifier
	Customer Name
	Customer Type
	Customer Zip Code
	Customer Years
Product	Product Identifier
	Product Description
	Product Finish
	Product Price
	Product Cost
	Product Prior Year Sales Goal
	Product Current Year Sales Goal
	Product Line Name
Product Line	Product Line Name
	Product Line Prior Year Sales Goal
	Product Line Current Year Sales Goal
Order	Order Number
	Order Placement Date
	Order Fulfillment Date
	Order Number of Shipments
	Customer Identifier
Ordered Product	Order Number
	Product Identifier
	Order Quantity
Invoice	Invoice Number
	Order Number
	Invoice Date
Payment	Invoice Number
	Payment Date
	Payment Amount

Designing the Database

Because Chris is following a prototyping methodology and the first two sessions with Helen quickly identified the data Helen might need, Chris is now ready to build a prototype. His first step is to create a project data model like the one shown in Figure 1-15. Notice the following characteristics of the project data model:

1. It is a model of the organization that provides valuable information about how the organization functions, as well as important constraints.
2. The project data model focuses on entities, relationships, and business rules. It also includes attribute labels for each piece of data that will be stored in each entity.

Second, Chris translates the data model into a set of tables for which the columns are data attributes and the rows are different sets of values for those attributes. Tables are the basic building blocks of a relational database (we will learn about this in Chapter 4),

FIGURE 1-15   Project data model for Home Office product line marketing support system

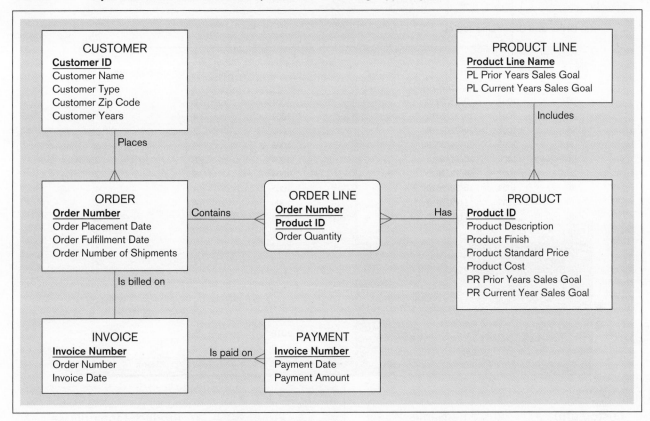

which is the database style for Microsoft Access. Figure 1-16 shows four tables with sample data: Customer, Product, Order, and OrderLine. Notice that these tables represent the four entities shown in the project data model (Figure 1-15). Each column of a table represents an attribute (or characteristic) of an entity. For example, the attributes shown for Customer are CustomerID and CustomerName. Each row of a table represents an instance (or occurrence) of the entity. The design of the database also required Chris to specify the format, or properties, for each attribute (MS Access calls attributes *fields*). These design decisions were easy in this case because most of the attributes were already specified in the corporate data dictionary.

The tables shown in Figure 1-16 were created using SQL (you will learn about this in Chapters 6 and 7). Figures 1-17 and 1-18 show the SQL statements that Chris would have likely used to create the structure of the ProductLine and Product tables. It is customary to add the suffix _T to a table name. Also note that because Access does not allow for spaces between names, the individual words in the attributes from the data model have now been concatenated. Hence, Product Description in the data model has become ProductDescription in the table. Chris did this translation so that each table had an attribute, called the table's "primary key," which will be distinct for each row in the table. The other major properties of each table are that there is only one value for each attribute in each row; if we know the value of the identifier, there can be only one value for each of the other attributes. For example, for any product line, there can be only one value for the current year's sales goal.

A final key characteristic of the relational model is that it represents relationships between entities by values stored in the columns of the corresponding tables. For example, notice that CustomerID is an attribute of both the Customer table and the Order table. As a result, we can easily link an order to its associated customer. For example, we can determine that OrderID 1003 is associated with CustomerID 1. Can you determine which ProductIDs are associated with OrderID 1004? In Chapters 6 and 7, you will also learn how to retrieve data from these tables by using SQL, which exploits these linkages.

The other major decision Chris has to make about database design is how to physically organize the database to respond as fast as possible to the queries Helen

FIGURE 1-16 Four relations (Pine Valley Furniture Company)

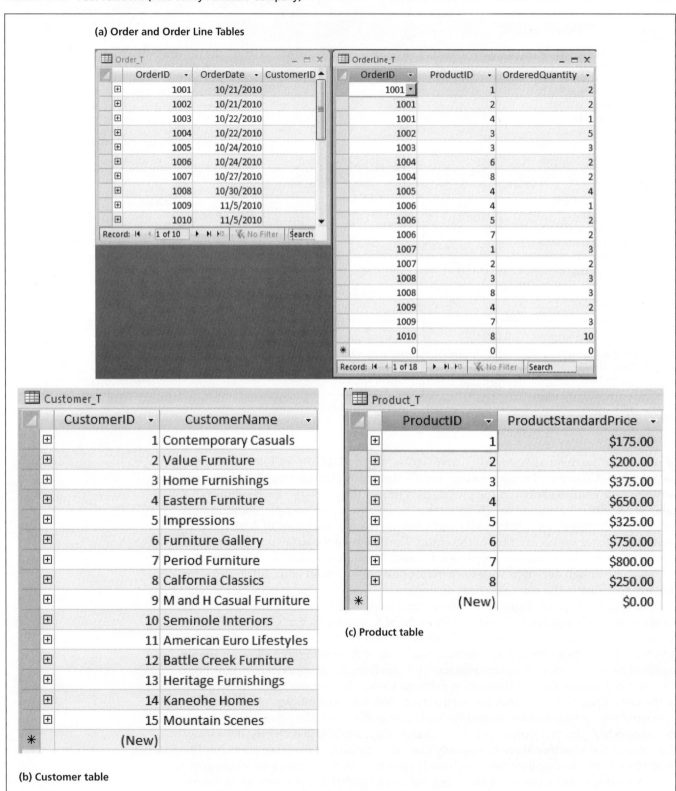

(a) Order and Order Line Tables

(b) Customer table

(c) Product table

will write. The key physical database design decision that SQL allows a database designer to make is on which attributes to create indexes. All primary key attributes (such as OrderNumber for the Order_T table)—those with unique values across the rows of the table—are indexed. In addition to this, Chris uses a general rule of thumb: Create an index for any attribute that has more than 10 different values and that Helen might use to segment the database.

```
CREATE TABLE ProductLine_T

(ProductLineID        VARCHAR (40) NOT NULL PRIMARY KEY,

PlPriorYearGoal       DECIMAL,

PlCurrentYearGoal     DECIMAL);
```

FIGURE 1-17 SQL definition of ProductLine table

```
CREATE TABLE Product_T

(ProductID              NUMBER(11,0) NOT NULL PRIMARY KEY

ProductDescription      VARCHAR (50),

ProductFinish           VARCHAR (20),

ProductStandardPrice    DECIMAL(6,2),

ProductCost             DECIMAL,

ProductPriorYearGoal    DECIMAL,

ProductCurrentYearGoal  DECIMAL,

ProductLineID           VARCHAR (40),

FOREIGN KEY             (ProductLineID) REFERENCES ProductLine_T (ProductLineID));
```

FIGURE 1-18 SQL definition of Product table

Using the Database

Helen will use the database Chris has built mainly for ad hoc questions, so Chris will train her so that she can access the database and build queries to answer her ad hoc questions. Helen has indicated a few standard questions she expects to ask periodically. Chris will develop several types of prewritten routines (forms, reports, and queries) that can make it easier for Helen to answer these standard questions (so she does not have to program these questions from scratch). One of the standard sets of information Helen says she wants is a list of each of the products in the Home Office product line showing each product's total sales to date compared with its current year sales goal. Helen may want the results of this query to be displayed in a more stylized fashion—an opportunity to use a report—but for now Chris will present this feature to Helen only as a query.

The query to produce this list of products appears in Figure 1-19, with sample output in Figure 1-20. The query in Figure 1-19 uses SQL. You can see three of the six

```
SELECT Product.ProductID, Product.ProductDescription, Product.PRCurrentYearSalesGoal,

       (OrderQuantity * ProductPrice) AS SalesToDate

FROM Order.OrderLine, Product.ProductLine

WHERE Order.OrderNumber = OrderLine.OrderNumber

AND Product.ProductID = OrderedProduct.ProductID

AND Product.ProductID = ProductLine.ProductID

AND Product.ProductLineName = "Home Office";
```

FIGURE 1-19 SQL query for Home Office sales-to-goal comparison

FIGURE 1-20   Home Office product line sales comparison

Home Office Sales to Date : Select Query			
Product ID	Product Description	PR Current Year Sales Goal	Sales to Date
3	Computer Desk	$23,500.00	5625
10	96" Bookcase	$22,500.00	4400
5	Writer's Desk	$26,500.00	650
3	Computer Desk	$23,500.00	3750
7	48" Bookcase	$17,000.00	2250
5	Writer's Desk	$26,500.00	3900

standard SQL clauses in this query: SELECT, FROM, and WHERE. SELECT indicates which attributes will be shown in the result. One calculation is also included and given the label "Sales to Date." FROM indicates which tables must be accessed to retrieve data. WHERE defines the links between the tables and indicates that results from only the Home Office product line are to be included. Only limited data are included for this example, so the Total Sales results in Figure 1-20 are fairly small, but the format is the result of the query in Figure 1-19.

Chris is now ready to meet with Helen again to see if the prototype is beginning to meet her needs. Chris shows Helen the system. As Helen makes suggestions, Chris is able to make a few changes online, but many of Helen's observations will have to wait for more careful work at his desk.

Space does not permit us to review the whole project to develop the Home Office marketing support system. Chris and Helen ended up meeting about a dozen times before Helen was satisfied that all the attributes she needed were in the database; that the standard queries, forms, and reports Chris wrote were of use to her; and that she knew how to write queries for unanticipated questions. Chris will be available to Helen at any time to provide consulting support when she has trouble with the system, including writing more complex queries, forms, or reports. One final decision that Chris and Helen made was that the performance of the final prototype was efficient enough that the prototype did not have to be rewritten or redesigned. Helen was now ready to use the system.

Administering the Database

The administration of the Home Office marketing support system is fairly simple. Helen decided that she could live with weekly downloads of new data from Pine Valley's operational databases into her MS Access database. Chris wrote a C# program with SQL commands embedded in it to perform the necessary extracts from the corporate databases and wrote an MS Access program in Visual Basic to rebuild the Access tables from these extracts; he scheduled these jobs to run every Sunday evening. Chris also updated the corporate information systems architecture model to include the Home Office marketing support system. This step was important so that when changes occurred to formats for data included in Helen's system, the corporate CASE tool could alert Chris that changes might also have to be made in her system.

Future of Databases at Pine Valley

Although the databases currently in existence at Pine Valley adequately support the daily operations of the company, requests such as the one made by Helen have highlighted that the current databases are often inadequate for decision support applications. For example, following are some types of questions that cannot be easily answered:

1. What is the pattern of furniture sales this year, compared with the same period last year?

2. Who are our 10 largest customers, and what are their buying patterns?
3. Why can't we easily obtain a consolidated view of any customer who orders through different sales channels, rather than viewing each contact as representing a separate customer?

To answer these and other questions, an organization often needs to build a separate database that contains historical and summarized information. Such a database is usually called a *data warehouse* or, in some cases, a *data mart*. Also, analysts need specialized decision support tools to query and analyze the database. One class of tools used for this purpose is called online analytical processing (OLAP) tools. We describe data warehouses, data marts, and related decision support tools in Chapter 9. There you will learn of the interest in building a data warehouse that is now growing within Pine Valley Furniture Company.

Summary

Over the past two decades, there has been enormous growth in the number and importance of database applications. Databases are used to store, manipulate, and retrieve data in every type of organization. In the highly competitive environment of today, there is every indication that database technology will assume even greater importance. A course in modern database management is one of the most important courses in the information systems curriculum.

A database is an organized collection of logically related data. We define *data* as stored representations of objects and events that have meaning and importance in the user's environment. Information is data that have been processed in such a way that the knowledge of the person who uses the data increases. Both data and information may be stored in a database.

Metadata are data that describe the properties or characteristics of end-user data and the context of that data. A database management system (DBMS) is a software system that is used to create, maintain, and provide controlled access to user databases. A DBMS stores metadata in a repository, which is a central storehouse for all data definitions, data relationships, screen and report formats, and other system components.

Computer file processing systems were developed early in the computer era so that computers could store, manipulate, and retrieve large files of data. These systems (still in use today) have a number of important limitations such as dependence between programs and data, data duplication, limited data sharing, and lengthy development times. The database approach was developed to overcome these limitations. This approach emphasizes the integration and sharing of data across the organization. Advantages of this approach include program-data independence, improved data sharing, minimal data redundancy, and improved productivity of application development.

Database applications can be arranged into the following categories: personal databases, two-tier databases, multitier databases, and enterprise databases. Enterprise databases include data warehouses and integrated decision support databases whose content is derived from the various operational databases. Enterprise resource planning (ERP) systems rely heavily on enterprise databases. A modern database and the applications that use it may be located on multiple computers. Although any number of tiers may exist (from one to many), three tiers of computers relate to the client/server architecture for database processing: (1) the client tier, where database contents are presented to the user; (2) the application/Web server tier, where analyses on database contents are made and user sessions are managed; and (3) the enterprise server tier, where the data from across the organization are merged into an organizational asset.

Database development begins with enterprise data modeling, during which the range and general contents of organizational databases are established. In addition to the relationships among the data entities themselves, their relationship to other organizational planning objects, such as organizational units, locations, business functions, and information systems, also need to be established. Relationships between data entities and the other organizational planning objects can be represented at a high level by planning matrixes, which can be manipulated to understand patterns of relationships. Once the need for a database is identified, either from a planning exercise or from a specific request (such as the one from Helen Jarvis for a Home Office products marketing support system), a project team is formed to develop all elements. The project team follows a systems development process, such as the systems development life cycle (SDLC) or prototyping. The SDLC can be represented by five methodical steps: (1) planning, (2) analysis, (3) design, (4) implementation, and (5) maintenance. Database development activities occur in each of these overlapping phases, and feedback may occur that causes a project to return to a prior phase. In prototyping, a database and its applications are iteratively refined through a close interaction of systems developers and users. Prototyping works best when the database application is small and stand-alone, and a small number of users exist.

Those working on a database development project deal with three views, or schemas, for a database: (1) a conceptual schema, which provides a complete, technology-independent picture of the database; (2) an internal schema, which specifies the complete database as it will be stored in computer secondary memory in terms of a logical schema and a physical schema; and (3) an external schema or user view, which describes the database relevant to a specific set of users in terms of a set of user views combined with the enterprise data model.

We closed the chapter with the review of a hypothetical database development project at Pine Valley Furniture Company. This system to support marketing a Home Office furniture product line illustrated the use of a personal database management system and SQL coding for developing a retrieval-only database. The database in this application contained data extracted from the enterprise databases and then stored in a separate database on the client tier. Prototyping was used to develop this database application because the user, Helen Jarvis, had rather unstructured needs that could best be discovered through an iterative process of developing and refining the system. Also, her interest and ability to work closely with Chris was limited.

Chapter Review

Key Terms

Agile software development 21
Computer-aided software engineering (CASE) tools 14
Conceptual schema 18
Constraint 12
Data 4
Data administration 12
Data independence 11
Data model 8
Data warehouse 27
Database 4
Database administration 12
Database application 7
Database management system (DBMS) 10
Enterprise data modeling 16
Enterprise resource planning (ERP) 27
Entity 8
Information 5
Logical schema 18
Metadata 6
Physical schema 19
Prototyping 20
Relational database 10
Repository 15
Systems development life cycle (SDLC) 17
User view 12

Review Questions

1. Define each of the following terms:
   a. data
   b. information
   c. metadata
   d. database application
   e. data warehouse
   f. constraint
   g. database
   h. entity
   i. database management system
   j. client/server architecture
   k. systems development life cycle (SDLC)
   l. agile software development
   m. enterprise data model
   n. conceptual data model
   o. logical data model
   p. physical data model

2. Match the following terms and definitions:
   _____ data
   _____ database application
   _____ constraint
   _____ repository
   _____ metadata
   _____ data warehouse
   _____ information
   _____ user view
   _____ database management system
   _____ data independence
   _____ database
   _____ enterprise resource planning (ERP)
   _____ systems development life cycle (SDLC)
   _____ prototyping
   _____ enterprise data model
   _____ conceptual schema
   _____ internal schema
   _____ external schema

   a. data placed in context or summarized
   b. application program(s)
   c. facts, text, graphics, images, etc.
   d. a graphical model that shows the high-level entities for the organization and the relationships among those entities
   e. organized collection of related data
   f. includes data definitions and constraints
   g. centralized storehouse for all data definitions
   h. separation of data description from programs
   i. a business management system that integrates all functions of the enterprise
   j. logical description of portion of database
   k. a software application that is used to create, maintain, and provide controlled access to user databases
   l. a rule that cannot be violated by database users
   m. integrated decision support database
   n. consist of the enterprise data model and multiple user views
   o. a rapid approach to systems development
   p. consists of two data models: a logical model and a physical model
   q. a comprehensive description of business data
   r. a structured, step-by-step approach to systems development

3. Contrast the following terms:
   a. data dependence; data independence
   b. structured data; unstructured data
   c. data; information
   d. repository; database
   e. entity; enterprise data model
   f. data warehouse; ERP system
   g. two-tier databases; multitier databases
   h. systems development life cycle; prototyping
   i. enterprise data model; conceptual data model
   j. prototyping; agile software development
4. List five disadvantages of file processing systems.
5. List the nine major components in a database system environment.
6. How are relationships between tables expressed in a relational database?
7. What does the term *data independence* mean, and why is it an important goal?
8. List 10 potential benefits of the database approach over conventional file systems.
9. List five costs or risks associated with the database approach.
10. Define a three-tiered database architecture.
11. In the three-tiered database architecture, is it possible for there to be no database on a particular tier? If not, why? If yes, give an example.
12. Name the five phases of the traditional systems development life cycle (SDLC), and explain the purpose and deliverables of each phase.
13. In which of the five phases of the SDLC do database development activities occur?
14. Are there procedures and processes that are common to the use of SDLC, prototyping, and agile methodologies? Explain any that you can identify and then indicate why the methodologies are considered to be different even though fundamental procedures and processes are still included.
15. Explain the differences between user views, a conceptual schema, and an internal schema as different perspectives of the same database.
16. In the three-schema architecture:
   a. The view of a manager or other type of user is called the _____ schema.
   b. The view of the data architect or data administrator is called the _____ schema.
   c. The view of the database administrator is called the _____ schema.
17. Revisit the section titled "Developing a Database Application for Pine Valley Furniture Company." What phase(s) of the database development process (Figure 1-8) do the activities that Chris performs in the following sub-sections correspond to:
   a. Project planning
   b. Analyzing database requirements
   c. Designing the database
   d. Using the database
   e. Administering the database
18. Why might Pine Valley Furniture Company need a data warehouse?
19. As the ability to handle large amounts of data improves, describe three business areas where these very large databases are being used effectively.

Problems and Exercises

1. For each of the following pairs of related entities, indicate whether (under typical circumstances) there is a one-to-many or a many-to-many relationship. Then, using the shorthand notation introduced in the text, draw a diagram for each of the relationships.
   a. STUDENT and COURSE (students register for courses)
   b. BOOK and BOOK COPY (books have copies)
   c. COURSE and SECTION (courses have sections)
   d. SECTION and ROOM (sections are scheduled in rooms)
   e. INSTRUCTOR and COURSE
2. Reread the definitions for *data* and *database* in this chapter. Database management systems only recently began to include the capability to store and retrieve more than numeric and textual data. What special data storage, retrieval, and maintenance capabilities do images, sound, video, and other advanced data types require that are not required or are simpler with numeric and textual data?
3. Table 1-1 shows example metadata for a set of data items. Identify three other columns for these data (i.e., three other metadata characteristics for the listed attributes) and complete the entries of the table in Table 1-1 for these three additional columns.
4. In the section "Disadvantages of File Processing Systems," the statement is made that the disadvantages of file processing systems can also be limitations of databases, depending on how an organization manages its databases. First, why do organizations create multiple databases, not just one all-inclusive database supporting all data processing needs? Second, what organizational and personal factors are at work that might lead an organization to have multiple, independently managed databases (and, hence, not completely follow the database approach)?
5. Consider a student club or organization in which you are a member. What are the data entities of this enterprise? List and define each entity. Then, develop an enterprise data model (such as Figure 1-3a) showing these entities and important relationships between them.
6. A driver's license bureau maintains a database of licensed drivers. State whether each of the following represents data or metadata. If it represents data, state whether it is structured or unstructured data. If it represents metadata, state whether it is a fact describing a property of data or a fact describing the context of data.
   a. Driver's name, address, and birth date
   b. The fact that the driver's name is a 30-character field
   c. A photo image of the driver
   d. An image of the driver's fingerprint
   e. The make and serial number of the scanning device that was used to scan the fingerprint
   f. The resolution (in megapixels) of the camera that was used to photograph the driver
   g. The fact that the driver's birth date must precede today's date by at least 16 years
7. Great Lakes Insurance would like to implement a relational database for both its in-house and outside agents. The

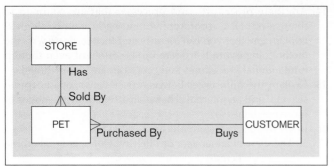

FIGURE 1-21   Data model for Problem and Exercise 8

outside agents will use notebook computers to keep track of customers and policy information. Based on what you have learned in this chapter, what type (or types) of database(s) would you recommend for this application?

8. Figure 1-21 shows an enterprise data model for a pet store.
   a. What is the relationship between Pet and Store (one-to-one, many-to-many, or one-to-many)?
   b. What is the relationship between Customer and Pet?
   c. Do you think there should be a relationship between Customer and Store?

9. Consider Figure 1-12, which depicts a hypothetical three-tiered database architecture. Identify potential duplications of data across all the databases listed on this figure. What problems might arise because of this duplication? Does this duplication violate the principles of the database approach outlined in this chapter? Why or why not?

10. What is your reaction to the representation of the systems development life cycle included in this chapter? Explain any problems you have with it.

11. List three additional entities that might appear in an enterprise data model for Pine Valley Furniture Company (Figure 1-3a).

12. Consider your business school or other academic unit as a business enterprise.
   a. Define several major data entity types and draw a preliminary enterprise data model (similar in notation to Figure 1-3a).
   b. Would your business school or academic unit benefit from a multitiered architecture for data? Why or why not?

13. The objective of the prototyping systems development methodology is to rapidly build and rebuild an information system as the user and systems analyst learn from use of the prototype what features should be included in the evolving information system. Because the final prototype does not have to become the working system, where do you think would be an ideal location to develop a prototype: on a personal computer, department server, or enterprise server? Does your answer depend on any assumptions?

14. Explain the differences between an enterprise data model and a conceptual data model. How many databases does each represent? What scope of the organization does each address? What are other salient differences?

15. Consider Figure 1-14. Explain the meaning of the line that connects ORDER to INVOICE and the line that connects INVOICE to PAYMENT. What does this say about how Pine Valley Furniture Company does business with its customers?

16. Answer the following questions concerning Figures 1-17 and 1-18:
   a. What will be the field size for the ProductLineName field in the Product table? Why?
   b. In Figure 1-18, how is the ProductID field in the Product table specified to be required? Why is it a required attribute?
   c. In Figure 1-18, explain the function of the FOREIGN KEY definition.

17. Consider the SQL query in Figure 1-19.
   a. How is Sales to Date calculated?
   b. How would the query have to change if Helen Jarvis wanted to see the results for all of the product lines, not just the Home Office product line?

18. Helen Jarvis wants to determine the most important customers for Home Office products. She requests a listing of total dollar sales year-to-date for each customer who bought these products, as revealed by invoiced payments. The list is to be sorted in descending order, so that the largest customer heads the list.
   a. Look at Figure 1-15 and determine what entities are required to produce this list.
   b. Which entities will be involved in the SQL query that will give Helen the information she needs?

References

Fowler, M. 2005. "The New Methodology" available at **www.martinfowler.com/articles/newMethodology.html** (access verified November 27, 2011).

Hoffer, J. A., J. F. George, and J. S. Valacich. 2011. *Modern Systems Analysis and Design*, 6th ed. Upper Saddle River, NJ: Prentice Hall.

Jordan, A. 1996. "Data Warehouse Integrity: How Long and Bumpy the Road?" *Data Management Review* 6,3 (March): 35–37.

Long, D. 2005. Presentation. ".Net Overview," Tampa Bay Technology Leadership Association, May 19, 2005.

Mullins, C. S. 2002. *Database Administration: The Complete Guide to Practices and Procedures*. New York: Addison-Wesley.

Ritter, D. 1999. "Don't Neglect Your Legacy." *Intelligent Enterprise* 2,5 (March 30): 70–72.

Winter, R. 1997. "What, After All, Is a Very Large Database?" *Database Programming & Design* 10,1 (January): 23–26.

Further Reading

Ballou, D. P., and G. K. Tayi. 1999. "Enhancing Data Quality in Data Warehouse Environments." *Communications of the ACM* 42,1 (January): 73–78.

Codd, E. F. 1970. "A Relational Model of Data for Large Shared Data Banks." *Communications of the ACM* 13,6 (June): 377–87.

Date, C. J. 1998. "The Birth of the Relational Model, Part 3." *Intelligent Enterprise* 1,4 (December 10): 45–48.

Grimes, S. 1998. "Object/Relational Reality Check." *Database Programming & Design* 11,7 (July): 26–33.

IBM. 2011. "The Essential CIO: Insights from the 2011 IBM Global CIO Study."

Kimball, R., and M. Ross. 2002. *The Data Warehouse Toolkit: The Complete Guide to Dimensional Data Modeling*, 2d ed. New York: Wiley.

Ritter, D. 1999. "The Long View." *Intelligent Enterprise* 2,12 (August 24): 58–67.

Silverston, L. 2001a. *The Data Model Resource Book, Vol. 1: A Library of Universal Data Models for all Enterprises*. New York: Wiley.

Silverston, L. 2001b. *The Data Model Resource Book, Vol 2: A Library of Data Models for Specific Industries*. New York: Wiley.

Web Resources

www.dbazine.com An online portal for database issues and solutions.

www.webopedia.com An online dictionary and search engine for computer terms and Internet technology.

www.techrepublic.com A portal site for information technology professionals that users can customize to their own particular interests.

www.zdnet.com A portal site where users can review recent articles on information technology subjects.

www.information-management.com *DM Review* magazine Web site, with the tagline "Covering Business Intelligence, Integration and Analytics." Provides a comprehensive list of links to relevant resource portals in addition to providing many of the magazine articles online.

www.dbta.com *Data Base Trends and Applications* magazine Web site. Addresses enterprise-level information issues.

http://databases.about.com A comprehensive site with many feature articles, links, interactive forum, chat rooms, and so forth.

http://thecaq.aicpa.org/Resources/Sarbanes+Oxley AICPA site for current information regarding Sarbanes-Oxley legislation.

www.basel.int United Nations page offering an overview of the Basel Convention, which addresses global waste issues.

www.usdoj.gov/jmd/irm/lifecycle/table.htm The Department of Justice Systems Development Life Cycle Guidance Document. This is an example of a systems methodology that you may want to look over.

http://groups.google.com/group/comp.software-eng? lnk=gsch&hl=en The software engineering archives for a Google group that focuses on software engineering and related topics. This site contains many links that you may want to explore.

www.acinet.org/acinet America's Career InfoNet, which provides information about careers, outlook, requirements, and so forth.

www.collegegrad.com/salaries/index.shtml A site for finding recent salary information for a wide range of careers, including database-related careers.

www.essentialstrategies.com/publications/methodology /zachman.htm David Hay's Web site, which has considerable information on universal data models as well as how database development fits into the Zachman information systems architecture.

www.inmondatasystems.com Web site for one of the pioneers of data warehousing.

www.agilemanifesto.org Web site that explains the viewpoints of those who created The Manifesto for Agile Software Development.

PART II

Database Analysis

AN OVERVIEW OF PART TWO

The first step in database development is database analysis, in which we determine user requirements for data and develop data models to represent those requirements. The two chapters in Part II describe in depth the de facto standard for conceptual data modeling—entity-relationship diagramming. A conceptual data model represents data from the viewpoint of the organization, independent of any technology that will be used to implement the model.

Chapter 2 ("Modeling Data in the Organization") begins by describing business rules, which are the policies and rules about the operation of a business that a data model represents. Characteristics of good business rules are described, and the process of gathering business rules is discussed. General guidelines for naming and defining elements of a data model are presented within the context of business rules.

Chapter 2 introduces the notations and main constructs of this modeling technique, including entities, relationships, and attributes; for each construct, we provide specific guidelines for naming and defining these elements of a data model. We distinguish between strong and weak entity types and the use of identifying relationships. We describe different types of attributes, including required versus optional attributes, simple versus composite attributes, single-valued versus multivalued attributes, derived attributes, and identifiers. We contrast relationship types and instances and introduce associative entities. We describe and illustrate relationships of various degrees, including unary, binary, and ternary relationships. We also describe the various relationship cardinalities that arise in modeling situations. We discuss the common problem of how to model time-dependent data. Finally, we describe the situation in which multiple relationships are defined between a given set of entities. The E-R modeling concepts are illustrated with an extended example for Pine Valley Furniture Company. This final example, as well as a few other examples throughout the chapter, is presented using Microsoft Visio, which shows how many data modeling tools represent data models.

Chapter 3 ("The Enhanced E-R Model") presents advanced concepts in E-R modeling; these additional modeling features are often required to cope with the increasingly complex business environment encountered in organizations today.

The most important modeling construct incorporated in the enhanced entity-relationship (EER) diagram is supertype/subtype relationships. This facility allows us to model a general entity type (called a supertype) and then subdivide it into several specialized entity types called subtypes. For example, sports cars and sedans are subtypes of automobiles. We introduce a simple notation for representing supertype/subtype relationships and several refinements. We also introduce generalization and specialization as two contrasting techniques for identifying supertype/subtype relationships. Supertype/subtype notation is necessary for the increasingly popular universal data model, which is motivated and explained in Chapter 3.

The concept of patterns has become a central element of many information systems development methodologies. The notion is that there are reusable component designs that can be combined and tailored to meet new information system requests. In the database world, these patterns are called universal data models, prepackaged data models, or logical data models. These patterns can be purchased or may be inherent in a commercial off-the-shelf package, such as an ERP or CRM application. Increasingly, it is from these patterns that new databases are designed. In Chapter 3, we describe the usefulness of such patterns and outline a modification of the database development process when such patterns are the starting point. Universal industry or business function data models extensively use the extended entity-relationship diagramming notations introduced in this chapter.

The conceptual data modeling concepts presented in the two chapters in Part II provide the foundation for your career in database analysis and design. As a database analyst, you will be expected to apply the E-R notation in modeling user requirements for data and information.

CHAPTER 2

Modeling Data in the Organization

LEARNING OBJECTIVES

After studying this chapter, you should be able to:

- Concisely define each of the following key terms: **entity-relationship model (E-R model), entity-relationship diagram (E-R diagram, or ERD), business rule, entity, entity type, entity instance, strong entity type, weak entity type, identifying owner, identifying relationship, attribute, required attribute, optional attribute, composite attribute, simple (or atomic) attribute, multivalued attribute, derived attribute, identifier, composite identifier, relationship type, relationship instance, associative entity, degree, unary relationship, binary relationship, ternary relationship, cardinality constraint, minimum cardinality, maximum cardinality,** and **time stamp.**
- State reasons why many system developers believe that data modeling is the most important part of the systems development process.
- Write good names and definitions for entities, relationships, and attributes.
- Distinguish unary, binary, and ternary relationships and give a common example of each.
- Model each of the following constructs in an E-R diagram: composite attribute, multivalued attribute, derived attribute, associative entity, identifying relationship, and minimum and maximum cardinality constraints.
- Draw an E-R diagram to represent common business situations.
- Convert a many-to-many relationship to an associative entity type.
- Model simple time-dependent data using time stamps and relationships in an E-R diagram.

Visit www.pearsonhighered.com/ hoffer to view the accompanying video for this chapter.

INTRODUCTION

You have already been introduced to modeling data and the entity-relationship (E-R) data model through simplified examples in Chapter 1. (You may want to review, for example, the E-R models in Figures 1-3 and 1-4.) In this chapter, we formalize data modeling based on the powerful concept of business rules and describe the E-R data model in detail. This chapter begins your journey of learning how to design and use databases. It is exciting to create information systems that run organizations and help people do their jobs well.

Business rules, the foundation of data models, are derived from policies, procedures, events, functions, and other business objects, and they state constraints on the organization. Business rules represent the language and fundamental structure of an organization (Hay, 2003). Business rules formalize the understanding of the organization by organization owners, managers, and leaders with that of information systems architects.

Business rules are important in data modeling because they govern how data are handled and stored. Examples of basic business rules are data names and definitions. This chapter explains guidelines for the clear naming and definition of data objects in a business. In terms of conceptual data modeling, names and definitions must be provided for the main data objects: entity types (e.g., Customer), attributes (Customer Name), and relationships (Customer Places Orders). Other business rules may state constraints on these data objects. These constraints can be captured in a data model, such as an entity-relationship diagram, and associated documentation. Additional business rules govern the people, places, events, processes, networks, and objectives of the organization, which are all linked to the data requirements through other system documentation.

After decades of use, the E-R model remains the mainstream approach for conceptual data modeling. Its popularity stems from factors such as relative ease of use, widespread computer-aided software engineering (CASE) tool support, and the belief that entities and relationships are natural modeling concepts in the real world.

The E-R model is most used as a tool for communications between database designers and end users during the analysis phase of database development (described in Chapter 1). The E-R model is used to construct a conceptual data model, which is a representation of the structure and constraints of a database that is independent of software (such as a database management system).

Some authors introduce terms and concepts peculiar to the relational data model when discussing E-R modeling; the relational data model is the basis for most database management systems in use today. In particular, they recommend that the E-R model be completely normalized, with full resolution of primary and foreign keys. However, we believe that this forces a premature commitment to the relational data model. In today's database environment, the database may be implemented with object-oriented technology or with a mixture of object-oriented and relational technology. Therefore, we defer discussion of normalization concepts to Chapter 4.

The E-R model continues to evolve, but unfortunately there is not yet a standard notation for E-R modeling. Song et al. (1995) present a side-by-side comparison of 10 different E-R modeling notations, explaining the major advantages and disadvantages of each approach. Because data modeling software tools are now commonly used by professional data modelers, we adopt for use in this text a variation of the notation used in professional modeling tools.

In an actual work environment, you may not have to develop a data model from scratch. Because of the increased acceptance of packaged software (for example, enterprise resource planning with a predefined data model) and purchased business area or industry data models (which we discuss in Chapter 3), your job of data modeling has a jump start. This is good because such components and patterns give you a starting point based on generally accepted practices. However, your job is not done for several reasons:

1. There are still many times when a new, custom-built application is being developed along with the associated database. The business rules for the business area supported by this application need to be modeled.
2. Purchased applications and data models need to be customized for your particular setting. Predefined data models tend to be very extensive and complex; hence, they require significant data modeling skill to tailor the models to be effective and efficient in a given organization. Although this effort can be much faster, thorough, and accurate than starting from scratch, the ability to understand a particular organization to match the data model to its business rules is an essential task.

In this chapter, we present the main features of E-R modeling, using common notation and conventions. We begin with a sample E-R diagram, including the basic constructs of the E-R model—entities, attributes, and relationships—and then we introduce the concept of business rules, which is the foundation for all the data modeling constructs. We define three types of entities that are common in E-R modeling: strong entities, weak entities, and associative; a few more entity types are defined in Chapter 3. We also define several important types of attributes, including required and optional attributes, single- and multivalued attributes, derived attributes, and composite attributes. We then introduce three important concepts associated with relationships: the degree of a relationship, the cardinality of a relationship, and participation constraints in a relationship. We conclude with an extended example of an E-R diagram for Pine Valley Furniture Company.

THE E-R MODEL: AN OVERVIEW

An **entity-relationship model (E-R model)** is a detailed, logical representation of the data for an organization or for a business area. The E-R model is expressed in terms of entities in the business environment, the relationships (or associations) among those entities, and the attributes (or properties) of both the entities and their relationships. An E-R model is normally expressed as an **entity-relationship diagram (E-R diagram, or ERD)**, which is a graphical representation of an E-R model.

Entity-relationship model (E-R model)

A logical representation of the data for an organization or for a business area, using entities for categories of data and relationships for associations between entities.

Entity-relationship diagram (E-R diagram, or ERD)

A graphical representation of an entity-relationship model.

Sample E-R Diagram

To jump-start your understanding of E-R diagrams, Figure 2-1 presents a simplified E-R diagram for a small furniture manufacturing company, Pine Valley Furniture Company. (This figure, which does not include attributes, is often called an *enterprise data model*,

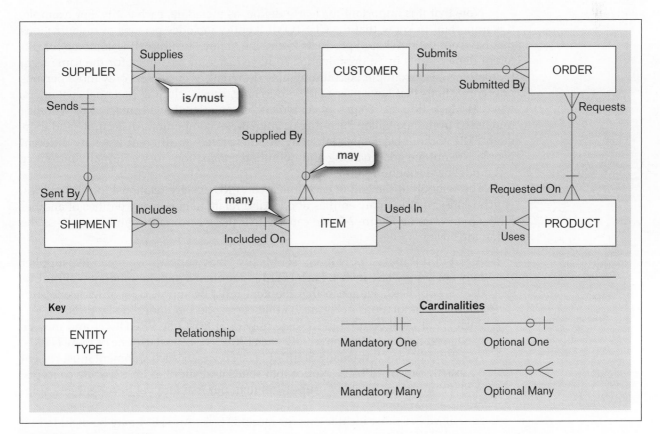

FIGURE 2-1   Sample E-R diagram

which we introduced Chapter 1.) A number of suppliers supply and ship different items to Pine Valley Furniture. The items are assembled into products that are sold to customers who order the products. Each customer order may include one or more lines corresponding to the products appearing on that order.

The diagram in Figure 2-1 shows the entities and relationships for this company. (Attributes are omitted to simplify the diagram for now.) Entities (the objects of the organization) are represented by the rectangle symbol, whereas relationships between entities are represented by lines connecting the related entities. The entities in Figure 2-1 include the following:

CUSTOMER	A person or an organization that has ordered or might order products. *Example*: L. L. Fish Furniture.
PRODUCT	A type of furniture made by Pine Valley Furniture that may be ordered by customers. Note that a product is not a specific bookcase, because individual bookcases do not need to be tracked. *Example*: A 6-foot, 5-shelf, oak bookcase called O600.
ORDER	The transaction associated with the sale of one or more products to a customer and identified by a transaction number from sales or accounting. *Example*: The event of L. L. Fish buying one product O600 and four products O623 on September 10, 2010.
ITEM	A type of component that goes into making one or more products and can be supplied by one or more suppliers. *Example*: A 4-inch ball-bearing caster called I-27–4375.
SUPPLIER	Another company that may provide items to Pine Valley Furniture. *Example*: Sure Fasteners, Inc.
SHIPMENT	The transaction associated with items received in the same package by Pine Valley Furniture from a supplier. All items in a shipment appear on one bill-of-lading document. *Example*: The receipt of 300 I-27-4375 and 200 I-27-4380 items from Sure Fasteners, Inc., on September 9, 2010.

Note that it is important to clearly define, as metadata, each entity. For example, it is important to know that the CUSTOMER entity includes persons or organizations that have not yet purchased products from Pine Valley Furniture. It is common for different departments in an organization to have different meanings for the same term (homonyms). For example, Accounting may designate as customers only those persons or organizations that have ever made a purchase, thus excluding potential customers, whereas Marketing designates as customers anyone they have contacted or who has purchased from Pine Valley Furniture or any known competitor. An accurate and thorough ERD without clear metadata may be interpreted in different ways by different people. We outline good naming and definition conventions as we formally introduce E-R modeling throughout this chapter.

The symbols at the end of each line on an ERD specify relationship cardinalities, which represent how many entities of one kind relate to how many entities of another kind. On examining Figure 2-1, we can see that these cardinality symbols express the following business rules:

1. A SUPPLIER <u>may</u> supply <u>many</u> ITEMs (by "may supply," we mean the supplier may not supply any items). Each ITEM <u>is</u> supplied by any number of SUPPLIERs (by "is supplied," we mean that the item <u>must</u> be supplied by at least one supplier). See annotations in Figure 2-1 that correspond to underlined words.
2. Each ITEM must be used in the assembly of at least one PRODUCT and may be used in many products. Conversely, each PRODUCT must use one or more ITEMs.
3. A SUPPLIER may send many SHIPMENTs. However, each shipment must be sent by exactly one SUPPLIER. Notice that sends and supplies are separate concepts. A SUPPLIER may be able to supply an item but may not yet have sent any shipments of that item.
4. A SHIPMENT must include one (or more) ITEMs. An ITEM may be included on several SHIPMENTs.

5. A CUSTOMER may submit any number of ORDERs. However, each ORDER must be submitted by exactly one CUSTOMER. Given that a CUSTOMER may not have submitted any ORDERs, some CUSTOMERs must be potential, inactive, or some other customer possibly without any related ORDERs.

6. An ORDER must request one (or more) PRODUCTs. A given PRODUCT may not be requested on any ORDER or may be requested on one or more orders.

There are actually two business rules for each relationship, one for each direction from one entity to the other. Note that each of these business rules roughly follows a certain grammar:

<entity> <minimum cardinality> <relationship> <maximum cardinality> <entity>

For example, rule 5 is

<CUSTOMER> <may> <Submit> <any number> <ORDER>

This grammar gives you a standard way to put each relationship into a natural English business rule statement.

E-R Model Notation

The notation we use for E-R diagrams is shown in Figure 2-2. As indicated in the previous section, there is no industry-standard notation (in fact, you saw a slightly simpler

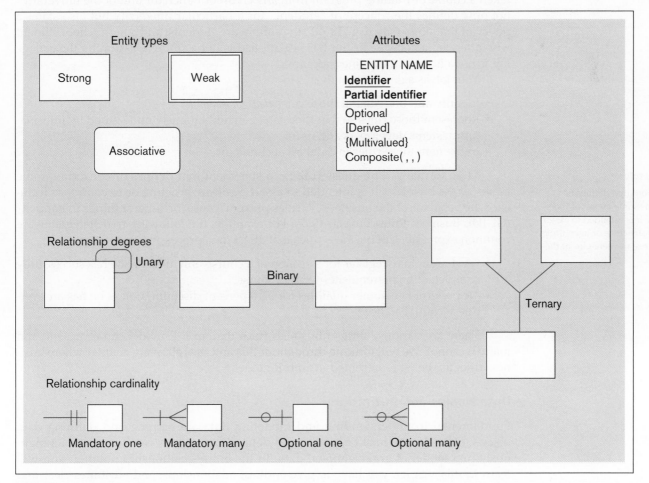

FIGURE 2-2   Basic E-R notation

notation in Chapter 1). The notation in Figure 2-2 combines most of the desirable features of the different notations that are commonly used in E-R drawing tools today and also allows us to model accurately most situations that are encountered in practice. We introduce additional notation for enhanced entity-relationship models (including class-subclass relationships) in Chapter 3.

In many situations, however, a simpler E-R notation is sufficient. Most drawing tools, either stand-alone ones such as Microsoft Visio or SmartDraw (which we use in the video associated with this chapter) or those in CASE tools such as Oracle Designer, CA ERwin, or PowerDesigner, do not show all the entity and attribute types we use. It is important to note that any notation requires special annotations, not always present in a diagramming tool, to show all the business rules of the organizational situation you are modeling. We will use the Visio notation for a few examples throughout the chapter and at the end of the chapter so that you can see the differences.

MODELING THE RULES OF THE ORGANIZATION

Now that you have an example of a data model in mind, let's step back and consider more generally what a data model is representing. We will see in this and the next chapter how to use data models, in particular the entity-relationship notation, to document rules and policies of an organization. *In fact, documenting rules and policies of an organization that govern data is exactly what data modeling is all about.* Business rules and policies govern creating, updating, and removing data in an information processing and storage system; thus, they must be described along with the data to which they are related. For example, the policy "every student in the university must have a faculty adviser" forces data (in a database) about each student to be associated with data about some student adviser. Also, the statement "a student is any person who has applied for admission or taken a course or training program from any credit or noncredit unit of the university" not only defines the concept of "student" for a particular university but also states a policy of that university (e.g., implicitly, alumni are students, and a high school student who attended a college fair but has not applied is not a student, assuming the college fair is not a noncredit training program).

Your job as a database analyst is to

- Identify and understand those rules *that govern data*
- Represent those rules so that they can be unambiguously understood by information systems developers and users
- Implement those rules in database technology

Business rule

A statement that defines or constrains some aspect of the business. It is intended to assert business structure or to control or influence the behavior of the business.

More formally, a **business rule** is "a statement that defines or constrains some aspect of the business. It is intended to assert business structure or to control or influence the behavior of the business . . . rules prevent, cause, or suggest things to happen" (GUIDE Business Rules Project, 1997). For example, the following two statements are common expressions of business rules that affect data processing and storage:

- "A student may register for a section of a course only if he or she has successfully completed the prerequisites for that course."
- "A preferred customer qualifies for a 10 percent discount, unless he has an overdue account balance."

There are various kinds of business rules that an E-R model can represent, and many it cannot. We will indicate throughout this and the following chapter where business rules are being represented in an E-R model.

Data Names and Definitions

Fundamental to understanding and modeling data are naming and defining data objects. Data objects must be named and defined before they can be used unambiguously in a model of organizational data. In the entity-relationship notation you will learn in this chapter, you have to give entities, relationships, and attributes clear and distinct names and definitions.

DATA NAMES   We will provide specific guidelines for naming entities, relationships, and attributes as we develop the entity-relationship data model, but there are some general guidelines about naming any data object. Data names should (Salin, 1990; ISO/IEC, 2005)

- *Relate to business, not technical (hardware or software), characteristics;*   so, Customer is a good name, but File10, Bit7, and Payroll Report Sort Key are not good names.
- *Be meaningful,*   almost to the point of being self-documenting (i.e., the definition will refine and explain the name without having to state the essence of the object's meaning); you should avoid using generic words such as *has, is, person,* or *it.*
- *Be unique,*   from the name used for every other distinct data object; words should be included in a data name if they distinguish the data object from other similar data objects (e.g., Home Address versus Campus Address).
- *Be readable,*   so that the name is structured as the concept would most naturally be said (e.g., Grade Point Average is a good name, whereas Average Grade Relative To A, although possibly accurate, is an awkward name).
- *Be composed of words taken from an approved list;*   each organization often chooses a vocabulary from which significant words in data names must be chosen (e.g., maximum is preferred, never upper limit, ceiling, or highest); alternative, or alias names, also can be used as can approved abbreviations (e.g., CUST for CUSTOMER), and you may be encouraged to use the abbreviations so that data names are short enough to meet maximum length limits of database technology.
- *Be repeatable,*   meaning that different people or the same person at different times should develop exactly or almost the same name; this often means that there is a standard hierarchy or pattern for names (e.g., the birth date of a student would be Student Birth Date and the birth date of an employee would be Employee Birth Date).
- *Follow a standard syntax,*   meaning that the parts of the name should follow a standard arrangement adopted by the organization.

Salin (1990) suggests that you develop data names by

1. Preparing a definition of the data. (We talk about definitions next.)
2. Removing insignificant or illegal words (words not on the approved list for names); note that the presence of AND and OR in the definition may imply that two or more data objects are combined, and you may want to separate the objects and assign different names.
3. Arranging the words in a meaningful, repeatable way.
4. Assigning a standard abbreviation for each word.
5. Determining whether the name already exists, and if so, adding other qualifiers that make the name unique.

We will see examples of good data names as we develop a data modeling notation in this chapter.

DATA DEFINITIONS   A definition (sometimes called a *structural assertion*) is considered a type of business rule (GUIDE Business Rules Project, 1997). A definition is an explanation of a concept or association between concepts. Examples of concepts are *course, section, rental car, flight, reservation,* and *passenger.* A definition can relate several concepts, such as:

- "A <u>course</u> is a module of instruction in a particular subject area." This definition associates two concepts: *module of instruction* and *subject area.* We assume that these are common terms that do not need to be further defined.

GOOD DATA DEFINITIONS   We will illustrate good definitions for entities, relationships, and attributes as we develop the entity-relationship notation in this and the next chapters. There are, however, some general guidelines to follow (Aranow, 1989; ISO/IEC, 2004):

- Definitions (and all other types of business rules) are gathered from the same sources as all requirements for information systems. Thus, systems and data analysts should be looking for data objects and their definitions as these sources of information systems requirements are studied.
- Definitions will usually be accompanied by diagrams, such as entity-relationship diagrams. The definition does not need to repeat what is shown on the diagram but rather supplement the diagram.
- Definitions will be stated in the singular and explain what the data element is, not what it is not. A definition will use commonly understood terms and abbreviations and stand alone in its meaning and not embed other definitions within it. It should be concise and concentrate on the essential meaning of the data, but it may also state such characteristics of a data object as
  - Subtleties
  - Special or exceptional conditions
  - Examples
  - Where, when, and how the data are created or calculated in the organization
  - Whether the data are static or change over time
  - Whether the data are singular or plural in their atomic form
  - Who determines the value for the data
  - Who owns the data (i.e., who controls the definition and usage)
  - Whether the data are optional or whether empty (what we will call null) values are allowed
  - Whether the data can be broken down into more atomic parts or are often combined with other data into some more composite or aggregate form

  If not included in a data definition, these characteristics need to be documented elsewhere, where other metadata are stored.
- A data object should not be added to a data model, such as an entity-relationship diagram, until after it has been carefully defined (and named) and there is agreement on this definition. But expect the definition of the data to change once you place the object on the diagram because the process of developing a data model tests your understanding of the meaning of data. (In other words, *modeling data is an iterative process*.)

There is an unattributed phrase in data modeling that highlights the importance of good data definitions: "The person who controls the meaning of data controls the data." It might seem that obtaining concurrence in an organization on the definitions to be used for the various terms and facts should be relatively easy. However, this is usually far from the case. In fact, it is likely to be one of the most difficult challenges you will face in data modeling or, for that matter, in any other endeavor. It is not unusual for an organization to have multiple definitions (perhaps a dozen or more) for common terms such as *customer* or *order*.

To illustrate the problems inherent in developing definitions, consider a data object of Student found in a typical university. A sample definition for Student is "a person who has been admitted to the school and who has registered for at least one course during the past year." This definition is certain to be challenged, because it is probably too narrow. A person who is a student typically proceeds through several stages in relationship with the school, such as the following:

1. Prospect—some formal contact, indicating an interest in the school
2. Applicant—applies for admission
3. Admitted applicant—admitted to the school and perhaps to a degree program
4. Matriculated student—registers for at least one course
5. Continuing student—registers for courses on an ongoing basis (no substantial gaps)
6. Former student—fails to register for courses during some stipulated period (now may reapply)
7. Graduate—satisfactorily completes some degree program (now may apply for another program)

Imagine the difficulty of obtaining consensus on a single definition in this situation! It would seem you might consider three alternatives:

1. *Use multiple definitions to cover the various situations.* This is likely to be highly confusing if there is only one entity type, so this approach is not recommended (multiple definitions are not good definitions).
2. *Use a very general definition that will cover most situations.* This approach may necessitate adding additional data about students to record a given student's actual status.
3. *Consider using multiple, related data objects for Student.* For example, we could create a general entity type for Student and then other specific entity types for kinds of students with unique characteristics. We describe the conditions that suggest this approach in Chapter 3.

MODELING ENTITIES AND ATTRIBUTES

The basic constructs of the E-R model are entities, relationships, and attributes. As shown in Figure 2-2, the model allows numerous variations for each of these constructs. The richness of the E-R model allows designers to model real-world situations accurately and expressively, which helps account for the popularity of the model.

Entities

An **entity** is a person, a place, an object, an event, or a concept in the user environment about which the organization wishes to maintain data. Thus, an entity has a noun name. Some examples of each of these *kinds* of entities follow:

Person:	EMPLOYEE, STUDENT, PATIENT
Place:	STORE, WAREHOUSE, STATE
Object:	MACHINE, BUILDING, AUTOMOBILE
Event:	SALE, REGISTRATION, RENEWAL
Concept:	ACCOUNT, COURSE, WORK CENTER

Entity
A person, a place, an object, an event, or a concept in the user environment about which the organization wishes to maintain data.

ENTITY TYPE VERSUS ENTITY INSTANCE There is an important distinction between entity types and entity instances. An **entity type** is a collection of entities that share common properties or characteristics. Each entity type in an E-R model is given a name. Because the name represents a collection (or set) of items, it is always singular. We use capital letters for names of entity type(s). In an E-R diagram, the entity name is placed inside the box representing the entity type (see Figure 2-1).

Entity type
A collection of entities that share common properties or characteristics.

An **entity instance** is a single occurrence of an entity type. Figure 2-3 illustrates the distinction between an entity type and two of its instances. An entity type is described just once (using metadata) in a database, whereas many instances of that entity type may

Entity instance
A single occurrence of an entity type.

Entity type: EMPLOYEE

Attributes	Attribute Data Type	Example Instance	Example Instance
Employee Number	CHAR (10)	642-17-8360	534-10-1971
Name	CHAR (25)	Michelle Brady	David Johnson
Address	CHAR (30)	100 Pacific Avenue	450 Redwood Drive
City	CHAR (20)	San Francisco	Redwood City
State	CHAR (2)	CA	CA
Zip Code	CHAR (9)	98173	97142
Date Hired	DATE	03-21-1992	08-16-1994
Birth Date	DATE	06-19-1968	09-04-1975

FIGURE 2-3 Entity type EMPLOYEE with two instances

be represented by data stored in the database. For example, there is one EMPLOYEE entity type in most organizations, but there may be hundreds (or even thousands) of instances of this entity type stored in the database. We often use the single term *entity* rather than *entity instance* when the meaning is clear from the context of our discussion.

ENTITY TYPE VERSUS SYSTEM INPUT, OUTPUT, OR USER A common mistake people make when they are learning to draw E-R diagrams, especially if they are already familiar with data process modeling (such as data flow diagramming), is to confuse data entities with other elements of an overall information systems model. A simple rule to avoid such confusion is that *a true data entity will have many possible instances, each with a distinguishing characteristic, as well as one or more other descriptive pieces of data.*

Consider Figure 2-4a, which might be drawn to represent a database needed for a college sorority's expense system. (For simplicity in this and some other figures, we show only one name for a relationship.) In this situation, the sorority treasurer manages accounts, receives expense reports, and records expense transactions against each account. However, do we need to keep track of data about the Treasurer (the TREASURER entity type) and her supervision of accounts (the Manages relationship) and receipt of reports (the Receives relationship)? The Treasurer is the person entering data about accounts and expenses and receiving expense reports. That is, she is a user of the database. Because there is only one Treasurer, TREASURER data do not need to be kept. Further, is the EXPENSE REPORT entity necessary? Because an expense report is computed from expense transactions and account balances, it is the result of extracting data from the database and received by the Treasurer. Even though there will be multiple instances of expense reports given to the Treasurer over time, data needed to compute the report contents each time are already represented by the ACCOUNT and EXPENSE entity types.

Another key to understanding why the ERD in Figure 2-4a might be in error is the nature of the *relationship names*, Receives and Summarizes. These relationship names refer to business activities that transfer or translate data, not to simply the association of one kind of data with another kind of data. The simple E-R diagram in Figure 2-4b shows entities and a relationship that would be sufficient to handle the sorority expense system as described here. See Problem and Exercise 21 for a variation on this situation.

FIGURE 2-4 **Example of inappropriate entities (a) System user (Treasurer) and output (Expense Report) shown as entities**

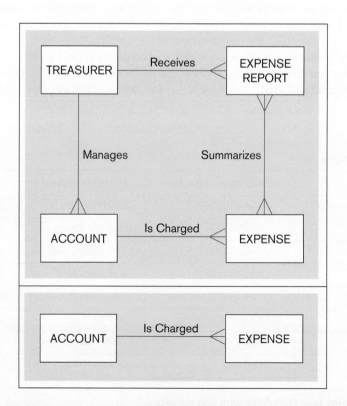

(b) E-R diagram with only the necessary entities

STRONG VERSUS WEAK ENTITY TYPES   Most of the basic entity types to identify in an organization are classified as strong entity types. A **strong entity type** is one that exists independently of other entity types. (Some data modeling software, in fact, use the term *independent entity*.) Examples include STUDENT, EMPLOYEE, AUTOMOBILE, and COURSE. Instances of a strong entity type always have a unique characteristic (called an *identifier*)—that is, an attribute or a combination of attributes that uniquely distinguish each occurrence of that entity.

In contrast, a **weak entity type** is an entity type whose existence depends on some other entity type. (Some data modeling software, in fact, use the term *dependent entity*.) A weak entity type has no business meaning in an E-R diagram without the entity on which it depends. The entity type on which the weak entity type depends is called the **identifying owner** (or simply *owner* for short). A weak entity type does not typically have its own identifier. Generally, on an E-R diagram, a weak entity type has an attribute that serves as a *partial* identifier. During a later design stage (described in Chapter 4 a full identifier will be formed for the weak entity by combining the partial identifier with the identifier of its owner or by creating a surrogate identifier attribute.

An example of a weak entity type with an identifying relationship is shown in Figure 2-5. EMPLOYEE is a strong entity type with identifier Employee ID (we note the identifier attribute by underlining it). DEPENDENT is a weak entity type, as indicated by the double-lined rectangle. The relationship between a weak entity type and its owner is called an **identifying relationship.** In Figure 2-5, Carries is the identifying relationship (indicated by the double line). The attribute Dependent Name serves as a *partial* identifier. (Dependent Name is a composite attribute that can be broken into component parts, as we describe later.) We use a double underline to indicate a partial identifier. During a later design stage, Dependent Name will be combined with Employee ID (the identifier of the owner) to form a full identifier for DEPENDENT. Some additional examples of strong and weak entity pairs are: BOOK–BOOK COPY, PRODUCT–SERIAL PRODUCT, and COURSE–COURSE OFFERING.

NAMING AND DEFINING ENTITY TYPES   In addition to the general guidelines for naming and defining data objects, there are a few special guidelines for *naming* entity types, which follow:

- An entity type name is a *singular noun* (such as CUSTOMER, STUDENT, or AUTOMOBILE); an entity is a person, a place, an object, an event, or a concept, and the name is for the entity type, which represents a set of entity instances (i.e., STUDENT represents students Hank Finley, Jean Krebs, and so forth). It is common to also specify the plural form (possibly in a CASE tool repository accompanying the E-R diagram), because sometimes the E-R diagram is read best by using plurals. For example, in Figure 2-1, we would say that a SUPPLIER may supply ITEMs. Because plurals are not always formed by adding an *s* to the singular noun, it is best to document the exact plural form.

Strong entity type

An entity that exists independently of other entity types.

Weak entity type

An entity type whose existence depends on some other entity type.

Identifying owner

The entity type on which the weak entity type depends.

Identifying relationship

The relationship between a weak entity type and its owner.

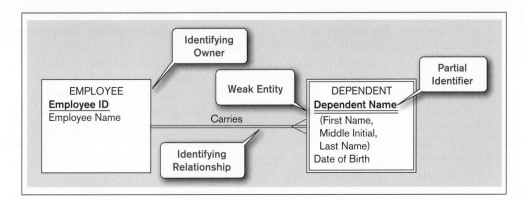

FIGURE 2-5   Example of a weak entity and its identifying relationship

- An entity type name should be *specific to the organization*. Thus, one organization may use the entity type name CUSTOMER, and another organization may use the entity type name CLIENT (this is one task, for example, done to customize a purchased data model). The name should be descriptive for everyone in the organization and distinct from all other entity type names within that organization. For example, a PURCHASE ORDER for orders placed with suppliers is distinct from CUSTOMER ORDER for orders placed with a company by its customers. Both of these entity types cannot be named ORDER.
- An entity type name should be *concise*, using as few words as possible. For example, in a university database, an entity type REGISTRATION for the event of a student registering for a class is probably a sufficient name for this entity type; STUDENT REGISTRATION FOR CLASS, although precise, is probably too wordy because the reader will understand REGISTRATION from its use with other entity types.
- An *abbreviation*, or a *short name*, should be specified for each entity type name, and the abbreviation may be sufficient to use in the E-R diagram; abbreviations must follow all of the same rules as do the full entity names.
- *Event entity types* should be named for the result of the event, not the activity or process of the event. For example, the event of a project manager assigning an employee to work on a project results in an ASSIGNMENT, and the event of a student contacting his or her faculty adviser seeking some information is a CONTACT.
- The *name* used for the same entity type *should be the same* on all E-R diagrams on which the entity type appears. Thus, as well as being specific to the organization, the name used for an entity type should be a standard, adopted by the organization for all references to the same kind of data. However, some entity types will have aliases, or alternative names, which are synonyms used in different parts of the organization. For example, the entity type ITEM may have aliases of MATERIAL (for production) and DRAWING (for engineering). Aliases are specified in documentation about the database, such as the repository of a CASE tool.

There are also some specific guidelines for *defining* entity types, which follow:

- *An entity type definition usually starts with* "An X is. . . ." This is the most direct and clear way to state the meaning of an entity type.
- An entity type definition should *include a statement of what the unique characteristic is for each instance of the entity type*. In many cases, stating the identifier for an entity type helps convey the meaning of the entity. An example for Figure 2-4b is "An expense is a payment for the purchase of some good or service. An expense is identified by a journal entry number."
- An entity type definition should make it clear what *entity instances are included and not included* in the entity type; often, it is necessary to list the kinds of entities that are excluded. For example, "A customer is a person or organization that has placed an order for a product from us or one that we have contacted to advertise or promote our products. A customer does not include persons or organizations that buy our products only through our customers, distributors, or agents."
- An entity type definition often includes a description of *when an instance of the entity type is created and deleted*. For example, in the previous bullet point, a customer instance is implicitly created when the person or organization places its first order; because this definition does not specify otherwise, implicitly a customer instance is never deleted, or it is deleted based on general rules that are specified about the purging of data from the database. A statement about when to delete an entity instance is sometimes referred to as the retention of the entity type. A possible deletion statement for a customer entity type definition might be "A customer ceases to be a customer if it has not placed an order for more than three years."
- For some entity types, the definition must specify *when an instance might change into an instance of another entity type*. For example, consider the situation of a construction company for which bids accepted by potential customers become contracts. In this case, a bid might be defined by "A bid is a legal offer by our organization to do work for a customer. A bid is created when an officer of our

company signs the bid document; a bid becomes an instance of contract when we receive a copy of the bid signed by an officer of the customer." This definition is also a good example to note how one definition can use other entity type names (in this case, the definition of bid uses the entity type name CUSTOMER).

- For some entity types, the definition must specify *what history is to be kept about instances of the entity type*. For example, the characteristics of an ITEM in Figure 2-1 may change over time, and we may need to keep a complete history of the individual values and when they were in effect. As we will see in some examples later, such statements about keeping history may have ramifications about how we represent the entity type on an E-R diagram and eventually how we store data for the entity instances.

Attributes

Each entity type has a set of attributes associated with it. An **attribute** is a property or characteristic of an entity type that is of interest to the organization. (Later, we will see that some types of relationships may also have attributes.) Thus, an attribute has a noun name. Following are some typical entity types and their associated attributes:

Attribute

A property or characteristic of an entity or relationship type that is of interest to the organization.

STUDENT	Student ID, Student Name, Home Address, Phone Number, Major
AUTOMOBILE	Vehicle ID, Color, Weight, Horsepower
EMPLOYEE	Employee ID, Employee Name, Payroll Address, Skill

In naming attributes, we use an initial capital letter followed by lowercase letters. If an attribute name consists of more than one word, we use a space between the words and we start each word with a capital letter, for example, Employee Name or Student Home Address. In E-R diagrams, we represent an attribute by placing its name in the entity it describes. Attributes may also be associated with relationships, as described later. Note that an attribute is associated with exactly one entity or relationship.

Notice in Figure 2-5 that all of the attributes of DEPENDENT are characteristics only of an employee's dependent, not characteristics of an employee. In traditional E-R notation, an entity type (not just weak entities but any entity) does not include attributes of entities to which it is related (what might be called foreign attributes). For example, DEPENDENT does not include any attribute that indicates to which employee this dependent is associated. This nonredundant feature of the E-R data model is consistent with the shared data property of databases. Because of relationships, which we discuss shortly, someone accessing data from a database will be able to associate attributes from related entities (e.g., show on a display screen a Dependent Name and the associated Employee Name).

REQUIRED VERSUS OPTIONAL ATTRIBUTES Each entity (or instance of an entity type) potentially has a value associated with each of the attributes of that entity type. An attribute that must be present for each entity instance is called a **required attribute**, whereas an attribute that may not have a value is called an **optional attribute**. For example, Figure 2-6 shows two STUDENT entities (instances) with their respective attribute values. The only optional attribute for STUDENT is Major. (Some students, specifically Melissa Kraft in this example, have not chosen a major yet; MIS would, of course, be a great career choice!) However, every student must, by the rules of the organization, have values for all the other attributes; *that is, we cannot store any data about a student in a STUDENT entity instance unless there are values for all the required attributes.* In various E-R diagramming notations, a symbol might appear in front of each attribute to indicate whether it is required (e.g., *) or optional (e.g., o), or required attributes will be in **boldface**, whereas optional attributes will be in normal font (the format we use in this text); in many cases, required or optional is indicated within supplemental documentation. In Chapter 3, when we consider entity supertypes and subtypes, we will see

Required attribute

An attribute that must have a value for every entity (or relationship) instance with which it is associated.

Optional attribute

An attribute that may not have a value for every entity (or relationship) instance with which it is associated.

FIGURE 2-6 Entity type
STUDENT with required and
optional attributes

Entity type: STUDENT				
Attributes	Attribute Data Type	Required or Optional	Example Instance	Example Instance
Student ID	CHAR (10)	Required	876-24-8217	822-24-4456
Student Name	CHAR (40)	Required	Michael Grant	Melissa Kraft
Home Address	CHAR (30)	Required	314 Baker St.	1422 Heft Ave
Home City	CHAR (20)	Required	Centerville	Miami
Home State	CHAR (2)	Required	OH	FL
Home Zip Code	CHAR (9)	Required	45459	33321
Major	CHAR (3)	Optional	MIS	

how sometimes optional attributes imply that there are different types of entities. (For example, we may want to consider students who have not declared a major as a subtype of the student entity type.) An attribute without a value is said to be null. Thus, each entity has an identifying attribute, which we discuss in a subsequent section, plus one or more other attributes. If you try to create an entity that has only an identifier, that entity is likely not legitimate. Such a data structure may simply hold a list of legal values for some attribute, which is better kept outside the database.

SIMPLE VERSUS COMPOSITE ATTRIBUTES   Some attributes can be broken down into meaningful component parts (detailed attributes). A common example is Name, which we saw in Figure 2-5; another is Address, which can usually be broken down into the following component attributes: Street Address, City, State, and Postal Code. A **composite attribute** is an attribute, such as Address, that has meaningful component parts, which are more detailed attributes. Figure 2-7 shows the notation that we use for composite attributes applied to this example. Most drawing tools do not have a notation for composite attributes, so you simply list all the component parts.

Composite attributes provide considerable flexibility to users, who can either refer to the composite attribute as a single unit or else refer to individual components of that attribute. Thus, for example, a user can either refer to Address or refer to one of its components, such as Street Address. The decision about whether to subdivide an attribute into its component parts depends on whether users will need to refer to those individual components, and hence, they have organizational meaning. Of course, the designer must always attempt to anticipate possible future usage patterns for the database.

A **simple (or atomic) attribute** is an attribute that cannot be broken down into smaller components that are meaningful for the organization. For example, all the attributes associated with AUTOMOBILE are simple: Vehicle ID, Color, Weight, and Horsepower.

Composite attribute

An attribute that has meaningful component parts (attributes).

Simple (or atomic) attribute

An attribute that cannot be broken down into smaller components that are meaningful to the organization.

FIGURE 2-7   A composite attribute

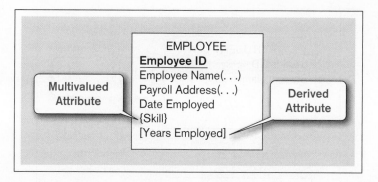

SINGLE-VALUED VERSUS MULTIVALUED ATTRIBUTES Figure 2-6 shows two entity instances with their respective attribute values. For each entity instance, each of the attributes in the figure has one value. It frequently happens that there is an attribute that may have more than one value for a given instance. For example, the EMPLOYEE entity type in Figure 2-8 has an attribute named Skill, whose values record the skill (or skills) for that employee. Of course, some employees may have more than one skill, such as PHP Programmer and C++ Programmer. A **multivalued attribute** is an attribute that may take on more than one value for a given entity (or relationship) instance. In this text, we indicate a multivalued attribute with curly brackets around the attribute name, as shown for the Skill attribute in the EMPLOYEE example in Figure 2-8. In Microsoft Visio, once an attribute is placed in an entity, you can edit that attribute (column), select the Collection tab, and choose one of the options. (Typically, MultiSet will be your choice, but one of the other options may be more appropriate for a given situation.) Other E-R diagramming tools may use an asterisk (*) after the attribute name, or you may have to use supplemental documentation to specify a multivalued attribute.

Multivalued and composite are different concepts, although beginner data modelers often confuse these terms. Skill, a multivalued attribute, may occur multiple times for each employee; Employee Name and Payroll Address are both likely composite attributes, each of which occurs once for each employee, but which have component, more atomic attributes, which are not shown in Figure 2-8 for simplicity. See Problem and Exercise 16 to review the concepts of composite and multivalued attributes.

STORED VERSUS DERIVED ATTRIBUTES Some attribute values that are of interest to users can be calculated or derived from other related attribute values that are stored in the database. For example, suppose that for an organization, the EMPLOYEE entity type has a Date Employed attribute. If users need to know how many years a person has been employed, that value can be calculated using Date Employed and today's date. A **derived attribute** is an attribute whose values can be calculated from related attribute values (plus possibly data not in the database, such as today's date, the current time, or a security code provided by a system user). We indicate a derived attribute in an E-R diagram by using square brackets around the attribute name, as shown in Figure 2-8 for the Years Employed attribute. Some E-R diagramming tools use a notation of a forward slash (/) in front of the attribute name to indicate that it is derived. (This notation is borrowed from UML for a virtual attribute.)

In some situations, the value of an attribute can be derived from attributes in related entities. For example, consider an invoice created for each customer at Pine Valley Furniture Company. Order Total would be an attribute of the INVOICE entity, which indicates the total dollar amount that is billed to the customer. The value of Order Total can be computed by summing the Extended Price values (unit price times quantity sold) for the various line items that are billed on the invoice. Formulas for computing values such as this are one type of business rule.

IDENTIFIER ATTRIBUTE An **identifier** is an attribute (or combination of attributes) whose value distinguishes individual instances of an entity type. That is, no two instances of the entity type may have the same value for the identifier attribute. The

Multivalued attribute
An attribute that may take on more than one value for a given entity (or relationship) instance.

Derived attribute
An attribute whose values can be calculated from related attribute values.

Identifier
An attribute (or combination of attributes) whose value distinguishes instances of an entity type.

FIGURE 2-9 Simple and
composite identifier attributes
(a) Simple identifier attribute

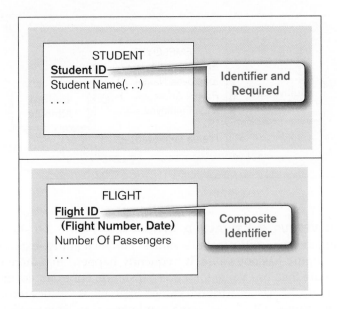

(b) Composite identifier attribute

identifier for the STUDENT entity type introduced earlier is Student ID, whereas the identifier for AUTOMOBILE is Vehicle ID. Notice that an attribute such as Student Name is not a candidate identifier, because many students may potentially have the same name, and students, like all people, can change their names. To be a candidate identifier, each entity instance must have a single value for the attribute and the attribute must be associated with the entity. We underline identifier names on the E-R diagram, as shown in the STUDENT entity type example in Figure 2-9a. To be an identifier, the attribute is also required (so the distinguishing value must exist), so an identifier is also in bold. Some E-R drawing software will place a symbol, called a stereotype, in front of the identifier (e.g., <<ID>> or <<PK>>).

For some entity types, there is no single (or atomic) attribute that can serve as the identifier (i.e., that will ensure uniqueness). However, two (or more) attributes used in combination may serve as the identifier. A **composite identifier** is an identifier that consists of a composite attribute. Figure 2-9b shows the entity FLIGHT with the composite identifier Flight ID. Flight ID in turn has component attributes Flight Number and Date. This combination is required to identify uniquely individual occurrences of FLIGHT. We use the convention that the composite attribute (Flight ID) is underlined to indicate it is the identifier, whereas the component attributes are not underlined. Some data modelers think of a composite identifier as "breaking a tie" created by a simple identifier. Even with Flight ID, a data modeler would ask a question, such as "Can two flights with the same number occur on the same date?" If so, yet another attribute is needed to form the composite identifier and to break the tie.

Some entities may have more than one candidate identifier. If there is more than one candidate identifier, the designer must choose one of them as the identifier. Bruce (1992) suggests the following criteria for selecting identifiers:

1. Choose an identifier that will not change its value over the life of each instance of the entity type. For example, the combination of Employee Name and Payroll Address (even if unique) would be a poor choice as an identifier for EMPLOYEE because the values of Employee Name and Payroll Address could easily change during an employee's term of employment.
2. Choose an identifier such that for each instance of the entity, the attribute is guaranteed to have valid values and not be null (or unknown). If the identifier is a composite attribute, such as Flight ID in Figure 2-9b, make sure that all parts of the identifier will have valid values.
3. Avoid the use of so-called intelligent identifiers (or keys), whose structure indicates classifications, locations, and so on. For example, the first two digits of an identifier value may indicate the warehouse location. Such codes are often changed as conditions change, which renders the identifier values invalid.

Composite identifier

An identifier that consists
of a composite attribute.

4. Consider substituting single-attribute surrogate identifiers for large composite identifiers. For example, an attribute called Game Number could be used for the entity type GAME instead of the combination of Home Team and Visiting Team.

NAMING AND DEFINING ATTRIBUTES In addition to the general guidelines for naming data objects, there are a few special guidelines for naming attributes, which follow:

- An attribute name is a *singular noun or noun phrase* (such as Customer ID, Age, Product Minimum Price, or Major). Attributes, which materialize as data values, are concepts or physical characteristics of entities. Concepts and physical characteristics are described by nouns.
- An attribute name should be *unique*. No two attributes of the same entity type may have the same name, and it is desirable, for clarity purposes, that no two attributes across all entity types have the same name.
- To make an attribute name unique and for clarity purposes, *each attribute name should follow a standard format*. For example, your university may establish Student GPA, as opposed to GPA of Student, as an example of the standard format for attribute naming. The format to be used will be established by each organization. A common format is [Entity type name { [Qualifier] }] Class, where [. . .] is an optional clause, and { . . . } indicates that the clause may repeat. *Entity type name* is the name of the entity with which the attribute is associated. *Class* is a phrase from a list of phrases defined by the organization that are the permissible characteristics or properties of entities (or abbreviations of these characteristics). For example, permissible values (and associated approved abbreviations) for Class might be Name (Nm), Identifier (ID), Date (Dt), or Amount (Amt). *Qualifier* is a phrase from a list of phrases defined by the organization that are used to place constraints on classes. Sometimes a qualifier is necessary. For example, Employee Birth Date and Employee Hire Date are two attributes of Employee that require one qualifier.
- *Similar attributes* of different entity types *should use the same qualifiers and classes*, as long as those are the names used in the organization. For example, the city of residence for faculty and students should be, respectively, Faculty Residence City Name and Student Residence City Name.

There are also some specific guidelines for defining attributes, which follow:

- An attribute definition states *what the attribute is and possibly why it is important*. The definition will often parallel the attribute's name; for example, Student Residence City Name could be defined as "The name of the city in which a student maintains his or her permanent residence."
- An attribute definition should make it clear *what is included and not included* in the attribute's value; for example, "Employee Monthly Salary Amount is the amount of money paid each month in the currency of the country of residence of the employee exclusive of any benefits, bonuses, reimbursements, or special payments."
- Any *aliases*, or alternative names, for the attribute can be specified in the definition or may be included elsewhere in documentation about the attribute, possibly stored in the repository of a CASE tool used to maintain data definitions.
- It may also be desirable to state in the definition *the source of values for the attribute*. Stating the source may make the meaning of the data clearer. For example, "Customer Standard Industrial Code is an indication of the type of business for the customer. Values for this code come from a standard set of values provided by the Federal Trade Commission and are found on a CD we purchase named SIC provided annually by the FTC."
- An attribute definition (or other specification in a CASE tool repository) also should indicate *if a value for the attribute is required or optional*. This business rule about an attribute is important for maintaining data integrity. For example, "Employee Department ID is the identifier of the department to which the employee is assigned. An employee may not be assigned to a department when hired (so this attribute is initially optional), but once an employee is assigned to a department, the employee must always be assigned to some department."

- An attribute definition (or other specification in a CASE tool repository) may also indicate *whether a value for the attribute may change* once a value is provided and before the entity instance is deleted. This business rule also controls data integrity. Nonintelligent identifiers may not change values over time. To assign a new nonintelligent identifier to an entity instance, that instance must first be deleted and then re-created.

- For a multivalued attribute, the attribute definition should indicate *the maximum and minimum number of occurrences of an attribute value for an entity instance*. For example, "Employee Skill Name is the name of a skill an employee possesses. Each employee must possess at least one skill, and an employee can choose to list at most 10 skills." The reason for a multivalued attribute may be that a history of the attribute needs to be kept. For example, "Employee Yearly Absent Days Number is the number of days in a calendar year the employee has been absent from work. An employee is considered absent if he or she works less than 50 percent of the scheduled hours in the day. A value for this attribute should be kept for each year in which the employee works for our company."

- An attribute definition may also indicate *any relationships that attribute has with other attributes*. For example, "Employee Vacation Days Number is the number of days of paid vacation for the employee. If the employee has a value of 'Exempt' for Employee Type, then the maximum value for Employee Vacation Days Number is determined by a formula involving the number of years of service for the employee."

MODELING RELATIONSHIPS

Relationships are the glue that holds together the various components of an E-R model. Intuitively, a *relationship* is an association representing an interaction among the instances of one or more entity types that is of interest to the organization. Thus, a relationship has a verb phrase name. Relationships and their characteristics (degree and cardinality) represent business rules, and usually relationships represent the most complex business rules shown in an ERD. In other words, this is where data modeling gets really interesting and fun, as well as crucial for controlling the integrity of a database.

To understand relationships more clearly, we must distinguish between relationship types and relationship instances. To illustrate, consider the entity types EMPLOYEE and COURSE, where COURSE represents training courses that may be taken by employees. To track courses that have been completed by particular employees, we define a relationship called Completes between the two entity types (see Figure 2-10a). This is a many-to-many relationship, because each employee may complete any number of courses (zero, one, or many courses), whereas a given course may be completed by any number of employees (nobody, one employee, many employees). For example, in Figure 2-10b, the employee Melton has completed three courses (C++, COBOL, and Perl). The SQL course has been completed by two employees (Celko and Gosling), and the Visual Basic course has not been completed by anyone.

In this example, there are two entity types (EMPLOYEE and COURSE) that participate in the relationship named Completes. In general, any number of entity types (from one to many) may participate in a relationship.

We frequently use in this and subsequent chapters the convention of a single verb phrase label to represent a relationship. Because relationships often occur due to an organizational event, entity instances are related because an action was taken; thus, a verb phrase is appropriate for the label. This verb phrase should be in the present tense and descriptive. There are, however, many ways to represent a relationship. Some data modelers prefer the format with two relationship names, one to name the relationship in each direction. One or two verb phrases have the same structural meaning, so you may use either format as long as the meaning of the relationship in each direction is clear.

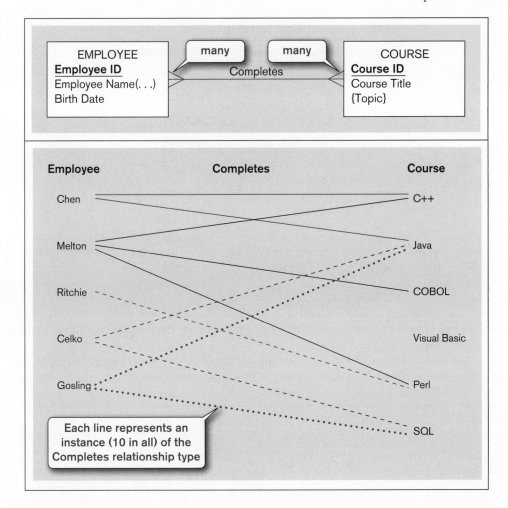

FIGURE 2-10 Relationship type
and instances
(a) Relationship type (Complete)

(b) Relationship instances

Basic Concepts and Definitions in Relationships

A **relationship type** is a meaningful association between (or among) entity types. The phrase *meaningful association* implies that the relationship allows us to answer questions that could not be answered given only the entity types. A relationship type is denoted by a line labeled with the name of the relationship, as in the example shown in Figure 2-10a, or with two names, as in Figure 2-1. We suggest you use a short, descriptive verb phrase that is meaningful to the user in naming the relationship. (We say more about naming and defining relationships later in this section.)

A **relationship instance** is an association between (or among) entity instances, where each relationship instance associates exactly one entity instance from each participating entity type (Elmasri and Navathe, 1994). For example, in Figure 2-10b, each of the 10 lines in the figure represents a relationship instance between one employee and one course, indicating that the employee has completed that course. For example, the line between Employee Ritchie to Course Perl is one relationship instance.

ATTRIBUTES ON RELATIONSHIPS It is probably obvious to you that entities have attributes, but attributes may be associated with a many-to-many (or one-to-one) relationship, too. For example, suppose the organization wishes to record the date (month and year) when an employee completes each course. This attribute is named Date Completed. For some sample data, see Table 2-1.

Where should the attribute Date Completed be placed on the E-R diagram? Referring to Figure 2-10a, you will notice that Date Completed has not been associated with either the EMPLOYEE or COURSE entity. That is because Date Completed is a property of the relationship Completes, rather than a property of either entity. In other words, for each instance of the relationship Completes, there is a value for Date

Relationship type

A meaningful association between (or among) entity types.

Relationship instance

An association between (or among) entity instances where each relationship instance associates exactly one entity instance from each participating entity type.

Part II • Database Analysis

TABLE 2-1 Instances Showing Date Completed

Employee Name	Course Title	Date Completed
Chen	C++	06/2009
Chen	Java	09/2009
Melton	C++	06/2009
Melton	COBOL	02/2010
Melton	SQL	03/2009
Ritchie	Perl	11/2009
Celko	Java	03/2009
Celko	SQL	03/2010
Gosling	Java	09/2009
Gosling	Perl	06/2009

Completed. One such instance (for example) shows that the employee named Melton completed the course titled C++ in 06/2009.

A revised version of the ERD for this example is shown in Figure 2-11a. In this diagram, the attribute Date Completed is in a rectangle connected to the Completes

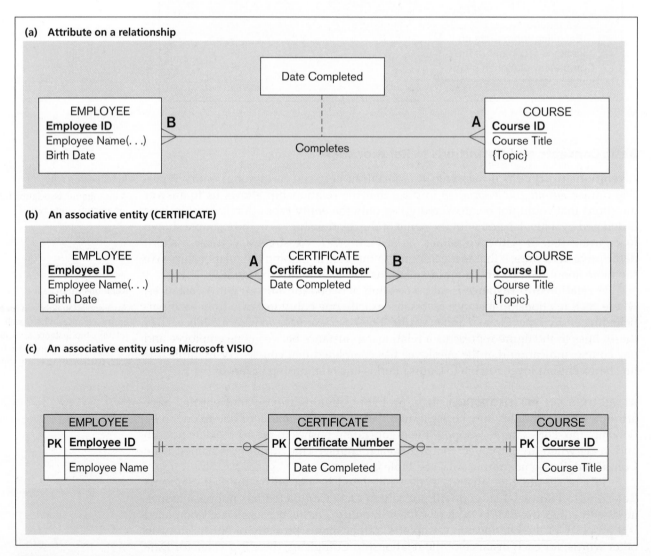

FIGURE 2-11 An associative entity

relationship line. Other attributes might be added to this relationship if appropriate, such as Course Grade, Instructor, and Room Location.

It is interesting to note that an attribute cannot be associated with a one-to-many relationship, such as Carries in Figure 2-5. For example, consider Dependent Date, similar to Date Completed above, for when the DEPENDENT begins to be carried by the EMPLOYEE. Because each DEPENDENT is associated with only one EMPLOYEE, such a date is unambiguously a characteristic of the DEPENDENT (i.e., for a given DEPENDENT, Dependent Date cannot vary by EMPLOYEE). So, if you ever have the urge to associate an attribute with a one-to-many relationship, "step away from the relationship!"

ASSOCIATIVE ENTITIES   The presence of one or more attributes on a relationship suggests to the designer that the relationship should perhaps instead be represented as an entity type. To emphasize this point, most E-R drawing tools require that such attributes be placed in an entity type. An **associative entity** is an entity type that associates the instances of one or more entity types and contains attributes that are peculiar to the relationship between those entity instances. The associative entity CERTIFICATE is represented with the rectangle with rounded corners, as shown in Figure 2-11b. Most E-R drawing tools do not have a special symbol for an associative entity. Associative entities are sometimes referred to as gerunds, because the relationship name (a verb) is usually converted to an entity name that is a noun. Note in Figure 2-11b that there are no relationship names on the lines between an associative entity and a strong entity. This is because the associative entity represents the relationship. Figure 2-11c shows how associative entities are drawn using Microsoft Visio, which is representative of how you would draw an associative entity with most E-R diagramming tools. In Visio, the relationship lines are dashed because CERTIFICATE does not include the identifiers of the related entities in its identifier. (Certificate Number is sufficient.)

> **Associative entity**
> An entity type that associates the instances of one or more entity types and contains attributes that are peculiar to the relationship between those entity instances.

How do you know whether to convert a relationship to an associative entity type? Following are four conditions that should exist:

1. All the relationships for the participating entity types are "many" relationships.
2. The resulting associative entity type has independent meaning to end users and, preferably, can be identified with a single-attribute identifier.
3. The associative entity has one or more attributes in addition to the identifier.
4. The associative entity participates in one or more relationships independent of the entities related in the associated relationship.

Figure 2-11b shows the relationship Completes converted to an associative entity type. In this case, the training department for the company has decided to award a certificate to each employee who completes a course. Thus, the entity is named CERTIFICATE, which certainly has independent meaning to end users. Also, each certificate has a number (Certificate Number) that serves as the identifier. The attribute Date Completed is also included. Note also in Figure 2-11b and the Visio version of Figure 2-11c that both EMPLOYEE and COURSE are mandatory participants in the two relationships with CERTIFICATE. This is exactly what occurs when you have to represent a many-to-many relationship (Completes in Figure 2-11a) as two one-to-many relationships (the ones associated with CERTIFICATE in Figures 2-11b and 2-11c).

Notice that converting a relationship to an associative entity has caused the relationship notation to move. That is, the "many" cardinality now terminates at the associative entity, rather than at each participating entity type. In Figure 2-11, this shows that an employee, who may complete one or more courses (notation A in Figure 2-11a), may be awarded more than one certificate (notation A in Figure 2-11b); and that a course, which may have one or more employees complete it (notation B in Figure 2-11a), may have many certificates awarded (notation B in Figure 2-11b). See Problem and Exercise 20 for an interesting variation on Figure 2-11a, which emphasizes the rules for when to convert a many-to-many relationship, such as Completes, into an associative entity.

Degree of a Relationship

Degree

The number of entity types that participate in a relationship.

The **degree** of a relationship is the number of entity types that participate in that relationship. Thus, the relationship Completes in Figure 2-11 is of degree 2, because there are two entity types: EMPLOYEE and COURSE. The three most common relationship degrees in E-R models are unary (degree 1), binary (degree 2), and ternary (degree 3). Higher-degree relationships are possible, but they are rarely encountered in practice, so we restrict our discussion to these three cases. Examples of unary, binary, and ternary relationships appear in Figure 2-12. (Attributes are not shown in some figures for simplicity.)

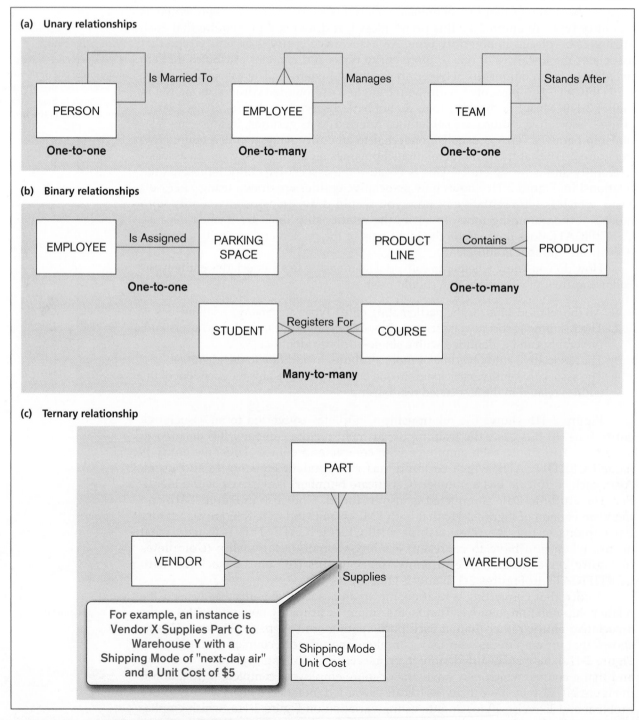

FIGURE 2-12   Examples of relationships of different degrees

As you look at Figure 2-12, understand that any particular data model represents a specific situation, not a generalization. For example, consider the Manages relationship in Figure 2-12a. In some organizations, it may be possible for one employee to be managed by many other employees (e.g., in a matrix organization). It is important when you develop an E-R model that you understand the business rules of the particular organization you are modeling.

UNARY RELATIONSHIP   A **unary relationship** is a relationship between the instances of a *single* entity type. (Unary relationships are also called *recursive relationships*.) Three examples are shown in Figure 2-12a. In the first example, Is Married To is shown as a one-to-one relationship between instances of the PERSON entity type. Because this is a one-to-one relationship, this notation indicates that only the current marriage, if one exists, needs to be kept about a person. What would change if we needed to retain the history of marriages for each person? See Problem and Exercise 12 for other business rules and their effect on the Is Married To relationship representation. In the second example, Manages is shown as a one-to-many relationship between instances of the EMPLOYEE entity type. Using this relationship, we could identify, for example, the employees who report to a particular manager. The third example is one case of using a unary relationship to represent a sequence, cycle, or priority list. In this example, sports teams are related by their standing in their league (the Stands After relationship). (Note: In these examples, we ignore whether these are mandatory- or optional-cardinality relationships or whether the same entity instance can repeat in the same relationship instance; we will introduce mandatory and optional cardinality in a later section of this chapter.)

Figure 2-13 shows an example of another unary relationship, called a *bill-of-materials structure*. Many manufactured products are made of assemblies, which in turn are composed of subassemblies and parts, and so on. As shown in Figure 2-13a, we can represent this structure as a many-to-many unary relationship. In this figure, the entity type ITEM is used to represent all types of components, and we use Has Components for the name of the relationship type that associates lower-level items with higher-level items.

Two occurrences of this bill-of-materials structure are shown in Figure 2-13b. Each of these diagrams shows the immediate components of each item as well as the quantities of that component. For example, item TX100 consists of item BR450 (quantity 2) and item DX500 (quantity 1). You can easily verify that the associations are in fact many-to-many. Several of the items have more than one component type (e.g., item MX300 has three immediate component types: HX100, TX100, and WX240). Also, some of the components are used in several higher-level assemblies. For example, item WX240 is used in both item MX300 and item WX340, even at different levels of the bill-of-materials. The many-to-many relationship guarantees that, for example, the same subassembly structure of WX240 (not shown) is used each time item WX240 goes into making some other item.

The presence of the attribute Quantity on the relationship suggests that the analyst consider converting the relationship Has Components to an associative entity. Figure 2-13c shows the entity type BOM STRUCTURE, which forms an association between instances of the ITEM entity type. A second attribute (named Effective Date) has been added to BOM STRUCTURE to record the date when this component was first used in the related assembly. Effective dates are often needed when a history of values is required. Other data model structures can be used for unary relationships involving such hierarchies; we show some of these other structures in Chapter 9.

BINARY RELATIONSHIP   A **binary relationship** is a relationship between the instances of two entity types and is the most common type of relationship encountered in data modeling. Figure 2-12b shows three examples. The first (one-to-one) indicates that an employee is assigned one parking place, and that each parking place is assigned to one employee. The second (one-to-many) indicates that a product line may contain several products, and that each product belongs to only one product line. The third (many-to-many) shows that a student may register for more than one course, and that each course may have many student registrants.

Unary relationship
A relationship between instances of a single entity type.

Binary relationship
A relationship between the instances of two entity types.

FIGURE 2-13 Representing a bill-of-materials structure

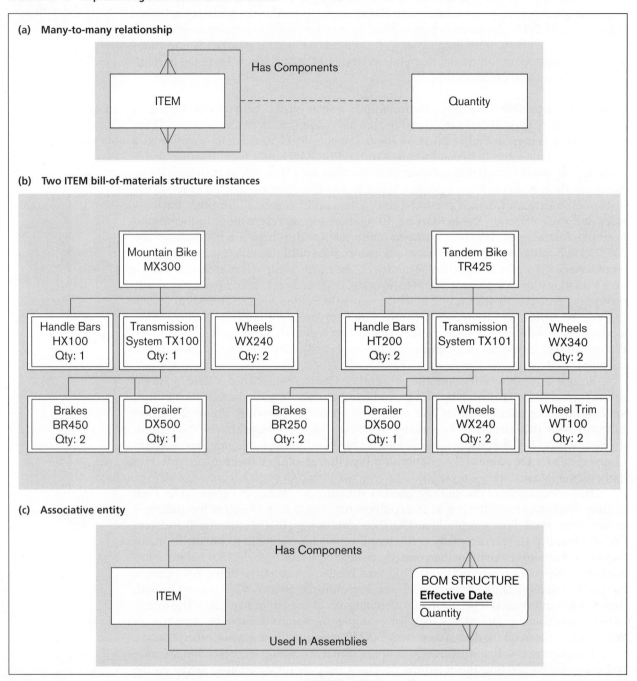

Ternary relationship

A simultaneous relationship among the instances of three entity types.

TERNARY RELATIONSHIP A **ternary relationship** is a *simultaneous* relationship among the instances of three entity types. A typical business situation that leads to a ternary relationship is shown in Figure 2-12c. In this example, vendors can supply various parts to warehouses. The relationship Supplies is used to record the specific parts that are supplied by a given vendor to a particular warehouse. Thus, there are three entity types: VENDOR, PART, and WAREHOUSE. There are two attributes on the relationship Supplies: Shipping Mode and Unit Cost. For example, one instance of Supplies might record the fact that vendor X can ship part C to warehouse Y, that the shipping mode is next-day air, and that the cost is $5 per unit.

Don't be confused: A ternary relationship is not the same as three binary relationships. For example, Unit Cost is an attribute of the Supplies relationship in Figure 2-12c. Unit Cost cannot be properly associated with any one of the three possible binary relationships among the three entity types, such as that between PART and WAREHOUSE.

FIGURE 2-14 Ternary relationship as an associative entity

Thus, for example, if we were told that vendor X can ship part C for a unit cost of $8, those data would be incomplete because they would not indicate to which warehouse the parts would be shipped.

As usual, the presence of an attribute on the relationship Supplies in Figure 2-12c suggests converting the relationship to an associative entity type. Figure 2-14 shows an alternative (and preferable) representation of the ternary relationship shown in Figure 2-12c. In Figure 2-14, the (associative) entity type SUPPLY SCHEDULE is used to replace the Supplies relationship from Figure 2-12c. Clearly, the entity type SUPPLY SCHEDULE is of independent interest to users. However, notice that an identifier has not yet been assigned to SUPPLY SCHEDULE. This is acceptable. If no identifier is assigned to an associative entity during E-R modeling, an identifier (or key) will be assigned during logical modeling (discussed in Chapter 4). This will be a composite identifier whose components will consist of the identifier for each of the participating entity types (in this example, PART, VENDOR, and WAREHOUSE). Can you think of other attributes that might be associated with SUPPLY SCHEDULE?

As noted earlier, we do not label the lines from SUPPLY SCHEDULE to the three entities. This is because these lines do not represent binary relationships. To keep the same meaning as the ternary relationship of Figure 2-12c, we cannot break the Supplies relationship into three binary relationships, as we have already mentioned.

So, here is a guideline to follow: Convert all ternary (or higher) relationships to associative entities, as in this example. Song et al. (1995) show that participation constraints (described in a following section on cardinality constraints) cannot be accurately represented for a ternary relationship, given the notation with attributes on the relationship line. However, by converting to an associative entity, the constraints can be accurately represented. Also, many E-R diagram drawing tools, including most CASE tools, cannot represent ternary (or higher order) relationships. So, although not semantically accurate, you must use these tools to represent the ternary relationship with an associative entity and three binary relationships, which have a mandatory association with each of the three related entity types.

Attributes or Entity?

Sometimes you will wonder if you should represent data as an attribute or an entity; this is a common dilemma. Figure 2-15 includes three examples of situations when an attribute could be represented via an entity type. We use this text's E-R notation in the left column and the notation from Microsoft Visio in the right column; it is important that you learn how to read ERDs in several notations because you will encounter various styles in different publications and organizations. In Figure 2-15a, the potentially multiple prerequisites of a course (shown as a multivalued attribute in the Attribute cell) are also courses (and a course may be a prerequisite for many other courses). Thus, prerequisite could be viewed as a bill-of-materials structure

FIGURE 2-15 Using relationships and entities to link related attributes

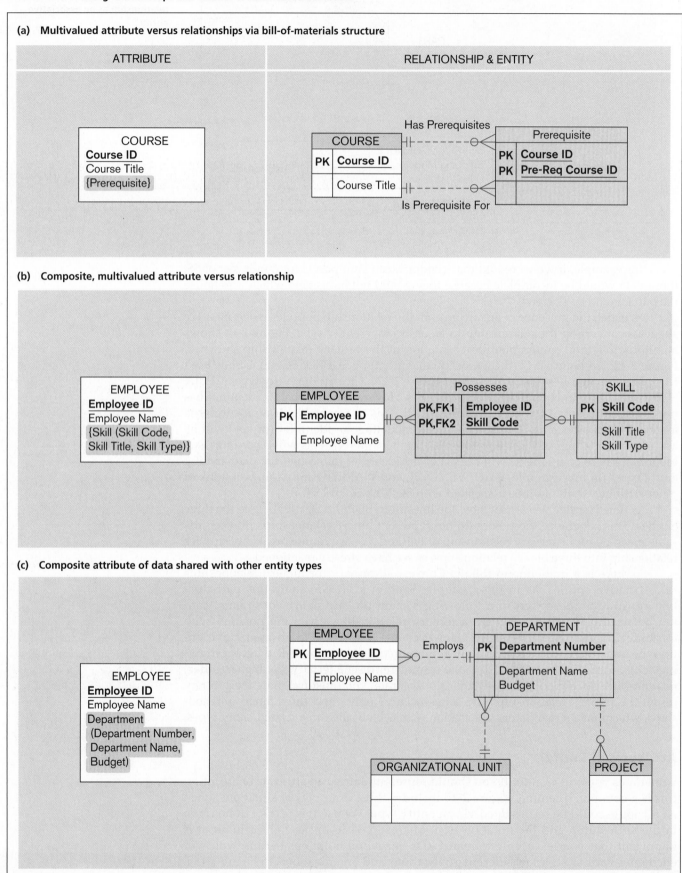

(shown in the Relationship & Entity cell) between courses, not a multivalued attribute of COURSE. Representing prerequisites via a bill-of-materials structure also means that finding the prerequisites of a course and finding the courses for which a course is prerequisite both deal with relationships between entity types. When a prerequisite is a multivalued attribute of COURSE, finding the courses for which a course is a prerequisite means looking for a specific value for a prerequisite across all COURSE instances. As was shown in Figure 2-13a, such a situation could also be modeled as a unary relationship among instances of the COURSE entity type. In Visio, this specific situation requires creating the equivalent of an associative entity (see the Relationship & Entity cell in Figure 2-15a; Visio does not use the rectangle with rounded corners symbol). By creating the associative entity, it is now easy to add characteristics to the relationship, such as a minimum grade required. Also note that Visio shows the identifier (in this case compound) with a PK stereotype symbol and boldface on the component attribute names, signifying these are required attributes.

In Figure 2-15b, employees potentially have multiple skills (shown in the Attribute cell), but skill could be viewed instead as an entity type (shown in the Relationship & Entity cell as the equivalent of an associative entity) about which the organization wants to maintain data (the unique code to identify each skill, a descriptive title, and the type of skill, for example, technical or managerial). An employee has skills, which are not viewed as attributes, but rather as instances of a related entity type. In the cases of Figures 2-15a and 2-15b, representing the data as a multivalued attribute rather than via a relationship with another entity type may, in the view of some people, simplify the diagram. On the other hand, the right-hand drawings in these figures are closer to the way the database would be represented in a standard relational database management system, the most popular type of DBMS in use today. Although we are not concerned with implementation during conceptual data modeling, there is some logic for keeping the conceptual and logical data models similar. Further, as we will see in the next example, there are times when an attribute, whether simple, composite, or multivalued, should be in a separate entity.

So, when *should* an attribute be linked to an entity type via a relationship? The answer is when the attribute is the identifier or some other characteristic of an entity type in the data model and multiple entity instances need to share these same attributes. Figure 2-15c represents an example of this rule. In this example, EMPLOYEE has a composite attribute of Department. Because Department is a concept of the business, and multiple employees will share the same department data, department data could be represented (nonredundantly) in a DEPARTMENT entity type, with attributes for the data about departments that all other related entity instances need to know. With this approach, not only can different employees share the storage of the same department data, but projects (which are assigned to a department) and organizational units (which are composed of departments) also can share the storage of this same department data.

Cardinality Constraints

There is one more important data modeling notation for representing common and important business rules. Suppose there are two entity types, A and B, that are connected by a relationship. A **cardinality constraint** specifies the number of instances of entity B that can (or must) be associated with each instance of entity A. For example, consider a video store that rents DVDs of movies. Because the store may stock more than one DVD for each movie, this is intuitively a one-to-many relationship, as shown in Figure 2-16a. Yet, it is also true that the store may not have any DVDs of a given movie in stock at a particular time (e.g., all copies may be checked out). We need a more precise notation to indicate the range of cardinalities for a relationship. This notation was introduced in Figure 2-2, which you may want to review at this time.

MINIMUM CARDINALITY The **minimum cardinality** of a relationship is the minimum number of instances of entity B that may be associated with each instance of entity A. In our DVD example, the minimum number of DVDs for a movie is zero. When the

Cardinality constraint

A rule that specifies the number of instances of one entity that can (or must) be associated with each instance of another entity.

Minimum cardinality

The minimum number of instances of one entity that may be associated with each instance of another entity.

FIGURE 2-16 Introducing
cardinality constraints
(a) Basic relationship

**(b) Relationship with cardinality
constraints**

minimum number of participants is zero, we say that entity type B is an optional participant in the relationship. In this example, DVD (a weak entity type) is an optional participant in the Is Stocked As relationship. This fact is indicated by the symbol zero through the line near the DVD entity in Figure 2-16b.

Maximum cardinality

The maximum number of
instances of one entity that may be
associated with each instance of
another entity.

MAXIMUM CARDINALITY The **maximum cardinality** of a relationship is the maximum number of instances of entity B that may be associated with each instance of entity A. In the video example, the maximum cardinality for the DVD entity type is "many"—that is, an unspecified number greater than one. This is indicated by the "crow's foot" symbol on the line next to the DVD entity symbol in Figure 2-16b. (You might find interesting the explanation of the origin of the crow's foot notation found in the Wikipedia entry about the entity-relationship model; this entry also shows the wide variety of notations used to represent cardinality; see **http://en.wikipedia.org/wiki /Entity-relationship_model.)**

A relationship is, of course, bidirectional, so there is also cardinality notation next to the MOVIE entity. Notice that the minimum and maximum are both one (see Figure 2-16b). This is called a *mandatory one* cardinality. In other words, each DVD of a movie must be a copy of exactly one movie. In general, participation in a relationship may be optional or mandatory for the entities involved. If the minimum cardinality is zero, participation is optional; if the minimum cardinality is one, participation is mandatory.

In Figure 2-16b, some attributes have been added to each of the entity types. Notice that DVD is represented as a weak entity. This is because a DVD cannot exist unless the owner movie also exists. The identifier of MOVIE is Movie Name. DVD does not have a unique identifier. However, Copy Number is a *partial* identifier, which together with Movie Name would uniquely identify an instance of DVD.

Some Examples of Relationships and Their Cardinalities

Examples of three relationships that show all possible combinations of minimum and maximum cardinalities appear in Figure 2-17. Each example states the business rule for each cardinality constraint and shows the associated E-R notation. Each example also shows some relationship instances to clarify the nature of the relationship. You should study each of these examples carefully. Following are the business rules for each of the examples in Figure 2-17:

1. *PATIENT Has Recorded PATIENT HISTORY (Figure 2-17a)*   Each patient has one or more patient histories. (The initial patient visit is always recorded as an instance of PATIENT HISTORY.) Each instance of PATIENT HISTORY "belongs to" exactly one PATIENT.

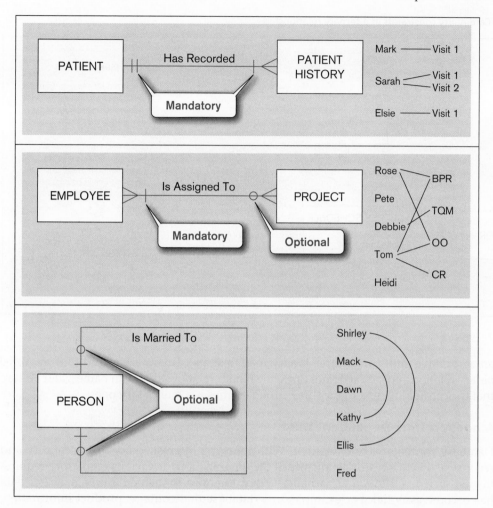

FIGURE 2-17 Examples of
cardinality constraints
(a) Mandatory cardinalities

(b) One optional, one mandatory
cardinality

(c) Optional cardinalities

2. *EMPLOYEE Is Assigned To PROJECT (Figure 2-17b)*   Each PROJECT has at
   least one EMPLOYEE assigned to it. (Some projects have more than one.) Each
   EMPLOYEE may or (optionally) may not be assigned to any existing PROJECT
   (e.g., employee Pete) or may be assigned to one or more PROJECTs.
3. *PERSON Is Married To PERSON (Figure 2-17c)*   This is an optional zero or one
   cardinality in both directions, because a person may or may not be married at a
   given point in time.

It is possible for the maximum cardinality to be a fixed number, not an arbitrary
"many" value. For example, suppose corporate policy states that an employee may
work on at most five projects at the same time. We could show this business rule by
placing a 5 above or below the crow's foot next to the PROJECT entity in Figure 2-17b.

A TERNARY RELATIONSHIP   We showed the ternary relationship with the associative
entity type SUPPLY SCHEDULE in Figure 2-14. Now let's add cardinality constraints to
this diagram, based on the business rules for this situation. The E-R diagram, with the
relevant business rules, is shown in Figure 2-18. Notice that PART and WAREHOUSE
must relate to some SUPPLY SCHEDULE instance, and a VENDOR optionally may not
participate. The cardinality at each of the participating entities is a mandatory one, because each SUPPLY SCHEDULE instance must be related to exactly one instance of
each of these participating entity types. (Remember, SUPPLY SCHEDULE is an associative entity.)

   As noted earlier, a ternary relationship is not equivalent to three binary relationships. Unfortunately, you are not able to draw ternary relationships with many CASE
tools; instead, you are forced to represent ternary relationships as three binaries (i.e.,

FIGURE 2-18 Cardinality constraints in a ternary relationship

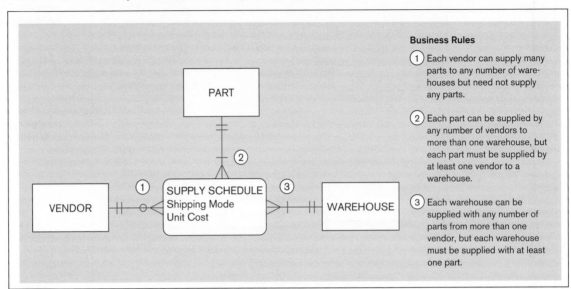

Business Rules

① Each vendor can supply many parts to any number of warehouses but need not supply any parts.

② Each part can be supplied by any number of vendors to more than one warehouse, but each part must be supplied by at least one vendor to a warehouse.

③ Each warehouse can be supplied with any number of parts from more than one vendor, but each warehouse must be supplied with at least one part.

an associative entity with three binary relationships). If you are forced to draw three binary relationships, then do not draw the binary relationships with names, and be sure that the cardinality next to the three strong entities is a mandatory one.

Modeling Time-Dependent Data

Database contents vary over time. With renewed interest today in traceability and reconstruction of a historical picture of the organization for various regulatory requirements, such as HIPAA and Sarbanes-Oxley, the need to include a time series of data has become essential. For example, in a database that contains product information, the unit price for each product may be changed as material and labor costs and market conditions change. If only the current price is required, Price can be modeled as a single-valued attribute. However, for accounting, billing, financial reporting, and other purposes, we are likely to need to preserve a history of the prices and the time period during which each was in effect. As Figure 2-19 shows, we can conceptualize this requirement as a series of prices and the effective date for each price. This results in the (composite) multivalued attribute named Price History, with components Price and Effective Date. An important characteristic of such a composite, multivalued attribute is that the component attributes go together. Thus, in Figure 2-19, each Price is paired with the corresponding Effective Date.

In Figure 2-19, each value of the attribute Price is time stamped with its effective date. A **time stamp** is simply a time value, such as date and time, that is associated with a data value. A time stamp may be associated with any data value that changes over time when we need to maintain a history of those data values. Time stamps may be recorded to indicate the time the value was entered (transaction time); the

Time stamp

A time value that is associated with a data value, often indicating when some event occurred that affected the data value.

FIGURE 2-19 Simple example of time stamping

time the value becomes valid or stops being valid; or the time when critical actions were performed, such as updates, corrections, or audits. This situation is similar to the employee skill diagrams in Figure 2-15b; thus, an alternative, not shown in Figure 2-19, is to make Price History a separate entity type, as was done with Skill using Microsoft Visio.

The use of simple time stamping (as in the preceding example) is often adequate for modeling time-dependent data. However, time can introduce subtler complexities to data modeling. For example, consider again Figure 2-17c. This figure is drawn for a given point in time, not to show history. If, on the other hand, we needed to record the full history of marriages for individuals, the Is Married To relationship would be an optional many-to-many relationship. Further, we might want to know the beginning and ending date (optional) of each marriage; these dates would be, similar to the bill-of-materials structure in Figure 2-13c, attributes of the relationship or associative entity.

We have discussed the problem of time-dependent data with managers in several organizations who are considered leaders in the use of data modeling and database management. Before the recent wave of financial reporting disclosure regulations, these discussions revealed that data models for operational databases were generally inadequate for handing time-dependent data, and that organizations often ignored this problem and hoped that the resulting inaccuracies balanced out. However, with these new regulations, you need to be alert to the complexities posed by time-dependent data as you develop data models in your organization. For a thorough explanation of time as a dimension of data modeling, see a series of articles by T. Johnson and R. Weis beginning in May 2007 in *DM Review* (now *Information Management*) and accessible from the Magazine Archives section of the Information Center at of **www.information-management.com.**

Modeling Multiple Relationships Between Entity Types

There may be more than one relationship between the same entity types in a given organization. Two examples are shown in Figure 2-20. Figure 2-20a shows two

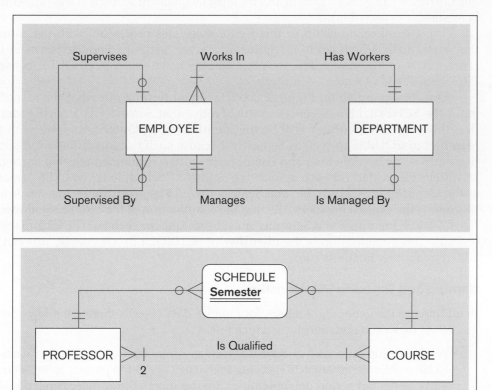

FIGURE 2-20 Examples of multiple relationships
(a) Employees and departments

(b) Professors and courses (fixed lower limit constraint)

relationships between the entity types EMPLOYEE and DEPARTMENT. In this figure, we use the notation with names for the relationship in each direction; this notation makes explicit what the cardinality is for each direction of the relationship (which becomes important for clarifying the meaning of the unary relationship on EMPLOYEE). One relationship associates employees with the department in which they work. This relationship is one-to-many in the Has Workers direction and is mandatory in both directions. That is, a department must have at least one employee who works there (perhaps the department manager), and each employee must be assigned to exactly one department. (Note: These are specific business rules we assume for this illustration. It is crucial when you develop an E-R diagram for a particular situation that you understand the business rules that apply for that setting. For example, if EMPLOYEE were to include retirees, then each employee may not be currently assigned to exactly one department; further, the E-R model in Figure 2-20a assumes that the organization needs to remember in which DEPARTMENT each EMPLOYEE currently works, rather than remembering the history of department assignments. Again, the structure of the data model reflects the information the organization needs to remember.)

The second relationship between EMPLOYEE and DEPARTMENT associates each department with the employee who manages that department. The relationship from DEPARTMENT to EMPLOYEE (called Is Managed By in that direction) is a mandatory one, indicating that a department must have exactly one manager. From EMPLOYEE to DEPARTMENT, the relationship (Manages) is optional because a given employee either is or is not a department manager.

Figure 2-20a also shows the unary relationship that associates each employee with his or her supervisor, and vice versa. This relationship records the business rule that each employee may have exactly one supervisor (Supervised By). Conversely, each employee may supervise any number of employees or may not be a supervisor.

The example in Figure 2-20b shows two relationships between the entity types PROFESSOR and COURSE. The relationship Is Qualified associates professors with the courses they are qualified to teach. A given course must have at a minimum two qualified instructors (an example of how to use a fixed value for a minimum or maximum cardinality). This might happen, for example, so that a course is never the "property" of one instructor. Conversely, each instructor must be qualified to teach at least one course (a reasonable expectation).

The second relationship in this figure associates professors with the courses they are actually scheduled to teach during a given semester. Because Semester is a characteristic of the relationship, we place an associative entity, SCHEDULE, between PROFESSOR and COURSE.

One final point about Figure 2-20b: Have you figured out what the identifier is for the SCHEDULE associative entity? Notice that Semester is a partial identifier; thus, the full identifier will be the identifier of PROFESSOR along with the identifier of COURSE as well as Semester. Because such full identifiers for associative entities can become long and complex, it is often recommended that surrogate identifiers be created for each associative entity; so, Schedule ID would be created as the identifier of SCHEDULE, and Semester would be an attribute. What is lost in this case is the explicit business rule that the combination of the PROFESSOR identifier, COURSE identifier, and Semester must be unique for each SCHEDULE instance (because this combination is the identifier of SCHEDULE). Of course, this can be added as another business rule.

Naming and Defining Relationships

In addition to the general guidelines for naming data objects, there are a few special guidelines for naming relationships, which follow:

- A relationship name is a *verb phrase* (such as Assigned To, Supplies, or Teaches). Relationships represent actions being taken, usually in the present tense, so transitive verbs (an action on something) are the most appropriate. A relationship name states the action taken, not the result of the action (e.g., use Assigned To, not

Assignment). The name states the essence of the interaction between the participating entity types, not the process involved (e.g., use an Employee is *Assigned To* a project, not an Employee is *Assigning* a project).

- You should *avoid vague names*, such as Has or Is Related To. Use descriptive, powerful verb phrases, often taken from the action verbs found in the definition of the relationship.

There are also some specific guidelines for defining relationships, which follow:

- A relationship definition *explains what action is being taken and possibly why it is important*. It may be important to state who or what does the action, but it is not important to explain how the action is taken. Stating the business objects involved in the relationship is natural, but because the E-R diagram shows what entity types are involved in the relationship and other definitions explain the entity types, you do not have to describe the business objects.

- It may also be important to *give examples to clarify the action*. For example, for a relationship of Registered For between student and course, it may be useful to explain that this covers both on-site and online registration and includes registrations made during the drop/add period.

- The definition should explain any *optional participation*. You should explain what conditions lead to zero associated instances, whether this can happen only when an entity instance is first created, or whether this can happen at any time. For example, "Registered For links a course with the students who have signed up to take the course, and the courses a student has signed up to take. A course will have no students registered for it before the registration period begins and may never have any registered students. A student will not be registered for any courses before the registration period begins and may not register for any classes (or may register for classes and then drop any or all classes)."

- A relationship definition should also *explain the reason for any explicit maximum cardinality* other than many. For example, "Assigned To links an employee with the projects to which that employee is assigned and the employees assigned to a project. Due to our labor union agreement, an employee may not be assigned to more than four projects at a given time." This example, typical of many upper-bound business rules, suggests that maximum cardinalities tend not to be permanent. In this example, the next labor union agreement could increase or decrease this limit. Thus, the implementation of maximum cardinalities must be done to allow changes.

- A relationship definition should *explain any mutually exclusive relationships*. Mutually exclusive relationships are ones for which an entity instance can participate in only one of several alternative relationships. We will show examples of this situation in Chapter 3. For now, consider the following example: "Plays On links an intercollegiate sports team with its student players and indicates on which teams a student plays. Students who play on intercollegiate sports teams cannot also work in a campus job (i.e., a student cannot be linked to both an intercollegiate sports team via Plays On and a campus job via the Works On relationship)." Another example of a mutually exclusive restriction is when an employee cannot both be Supervised By and be Married To the same employee.

- A relationship definition should *explain any restrictions on participation in the relationship*. Mutual exclusivity is one restriction, but there can be others. For example, "Supervised By links an employee with the other employees he or she supervises and links an employee with the other employee who supervises him or her. An employee cannot supervise him- or herself, and an employee cannot supervise other employees if his or her job classification level is below 4."

- A relationship definition should *explain the extent of history that is kept in the relationship*. For example, "Assigned To links a hospital bed with a patient. Only the current bed assignment is stored. When a patient is not admitted, that patient is not assigned to a bed, and a bed may be vacant at any given point in time." Another example of describing history for a relationship is "Places links a customer with the orders he or she has placed with our company and links an order with the associated customer. Only two years of orders are maintained in the database, so not all orders can participate in this relationship."

- A relationship definition should *explain whether an entity instance involved in a relationship instance can transfer participation to another relationship instance.* For example, "Places links a customer with the orders he or she has placed with our company and links an order with the associated customer. An order is not transferable to another customer." Another example is "Categorized As links a product line with the products sold under that heading and links a product to its associated product line. Due to changes in organization structure and product design features, products may be recategorized to a different product line. Categorized As keeps track of only the current product line to which a product is linked."

E-R MODELING EXAMPLE: PINE VALLEY FURNITURE COMPANY

Developing an E-R diagram can proceed from one (or both) of two perspectives. With a top-down perspective, the designer proceeds from basic descriptions of the business, including its policies, processes, and environment. This approach is most appropriate for developing a high-level E-R diagram with only the major entities and relationships and with a limited set of attributes (such as just the entity identifiers). With a bottom-up approach, the designer proceeds from detailed discussions with users, and from a detailed study of documents, screens, and other data sources. This approach is necessary for developing a detailed, "fully attributed" E-R diagram.

In this section, we develop a high-level ERD for Pine Valley Furniture Company, based largely on the first of these approaches (see Figure 2-21 for a Microsoft Visio version). For simplicity, we do not show any composite or multivalued attributes (e.g., skill is shown as a separate entity type associated with EMPLOYEE via an associative entity, which allows an employee to have many skills and a skill to be held by many employees).

Figure 2-21 provides many examples of common E-R modeling notations, and hence, it can be used as an excellent review of what you have learned in this chapter. In a moment, we will explain the business rules that are represented in this figure. However, before you read that explanation, one way to use Figure 2-21 is to search for typical E-R model constructs in it, such as one-to-many, binary, or unary relationships. Then, ask yourself why the business data was modeled this way. For example, ask yourself

- Where is a unary relationship, what does it mean, and for what reasons might the cardinalities on it be different in other organizations?
- Why is Includes a one-to many relationship, and why might this ever be different in some other organization?
- Does Includes allow for a product to be represented in the database before it is assigned to a product line (e.g., while the product is in research and development)?
- If there were a different customer contact person for each sales territory in which a customer did business, where in the data model would we place this person's name?
- What is the meaning of the Does Business In associative entity, and why does each Does Business In instance have to be associated with exactly one SALES TERRITORY and one CUSTOMER?
- In what way might Pine Valley change the way it does business that would cause the Supplies associative entity to be eliminated and the relationships around it to change?

Each of these questions is included in Problem and Exercise 3 at the end of the chapter, but we suggest you use these now as a way to review your understanding of E-R diagramming.

FIGURE 2-21 Data model for Pine Valley Furniture Company in Microsoft Visio notation

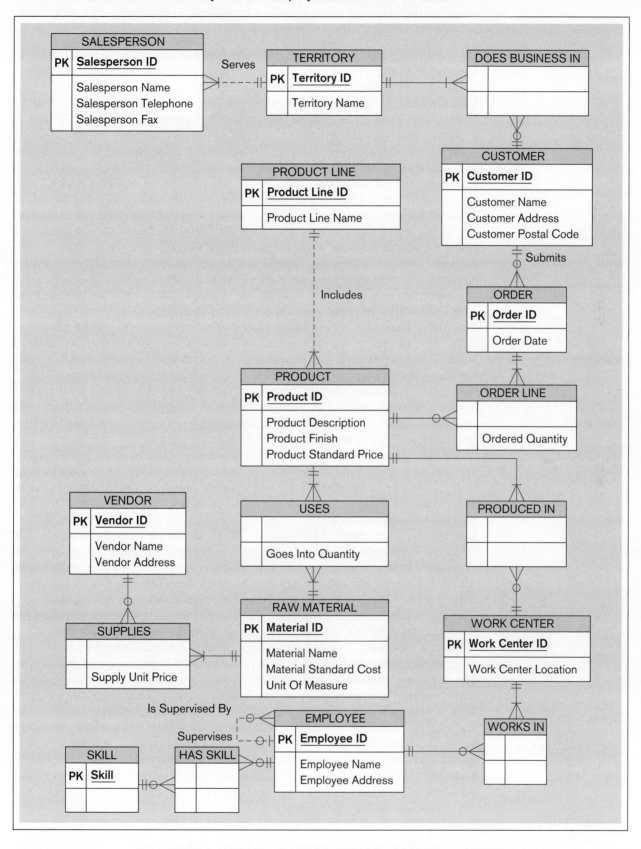

From a study of the business processes at Pine Valley Furniture Company, we have identified the following entity types. An identifier is also suggested for each entity, together with selected important attributes:

- The company sells a number of different furniture products. These products are grouped into several product lines. The identifier for a product is Product ID, whereas the identifier for a product line is Product Line ID. We identify the following additional attributes for product: Product Description, Product Finish, and Product Standard Price. Another attribute for product line is Product Line Name. A product line may group any number of products but must group at least one product. Each product must belong to exactly one product line.
- Customers submit orders for products. The identifier for an order is Order ID, and another attribute is Order Date. A customer may submit any number of orders but need not submit any orders. Each order is submitted by exactly one customer. The identifier for a customer is Customer ID. Other attributes include Customer Name, Customer Address, and Customer Postal Code.
- A given customer order must request at least one product and only one product per order line item. Any product sold by Pine Valley Furniture may not appear on any order line item or may appear on one or more order line items. An attribute associated with each order line item is Ordered Quantity.
- Pine Valley Furniture has established sales territories for its customers. Each customer may do business in any number of these sales territories or may not do business in any territory. A sales territory has one to many customers. The identifier for a sales territory is Territory ID and an attribute is Territory Name.
- Pine Valley Furniture Company has several salespersons. The identifier for a salesperson is Salesperson ID. Other attributes include Salesperson Name, Salesperson Telephone, and Salesperson Fax. A salesperson serves exactly one sales territory. Each sales territory is served by one or more salespersons.
- Each product is assembled from a specified quantity of one or more raw materials. The identifier for the raw material entity is Material ID. Other attributes include Unit Of Measure, Material Name, and Material Standard Cost. Each raw material is assembled into one or more products, using a specified quantity of the raw material for each product.
- Raw materials are supplied by vendors. The identifier for a vendor is Vendor ID. Other attributes include Vendor Name and Vendor Address. Each raw material can be supplied by one or more vendors. A vendor may supply any number of raw materials or may not supply any raw materials to Pine Valley Furniture. Supply Unit Price is the unit price at which a particular vendor supplies a particular raw material.
- Pine Valley Furniture has established a number of work centers. The identifier for a work center is Work Center ID. Another attribute is Work Center Location. Each product is produced in one or more work centers. A work center may be used to produce any number of products or may not be used to produce any products.
- The company has more than 100 employees. The identifier for employee is Employee ID. Other attributes include Employee Name, Employee Address, and Skill. An employee may have more than one skill. Each employee may work in one or more work centers. A work center must have at least one employee working in that center but may have any number of employees. A skill may be possessed by more than one employee or possibly no employees.
- Each employee has exactly one supervisor; however, a manager has no supervisor. An employee who is a supervisor may supervise any number of employees, but not all employees are supervisors.

DATABASE PROCESSING AT PINE VALLEY FURNITURE

The purpose of the data model diagram in Figure 2-21 is to provide a conceptual design for the Pine Valley Furniture Company database. It is important to check the quality of such a design through frequent interaction with the persons who will use the database after it is implemented. An important and often performed type of quality check is to determine whether the E-R model can easily satisfy user requests for data and/or information. Employees at Pine Valley Furniture have many data retrieval and reporting requirements. In this section, we show how a few of these information requirements can be satisfied by database processing against the database shown in Figure 2-21.

We use the SQL database processing language (explained in Chapters 6 and 7) to state these queries. To fully understand these queries, you will need to understand concepts introduced in Chapter 4. However, a few simple queries in this chapter should help you understand the capabilities of a database to answer important organizational questions and give you a jump-start toward understanding SQL queries in Chapter 6 as well as in later chapters.

Showing Product Information

Many different users have a need to see data about the products Pine Valley Furniture produces (e.g., salespersons, inventory managers, and product managers). One specific need is for a salesperson who wants to respond to a request from a customer for a list of products of a certain type. An example of this query is

List all details for the various computer desks that are stocked by the company.

The data for this query are maintained in the PRODUCT entity (see Figure 2-21). The query scans this entity and displays all the attributes for products that contain the description Computer Desk.

The SQL code for this query is

```
SELECT *
FROM Product
WHERE ProductDescription LIKE "Computer Desk%";
```

Typical output for this query is

PRODUCTID	PRODUCTDESCRIPTION	PRODUCTFINISH	PRODUCTSTANDARDPRICE
3	Computer Desk 48″	Oak	375.00
8	Computer Desk 64″	Pine	450.00

SELECT * FROM Product says display all attributes of PRODUCT entities. The WHERE clause says to limit the display to only products whose description begins with the phrase Computer Desk.

Showing Product Line Information

Another common information need is to show data about Pine Valley Furniture product lines. One specific type of person who needs this information is a product manager. The following is a typical query from a territory sales manager:

List the details of products in product line 4.

The data for this query are maintained in the PRODUCT entity. As we explain in Chapter 4, the attribute Product Line ID will be added to the PRODUCT entity when a data model in Figure 2-21 is translated into a database that can be accessed via SQL. The query scans the PRODUCT entity and displays all attributes for products that are in the selected product line.

The SQL code for this query is

```
SELECT *
FROM Product
WHERE ProductLineID = 4;
```

Typical output for this query is

PRODUCTID	PRODUCTDESCRIPTION	PRODUCTFINISH	PRODUCTSTANDARDPRICE	PRODUCTONHAND	PRODUCTLINEID
18	Grandfather Clock	Oak	890.0000	0	4
19	Grandfather Clock	Oak	1100.0000	0	4

The explanation of this SQL query is similar to the explanation of the previous one.

Showing Customer Order Status

The previous two queries are relatively simple, involving data from only one table in each case. Often, data from multiple tables are needed in one information request. Although the previous query is simple, we did have to look through the whole database to find the entity and attributes needed to satisfy the request.

To simplify query writing and for other reasons, many database management systems support creating restricted views of a database suitable for the information needs of a particular user. For queries related to customer order status, Pine Valley utilizes such a user view called "Orders for customers," which is created from the segment of an E-R diagram for PVFC shown in Figure 2-22. This user view allows users to see only CUSTOMER and ORDER entities in the database, and only the attributes of these entities shown in the figure. For the user, there is only one (virtual) table, ORDERS FOR CUSTOMERS, with the listed attributes. As we explain in Chapter 4, the attribute Customer ID will be added to the ORDER entity (as shown in Figure 2-22). A typical order status query is

How many orders have we received from Value Furniture?

Assuming that all the data we need are pulled together into this one user view, or virtual entity, called OrdersForCustomers, we can simply write the query as follows:

```
SELECT COUNT(Order ID)
FROM OrdersForCustomers
WHERE CustomerName = "Value Furniture";
```

Without the user view, we can write the SQL code for this query in several ways. The way we have chosen is to compose a query within a query, called a *subquery*. (We will explain subqueries in Chapter 7, with some diagramming techniques to assist you in composing the query.) The query is performed in two steps. First, the subquery (or inner query) scans the CUSTOMER entity to determine the Customer ID for the customer named Value Furniture. (The ID for this customer is 5, as shown in the output for the previous query.) Then the query (or outer query) scans the ORDER entity and counts the order instances for this customer.

FIGURE 2-22 User view: Orders for customer

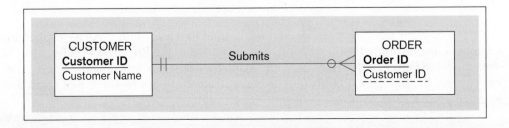

The SQL code for this query without the "Orders for customer" user view is as follows:

```
SELECT COUNT (OrderID)
FROM Order
WHERE CustomerID =
    (SELECT CustomerID
    FROM Customer
    WHERE CustomerName = "Value Furniture");
```

For this example query, using a subquery rather than a view did not make writing the query much more complex.

Typical output for this query using either of the query approaches above is

```
COUNT(ORDERID)
        4
```

Summary

This chapter has described the fundamentals of modeling data in the organization. Business rules, derived from policies, procedures, events, functions, and other business objects, state constraints that govern the organization and, hence, how data are handled and stored. Using business rules is a powerful way to describe the requirements for an information system, especially a database. The power of business rules results from business rules being core concepts of the business; being able to be expressed in terms familiar to end users; being highly maintainable; and being able to be enforced through automated means, mainly through a database.

Examples of basic business rules are data names and definitions. This chapter explained guidelines for the clear naming and definition of data objects in a business. In terms of conceptual data modeling, names and definitions must be provided for entity types, attributes, and relationships. Other business rules may state constraints on these data objects. These constraints can be captured in a data model and associated documentation.

The data modeling notation most frequently used today is the entity-relationship data model. An E-R model is a detailed, logical representation of the data for an organization. An E-R model is usually expressed in the form of an E-R diagram, which is a graphical representation of an E-R model. At the present time, there is no standard notation for E-R modeling. Notations such as those found in Microsoft Visio are used in many CASE tools.

The basic constructs of an E-R model are entity types, relationships, and related attributes. An entity is a person, a place, an object, an event, or a concept in the user environment about which the organization wishes to maintain data. An entity type is a collection of entities that share common properties, whereas an entity instance is a single occurrence of an entity type. A strong entity type is an entity that has its own identifier and can exist without other entities. A weak entity type is an entity whose existence depends on the existence of a strong entity type. Weak entities do not have their own identifier, although they normally have a partial identifier. Weak entities are identified through an identifying relationship with their owner entity type.

An attribute is a property or characteristic of an entity or relationship that is of interest to the organization. There are several types of attributes. A required attribute must have a value for an entity instance, whereas an optional attribute value may be null. A simple attribute is one that has no component parts. A composite attribute is an attribute that can be broken down into component parts. For example, Person Name can be broken down into the parts First Name, Middle Initial, and Last Name.

A multivalued attribute is one that can have multiple values for a single instance of an entity. For example, the attribute College Degree might have multiple values for an individual. A derived attribute is one whose values can be calculated from other attribute values. For example, Average Salary can be calculated from values of Salary for all employees.

An identifier is an attribute that uniquely identifies individual instances of an entity type. Identifiers should be chosen carefully to ensure stability and ease of use. Identifiers may be simple attributes, or they may be composite attributes with component parts.

A relationship type is a meaningful association between (or among) entity types. A relationship instance is an association between (or among) entity instances. The degree of a relationship is the number of entity types that participate in the relationship. The most common relationship types are unary (degree 1), binary (degree 2), and ternary (degree 3).

In developing E-R diagrams, we sometimes encounter many-to-many (and one-to-one) relationships that have one or more attributes associated with the relationship, rather than with one of the participating entity types. In such cases, we might consider converting the relationship to an associative entity. This type of entity associates the instances of one or more entity types and contains attributes that are peculiar to the relationship. Associative entity types may have their own simple identifier, or they may be assigned a composite identifier during logical design.

A cardinality constraint is a constraint that specifies the number of instances of entity B that may (or must) be associated with each instance of entity A. Cardinality constraints normally specify the minimum and maximum number of instances. The possible constraints are mandatory one, mandatory many, optional one, optional many, and a specific number. The minimum cardinality constraint is also referred to as the participation constraint. A minimum cardinality of zero specifies optional participation, whereas a minimum cardinality of one specifies mandatory participation.

Because many databases need to store the value of data over time, modeling time-dependent data is an important part of data modeling. Data that repeat over time may be modeled as multivalued attributes or as separate entity instances; in each case, a time stamp is necessary to identify the relevant date and time for the data value. Sometimes separate relationships need to be included in the data model to represent associations at different points in time. The recent wave of financial reporting disclosure regulations have made it more important to include time-sensitive and historical data in databases.

Chapter Review

Key Terms

Associative entity *65*	Entity *53*	Identifying relationship *55*	Simple (or atomic) attribute *58*
Attribute *57*	Entity instance *53*	Maximum cardinality *72*	Strong entity type *55*
Binary relationship *67*	Entity-relationship diagram (E-R diagram) *47*	Minimum cardinality *71*	Ternary relationship *68*
Business rule *50*	Entity-relationship model (E-R model) *47*	Multivalued attribute *59*	Time stamp *74*
Cardinality constraint *71*		Optional attribute *57*	Unary relationship *67*
Composite attribute *58*	Entity type *53*	Relationship instance *63*	Weak entity type *55*
Composite identifier *60*	Identifier *59*	Relationship type *63*	
Degree *66*	Identifying owner *55*	Required attribute *57*	
Derived attribute *59*			

Review Questions

1. Define each of the following terms:
   a. entity type
   b. entity-relationship model
   c. entity instance
   d. attribute
   e. relationship type
   f. identifier
   g. multivalued attribute
   h. associative entity
   i. cardinality constraint
   j. weak entity
   k. identifying relationship
   l. derived attribute
   m. business rule

2. Match the following terms and definitions.

   ___composite attribute   a. uniquely identifies entity instances
   ___associative entity   b. relates instances of a single entity type
   ___unary relationship   c. specifies maximum and minimum
   ___weak entity   number of instances
   ___attribute   d. relationship modeled as an entity type
   ___entity   e. association between entity types
   ___relationship type   f. collection of similar entities
   ___cardinality constraint   g. number of participating entity types
   ___degree   in relationship
   ___identifier   h. property of an entity
   ___entity type   i. can be broken into component parts
   ___ternary   j. depends on the existence of another entity type
   ___bill-of-materials   k. relationship of degree 3
                                l. many-to-many unary relationship
                                m. person, place, object, concept, event

3. Contrast the following terms:
   a. stored attribute; derived attribute
   b. simple attribute; composite attribute
   c. entity type; relationship type
   d. strong entity type; weak entity type
   e. degree; cardinality
   f. required attribute; optional attribute
   g. composite attribute; multivalued attribute
   h. ternary relationship; three binary relationships

4. Give three reasons why many system designers believe that data modeling is the most important part of the systems development process.

5. Explain where you can find business rules in an organization.

6. State six general guidelines for naming data objects in a data model.

7. State four criteria for selecting identifiers for entities.

8. Why must some identifiers be composite rather than simple?

9. State three conditions that suggest the designer should model a relationship as an associative entity type.

10. List the four types of cardinality constraints, and draw an example of each.

11. Give an example, other than those described in this chapter, of a weak entity type. Why is it necessary to indicate an identifying relationship?
12. What is the degree of a relationship? List the three types of relationship degrees described in the chapter and give an example of each.
13. Give an example (other than those described in this chapter) for each of the following, and justify your answer:
    a. derived attribute
    b. multivalued attribute
    c. atomic attribute
    d. composite attribute
    e. required attribute
    f. optional attribute
14. Give an example of each of the following, other than those described in this chapter, and clearly explain why your example is this type of relationship and not of some other degree.
    a. ternary relationship
    b. unary relationship
15. Give an example of the use of effective (or effectivity) dates as attributes of an entity.
16. What are the special guidelines for naming relationships?
17. In addition to explaining what action is being taken, what else should a relationship definition explain?
18. For the Manages relationship in Figure 2-12a, describe one or more situations that would result in different cardinalities on the two ends of this unary relationship. Based on your description for this example, do you think it is always clear simply from an E-R diagram what the business rule is that results in certain cardinalities? Justify your answer.
19. Explain the distinction between entity type and entity instance.
20. Why is it recommended that all ternary relationships be converted into an associative entity?

Problems and Exercises

1. A cellular operator needs a database to keep track of its customers, their subscription plans, and the handsets (mobile phones) that they are using. The E-R diagram in Figure 2-23 illustrates the key entities of interest to the operator and the relationships between them. Based on the figure, answer the following questions and explain the rationale for your response. For each question, identify the element(s) in the E-R diagram that you used to determine your answer.
   a. Can a customer have an unlimited number of plans?
   b. Can a customer exist without a plan?
   c. Is it possible to create a plan without knowing who the customer is?
   d. Does the operator want to limit the types of handsets that can be linked to a specific plan type?
   e. Is it possible to maintain data regarding a handset without connecting it to a plan?
   f. Can a handset be associated with multiple plans?
   g. Assume a handset type exists that can utilize multiple operating systems. Could this situation be accommodated within the model included in Figure 2-23?
   h. Is the company able to track a manufacturer without maintaining information about its handsets?
   i. Can the same operating system be used on multiple handset types?
   j. There are two relationships between Customer and Plan. Explain how they differ.
   k. Characterize the degree and the cardinalities of the relationship that connects Customer to itself. Explain its meaning.
   l. Is it possible to link a handset to a specific customer in a plan with multiple customers?
   m. Can the company track a handset without identifying its operating system?
2. For each of the descriptions below, perform the following tasks:
   i. Identify the degree and cardinalities of the relationship.
   ii. Express the relationships in each description graphically with an E-R diagram.

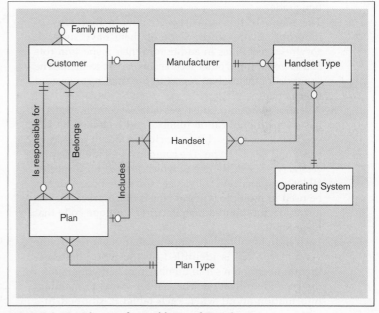

FIGURE 2-23 Diagram for Problem and Exercise 1

   a. A book is identified by its ISBN number, and it has a title, a price, and a date of publication. It is published by a publisher, which has its own ID number and a name. Each book has exactly one publisher, but one publisher typically publishes multiple books over time.
   b. A book (see 2a) is written by one or multiple authors. Each author is identified by an author number and has a name and date of birth. Each author has either one or multiple books; in addition, occasionally data are needed regarding prospective authors who have not yet published any books.
   c. In the context specified in 2a and 2b, better information is needed regarding the relationship between a book and

its authors. Specifically, it is important to record the percentage of the royalties that belongs to a specific author, whether or not a specific author is a lead author of the book, and each author's position in the sequence of the book's authors.

d. A book (see 2a) can be part of a series, which is also identified as a book and has its own ISBN number. One book can belong to several sets, and a set consists of at least one but potentially many books.

e. A piano manufacturer wants to keep track of all the pianos it makes individually. Each piano has an identifying serial number and a manufacturing completion date. Each instrument represents exactly one piano model, all of which have an identification number and a name. In addition, the company wants to maintain information about the designer of the model. Over time, the company often manufactures thousands of pianos of a certain model, and the model design is specified before any single piano exists.

f. A piano manufacturer (see 2e) employs piano technicians who are responsible for inspecting the instruments before they are shipped to the customers. Each piano is inspected by at least two technicians (identified by their employee number). For each separate inspection, the company needs to record its date and a quality evaluation grade.

g. The piano technicians (see 2f) have a hierarchy of reporting relationships: Some of them have supervisory responsibilities in addition to their inspection role and have multiple other technicians report to them. The supervisors themselves report to the chief technician of the company.

h. A vendor builds multiple types of tablet computers. Each has a type identification number and a name. The key specifications for each type include amount of storage space and display type. The company uses multiple processor types, exactly one of which is used for a specific tablet computer type; obviously, the same processor can be used in multiple types of tablets. Each processor has a manufacturer and a manufacturer's unique code that identifies it.

i. Each individual tablet computer manufactured by the vendor (see 2h) is identified by the type identification number and a serial number that is unique within the type identification. The vendor wants to maintain information about when each tablet is shipped to a customer.

j. Each of the tablet computer types (see 2h) has a specific operating system. Each technician the company employs is certified to assemble a specific tablet type–operating system combination. The validity of a certification starts on the day the employee passes a certification examination for the combination, and the certification is valid for

a specific period of time that varies depending on tablet type–operating system combination.

3. Answer the following questions concerning Figure 2-21:
a. Where is a unary relationship, what does it mean, and for what reasons might the cardinalities on it be different in other organizations?
b. Why is Includes a one-to many relationship, and why might this ever be different in some other organization?
c. Does Includes allow for a product to be represented in the database before it is assigned to a product line (e.g., while the product is in research and development)?
d. If there is a rating of the competency for each skill an employee possesses, where in the data model would we place this rating?
e. What is the meaning of the DOES BUSINESS IN associative entity, and why does each DOES BUSINESS IN instance have to be associated with exactly one TERRITORY and one CUSTOMER?
f. In what way might Pine Valley change the way it does business that would cause the Supplies associative entity to be eliminated and the relationships around it to change?

4. There is a bulleted list associated with Figure 2-21 that describes the entities and their relationships in Pine Valley Furniture. For each of the 10 points in the list, identify the subset of Figure 2-21 described by that point.

5. You may have been assigned a CASE or a drawing tool to develop conceptual data models. Using this tool, attempt to redraw all the E-R diagrams in this chapter. What difficulties did you encounter? What E-R notations did not translate well to your tool? How did you incorporate the E-R notation that did not directly translate into the tool's notation?

6. Consider the two E-R diagrams in Figure 2-24, which represent a database of community service agencies and volunteers in two different cities (A and B). For each of the following three questions, place a check mark under City A, City B, or Can't Tell for the choice that is the best answer.

	City A	City B	Can't Tell
a. Which city maintains data about only those volunteers who currently assist agencies?			
b. In which city would it be possible for a volunteer to assist more than one agency?			
c. In which city would it be possible for a volunteer to change which agency or agencies he or she assists?			

FIGURE 2-24 **Diagram for Problem and Exercise 6**

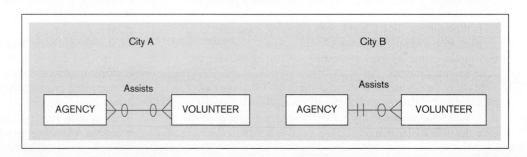

FIGURE 2-25   Grade report

```
MILLENNIUM COLLEGE
GRADE REPORT
FALL SEMESTER 200X

NAME:              Emily Williams        ID: 268300458
CAMPUS ADDRESS:    208 Brooks Hall
MAJOR:             Information Systems
```

COURSE ID	TITLE	INSTRUCTOR NAME	INSTRUCTOR LOCATION	GRADE
IS 350	Database Mgt.	Codd	B104	A
IS 465	System Analysis	Parsons	B317	B

7. The entity type STUDENT has the following attributes: Student Name, Address, Phone, Age, Activity, and No of Years. Activity represents some campus-based student activity, and No of Years represents the number of years the student has engaged in this activity. A given student may engage in more than one activity. Draw an ERD for this situation. What attribute or attributes did you designate as the identifier for the STUDENT entity? Why?

8. Are associative entities also weak entities? Why or why not? If yes, is there anything special about their "weakness"?

9. Because Visio does not explicitly show associative entities, it is not clear in Figure 2-21 which entity types are associative. List the associative entities in this figure. Why are there so many associative entities in Figure 2-21?

10. Figure 2-25 shows a grade report that is mailed to students at the end of each semester. Prepare an ERD reflecting the data contained in the grade report. Assume that each course is taught by one instructor. Also, draw this data model using the tool you have been told to use in the course. Explain what you chose for the identifier of each entity type on your ERD.

11. Add minimum and maximum cardinality notation to each of the following figures, as appropriate:
    a. Figure 2-5
    b. Figure 2-10a
    c. Figure 2-11b
    d. Figure 2-12 (all parts)
    e. Figure 2-13c
    f. Figure 2-14

12. The Is Married To relationship in Figure 2-12a would seem to have an obvious answer in Problem and Exercise 11d—that is, until time plays a role in modeling data. Draw a data model for the PERSON entity type and the Is Married To relationship for each of the following variations by showing the appropriate cardinalities and including, if necessary, any attributes:
    a. All we need to know is who a person is currently married to, if anyone. (This is likely what you represented in your answer to Problem and Exercise 11d.)
    b. We need to know who a person has ever been married to, if anyone.
    c. We need to know who a person has ever been married to, if anyone, as well as the date of their marriage and the date, if any, of the dissolution of their marriage.
    d. The same situation as in c, but now assume (which you likely did not do in c) that the same two people can

remarry each other after a dissolution of a prior marriage to each other.
    e. In history, and even in some cultures today, there may be no legal restriction on the number of people to whom one can be currently married. Does your answer to part c of this Problem and Exercise handle this situation or must you make some changes (if so, draw a new ERD).

13. Figure 2-26 represents a situation of students who attend and work in schools and who also belong to certain clubs that are located in different schools. Study this diagram carefully to try to discern what business rules are represented.
    a. You will notice that cardinalities are not included on the Works For relationship. State a business rule for this relationship, and then represent this rule with the cardinalities that match your rule.
    b. State a business rule that would make the Located In relationship redundant (i.e., where the school in which a club is located can be surmised or derived in some way from other relationships).
    c. Suppose a student could work for only a school that student attends but might not work. Would the Works For relationship still be necessary, or could you represent whether a student works for the school she attends in some other way (if so, how)?

14. Figure 2-27 shows two diagrams (A and B), both of which are legitimate ways to represent that a stock has a history of many prices. Which of the two diagrams do you consider a better way to model this situation and why?

15. Modify Figure 2-11a to model the following additional information requirements: The training director decides for

FIGURE 2-26   E-R diagram for Problem and Exercise 13

FIGURE 2-27 E-R diagram for
Problem and Exercise 14

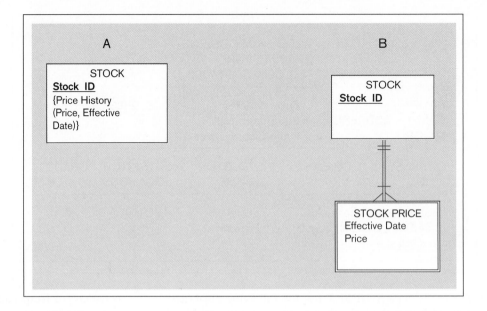

each employee who completes each class who (what employees) should be notified of the course completion. The training director needs to keep track of which employees are notified about each course completion by a student. The date of notification is the only attribute recorded about this notification.

16. Review Figure 2-8 and Figure 2-21.
    a. Identify any attributes in Figure 2-21 that might be composite attributes but are not shown that way. Justify your suggestions. Redraw the ERD to reflect any changes you suggest.
    b. Identify any attributes in Figure 2-21 that might be multivalued attributes but are not shown that way. Justify your suggestions. Redraw the ERD to reflect any changes you suggest.
    c. Is it possible for the same attribute to be both composite and multivalued? If no, justify your answer; if yes, give an example (Hint: Consider the CUSTOMER attributes in Figure 2-21).

17. Draw an ERD for each of the following situations. (If you believe that you need to make additional assumptions, clearly state them for each situation.) Draw the same situation using the tool you have been told to use in the course.
    a. A company has a number of employees. The attributes of EMPLOYEE include Employee ID (identifier), Name, Address, and Birthdate. The company also has several projects. Attributes of PROJECT include Project ID (identifier), Project Name, and Start Date. Each employee may be assigned to one or more projects or may not be assigned to a project. A project must have at least one employee assigned and may have any number of employees assigned. An employee's billing rate may vary by project, and the company wishes to record the applicable billing rate (Billing Rate) for each employee when assigned to a particular project. Do the attribute names in this description follow the guidelines for naming attributes? If not, suggest better names. Do you have any associative entities on your ERD? If so, what are the identifiers for those associative entities? Does your ERD allow a project to be created before it has any employees assigned to it? Explain. How would you change your ERD if the Billing Rate could change in the middle of a project?

    b. A laboratory has several chemists who work on one or more projects. Chemists also may use certain kinds of equipment on each project. Attributes of CHEMIST include Employee ID (identifier), Name, and Phone No. Attributes of PROJECT include Project ID (identifier) and Start Date. Attributes of EQUIPMENT include Serial No and Cost. The organization wishes to record Assign Date—that is, the date when a given equipment item was assigned to a particular chemist working on a specified project. A chemist must be assigned to at least one project and one equipment item. A given equipment item need not be assigned, and a given project need not be assigned either a chemist or an equipment item. Provide good definitions for all of the relationships in this situation.

    c. A college course may have one or more scheduled sections or may not have a scheduled section. Attributes of COURSE include Course ID, Course Name, and Units. Attributes of SECTION include Section Number and Semester ID. Semester ID is composed of two parts: Semester and Year. Section Number is an integer (such as 1 or 2) that distinguishes one section from another for the same course but does not uniquely identify a section. How did you model SECTION? Why did you choose this way versus alternative ways to model SECTION?

    d. A hospital has a large number of registered physicians. Attributes of PHYSICIAN include Physician ID (the identifier) and Specialty. Patients are admitted to the hospital by physicians. Attributes of PATIENT include Patient ID (the identifier) and Patient Name. Any patient who is admitted must have exactly one admitting physician. A physician may optionally admit any number of patients. Once admitted, a given patient must be treated by at least one physician. A particular physician may treat any number of patients, or may not treat any patients. Whenever a patient is treated by a physician, the hospital wishes to record the details of the treatment (Treatment Detail). Components of Treatment Detail include Date, Time, and Results. Did you draw more than one relationship between physician and patient? Why or why not? Did you include hospital as an entity type? Why or why not? Does your ERD allow for the same patient to be admitted by different physicians over time? How would you include on the ERD the need to represent the date on which a patient is admitted for each time he or she is admitted?

e. The loan office in a bank receives from various parties requests to investigate the credit status of a customer. Each credit request is identified by a Request ID and is described by a Request Date and Requesting Party Name. The loan office also received results of credit checks. A credit check is identified by a Credit Check ID and is described by the Credit Check Date and the Credit Rating. The loan office matches credit requests with credit check results. A credit request may be recorded before its result arrives; a particular credit result may be used in support of several credit requests. Draw an ERD for this situation. Now, assume that credit results may not be reused for multiple credit requests. Redraw the ERD for this new situation using two entity types, and then redraw it again using one entity type. Which of these two versions do you prefer, and why?

f. Companies, identified by Company ID and described by Company Name and Industry Type, hire consultants, identified by Consultant ID and described by Consultant Name and Consultant Specialty, which is multivalued. Assume that a consultant can work for only one company at a time, and we need to track only current consulting engagements. Draw an ERD for this situation. Now, consider a new attribute, Hourly Rate, which is the rate a consultant charges a company for each hour of his or her services. Redraw the ERD to include this new attribute. Now, consider that each time a consultant works for a company, a contract is written describing the terms for this consulting engagement. Contract is identified by a composite identifier of Company ID, Consultant ID, and Contract Date. Assuming that a consultant can still work for only one company at a time, redraw the ERD for this new situation. Did you move any attributes to different entity types in this latest situation? As a final situation, now consider that although a consultant can work for only one company at a time, we now need to keep the complete history of all consulting engagements for each consultant and company. Draw an ERD for this final situation. Explain why these different changes to the situation led to different data models, if they did.

g. An art museum owns a large volume of works of art. Each work of art is described by an item code (identifier), title, type, and size; size is further composed of height, width, and weight. A work of art is developed by an artist, but the artist for some works is unknown. An artist is described by an artist ID (identifier), name, date of birth, and date of death (which is null for still living artists). Only data about artists for works currently owned by the museum are kept in the database. At any point in time, a work of art is either on display at the museum, held in storage, away from the museum as part of a traveling show, or on loan to another gallery. If on display at the museum, a work of art is also described by its location within the museum. A traveling show is described by a show ID (identifier), the city in which the show is currently appearing, and the start and end dates of the show. Many of the museum works may be part of a given show, and only active shows with at least one museum work of art need be represented in the database. Finally, another gallery is described by a gallery ID (identifier), name, and city. The museum wants to retain a complete history of loaning a work of art to other galleries, and each time a work is loaned, the museum wants to know the date the work was loaned and the date it was returned. As you develop the ERD for this problem, follow good data naming guidelines.

h. Each case handled by the law firm of Dewey, Cheetim, and Howe has a unique case number; a date opened, date closed, and judgment description are also kept on each case. A case is brought by one or more plaintiffs, and the same plaintiff may be involved in many cases. A plaintiff has a requested judgment characteristic. A case is against one or more defendants, and the same defendant may be involved in many cases. A plaintiff or defendant may be a person or an organization. Over time, the same person or organization may be a defendant or a plaintiff in cases. In either situation, such legal entities are identified by an entity number, and other attributes are name and net worth. As you develop the ERD for this problem, follow good data naming guidelines.

i. Each publisher has a unique name; a mailing address and telephone number are also kept on each publisher. A publisher publishes one or more books; a book is published by exactly one publisher. A book is identified by its ISBN, and other attributes are title, price, and number of pages. Each book is written by one or more authors; an author writes one or more books, potentially for different publishers. Each author is uniquely described by an author ID, and we know each author's name and address. Each author is paid a certain royalty rate on each book he or she authors, which potentially varies for each book and for each author. An author receives a separate royalty check for each book he or she writes. Each check is identified by its check number, and we also keep track of the date and amount of each check. As you develop the ERD for this problem, follow good data naming guidelines.

18. Assume that at Pine Valley Furniture, each product (described by product number, description, and cost) is composed of three components (described by component number, description, and unit of measure), and components are used to make one or many products. In addition, assume that components are used to make other components, and that raw materials are also considered to be components. In both cases of components, we need to keep track of how many components go into making something else. Draw an ERD for this situation, and place minimum and maximum cardinalities on the diagram. Also, draw a data model for this situation using the tool you have been told to use in your course.

19. Emerging Electric wishes to create a database with the following entities and attributes:
   • Customer, with attributes Customer ID, Name, Address (Street, City, State, Zip Code), and Telephone
   • Location, with attributes Location ID, Address (Street, City, State, Zip Code), and Type (values of Business or Residential)
   • Rate, with attributes Rate Class and RatePerKWH

   After interviews with the owners, you have come up with the following business rules:
   • Customers can have one or more locations.
   • Each location can have one or more rates, depending on the time of day.

Draw an ERD for this situation and place minimum and maximum cardinalities on the diagram. Also, draw a data model for this situation using the tool you have been told to use in your course. State any assumptions that you have made.

20. Each semester, each student must be assigned an adviser who counsels students about degree requirements and helps students register for classes. Each student must register for classes with the help of an adviser, but if the student's assigned adviser is not available, the student may register with any adviser. We must keep track of students, the assigned adviser for each, and the name of the adviser with whom the student registered for the current term. Represent this situation of students and advisers with an E-R diagram. Also, draw a data model for this situation using the tool you have been told to use in your course.

21. In the chapter, when describing Figure 2-4a, it was argued that the Received and Summarizes relationships and TREASURER entity were not necessary. Within the context of this explanation, this is true. Now, consider a slightly different situation. Suppose it is necessary, for compliance purposes (e.g., Sarbanes-Oxley compliance), to know when each expense report was produced and which officers (not just the treasurer) received each expense report and when each signed off on that report. Redraw Figure 2-4a, now including any attributes and relationships required for this revised situation.

22. Prepare an ERD for a real estate firm that lists property for sale. Also prepare a definition for each entity type, attribute, and relationship on your diagram. In addition, draw a data model for this situation using the tool you have been told to use in your course. The following describes this organization:
    - The firm has a number of sales offices in several states. Attributes of sales office include Office Number (identifier) and Location.
    - Each sales office is assigned one or more employees. Attributes of employee include Employee ID (identifier) and Employee Name. An employee must be assigned to only one sales office.
    - For each sales office, there is always one employee assigned to manage that office. An employee may manage only the sales office to which he or she is assigned.

- The firm lists property for sale. Attributes of property include Property ID (identifier) and Location. Components of Location include Address, City, State, and Zip Code.
- Each unit of property must be listed with one (and only one) of the sales offices. A sales office may have any number of properties listed or may have no properties listed.
- Each unit of property has one or more owners. Attributes of owners are Owner ID (identifier) and Owner Name. An owner may own one or more units of property. An attribute of the relationship between property and owner is Percent Owned.

23. After completing a course in database management, you are asked to develop a preliminary ERD for a symphony orchestra. You discover the entity types that should be included as shown in Table 2-2.
    During further discussions you discover the following:
    - A concert season schedules one or more concerts. A particular concert is scheduled for only one concert season.
    - A concert includes the performance of one or more compositions. A composition may be performed at one or more concerts or may not be performed.
    - For each concert there is one conductor. A conductor may conduct any number of concerts or may not conduct any concerts.
    - Each composition may require one or more soloists or may not require a soloist. A soloist may perform one or more compositions at a given concert or may not perform any composition. The symphony orchestra wishes to record the date when a soloist last performed a given composition (Date Last Performed).
    Draw an ERD to represent what you have discovered. Identify a business rule in this description and explain how this business rule is modeled on the E-R diagram. Also draw a data model for this situation using the tool you have been told to use in your course.

24. Draw an ERD for the following situation. (State any assumptions you believe you have to make in order to develop a complete diagram.) Also, draw a data model for this situation using the tool you have been told to use in your course: Stillwater Antiques buys and sells one-of-a-kind antiques of all kinds (e.g., furniture, jewelry,

TABLE 2-2 Entity Types for Problem and Exercise 23

CONCERT SEASON	The season during which a series of concerts will be performed. Identifier is Opening Date, which includes Month, Day, and Year.
CONCERT	A given performance of one or more compositions. Identifier is Concert Number. Another important attribute is Concert Date, which consists of the following: Month, Day, Year, and Time. Each concert typically has more than one concert date.
COMPOSITION	Compositions to be performed at each concert. Identifier is Composition ID, which consists of the following: Composer Name and Composition Name. Another attribute is Movement ID, which consists of two parts: Movement Number and Movement Name. Many, but not all, compositions have multiple movements.
CONDUCTOR	Person who will conduct the concert. Identifier is Conductor ID. Another attribute is Conductor Name.
SOLOIST	Solo artist who performs a given composition on a particular concert. Identifier is Soloist ID. Another attribute is Soloist Name.

china, and clothing). Each item is uniquely identified by an item number and is also characterized by a description, asking price, condition, and open-ended comments. Stillwater works with many different individuals, called clients, who sell items to and buy items from the store. Some clients only sell items to Stillwater, some only buy items, and some others both sell and buy. A client is identified by a client number and is also described by a client name and client address. When Stillwater sells an item in stock to a client, the owners want to record the commission paid, the actual selling price, sales tax (tax of zero indicates a tax exempt sale), and date sold. When Stillwater buys an item from a client, the owners want to record the purchase cost, date purchased, and condition at time of purchase.

25. Draw an ERD for the following situation. (State any assumptions you believe you have to make in order to develop a complete diagram.) Also, draw a data model for this situation using the tool you have been told to use in your course: The A. M. Honka School of Business operates international business programs in 10 locations throughout Europe. The school had its first class of 9,000 graduates in 1965. The school keeps track of each graduate's student number, name when a student, country of birth, current country of citizenship, current name, and current address, as well as the name of each major the student completed. (Each student has one or two majors.) To maintain strong ties to its alumni, the school holds various events around the world. Events have a title, date, location, and type (e.g., reception, dinner, or seminar). The school needs to keep track of which graduates have attended which events. For an attendance by a graduate at an event, a comment is recorded about information school officials learned from that graduate at that event. The school also keeps in contact with graduates by mail, e-mail, telephone, and fax interactions. As with events, the school records information learned from the graduate from each of these contacts. When a school official knows that he or she will be meeting or talking to a graduate, a report is produced showing the latest information about that graduate and the information learned during the past two years from that graduate from all contacts and events the graduate attended.

26. Wally Los Gatos, owner of Wally's Wonderful World of Wallcoverings, has hired you as a consultant to design a database management system for his chain of three stores that sells wallpaper and accessories. He would like to track sales, customers, and employees. After an initial meeting with Wally, you have developed a list of business rules and specifications to begin the design of an E-R model:

- Customers place orders through a branch.
- Wally would like to track the following about customers: Name, Address, City, State, Zip Code, Telephone, Date of Birth, and Primary Language.
- A customer may place many orders.
- A customer does not always have to order through the same branch all the time.
- Customers may have one or more accounts, although they may also have no accounts.
- The following information needs to be recorded about accounts: Balance, Last payment date, Last payment amount, and Type.

- A branch may have many customers.
- The following information about each branch needs to be recorded: Branch Number, Location (Address, City, State, Zip Code), and Square Footage.
- A branch may sell all items or may only sell certain items.
- Orders are composed of one or more items.
- The following information about each order needs to be recorded: Order Date and Credit Authorization Status.
- Items may be sold by one or more branches.
- We wish to record the following about each item: Description, Color, Size, Pattern, and Type.
- An item can be composed of multiple items; for example, a dining room wallcovering set (item 20) may consist of wallpaper (item 22) and borders (item 23).
- Wally employs 56 employees.
- He would like to track the following information about employees: Name, Address (Street, City, State, Zip Code), Telephone, Date of Hire, Title, Salary, Skill, and Age.
- Each employee works in one and only one branch.
- Each employee may have one or more dependents. We wish to record the name of the dependent as well as the age and relationship.
- Employees can have one or more skills.

Based upon this information, draw an E-R model. Indicate any assumptions that you have made. Also, draw a data model for this situation using the tool you have been told to use in your course.

27. Our friend Wally Los Gatos (see Problem and Exercise 26), realizing that his wallcovering business had a few wrinkles in it, decided to pursue a law degree at night. After graduating, he has teamed up with Lyla El Pàjaro to form Peck and Paw, Attorneys at Law. Wally and Lyla have hired you to design a database system based upon the following set of business rules. It is in your best interest to perform a thorough analysis, to avoid needless litigation. Create an ERD based upon the following set of rules:

- An ATTORNEY is retained by one or more CLIENTS for each CASE.
- Attributes of ATTORNEY are Attorney ID, Name, Address, City, State, Zip Code, Specialty (may be more than one), and Bar (may be more than one).
- A CLIENT may have more than one ATTORNEY for each CASE.
- Attributes of CLIENT are Client ID, Name, Address, City, State, Zip Code, Telephone, and Date of Birth.
- A CLIENT may have more than one CASE.
- Attributes of CASE are Case ID, Case Description, and Case Type.
- An ATTORNEY may have more than one CASE.
- Each CASE is assigned to one and only one COURT.
- Attributes of COURT are Court ID, Court Name, City, State, and Zip Code.
- Each COURT has one or more JUDGES assigned to it.
- Attributes of JUDGE are Judge ID, Name, and Years In Practice.
- Each JUDGE is assigned to exactly one court.

State any assumptions that you have made. Also, draw a data model for this situation using the tool you have been told to use in your course.

References

Aranow, E. B. 1989. "Developing Good Data Definitions." *Database Programming & Design* 2,8 (August): 36–39.

Bruce, T. A. 1992. *Designing Quality Databases with IDEF1X Information Models*. New York: Dorset House.

Elmasri, R., and S. B. Navathe. 1994. *Fundamentals of Database Systems*. 2d ed. Menlo Park, CA: Benjamin/Cummings.

Hay, D. C. 2003. "What Exactly IS a Data Model?" Parts 1, 2, and 3. *DM Review* 13,2 (February: 24–26), 3 (March: 48–50), and 4 (April: 20–22, 46).

GUIDE. 1997 (October)."GUIDE Business Rules Project." Final Report, revision 1.2.

ISO/IEC. 2004. "Information Technology—Metadata Registries (MDR)—Part 4: Formulation of Data Definitions." July. Switzerland. Available at **http://metadata-standards.org/ 11179**.

ISO/IEC. 2005. "Information Technology—Metadata Registries (MDR)—Part 5: Naming and Identification Principles." September. Switzerland. Available at **http://metadata-standards.org/11179**.

Johnson, T. and R. Weis. 2007. "Time and Time Again: Managing Time in Relational Databases, Part 1." May. *DM Review*. Available from Magazine Archives section in the Information Center of **www.information-management.com**. See whole series of articles called "Time and Time Again" in subsequent issues.

Salin, T. 1990. "What's in a Name?" *Database Programming & Design* 3,3 (March): 55–58.

Song, I.-Y., M. Evans, and E. K. Park. 1995. "A Comparative Analysis of Entity-Relationship Diagrams." *Journal of Computer & Software Engineering* 3,4: 427–59.

Further Reading

Batini, C., S. Ceri, and S. B. Navathe. 1992. *Conceptual Database Design: An Entity-Relationship Approach*. Menlo Park, CA: Benjamin/Cummings.

Bodart, F., A. Patel, M. Sim, and R. Weber. 2001. "Should Optional Properties Be Used in Conceptual Modelling? A Theory and Three Empirical Tests." *Information Systems Research* 12,4 (December): 384–405.

Carlis, J., and J. Maguire. 2001. *Mastering Data Modeling: A User-Driven Approach*. Upper Saddle River, NJ: Prentice Hall.

Chen, P. P.-S. 1976. "The Entity-Relationship Model—Toward a Unified View of Data." *ACM Transactions on Database Systems* 1,1 (March): 9–36.

Gottesdiener, E. 1997. "Business Rules Show Power, Promise." *Application Development Trends* 4,3 (March): 36–54.

Gottesdiener, E. 1999. "Turning Rules into Requirements." *Application Development Trends* 6,7 (July): 37–50.

Hoffer, J. A., J. F. George, and J. S. Valacich. 2011. *Modern Systems Analysis and Design*. 6th ed. Upper Saddle River, NJ: Prentice Hall.

Keuffel, W. 1996. "Battle of the Modeling Techniques." *DBMS* 9,8 (August): 83, 84, 86, 97.

Moriarty, T. 2000. "The Right Tool for the Job." *Intelligent Enterprise* 3,9 (June 5): 68, 70–71.

Moody, D. 1996. "The Seven Habits of Highly Effective Data Modelers." *Database Programming & Design* 9,10 (October): 57, 58, 60–62, 64.

Owen, J. 2004. "Putting Rules Engines to Work." *InfoWorld* (June 28): 35–41.

Plotkin, D. 1999. "Business Rules Everywhere." *Intelligent Enterprise* 2,4 (March 30): 37–44.

Storey, V. C. 1991. "Relational Database Design Based on the Entity-Relationship Model." *Data and Knowledge Engineering* 7: 47–83.

Teorey, T. 1999. *Database Modeling & Design*. 3d ed. San Francisco, CA: Morgan Kaufman.

Teorey, T. J., D. Yang, and J. P. Fry. 1986. "A Logical Design Methodology for Relational Databases Using the Extended Entity-Relationship Model." *Computing Surveys* 18, 2 (June): 197–221.

Tillman, G. 1994. "Should You Model Derived Data?" *DBMS* 7,11 (November): 88, 90.

Tillman, G. 1995. "Data Modeling Rules of Thumb." *DBMS* 8,8 (August): 70, 72, 74, 76, 80–82, 87.

von Halle, B. 1997. "Digging for Business Rules." *Database Programming & Design* 8,11: 11–13.

Web Resources

http://dwr.ais.columbia.edu/info/Data%20Naming%20Standards.html Web site that provides guidelines for naming entities, attributes, and relationships similar to those suggested in this chapter.

www.adtmag.com Web site of *Application Development Trends*, a leading publication on the practice of information systems development.

www.axisboulder.com Web site for one vendor of business rules software.

www.businessrulesgroup.org Web site of the Business Rules Group, formerly part of GUIDE International, which formulates and supports standards about business rules.

http://en.wikipedia.org/wiki/Entity-relationship_model The Wikipedia entry for entity-relationship model, with an explanation of the origins of the crow's foot notation, which is used in this book.

http://ss64.com/ora/syntax-naming.html Web site that suggests naming conventions for entities, attributes, and relationships within an Oracle database environment.

www.tdan.com Web site of *The Data Administration Newsletter*, an online journal that includes articles on a wide variety of data management topics. This Web site is considered a "must follow" Web site for data management professionals.

The Enhanced E-R Model

LEARNING OBJECTIVES

After studying this chapter, you should be able to:

- Concisely define each of the following key terms: **enhanced entity-relationship (EER) model, subtype, supertype, attribute inheritance, generalization, specialization, completeness constraint, total specialization rule, partial specialization rule, disjointness constraint, disjoint rule, overlap rule, subtype discriminator, supertype/ subtype hierarchy,** and **universal data model.**
- Recognize when to use supertype/subtype relationships in data modeling.
- Use both specialization and generalization as techniques for defining supertype/ subtype relationships.
- Specify both completeness constraints and disjointness constraints in modeling supertype/subtype relationships.
- Develop a supertype/subtype hierarchy for a realistic business situation.
- Explain the major features and data modeling structures of a universal (packaged) data model.
- Describe the special features of a data modeling project when using a packaged data model.

Visit www.pearsonhighered.com/ hoffer to view the accompanying video for this chapter.

INTRODUCTION

The basic E-R model described in Chapter 2 was first introduced during the mid-1970s. It has been suitable for modeling most common business problems and has enjoyed widespread use. However, the business environment has changed dramatically since that time. Business relationships are more complex, and as a result, business data are much more complex as well. For example, organizations must be prepared to segment their markets and to customize their products, which places much greater demands on organizational databases.

To cope better with these changes, researchers and consultants have continued to enhance the E-R model so that it can more accurately represent the complex data encountered in today's business environment. The term **enhanced entity-relationship (EER) model** is used to identify the model that has resulted from extending the original E-R model with these new modeling constructs.

The most important modeling construct incorporated in the EER model is supertype/subtype relationships. This facility enables us to model a general entity type (called the *supertype*) and then subdivide it into several specialized entity types (called *subtypes*). Thus, for example, the entity type CAR can be modeled as a supertype, with subtypes SEDAN, SPORTS CAR, COUPE, and so on. Each subtype inherits attributes from its supertype and in addition may have special attributes and be involved in relationships of its own. Adding new notation for modeling

Enhanced entity-relationship (EER) model

A model that has resulted from extending the original E-R model with new modeling constructs.

supertype/subtype relationships has greatly improved the flexibility of the basic E-R model.

As introduced in Chapter 2, universal and industry-specific generalizable data models, which extensively utilized EER capabilities, have become very important for contemporary data modelers. These packaged data models and data model patterns have made data modelers more efficient and produce data models of higher quality. The EER features of supertypes/subtypes are essential to create generalizable data models; additional generalizing constructs, such as typing entities and relationships, are also employed. It has become very important for data modelers to know how to customize a data model pattern or data model for a major software package (e.g., enterprise resource planning or customer relationship management), just as it has become commonplace for information system builders to customize off-the-shelf software packages and software components.

REPRESENTING SUPERTYPES AND SUBTYPES

Recall from Chapter 2 that an entity type is a collection of entities that share common properties or characteristics. Although the entity instances that comprise an entity type are similar, we do not expect them to have exactly the same attributes. For example, recall required and optional attributes from Chapter 2. One of the major challenges in data modeling is to recognize and clearly represent entities that are almost the same, that is, entity types that share common properties but also have one or more distinct properties that are of interest to the organization.

Subtype

A subgrouping of the entities in an entity type that is meaningful to the organization and that shares common attributes or relationships distinct from other subgroupings.

Supertype

A generic entity type that has a relationship with one or more subtypes.

For this reason, the E-R model has been extended to include supertype/subtype relationships. A **subtype** is a subgrouping of the entities in an entity type that is meaningful to the organization. For example, STUDENT is an entity type in a university. Two subtypes of STUDENT are GRADUATE STUDENT and UNDERGRADUATE STUDENT. In this example, we refer to STUDENT as the supertype. A **supertype** is a generic entity type that has a relationship with one or more subtypes.

In the E-R diagramming we have done so far, supertypes and subtypes have been hidden. For example, consider again Figure 2-21, which is the E-R diagram (in Microsoft Visio) for Pine Valley Furniture Company. Notice that it is possible for a customer to not do business in any territory (i.e., no associated instances of the DOES BUSINESS IN associative entity). Why is this? One possible reason is that there are two types of customers—national account customers and regular customers—and only regular customers are assigned to a sales territory. Thus, in that figure, the reason for the optional cardinality next to the DOES BUSINESS IN associative entity coming from CUSTOMER is obscured. Explicitly drawing a customer entity supertype and several entity subtypes will help us make the E-R diagram more meaningful. Later in this chapter, we show a revised E-R diagram for Pine Valley Furniture, which demonstrates several EER notations to make vague aspects of Figure 2-21 more explicit.

Basic Concepts and Notation

The notation that is used for supertype/subtype relationships in this text is shown in Figure 3-1a. The supertype is connected with a line to a circle, which in turn is connected with a line to each subtype that has been defined. The U-shaped symbol on each line connecting a subtype to the circle emphasizes that the subtype is a subset of the supertype. It also indicates the direction of the subtype/supertype relationship. (This U is optional because the meaning and direction of the supertype/subtype relationship is usually obvious; in most examples, we will not include this symbol.) Figure 3-1b shows the type of EER notation used by Microsoft Visio (which is very similar to that used in this text), and Figure 3-1c shows the type of EER notation used by some CASE tools (e.g., Oracle Designer); the notation in Figure 3-1c is also the form often used for universal and industry-specific data models. These different formats have identical basic features, and you should easily become comfortable using any of these forms. We primarily use the text notation for examples in this chapter because advanced EER features are more standard with this format.

FIGURE 3-1 Basic notation for supertype/subtype relationships
(a) EER notation

(b) Microsoft Visio notation

(Figure 3-1 continues on the next page)

Attributes that are shared by all entities (including the identifier) are associated with the supertype. Attributes that are unique to a particular subtype are associated with that subtype. The same is true for relationships. Other components will be added to this notation to provide additional meaning in supertype/subtype relationships as we proceed through the remainder of this chapter.

AN EXAMPLE OF A SUPERTYPE/SUBTYPE RELATIONSHIP   Let us illustrate supertype/ subtype relationships with a simple, yet common, example. Suppose that an organization has three basic types of employees: hourly employees, salaried employees, and contract consultants. The following are some of the important attributes for each of these types of employees:

- *Hourly employees*   Employee Number, Employee Name, Address, Date Hired, Hourly Rate
- *Salaried employees*   Employee Number, Employee Name, Address, Date Hired, Annual Salary, Stock Option
- *Contract consultants*   Employee Number, Employee Name, Address, Date Hired, Contract Number, Billing Rate

Notice that all of the employee types have several attributes in common: Employee Number, Employee Name, Address, and Date Hired. In addition, each type has one or

FIGURE 3-1 (*continued*)
(c) Subtypes inside
supertypes notation

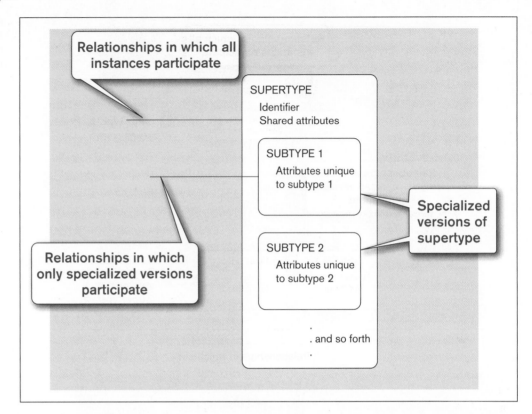

more attributes distinct from the attributes of other types (e.g., Hourly Rate is unique to hourly employees). If you were developing a conceptual data model in this situation, you might consider three choices:

1. Define a single entity type called EMPLOYEE. Although conceptually simple, this approach has the disadvantage that EMPLOYEE would have to contain all of the attributes for the three types of employees. For an instance of an hourly employee (for example), attributes such as Annual Salary and Contract Number would not apply (optional attributes) and would be null or not used. When taken to a development environment, programs that use this entity type would necessarily need to be quite complex to deal with the many variations.
2. Define a separate entity type for each of the three entities. This approach would fail to exploit the common properties of employees, and users would have to be careful to select the correct entity type when using the system.
3. Define a supertype called EMPLOYEE with subtypes HOURLY EMPLOYEE, SALARIED EMPLOYEE, and CONSULTANT. This approach exploits the common properties of all employees, yet it recognizes the distinct properties of each type.

Figure 3-2 shows a representation of the EMPLOYEE supertype with its three subtypes, using enhanced E-R notation. Attributes shared by all employees are associated with the EMPLOYEE entity type. Attributes that are peculiar to each subtype are included with that subtype only.

ATTRIBUTE INHERITANCE   A subtype is an entity type in its own right. An entity instance of a subtype represents the same entity instance of the supertype. For example, if "Therese Jones" is an occurrence of the CONSULTANT subtype, then this same person is necessarily an occurrence of the EMPLOYEE supertype. As a consequence, an entity in a subtype must possess not only values for its own attributes, but also values for its attributes as a member of the supertype, including the identifier.

   Attribute inheritance is the property by which subtype entities inherit values of all attributes and instances of all relationships of their supertype. This important property makes it unnecessary to include supertype attributes or relationships redundantly with the subtypes (remember, when it comes to data modeling, redundancy = bad, simplicity =

Attribute inheritance

A property by which subtype entities inherit values of all attributes and instances of all relationships of their supertype.

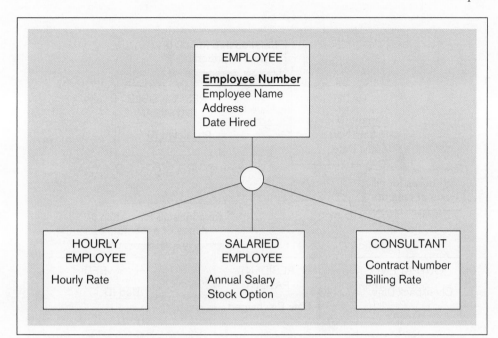

FIGURE 3-2 Employee
supertype with three
subtypes

good). For example, Employee Name is an attribute of EMPLOYEE (Figure 3-2) but
not of the subtypes of EMPLOYEE. Thus, the fact that the employee's name is "Therese
Jones" is inherited from the EMPLOYEE supertype. However, the Billing Rate for this
same employee is an attribute of the subtype CONSULTANT.

We have established that a member of a subtype must be a member of the supertype. Is the converse also true—that is, is a member of the supertype also a member of
one (or more) of the subtypes? This may or may not be true, depending on the business
situation. (Sure, "it depends" is the classic academic answer, but it's true in this case.)
We discuss the various possibilities later in this chapter.

WHEN TO USE SUPERTYPE/SUBTYPE RELATIONSHIPS So, how do you know when to use
a supertype/subtype relationship? You should consider using subtypes when either (or
both) of the following conditions are present:

1. There are attributes that apply to some (but not all) instances of an entity type. For
   example, see the EMPLOYEE entity type in Figure 3-2.
2. The instances of a subtype participate in a relationship unique to that subtype.

Figure 3-3 is an example of the use of subtype relationships that illustrates both
of these situations. The hospital entity type PATIENT has two subtypes: OUTPATIENT
and RESIDENT PATIENT. (The identifier is Patient ID.) All patients have an Admit Date
attribute, as well as a Patient Name. Also, every patient is cared for by a RESPONSIBLE
PHYSICIAN who develops a treatment plan for the patient.

Each subtype has an attribute that is unique to that subtype. Outpatients have
Checkback Date, whereas resident patients have Date Discharged. Also, resident patients have a unique relationship that assigns each patient to a bed. (Notice that this is a
mandatory relationship; it would be optional if it were attached to PATIENT.) Each bed
may or may not be assigned to a patient.

Earlier we discussed the property of attribute inheritance. Thus, each outpatient
and each resident patient inherits the attributes of the parent supertype PATIENT:
Patient ID, Patient Name, and Admit Date. Figure 3-3 also illustrates the principle of
relationship inheritance. OUTPATIENT and RESIDENT PATIENT are also instances of
PATIENT; therefore, each Is Cared For by a RESPONSIBLE PHYSICIAN.

Representing Specialization and Generalization

We have described and illustrated the basic principles of supertype/subtype relationships, including the characteristics of "good" subtypes. But in developing real-world

FIGURE 3-3 Supertype/subtype
relationships in a hospital

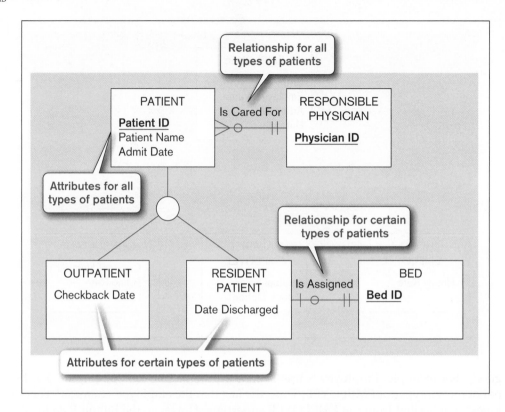

Generalization

The process of defining a more
general entity type from a set of
more specialized entity types.

data models, how can you recognize opportunities to exploit these relationships? There
are two processes—generalization and specialization—that serve as mental models in
developing supertype/subtype relationships.

GENERALIZATION   A unique aspect of human intelligence is the ability and propensity
to classify objects and experiences and to generalize their properties. In data modeling,
generalization is the process of defining a more general entity type from a set of more
specialized entity types. Thus, generalization is a bottom-up process.

An example of generalization is shown in Figure 3-4. In Figure 3-4a, three entity types have been defined: CAR, TRUCK, and MOTORCYCLE. At this stage, the
data modeler intends to represent these separately on an E-R diagram. However, on
closer examination, we see that the three entity types have a number of attributes in
common: Vehicle ID (identifier), Vehicle Name (with components Make and Model),
Price, and Engine Displacement. This fact (reinforced by the presence of a common
identifier) suggests that each of the three entity types is really a version of a more
general entity type.

This more general entity type (named VEHICLE), together with the resulting
supertype/subtype relationships, is shown in Figure 3-4b. The entity CAR has the specific attribute No Of Passengers, whereas TRUCK has two specific attributes: Capacity
and Cab Type. Thus, generalization has allowed us to group entity types along with their
common attributes and at the same time preserve specific attributes that are peculiar
to each subtype.

Notice that the entity type MOTORCYCLE is not included in the relationship.
Is this simply an omission? No. Instead, it is deliberately not included because it does
not satisfy the conditions for a subtype discussed earlier. Comparing Figure 3-4
parts a and b, you will notice that the only attributes of MOTORCYCLE are those
that are common to all vehicles; there are no attributes specific to motorcycles.
Furthermore, MOTORCYCLE does not have a relationship to another entity type.
Thus, there is no need to create a MOTORCYCLE subtype.

The fact that there is no MOTORCYCLE subtype suggests that it must be possible
to have an instance of VEHICLE that is not a member of any of its subtypes. We discuss
this type of constraint in the section on specifying constraints.

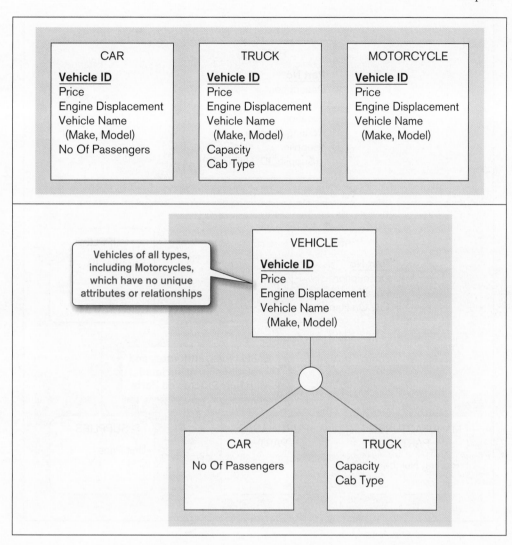

FIGURE 3-4 Example of generalization

(a) Three entity types: CAR, TRUCK, and MOTORCYCLE

(b) Generalization to VEHICLE supertype

SPECIALIZATION As we have seen, generalization is a bottom-up process. **Specialization** is a top-down process, the direct reverse of generalization. Suppose that we have defined an entity type with its attributes. Specialization is the process of defining one or more subtypes of the supertype and forming supertype/subtype relationships. Each subtype is formed based on some distinguishing characteristic, such as attributes or relationships specific to the subtype.

An example of specialization is shown in Figure 3-5. Figure 3-5a shows an entity type named PART, together with several of its attributes. The identifier is Part No, and other attributes are Description, Unit Price, Location, Qty On Hand, Routing Number, and Supplier. (The last attribute is multivalued and composite because there may be more than one supplier with an associated unit price for a part.)

In discussions with users, we discover that there are two possible sources for parts: Some are manufactured internally, whereas others are purchased from outside suppliers. Further, we discover that some parts are obtained from both sources. In this case, the choice depends on factors such as manufacturing capacity, unit price of the parts, and so on.

Some of the attributes in Figure 3-5a apply to all parts, regardless of source. However, others depend on the source. Thus, Routing Number applies only to manufactured parts, whereas Supplier ID and Unit Price apply only to purchased parts. These factors suggest that PART should be specialized by defining the subtypes MANUFACTURED PART and PURCHASED PART (Figure 3-5b).

In Figure 3-5b, Routing Number is associated with MANUFACTURED PART. The data modeler initially planned to associate Supplier ID and Unit Price with

Specialization

The process of defining one or more subtypes of the supertype and forming supertype/subtype relationships.

FIGURE 3-5 Example of specialization
(a) Entity type PART

(b) Specialization to MANUFACTURED PART and PURCHASED PART

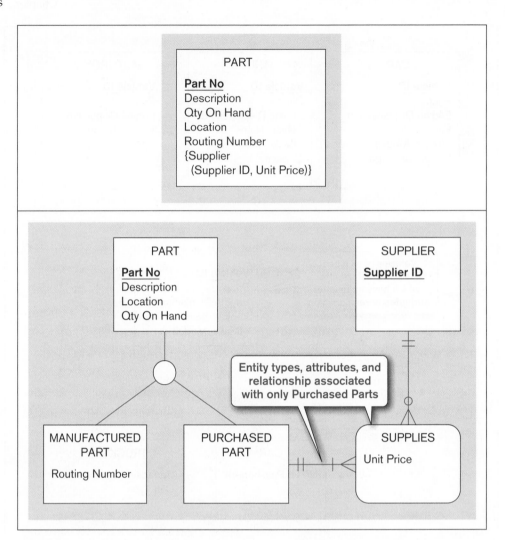

PURCHASED PART. However, in further discussions with users, the data modeler suggested instead that they create a SUPPLIER entity type and an associative entity linking PURCHASED PART with SUPPLIER. This associative entity (named SUPPLIES in Figure 3-5b) allows users to more easily associate purchased parts with their suppliers. Notice that the attribute Unit Price is now associated with the associative entity so that the unit price for a part may vary from one supplier to another. In this example, specialization has permitted a preferred representation of the problem domain.

COMBINING SPECIALIZATION AND GENERALIZATION Specialization and generalization are both valuable techniques for developing supertype/subtype relationships. The technique you use at a particular time depends on several factors, such as the nature of the problem domain, previous modeling efforts, and personal preference. You should be prepared to use both approaches and to alternate back and forth as dictated by the preceding factors.

SPECIFYING CONSTRAINTS IN SUPERTYPE/SUBTYPE RELATIONSHIPS

So far we have discussed the basic concepts of supertype/subtype relationships and introduced some basic notation to represent these concepts. We have also described the processes of generalization and specialization, which help a data modeler recognize opportunities for exploiting these relationships. In this section, we introduce additional notation to represent constraints on supertype/subtype relationships. These constraints allow us to capture some of the important business rules that apply to these relationships. The two most important types of constraints that are described in this section are completeness and disjointness constraints (Elmasri and Navathe, 1994).

Specifying Completeness Constraints

A **completeness constraint** addresses the question of whether an instance of a supertype must also be a member of at least one subtype. The completeness constraint has two possible rules: total specialization and partial specialization. The **total specialization rule** specifies that each entity instance of the supertype must be a member of some subtype in the relationship. The **partial specialization rule** specifies that an entity instance of the supertype is allowed not to belong to any subtype. We illustrate each of these rules with earlier examples from this chapter (see Figure 3-6).

TOTAL SPECIALIZATION RULE Figure 3-6a repeats the example of PATIENT (Figure 3-3) and introduces the notation for total specialization. In this example, the business rule is the following: A patient must be either an outpatient or a resident patient. (There are no other types of patient in this hospital.) Total specialization is indicated by the *double* line extending from the PATIENT entity type to the circle. (In the Microsoft Visio notation, total specialization is called "Category is complete" and is shown also by a *double* line under the category circle between the supertype and associated subtypes.)

In this example, every time a new instance of PATIENT is inserted into the supertype, a corresponding instance is inserted into either OUTPATIENT or RESIDENT PATIENT. If the instance is inserted into RESIDENT PATIENT, an instance of the relationship Is Assigned is created to assign the patient to a hospital bed.

PARTIAL SPECIALIZATION RULE Figure 3-6b repeats the example of VEHICLE and its subtypes CAR and TRUCK from Figure 3-4. Recall that in this example, motorcycle is a type of vehicle, but it is not represented as a subtype in the data model. Thus, if a vehicle is a car, it must appear as an instance of CAR, and if it is a truck, it must appear as an instance of TRUCK. However, if the vehicle is a motorcycle, it cannot appear as an instance of any subtype. This is an example of partial specialization, and it is specified by the single line from the VEHICLE supertype to the circle.

Specifying Disjointness Constraints

A **disjointness constraint** addresses whether an instance of a supertype may simultaneously be a member of two (or more) subtypes. The disjointness constraint has two possible rules: the disjoint rule and the overlap rule. The disjoint rule specifies that if an entity instance (of the supertype) is a member of one subtype, it cannot simultaneously be a member of any other subtype. The overlap rule specifies that an entity instance can

Completeness constraint

A type of constraint that addresses whether an instance of a supertype must also be a member of at least one subtype.

Total specialization rule

A rule that specifies that each entity instance of a supertype must be a member of some subtype in the relationship.

Partial specialization rule

A rule that specifies that an entity instance of a supertype is allowed not to belong to any subtype.

Disjointness constraint

A constraint that addresses whether an instance of a supertype may simultaneously be a member of two (or more) subtypes.

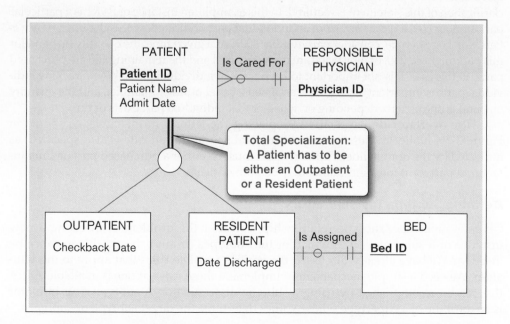

FIGURE 3-6 Examples of completeness constraints (a) Total specialization rule

(Figure 3-6 continues on the next page)

FIGURE 3-6 (*continued*)
(b) Partial specialization rule

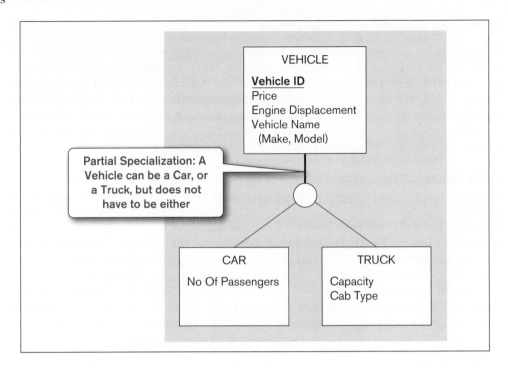

simultaneously be a member of two (or more) subtypes. An example of each of these rules is shown in Figure 3-7.

DISJOINT RULE Figure 3-7a shows the PATIENT example from Figure 3-6a. The business rule in this case is the following: *At any given time*, a patient must be either an outpatient or a resident patient, but cannot be both. This is the **disjoint rule**, as specified by the letter *d* in the circle joining the supertype and its subtypes. Note in this figure, the subclass of a PATIENT may change over time, but at a given time, a PATIENT is of only one type. (The Microsoft Visio notation does not have a way to designate disjointness or overlap; however, you can place a *d* or an *o* inside the category circle using the Text tool.)

OVERLAP RULE Figure 3-7b shows the entity type PART with its two subtypes, MANUFACTURED PART and PURCHASED PART (from Figure 3-5b). Recall from our discussion of this example that some parts are both manufactured and purchased. Some clarification of this statement is required. In this example, an instance of PART is a particular part number (i.e., a *type of part*), not an individual part (indicated by the identifier, which is Part No). For example, consider part number 4000. At a given time, the quantity on hand for this part might be 250, of which 100 are manufactured and the remaining 150 are purchased parts. In this case, it is not important to keep track of individual parts. When tracking individual parts is important, each part is assigned a serial number identifier, and the quantity on hand is one or zero, depending on whether that individual part exists or not.

The **overlap rule** is specified by placing the letter *o* in the circle, as shown in Figure 3-7b. Notice in this figure that the total specialization rule is also specified, as indicated by the double line. Thus, any part must be either a purchased part or a manufactured part, or it may simultaneously be both of these.

Defining Subtype Discriminators

Given a supertype/subtype relationship, consider the problem of inserting a new instance of a supertype. Into which of the subtypes (if any) should this instance be inserted? We have already discussed the various possible rules that apply to this situation. We need a simple mechanism to implement these rules, if one is available. Often this can be accomplished by using a subtype discriminator. A **subtype discriminator** is an attribute of a supertype whose values determine the target subtype or subtypes.

Disjoint rule

A rule that specifies that an instance of a supertype may not simultaneously be a member of two (or more) subtypes.

Overlap rule

A rule that specifies that an instance of a supertype may simultaneously be a member of two (or more) subtypes.

Subtype discriminator

An attribute of a supertype whose values determine the target subtype or subtypes.

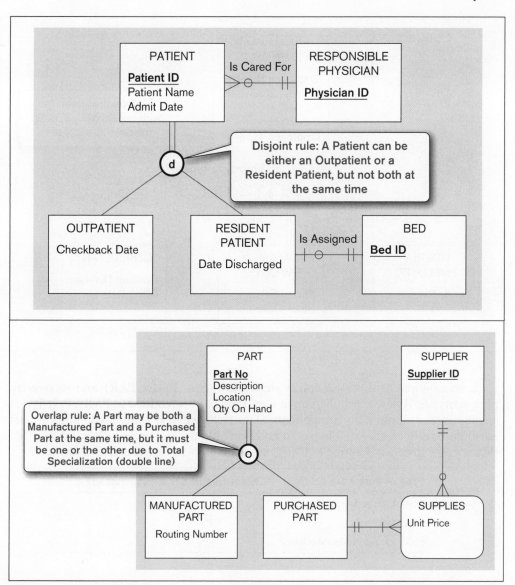

FIGURE 3-7 Examples of disjointness constraints
(a) Disjoint rule

(b) Overlap rule

DISJOINT SUBTYPES An example of the use of a subtype discriminator is shown in Figure 3-8. This example is for the EMPLOYEE supertype and its subtypes, introduced in Figure 3-2. Notice that the following constraints have been added to this figure: total specialization and disjoint subtypes. Thus, each employee must be either hourly, salaried, or a consultant.

A new attribute (Employee Type) has been added to the supertype to serve as a subtype discriminator. When a new employee is added to the supertype, this attribute is coded with one of three values, as follows: "H" (for Hourly), "S" (for Salaried), or "C" (for Consultant). Depending on this code, the instance is then assigned to the appropriate subtype. (An attribute of the supertype may be selected in the Microsoft Visio notation as a discriminator, which is shown similarly next to the category symbol.)

The notation we use to specify the subtype discriminator is also shown in Figure 3-8. The expression Employee Type= (which is the left side of a condition statement) is placed next to the line leading from the supertype to the circle. The value of the attribute that selects the appropriate subtype (in this example, either "H," "S," or "C") is placed adjacent to the line leading to that subtype. Thus, for example, the condition Employee Type="S" causes an entity instance to be inserted into the SALARIED EMPLOYEE subtype.

OVERLAPPING SUBTYPES When subtypes overlap, a slightly modified approach must be applied for the subtype discriminator. The reason is that a given instance of the supertype may require that we create an instance in more than one subtype.

FIGURE 3-8 Introducing a subtype discriminator (disjoint rule)

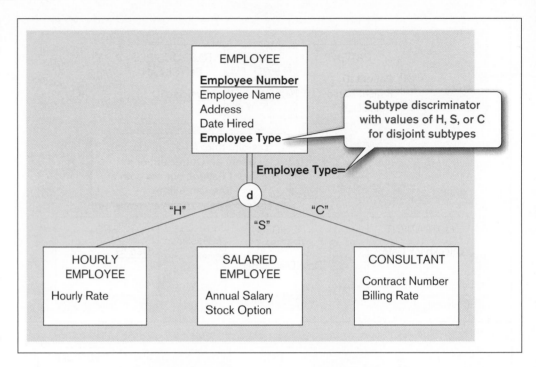

An example of this situation is shown in Figure 3-9 for PART and its overlapping subtypes. A new attribute named Part Type has been added to PART. Part Type is a composite attribute with components Manufactured? and Purchased? Each of these attributes is a Boolean variable (i.e., it takes on only the values yes, "Y," and no, "N"). When a new instance is added to PART, these components are coded as follows:

Type of Part	Manufactured?	Purchased?
Manufactured only	"Y"	"N"
Purchased only	"N"	"Y"
Purchased and manufactured	"Y"	"Y"

FIGURE 3-9 Subtype discriminator (overlap rule)

The method for specifying the subtype discriminator for this example is shown in Figure 3-9. Notice that this approach can be used for any number of overlapping subtypes.

Defining Supertype/Subtype Hierarchies

We have considered a number of examples of supertype/subtype relationships in this chapter. It is possible for any of the subtypes in these examples to have other subtypes defined on it (in which case the subtype becomes a supertype for the newly defined subtypes). A **supertype/subtype hierarchy** is a hierarchical arrangement of supertypes and subtypes, where each subtype has only one supertype (Elmasri and Navathe, 1994).

We present an example of a supertype/subtype hierarchy in this section in Figure 3-10. (For simplicity, we do not show subtype discriminators in this and most subsequent examples. See Problems and Exercises 2 and 3.) This example includes most of the concepts and notation we have used in this chapter to this point. It also presents a methodology (based on specialization) that you can use in many data modeling situations.

AN EXAMPLE OF A SUPERTYPE/SUBTYPE HIERARCHY   Suppose that you are asked to model the human resources in a university. Using specialization (a top-down approach), you might proceed as follows: Starting at the top of a hierarchy, model the most general entity type first. In this case, the most general entity type is PERSON. List and associate all attributes of PERSON. The attributes shown in Figure 3-10 are SSN (identifier), Name, Address, Gender, and Date Of Birth. The entity type at the top of a hierarchy is sometimes called the *root*.

Supertype/subtype hierarchy
A hierarchical arrangement of supertypes and subtypes in which each subtype has only one supertype.

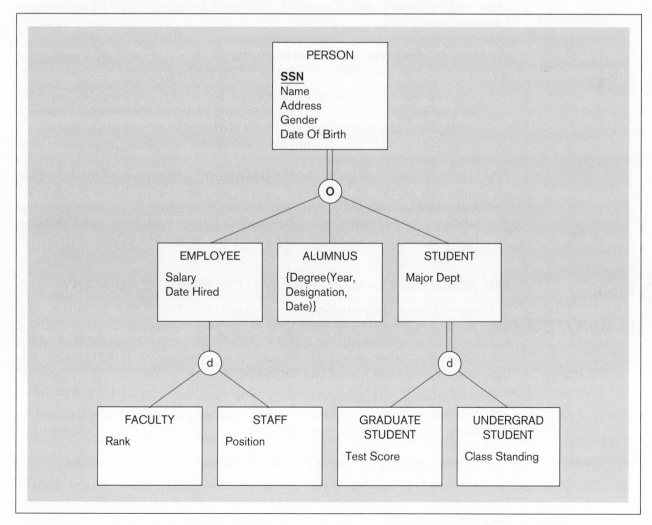

FIGURE 3-10   Example of supertype/subtype hierarchy

Next, define all major subtypes of the root. In this example, there are three subtypes of PERSON: EMPLOYEE (persons who work for the university), STUDENT (persons who attend classes), and ALUMNUS (persons who have graduated). Assuming that there are no other types of persons of interest to the university, the total specialization rule applies, as shown in the figure. A person might belong to more than one subtype (e.g., ALUMNUS and EMPLOYEE), so the overlap rule is used. Note that overlap allows for any overlap. (A PERSON may be simultaneously in any pair or in all three subtypes.) If certain combinations are not allowed, a more refined supertype/subtype hierarchy would have to be developed to eliminate the prohibited combinations.

Attributes that apply specifically to each of these subtypes are shown in the figure. Thus, each instance of EMPLOYEE has a value for Date Hired and Salary. Major Dept is an attribute of STUDENT, and Degree (with components Year, Designation, and Date) is a multivalued, composite attribute of ALUMNUS.

The next step is to evaluate whether any of the subtypes already defined qualify for further specialization. In this example, EMPLOYEE is partitioned into two subtypes: FACULTY and STAFF. FACULTY has the specific attribute Rank, whereas STAFF has the specific attribute Position. Notice that in this example the subtype EMPLOYEE becomes a supertype to FACULTY and STAFF. Because there may be types of employees other than faculty and staff (such as student assistants), the partial specialization rule is indicated. However, an employee cannot be both faculty and staff at the same time. Therefore, the disjoint rule is indicated in the circle.

Two subtypes are also defined for STUDENT: GRADUATE STUDENT and UNDERGRAD STUDENT. UNDERGRAD STUDENT has the attribute Class Standing, whereas GRADUATE STUDENT has the attribute Test Score. Notice that total specialization and the disjoint rule are specified; you should be able to state the business rules for these constraints.

SUMMARY OF SUPERTYPE/SUBTYPE HIERARCHIES We note two features concerning the attributes contained in the hierarchy shown in Figure 3-10:

1. Attributes are assigned at the highest logical level that is possible in the hierarchy. For example, because SSN (i.e., Social Security Number) applies to all persons, it is assigned to the root. In contrast, Date Hired applies only to employees, so it is assigned to EMPLOYEE. This approach ensures that attributes can be shared by as many subtypes as possible.
2. Subtypes that are lower in the hierarchy inherit attributes not only from their immediate supertype, but from all supertypes higher in the hierarchy, up to the root. Thus, for example, an instance of faculty has values for all of the following attributes: SSN, Name, Address, Gender, and Date Of Birth (from PERSON); Date Hired and Salary (from EMPLOYEE); and Rank (from FACULTY).

EER MODELING EXAMPLE: PINE VALLEY FURNITURE COMPANY

In Chapter 2, we presented a sample E-R diagram for Pine Valley Furniture. (This diagram, developed using Microsoft Visio, is repeated in Figure 3-11.) After studying this diagram, you might use some questions to help you clarify the meaning of entities and relationships. Three such areas of questions are (see annotations in Figure 3-11 that indicate the source of each question) the following:

1. Why do some customers not do business in one or more sales territories?
2. Why do some employees not supervise other employees, and why are they not all supervised by another employee? And why do some employees not work in a work center?
3. Why do some vendors not supply raw materials to Pine Valley Furniture?

You may have other questions, but we will concentrate on these three to illustrate how supertype/subtype relationships can be used to convey a more specific (semantically rich) data model.

FIGURE 3-11 E-R diagram for Pine Valley Furniture Company

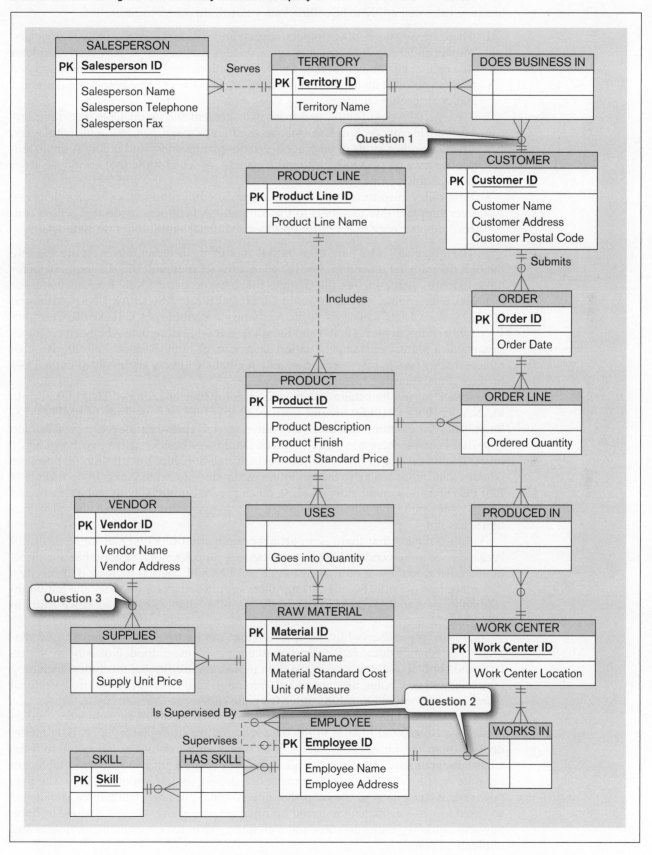

After some investigation into these three questions, we discover the following business rules that apply to how Pine Valley Furniture does business:

1. There are two types of customers: regular and national account. Only regular customers do business in sales territories. A sales territory exists only if it has at least one regular customer associated with it. A national account customer is associated with an account manager. It is possible for a customer to be both a regular and a national account customer.

2. Two special types of employees exist: management and union. Only union employees work in work centers, and a management employee supervises union employees. There are other kinds of employees besides management and union. A union employee may be promoted into management, at which time that employee stops being a union employee.

3. Pine Valley Furniture keeps track of many different vendors, not all of which have ever supplied raw materials to the company. A vendor is associated with a contract number once that vendor becomes an official supplier of raw materials.

These business rules have been used to modify the E-R diagram in Figure 3-11 into the EER diagram in Figure 3-12. (We have left most attributes off this diagram except for those that are essential to see the changes that have occurred.) Rule 1 means that there is a total, overlapping specialization of CUSTOMER into REGULAR CUSTOMER and NATIONAL ACCOUNT CUSTOMER. A composite attribute of CUSTOMER, Customer Type (with components National and Regular), is used to designate whether a customer instance is a regular customer, a national account, or both. Because only regular customers do business in sales territories, only regular customers are involved in the Does Business In relationship (associative entity).

Rule 2 means that there is a partial, disjoint specialization of EMPLOYEE into MANAGEMENT EMPLOYEE and UNION EMPLOYEE. An attribute of EMPLOYEE, Employee Type, discriminates between the two special types of employees. Specialization is partial because there are other kinds of employees besides these two types. Only union employees are involved in the Works In relationship, but all union employees work in some work center, so the minimum cardinality of next to Works In from UNION EMPLOYEE is now mandatory. Because an employee cannot be both management and union at the same time (although he or she can change status over time), the specialization is disjoint.

Rule 3 means that there is a partial specialization of VENDOR into SUPPLIER because only some vendors become suppliers. A supplier, not a vendor, has a contract number. Because there is only one subtype of VENDOR, there is no reason to specify a disjoint or overlap rule. Because all suppliers supply some raw material, the minimum cardinality next to RAW MATERIAL in the Supplies relationship (associative entity in Visio) now is one.

This example shows how an E-R diagram can be transformed into an EER diagram once generalization/specialization of entities is understood. Not only are supertype and subtype entities now in the data model, but additional attributes, including discriminating attributes, also are added; minimum cardinalities change (from optional to mandatory), and relationships move from the supertype to a subtype.

This is a good time to emphasize a point made earlier about data modeling. A data model is a conceptual picture of the data required by an organization. A data model does not map one-for-one to elements of an implemented database. For example, a database designer may choose to put all customer instances into one database table, not separate ones for each type of customer. Such details are not important now. The purpose now is to explain all the rules that govern data, not how data will be stored and accessed to achieve efficient, required information processing. We will address technology and efficiency issues in subsequent chapters when we cover database design and implementation.

Although the EER diagram in Figure 3-12 clarifies some questions and makes the data model in Figure 3-11 more explicit, it still can be difficult for some people to comprehend. Some people will not be interested in all types of data, and some may not need

FIGURE 3-12   EER diagram for Pine Valley Furniture Company using Microsoft Visio

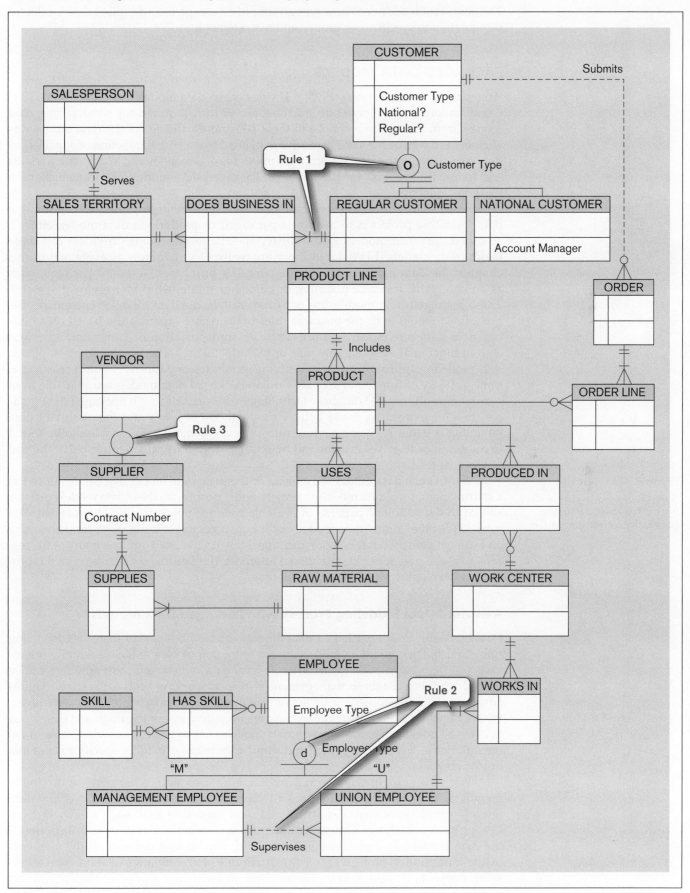

to see all the details in the EER diagram to understand what the database will cover. The next section addresses how we can simplify a complete and explicit data model for presentation to specific user groups and management.

PACKAGED DATA MODELS

According to Len Silverston (1998), "The age of the data modeler as artisan is passing. Organizations can no longer afford the labor or time required for handcrafting data models from scratch. In response to these constraints, the age of the data modeler as engineer is dawning." As one executive explained to us, "the acquisition of a [packaged data model] was one of the key strategic things his organization did to gain quick results and long-term success" for the business. Packaged data models are a game-changer for data modeling.

As introduced in Chapter 2, an increasingly popular approach to beginning a data modeling project is to acquire a packaged or predefined data model, either a so-called universal model or an industry-specific model (some providers call these logical data models [LDMs], but these are really EER diagrams as explained in this chapter; the data model may also be part of a purchased software package, such as an enterprise resource planning or customer relationship management system). These packaged data models are not fixed; rather, the data modeler customizes the predefined model to fit the business rules of his or her organization based on a best-practices data model for the industry (e.g., transportation or communications) or chosen functional area (e.g., finance or manufacturing). The key assumption of this data modeling approach is that underlying structures or patterns of enterprises in the same industry or functional area are similar. Packaged data models are available from various consultants and database technology vendors. Although packaged data models are not inexpensive, many believe the total cost is lower and the quality of data modeling is better by using such resources. Some generic data models can be found in publications (e.g., see articles and books by Hay and by Silverston listed at the end of this chapter).

Universal data model

A generic or template data model that can be reused as a starting point for a data modeling project.

A **universal data model** is a generic or template data model that can be reused as a starting point for a data modeling project. Some people call these data model patterns, similar to the notion of patterns of reusable code for programming. A universal data model is not the "right" data model, but it is a successful starting point for developing an excellent data model for an organization. Hoberman (2006) outlines many of the reasons why the prepackaged data model approach has become a prominent method for quickly developing and evolving a database.

A Revised Data Modeling Process with Packaged Data Models

Data modeling from a packaged data model requires no less skill than data modeling from scratch. Packaged data models are not going to put data modelers out of work (or keep you from getting that job as an entry-level data analyst you want now that you've started studying database management!). In fact, working with a package requires advanced skills, like those you are learning in this chapter and Chapter 2. As we will see, the packaged data models are rather complex because they are thorough and developed to cover all possible circumstances. A data modeler has to be very knowledgeable of the organization as well as the package to customize the package to fit the specific rules of that organization.

What do you get when you purchase a data model? What you are buying is metadata. You receive, usually on a CD, a fully populated description of the data model, usually specified in a structured data modeling tool, such as ERwin from Computer Associates or Oracle Designer from Oracle Corporation. The supplier of the data model has drawn the EER diagram; named and defined all the elements of the data model; and given all the attributes characteristics of data type (character, numeric, image), length, format, and so forth. You can print the data model and various reports about its contents to support the customization process. Once you customize the model, you can then use the data modeling tool to automatically generate the SQL commands to define the database to a variety of database management systems.

How is the data modeling process different when starting with a purchased solution? The following are the key differences (our understanding of these differences are enhanced by the interviews we conducted at Overstock.com):

- Because a purchased data model is extensive, you begin by identifying the parts of the data model that apply to your data modeling situation. Concentrate on these parts first and in the most detail. Start, as with most data modeling activities, first with entities, then attributes, and finally relationships. Consider how your organization will operate in the future, not just today.

- You then rename the identified data elements to terms local to the organization rather than the generic names used in the package.

- In many cases, the packaged data model will be used in new information systems that replace existing databases as well as to extend into new areas. So the next step is to map the data to be used from the package to data in current databases. One way this mapping will be used is to design migration plans to convert existing databases to the new structures. The following are some key points about this mapping process:

  - There will be data elements from the package that are not in current systems, and there will be some data elements in current databases not in the package. Thus, some elements won't map between the new and former environments. This is to be expected because the package anticipates information needs you have not, yet, satisfied by your current databases and because you do some special things in your organization that you want to retain but that are not standard practices. However, be sure that each non-mapped data element is really unique and needed. For example, it is possible that a data element in a current database may actually be derived from other more atomic data in the purchased data model. Also, you need to decide if data elements unique to the purchased data model are needed now or can be added on when you are ready to take advantage of these capabilities in the future.

  - In general, the business rules embedded in the purchased data model cover all possible circumstances (e.g., the maximum number of customers associated with a customer order). The purchased data model allows for great flexibility, but a general-purpose business rule may be too weak for your situation (e.g., you are sure you will never allow more than one customer per customer order). As you will see in the next section, the flexibility and generalizability of a purchased data model results in complex relationships and many entity types. Although the purchased model alerts you to what is possible, you need to decide if you really need this flexibility and if the complexity is worthwhile.

  - Because you are starting with a prototypical data model, it is possible to engage users and managers to be supported by the new database early and often in the data modeling project. Interviews, JAD sessions, and other requirements gathering activities are based on concrete ERDs rather than wish lists. The purchased data model essentially suggests specific questions to be asked or issues to discuss (e.g., "Would we ever have a customer order with more than one customer associated with it?" or "Might an employee also be a customer?"). The purchased model in a sense provides a visual checklist of items to discuss (e.g., Do we need these data? Is this business rule right for us?); further, it is comprehensive, so it is less likely that an important requirement will be missed.

  - Because the purchased data model is comprehensive, there is no way you will be able to build and populate the full database or even customize the whole data model in one project. However, you don't want to miss the opportunity to visualize future requirements shown in the full data model. Thus, you will get to a point where you have to make a decision on what will be built first and possible future phases to build out as much of the purchased data model as will make sense.

You will learn in subsequent chapters of this book important database modeling and design concepts and skills that are important in any database development effort, including those based on purchased data models. There are, however, some important things to note about projects involving purchased data models. Some of these involve using existing databases to guide how to customize a purchased data model, including the following:

- Over time the same attribute may have been used for different purposes—what people call overloaded columns in current systems. This means that the data values in existing databases may not have uniform meaning for the migration to the new database. Oftentimes these multiple uses are not documented and are not known until the migration begins. Some data may no longer be needed (maybe used for a special business project), or there may be hidden requirements that were not formally incorporated into the database design. More on how to deal with this in a moment.

- Similarly, some attributes may be empty (i.e., have no values), at least for some periods of time. For example, some employee home addresses could be missing, or product engineering attributes for a given product line might be absent for products developed a few years ago. This could have occurred because of application software errors, human data entry mistakes, or other reasons. As we have studied, missing data may suggest optional data, and the need for entity subtypes. So missing data need to be studied to understand why the data are sparse.

- A good method for understanding hidden meaning and identifying inconsistencies in existing data models, and hence data and business rules that need to be included in the customized purchased data model, is data profiling. Profiling is a way to statistically analyze data to uncover hidden patterns and flaws. Profiling can find outliers, identify shifts in data distribution over time, and identify other phenomena. Each perturbation of the distribution of data may tell a story, such as showing when major application system changes occurred, or when business rules changed. Often these patterns suggest poorly designed databases (e.g., data for separate entities were combined to improve processing speed for a special set of queries but the better structure was never restored). Data profiling can also be used to assess how accurate current data are and anticipate the clean-up effort that will be needed to populate the purchased data model with high-quality data.

- Arguably the most important challenge of customizing a purchased data model is determining the business rules that will be established through the data model. A purchased data model will anticipate the vast majority of the needed rules, but each rule must be verified for your organization. Fortunately, you don't have to guess which ones to address; each is laid out by the entities, attributes, and relationships with their metadata (names, definitions, data types, formats, lengths, etc.) in the purchased model. It simply takes time to go through each of these data elements with the right subject matter experts to make sure you have the relationship cardinalities and all other aspects of the data model right.

Summary of Prepackaged Data Models

Essentially any existing data model can be a starting point for a new data modeling project. The best prepackaged data models are comprehensive, utilizing extensive EER features. True prepackaged data models are so extensive that examples are beyond the scope of this chapter. However, if you master an understanding of EER concepts and notations, you should be able to read and work with most universal data models.

Summary

This chapter has described how the basic E-R model has been extended to include supertype/subtype relationships. A *supertype* is a generic entity type that has a relationship with one or more subtypes. A *subtype* is a grouping of the entities in an entity type that is meaningful to the organization. For example, the entity type PERSON is frequently modeled as a supertype. Subtypes of PERSON may include EMPLOYEE, VOLUNTEER, and CLIENT. Subtypes inherit the attributes and relationships associated with their supertype.

Supertype/subtype relationships should normally be considered in data modeling with either (or both) of the following conditions present: First, there are attributes that apply to some (but not all) of the instances of an entity type. Second, the instances of a subtype participate in a relationship unique to that subtype.

The techniques of generalization and specialization are important guides in developing supertype/subtype relationships. Generalization is the bottom-up process of defining a generalized entity type from a set of more specialized entity types. Specialization is the top-down process of defining one or more subtypes of a supertype that has already been defined.

The EER notation allows us to capture the important business rules that apply to supertype/subtype relationships. The completeness constraint allows us to specify whether an instance of a supertype must also be a member of at least one subtype. There are two cases: With total specialization, an instance of the supertype must be a member of at least one subtype. With partial specialization, an instance of a supertype may or may not be a member of any subtype. The disjointness constraint allows us to specify whether an instance of a supertype may simultaneously be a member of two or more subtypes. Again, there are two cases. With the disjoint rule, an instance can be a member of only one subtype at a given time. With the overlap rule, an entity instance can simultaneously be a member of two (or more) subtypes.

A subtype discriminator is an attribute of a supertype whose values determine to which subtype (or subtypes) a supertype instance belongs. A supertype/subtype hierarchy is a hierarchical arrangement of supertypes and subtypes, where each subtype has only one supertype.

Packaged data models, so called universal and industry-specific data models, extensively utilize EER features. These generalizable data models often use multiple level supertype/subtype hierarchies and associative entities. Subjects and the roles subjects play are separated, creating many entity types; this complexity can be simplified when customized for a given organization, and entity clusters can be used to present simpler views of the data model to different audiences.

The use of packaged data models can save considerable time and cost in data modeling. The skills required for a data modeling project with a packaged data model are quite advanced and are built on the data modeling principles covered in this text. You have to consider not only current needs but also future requirements to customize the general-purpose package. Data elements must be renamed to local terms, and current data need to be mapped to the target database design. This mapping can be challenging due to various forms of mismatches between the data in current databases with those found in the best-practices purchased database model. Fortunately, having actual data models "right out of the box" helps structure the customization process for completeness and ease of communication with subject-matter experts. Overloaded columns, poor metadata, and abuses of the structure of current databases can make the customization and migration processes challenging. Data profiling can be used to understand the current data and uncover hidden meanings and business rules in data for your organization.

Chapter Review

Key Terms

Attribute inheritance 96	Enhanced entity-relationship (EER) model 93	Partial specialization rule 101	Supertype 94
Completeness constraint 101		Specialization 99	Supertype/subtype hierarchy 105
Disjoint rule 102	Generalization 98	Subtype 94	Total specialization rule 101
Disjointness constraint 101	Overlap rule 102	Subtype discriminator 102	Universal data model 110

Review Questions

1. Define each of the following terms:
   a. supertype
   b. subtype
   c. specialization
   d. attribute inheritance
   e. completeness constraint
   f. enhanced entity-relationship (EER) model
   g. subtype discriminator
   h. total specialization rule
   i. generalization
   j. disjoint rule
   k. overlap rule
   l. partial specialization rule
   m. universal data model

2. Match the following terms and definitions:
   _____ supertype   a. subset of supertype
   _____ subtype   b. entity belongs to two subtypes
   _____ specialization c. subtype gets supertype attributes
   _____ subtype   d. generalized entity type
            discriminator e. creating subtypes for an entity type
   _____ attribute   f. locates target subtype for an entity
            inheritance
   _____ overlap rule

3. Contrast the following terms:
   a. supertype; subtype
   b. generalization; specialization
   c. disjoint rule; overlap rule
   d. total specialization rule; partial specialization rule

4. State two conditions that indicate when a database designer should consider using supertype/subtype relationships.
5. Give an example (other than those discussed in the chapter) of a supertype/subtype relationship.
6. What is attribute inheritance? Why is it important?
7. Give an example of each of the following:
   a. a supertype/subtype relationship where the disjoint rule applies
   b. a supertype/subtype relationship where the overlap rule applies
8. What types of business rules are normally captured in an EER diagram?
9. What is the purpose of a subtype discriminator?
10. When would a packaged data model be useful?
11. In what ways is starting a data modeling project with a packaged data model different from starting a data modeling project with a clean sheet of paper?
12. Does a data modeling project using a packaged data model require less or greater skill than a project not using a packaged data model? Why or why not?
13. What do you purchase when you acquire a packaged data model?
14. When might a supertype/subtype hierarchy be useful?
15. When is a member of a supertype always a member of at least one subtype?

Problems and Exercises

1. Examine the hierarchy for the university EER diagram (Figure 3-10). As a student, you are an instance of one of the subtypes: either UNDERGRAD STUDENT or GRADUATE STUDENT. List the names of all the attributes that apply to you. For each attribute, record the data value that applies to you.
2. Add a subtype discriminator for each of the supertypes shown in Figure 3-10. Show the discriminator values that assign instances to each subtype. Use the following subtype discriminator names and values:
   a. PERSON: Person Type (Employee? Alumnus? Student?)
   b. EMPLOYEE: Employee Type (Faculty, Staff)
   c. STUDENT: Student Type (Grad, Undergrad)
3. For simplicity, subtype discriminators were left off many figures in this chapter. Add subtype discriminator notation in each figure listed below. If necessary, create a new attribute for the discriminator.
   a. Figure 3-2
   b. Figure 3-3
   c. Figure 3-4b
   d. Figure 3-7a
   e. Figure 3-7b
4. Refer to the employee EER diagram in Figure 3-2. Make any assumptions that you believe are necessary. Develop a sample definition for each entity type, attribute, and relationship in the diagram.
5. Refer to the EER diagram for patients in Figure 3-3. Make any assumptions you believe are necessary. Develop sample definitions for each entity type, attribute, and relationship in the diagram.
6. A rental car agency classifies the vehicles it rents into four categories: compact, midsize, full size, and sport utility. The agency wants to record the following data for all vehicles: Vehicle ID, Make, Model, Year, and Color. There are no unique attributes for any of the four classes of vehicle. The entity type vehicle has a relationship (named Rents) with a customer entity type. None of the four vehicle classes has a unique relationship with an entity type. Would you consider creating a supertype/subtype relationship for this problem? Why or why not?
7. For a library, the entity type HOLDING has four subtypes: BOOK, AUDIO BOOK, DVD, and SOFTWARE. Draw a separate EER diagram segment for each of the following situations:
   a. At a given time, a holding must be exactly one of these subtypes.
   b. A holding may or may not be one of these subtypes. However, a holding that is one of these subtypes cannot at the same time be one of the other subtypes.
   c. A holding may or may not be one of these subtypes. On the other hand, a holding may be any two (or even four) of these subtypes at the same time.
   d. At a given time, a holding must be at least one of these subtypes.
8. A bank has three types of accounts: checking, savings, and loan. Following are the attributes for each type of account:

   CHECKING: Acct No, Date Opened, Balance, Service Charge
   SAVINGS: Acct No, Date Opened, Balance, Interest Rate
   LOAN: Acct No, Date Opened, Balance, Interest Rate, Payment

   Assume that each bank account must be a member of exactly one of these subtypes. Using generalization, develop an EER model segment to represent this situation using the traditional EER notation, the Visio notation, or the subtypes inside supertypes notation, as specified by your instructor. Remember to include a subtype discriminator.
9. Draw an EER diagram for the following problem using this text's EER notation, the Visio notation, or the subtypes inside supertypes notation, as specified by your instructor.

   A nonprofit organization depends on a number of different types of persons for its successful operation. The organization is interested in the following attributes for all of these persons: SSN, Name, Address, City/State/Zip, and Telephone. Three types of persons are of greatest interest: employees, volunteers, and donors. Employees have only a Date Hired attribute, and volunteers have only a Skill attribute. Donors have only a relationship (named Donates) with an Item entity type. A donor must have donated one or more items, and an item may have no donors, or one or more donors.

   There are persons other than employees, volunteers, and donors who are of interest to the organization so that a person need not belong to any of these three groups. On the other hand, at a given time a person may belong to two or more of these groups (e.g., employee and donor).

10. Add a subtype discriminator (named Person Type) to the diagram you created in Problem and Exercise 9.

11. Develop an EER model for the following situation, using the traditional EER notation, the Visio notation, or the subtypes inside supertypes notation, as specified by your instructor:

A technology company provides offerings to its customers. Offerings are of two separate types: products and services. Offerings are identified by an offering ID and an attribute of description. In addition, products are described by product name, standard price, and date of first release; services are described by name of the company's unit responsible for the service and conditions of service. There are repair, maintenance, and other types of services. A repair service has a cost and is the repair of some product; a maintenance service has an hourly rate. Fortunately, some products never require repair. However, there are many potential repair services for a product. A customer may purchase an offering, and the company needs to keep track of when the offering was purchased and the contact person for that offering with the customer. Unfortunately, not all offerings are purchased. Customers are identified by customer ID and have descriptive data of name, address, and phone number. When a service is performed, that service is billed to some customer. Because some customers purchase offerings for their clients, a customer may be billed for services he or she did not purchase, as well as for ones that were purchased. When a customer is billed for a service (although some may never require a service of any type), the company needs to keep track of the date the service was performed, the date the bill is due, and the amount due.

12. Draw an EER diagram for the following description of a law firm:

Each case handled by the firm has a unique case number; a date opened, date closed, and judgment description are also kept on each case. A case is brought by one or more plaintiffs, and the same plaintiff may be involved in many cases. A plaintiff has a requested judgment characteristic. A case is against one or more defendants, and the same defendant may be involved in many cases. A plaintiff or defendant may be a person or an organization. Over time, the same person or organization may be a defendant or a plaintiff in cases. In either situation, such legal entities are identified by an entity number, and other attributes are name and net worth.

13. Develop an EER model for the following situation using the traditional EER notation, the Visio notation, or the subtypes inside supertypes notation, as specified by your instructor:

An international school of technology has hired you to create a database management system to assist in scheduling classes. After several interviews with the president, you have come up with the following list of entities, attributes, and initial business rules:

- Room is identified by Building ID and Room No and also has a Capacity. A room can be either a lab or a classroom. If it is a classroom, it has an additional attribute called Board Type.
- Media is identified by MType ID and has attributes of Media Type and Type Description. Note: Here we are tracking type of media (such as a VCR, projector, etc.), not the individual piece of equipment. Tracking of equipment is outside of the scope of this project.

- Computer is identified by CType ID and has attributes Computer Type, Type Description, Disk Capacity, and Processor Speed. Please note: As with Media Type, we are tracking only the type of computer, not an individual computer. You can think of this as a class of computers (e.g., Core™ i7 2.6GHz).
- Instructor has identifier Emp ID and has attributes Name, Rank, and Office Phone.
- Timeslot has identifier TSIS and has attributes Day Of Week, Start Time, and End Time.
- Course has identifier Course ID and has attributes Course Description and Credits. Courses can have one, none, or many prerequisites. Courses also have one or more sections.
- Section has identifier Section ID and attribute Enrollment Limit.

After some further discussions, you have come up with some additional business rules to help you create the initial design:

- An instructor teaches one, none, or many sections of a course in a given semester.
- An instructor specifies preferred time slots.
- Scheduling data are kept for each semester, uniquely identified by semester and year.
- A room can be scheduled for one section or no section during one time slot in a given semester of a given year. However, one room can participate in many schedules, one schedule, or no schedules; one time slot can participate in many schedules, one schedule, or no schedules; one section can participate in many schedules, one schedule, or no schedules. Hint: Can you associate this to anything that you have seen before?
- A room can have one type of media, several types of media, or no media.
- Instructors are trained to use one, none, or many types of media.
- A lab has one or more computer types. However, a classroom does not have any computers.
- A room cannot be both a classroom and a lab. There also are no other room types to be incorporated into the system.

14. Develop an EER model for the following situation using the traditional EER notation, the Visio notation, or the subtypes inside supertypes notation, as specified by your instructor:

Wally Los Gatos and his partner Henry Chordate have formed a new limited partnership, Fin and Finicky Security Consultants. Fin and Finicky consults with corporations to determine their security needs. You have been hired by Wally and Henry to design a database management system to help them manage their business.

Due to a recent increase in business, Fin and Finicky has decided to automate its client tracking system. You and your team have done a preliminary analysis and come up with the following set of entities, attributes, and business rules:

Consultant

There are two types of consultants: business consultants and technical consultants. Business consultants are contacted by a business in order to first determine security needs and provide an estimate for the actual services to be performed. Technical consultants perform services according to the specifications developed by the business consultants.

Attributes of business consultant are the following: Employee ID (identifier), Name, Address (which is composed of Street, City, State, and Zip Code), Telephone, Date Of Birth, Age, Business Experience (which is composed of Number of Years, Type of Business [or businesses], and Degrees Received).

Attributes of technical consultant are the following: Employee ID (identifier), Name, Address (which is composed of Street, City, State, and Zip Code), Telephone, Date Of Birth, Age, Technical Skills, and Degrees Received.

Customer

Customers are businesses that have asked for consulting services. Attributes of customer are Customer ID (identifier), Company Name, Address (which is composed of Street, City, State, and Zip Code), Contact Name, Contact Title, Contact Telephone, Business Type, and Number Of Employees.

Location

Customers can have multiple locations. Attributes of location are Customer ID (identifier), Location ID (which is unique only for each Customer ID), Address (which is composed of Street, City, State, and Zip Code), Telephone, and Building Size.

Service

A security service is performed for a customer at one or more locations. Before services are performed, an estimate is prepared. Attributes of service are Service ID (identifier), Description, Cost, Coverage, and Clearance Required.

Additional Business Rules

In addition to the entities outlined previously, the following information will need to be stored to tables and should be shown in the model. These may be entities, but they also reflect a relationship between more than one entity:

- Estimates, which have characteristics of Date, Amount, Business Consultant, Services, and Customer
- Services Performed, which have characteristics of Date, Amount, Technical Consultant, Services, and Customer

In order to construct the EER diagram, you may assume the following:

A customer can have many consultants providing many services. You wish to track both actual services performed as well as services offered. Therefore, there should be two relationships between customer, service, and consultant, one to show services performed and one to show services offered as part of the estimate.

15. Based on the EER diagram constructed for Problem and Exercise 14, develop a sample definition for each entity type, attribute, and relationship in the diagram.

16. Draw an EER diagram for the following situation:

You are working for a large country club. This country club wants to keep a database on its members and their guests. For each member, the club keeps mail and telephone contact information, name, and membership number. When you join this club, you can join as a social member (which allows you two rounds of golf a year as well as privileges to the swimming pool and weight room), a tennis member (which allows you all the privileges of a social member as well as use of the tennis courts and four rounds of golf), or a golfing member (which allows you all the privileges of a tennis member and unlimited use of the golf course). This database needs to track how often a member (who has limited use of the golf course; all golfing members have unlimited use of the golf course) has used the golf course, and how many guests any and each member has brought to the club. All members have guest privileges. The club also wants to attract new members by mailing to all those who came to the club as guests and live in the state. The mailing includes information about their visits (i.e., date of visit and which member was their host for each visit). Once a person becomes a member of any type, information about him or her as a guest is no longer important to retain.

17. Draw an EER diagram for the following situation:

TomKat Entertainment is a chain of theaters owned by former husband and wife actors/entertainers who, for some reason, can't get a job performing anymore. The owners want a database to track what is playing or has played on each screen in each theater of their chain at different times of the day. A theater (identified by a Theater ID and described by a theater name and location) contains one or more screens for viewing various movies. Within each theater each screen is identified by its number and is described by the seating capacity for viewing the screen. Movies are scheduled for showing in time slots each day. Each screen can have different time slots on different days (i.e., not all screens in the same theater have movies starting at the same time, and even on different days the same movie may play at different times on the same screen). For each time slot, the owners also want to know the end time of the time slot (assume all slots end on the same day the slot begins), attendance during that time slot, and the price charged for attendance in that time slot. Each movie (which can be either a trailer, feature, or commercial) is identified by a Movie ID and further described by its title, duration, and type (i.e., trailer, feature, or commercial). In each time slot, one or more movies are shown. The owners want to also keep track of in what sequence the movies are shown (e.g., in a time slot there might be two trailers, followed by two commercials, followed by a feature film, and closed with another commercial).

References

Elmasri, R., and S. B. Navathe. 1994. *Fundamentals of Database Systems*. Menlo Park, CA: Benjamin/Cummings.

Hay, D. C. 1996. *Data Model Patterns: Conventions of Thought.* New York: Dorset House Publishing.

Hoberman, S. 2006. "Industry Logical Data Models." *Teradata Magazine*. Available at www.teradata.com.

Silverston, L. 1998. "Is Your Organization Too Unique to Use Universal Data Models?" *DM Review* 8,8 (September),

accessed at www.information-management.com/issues/19980901/425-1.html.

Silverston, L. 2001a. *The Data Model Resource Book, Volume 1*, Rev. ed. New York: Wiley.

Silverston, L. 2001b. *The Data Model Resource Book, Volume 2*, Rev. ed. New York: Wiley.

Silverston, L. 2002. "A Universal Data Model for Relationship Development." *DM Review* 12,3 (March): 44–47, 65.

Further Reading

Frye, C. 2002. "Business Rules Are Back." *Application Development Trends* 9, 7 (July): 29–35.

Gottesdiener, E. 1997. "Business Rules Show Power, Promise." *Application Development Trends* 4,3 (March): 36–54.

GUIDE. 1997 (October). "GUIDE Business Rules Project." Final Report, revision 1.2.

Hoffer, J. A., J. F. George, and J. S. Valacich. 2011. *Modern Systems Analysis and Design*. 6th ed. Upper Saddle River, NJ: Prentice Hall.

Moriarty, T. 1993. "Using Scenarios in Information Modeling: Bringing Business Rules to Life." *Database Programming & Design* 6, 8 (August): 65–67.

Ross, R. G. 1997. *The Business Rule Book*. Version 4. Boston: Business Rule Solutions, Inc.

Ross, R. G. 1998. *Business Rule Concepts: The New Mechanics of Business Information Systems*. Boston: Business Rule Solutions, Inc.

Ross, R. G. 2003. *Principles of the Business Rule Approach*. Boston: Addison-Wesley.

Schmidt, B. 1997. "A Taxonomy of Domains." *Database Programming & Design* 10, 9 (September): 95, 96, 98, 99.

Silverston, L. 2002. Silverston has a series of articles in *DM Review* that discuss universal data models in different settings. See in particular Vol. 12 issues 1 (January) on clickstream analysis, 5 (May) on health care, 7 (July) on financial services, and 12 (December) on manufacturing.

Teorey, T. 1999. *Database Modeling & Design*. San Francisco: Morgan Kaufman Publishers.

von Halle, B. 1996. "Object-Oriented Lessons." *Database Programming & Design* 9,1 (January): 13–16.

von Halle, B. 2001. von Halle has a series of articles in *DM Review* on building a business rules system. These articles are in Vol. 11, issues 1–5 (January–May).

von Halle, B., and R. Kaplan. 1997. "Is IT Falling Short?" *Database Programming & Design* 10, 6 (June): 15–17.

Web Resources

www.adtmag.com Web site of *Application Development Trends*, a leading publication on the practice of information systems development.

www.brsolutions.com Web site of Business Rule Solutions, the consulting company of Ronald Ross, a leader in the development of a business rule methodology. Or you can check out **www.BRCommunity.com**, which is a virtual community site for people interested in business rules (sponsored by Business Rule Solutions).

www.businessrulesgroup.org Web site of the Business Rules Group, formerly part of GUIDE International, which formulates and supports standards about business rules.

www.databaseanswers.org/data_models A fascinating site that shows more than 100 sample E-R diagrams for a wide variety of applications and organizations. A variety of notations are used, so this a good site to also learn about variations in E-R diagramming.

www.kpiusa.com The homepage for Knowledge Partners International, founded by Barbara von Halle. This site has some interesting case studies and white papers about business rules.

http://researchlibrary.theserverside.net/detail/RES/1214505974 _136.html Link to the white paper "Modeling Unstructured Data" by Steve Hoberman. Unstructured data (e.g., e-mails, images, sounds) is an emerging area for databases, and there are some special issues in data modeling for unstructured data.

www.tdan.com Web site of *The Data Administration Newsletter*, which regularly publishes new articles, special reports, and news on a variety of data modeling and administration topics.

www.teradatauniversitynetwork.com Web site for Teradata University Network, a free resource for a wide variety of information about database management and related topics. Go to this site and search on "entity relationship" to see many articles and assignments related to EER data modeling.

PART III

Database Design

AN OVERVIEW OF PART THREE

By the end of the database analysis phase of database development, systems and database analysts have a fairly clear understanding of data storage and access requirements. However, the data model developed during analysis explicitly avoids any ties to database technologies. Before we can implement a database, the conceptual data model must be mapped into a data model that is compatible with the database management system to be used.

The activities of database design transform the requirements for data storage developed during database analysis into specifications to guide database implementation. There are two forms of specifications:

1. Logical specifications, which map the conceptual requirements into the data model associated with a specific database management system.
2. Physical specifications, which indicate all the parameters for data storage that are then used as input for database implementation. During this phase, a database is actually defined using a data definition language.

In Chapter 4 ("Logical Database Design and the Relational Model"), we describe logical database design, with special emphasis on the relational data model. Logical database design is the process of transforming the conceptual data model (described in Chapters 2 and 3) into a logical data model. Most database management systems in use today are based on the relational data model, so this data model is the basis for our discussion of logical database design.

In Chapter 4, we first define the important terms and concepts for this model, including *relation*, *primary key* and *surrogate primary key*, *foreign key*, *anomaly*, *normal form*, *normalization*, *functional dependency*, *partial functional dependency*, and *transitive dependency*. We next describe and illustrate the process of transforming an E-R model to the relational model. Many modeling tools support this transformation; however, it is important that you understand the underlying principles and procedures. We then describe and illustrate in detail the important concepts of normalization (the process of designing well-structured relations). Finally, we describe how to merge relations from separate logical design activities (e.g., different groups within a large project team) while avoiding common pitfalls that may occur in this process.

The purpose of physical database design, the topic of Chapter 5 ("Physical Database Design and Performance"), is to translate the logical description of data into the technical specifications for storing and retrieving data. The goal is to create a design for storing data that will provide adequate performance and ensure database integrity, security, and recoverability. Physical database design produces the technical specifications that programmers and others involved in information systems construction will use during the implementation phase, which we discuss in Chapters 6 through 9.

In Chapter 5, you will learn key terms and concepts for physical database design, including *data type*, *page*, *pointer*, *denormalization*, *indexed file organization*, and *hashed file organization*. You will study the basic steps in developing an efficient physical database design. You will learn about choices for storing attribute values and how to select among these choices. You will also learn why normalized tables do not always form the best physical data files and how you can, if necessary, denormalize the data to achieve data retrieval speed improvements. You will learn about different file organizations and different types of indexes, which are important in speeding the retrieval of data. In addition, you will learn how physical database design choices that improve data quality affect the process of validating the accuracy of financial reporting. These are essential issues today because of government regulations, such as Sarbanes-Oxley, and because of the growing realization that ensuring high data quality makes business sense.

You must carefully perform physical database design because decisions made during this stage have a major impact on data accessibility, response times, security, user friendliness, information quality, and similarly important information system design factors.

Logical Database Design and the Relational Model

LEARNING OBJECTIVES

After studying this chapter, you should be able to:

- Concisely define each of the following key terms: **relation, primary key, composite key, foreign key, null, entity integrity rule, referential integrity constraint, well-structured relation, anomaly, surrogate primary key, recursive foreign key, normalization, normal form, functional dependency, determinant, candidate key, first normal form, second normal form, partial functional dependency, third normal form, transitive dependency, synonym, alias,** and **homonym.**

- List five properties of relations.

- State two essential properties of a candidate key.

- Give a concise definition of each of the following: first normal form, second normal form, and third normal form.

- Briefly describe four problems that may arise when merging relations.

- Transform an E-R (or EER) diagram into a logically equivalent set of relations.

- Create relational tables that incorporate entity integrity and referential integrity constraints.

- Use normalization to decompose a relation with anomalies into well-structured relations.

Visit www.pearsonhighered.com/
hoffer to view the accompanying
video for this chapter.

INTRODUCTION

In this chapter, we describe logical database design, with special emphasis on the relational data model. Logical database design is the process of transforming the conceptual data model (described in Chapters 2 and 3) into a logical data model—one that is consistent and compatible with a specific type of database technology. An experienced database designer often will do logical database design in parallel with conceptual data modeling if he or she knows the type of database technology that will be used. It is, however, important to treat these as separate steps so that you concentrate on each important part of database development. Conceptual data modeling is about understanding the organization—getting the requirements right. Logical database design is about creating stable database structures—correctly expressing the requirements in a technical language. Both are important steps that must be performed carefully.

Although there are other logical data models, we have two reasons for emphasizing the relational data model in this chapter. First, the relational data model is by far the one most commonly used in contemporary database applications. Second, some of the principles of logical database design for the relational model apply to the other logical models as well.

We have introduced the relational data model informally through simple examples in earlier chapters. It is important, however, to note that the relational data model is a form of logical data model, and as such it is different from the conceptual data models. Thus, an E-R data model is not a relational data model, and an E-R model may not obey the rules for a well-structured relational data model, called *normalization*, which we explain in this chapter. That is okay, because the E-R model was developed for other purposes—understanding data requirements and business rules about the data—not structuring the data for sound database processing, which is the goal of logical database design.

In this chapter, we first define the important terms and concepts for the relational data model. (We often use the abbreviated term *relational model* when referring to the relational data model.) We next describe and illustrate the process of transforming an EER model into the relational model. Many CASE tools support this transformation today at the technical level. It is, however, important that you understand the underlying principles and procedures. We then describe the concepts of normalization in detail. Normalization, which is the process of designing well-structured relations, is an important component of logical design for the relational model. Finally, we describe how to merge relations while avoiding common pitfalls that may occur in this process.

The objective of logical database design is to translate the conceptual design (which represents an organization's requirements for data) into a logical database design that can be implemented via a chosen database management system. The resulting databases must meet user needs for data sharing, flexibility, and ease of access. The concepts presented in this chapter are essential to your understanding of the database development process.

THE RELATIONAL DATA MODEL

The relational data model was first introduced in 1970 by E. F. Codd, then of IBM (Codd, 1970). Two early research projects were launched to prove the feasibility of the relational model and to develop prototype systems. The first of these, at IBM's San Jose Research Laboratory, led to the development of System R (a prototype relational DBMS [RDBMS]) during the late 1970s. The second, at the University of California at Berkeley, led to the development of Ingres, an academically oriented RDBMS. Commercial RDBMS products from numerous vendors started to appear about 1980. (See the Web site for this text for links to RDBMS and other DBMS vendors.) Today, RDBMSs have become the dominant technology for database management, and there are literally hundreds of RDBMS products for computers ranging from smartphones and personal computers to mainframes.

Basic Definitions

The relational data model represents data in the form of tables. The relational model is based on mathematical theory and therefore has a solid theoretical foundation. However, we need only a few simple concepts to describe the relational model. Therefore, it can be easily understood and used even by those unfamiliar with the underlying theory. The relational data model consists of the following three components (Fleming and von Halle, 1989):

1. *Data structure* Data are organized in the form of tables, with rows and columns.
2. *Data manipulation* Powerful operations (typically implemented using the SQL language) are used to manipulate data stored in the relations.
3. *Data integrity* The model includes mechanisms to specify business rules that maintain the integrity of data when they are manipulated.

FIGURE 4-1 EMPLOYEE1 relation with sample data

EMPLOYEE1

EmpID	Name	DeptName	Salary
100	Margaret Simpson	Marketing	48,000
140	Allen Beeton	Accounting	52,000
110	Chris Lucero	Info Systems	43,000
190	Lorenzo Davis	Finance	55,000
150	Susan Martin	Marketing	42,000

We discuss data structure and data integrity in this section. Data manipulation is discussed in Chapters 6, 7, and 8.

RELATIONAL DATA STRUCTURE A **relation** is a named, two-dimensional table of data. Each relation (or table) consists of a set of named columns and an arbitrary number of unnamed rows. An attribute, consistent with its definition in Chapter 2, is a named column of a relation. Each row of a relation corresponds to a record that contains data (attribute) values for a single entity. Figure 4-1 shows an example of a relation named EMPLOYEE1. This relation contains the following attributes describing employees: EmpID, Name, DeptName, and Salary. The five rows of the table correspond to five employees. It is important to understand that the sample data in Figure 4-1 are intended to illustrate the structure of the EMPLOYEE1 relation; they are not part of the relation itself. Even if we add another row of data to the figure or change any of the data in the existing rows, it is still the same EMPLOYEE1 relation. Nor does deleting a row change the relation. In fact, we could delete all of the rows shown in Figure 4-1, and the EMPLOYEE1 relation would still exist. In other words, Figure 4-1 is an instance of the EMPLOYEE1 relation.

Relation

A named two-dimensional table of data.

We can express the structure of a relation by using a shorthand notation in which the name of the relation is followed (in parentheses) by the names of the attributes in that relation. For EMPLOYEE1, we would have

EMPLOYEE1(EmpID, Name, DeptName, Salary)

RELATIONAL KEYS We must be able to store and retrieve a row of data in a relation, based on the data values stored in that row. To achieve this goal, every relation must have a primary key. A **primary key** is an attribute or a combination of attributes that uniquely identifies each row in a relation. We designate a primary key by underlining the attribute name(s). For example, the primary key for the relation EMPLOYEE1 is EmpID. Notice that this attribute is underlined in Figure 4-1. In shorthand notation, we express this relation as follows:

Primary key

An attribute or a combination of attributes that uniquely identifies each row in a relation.

EMPLOYEE1(EmpID, Name, DeptName, Salary)

The concept of a primary key is related to the term *identifier* defined in Chapter 2. The attribute or a collection of attributes indicated as an entity's identifier in an E-R diagram may be the same attributes that comprise the primary key for the relation representing that entity. There are exceptions: For example, associative entities do not have to have an identifier, and the (partial) identifier of a weak entity forms only part of a weak entity's primary key. In addition, there may be several attributes of an entity that may serve as the associated relation's primary key. All of these situations will be illustrated later in this chapter.

A **composite key** is a primary key that consists of more than one attribute. For example, the primary key for a relation DEPENDENT would likely consist of the combination EmpID and DependentName. We show several examples of composite keys later in this chapter.

Composite key

A primary key that consists of more than one attribute.

Often we must represent the relationship between two tables or relations. This is accomplished through the use of foreign keys. A **foreign key** is an attribute (possibly composite) in a relation that serves as the primary key of another relation. For example, consider the relations EMPLOYEE1 and DEPARTMENT:

Foreign key

An attribute in a relation that serves as the primary key of another relation in the same database.

EMPLOYEE1(EmpID, Name, DeptName, Salary)
DEPARTMENT(DeptName, Location, Fax)

The attribute DeptName is a foreign key in EMPLOYEE1. It allows a user to associate any employee with the department to which he or she is assigned. Some authors emphasize the fact that an attribute is a foreign key by using a dashed underline, like this:

EMPLOYEE1(EmpID, Name, DeptName, Salary)

We provide numerous examples of foreign keys in the remainder of this chapter and discuss the properties of foreign keys under the heading "Referential Integrity."

PROPERTIES OF RELATIONS We have defined relations as two-dimensional tables of data. However, not all tables are relations. Relations have several properties that distinguish them from non-relational tables. We summarize these properties next:

1. Each relation (or table) in a database has a unique name.
2. An entry at the intersection of each row and column is atomic (or single valued). There can be only one value associated with each attribute on a specific row of a table; no multivalued attributes are allowed in a relation.
3. Each row is unique; no two rows in a relation can be identical.
4. Each attribute (or column) within a table has a unique name.
5. The sequence of columns (left to right) is insignificant. The order of the columns in a relation can be changed without changing the meaning or use of the relation.
6. The sequence of rows (top to bottom) is insignificant. As with columns, the order of the rows of a relation may be changed or stored in any sequence.

REMOVING MULTIVALUED ATTRIBUTES FROM TABLES The second property of relations listed in the preceding section states that no multivalued attributes are allowed in a relation. Thus, a table that contains one or more multivalued attributes is not a relation. For example, Figure 4-2a shows the employee data from the EMPLOYEE1 relation extended to include courses that may have been taken by those employees. Because a given employee may have taken more than one course, CourseTitle and DateCompleted are multivalued attributes. For example, the employee with EmpID 100 has taken two courses. If an employee has not taken any courses, the CourseTitle and DateCompleted attribute values are null. (See the employee with EmpID 190 for an example.)

We show how to eliminate the multivalued attributes in Figure 4-2b by filling the relevant data values into the previously vacant cells of Figure 4-2a. As a result, the table in Figure 4-2b has only single-valued attributes and now satisfies the atomic property of relations. The name EMPLOYEE2 is given to this relation to distinguish it from EMPLOYEE1. However, as you will see, this new relation does have some undesirable properties.

Sample Database

A relational database may consist of any number of relations. The structure of the database is described through the use of a schema (defined in Chapter 1), which is a description of the overall logical structure of the database. There are two common methods for expressing a schema:

1. Short text statements, in which each relation is named and the names of its attributes follow in parentheses. (See the EMPLOYEE1 and DEPARTMENT relations defined earlier in this chapter.)

FIGURE 4-2 Eliminating multivalued attributes

(a) Table with repeating groups

EmpID	Name	DeptName	Salary	CourseTitle	DateCompleted
100	Margaret Simpson	Marketing	48,000	SPSS	6/19/201X
				Surveys	10/7/201X
140	Alan Beeton	Accounting	52,000	Tax Acc	12/8/201X
110	Chris Lucero	Info Systems	43,000	Visual Basic	1/12/201X
				C++	4/22/201X
190	Lorenzo Davis	Finance	55,000		
150	Susan Martin	Marketing	42,000	SPSS	6/16/201X
				Java	8/12/201X

(b) EMPLOYEE2 relation

EMPLOYEE2

EmpID	Name	DeptName	Salary	CourseTitle	DateCompleted
100	Margaret Simpson	Marketing	48,000	SPSS	6/19/201X
100	Margaret Simpson	Marketing	48,000	Surveys	10/7/201X
140	Alan Beeton	Accounting	52,000	Tax Acc	12/8/201X
110	Chris Lucero	Info Systems	43,000	Visual Basic	1/12/201X
110	Chris Lucero	Info Systems	43,000	C++	4/22/201X
190	Lorenzo Davis	Finance	55,000		
150	Susan Martin	Marketing	42,000	SPSS	6/19/201X
150	Susan Martin	Marketing	42,000	Java	8/12/201X

2. A graphical representation, in which each relation is represented by a rectangle containing the attributes for the relation.

Text statements have the advantage of simplicity. However, a graphical representation provides a better means of expressing referential integrity constraints (as you will see shortly). In this section, we use both techniques for expressing a schema so that you can compare them.

A schema for four relations at Pine Valley Furniture Company is shown in Figure 4-3. The four relations shown in this figure are CUSTOMER, ORDER, ORDER LINE, and PRODUCT. The key attributes for these relations are underlined, and other important attributes are included in each relation. We show how to design these relations using the techniques of normalization later in this chapter.

Following is a text description of these relations:

PINE VALLEY FURNITURE

CUSTOMER(CustomerID, CustomerName, CustomerAddress,
    CustomerCity, CustomerState, CustomerPostalCode)
ORDER(OrderID, OrderDate, CustomerID)
ORDER LINE(OrderID, ProductID, OrderedQuantity)
PRODUCT(ProductID, ProductDescription, ProductFinish,
    ProductStandardPrice, ProductLineID)

Notice that the primary key for ORDER LINE is a composite key consisting of the attributes OrderID and ProductID. Also, CustomerID is a foreign key in the ORDER relation; this allows the user to associate an order with the customer who submitted the

FIGURE 4-3   Schema for four
relations (Pine Valley Furniture
Company)

CUSTOMER

CustomerID	CustomerName	CustomerAddress	CustomerCity*	CustomerState*	CustomerPostalCode

ORDER

OrderID	OrderDate	CustomerID

ORDER LINE

OrderID	ProductID	OrderedQuantity

PRODUCT

ProductID	ProductDescription	ProductFinish	ProductStandardPrice	ProductLineID

* Not in Figure 2-21 for simplicity.

order. ORDER LINE has two foreign keys: OrderID and ProductID. These keys allow the user to associate each line on an order with the relevant order and product.

An instance of this database is shown in Figure 4-4. This figure shows four tables with sample data. Notice how the foreign keys allow us to associate the various tables. It is a good idea to create an instance of your relational schema with sample data for four reasons:

1. The sample data allow you to test your assumptions regarding the design.
2. The sample data provide a convenient way to check the accuracy of your design.
3. The sample data help improve communications with users in discussing your design.
4. The sample data can be used to develop prototype applications and to test queries.

INTEGRITY CONSTRAINTS

The relational data model includes several types of constraints, or rules limiting acceptable values and actions, whose purpose is to facilitate maintaining the accuracy and integrity of data in the database. The major types of integrity constraints are domain constraints, entity integrity, and referential integrity.

Domain Constraints

All of the values that appear in a column of a relation must be from the same domain. A domain is the set of values that may be assigned to an attribute. A domain definition usually consists of the following components: domain name, meaning, data type, size (or length), and allowable values or allowable range (if applicable). Table 4-1 (page 128) shows domain definitions for the domains associated with the attributes in Figures 4-3 and 4-4.

Entity Integrity

The entity integrity rule is designed to ensure that every relation has a primary key and that the data values for that primary key are all valid. In particular, it guarantees that every primary key attribute is non-null.

In some cases, a particular attribute cannot be assigned a data value. There are two situations in which this is likely to occur: Either there is no applicable data value or the applicable data value is not known when values are assigned. Suppose, for example, that you fill out an employment form that has a space reserved for a fax number. If you have no fax number, you leave this space empty because it does not apply to you. Or suppose that you are asked to fill in the telephone number of your previous employer. If you do not recall this number, you may leave it empty because that information is not known.

FIGURE 4-4   Instance of a relational schema (Pine Valley Furniture Company)

Customer_T

CustomerID	CustomerName	CustomerAddress	CustomerCity	CustomerState	CustomerPostalCode
1	Contemporary Casuals	1355 S Hines Blvd	Gainesville	FL	32601-2871
2	Value Furniture	15145 S.W. 17th St.	Plano	TX	75094-7743
3	Home Furnishings	1900 Allard Ave.	Albany	NY	12209-1125
4	Eastern Furniture	1925 Beltline Rd.	Carteret	NJ	07008-3188
5	Impressions	5585 Westcott Ct.	Sacramento	CA	94206-4056
6	Furniture Gallery	325 Flatiron Dr.	Boulder	CO	80514-4432
7	Period Furniture	394 Rainbow Dr.	Seattle	WA	97954-5589
8	Calfornia Classics	816 Peach Rd.	Santa Clara	CA	96915-7754
9	M and H Casual Furniture	370...			...620-2314
10	Seminole Interiors	240			...546-4423
11	American Euro Lifestyles	242			...508-5621
12	Battle Creek Furniture	345			...015-3401
13	Heritage Furnishings	667			...013-8834
14	Kaneohe Homes	112			...744-2537
15	Mountain Scenes	413			...403-4432

Record: 1 of 15   No Filter   Search

OrderLine_T

OrderID	ProductID	OrderedQuantity
1001	1	2
1001	2	2
1001	4	1
1002	3	5
1003	3	3
1004	6	2
1004	8	2
1005	4	4
1006	4	1
1006	5	2
1006	7	2
1007	1	3
1007	2	2
1008	3	3
1008	8	3
1009	4	2
1009	7	3
1010	8	10

Record: 1 of 18   No Filter   Search

Order_T

OrderID	OrderDate	CustomerID
1001	10/21/2010	1
1002	10/21/2010	8
1003	10/22/2010	15
1004	10/22/2010	5
1005	10/24/2010	3
1006	10/24/2010	2
1007	10/27/2010	11
1008	10/30/2010	12
1009	11/5/2010	4
1010	11/5/2010	1

Record: 1 of 10   No Filter   Search

Product_T

ProductID	ProductDescription	ProductFinish	ProductStandardPrice	ProductLineID
1	End Table	Cherry	$175.00	1
2	Coffe Table	Natural Ash	$200.00	2
3	Computer Desk	Natural Ash	$375.00	2
4	Entertainment Center	Natural Maple	$650.00	3
5	Writers Desk	Cherry	$325.00	1
6	8-Drawer Desk	White Ash	$750.00	2
7	Dining Table	Natural Ash	$800.00	2
8	Computer Desk	Walnut	$250.00	3

Record: 1 of 8   No Filter   Search

The relational data model allows us to assign a null value to an attribute in the just described situations. A **null** is a value that may be assigned to an attribute when no other value applies or when the applicable value is unknown. In reality, a null is not a value, but rather it indicates the absence of a value. For example, it is not the same as a numeric zero or a string of blanks. The inclusion of nulls in the relational model is somewhat controversial, because it sometimes leads to anomalous results (Date, 2003). However, Codd, the inventor of the relational model, advocates the use of nulls for missing values (Codd, 1990).

Everyone agrees that primary key values must not be allowed to be null. Thus, the **entity integrity rule** states the following: No primary key attribute (or component of a primary key attribute) may be null.

Null

A value that may be assigned to an attribute when no other value applies or when the applicable value is unknown.

Entity integrity rule

A rule that states that no primary key attribute (or component of a primary key attribute) may be null.

TABLE 4-1   Domain Definitions for INVOICE Attributes

Attribute	Domain Name	Description	Domain
CustomerID	Customer IDs	Set of all possible customer IDs	character: size 5
CustomerName	Customer Names	Set of all possible customer names	character: size 25
CustomerAddress	Customer Addresses	Set of all possible customer addresses	character: size 30
CustomerCity	Cities	Set of all possible cities	character: size 20
CustomerState	States	Set of all possible states	character: size 2
CustomerPostalCode	Postal Codes	Set of all possible postal zip codes	character: size 10
OrderID	Order IDs	Set of all possible order IDs	character: size 5
OrderDate	Order Dates	Set of all possible order dates	date: format mm/dd/yy
ProductID	Product IDs	Set of all possible product IDs	character: size 5
ProductDescription	Product Descriptions	Set of all possible product descriptions	character: size 25
ProductFinish	Product Finishes	Set of all possible product finishes	character: size 15
ProductStandardPrice	Unit Prices	Set of all possible unit prices	monetary: 6 digits
ProductLineID	Product Line IDs	Set of all possible product line IDs	integer: 3 digits
OrderedQuantity	Quantities	Set of all possible ordered quantities	integer: 3 digits

Referential Integrity

In the relational data model, associations between tables are defined through the use of foreign keys. For example, in Figure 4-4, the association between the CUSTOMER and ORDER tables is defined by including the CustomerID attribute as a foreign key in ORDER. This of course implies that before we insert a new row in the ORDER table, the customer for that order must already exist in the CUSTOMER table. If you examine the rows in the ORDER table in Figure 4-4, you will find that every customer number for an order already appears in the CUSTOMER table.

Referential integrity constraint

A rule that states that either each foreign key value must match a primary key value in another relation or the foreign key value must be null.

A **referential integrity constraint** is a rule that maintains consistency among the rows of two relations. The rule states that if there is a foreign key in one relation, either each foreign key value must match a primary key value in another relation or the foreign key value must be null. You should examine the tables in Figure 4-4 to check whether the referential integrity rule has been enforced.

The graphical version of the relational schema provides a simple technique for identifying associations where referential integrity must be enforced. Figure 4-5 shows the schema for the relations introduced in Figure 4-3. An arrow has been drawn from each foreign key to the associated primary key. A referential integrity constraint must be defined for each of these arrows in the schema.

How do you know whether a foreign key is allowed to be null? If each order must have a customer (a mandatory relationship), then the foreign key CustomerID cannot be null in the ORDER relation. If the relationship is optional, then the foreign key could be null. Whether a foreign key can be null must be specified as a property of the foreign key attribute when the database is defined.

Actually, whether a foreign key can be null is more complex to model on an E-R diagram and to determine than we have shown so far. For example, what happens to order data if we choose to delete a customer who has submitted orders? We may want to see sales even if we do not care about the customer any more. Three choices are possible:

1. Delete the associated orders (called a cascading delete), in which case we lose not only the customer but also all the sales history.
2. Prohibit deletion of the customer until all associated orders are first deleted (a safety check).

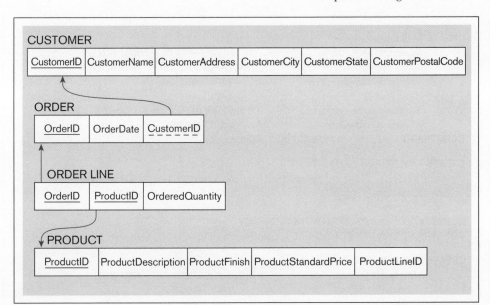

FIGURE 4-5 Referential integrity constraints (Pine Valley Furniture Company)

3. Place a null value in the foreign key (an exception stating that although an order must have a CustomerID value when the order is created, CustomerID can become null later if the associated customer is deleted).

We will see how each of these choices is implemented when we describe the SQL database query language in Chapter 6. Please note that in practice, organizational rules and various regulations regarding data retention often determine what data can be deleted and when, and they therefore govern the choice between various deletion options.

Creating Relational Tables

In this section, we create table definitions for the four tables shown in Figure 4-5. These definitions are created using the **CREATE TABLE** statements of the SQL data definition language. In practice, these table definitions are actually created during the implementation phase later in the database development process. However, we show these sample tables in this chapter for continuity and especially to illustrate the way the integrity constraints described previously are implemented in SQL.

The SQL table definitions are shown in Figure 4-6. One table is created for each of the four relations shown in the relational schema (Figure 4-5). Each attribute for a table is then defined. Notice that the data type and length for each attribute are taken from the domain definitions (Table 4-1). For example, the attribute CustomerName in the Customer_T table is defined as VARCHAR (variable character) data type with length 25. By specifying **NOT NULL**, each attribute can be constrained from being assigned a null value.

The primary key is specified for each table using the **PRIMARY KEY** clause at the end of each table definition. The OrderLine_T table illustrates how to specify a primary key when that key is a composite attribute. In this example, the primary key of OrderLine_T is the combination of OrderID and ProductID. Each primary key attribute in the four tables is constrained with **NOT NULL**. This enforces the entity integrity constraint described in the previous section. Notice that the **NOT NULL** constraint can also be used with non-primary-key attributes.

Referential integrity constraints are easily defined, based on the graphical schema shown in Figure 4-5. An arrow originates from each foreign key and points to the related primary key in the associated relation. In the SQL table definition, a **FOREIGN KEY REFERENCES** statement corresponds to each of these arrows. Thus, for the table Order_T, the foreign key CustomerID references the primary key of Customer_T, which is also called CustomerID. Although in this instance, the foreign key and primary key have the same name, this need not be the case. For example, the foreign key attribute could be named CustNo instead of CustomerID. However, the foreign and primary keys must be from the same domain.

```
CREATE TABLE Customer_T
    (CustomerID                    NUMBER(11,0)      NOT NULL,
    CustomerName                   VARCHAR2(25)      NOT NULL,
    CustomerAddress                VARCHAR2(30),
    CustomerCity                   VARCHAR2(20),
    CustomerState                  CHAR(2),
    CustomerPostalCode             VARCHAR2(9),
CONSTRAINT Customer_PK PRIMARY KEY (CustomerID));

CREATE TABLE Order_T
    (OrderID                       NUMBER(11,0)      NOT NULL,
    OrderDate                      DATE DEFAULT SYSDATE,
    CustomerID                     NUMBER(11,0),
CONSTRAINT Order_PK PRIMARY KEY (OrderID),
CONSTRAINT Order_FK FOREIGN KEY (CustomerID) REFERENCES Customer_T (CustomerID));

CREATE TABLE Product_T
    (ProductID                     NUMBER(11,0)      NOT NULL,
    ProductDescription             VARCHAR2(50),
    ProductFinish                  VARCHAR2(20),
    ProductStandardPrice           DECIMAL(6,2),
    ProductLineID                  NUMBER(11,0),
CONSTRAINT Product_PK PRIMARY KEY (ProductID));

CREATE TABLE OrderLine_T
    (OrderID                       NUMBER(11,0)      NOT NULL,
    ProductID                      NUMBER(11,0)      NOT NULL,
    OrderedQuantity                NUMBER(11,0),
CONSTRAINT OrderLine_PK PRIMARY KEY (OrderID, ProductID),
CONSTRAINT OrderLine_FK1 FOREIGN KEY (OrderID) REFERENCES Order_T (OrderID),
CONSTRAINT OrderLine_FK2 FOREIGN KEY (ProductID) REFERENCES Product_T (ProductID));
```

The OrderLine_T table provides an example of a table that has two foreign keys. Foreign keys in this table reference the Order_T and Product_T tables, respectively.

Well-Structured Relations

To prepare for our discussion of normalization, we need to address the following question: What constitutes a well-structured relation? Intuitively, a **well-structured relation** contains minimal redundancy and allows users to insert, modify, and delete the rows in a table without errors or inconsistencies. EMPLOYEE1 (Figure 4-1) is such a relation. Each row of the table contains data describing one employee, and any modification to an employee's data (such as a change in salary) is confined to one row of the table. In contrast, EMPLOYEE2 (Figure 4-2b) is not a well-structured relation. If you examine the sample data in the table, you will notice considerable redundancy. For example, values for EmpID, Name, DeptName, and Salary appear in two separate rows for employees 100, 110, and 150. Consequently, if the salary for employee 100 changes, we must record this fact in two rows (or more, for some employees).

Redundancies in a table may result in errors or inconsistencies (called **anomalies**) when a user attempts to update the data in the table. We are typically concerned about three types of anomalies:

1. *Insertion anomaly* Suppose that we need to add a new employee to EMPLOYEE2. The primary key for this relation is the combination of EmpID and CourseTitle (as noted earlier). Therefore, to insert a new row, the user must supply values for both EmpID and CourseTitle (because primary key values cannot be null or nonexistent). This is an anomaly because the user should be able to enter employee data without supplying course data.

2. *Deletion anomaly* Suppose that the data for employee number 140 are deleted from the table. This will result in losing the information that this employee completed a

Well-structured relation

A relation that contains minimal redundancy and allows users to insert, modify, and delete the rows in a table without errors or inconsistencies.

Anomaly

An error or inconsistency that may result when a user attempts to update a table that contains redundant data. The three types of anomalies are insertion, deletion, and modification anomalies.

FIGURE 4-7   EMP COURSE

EmpID	CourseTitle	DateCompleted
100	SPSS	6/19/201X
100	Surveys	10/7/201X
140	Tax Acc	12/8/201X
110	Visual Basic	1/12/201X
110	C++	4/22/201X
150	SPSS	6/19/201X
150	Java	8/12/201X

course (Tax Acc) on 12/8/201X. In fact, it results in losing the information that this course had an offering that completed on that date.

3. *Modification anomaly*   Suppose that employee number 100 gets a salary increase. We must record the increase in each of the rows for that employee (two occurrences in Figure 4-2); otherwise, the data will be inconsistent.

These anomalies indicate that EMPLOYEE2 is not a well-structured relation. The problem with this relation is that it contains data about two entities: EMPLOYEE and COURSE. We will use normalization theory (described later in this chapter) to divide EMPLOYEE2 into two relations. One of the resulting relations is EMPLOYEE1 (Figure 4-1). The other we will call EMP COURSE, which appears with sample data in Figure 4-7. The primary key of this relation is the combination of EmpID and CourseTitle, and we underline these attribute names in Figure 4-7 to highlight this fact. Examine Figure 4-7 to verify that EMP COURSE is free of the types of anomalies described previously and is therefore well structured.

TRANSFORMING EER DIAGRAMS INTO RELATIONS

During logical design, you transform the E-R (and EER) diagrams that were developed during conceptual design into relational database schemas. The inputs to this process are the entity-relationship (and enhanced E-R) diagrams that you studied in Chapters 2 and 3. The outputs are the relational schemas described in the first two sections of this chapter.

Transforming (or mapping) EER diagrams into relations is a relatively straight-forward process with a well-defined set of rules. In fact, many CASE tools can auto-matically perform many of the conversion steps. However, it is important that you understand the steps in this process for four reasons:

1. CASE tools often cannot model more complex data relationships such as ternary relationships and supertype/subtype relationships. In these situations, you may have to perform the steps manually.
2. There are sometimes legitimate alternatives for which you will need to choose a particular solution.
3. You must be prepared to perform a quality check on the results obtained with a CASE tool.
4. Understanding the transformation process helps you understand why conceptual data modeling (modeling the real-world domain) is truly a different activity from representing the results of the conceptual data modeling process in a form that can be implemented using a DBMS.

In the following discussion, we illustrate the steps in the transformation with examples taken from Chapters 2 and 3. It will help for you to recall that we discussed three types of entities in those chapters:

1. *Regular entities*   are entities that have an independent existence and generally represent real-world objects, such as persons and products. Regular entity types are represented by rectangles with a single line.
2. *Weak entities*   are entities that cannot exist except with an identifying relation-ship with an owner (regular) entity type. Weak entities are identified by a rect-angle with a double line.

FIGURE 4-8 Example of
mapping a regular entity
(a) CUSTOMER entity type

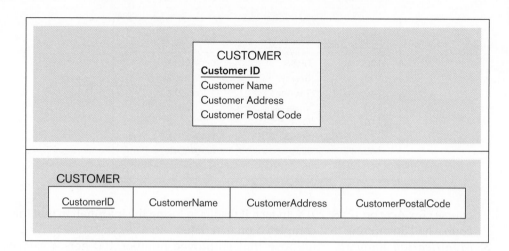

(b) CUSTOMER relation

3. *Associative entities* (also called gerunds) are formed from many-to-many relationships between other entity types. Associative entities are represented by a
rectangle with rounded corners.

Step 1: Map Regular Entities

Each regular entity type in an E-R diagram is transformed into a relation. The name
given to the relation is generally the same as the entity type. Each simple attribute of the
entity type becomes an attribute of the relation. The identifier of the entity type becomes
the primary key of the corresponding relation. You should check to make sure that this
primary key satisfies the desirable properties of identifiers outlined in Chapter 2.

Figure 4-8a shows a representation of the CUSTOMER entity type for Pine Valley
Furniture Company from Chapter 2 (see Figure 2-21). The corresponding CUSTOMER
relation is shown in graphical form in Figure 4-8b. In this figure and those that follow in this section, we show only a few key attributes for each relation to simplify the
figures.

COMPOSITE ATTRIBUTES   When a regular entity type has a composite attribute, only the
simple components of the composite attribute are included in the new relation as its
attributes. Figure 4-9 shows a variation on the example in Figure 4-8, where Customer
Address is represented as a composite attribute with components Street, City, and State
(see Figure 4-9a). This entity is mapped to the CUSTOMER relation, which contains the
simple address attributes, as shown in Figure 4-9b. Although Customer Name is modeled as a simple attribute in Figure 4-9a, you are aware that it instead could have been
modeled as a composite attribute with components Last Name, First Name, and Middle
Initial. In designing the CUSTOMER relation (Figure 4-9b), you may choose to use these

FIGURE 4-9 Example of mapping
a composite attribute
(a) CUSTOMER entity type
with composite attribute

CUSTOMER

| **Customer ID** |
| Customer Name |
| Customer Address |
| (Customer Street, Customer City, Customer State) |
| Customer Postal Code |

(b) CUSTOMER relation with
address detail

CUSTOMER

| CustomerID | CustomerName | CustomerStreet | CustomerCity | CustomerState | CustomerPostalCode |

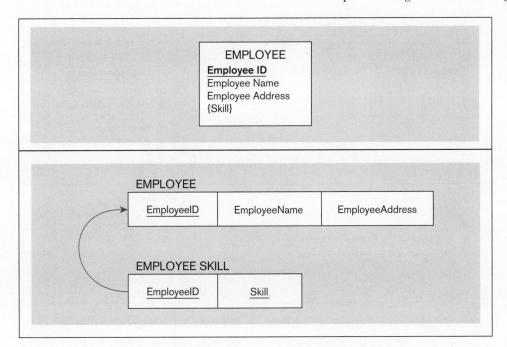

FIGURE 4-10 Example of mapping an entity with a multivalued attribute
(a) EMPLOYEE entity type with multivalued attribute

(b) EMPLOYEE and EMPLOYEE SKILL relations

simple attributes instead of CustomerName. Compared to composite attributes, simple attributes improve data accessibility and facilitate maintaining data quality.

MULTIVALUED ATTRIBUTES   When the regular entity type contains a multivalued attribute, two new relations (rather than one) are created. The first relation contains all of the attributes of the entity type except the multivalued attribute. The second relation contains two attributes that form the primary key of the second relation. The first of these attributes is the primary key from the first relation, which becomes a foreign key in the second relation. The second is the multivalued attribute. The name of the second relation should capture the meaning of the multivalued attribute.

An example of this procedure is shown in Figure 4-10. This is the EMPLOYEE entity type for Pine Valley Furniture Company. As shown in Figure 4-10a, EMPLOYEE has Skill as a multivalued attribute. Figure 4-10b shows the two relations that are created. The first (called EMPLOYEE) has the primary key EmployeeID. The second relation (called EMPLOYEE SKILL) has the two attributes, EmployeeID and Skill, which form the primary key. The relationship between foreign and primary keys is indicated by the arrow in the figure.

The relation EMPLOYEE SKILL contains no nonkey attributes (also called *descriptors*). Each row simply records the fact that a particular employee possesses a particular skill. This provides an opportunity for you to suggest to users that new attributes can be added to this relation. For example, the attributes YearsExperience and/or CertificationDate might be appropriate new values to add to this relation. (See Figure 2-15b for another variation on employee skills.)

If an entity type contains multiple multivalued attributes, each of them will be converted to a separate relation.

Step 2: Map Weak Entities

Recall that a weak entity type does not have an independent existence but exists only through an identifying relationship with another entity type called the *owner*. A weak entity type does not have a complete identifier but must have an attribute called a partial identifier that permits distinguishing the various occurrences of the weak entity for each owner entity instance.

The following procedure assumes that you have already created a relation corresponding to the identifying entity type during Step 1. If you have not, you should create that relation now, using the process described in Step 1.

FIGURE 4-11 Example of
mapping a weak entity
(a) Weak entity DEPENDENT

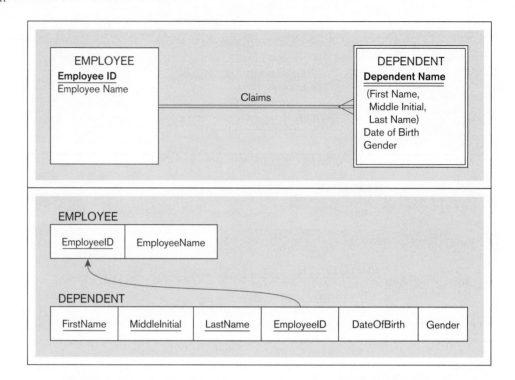

**(b) Relations resulting from
weak entity**

For each weak entity type, create a new relation and include all of the simple attributes (or simple components of composite attributes) as attributes of this relation. Then include the primary key of the *identifying* relation as a foreign key attribute in this new relation. The primary key of the new relation is the combination of this primary key of the identifying and the partial identifier of the weak entity type.

An example of this process is shown in Figure 4-11. Figure 4-11a shows the weak entity type DEPENDENT and its identifying entity type EMPLOYEE, linked by the identifying relationship Claims (see Figure 2-5). Notice that the attribute Dependent Name, which is the partial identifier for this relation, is a composite attribute with components First Name, Middle Initial, and Last Name. Thus, we assume that, *for a given employee*, these items will uniquely identify a dependent (a notable exception being the case of prizefighter George Foreman, who has named all his sons after himself).

Figure 4-11b shows the two relations that result from mapping this E-R segment. The primary key of DEPENDENT consists of four attributes: EmployeeID, FirstName, MiddleInitial, and LastName. DateOfBirth and Gender are the nonkey attributes. The foreign key relationship with its primary key is indicated by the arrow in the figure.

In practice, an alternative approach is often used to simplify the primary key of the DEPENDENT relation: Create a new attribute (called Dependent#), which will be used as a **surrogate primary key** in Figure 4-11b. With this approach, the relation DEPENDENT has the following attributes:

Surrogate primary key

A serial number or other system-assigned primary key for a relation.

DEPENDENT(<u>Dependent#</u>, *EmployeeID*, FirstName, MiddleInitial, LastName, DateOfBirth, Gender)

Dependent# is simply a serial number that is assigned to each dependent of an employee. Notice that this solution will ensure unique identification for each dependent (even for those of George Foreman!).

WHEN TO CREATE A SURROGATE KEY A surrogate key is usually created to simplify the key structures. According to Hoberman (2006), a surrogate key should be created when any of the following conditions hold:

• There is a composite primary key, as in the case of the DEPENDENT relation shown previously with the four-component primary key.

- The natural primary key (i.e., the key used in the organization and recognized in conceptual data modeling as the identifier) is inefficient (e.g., it may be very long and hence costly for database software to handle if it is used as a foreign key that references other tables).
- The natural primary key is recycled (i.e., the key is reused or repeated periodically, so it may not actually be unique over time); a more general statement of this condition is when the natural primary key cannot, in fact, be guaranteed to be unique over time (e.g., there could be duplicates, such as with names or titles).

Whenever a surrogate key is created, the natural key is always kept as nonkey data in the same relation because the natural key has organizational meaning that has to be captured in the database. In fact, surrogate keys mean nothing to users, so they are usually never shown to the user; instead, the natural keys are used as identifiers in searches.

Step 3: Map Binary Relationships

The procedure for representing relationships depends on both the degree of the relationships (unary, binary, or ternary) and the cardinalities of the relationships. We describe and illustrate the important cases in the following discussion.

MAP BINARY ONE-TO-MANY RELATIONSHIPS For each binary 1:*M* relationship, first create a relation for each of the two entity types participating in the relationship, using the procedure described in Step 1. Next, include the primary key attribute (or attributes) of the entity on the one-side of the relationship as a foreign key in the relation that is on the many-side of the relationship. (A mnemonic you can use to remember this rule is this: The primary key migrates to the many side.)

To illustrate this simple process, we use the Submits relationship between customers and orders for Pine Valley Furniture Company (see Figure 2-21). This 1:*M* relationship is illustrated in Figure 4-12a. (Again, we show only a few attributes for simplicity.) Figure 4-12b shows the result of applying this rule to map the entity types with the 1:*M* relationship. The primary key CustomerID of CUSTOMER (the one side) is included as a foreign key in ORDER (the many side). The foreign key relationship is indicated with an arrow.

MAP BINARY MANY-TO-MANY RELATIONSHIPS Suppose that there is a binary many-to-many (*M:N*) relationship between two entity types, A and B. For such a relationship, create a new relation, C. Include as foreign key attributes in C the primary key for each

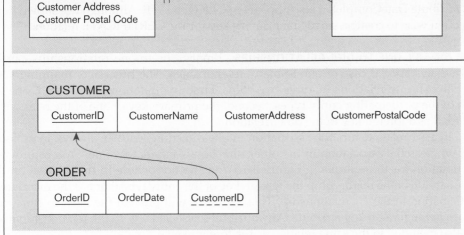

FIGURE 4-12 Example of mapping a 1:*M* relationship
(a) Relationship between CUSTOMER and ORDER entities

(b) CUSTOMER and ORDER relations with a foreign key in ORDER

FIGURE 4-13 Example of mapping a *M:N* relationship (a) Completes relationship (*M:N*)

(b) Three resulting relations

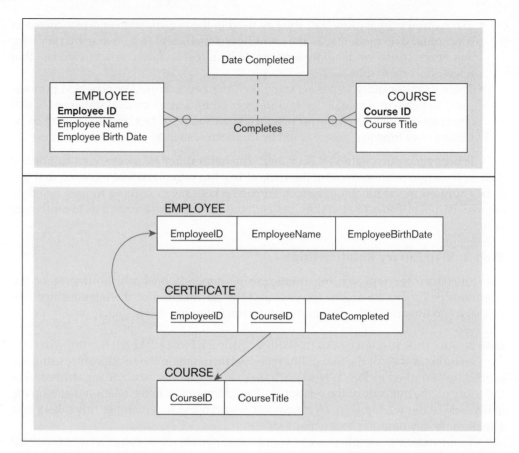

of the two participating entity types. These attributes together become the primary key of C. Any nonkey attributes that are associated with the *M:N* relationship are included with the relation C.

Figure 4-13 shows an example of applying this rule. Figure 4-13a shows the Completes relationship between the entity types EMPLOYEE and COURSE from Figure 2-11a. Figure 4-13b shows the three relations (EMPLOYEE, COURSE, and CERTIFICATE) that are formed from the entity types and the Completes relationship. If Completes had been represented as an associative entity, as is done in Figure 2-11b, a similar result would occur, but we will deal with associative entities in a subsequent section. In the case of an *M:N* relationship, first, a relation is created for each of the two regular entity types EMPLOYEE and COURSE. Then a new relation (named CERTIFICATE in Figure 4-13b) is created for the Completes relationship. The primary key of CERTIFICATE is the combination of EmployeeID and CourseID, which are the respective primary keys of EMPLOYEE and COURSE. As indicated in the diagram, these attributes are foreign keys that "point to" the respective primary keys. The nonkey attribute DateCompleted also appears in CERTIFICATE. Although not shown here, it is often wise to create a surrogate primary key for the CERTIFICATE relation.

MAP BINARY ONE-TO-ONE RELATIONSHIPS Binary one-to-one relationships can be viewed as a special case of one-to-many relationships. The process of mapping such a relationship to relations requires two steps. First, two relations are created, one for each of the participating entity types. Second, the primary key of one of the relations is included as a foreign key in the other relation.

In a 1:1 relationship, the association in one direction is nearly always an optional one, whereas the association in the other direction is mandatory one. (You can review the notation for these terms in Figure 2-1.) You should include in the relation on the optional side of the relationship the foreign key of the entity type that has the mandatory participation in the 1:1 relationship. This approach will prevent the need to store null values in the foreign key attribute. Any attributes associated with the relationship itself are also included in the same relation as the foreign key.

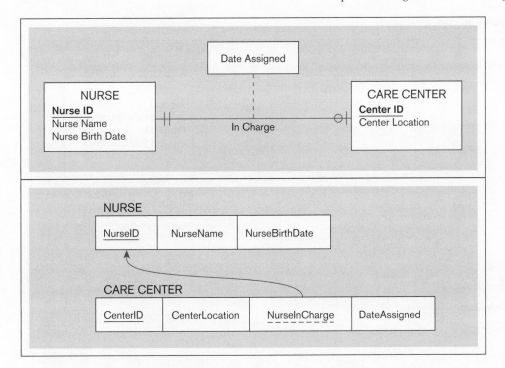

FIGURE 4-14 Example of mapping a binary 1:1 relationship
(a) In Charge relationship (binary 1:1)

(b) Resulting relations

An example of applying this procedure is shown in Figure 4-14. Figure 4-14a shows a binary 1:1 relationship between the entity types NURSE and CARE CENTER. Each care center must have a nurse who is in charge of that center. Thus, the association from CARE CENTER to NURSE is a mandatory one, whereas the association from NURSE to CARE CENTER is an optional one (since any nurse may or may not be in charge of a care center). The attribute Date Assigned is attached to the In Charge relationship.

The result of mapping this relationship to a set of relations is shown in Figure 4-14b. The two relations NURSE and CARE CENTER are created from the two entity types. Because CARE CENTER is the optional participant, the foreign key is placed in this relation. In this case, the foreign key is NurseInCharge. It has the same domain as NurseID, and the relationship with the primary key is shown in the figure. The attribute DateAssigned is also located in CARE CENTER and would not be allowed to be null.

Step 4: Map Associative Entities

As explained in Chapter 2, when a data modeler encounters a many-to-many relationship, he or she may choose to model that relationship as an associative entity in the E-R diagram. This approach is most appropriate when the end user can best visualize the relationship as an entity type rather than as an *M:N* relationship. Mapping the associative entity involves essentially the same steps as mapping an *M:N* relationship, as described in Step 3.

The first step is to create three relations: one for each of the two participating entity types and a third for the associative entity. We refer to the relation formed from the associative entity as the *associative relation*. The second step then depends on whether on the E-R diagram an identifier was assigned to the associative entity.

IDENTIFIER NOT ASSIGNED If an identifier was not assigned, the default primary key for the associative relation consists of the two primary key attributes from the other two relations. These attributes are then foreign keys that reference the other two relations.

An example of this case is shown in Figure 4-15. Figure 4-15a shows the associative entity ORDER LINE that links the ORDER and PRODUCT entity types at Pine Valley Furniture Company (see Figure 2-21). Figure 4-15b shows the three relations that result from this mapping. Note the similarity of this example to that of an *M:N* relationship shown in Figure 4-13.

FIGURE 4-15 Example of mapping an associative entity

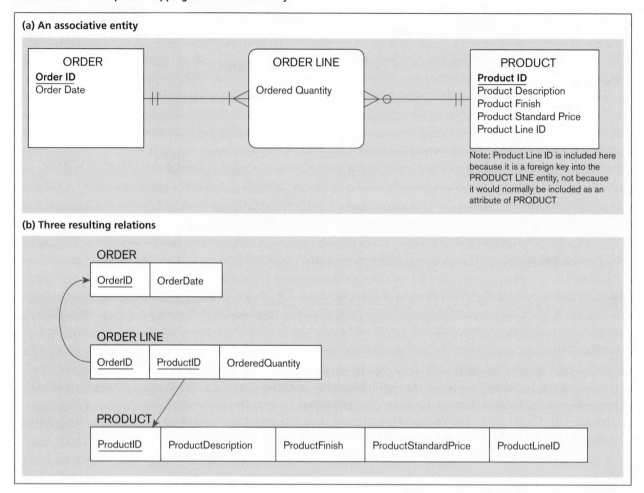

(a) An associative entity

ORDER
Order ID
Order Date

ORDER LINE

Ordered Quantity

PRODUCT
Product ID
Product Description
Product Finish
Product Standard Price
Product Line ID

Note: Product Line ID is included here because it is a foreign key into the PRODUCT LINE entity, not because it would normally be included as an attribute of PRODUCT

(b) Three resulting relations

ORDER

OrderID	OrderDate

ORDER LINE

OrderID	ProductID	OrderedQuantity

PRODUCT

ProductID	ProductDescription	ProductFinish	ProductStandardPrice	ProductLineID

IDENTIFIER ASSIGNED Sometimes a data modeler will assign a single-attribute identifier to the associative entity type on the E-R diagram. Two reasons may have motivated the data modeler to assign a single-attribute key during conceptual data modeling:

1. The associative entity type has a natural single-attribute identifier that is familiar to end users.
2. The default identifier (consisting of the identifiers for each of the participating entity types) may not uniquely identify instances of the associative entity.

These motivations are in addition to the reasons mentioned earlier in this chapter to create a surrogate primary key.

The process for mapping the associative entity in this case is now modified as follows: As before, a new (associative) relation is created to represent the associative entity. However, the primary key for this relation is the identifier assigned on the E-R diagram (rather than the default key). The primary keys for the two participating entity types are then included as foreign keys in the associative relation.

An example of this process is shown in Figure 4-16. Figure 4-16a shows the associative entity type SHIPMENT that links the CUSTOMER and VENDOR entity types. Shipment ID has been chosen as the identifier for SHIPMENT for two reasons:

1. Shipment ID is a natural identifier for this entity that is very familiar to end users.
2. The default identifier consisting of the combination of Customer ID and Vendor ID does not uniquely identify the instances of SHIPMENT. In fact, a given vendor typically makes many shipments to a given customer. Even including the attribute Date does not guarantee uniqueness, since there may be more than one shipment by a particular vendor on a given date. The surrogate key ShipmentID will, however, uniquely identify each shipment.

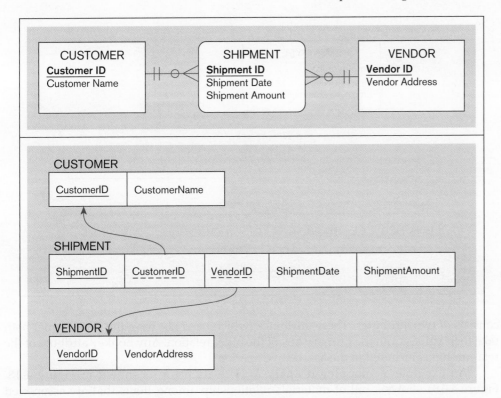

FIGURE 4-16 Example of mapping an associative entity with an identifier
(a) SHIPMENT associative entity

(b) Three resulting relations

Two nonkey attributes associated with the SHIPMENT associative entity are Shipment Date and Shipment Amount.

The result of mapping this entity to a set of relations is shown in Figure 4-16b. The new associative relation is named SHIPMENT. The primary key is ShipmentID. CustomerID and VendorID are included as foreign keys in this relation, and ShipmentDate and ShipmentAmount are nonkey attributes.

Step 5: Map Unary Relationships

In Chapter 2, we defined a unary relationship as a relationship between the instances of a single entity type. Unary relationships are also called *recursive relationships*. The two most important cases of unary relationships are one-to-many and many-to-many relationships. We discuss these two cases separately because the approach to mapping is somewhat different for the two types.

UNARY ONE-TO-MANY RELATIONSHIPS   The entity type in the unary relationship is mapped to a relation using the procedure described in Step 1. Then a foreign key attribute is added to the same relation; this attribute references the primary key values in the same relation. (This foreign key must have the same domain as the primary key.) This type of a foreign key is called a **recursive foreign key**.

Figure 4-17a shows a unary one-to-many relationship named Manages that associates each employee of an organization with another employee who is his or her manager. Each employee may have one manager; a given employee may manage zero to many employees.

The EMPLOYEE relation that results from mapping this entity and relationship is shown in Figure 4-17b. The (recursive) foreign key in the relation is named ManagerID. This attribute has the same domain as the primary key EmployeeID. Each row of this relation stores the following data for a given employee: EmployeeID, EmployeeName, EmployeeDateOfBirth, and ManagerID (i.e., EmployeeID for this employee's manager). Notice that because it is a foreign key, ManagerID references EmployeeID.

UNARY MANY-TO-MANY RELATIONSHIPS   With this type of relationship, two relations are created: one to represent the entity type in the relationship and an associative relation to represent the *M:N* relationship itself. The primary key of the associative relation

Recursive foreign key

A foreign key in a relation that references the primary key values of the same relation.

FIGURE 4-17 Example of
mapping a unary 1:*M* relationship
(a) EMPLOYEE entity with unary
relationship

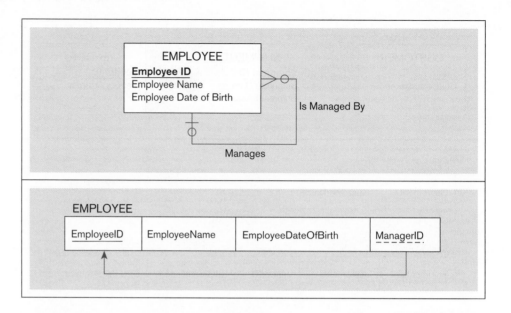

**(b) EMPLOYEE relation with
recursive foreign key**

consists of two attributes. These attributes (which need not have the same name) both
take their values from the primary key of the other relation. Any nonkey attribute of the
relationship is included in the associative relation.

An example of mapping a unary *M:N* relationship is shown in Figure 4-18.
Figure 4-18a shows a bill-of-materials relationship among items that are assembled
from other items or components. (This structure was described in Chapter 2, and an
example appears in Figure 2-13.) The relationship (called Contains) is *M:N* because a
given item can contain numerous component items, and, conversely, an item can be
used as a component in numerous other items.

The relations that result from mapping this entity and its relationship are shown
in Figure 4-18b. The ITEM relation is mapped directly from the same entity type.
COMPONENT is an associative relation whose primary key consists of two attributes
that are arbitrarily named ItemNo and ComponentNo. The attribute Quantity is a

FIGURE 4-18 Example
of mapping a unary *M:N*
relationship
(a) Bill-of-materials relationship
Contains (*M:N*)

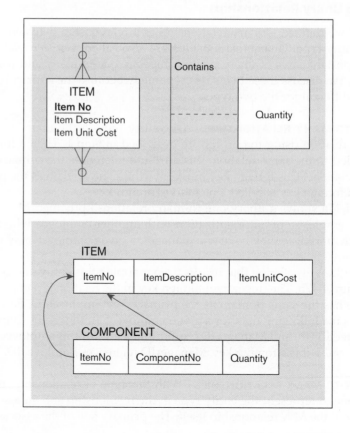

**(b) ITEM and COMPONENT
relations**

nonkey attribute of this relation that, for a given item, records the quantity of a particular component item used in that item. Notice that both ItemNo and ComponentNo reference the primary key (ItemNo) of the ITEM relation.

We can easily query these relations to determine, for example, the components of a given item. The following SQL query will list the immediate components (and their quantity) for item number 100:

```
SELECT ComponentNo, Quantity
FROM Component_T
WHERE ItemNo = 100;
```

Step 6: Map Ternary (and *n*-ary) Relationships

Recall from Chapter 2 that a ternary relationship is a relationship among three entity types. In that chapter, we recommended that you convert a ternary relationship to an associative entity to represent participation constraints more accurately.

To map an associative entity type that links three regular entity types, we create a new associative relation. The default primary key of this relation consists of the three primary key attributes for the participating entity types. (In some cases, additional attributes are required to form a unique primary key.) These attributes then act in the role of foreign keys that reference the individual primary keys of the participating entity types. Any attributes of the associative entity type become attributes of the new relation.

An example of mapping a ternary relationship (represented as an associative entity type) is shown in Figure 4-19. Figure 4-19a is an E-R segment (or view) that represents a *patient* receiving a *treatment* from a *physician*. The associative entity type PATIENT TREATMENT has the attributes PTreatment Date, PTreatment Time, and PTreatment Results; values are recorded for these attributes for each instance of PATIENT TREATMENT.

The result of mapping this view is shown in Figure 4-19b. The primary key attributes PatientID, PhysicianID, and TreatmentCode become foreign keys in PATIENT TREATMENT. The foreign key into TREATMENT is called PTreatmentCode in PATIENT TREATMENT. We are using this column name to illustrate that the foreign key name does not have to be the same as the name of the primary key to which it refers, as long as the values come from the same domain. These three attributes are components of the primary key of PATIENT TREATMENT. However, they do not uniquely identify a given treatment, because a patient may receive the same treatment from the same physician on more than one occasion. Does including the attribute Date as part of the primary key (along with the other three attributes) result in a primary key? This would be so if a given patient receives only one treatment from a particular physician on a given date. However, this is not likely to be the case. For example, a patient may receive a treatment in the morning, then the same treatment again in the afternoon. To resolve this issue, we include PTreatmentDate and PTreatmentTime as part of the primary key. Therefore, the primary key of PATIENT TREATMENT consists of the five attributes shown in Figure 4-19b: PatientID, PhysicianID, TreatmentCode, PTreatmentDate, and PTreatmentTime. The only nonkey attribute in the relation is PTreatmentResults.

Although this primary key is technically correct, it is complex and therefore difficult to manage and prone to errors. A better approach is to introduce a surrogate key, such as PTreatmentID, that is, a serial number that uniquely identifies each treatment. In this case, each of the former primary key attributes except for PTreatmentDate and PTreatmentTime becomes a foreign key in the PATIENT TREATMENT relation.

Step 7: Map Supertype/Subtype Relationships

The relational data model does not yet directly support supertype/subtype relationships. Fortunately, there are various strategies that database designers can use

FIGURE 4-19 Example of mapping a ternary relationship

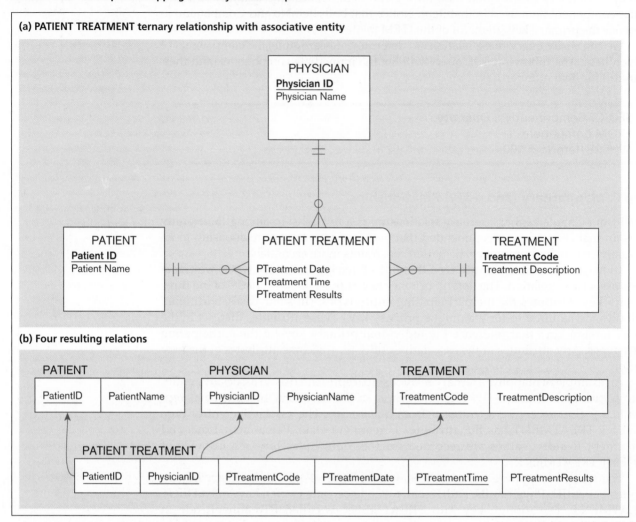

(a) PATIENT TREATMENT ternary relationship with associative entity

(b) Four resulting relations

to represent these relationships with the relational data model (Chouinard, 1989). For our purposes, we use the following strategy, which is the one most commonly employed:

1. Create a separate relation for the supertype and for each of its subtypes.
2. Assign to the relation created for the supertype the attributes that are common to all members of the supertype, including the primary key.
3. Assign to the relation for each subtype the primary key of the supertype and only those attributes that are unique to that subtype.
4. Assign one (or more) attributes of the supertype to function as the subtype discriminator. (The role of the subtype discriminator was discussed in Chapter 3.)

An example of applying this procedure is shown in Figures 4-20 and 4-21. Figure 4-20 shows the supertype EMPLOYEE with subtypes HOURLY EMPLOYEE, SALARIED EMPLOYEE, and CONSULTANT. (This example is described in Chapter 3, and Figure 4-20 is a repeat of Figure 3-8.) The primary key of EMPLOYEE is Employee Number, and the attribute Employee Type is the subtype discriminator.

The result of mapping this diagram to relations using these rules is shown in Figure 4-21. There is one relation for the supertype (EMPLOYEE) and one for each of the three subtypes. The primary key for each of the four relations is EmployeeNumber. A prefix is used to distinguish the name of the primary key for each subtype. For example, SEmployeeNumber is the name for the primary key of the relation SALARIED EMPLOYEE. Each of these attributes is a foreign key that references the supertype

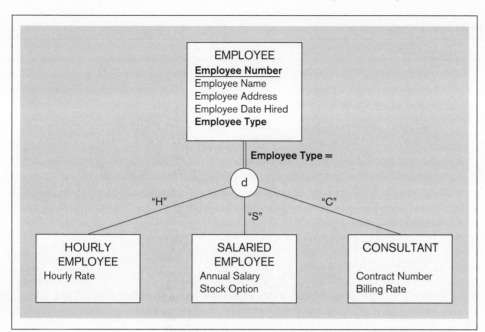

FIGURE 4-20 Supertype/subtype relationships

primary key, as indicated by the arrows in the diagram. Each subtype relation contains only those attributes unique to the subtype.

For each subtype, a relation can be produced that contains all of the attributes of that subtype (both specific and inherited) by using an SQL command that joins the subtype with its supertype. For example, suppose that we want to display a table that contains all of the attributes for SALARIED EMPLOYEE. The following command is used:

```
SELECT *
FROM Employee_T, SalariedEmployee_T
WHERE EmployeeNumber = SEmployeeNumber;
```

Summary of EER-to-Relational Transformations

The steps provide a comprehensive explanation of how each element of an EER diagram is transformed into parts of a relational data model. Table 4-2 is a quick reference to these steps and the associated figures that illustrate each type of transformation.

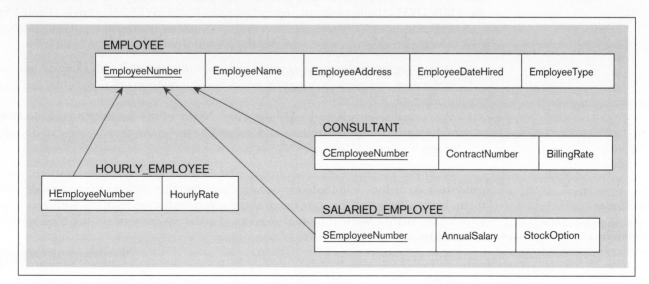

FIGURE 4-21 Mapping supertype/subtype relationships to relations

TABLE 4-2 Summary of EER-to-Relational Transformations

EER Structure	Relational Representation (Sample Figure)
Regular entity	Create a relation with primary key and nonkey attributes (Figure 4-8)
Composite attribute	Each component of a composite attribute becomes a separate attribute in the target relation (Figure 4-9)
Multivalued attribute	Create a separate relation for multivalued attribute with composite primary key, including the primary key of the entity (Figure 4-10)
Weak entity	Create a relation with a composite primary key (which includes the primary key of the entity on which this entity depends) and nonkey attributes (Figure 4-11)
Binary or unary 1:*M* relationship	Place the primary key of the entity on the one side of the relationship as a foreign key in the relation for the entity on the many side (Figure 4-12; Figure 4-17 for unary relationship)
Binary or unary *M:N* relationship or associative entity without its own key	Create a relation with a composite primary key using the primary keys of the related entities plus any nonkey attributes of the relationship or associative entity (Figure 4-13, Figure 4-15 for associative entity, Figure 4-18 for unary relationship)
Binary or unary 1:1 relationship	Place the primary key of either entity in the relation for the other entity; if one side of the relationship is optional, place the foreign key of the entity on the mandatory side in the relation for the entity on the optional side (Figure 4-14)
Binary or unary *M:N* relationship or associative entity with its own key	Create a relation with the primary key associated with the associative entity plus any nonkey attributes of the associative entity and the primary keys of the related entities as foreign keys (Figure 4-16)
Ternary and *n*-ary relationships	Same as binary *M:N* relationships above; without its own key, include as part of primary key of relation for the relationship or associative entity the primary keys from all related entities; with its own surrogate key, the primary keys of the associated entities are included as foreign keys in the relation for the relationship or associative entity (Figure 4-19)
Supertype/subtype relationship	Create a relation for the superclass, which contains the primary and all nonkey attributes in common with all subclasses, plus create a separate relation for each subclass with the same primary key (with the same or local name) but with only the nonkey attributes related to that subclass (Figure 4-20 and 4-21)

INTRODUCTION TO NORMALIZATION

Following the steps outlined previously for transforming EER diagrams into relations often results in well-structured relations. However, there is no guarantee that all anomalies are removed by following these steps. Normalization is a formal process for deciding which attributes should be grouped together in a relation so that all anomalies are removed. For example, we used the principles of normalization to convert the EMPLOYEE2 table (with its redundancy) to EMPLOYEE1 (Figure 4-1) and EMP COURSE (Figure 4-7). There are two major occasions during the overall database development process when you can usually benefit from using normalization:

1. *During logical database design (described in this chapter)* You should use normalization concepts as a quality check for the relations that are obtained from mapping E-R diagrams.
2. *When reverse-engineering older systems* Many of the tables and user views for older systems are redundant and subject to the anomalies we describe in this chapter.

So far we have presented an intuitive discussion of well-structured relations; however, we need formal definitions of such relations, together with a process for designing them. **Normalization** is the process of successively reducing relations with anomalies to produce smaller, well-structured relations. Following are some of the main goals of normalization:

1. Minimize data redundancy, thereby avoiding anomalies and conserving storage space.
2. Simplify the enforcement of referential integrity constraints.

Normalization

The process of decomposing relations with anomalies to produce smaller, well-structured relations.

3. Make it easier to maintain data (insert, update, and delete).
4. Provide a better design that is an improved representation of the real world and a stronger basis for future growth.

Normalization makes no assumptions about how data will be used in displays, queries, or reports. Normalization, based on what we will call *normal forms* and *functional dependencies*, defines rules of the business, not data usage. Further, remember that data are normalized by the end of logical database design. Thus, normalization, as we will see in Chapter 5, places no constraints on how data can or should be physically stored or, therefore, on processing performance. Normalization is a logical data-modeling technique used to ensure that data are well structured from an organization-wide view.

Steps in Normalization

Normalization can be accomplished and understood in stages, each of which corresponds to a normal form (see Figure 4-22). A **normal form** is a state of a relation that requires that certain rules regarding relationships between attributes (or functional dependencies) are satisfied. We describe these rules briefly in this section and illustrate them in detail in the following sections:

Normal form

A state of a relation that requires that certain rules regarding relationships between attributes (or functional dependencies) are satisfied.

1. *First normal form*   Any multivalued attributes (also called *repeating groups*) have been removed, so there is a single value (possibly null) at the intersection of each row and column of the table (as in Figure 4-2b).
2. *Second normal form*   Any partial functional dependencies have been removed (i.e., nonkey attributes are identified by the whole primary key).
3. *Third normal form*   Any transitive dependencies have been removed (i.e., nonkey attributes are identified by only the primary key).

We describe and illustrate the first through the third normal forms in this chapter. There are additional normal forms that are beyond the scope of this book.

FIGURE 4-22   Steps in normalization

Functional Dependencies and Keys

The first stages of normalization are based on the analysis of functional dependencies. A **functional dependency** is a constraint between two attributes or two sets of attributes. For any relation R, attribute B is functionally dependent on attribute A if, for every valid instance of A, that value of A uniquely determines the value of B (Dutka and Hanson, 1989). The functional dependency of B on A is represented by an arrow, as follows: A → B. A functional dependency is not a mathematical dependency: B cannot be computed from A. Rather, if you know the value of A, there can be only one value for B. An attribute may be functionally dependent on a combination of two (or more) attributes rather than on a single attribute. For example, consider the relation EMP COURSE (EmpID, CourseTitle, DateCompleted) shown in Figure 4-7. We represent the functional dependency in this relation as follows:

EmpID, CourseTitle → DateCompleted

The comma between EmpID and CourseTitle stands for the logical AND operator, because DateCompleted is functionally dependent on EmpID and CourseTitle in combination.

The functional dependency in this statement implies that the date a course is completed is determined by the identity of the employee and the title of the course. Typical examples of functional dependencies are the following:

1. *SSN → Name, Address, Birthdate*   A person's name, address, and birth date are functionally dependent on that person's Social Security number (in other words, there can be only one Name, one Address, and one Birthdate for each SSN).
2. *VIN → Make, Model, Color*   The make, model, and color of a vehicle are functionally dependent on the vehicle identification number (as above, there can be only one value of Make, Model, and Color associated with each VIN).
3. *ISBN → Title, FirstAuthorName, Publisher*   The title of a book, the name of the first author, and the publisher are functionally dependent on the book's international standard book number (ISBN).

DETERMINANTS   The attribute on the left side of the arrow in a functional dependency is called a **determinant**. SSN, VIN, and ISBN are determinants in the preceding three examples. In the EMP COURSE relation (Figure 4-7), the combination of EmpID and CourseTitle is a determinant.

CANDIDATE KEYS   A **candidate key** is an attribute, or combination of attributes, that uniquely identifies a row in a relation. A candidate key must satisfy the following properties (Dutka and Hanson, 1989), which are a subset of the six properties of a relation previously listed:

1. *Unique identification*   For every row, the value of the key must uniquely identify that row. This property implies that each nonkey attribute is functionally dependent on that key.
2. *Nonredundancy*   No attribute in the key can be deleted without destroying the property of unique identification.

Let's apply the preceding definition to identify candidate keys in two of the relations described in this chapter. The EMPLOYEE1 relation (Figure 4-1) has the following schema: EMPLOYEE1(EmpID, Name, DeptName, Salary). EmpID is the only determinant in this relation. All of the other attributes are functionally dependent on EmpID. Therefore, EmpID is a candidate key and (because there are no other candidate keys) also is the primary key.

We represent the functional dependencies for a relation using the notation shown in Figure 4-23. Figure 4-23a shows the representation for EMPLOYEE1. The horizontal

FIGURE 4-23 **Representing functional dependencies**

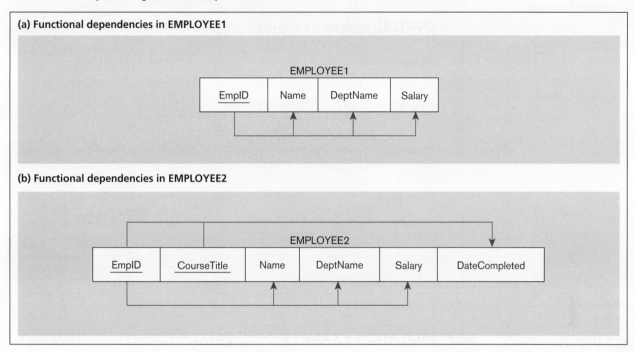

line in the figure portrays the functional dependencies. A vertical line drops from the primary key (EmpID) and connects to this line. Vertical arrows then point to each of the nonkey attributes that are functionally dependent on the primary key.

For the relation EMPLOYEE2 (Figure 4-2b), notice that (unlike EMPLOYEE1) EmpID does not uniquely identify a row in the relation. For example, there are two rows in the table for EmpID number 100. There are two types of functional dependencies in this relation:

1. EmpID → Name, DeptName, Salary
2. EmpID, CourseTitle → DateCompleted

The functional dependencies indicate that the combination of EmpID and CourseTitle is the only candidate key (and therefore the primary key) for EMPLOYEE2. In other words, the primary key of EMPLOYEE2 is a composite key. Neither EmpID nor CourseTitle uniquely identifies a row in this relation and therefore (according to property 1) cannot by itself be a candidate key. Examine the data in Figure 4-2b to verify that the combination of EmpID and CourseTitle does uniquely identify each row of EMPLOYEE2. We represent the functional dependencies in this relation in Figure 4-23b. Notice that DateCompleted is the only attribute that is functionally dependent on the full primary key consisting of the attributes EmpID and CourseTitle.

We can summarize the relationship between determinants and candidate keys as follows: A candidate key is always a determinant, whereas a determinant may or may not be a candidate key. For example, in EMPLOYEE2, EmpID is a determinant but not a candidate key. A candidate key is a determinant that uniquely identifies the remaining (nonkey) attributes in a relation. A determinant may be a candidate key (such as EmpID in EMPLOYEE1), part of a composite candidate key (such as EmpID in EMPLOYEE2), or a nonkey attribute. We will describe examples of this shortly.

As a preview to the following illustration of what normalization accomplishes, normalized relations have as their primary key the determinant for each of the nonkeys, and within that relation there are no other functional dependencies.

FIGURE 4-24 Invoice (Pine Valley Furniture Company)

PVFC Customer Invoice

Customer ID	2		Order ID	1006
Customer Name	Value Furniture		Order Date	10/24/2010
Address	15145 S.W. 17th St. Plano TX 75022			

Product ID	Product Description	Finish	Quantity	Unit Price	Extended Price
7	Dining Table	Natural Ash	2	$800.00	$1,600.00
5	Writer's Desk	Cherry	2	$325.00	$650.00
4	Entertainment Center	Natural Maple	1	$650.00	$650.00
				Total	$2,900.00

NORMALIZATION EXAMPLE: PINE VALLEY FURNITURE COMPANY

Now that we have examined functional dependencies and keys, we are ready to describe and illustrate the steps of normalization. If an EER data model has been transformed into a comprehensive set of relations for the database, then each of these relations needs to be normalized. In other cases in which the logical data model is being derived from user interfaces, such as screens, forms, and reports, you will want to create relations for each user interface and normalize those relations.

For a simple illustration, we use a customer invoice from Pine Valley Furniture Company (see Figure 4-24.)

Step 0: Represent the View in Tabular Form

The first step (preliminary to normalization) is to represent the user view (in this case, an invoice) as a single table, or relation, with the attributes recorded as column headings. Sample data should be recorded in the rows of the table, including any repeating groups that are present in the data. The table representing the invoice is shown in Figure 4-25. Notice that data for a second order (OrderID 1007) are included in Figure 4-25 to clarify further the structure of this data.

OrderID	Order Date	Customer ID	Customer Name	Customer Address	ProductID	Product Description	Product Finish	Product StandardPrice	Ordered Quantity
1006	10/24/2010	2	Value Furniture	Plano, TX	7	Dining Table	Natural Ash	800.00	2
					5	Writer's Desk	Cherry	325.00	2
					4	Entertainment Center	Natural Maple	650.00	1
1007	10/25/2010	6	Furniture Gallery	Boulder, CO	11	4–Dr Dresser	Oak	500.00	4
					4	Entertainment Center	Natural Maple	650.00	3

FIGURE 4-25 INVOICE data (Pine Valley Furniture Company)

Step 1: Convert to First Normal Form

A relation is in **first normal form (1NF)** if the following two constraints both apply:

1. There are no repeating groups in the relation (thus, there is a single fact at the intersection of each row and column of the table).
2. A primary key has been defined, which uniquely identifies each row in the relation.

REMOVE REPEATING GROUPS As you can see, the invoice data in Figure 4-25 contain a repeating group for each product that appears on a particular order. Thus, OrderID 1006 contains three repeating groups, corresponding to the three products on that order.

In a previous section, we showed how to remove repeating groups from a table by filling relevant data values into previously vacant cells of the table (see Figures 4-2a and 4-2b). Applying this procedure to the invoice table yields the new relation (named INVOICE) shown in Figure 4-26.

SELECT THE PRIMARY KEY There are four determinants in INVOICE, and their functional dependencies are the following:

OrderID → OrderDate, CustomerID, CustomerName, CustomerAddress
CustomerID → CustomerName, CustomerAddress
ProductID → ProductDescription, ProductFinish, ProductStandardPrice
OrderID, ProductID → OrderedQuantity

Why do we know these are the functional dependencies? These business rules come from the organization. We know these from studying the nature of the Pine Valley Furniture Company business. We can also see that no data in Figure 4-26 violates any of these functional dependencies. But because we don't see all possible rows of this table, we cannot be sure that there wouldn't be some invoice that would violate one of these functional dependencies. Thus, we must depend on our understanding of the rules of the organization.

As you can see, the only candidate key for INVOICE is the composite key consisting of the attributes OrderID and ProductID (because there is only one row in the table for any combination of values for these attributes). Therefore, OrderID and ProductID are underlined in Figure 4-26, indicating that they compose the primary key.

When forming a primary key, you must be careful not to include redundant (and therefore unnecessary) attributes. Thus, although CustomerID is a determinant in INVOICE, it is not included as part of the primary key because all of the nonkey attributes are identified by the combination of OrderID and ProductID. We will see the role of CustomerID in the normalization process that follows.

OrderID	Order Date	Customer ID	Customer Name	Customer Address	ProductID	Product Description	Product Finish	Product StandardPrice	Ordered Quantity
1006	10/24/2010	2	Value Furniture	Plano, TX	7	Dining Table	Natural Ash	800.00	2
1006	10/24/2010	2	Value Furniture	Plano, TX	5	Writer's Desk	Cherry	325.00	2
1006	10/24/2010	2	Value Furniture	Plano, TX	4	Entertainment Center	Natural Maple	650.00	1
1007	10/25/2010	6	Furniture Gallery	Boulder, CO	11	4–Dr Dresser	Oak	500.00	4
1007	10/25/2010	6	Furniture Gallery	Boulder, CO	4	Entertainment Center	Natural Maple	650.00	3

FIGURE 4-26 INVOICE relation (1NF) (Pine Valley Furniture Company)

FIGURE 4-27 Functional dependency diagram for INVOICE

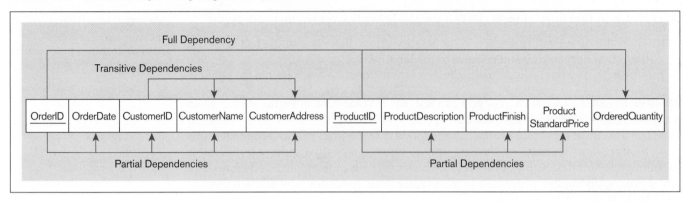

A diagram that shows these functional dependencies for the INVOICE relation is shown in Figure 4-27. This diagram is a horizontal list of all the attributes in INVOICE, with the primary key attributes (OrderID and ProductID) underlined. Notice that the only attribute that depends on the full key is OrderedQuantity. All of the other functional dependencies are either partial dependencies or transitive dependencies (both are defined next).

ANOMALIES IN 1NF   Although repeating groups have been removed, the data in Figure 4-26 still contain considerable redundancy. For example, CustomerID, CustomerName, and CustomerAddress for Value Furniture are recorded in three rows (at least) in the table. As a result of these redundancies, manipulating the data in the table can lead to anomalies such as the following:

1. *Insertion anomaly*   With this table structure, the company is not able to introduce a new product (say, Breakfast Table with ProductID 8) and add it to the database before it is ordered the first time: No entries can be added to the table without both ProductID *and* OrderID. As another example, if a customer calls and requests another product be added to his OrderID 1007, a new row must be inserted in which the order date and all of the customer information must be repeated. This leads to data replication and potential data entry errors (e.g., the customer name may be entered as "Valley Furniture").
2. *Deletion anomaly*   If a customer calls and requests that the Dining Table be deleted from her OrderID 1006, this row must be deleted from the relation, and we lose the information concerning this item's finish (Natural Ash) and price ($800.00).
3. *Update anomaly*   If Pine Valley Furniture (as part of a price adjustment) increases the price of the Entertainment Center (ProductID 4) to $750.00, this change must be recorded in all rows containing that item. (There are two such rows in Figure 4-26.)

Step 2: Convert to Second Normal Form

Second normal form (2NF)

A relation in first normal form in which every nonkey attribute is fully functionally dependent on the primary key.

Partial functional dependency

A functional dependency in which one or more nonkey attributes are functionally dependent on part (but not all) of the primary key.

We can remove many of the redundancies (and resulting anomalies) in the INVOICE relation by converting it to second normal form. A relation is in **second normal form (2NF)** if it is in first normal form and contains no partial functional dependencies. A **partial functional dependency** exists when a nonkey attribute is functionally dependent on part (but not all) of the primary key. As you can see, the following partial dependencies exist in Figure 4-27:

OrderID → OrderDate, CustomerID, CustomerName, CustomerAddress
ProductID → ProductDescription, ProductFinish, ProductStandardPrice

The first of these partial dependencies (for example) states that the date on an order is uniquely determined by the order number and has nothing to do with the ProductID.

FIGURE 4-28 Removing partial dependencies

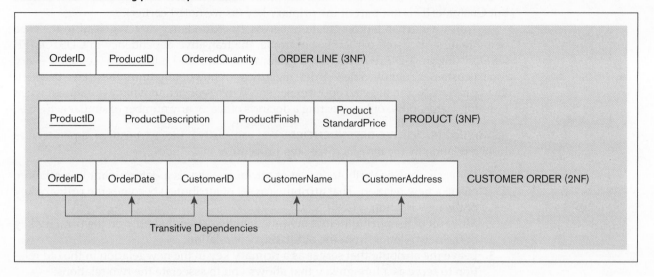

To convert a relation with partial dependencies to second normal form, the following steps are required:

1. Create a new relation for each primary key attribute (or combination of attributes) that is a determinant in a partial dependency. That attribute is the primary key in the new relation.
2. Move the nonkey attributes that are only dependent on this primary key attribute (or attributes) from the old relation to the new relation.

The results of performing these steps for the INVOICE relation are shown in Figure 4-28. Removal of the partial dependencies results in the formation of two new relations: PRODUCT and CUSTOMER ORDER. The INVOICE relation is now left with just the primary key attributes (OrderID and ProductID) and OrderedQuantity, which is functionally dependent on the whole key. We rename this relation ORDER LINE, because each row in this table represents one line item on an order.

As indicated in Figure 4-28, the relations ORDER LINE and PRODUCT are in third normal form. However, CUSTOMER ORDER contains transitive dependencies and therefore (although in second normal form) is not yet in third normal form.

A relation that is in first normal form will be in second normal form if any one of the following conditions applies:

1. The primary key consists of only one attribute (e.g., the attribute ProductID in the PRODUCT relation in Figure 4-28). By definition, there cannot be a partial dependency in such a relation.
2. No nonkey attributes exist in the relation (thus all of the attributes in the relation are components of the primary key). There are no functional dependencies in such a relation.
3. Every nonkey attribute is functionally dependent on the full set of primary key attributes (e.g., the attribute OrderedQuantity in the ORDER LINE relation in Figure 4-28).

Step 3: Convert to Third Normal Form

A relation is in **third normal form (3NF)** if it is in second normal form and no transitive dependencies exist. A **transitive dependency** in a relation is a functional dependency between the primary key and one or more nonkey attributes that are dependent on the primary key via another nonkey attribute. For example, there are two transitive dependencies in the CUSTOMER ORDER relation shown in Figure 4-28:

OrderID → CustomerID → CustomerName
OrderID → CustomerID → CustomerAddress

Third normal form (3NF)

A relation that is in second normal form and has no transitive dependencies.

Transitive dependency

A functional dependency between the primary key and one or more nonkey attributes that are dependent on the primary key via another nonkey attribute.

In other words, both customer name and address are uniquely identified by CustomerID, but CustomerID is not part of the primary key (as we noted earlier).

Transitive dependencies create unnecessary redundancy that may lead to the type of anomalies discussed earlier. For example, the transitive dependency in CUSTOMER ORDER (Figure 4-28) requires that a customer's name and address be reentered every time a customer submits a new order, regardless of how many times they have been entered previously. You have no doubt experienced this type of annoying requirement when ordering merchandise online, visiting a doctor's office, or any number of similar activities.

REMOVING TRANSITIVE DEPENDENCIES   You can easily remove transitive dependencies from a relation by means of a three-step procedure:

1. For each nonkey attribute (or set of attributes) that is a determinant in a relation, create a new relation. That attribute (or set of attributes) becomes the primary key of the new relation.
2. Move all of the attributes that are functionally dependent only on the primary key of the new relation from the old to the new relation.
3. Leave the attribute that serves as a primary key in the new relation in the old relation to serve as a foreign key that allows you to associate the two relations.

The results of applying these steps to the relation CUSTOMER ORDER are shown in Figure 4-29. A new relation named CUSTOMER has been created to receive the components of the transitive dependency. The determinant CustomerID becomes the primary key of this relation, and the attributes CustomerName and CustomerAddress are moved to the relation. CUSTOMER ORDER is renamed ORDER, and the attribute CustomerID remains as a foreign key in that relation. This allows us to associate an order with the customer who submitted the order. As indicated in Figure 4-29, these relations are now in third normal form.

Normalizing the data in the INVOICE view has resulted in the creation of four relations in third normal form: CUSTOMER, PRODUCT, ORDER, and ORDER LINE. A relational schema showing these four relations and their associations (developed using Microsoft Visio) is shown in Figure 4-30. Note that CustomerID is a foreign key in ORDER, and OrderID and ProductID are foreign keys in ORDER LINE. (Foreign keys are shown in Visio for logical, but not conceptual, data models.) Also note that minimum cardinalities are shown on the relationships even though the normalized relations provide no evidence of what the minimum cardinalities should be. Sample data for the relations might include, for example, a customer with no orders, thus providing evidence of the optional cardinality for the relationship Places. However, even if there were an order for every customer in a sample data set, this would not prove mandatory cardinality. Minimum cardinalities must be determined from business rules, not illustrations of reports, screens, and transactions. The same statement is true for specific maximum cardinalities (e.g., a business rule that no order may contain more than 100 line items).

Determinants and Normalization

We demonstrated normalization through 3NF in steps. There is an easy shortcut, however. If you look back at the original set of four determinants and the associated functional dependencies for the invoice user view, each of these corresponds to one of the relations in Figure 4-30, with each determinant being the primary key of a relation,

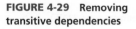

FIGURE 4-29 **Removing transitive dependencies**

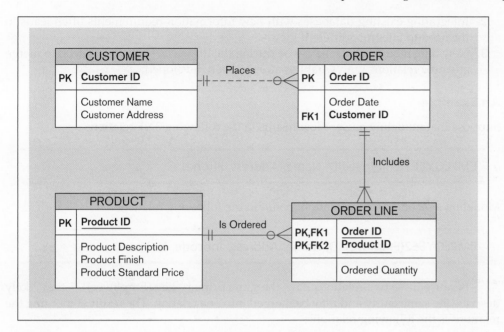

FIGURE 4-30 Relational schema for INVOICE data (Microsoft Visio notation)

and the nonkeys of each relation are those attributes that are functionally dependent on each determinant. There is a subtle but important difference: Because OrderID determines CustomerID, CustomerName, and CustomerAddress and CustomerID determines its dependent attributes, CustomerID becomes a foreign key in the ORDER relation, which is where CustomerName and CustomerAddress are represented. The point is, if you can determine determinants that have no overlapping dependent attributes, then you have defined the relations. Thus, you can do normalization step by step as illustrated for the Pine Valley Furniture invoice, or you can create relations in 3NF straight from determinants' functional dependencies.

After completing Steps 0 through 3, all nonkeys will be dependent on the primary key, the whole primary key, and nothing but the primary key ("so help you Codd!"). Actually, normal forms are rules about functional dependencies and, hence, are the result of finding determinants and their associated nonkeys. The steps we outlined above are an aid in creating a relation for each determinant and its associated nonkeys.

MERGING RELATIONS

In a previous section, we described how to transform EER diagrams into relations. This transformation occurs when we take the results of a top-down analysis of data requirements and begin to structure them for implementation in a database. We then described how to check the resulting relations to determine whether they are in third (or higher) normal form and perform normalization steps if necessary.

As part of the logical design process, normalized relations may have been created from a number of separate EER diagrams and (possibly) other user views (i.e., there may be bottom-up or parallel database development activities for different areas of the organization as well as top-down ones). For example, besides the invoice used in the prior section to illustrate normalization, there may be an order form, an account balance report, production routing, and other user views, each of which has been normalized separately. The three-schema architecture for databases (see Chapter 1) encourages the simultaneous use of both top-down and bottom-up database development processes. In reality, most medium-to-large organizations have many reasonably independent systems development activities that at some point need to come together to create a shared database. The result is that some of the relations generated from these various processes may be redundant; that is, they may refer to the same entities. In such cases, we should merge those relations to remove the redundancy. This section describes merging relations (also called *view integration*). An understanding of how to merge relations is important for three reasons:

1. On large projects, the work of several subteams comes together during logical design, so there is often a need to merge relations.

2. Integrating existing databases with new information requirements often leads to the need to integrate different views.
3. New data requirements may arise during the life cycle, so there is a need to merge any new relations with what has already been developed.

An Example

Suppose that modeling a user view results in the following 3NF relation:

EMPLOYEE1(<u>EmployeeID</u>, Name, Address, Phone)

Modeling a second user view might result in the following relation:

EMPLOYEE2(<u>EmployeeID</u>, Name, Address, Jobcode, NoYears)

Because these two relations have the same primary key (EmployeeID), they likely describe the same entity and may be merged into one relation. The result of merging the relations is the following relation:

EMPLOYEE(<u>EmployeeID</u>, Name, Address, Phone, Jobcode, NoYears)

Notice that an attribute that appears in both relations (e.g., Name in this example) appears only once in the merged relation.

View Integration Problems

When integrating relations as in the preceding example, a database analyst must understand the meaning of the data and must be prepared to resolve any problems that may arise in that process. In this section, we describe and briefly illustrate four problems that arise in view integration: *synonyms, homonyms, transitive dependencies*, and *supertype/ subtype relationships*.

Synonyms

Two (or more) attributes that have different names but the same meaning.

SYNONYMS In some situations, two (or more) attributes may have different names but the same meaning (e.g., when they describe the same characteristic of an entity). Such attributes are called **synonyms**. For example, EmployeeID and EmployeeNo may be synonyms. When merging the relations that contain synonyms, you should obtain agreement (if possible) from users on a single, standardized name for the attribute and eliminate any other synonyms. (Another alternative is to choose a third name to replace the synonyms.) For example, consider the following relations:

STUDENT1(<u>StudentID</u>, Name)
STUDENT2(<u>MatriculationNo</u>, Name, Address)

In this case, the analyst recognizes that both StudentID and MatriculationNo are synonyms for a person's student identity number and are identical attributes. (Another possibility is that these are both candidate keys, and only one of them should be selected as the primary key.) One possible resolution would be to standardize on one of the two attribute names, such as StudentID. Another option is to use a new attribute name, such as StudentNo, to replace both synonyms. Assuming the latter approach, merging the two relations would produce the following result:

STUDENT(<u>StudentNo</u>, Name, Address)

Often when there are synonyms, there is a need to allow some database users to refer to the same data by different names. Users may need to use familiar names that are consistent with terminology in their part of the organization. An **alias** is an alternative name used for an attribute. Many database management systems allow the definition of an alias that may be used interchangeably with the primary attribute label.

HOMONYMS An attribute name that may have more than one meaning is called a **homonym**. For example, the term *account* might refer to a bank's checking account, savings account, loan account, or other type of account (and therefore *account* refers to different data, depending on how it is used).

You should be on the lookout for homonyms when merging relations. Consider the following example:

STUDENT1(<u>StudentID</u>, Name, Address)
STUDENT2(<u>StudentID</u>, Name, PhoneNo, Address)

In discussions with users, an analyst may discover that the attribute Address in STUDENT1 refers to a student's campus address, whereas in STUDENT2 the same attribute refers to a student's permanent (or home) address. To resolve this conflict, we would probably need to create new attribute names, so that the merged relation would become

STUDENT(<u>StudentID</u>, Name, PhoneNo, CampusAddress, PermanentAddress)

TRANSITIVE DEPENDENCIES When two 3NF relations are merged to form a single relation, transitive dependencies (described earlier in this chapter) may result. For example, consider the following two relations:

STUDENT1(<u>StudentID</u>, MajorName)
STUDENT2(<u>StudentID</u>, Advisor)

Because STUDENT1 and STUDENT2 have the same primary key, the two relations can be merged:

STUDENT(<u>StudentID</u>, MajorName, Advisor)

However, suppose that each major has exactly one advisor. In this case, Advisor is functionally dependent on Major Name:

MajorName → Advisor

If the preceding functional dependency exists, then STUDENT is in 2NF but not in 3NF, because it contains a transitive dependency. The analyst can create 3NF relations by removing the transitive dependency. Major Name becomes a foreign key in STUDENT:

STUDENT(<u>StudentID</u>, MajorName)
MAJOR (<u>MajorName</u>, Advisor)

SUPERTYPE/SUBTYPE RELATIONSHIPS   These relationships may be hidden in user views or relations. Suppose that we have the following two hospital relations:

PATIENT1(<u>PatientID</u>, Name, Address)
PATIENT2(<u>PatientID</u>, RoomNo)

Initially, it appears that these two relations can be merged into a single PATIENT relation. However, the analyst correctly suspects that there are two different types of patients: resident patients and outpatients. PATIENT1 actually contains attributes common to all patients. PATIENT2 contains an attribute (RoomNo) that is a characteristic only of resident patients. In this situation, the analyst should create supertype/subtype relationships for these entities:

PATIENT(<u>PatientID</u>, Name, Address)
RESIDENT PATIENT(<u>PatientID</u>, RoomNo)
OUTPATIENT(<u>PatientID</u>, DateTreated)

We have created the OUTPATIENT relation to show what it might look like if it were needed, but it is not necessary, given only PATIENT1 and PATIENT2 user views. For an extended discussion of view integration in database design, see Navathe et al. (1986).

Summary

Logical database design is the process of transforming the conceptual data model into a logical data model. The emphasis in this chapter has been on the relational data model, because of its importance in contemporary database systems. The relational data model represents data in the form of tables called relations. A relation is a named, two-dimensional table of data. A key property of relations is that they cannot contain multivalued attributes.

In this chapter, we described the major steps in the logical database design process. This process is based on transforming EER diagrams into normalized relations. This process has three steps: Transform EER diagrams into relations, normalize the relations, and merge the relations. The result of this process is a set of relations in third normal form that can be implemented using any contemporary relational database management system.

Each entity type in the EER diagram is transformed into a relation that has the same primary key as the entity type. A one-to-many relationship is represented by adding a foreign key to the relation that represents the entity on the many side of the relationship. (This foreign key is the primary key of the entity on the one side of the relationship.) A many-to-many relationship is represented by creating a separate relation. The primary key of this relation is a composite key, consisting of the primary key of each of the entities that participate in the relationship.

The relational model does not directly support supertype/subtype relationships, but we can model these relationships by creating a separate table (or relation) for the supertype and for each subtype. The primary key of each subtype is the same (or at least from the same domain) as for the supertype. The supertype must have an attribute called the subtype discriminator that indicates to which subtype (or subtypes) each instance of the supertype belongs.

The purpose of normalization is to derive well-structured relations that are free of anomalies (inconsistencies or errors) that would otherwise result when the relations are updated or modified. Normalization is based on the analysis of functional dependencies, which are constraints between two attributes (or two sets of attributes). It may be accomplished in several stages. Relations in first normal form (1NF) contain no multivalued attributes or repeating groups. Relations in second normal form (2NF) contain no partial dependencies, and relations in third normal form (3NF) contain no transitive dependencies. We can use diagrams that show the functional dependencies in a relation to help decompose that relation (if necessary) to obtain relations in 3NF. Higher normal forms (beyond 3NF) have also been defined.

We must be careful when combining relations to deal with problems such as synonyms, homonyms, transitive dependencies, and supertype/subtype relationships. In addition, before relations are defined to the database management system, all primary keys should be described as single-attribute nonintelligent keys.

Chapter Review

Key Terms

Alias *155*
Anomaly *130*
Candidate key *146*
Composite key *123*
Determinant *146*
Entity integrity rule *127*
First normal form
 (1NF) *149*

Foreign key *124*
Functional
 dependency *146*
Homonym *155*
Normal form *145*
Normalization *144*
Null *127*
Partial functional
 dependency *150*

Primary key *123*
Recursive foreign key *139*
Referential integrity
 constraint *128*
Relation *123*
Second normal form
 (2NF) *150*
Surrogate primary
 key *134*

Synonyms *154*
Third normal form
 (3NF) *151*
Transitive dependency *151*
Well-structured
 relation *130*

Review Questions

1. Define each of the following terms:
   a. determinant
   b. functional dependency
   c. transitive dependency
   d. recursive foreign key
   e. normalization
   f. composite key
   g. relation
   h. normal form
   i. partial functional dependency
   j. surrogate primary key
2. Match the following terms to the appropriate definitions:

   _____ well-structured relation
   _____ anomaly
   _____ functional dependency
   _____ determinant
   _____ composite key
   _____ 1NF
   _____ 2NF
   _____ 3NF
   _____ recursive foreign key
   _____ relation
   _____ transitive dependency

   a. constraint between two attributes
   b. functional dependency between the primary key and a nonkey attribute via another nonkey attribute
   c. references the primary key in the same relation
   d. multivalued attributes removed
   e. inconsistency or error
   f. contains little redundancy
   g. contains two (or more) attributes
   h. contains no partial functional dependencies
   i. transitive dependencies eliminated
   j. attribute on left side of functional dependency
   k. named two-dimensional table of data
3. Contrast the following terms:
   a. normal form; normalization
   b. candidate key; primary key
   c. partial dependency; transitive dependency
   d. composite key; recursive foreign key
   e. determinant; candidate key
   f. foreign key; primary key

4. Describe the primary differences between the conceptual and logical data models.
5. Summarize six important properties of relations.
6. Describe two properties that each candidate key must satisfy.
7. Describe three types of anomalies that can arise in a table and the negative consequences of each.
8. Fill in the blanks in each of the following statements:
   a. A relation that has no partial functional dependencies is in _____ normal form.
   b. A relation that has no transitive dependencies is in _____ normal form.
   c. A relation that has no multivalued attributes is in _____ normal form.
9. What is a well-structured relation? Why are well-structured relations important in logical database design?
10. Describe the primary way in which relationships in an E-R diagram are expressed in a corresponding relational data model.
11. Describe how the following components of an E-R diagram are transformed into relations:
    a. regular entity type
    b. relationship (1:*M*)
    c. relationship (*M:N*)
    d. relationship (supertype/subtype)
    e. multivalued attribute
    f. weak entity
    g. composite attribute
12. What is the primary purpose of normalization?
13. Briefly describe four typical problems that often arise in merging relations and common techniques for addressing those problems.
14. List three conditions that you can apply to determine whether a relation that is in first normal form is also in second normal form.
15. Explain how each of the following types of integrity constraints is enforced in the SQL CREATE TABLE commands:
    a. entity integrity
    b. referential integrity
16. What are the benefits of enforcing the integrity constraints as part of the database design and implementation process (instead of doing it in application design)?
17. How are relationships between entities represented in the relational data model?
18. How do you represent a 1:*M* unary relationship in a relational data model?

19. How do you represent an *M:N* ternary relationship in a relational data model?
20. How do you represent an associative entity in a relational data model?
21. What is the relationship between the primary key of a relation and the functional dependencies among all attributes within that relation?
22. Under what conditions must a foreign key not be null?

23. Explain what can be done with primary keys to eliminate key ripple effects as a database evolves.
24. Describe the difference between how a 1:*M* unary relationship and an *M:N* unary relationship are implemented in a relational data model.
25. Explain three conditions that suggest a surrogate key should be created for the primary key of a relation.

Problems and Exercises

1. For each of the following E-R diagrams from Chapter 2:
   I. Transform the diagram to a relational schema that shows referential integrity constraints (see Figure 4-5 for an example of such a schema):
   II. For each relation, diagram the functional dependencies (see Figure 4-23 for an example).
   III. If any of the relations are not in 3NF, transform them to 3NF.
      a. Figure 2-8
      b. Figure 2-9b
      c. Figure 2-11a
      d. Figure 2-11b
      e. Figure 2-15a (relationship version)
      f. Figure 2-15b (attribute version)
      g. Figure 2-16b
      h. Figure 2-19
2. For each of the following EER diagrams from Chapter 3:
   I. Transform the diagram into a relational schema that shows referential integrity constraints (see Figure 4-5 for an example of such a schema).
   II. For each relation, diagram the functional dependencies (see Figure 4-23 for an example).
   III. If any of the relations are not in 3NF, transform them to 3NF.
      a. Figure 3-6b
      b. Figure 3-7a
      c. Figure 3-9
      d. Figure 3-10
      e. Figure 3-11
3. For each of the following relations, indicate the normal form for that relation. If the relation is not in third normal form, decompose it into 3NF relations. Functional dependencies (other than those implied by the primary key) are shown where appropriate.
   a. CLASS(CourseNo, SectionNo)
   b. CLASS(CourseNo, SectionNo, Room)
   c. CLASS(CourseNo, SectionNo, Room, Capacity) [FD: Room → Capacity]
   d. CLASS(CourseNo, SectionNo, CourseName, Room, Capacity) [FD: CourseNo → CourseName; FD: Room → Capacity]
4. For your answers to the following Problems and Exercises from prior chapters, transform the EER diagrams into a set of relational schemas, diagram the functional dependencies, and convert all the relations to third normal form:
   a. Chapter 2, Problem and Exercise 17b
   b. Chapter 2, Problem and Exercise 17g
   c. Chapter 2, Problem and Exercise 17h
   d. Chapter 2, Problem and Exercise 17i
   e. Chapter 2, Problem and Exercise 23
   f. Chapter 2, Problem and Exercise 24

```
              MILLENNIUM COLLEGE
              CLASS LIST
              FALL SEMESTER 201X

COURSE NO.:  IS 460
COURSE TITLE:  DATABASE
INSTRUCTOR NAME:  NORMA L. FORM
INSTRUCTOR LOCATION:  B 104
```

STUDENT NO.	STUDENT NAME	MAJOR	GRADE
38214	Bright	IS	A
40875	Cortez	CS	B
51893	Edwards	IS	A

FIGURE 4-31 Class list (Millennium College)

5. Figure 4-31 shows a class list for Millennium College. Convert this user view to a set of 3NF relations. Assume the following:
   • An instructor has a unique location.
   • A student has a unique major.
   • A course has a unique title.
6. Figure 4-32 (page 159) shows an EER diagram for a simplified credit card environment. There are two types of card accounts: debit cards and credit cards. Credit card accounts accumulate charges with merchants. Each charge is identified by the date and time of the charge as well as the primary keys of merchant and credit card.
   a. Develop a relational schema.
   b. Show the functional dependencies.
   c. Develop a set of 3NF relations.
7. Table 4-3 (page 159) contains sample data for parts and for vendors who supply those parts. In discussing these data with users, we find that part numbers (but not descriptions) uniquely identify parts and that vendor names uniquely identify vendors.
   a. Convert this table to a relation (named PART SUPPLIER) in first normal form. Illustrate the relation with the sample data in the table.
   b. List the functional dependencies in PART SUPPLIER and identify a candidate key.
   c. For the relation PART SUPPLIER, identify each of the following: an insert anomaly, a delete anomaly, and a modification anomaly.
   d. Draw a relational schema for PART SUPPLIER and show the functional dependencies.
   e. In what normal form is this relation?
   f. Develop a set of 3NF relations from PART SUPPLIER.

FIGURE 4-32 EER diagram for bank cards

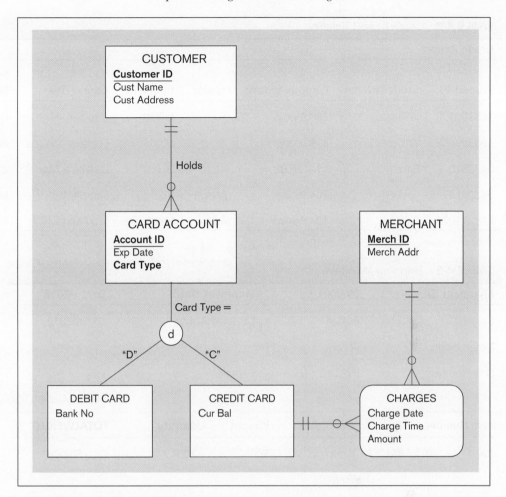

TABLE 4-3 Sample Data for Parts and Vendors

Part No	Description	Vendor Name	Address	Unit Cost
1234	Logic chip	Fast Chips	Cupertino	10.00
		Smart Chips	Phoenix	8.00
5678	Memory chip	Fast Chips	Cupertino	3.00
		Quality Chips	Austin	2.00
		Smart Chips	Phoenix	5.00

g. Show the 3NF relations using Microsoft Visio (or any other tool specified by your instructor).

8. Table 4-4 shows a relation called GRADE REPORT for a university. Your assignment is as follows:
   a. Draw a relational schema and diagram the functional dependencies in the relation.
   b. In what normal form is this relation?
   c. Decompose GRADE REPORT into a set of 3NF relations.
   d. Draw a relational schema for your 3NF relations and show the referential integrity constraints.
   e. Draw your answer to part d using Microsoft Visio (or any other tool specified by your instructor).

9. Table 4-5 shows a shipping manifest. Your assignment is as follows:
   a. Draw a relational schema and diagram the functional dependencies in the relation.

   b. In what normal form is this relation?
   c. Decompose MANIFEST into a set of 3NF relations.
   d. Draw a relational schema for your 3NF relations and show the referential integrity constraints.
   e. Draw your answer to part d using Microsoft Visio (or any other tool specified by your instructor).

10. Transform the relational schema developed in Problem and Exercise 9 into an EER diagram. State any assumptions that you have made.

11. For your answers to the following Problems and Exercises from prior chapters, transform the EER diagrams into a set of relational schemas, diagram the functional dependencies, and convert all the relations to third normal form.
    a. Chapter 3, Problem and Exercise 12
    b. Chapter 3, Problem and Exercise 17

TABLE 4-4 Grade Report Relation

Grade Report

StudentID	StudentName	CampusAddress	Major	CourseID	CourseTitle	Instructor Name	Instructor Location	Grade
168300458	Williams	208 Brooks	IS	IS 350	Database Mgt	Codd	B 104	A
168300458	Williams	208 Brooks	IS	IS 465	Systems Analysis	Parsons	B 317	B
543291073	Baker	104 Phillips	Acctg	IS 350	Database Mgt	Codd	B 104	C
543291073	Baker	104 Phillips	Acctg	Acct 201	Fund Acctg	Miller	H 310	B
543291073	Baker	104 Phillips	Acctg	Mkgt 300	Intro Mktg	Bennett	B 212	A

TABLE 4-5 Shipping Manifest

Shipment ID:	00-0001	Shipment Date:	01/10/2012
Origin:	Boston	Expected Arrival:	01/14/2012
Destination:	Brazil		
Ship Number:	39	Captain:	002-15
			Henry Moore

Item Number	Type	Description	Weight	Quantity	TOTALWEIGHT
3223	BM	Concrete Form	500	100	50,000
3297	BM	Steel Beam	87	2,000	174,000
				Shipment Total:	224,000

TABLE 4-6 Parking Tickets at Millennium College

Parking Ticket Table

St ID	L Name	F Name	Phone No	St Lic	Lic No	Ticket #	Date	Code	Fine
38249	Brown	Thomas	111-7804	FL	BRY 123	15634	10/17/12	2	$25
						16017	11/13/12	1	$15
82453	Green	Sally	391-1689	AL	TRE 141	14987	10/05/12	3	$100
						16293	11/18/12	1	$15
						17892	12/13/12	2	$25

12. Transform Figure 2-15a, attribute version, to 3NF relations. Transform Figure 2-15b, relationship version, to 3NF relations. Compare these two sets of 3NF relations with those in Figure 4-10. What observations and conclusions do you reach by comparing these different sets of 3NF relations?

13. The Public Safety office at Millennium College maintains a list of parking tickets issued to vehicles parked illegally on the campus. Table 4-6 shows a portion of this list for the fall semester. (Attribute names are abbreviated to conserve space.)

a. Convert this table to a relation in first normal form by entering appropriate data in the table. What are the determinants in this relation?

b. Draw a dependency diagram that shows all functional dependencies in the relation, based on the sample data shown.

c. Give an example of one or more anomalies that can result in using this relation.

d. Develop a set of relations in third normal form. Include a new column with the heading Violation in the appropriate table to explain the reason for each ticket. Values in this column are: expired parking meter (ticket code 1), no parking permit (ticket code 2), and handicap violation (ticket code 3).

e. Develop an E-R diagram with the appropriate cardinality notations.

14. The materials manager at Pine Valley Furniture Company maintains a list of suppliers for each of the material items purchased by the company from outside vendors. Table 4-7 shows the essential data required for this application.

a. Draw a dependency diagram for this data. You may assume the following:

- Each material item has one or more suppliers. Each supplier may supply one or more items or may not supply any items.
- The unit price for a material item may vary from one vendor to another.
- The terms code for a supplier uniquely identifies the terms of the sale (e.g., code 2 means 10 percent net 30 days). The terms for a supplier are the same for all material items ordered from that supplier.

b. Decompose this diagram into a set of diagrams in 3NF.

c. Draw an E-R diagram for this situation.

15. Table 4-8 shows a portion of a shipment table for a large manufacturing company. Each shipment (identified by Shipment#) uniquely identifies the shipment Origin, Destination, and Distance. The shipment Origin and Destination pair also uniquely identifies the Distance.

a. Develop a diagram that shows the functional dependencies in the SHIPMENT relation.

b. In what normal form is SHIPMENT? Why?

c. Convert SHIPMENT to third normal form if necessary. Show the resulting table(s) with the sample data presented in SHIPMENT.

16. Figure 4-33 shows an EER diagram for Vacation Property Rentals. This organization rents preferred properties

TABLE 4-7 Pine Valley Furniture Company Purchasing Data

Attribute Name	Sample Value
Material ID	3792
Material Name	Hinges 3" locking
Unit of Measure	each
Standard Cost	$5.00
Vendor ID	V300
Vendor Name	Apex Hardware
Unit Price	$4.75
Terms Code	1
Terms	COD

TABLE 4-8 Shipment Relation

Shipment#	Origin	Destination	Distance
409	Seattle	Denver	1,537
618	Chicago	Dallas	1,058
723	Boston	Atlanta	1,214
824	Denver	Los Angeles	975
629	Seattle	Denver	1,537

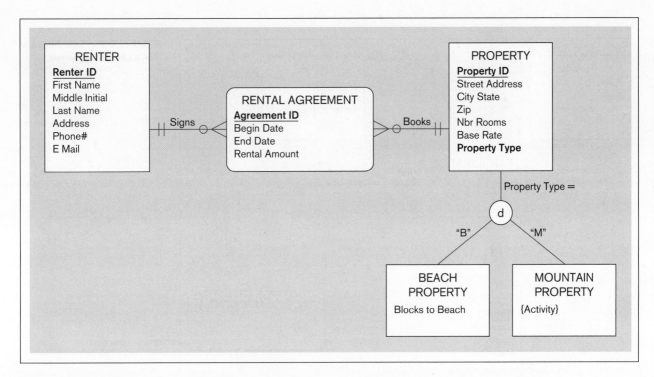

FIGURE 4-33   EER diagram for Vacation Property Rentals

in several states. As shown in the figure, there are two basic types of properties: beach properties and mountain properties.
  a. Transform the EER diagram to a set of relations and develop a relational schema.
  b. Diagram the functional dependencies and determine the normal form for each relation.
  c. Convert all relations to third normal form, if necessary, and draw a revised relational schema.
  d. Suggest an integrity constraint that would ensure that no property is rented twice during the same time interval.

17. For your answers to Problem and Exercise 13 from Chapter 3, transform the EER diagrams into a set of relational schemas, diagram the functional dependencies, and convert all the relations to third normal form.

18. Figure 4-34 includes an EER diagram describing a car racing league. Transform the diagram into a relational schema that shows referential integrity constraints (see Figure 4-5 for an example of such a schema). In addition, verify that the resulting relations are in 3NF.

19. Figure 4-35 includes an EER diagram for a medium-size software vendor. Transform the diagram into a relational schema that shows referential integrity constraints (see Figure 4-5 for an example of such a schema). In addition, verify that the resulting relations are in 3NF.

20. Examine the set of relations in Figure 4-36. What normal form are these in? How do you know this? If they are in 3NF, convert the relations into an EER diagram. What assumptions did you have to make to answer these questions?

21. A pet store currently uses a legacy flat file system to store all of its information. The owner of the store, Peter Corona, wants to implement a Web-enabled database application. This would enable branch stores to enter data regarding inventory levels, ordering, and so on. Presently, the data for inventory and sales tracking are stored in one file that has the following format:

StoreName, PetName, Pet Description, Price, Cost, SupplierName, ShippingTime, QuantityOnHand, DateOfLastDelivery, DateOfLastPurchase, DeliveryDate1, DeliveryDate2, DeliveryDate3, DeliveryDate4, PurchaseDate1, PurchaseDate2, PurchaseDate3, PurchaseDate4, LastCustomerName, CustomerName1, CustomerName2, CustomerName3, CustomerName4

Assume that you want to track all purchase and inventory data, such as who bought the fish, the date that it was purchased, the date that it was delivered, and so on. The present file format allows only the tracking of the last purchase and delivery as well as four prior purchases and deliveries. You can assume that a type of fish is supplied by one supplier.
  a. Show all functional dependencies.
  b. What normal form is this table in?
  c. Design a normalized data model for these data. Show that it is in 3NF.

22. For Problem and Exercise 21, draw the E-R diagram based on the normalized relations.

23. How would Problems and Exercises 21 and 22 change if a type of fish could be supplied by multiple suppliers?

24. Figure 4-37 shows an EER diagram for a university dining service organization that provides dining services to a major university.
  a. Transform the EER diagram to a set of relations and develop a relational schema.
  b. Diagram the functional dependencies and determine the normal form for each relation.
  c. Convert all relations to third normal form, if necessary, and draw a revised relational schema.

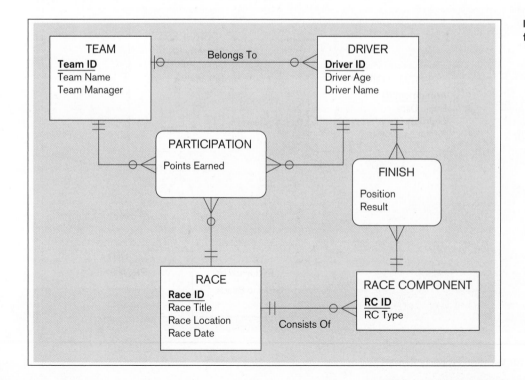

FIGURE 4-34 EER diagram for a car racing league

FIGURE 4-35   EER diagram for a middle-size software vendor

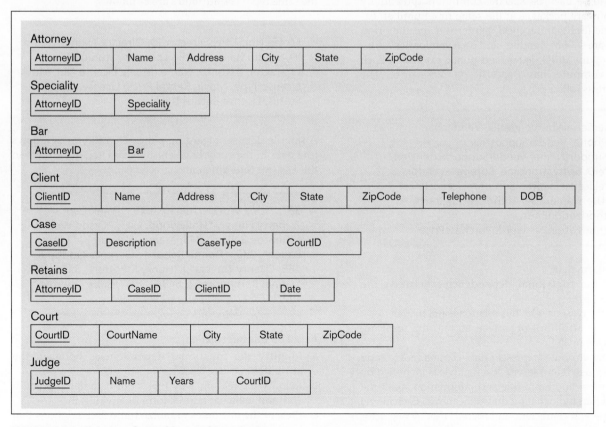

FIGURE 4-36   Relations for Problem and Exercise 20

FIGURE 4-37 **EER diagram for university dining services**

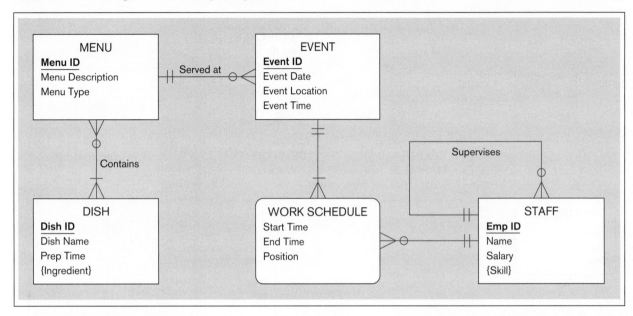

25. The following attributes form a relation that includes information about individual computers, their vendors, software packages running on the computers, computer users, and user authorizations. Users are authorized to use a specific software package on a specific computer during a specific time frame (characterized with attributes UserAuthorization Starts and UserAuthorizationEnds and secured with UserAuthorizationPassword). Software is licensed to be used on specific computers (potentially multiple software packages at the same time) until an expiration time (SoftwareLicenceExpires) at a specific price. Computers are sold by vendors, and each vendor has a support person with an ID, name, and phone extension. Each individual computer has a specific purchase price. The attributes are as follows:

> ComputerSerialNbr, VendorID, VendorName,
> VendorPhone, VendorSupportID,
> VendorSupportName, VendorSupportExtension,
> SoftwareID, SoftwareName, SoftwareVendor,
> SoftwareLicenceExpires, SoftwareLicencePrice,
> UserID, UserName, UserAuthorizationStarts,
> UserAuthorizationEnds,
> UserAuthorizationPassword, PurchasePrice

Based on this information,

a. Identify the functional dependencies between the attributes.

b. Identify the reasons why this relation is not in 3NF.

c. Present the attributes organized so that the resulting relations are in 3NF.

26. The following attributes represent data about a movie copy at an online video rental service. Each movie is identified by a movie number and has a title and information about the director and the studio that produced the movie. Each movie has one or several characters, and there is exactly one actor playing the role of each of the characters (but one actor can play multiple roles in each of the movies). The video rental service has multiple licenses for the same movie, and the service differentiates the licenses with a movie copy number, which is unique within a single movie but not unique between different movies. Each movie license has a rental status and return date; in addition, each license has a type (Regular or HD). The rental price depends on the movie and the license type, but the price is the same for all licenses of the same type. The attributes are as follows:

> Movie Nbr, Title, Director ID, Director Name, Studio ID, Studio Name, Studio Location, Studio CEO, Character, Actor ID, Name, Movie License Nbr, Movie License Type, Movie Rental Price, License Rental Status, License Return Date

A sample data set regarding a movie would be as follows (the data in the curly brackets are character/actor data, in this case for four different characters):

> 567, "It's a Wonderful Life", 25, "Frank Capra", 234, "Liberty Films", "Hollywood, CA", "Orson Wells", {"George Bailey", 245, "James Stewart" | "Mary Bailey", 236, "Donna Reed" | "Clarence Oddbody", 765, "Henry Travers" | "Henry F. Potter", 325, "Lionel Barrymore" }, 5434, "HD", 3.95, "Rented", "12/15/2012"

Based on this information,

a. Identify the functional dependencies between the attributes.

b. Identify the reasons why this set of data items is not in 3NF and tell what normal form (if any) it is in.

c. Present the attributes organized into 3NF relations that have been named appropriately.

27. A bus company is responsible for offering public transportation in the suburbs of a large metropolitan area. The company has significant data management requirements: It needs to keep track of its 150 vehicles, 400 drivers, 60 bus routes, and hundreds of scheduled departures every day. In addition, it is essential for the company to know which drivers are certified to drive which buses.

The data that the company has available include the following attributes:

RouteID, RouteStartPoint, RouteEndPoint, RouteStandardDrivingTime, ScheduleDate, ScheduledDepTime, ScheduledArrTime, DriverID, DriverFName, DriverLName, DateDriverJoinedCompany, DriverDOB, VehicleID, VehicleMake, VehicleModel, VehiclePassangerCapacity, DriverCertStartDate, DriverCertEndDate.

Sample data for this set of attributes are as follows:

28, Grand Avenue, Madison Street, 38, {9/12/2012, 8.30, 9.18, 8273, Mary, Smith, 5/2/2007, 3/23/1974, 1123, GreatTrucks, CityCoach, 58, 6/10/2012,

6/9/2013 | 9/12/2012, 9.30, 10.12, 7234, John, Jones, 10/12/2011, 12/15/1991, 5673, GreatTrucks, CityCoach 2, 62, 4/12/2012, 4/11/2013 | 9/12/2012, 10.30, 11.08, 2343, Pat, Moore, 2/24/1982, 1/19/1958, 4323, PowerTransport, MidiBus, 32, 8/20/2012, 8/19/2013}

Note that the information for specific bus schedules (starting with the attribute ScheduleDate) is repeated three times in the sample data set and is separated by the "|" symbol. Also, take into account that in this case, the certification is specific to a particular vehicle driver pair.

Based on the facts stated above,

a. Identify the functional dependencies between the attributes.
b. Identify the reasons why this set of data is not in 3NF and indicate the normal form (if any) it is in.
c. Including all intermediate stages, organize the attributes into a set of 3NF relations.
d. Draw an E-R diagram based on the normalized relations.
e. Based on the E-R diagram you just drew and the case narrative, explore the areas in which there could be opportunities to expand the data model to achieve better tracking of the company's operations or improved clarity, such as maintaining more detailed route information.

References

Chouinard, P. 1989. "Supertypes, Subtypes, and DB2." *Database Programming & Design* 2,10 (October): 50–57.

Codd, E. F. 1970. "A Relational Model of Data for Large Shared Data Banks." *Communications of the ACM* 13,6 (June): 77–87.

Codd, E. F. 1990. *The Relational Model for Database Management, Version 2.* Reading, MA: Addison-Wesley.

Date, C. J. 2003. *An Introduction to Database Systems.* 8th ed. Reading, MA: Addison-Wesley.

Dutka, A. F., and H. H. Hanson. 1989. *Fundamentals of Data Normalization.* Reading, MA: Addison-Wesley.

Fleming, C. C., and B. von Halle. 1989. *Handbook of Relational Database Design.* Reading, MA: Addison-Wesley.

Hoberman, S. 2006. "To Surrogate Key or Not." *DM Review* 16,8 (August): 29.

Navathe, S., R. Elmasri, and J. Larson. 1986. "Integrating User Views in Database Design." *Computer* 19,1 (January): 50–62.

Further Reading

Elmasri, R., and S. Navathe. 2010. *Fundamentals of Database Systems.* 6th ed. Reading, MA: Addison Wesley.

Hoffer, J. A., J. F. George, and J. S. Valacich. 2011. *Modern Systems Analysis and Design.* 6th ed. Upper Saddle River, NJ: Prentice Hall.

Johnston, T. 2000. "Primary Key Reengineering Projects: The Problem" and "Primary Key Reengineering Projects: The Solution." Available at **www.information-management.com.**

Russell, T., and R. Armstrong. 2002. "13 Reasons Why Normalized Tables Help Your Business." *Database Administrator,* April 20, 2002. Available at **http://searchoracle .techtarget.com/tip/13-reasons-why-normalized-tables -help-your-business**

Storey, V. C. 1991. "Relational Database Design Based on the Entity-Relationship Model." *Data and Knowledge Engineering* 7,1 (November): 47–83.

Web Resources

http://en.wikipedia.org/wiki/Database_normalization Wikipedia entry that provides a thorough explanation of all normal forms, including those that are not covered in this chapter.

www.bkent.net/Doc/simple5.htm Web site that presents a summary paper by William Kent titled "A Simple Guide to Five Normal Forms in Relational Database Theory."

http://www.stevehoberman.com/DesignChallengeSignUp .aspx Web site where Steve Hoberman, a leading consultant and lecturer on database design, periodically creates database design (conceptual and logical) problems and posts them. These are practical (based on real experiences or questions sent to him) situations that make for interesting puzzles to solve.

www.troubleshooters.com/codecorn/norm.htm Web page on normalization on Steve Litt's site that contains various troubleshooting tips for avoiding programming and systems development problems.

Physical Database Design and Performance

LEARNING OBJECTIVES

After studying this chapter, you should be able to:

- Concisely define each of the following key terms: **field, data type, denormalization, physical file, tablespace, extent, file organization, sequential file organization, indexed file organization, index, secondary key, join index, hashed file organization, hashing algorithm, pointer,** and **hash index table.**
- Describe the physical database design process, its objectives, and its deliverables.
- Choose storage formats for attributes from a logical data model.
- Select an appropriate file organization by balancing various important design factors.
- Describe three important types of file organization.
- Describe the purpose of indexes and the important considerations in selecting attributes to be indexed.
- Translate a relational data model into efficient database structures, including knowing when and how to denormalize the logical data model.

INTRODUCTION

In Chapters 2 through 4, you learned how to describe and model organizational data during the conceptual data modeling and logical database design phases of the database development process. You learned how to use EER notation, the relational data model, and normalization to develop abstractions of organizational data that capture the meaning of data. However, these notations do not explain how data will be processed or stored. The purpose of physical database design is to translate the logical description of data into the technical specifications for storing and retrieving data. The goal is to create a design for storing data that will provide adequate performance and ensure database integrity, security, and recoverability.

Physical database design does not include implementing files and databases (i.e., creating them and loading data into them). Physical database design produces the technical specifications that programmers, database administrators, and others involved in information systems construction will use during the implementation phase, which we discuss in Chapters 6 through 9.

In this chapter, you study the basic steps required to develop an efficient and high-integrity physical database design. We concentrate in this chapter on the design of a single, centralized database. You learn how to estimate the amount of data that users will require in the database and determine how data are likely to be used. You learn about choices for storing attribute values and how to select from among these choices to achieve efficiency and data quality. Because of recent U.S. and international regulations (e.g., Sarbanes-Oxley) on financial reporting by organizations, proper controls specified in physical database design are required as a sound foundation for compliance. Hence, we place special emphasis on data quality measures you can implement within the physical design. You will also learn why normalized tables are not always the basis for the best physical data files and how you can denormalize the data to improve the speed of data retrieval. Finally, you learn about the use of indexes, which are important in speeding up the retrieval of data. In essence, you learn in this chapter how to make databases really "hum."

You must carefully perform physical database design, because the decisions made during this stage have a major impact on data accessibility, response times, data quality, security, user friendliness, and similarly important information system design factors.

THE PHYSICAL DATABASE DESIGN PROCESS

To make life a little easier for you, many physical database design decisions are implicit or eliminated when you choose the database management technologies to use with the information system you are designing. Because many organizations have standards for operating systems, database management systems, and data access languages, you must deal only with those choices not implicit in the given technologies. Thus, this chapter covers those decisions that you will make most frequently, as well as other selected decisions that may be critical for some types of applications, such as online data capture and retrieval.

The primary goal of physical database design is data processing efficiency. Today, with ever-decreasing costs for computer technology per unit of measure (both speed and space), it is typically very important to design a physical database to minimize the time required by users to interact with the information system. Thus, we concentrate on how to make processing of physical files and databases efficient, with less attention on minimizing the use of space.

Designing physical files and databases requires certain information that should have been collected and produced during prior systems development phases. The information needed for physical file and database design includes these requirements:

- Normalized relations, including estimates for the range of the number of rows in each table
- Definitions of each attribute, along with physical specifications such as maximum possible length
- Descriptions of where and when data are used in various ways (entered, retrieved, deleted, and updated, including typical frequencies of these events)
- Expectations or requirements for response time and data security, backup, recovery, retention, and integrity
- Descriptions of the technologies (database management systems) used for implementing the database

Physical database design requires several critical decisions that will affect the integrity and performance of the application system. These key decisions include the following:

- Choosing the storage format (called *data type*) for each attribute from the logical data model. The format and associated parameters are chosen to maximize data integrity and to minimize storage space.
- Giving the database management system guidance regarding how to group attributes from the logical data model into *physical records*. You will discover that although the columns of a relational table as specified in the logical design are a natural definition for the contents of a physical record, this does not always form the foundation for the most desirable grouping of attributes in the physical design.

- Giving the database management system guidance regarding how to arrange similarly structured records in secondary memory (primarily hard disks), using a structure (called a *file organization*) so that individual and groups of records can be stored, retrieved, and updated rapidly. Consideration must also be given to protecting data and recovering data if errors are found.
- Selecting structures (including *indexes* and the overall *database architecture*) for storing and connecting files to make retrieving related data more efficient.
- Preparing strategies for handling queries against the database that will optimize performance and take advantage of the file organizations and indexes that you have specified. Efficient database structures will be beneficial only if queries and the database management systems that handle those queries are tuned to intelligently use those structures.

Physical Database Design as a Basis for Regulatory Compliance

One of the primary motivations for strong focus on physical database design is that it forms a foundation for compliance with new national and international regulations on financial reporting. Without careful physical design, an organization cannot demonstrate that its data are accurate and well protected. Laws and regulations such as the Sarbanes-Oxley Act (SOX) in the United States and Basel II for international banking are reactions to recent cases of fraud and deception by executives in major corporations and partners in public accounting firms. The purpose of SOX is to protect investors by improving the accuracy and reliability of corporate disclosures made pursuant to the securities laws, and for other purposes. SOX requires that every annual financial report include an internal control report. This is designed to show that not only are the company's financial data accurate, but also that the company has confidence in them because adequate controls are in place to safeguard financial data. Among these controls are ones that focus on database integrity.

SOX is the most recent regulation in a stream of efforts to improve financial data reporting. The Committee of Sponsoring Organizations (COSO) of the Treadway Commission is a voluntary private-sector organization dedicated to improving the quality of financial reporting through business ethics, effective internal controls, and corporate governance. COSO was originally formed in 1985 to sponsor the National Commission on Fraudulent Financial Reporting (NCFFR), an independent private-sector initiative that studied the factors that can lead to fraudulent financial reporting. Based on its research, COSO developed recommendations for public companies and their independent auditors, for the U.S. Securities and Exchange Commission (SEC) and other regulators, and for educational institutions. The Control Objectives for Information and Related Technology (COBIT) is an open standard published by the IT Governance Institute and the Information Systems Audit and Control Association. It is an IT control framework built in part upon the COSO framework. The IT Infrastructure Library (ITIL), published by the Office of Government Commerce in Great Britain, focuses on IT services and is often used to complement the COBIT framework.

These standards, guidelines, and rules focus on corporate governance, risk assessment, and security and controls of data. Although laws such as SOX and Basel II require comprehensive audits of all procedures that deal with financial data, compliance can be greatly enhanced by a strong foundation of basic data integrity controls. If designed into the database and enforced by the DBMS, such preventive controls are applied consistently and thoroughly. Therefore, field-level data integrity controls can be viewed very positively in compliance audits. Other DBMS features, such as triggers and stored procedures, discussed in Chapter 7, provide even further ways to ensure that only legitimate data values are stored in the database. However, even these control mechanisms are only as good as the underlying field-level data controls. Further, for full compliance, all data integrity controls must be thoroughly documented; defining these controls for the DBMS is a form of documentation. Finally, changes to these controls must occur through well-documented change control procedures (so that temporary changes cannot be used to bypass well-designed controls).

DESIGNING FIELDS

A **field** is the smallest unit of application data recognized by system software, such as a programming language or database management system. A field corresponds to a simple attribute in the logical data model, and so in the case of a composite attribute, a field represents a single component.

The basic decisions you must make in specifying each field concern the type of data (or storage type) used to represent values of this field, data integrity controls built into the database, and the mechanisms that the DBMS uses to handle missing values for the field. Other field specifications, such as display format, also must be made as part of the total specification of the information system, but we will not be concerned here with those specifications that are often handled by applications rather than the DBMS.

Choosing Data Types

A **data type** is a detailed coding scheme recognized by system software, such as a DBMS, for representing organizational data. The bit pattern of the coding scheme is usually transparent to you, but the space to store data and the speed required to access data are of consequence in physical database design. The specific DBMS you will use will dictate which choices are available to you. For example, Table 5-1 lists some of the data types available in the Oracle 11g DBMS, a typical DBMS that uses the SQL data definition and manipulation language. Additional data types might be available for currency, voice, image, and user defined for some DBMSs.

Selecting a data type involves four objectives that will have different relative levels of importance for different applications:

1. Represent all possible values.
2. Improve data integrity.
3. Support all data manipulations.
4. Minimize storage space.

An optimal data type for a field can, in minimal space, represent every possible value (while eliminating illegal values) for the associated attribute and can support

Field

The smallest unit of application data recognized by system software.

Data type

A detailed coding scheme recognized by system software, such as a DBMS, for representing organizational data.

TABLE 5-1 Commonly Used Data Types in Oracle 11g

Data Type	Description
VARCHAR2	Variable-length character data with a maximum length of 4,000 characters; you must enter a maximum field length (e.g., VARCHAR2(30) specifies a field with a maximum length of 30 characters). A string that is shorter than the maximum will consume only the required space.
CHAR	Fixed-length character data with a maximum length of 2,000 characters; default length is 1 character (e.g., CHAR(5) specifies a field with a fixed length of 5 characters, capable of holding a value from 0 to 5 characters long).
CLOB	Character large object, capable of storing up to (4 gigabytes – 1) * (database block size) of one variable-length character data field (e.g., to hold a medical instruction or a customer comment).
NUMBER	Positive or negative number in the range 10^{-130} to 10^{126}; can specify the precision (total number of digits to the left and right of the decimal point) and the scale (the number of digits to the right of the decimal point). For example, NUMBER(5) specifies an integer field with a maximum of 5 digits, and NUMBER(5,2) specifies a field with no more than 5 digits and exactly 2 digits to the right of the decimal point.
DATE	Any date from January 1, 4712 B.C., to December 31, 9999 A.D.; DATE stores the century, year, month, day, hour, minute, and second.
BLOB	Binary large object, capable of storing up to (4 gigabytes – 1) * (database block size) of binary data (e.g., a photograph or sound clip).

FIGURE 5-1 Example of a code lookup table (Pine Valley Furniture Company)

PRODUCT Table					PRODUCT FINISH Lookup Table	
ProductNo	Description	ProductFinish	...		Code	Value
B100	Chair	C			A	Birch
B120	Desk	A			B	Maple
M128	Table	C			C	Oak
T100	Bookcase	B				
...	...	...				

the required data manipulation (e.g., numeric data types for arithmetic operations and character data types for string manipulation). Any attribute domain constraints from the conceptual data model are helpful in selecting a good data type for that attribute. Achieving these four objectives can be subtle. For example, consider a DBMS for which a data type has a maximum width of 2 bytes. Suppose this data type is sufficient to represent a QuantitySold field. When QuantitySold fields are summed, the sum may require a number larger than 2 bytes. If the DBMS uses the field's data type for results of any mathematics on that field, the 2-byte length will not work. Some data types have special manipulation capabilities; for example, only the DATE data type allows true date arithmetic.

CODING TECHNIQUES   Some attributes have a sparse set of values or are so large that, given data volumes, considerable storage space will be consumed. A field with a limited number of possible values can be translated into a code that requires less space. Consider the example of the ProductFinish field illustrated in Figure 5-1. Products at Pine Valley Furniture come in only a limited number of woods: Birch, Maple, and Oak. By creating a code or translation table, each ProductFinish field value can be replaced by a code, a cross-reference to the lookup table, similar to a foreign key. This will decrease the amount of space for the ProductFinish field and hence for the PRODUCT file. There will be additional space for the PRODUCT FINISH lookup table, and when the ProductFinish field value is needed, an extra access (called a join) to this lookup table will be required. If the ProductFinish field is infrequently used or if the number of distinct ProductFinish values is very large, the relative advantages of coding may outweigh the costs. Note that the code table would not appear in the conceptual or logical model. The code table is a physical construct to achieve data processing performance improvements, not a set of data with business value.

Controlling Data Integrity   For many DBMSs, data integrity controls (i.e., controls on the possible value a field can assume) can be built into the physical structure of the fields and controls enforced by the DBMS on those fields. The data type enforces one form of data integrity control because it may limit the type of data (numeric or character) and the length of a field value. The following are some other typical integrity controls that a DBMS may support:

- *Default value*   A default value is the value a field will assume unless a user enters an explicit value for an instance of that field. Assigning a default value to a field can reduce data entry time because entry of a value can be skipped. It can also help to reduce data entry errors for the most common value.

- *Range control*   A range control limits the set of permissible values a field may assume. The range may be a numeric lower-to-upper bound or a set of specific values. Range controls must be used with caution because the limits of the range may change over time. A combination of range controls and coding led to the year 2000 problem that many organizations faced, in which a field for year was represented by only the numbers 00 to 99. It is better to implement any range controls through a DBMS because range controls in applications may be inconsistently enforced. It is also more difficult to find and change them in applications than in a DBMS.
- *Null value control*   A null value is an empty value. Each primary key must have an integrity control that prohibits a null value. Any other required field may also have a null value control placed on it if that is the policy of the organization. For example, a university may prohibit adding a course to its database unless that course has a title as well as a value of the primary key, CourseID. Many fields legitimately may have a null value, so this control should be used only when truly required by business rules.
- *Referential integrity*   The term *referential integrity* was defined in Chapter 4. Referential integrity on a field is a form of range control in which the value of that field must exist as the value in some field in another row of the same or (most commonly) a different table. That is, the range of legitimate values comes from the dynamic contents of a field in a database table, not from some pre-specified set of values. Note that referential integrity guarantees that only some existing cross-referencing value is used, not that it is the correct one. A coded field will have referential integrity with the primary key of the associated lookup table.

HANDLING MISSING DATA   When a field may be null, simply entering no value may be sufficient. For example, suppose a customer zip code field is null and a report summarizes total sales by month and zip code. How should sales to customers with unknown zip codes be handled? Two options for handling or preventing missing data have already been mentioned: using a default value and not permitting missing (null) values. Missing data are inevitable. According to Babad and Hoffer (1984), the following are some other possible methods for handling missing data:

- Substitute an estimate of the missing value. For example, for a missing sales value when computing monthly product sales, use a formula involving the mean of the existing monthly sales values for that product indexed by total sales for that month across all products. Such estimates must be marked so that users know that these are not actual values.
- Track missing data so that special reports and other system elements cause people to resolve unknown values quickly. This can be done by setting up a trigger in the database definition. A trigger is a routine that will automatically execute when some event occurs or time period passes. One trigger could log the missing entry to a file when a null or other missing value is stored, and another trigger could run periodically to create a report of the contents of this log file.
- Perform sensitivity testing so that missing data are ignored unless knowing a value might significantly change results (e.g., if total monthly sales for a particular salesperson are almost over a threshold that would make a difference in that person's compensation). This is the most complex of the methods mentioned and hence requires the most sophisticated programming. Such routines for handling missing data may be written in application programs. All relevant modern DBMSs now have more sophisticated programming capabilities, such as case expressions, user-defined functions, and triggers, so that such logic can be available in the database for all users without application-specific programming.

DENORMALIZING DATA

Modern database management systems have an increasingly important role in determining how the data are actually stored on the storage media. The efficiency of database processing is, however, significantly affected by how the logical relations are structured as database tables. The purpose of this section is to discuss denormalization as a mechanism that is often used to improve efficient processing of data and quick access to stored data. It first describes the best-known denormalization approach: combining several logical tables into one physical table to avoid the need to bring related data back together when they are retrieved from the database.

Denormalization

With the rapid decline in the costs of secondary storage per unit of data, the efficient use of storage space (reducing redundancy)—while still a relevant consideration—has become less important than it has been in the past. In most cases, the primary goal of physical record design—efficient data processing—dominates the design process. In other words, speed, not style, matters. As in your dorm room, as long as you can find your favorite sweatshirt when you need it, it doesn't matter how tidy the room looks. (We won't tell your Mom.)

Efficient processing of data, just like efficient accessing of books in a library, depends on how close together related data (books or indexes) are. Often all the attributes that appear within a relation are not used together, and data from different relations are needed together to answer a query or produce a report. Thus, although normalized relations solve data maintenance anomalies and minimize redundancies (and storage space), they may not yield efficient data processing, if implemented one for one as physical records.

A fully normalized database usually creates a large number of tables. For a frequently used query that requires data from multiple, related tables, the DBMS can spend considerable computer resources each time the query is submitted in matching up (called *joining*) related rows from each table required to build the query result. Because this joining work is so time-consuming, the processing performance difference between totally normalized and partially normalized databases can be dramatic. In an early study, Inmon (1988) reports on a study to quantify fully and partially normalized databases. A fully normalized database contained eight tables with about 50,000 rows each; another partially normalized database had four tables with roughly 25,000 rows each; and yet another partially normalized database had two tables. The result showed that the less-than-fully normalized databases could be as much as an order of magnitude faster than the fully normalized one. Although such results depend greatly on the database and the type of processing against it, you should still carefully consider whether the physical structure should exactly match the normalized relations for a database.

Denormalization

The process of transforming normalized relations into non-normalized physical record specifications.

Denormalization is the process of transforming normalized relations into non-normalized physical record specifications. We will review various forms of, reasons for, and cautions about denormalization in this section. In general, denormalization may partition a relation into several physical records, may combine attributes from several relations together into one physical record, or may do a combination of both.

OPPORTUNITIES FOR AND TYPES OF DENORMALIZATION   Rogers (1989) introduces several common denormalization opportunities (Figures 5-2 through 5-4 show examples of normalized and denormalized relations for each of these three situations):

1. *Two entities with a one-to-one relationship*   Even if one of the entities is an optional participant, it may be wise to combine these two relations into one record definition if the matching entity exists most of the time (especially if the access frequency between these two entity types is high). Figure 5-2 shows student data with optional data from a standard scholarship application a student may complete. In this case, one record could be formed with four fields from the STUDENT and SCHOLARSHIP APPLICATION normalized relations (assuming that ApplicationID is no longer needed). (Note: In this case, fields from the optional entity must have null values allowed.)

2. *A many-to-many relationship (associative entity) with nonkey attributes*   Rather than join three files to extract data from the two basic entities in the relationship, it may be advisable to combine attributes from one of the entities into the record representing the many-to-many relationship, thus avoiding one of the join operations. Again, this would be most advantageous if this joining occurs frequently. Figure 5-3 shows price quotes for different items from different vendors.

FIGURE 5-2   **A possible denormalization situation: two entities with a one-to-one relationship**

(*Note:* We assume that ApplicationID is not necessary when all fields are stored in one record, but this field can be included if it is required application data.)

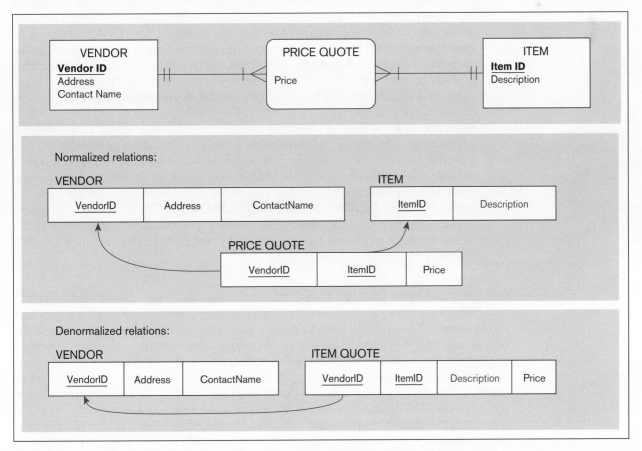

FIGURE 5-3   **A possible denormalization situation: a many-to-many relationship with nonkey attributes**

FIGURE 5-4   A possible
denormalization situation:
reference data

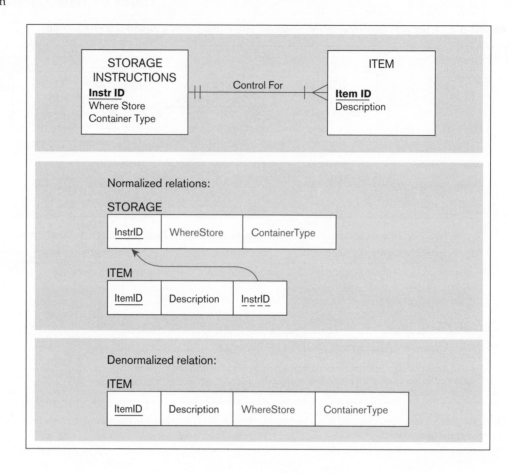

In this case, fields from ITEM and PRICE QUOTE relations might be combined
into one record to avoid having to join all three tables together. (Note: This may
create considerable duplication of data; in the example, the ITEM fields, such as
Description, would repeat for each price quote. This would necessitate excessive
updating if duplicated data changed. Careful analysis of a composite usage map
to study access frequencies and the number of occurrences of PRICE QUOTE per
associated VENDOR or ITEM would be essential to understand the consequences
of such denormalization.)

3. *Reference data*   Reference data exist in an entity on the one side of a one-to-many
   relationship, and this entity participates in no other database relationships. You
   should seriously consider merging the two entities in this situation into one record
   definition when there are few instances of the entity on the many side for each
   entity instance on the one side. See Figure 5-4, in which several ITEMs have the
   same STORAGE INSTRUCTIONS, and STORAGE INSTRUCTIONS relates only
   to ITEMs. In this case, the storage instructions data could be stored in the ITEM
   record to create, of course, redundancy and potential for extra data maintenance.
   (InstrID is no longer needed.)

DENORMALIZE WITH CAUTION   Denormalization has its critics. As Finkelstein (1988)
and Hoberman (2002) discuss, denormalization can increase the chance of errors and
inconsistencies (caused by reintroducing anomalies into the database) and can force the
reprogramming of systems if business rules change. For example, redundant copies of
the same data caused by a violation of second normal form are often not updated in a
synchronized way. And, if they are, extra programming is required to ensure that all
copies of exactly the same business data are updated together. Further, denormalization
optimizes certain data processing at the expense of other data processing, so if the
frequencies of different processing activities change, the benefits of denormalization
may no longer exist. Denormalization almost always leads to more storage space for raw
data and maybe more space for database overhead (e.g., indexes). Thus, denormalization

should be an explicit act to gain significant processing speed when other physical design actions are not sufficient to achieve processing expectations.

Pascal (2002a, 2002b) passionately reports of the many dangers of denormalization. The motivation for denormalization is that a normalized database often creates many tables, and joining tables slows database processing. Pascal argues that this is not necessarily true, so the motivation for denormalization may be without merit in some cases. Overall, performance does not depend solely on the number of tables accessed but rather also on how the tables are organized in the database (using *file organizations* and *clustering*), the proper design and implementation of queries, and the query optimization capabilities of the DBMS. Thus, to avoid problems associated with the data anomalies in denormalized databases, Pascal recommends first attempting to use these other means to achieve the necessary performance. This often will be sufficient, but in cases when further steps are needed, you must understand the opportunities for applying denormalization.

Hoberman (2002) has written a very useful two-part "denormalization survival guide," which summarizes the major factors (those outlined previously and a few others) in deciding whether to denormalize.

DESIGNING PHYSICAL DATABASE FILES

A **physical file** is a named portion of secondary memory (such as a magnetic tape or hard disk) allocated for the purpose of storing physical records. Some computer operating systems allow a physical file to be split into separate pieces, sometimes called *extents*. In subsequent sections, we will assume that a physical file is not split and that each record in a file has the same structure. That is, subsequent sections address how to store and link relational table rows from a single database in physical storage space. In order to optimize the performance of the database processing, the person who administers a database, the database administrator, often needs to know extensive details about how the database management system manages physical storage space. This knowledge is very DBMS specific, but the principles described in subsequent sections are the foundation for the physical data structures used by most relational DBMSs.

Most database management systems store many different kinds of data in one operating system file. By an *operating system file*, we mean a named file that would appear on a disk directory listing (e.g., a listing of the files in a folder on the C: drive of your personal computer). For example, an important logical structure for storage space in Oracle is a tablespace. A **tablespace** is a named logical storage unit in which data from one or more database tables, views, or other database objects may be stored. An instance of Oracle 11g includes many tablespaces—for example, two (SYSTEM and SYSAUX) for system data (data dictionary or data about data), one (TEMP) for temporary work space, one (UNDOTBS1) for undo operations, and one or several to hold user business data. A tablespace consists of one or several physical operating system files. Thus, Oracle has responsibility for managing the storage of data inside a tablespace, whereas the operating system has many responsibilities for managing a tablespace, but they are all related to its responsibilities related to the management of operating system files (e.g., handling file-level security, allocating space, and responding to disk read and write errors).

Because an instance of Oracle usually supports many databases for many users, a database administrator usually will create many user tablespaces, which helps achieve database security because the administrator can give each user selected rights to access each tablespace. Each tablespace consists of logical units called *segments* (consisting of one table, index, or partition), which, in turn, are divided into **extents**. These, finally, consist of a number of contiguous *data blocks*, which are the smallest units of storage. Each table, index, or other so-called schema object belongs to a single tablespace, but a tablespace may contain (and typically contains) one or more tables, indexes, and other schema objects. Physically, each tablespace can be stored in one or multiple data files, but each data file is associated with only one tablespace and only one database.

Physical file

A named portion of secondary memory (such as a hard disk) allocated for the purpose of storing physical records.

Tablespace

A named logical storage unit in which data from one or more database tables, views, or other database objects may be stored.

Extent

A contiguous section of disk storage space.

FIGURE 5-5 DBMS terminology in an Oracle 11g environment

Modern database management systems have an increasingly active role in managing the use of the physical devices and files on them; for example, the allocation of schema objects (e.g., tables and indexes) to data files is typically fully controlled by the DBMS. A database administrator does, however, have the ability to manage the disk space allocated to tablespaces and a number of parameters related to the way free space is managed within a database. Because this is not a text on Oracle, we do not cover specific details on managing tablespaces; however, the general principles of physical database design apply to the design and management of Oracle tablespaces as they do to whatever the physical storage unit is for any database management system. Figure 5-5 is an EER model that shows the relationships between various physical and logical database terms related to physical database design in an Oracle environment.

File Organizations

File organization

A technique for physically arranging the records of a file on secondary storage devices.

A **file organization** is a technique for physically arranging the records of a file on secondary storage devices. With modern relational DBMSs, you do not have to design file organizations, but you may be allowed to select an organization and its parameters for a table or physical file. In choosing a file organization for a particular file in a database, you should consider seven important factors:

1. Fast data retrieval
2. High throughput for processing data input and maintenance transactions
3. Efficient use of storage space
4. Protection from failures or data loss
5. Minimizing need for reorganization
6. Accommodating growth
7. Security from unauthorized use

Often these objectives are in conflict, and you must select a file organization that provides a reasonable balance among the criteria within resources available.

In this chapter, we consider the following families of basic file organizations: sequential, indexed, and hashed. Figure 5-6 illustrates each of these organizations, with the nicknames of some university sports teams.

FIGURE 5-6   Comparison of file organizations

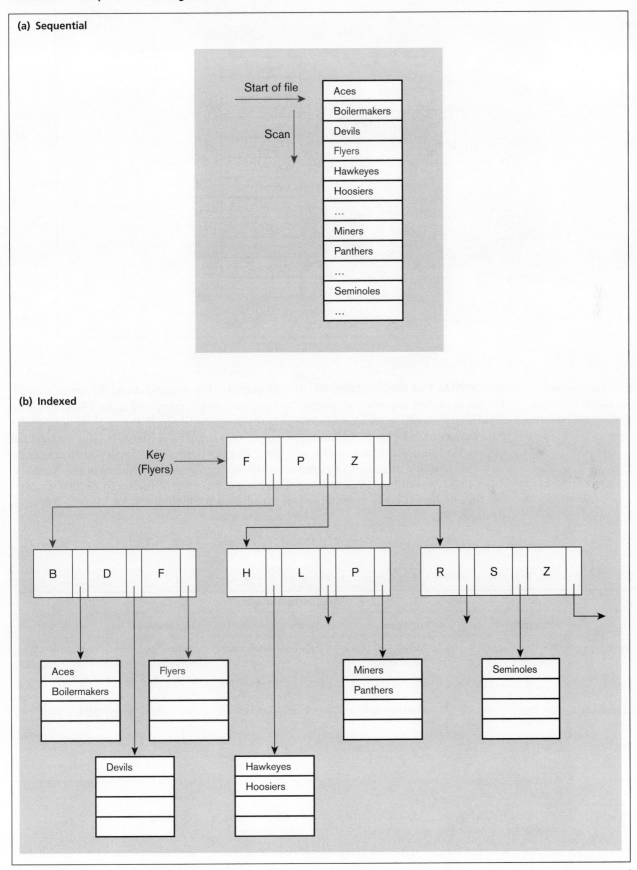

(a) Sequential

(b) Indexed

(Figure 5-6 continues on the next page)

FIGURE 5-6 (*continued*)

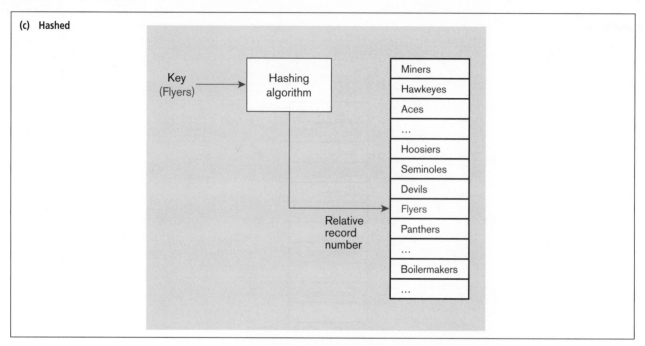

(c) Hashed

Sequential file organization

The storage of records in a file in sequence according to a primary key value.

SEQUENTIAL FILE ORGANIZATIONS In a **sequential file organization**, the records in the file are stored in sequence according to a primary key value (see Figure 5-6a). To locate a particular record, a program must normally scan the file from the beginning until the desired record is located. A common example of a sequential file is the alphabetical list of persons in the white pages of a telephone directory (ignoring any index that may be included with the directory). A comparison of the capabilities of sequential files with the other two types of files appears later in Table 5-2. Because of their inflexibility, sequential files are not used in a database but may be used for files that back up data from a database.

TABLE 5-2 Comparative Features of Different File Organizations

	File Organization		
Factor	**Sequential**	**Indexed**	**Hashed**
Storage space	No wasted space	No wasted space for data but extra space for index	Extra space may be needed to allow for addition and deletion of records after the initial set of records is loaded
Sequential retrieval on primary key	Very fast	Moderately fast	Impractical, unless using a hash index
Random retrieval on primary key	Impractical	Moderately fast	Very fast
Multiple-key retrieval	Possible but requires scanning whole file	Very fast with multiple indexes	Not possible unless using a hash index
Deleting records	Can create wasted space or require reorganizing	If space can be dynamically allocated, this is easy but requires maintenance of indexes	Very easy
Adding new records	Requires rewriting a file	If space can be dynamically allocated, this is easy but requires maintenance of indexes	Very easy, but multiple keys with the same address require extra work
Updating records	Usually requires rewriting a file	Easy but requires maintenance of indexes	Very easy

INDEXED FILE ORGANIZATIONS   In an **indexed file organization**, the records are stored either sequentially or nonsequentially, and an index is created that allows the application software to locate individual records (see Figure 5-6b). Like a card catalog in a library, an **index** is a table that is used to determine in a file the location of records that satisfy some condition. Each index entry matches a key value with one or more records. An index can point to unique records (a primary key index, such as on the ProductID field of a product record) or to potentially more than one record. An index that allows each entry to point to more than one record is called a **secondary key** index. Secondary key indexes are important for supporting many reporting requirements and for providing rapid ad hoc data retrieval. An example would be an index on the ProductFinish column of a Product table. Because indexes are extensively used with relational DBMSs, and the choice of what index and how to store the index entries matters greatly in database processing performance, we review indexed file organizations in more detail than the other types of file organizations.

Some index structures influence where table rows are stored, and other index structures are independent of where rows are located. Because the actual structure of an index does not influence database design and is not important in writing database queries, we will not address the actual physical structure of indexes in this chapter. Thus, Figure 5-6b should be considered a logical view of how an index is used, not a physical view of how data are stored in an index structure.

Transaction-processing applications require rapid response to queries that involve one or a few related table rows. For example, to enter a new customer order, an order entry application needs to rapidly find the specific customer table row, a few product table rows for the items being purchased, and possibly a few other product table rows based on the characteristics of the products the customer wants (e.g., product finish). Consequently, the application needs to add one customer order and order line rows to the respective tables. The types of indexes discussed so far work very well in an application that is searching for a few specific table rows.

Another increasingly popular type of index, especially in data warehousing and other decision support applications (see Chapter 9), is a join index. In decision support applications, the data accessing tends to want all rows that are related to one another (e.g., all the customers who have bought items from the same store) from very large tables. A **join index** is an index on columns from two or more tables that come from the same domain of values. For example, consider Figure 5-7a, which shows two tables, Customer and Store. Each of these tables has a column called City. The join index of the City column indicates the row identifiers for rows in the two tables that have the same City value. Because of the way many data warehouses are designed, there is a high frequency for queries to find data (facts) in common to a store and a customer in the same city (or similar intersections of facts across multiple dimensions). Figure 5-7b shows another possible application for a join index. In this case, the join index precomputes the matching of a foreign key in the Order table with the associated customer in the Customer table (i.e., the result of a relational join operator, which will be discussed in Chapter 6). Simply stated, a join says find rows in the same or different tables that have values that match some criterion.

A join index is created as rows are loaded into a database, so the index, like all other indexes previously discussed, is always up-to-date. Without a join index in the database of Figure 5-7a, any query that wants to find stores and customers in the same city would have to compute the equivalent of the join index each time the query is run. For very large tables, joining all the rows of one table with matching rows in another possibly large table can be very time consuming and can significantly delay responding to an online query. In Figure 5-7b, the join index provides one place for the DBMS to find information about related table rows. A join index, similar to any other index, saves query processing time by finding data meeting a prespecified qualification at the expense of the extra storage space and maintenance of the index. The use of databases for new applications, such as data warehousing and online decision support, is leading to the development of new types of indexes. We encourage you to investigate the indexing capabilities of the database management system you are using to understand fully when to apply each type of index and how to tune the performance of the index structures.

Indexed file organization

The storage of records either sequentially or nonsequentially with an index that allows software to locate individual records.

Index

A table or other data structure used to determine in a file the location of records that satisfy some condition.

Secondary key

One field or a combination of fields for which more than one record may have the same combination of values. Also called a nonunique key.

Join index

An index on columns from two or more tables that come from the same domain of values.

FIGURE 5-7 Join indexes
(a) Join index for common
nonkey columns

Customer

RowID	Cust#	CustName	City	State
10001	C2027	Hadley	Dayton	Ohio
10002	C1026	Baines	Columbus	Ohio
10003	C0042	Ruskin	Columbus	Ohio
10004	C3861	Davies	Toledo	Ohio
. . .				

Store

RowID	Store#	City	Size	Manager
20001	S4266	Dayton	K2	E2166
20002	S2654	Columbus	K3	E0245
20003	S3789	Dayton	K4	E3330
20004	S1941	Toledo	K1	E0874
. . .				

Join Index

CustRowID	StoreRowID	Common Value*
10001	20001	Dayton
10001	20003	Dayton
10002	20002	Columbus
10003	20002	Columbus
10004	20004	Toledo
. . .		

*This column may or may not be included, as needed. Join index could be sorted on any of the three columns. Sometimes two join indexes are created, one as above and one with the two RowID columns reversed.

(Figure 5-7 continues on the next page)

Hashed file organization

A storage system in which the address for each record is determined using a hashing algorithm.

Hashing algorithm

A routine that converts a primary key value into a relative record number or relative file address.

HASHED FILE ORGANIZATIONS In a **hashed file organization**, the address of each record is determined using a hashing algorithm (see Figure 5-6c). A **hashing algorithm** is a routine that converts a primary key value into a record address. Although there are several variations of hashed files, in most cases the records are located nonsequentially, as dictated by the hashing algorithm. Thus, sequential data processing is impractical.

A typical hashing algorithm uses the technique of dividing each primary key value by a suitable prime number and then using the remainder of the division as the relative storage location. For example, suppose that an organization has a set of approximately 1,000 employee records to be stored on magnetic disk. A suitable prime number would be 997, because it is close to 1,000. Now consider the record for employee 12396. When we divide this number by 997, the remainder is 432. Thus, this record is stored at location 432 in the file. Another technique (not discussed here) must be used to resolve duplicates (or overflow) that can occur with the division/remainder method when two or more keys hash to the same address (known as a "hash clash").

One of the severe limitations of hashing is that because data table row locations are dictated by the hashing algorithm, only one key can be used for hashing-based

Order

RowID	Order#	Order Date	Cust#(FK)
30001	O5532	10/01/2001	C3861
30002	O3478	10/01/2001	C1062
30003	O8734	10/02/2001	C1062
30004	O9845	10/02/2001	C2027
. . .			

Customer

RowID	Cust#(PK)	CustName	City	State
10001	C2027	Hadley	Dayton	Ohio
10002	C1062	Baines	Columbus	Ohio
10003	C0042	Ruskin	Columbus	Ohio
10004	C3861	Davies	Toledo	Ohio
. . .				

Join Index

CustRowID	OrderRowID	Cust#
10001	30004	C2027
10002	30002	C1062
10002	30003	C1062
10004	30001	C3861
. . .		

FIGURE 5-7 (*continued*)
(b) Join index for matching a foreign key (FK) and a primary key (PK)

(storage and) retrieval. Hashing and indexing can be combined into what is called a hash index table to overcome this limitation. A **hash index table** uses hashing to map a key into a location in an index (sometimes called a *scatter index table*), where there is a **pointer** (a field of data indicating a target address that can be used to locate a related field or record of data) to the actual data record matching the hash key. The index is the target of the hashing algorithm, but the actual data are stored separately from the addresses generated by hashing. Because the hashing results in a position in an index, the table rows can be stored independently of the hash address, using whatever file organization for the data table makes sense (e.g., sequential or first available space). Thus, as with other indexing schemes but unlike most pure hashing schemes, there can be several primary and secondary keys, each with its own hashing algorithm and index table, sharing one data table.

Also, because an index table is much smaller than a data table, the index can be more easily designed to reduce the likelihood of key collisions, or overflows, than can occur in the more space-consuming data table. Again, the extra storage space for the index adds flexibility and speed for data retrieval, along with the added expense of storing and maintaining the index space. Another use of a hash index table is found in some data warehousing database technologies that use parallel processing. In this situation, the DBMS can evenly distribute data table rows across all storage devices to fairly distribute work across the parallel processors, while using hashing and indexing to rapidly find on which processor the desired data are stored.

As stated earlier, the DBMS will handle the management of any hashing file organization. You do not have to be concerned with handling overflows, accessing

Hash index table

A file organization that uses hashing to map a key into a location in an index, where there is a pointer to the actual data record matching the hash key.

Pointer

A field of data indicating a target address that can be used to locate a related field or record of data.

indexes, or the hashing algorithm. What is important for you, as a database designer, is to understand the properties of different file organizations so that you can choose the most appropriate one for the type of database processing required in the database and application you are designing. Also, understanding the properties of the file organizations used by the DBMS can help a query designer write a query in a way that takes advantage of the file organization's properties. As you will see in Chapters 6 and 7, many queries can be written in multiple ways in SQL; different query structures, however, can result in vastly different steps by the DBMS to answer the query. If you know how the DBMS thinks about using a file organization (e.g., what indexes it uses when and how and when it uses a hashing algorithm), you can design better databases and more efficient queries.

The three families of file organizations cover most of the file organizations you will have at your disposal as you design physical files and databases. Although more complex structures can be built, you are unlikely to be able to use these with a database management system.

Table 5-2 summarizes the comparative features of sequential, indexed, and hashed file organizations. You should review this table and study Figure 5-6 to see why each comparative feature is true.

Designing Controls for Files

One additional aspect of a database file about which you may have design options is the types of controls you can use to protect the file from destruction or contamination or to reconstruct the file if it is damaged. Because a database file is stored in a proprietary format by the DBMS, there is a basic level of access control. You may require additional security controls on fields, files, or databases. It is likely that files will be damaged at some point during their lifetime, and, therefore, it is essential to be able to rapidly restore a damaged file. Backup procedures provide a copy of a file and of the transactions that have changed the file. When a file is damaged, the file copy or current file, along with the log of transactions, is used to recover the file to an uncontaminated state. In terms of security, the most effective method is to encrypt the contents of the file so that only programs with access to the decryption routine will be able to see the file contents.

USING AND SELECTING INDEXES

Most database manipulations require locating a row (or collection of rows) that satisfies some condition. Given the terabyte size of modern databases, locating data without some help would be like looking for the proverbial "needle in a haystack", or in more contemporary terms, it would be like searching the Internet without a powerful search engine. For example, we might want to retrieve all customers in a given zip code or all students with a particular major. Scanning every row in a table, looking for the desired rows, may be unacceptably slow, particularly when tables are large, as they often are in real-world applications. Using indexes, as described earlier, can greatly speed up this process, and defining indexes is an important part of physical database design.

As described in the section on indexes, indexes on a file can be created for either a primary or a secondary key or both. It is typical that an index would be created for the primary key of each table. The index is itself a table with two columns: the key and the address of the record or records that contain that key value. For a primary key, there will be only one entry in the index for each key value.

Creating a Unique Key Index

Assume a Customer table that has the primary key CustomerID. A unique key index would be created on this field using the following SQL command:

```
CREATE UNIQUE INDEX CustIndex_PK ON Customer_T(CustomerID);
```

In this command, CustIndex_PK is the name of the index file created to store the index entries. The ON clause specifies which table is being indexed and the column (or columns) that forms the index key. When this command is executed, any existing records in the Customer table would be indexed. If there are duplicate values of CustomerID, the CREATE INDEX command will fail. Once the index is created, the DBMS will reject any insertion or update of data in the CUSTOMER table that would violate the uniqueness constraint on CustomerIDs. Notice that every unique index creates overhead for the DBMS to validate uniqueness for each insertion or update of a table row on which there are unique indexes. We will return to this point later, when we review when to create an index.

When a composite unique key exists, you simply list all the elements of the unique key in the ON clause. For example, a table of line items on a customer order might have a composite unique key of OrderID and ProductID. The SQL command to create this index for the OrderLine_T table would be as follows:

```
CREATE UNIQUE INDEX LineIndex_PK ON OrderLine_T(OrderID, ProductID);
```

Creating a Secondary (Nonunique) Key Index

Database users often want to retrieve rows of a relation based on values for various attributes other than the primary key. For example, in a Product table, users might want to retrieve records that satisfy any combination of the following conditions:

- All table products (Description = "Table")
- All oak furniture (ProductFinish = "Oak")
- All dining room furniture (Room = "DR")
- All furniture priced below $500 (Price < 500)

To speed up such retrievals, we can define an index on each attribute that we use to qualify a retrieval. For example, we could create a nonunique index on the Description field of the Product table with the following SQL command:

```
CREATE INDEX DescIndex_FK ON Product_T(Description);
```

Notice that the term UNIQUE should not be used with secondary (nonunique) key attributes, because each value of the attribute may be repeated. As with unique keys, a secondary key index can be created on a combination of attributes.

When to Use Indexes

During physical database design, you must choose which attributes to use to create indexes. There is a trade-off between improved performance for retrievals through the use of indexes and degraded performance (because of the overhead for extensive index maintenance) for inserting, deleting, and updating the indexed records in a file. Thus, indexes should be used generously for databases intended primarily to support data retrieval, such as for decision support and data warehouse applications. Indexes should be used judiciously for databases that support transaction processing and other applications with heavy updating requirements, because the indexes impose additional overhead.

Following are some rules of thumb for choosing indexes for relational databases:

1. Indexes are most useful on larger tables.
2. Specify a unique index for the primary key of each table.
3. Indexes are most useful for columns that frequently appear in WHERE clauses of SQL commands either to qualify the rows to select (e.g., WHERE ProductFinish = "Oak," for which an index on ProductFinish would speed retrieval) or to link (join) tables (e.g., WHERE Product_T.ProductID = OrderLine_T.ProductID, for which a secondary key index on ProductID in the OrderLine_T table and a primary key index on ProductID in the Product_T table would improve retrieval performance). In the latter case, the index is on a foreign key in the OrderLine_T table that is used in joining tables.
4. Use an index for attributes referenced in ORDER BY (sorting) and GROUP BY (categorizing) clauses. You do have to be careful, though, about these clauses. Be sure that the DBMS will, in fact, use indexes on attributes listed in these clauses (e.g., Oracle uses indexes on attributes in ORDER BY clauses but not GROUP BY clauses).

5. Use an index when there is significant variety in the values of an attribute. Oracle suggests that an index is not useful when there are fewer than 30 different values for an attribute, and an index is clearly useful when there are 100 or more different values for an attribute. Similarly, an index will be helpful only if the results of a query that uses that index do not exceed roughly 20 percent of the total number of records in the file (Schumacher, 1997).

6. Before creating an index on a field with long values, consider first creating a compressed version of the values (coding the field with a surrogate key) and then indexing on the coded version (Catterall, 2005). Large indexes, created from long index fields, can be slower to process than small indexes.

7. If the key for the index is going to be used for determining the location where the record will be stored, then the key for this index should be a surrogate key so that the values cause records to be evenly spread across the storage space (Catterall, 2005). Many DBMSs create a sequence number so that each new row added to a table is assigned the next number in sequence; this is usually sufficient for creating a surrogate key.

8. Check your DBMS for the limit, if any, on the number of indexes allowable per table. Some systems permit no more than 16 indexes and may limit the size of an index key value (e.g., no more than 2,000 bytes for each composite value). If there is such a limit in your system, you will have to choose those secondary keys that will most likely lead to improved performance.

9. Be careful of indexing attributes that have null values. For many DBMSs, rows with a null value will not be referenced in the index (so they cannot be found from an *index search* based on the attribute value NULL). Such a search will have to be done by scanning the file.

Selecting indexes is arguably the most important physical database design decision, but it is not the only way you can improve the performance of a database. Other ways address such issues as reducing the costs to relocate records, optimizing the use of extra or so-called free space in files, and optimizing query processing algorithms. (See Lightstone, Teorey, and Nadeau, 2007, for a discussion of additional ways to enhance physical database design and efficiency.) We briefly discuss the topic of query optimization in the following section of this chapter because such optimization can be used to overrule how the DBMS would use certain database design options included because of their expected improvement in data processing performance in most instances.

DESIGNING A DATABASE FOR OPTIMAL QUERY PERFORMANCE

The primary purpose of physical database design is to optimize the performance of database processing. Database processing includes adding, deleting, and modifying a database, as well as a variety of data retrieval activities. For databases that have greater retrieval traffic than maintenance traffic, optimizing the database for query performance (producing online or off-line anticipated and ad hoc screens and reports for end users) is the primary goal. This chapter has already covered most of the decisions you can make to tune the database design to meet the need of database queries (indexes, file organizations, etc.).

The amount of work a database designer needs to put into optimizing query performance depends greatly on the DBMS. Because of the high cost of expert database developers, the less database and query design work developers have to do, the less costly the development and use of a database will be. Some DBMSs give very little control to the database designer or query writer over how a query is processed or the physical location of data for optimizing data reads and writes. Other systems give the application developers considerable control and often demand extensive work to tune the database design and the structure of queries to obtain acceptable performance. When the workload is fairly focused—say, for data warehousing, where there are a few batch updates and very complex queries requiring large segments of the database—performance can be well tuned either by smart query optimizers in the DBMS or by intelligent database and query design or a combination of both. For example, the Teradata DBMS is highly tuned for parallel processing in a data warehousing environment. In this case, only seldom can a database designer or query writer improve on the capabilities of the DBMS to store and process data. This situation is, however, rare, and therefore it is important for a database designer to consider options for improving database processing performance. Chapter 7 will provide additional guidelines for writing efficient queries.

Summary

During physical database design, you, the designer, translate the logical description of data into the technical specifications for storing and retrieving data. The goal is to create a design for storing data that will provide adequate performance and ensure database integrity, security, and recoverability. In physical database design, you consider normalized relations and data volume estimates, data definitions, data processing requirements and their frequencies, user expectations, and database technology characteristics to establish the specifications that are used to implement the database using a database management system.

A field is the smallest unit of application data, corresponding to an attribute in the logical data model. You must determine the data type and integrity controls and how to handle missing values for each field, among other factors. A data type is a detailed coding scheme for representing organizational data. Data may be coded to reduce storage space. Field integrity control includes specifying a default value, a range of permissible values, null value permission, and referential integrity.

A process of denormalization transforms normalized relations into non-normalized implementation specifications. Denormalization is done to improve the efficiency of input-output operations by specifying the database implementation structure so that data elements that are required together are also accessed together on the physical medium.

A physical file is a named portion of secondary memory allocated for the purpose of storing physical records. Data within a physical file are organized through a combination of sequential storage and pointers. A pointer is a field of data that can be used to locate a related field or record of data.

A file organization arranges the records of a file on a secondary storage device. The three major categories of file organizations are (1) sequential, which stores records in sequence according to a primary key value; (2) indexed, in which records are stored sequentially or nonsequentially and an index is used to keep track of where the records are stored; and (3) hashed, in which the address of each record is determined using an algorithm that converts a primary key value into a record address.

The indexed file organization is one of the most popular in use today. An index may be based on a unique key or a secondary (nonunique) key, which allows more than one record to be associated with the same key value. A join index indicates rows from two or more tables that have common values for related fields. A hash index table makes the placement of data independent of the hashing algorithm and permits the same data to be accessed via several hashing functions on different fields. Indexes are important in speeding up data retrieval, especially when multiple conditions are used for selecting, sorting, or relating data. Indexes are useful in a wide variety of situations, including for large tables, for columns that are frequently used to qualify the data to be retrieved, when a field has a large number of distinct values, and when data processing is dominated by data retrieval rather than data maintenance.

This chapter concludes the database design section of this book. Having developed complete physical data specifications, you are now ready to begin implementing the database with database technology. Implementation means defining the database and programming client and server routines to handle queries, reports, and transactions against the database. These are primary topics of the next five chapters, which cover relational database implementation on client platforms, server platforms, client/server environments, and data warehouse technologies.

Chapter Review

Key Terms

Data type *169*
Denormalization *172*
Extent *175*
Field *169*
File organization *176*

Hash index table *181*
Hashed file
  organization *180*
Hashing algorithm *180*
Index *179*

Indexed file
  organization *179*
Join index *179*
Physical file *175*
Pointer *181*

Secondary key *179*
Sequential file
  organization *178*
Tablespace *175*

Review Questions

1. Define each of the following terms:
   a. file organization
   b. sequential file organization
   c. indexed file organization
   d. hashed file organization
   e. denormalization
   f. composite key
   g. secondary key
   h. data type
   i. join index

2. Match the following terms to the appropriate definitions:

   _____ extent
   _____ hashing algorithm
   _____ index
   _____ physical record
   _____ pointer
   _____ data type
   _____ physical file

   a. a detailed coding scheme for representing organizational data
   b. a data structure used to determine in a file the location of a record/records
   c. a named area of secondary memory
   d. a contiguous section of disk storage space
   e. a field not containing business data
   f. converts a key value into an address
   g. adjacent fields

3. Contrast the following terms:
   a. physical file; tablespace
   b. normalization; denormalization
   c. range control; null control
   d. secondary key; primary key

4. What are the major inputs into physical database design?

5. What are the key decisions in physical database design?

6. What decisions have to be made to develop a field specification?

7. Explain how physical database design has an important role in forming a foundation for regulatory compliance.

8. What are the objectives of selecting a data type for a field?

9. Explain why you sometimes have to reserve much more space for a numeric field than any of the initial stored values requires.

10. Why are field values sometimes coded?

11. What options are available for controlling data integrity at the field level?

12. Describe three ways to handle missing field values.

13. Explain why normalized relations may not comprise an efficient physical implementation structure.

14. List three common situations that suggest that relations be denormalized before database implementation.

15. Explain the reasons why some observers are against the practice of denormalization.

16. List seven important criteria for selecting the best file organization.

17. What are the benefits of a hash index table?

18. State nine rules of thumb for choosing indexes.

19. One of the recommendations regarding indexes is to specify a unique index for each primary key. Explain the justification for this recommendation.

20. Explain why an index is useful only if there is sufficient variety in the values of an attribute.

21. Indexing can clearly be very beneficial. Why should you *not* create an index for every column of every table of your database?

Problems and Exercises

1. Consider the following two relations for Millennium College:

   STUDENT(StudentID, StudentName, CampusAddress, GPA)
   REGISTRATION(StudentID, CourseID, Grade)

   Following is a typical query against these relations:

   SELECT Student_T.StudentID, StudentName,
      CourseID, Grade
   FROM Student_T, Registration_T
      WHERE Student_T.StudentID =
         Registration_T.StudentID
      AND GPA > 3.0
   ORDER BY StudentName;

   a. On what attributes should indexes be defined to speed up this query? Give the reasons for each attribute selected.
   b. Write SQL commands to create indexes for each attribute you identified in part a.
   Problems and Exercises 2–5 have been written assuming that the DBMS you are using is Oracle. If that is not the case, feel *free to modify the question for the DBMS environment that you are familiar with. You can also compare and contrast answers for different DBMSs.*

2. Choose Oracle data types for the attributes in the normalized relations in Figure 5-3.

3. Choose Oracle data types for the attributes in the normalized relations that you created in Problem and Exercise 19 in Chapter 4.

4. Explain in your own words what the precision (p) and scale (s) parameters for the Oracle data type NUMBER mean.

5. Say that you are interested in storing the numeric value 3,456,349.2334. What will be stored, with each of the following Oracle data types:
   a. NUMBER(11)
   b. NUMBER(11,1)
   c. NUMBER(11,-2)
   d. NUMBER(6)
   e. NUMBER

6. Suppose you are designing a default value for the age field in a student record at your university. What possible values would you consider, and why? How might the default vary by other characteristics about the student, such as school within the university or degree sought?

7. When a student has not chosen a major at a university, the university often enters a value of "Undecided" for the major

field. Is "Undecided" a way to represent the null value? Should it be used as a default value? Justify your answer carefully.

8. Consider the following normalized relations from a database in a large retail chain:

STORE (StoreID, Region, ManagerID, SquareFeet)
EMPLOYEE (EmployeeID, WhereWork, EmployeeName, EmployeeAddress)
DEPARTMENT (DepartmentID, ManagerID, SalesGoal)
SCHEDULE (DepartmentID, EmployeeID, Date)

What opportunities might exist for denormalizing these relations when defining the physical records for this database? Under what circumstances would you consider creating such denormalized records?

9. Consider the following normalized relations for a sports league:

TEAM(TeamID, TeamName, TeamLocation)
PLAYER(PlayerID, PlayerFirstName, PlayerLastName, PlayerDateOfBirth, PlayerSpecialtyCode)
SPECIALTY(SpecialtyCode, SpecialtyDescription)
CONTRACT(TeamID, PlayerID, StartTime, EndTime, Salary)
LOCATION(LocationID, CityName, CityState, CityCountry, CityPopulation)
MANAGER(ManagerID, ManagerName, ManagerTeam)

What recommendations would you make regarding opportunities for denormalization? What additional information would you need to make fully informed denormalization decisions?

10. Is it possible with a sequential file organization to permit sequential scanning of the data, based on several sorted orders? If not, why not? If it is possible, how?

11. Suppose each record in a file were connected to the prior record and the next record in key sequence using pointers. Thus, each record might have the following format:
Primary key, other attributes, pointer to prior record, pointer to next record
   a. What would be the advantages of this file organization compared with a sequential file organization?
   b. In contrast with a sequential file organization, would it be possible to keep the records in multiple sequences? Why or why not?

12. Assume that a student table in a university database had an index on StudentID (the primary key) and indexes on Major, Age, MaritalStatus, and HomeZipCode (all secondary keys). Further, assume that the university wanted a list of students majoring in MIS or computer science, over age 25, and married OR students majoring in computer engineering, single, and from the 45462 zip code. How could indexes be used so that only records that satisfy this qualification are accessed?

13. Consider the relations specified in Problem and Exercise 9. Assume that the database has been implemented without denormalization. Further assume that the database is global in scope and covers thousands of leagues, tens of thousands of teams, and hundreds of thousands of players. In order to accommodate this, a new relation has been added:

LEAGUE(LeagueID, LeagueName, LeagueLocation)

In addition, TEAM has an additional attribute TeamLeague. The following database operations are typical:
- Adding new players
- Adding new player contracts
- Updating player specialty codes
- Updating city populations
- Reporting players by team
- Reporting players by team and specialty
- Reporting players ordered by salary
- Reporting teams and their players by city.
   a. Identify the foreign keys.
   b. Specify the types of indexes you would recommend for this situation. Explain how you used the list of operations described above to arrive at your recommendation.

14. Consider Figure 5-6b. Assuming that the empty rows in the leaves of this index show space where new records can be stored, explain where the record for Sooners would be stored. Where would the record for Flashes be stored? What might happen when one of the leaves is full and a new record needs to be added to that leaf?

15. Consider Figure 4-35 and your answer to Problem and Exercise 19 in Chapter 4. Assume that the most important reports that the organization needs are as follows:
- A list of the current developer's project assignments
- A list of the total costs for all projects
- For each team, a list of its membership history
- For each country, a list of all projects, with projected end dates, in which the country's developers are involved
- For each year separately, a list of all developers, in the order of their average assignment scores for all the assignments that were completed during that year

Based on this (admittedly limited) information, make a recommendation regarding the indexes that you would create for this database. Choose two of the indexes and provide the SQL command that you would use to create those indexes.

Problems and Exercises 16 and 17 refer to the large Pine Valley Furniture Company data set provided with the text.

16. Create a join index on the CustomerID fields of the Customer_T and Order_T tables in Figure 4-4.

17. Refer to Figure 4-4. For each of the following reports (with sample data), indicate any indexes that you feel would help the report run faster as well as the type of index:

   a. State, by products (user-specified period)

State, by Products Report, January 1, 2010, to March 31, 2010

State	Product Description	Total Quantity Ordered
CO	8-Drawer Dresser	1
CO	Entertainment Center	0
CO	Oak Computer Desk	1
CO	Writer's Desk	2
NY	Writer's Desk	1
VA	Writer's Desk	5

b. Most frequently sold product finish in a user-specified month

Most Frequently Sold Product Finish Report, March 1, 2010, to March 31, 2010

Product Finish	Units Sold
Cherry	13

c. All orders placed last month

Monthly Order Report, March 1, 2010, to March 31, 2010

Order ID	Order Date	Customer ID	Customer Name
19	3/5/10	4	Eastern Furniture

Associated Order Details:

Product Description	Quantity Ordered	Price	Extended Price
Cherry End Table	10	$75.00	$750.00
High Back Leather Chair	5	$362.00	$1,810.00

Order_ID	Order Date	Customer IDs	Customer Name
24	3/10/10	1	Contemporary Casuals

Associated Order Details:

Product Description	Quantity Ordered	Price	Extended Price
Bookcase	4	$69.00	$276.00

d. Total products sold, by product line (user-specified period)

Products Sold by Product Line, March 1, 2010, to March 31, 2010

Product Line	Quantity Sold
Basic	200
Antique	15
Modern	10
Classical	75

References

Babad, Y. M., and J. A. Hoffer. 1984. "Even No Data Has a Value." *Communications of the ACM* 27,8 (August): 748–56.

Catterall, R. 2005. "The Keys to the Database." *DB2 Magazine* 10,2 (Quarter 2): 49–51.

Finkelstein, R. 1988. "Breaking the Rules Has a Price." *Database Programming & Design* 1,6 (June): 11–14.

Hoberman, S. 2002. "The Denormalization Survival Guide—Parts I and II." Published in the online journal *The Data Administration Newsletter*, found in the April and July issues of Tdan.com; the two parts of this guide are available at **www.tdan.com/i020fe02.htm** and **www.tdan.com/i021ht03.htm**, respectively.

Inmon, W. H. 1988. "What Price Normalization." *ComputerWorld* (October 17): 27, 31.

Lightstone, S., T. Teorey, and T. Nadeau. 2007. *Physical Database Design*. San Francisco, CA: Morgan Kaufmann.

Pascal, F. 2002a. "The Dangerous Illusion: Denormalization, Performance and Integrity, Part 1." *DM Review* 12,6 (June): 52–53, 57.

Pascal, F. 2002b. "The Dangerous Illusion: Denormalization, Performance and Integrity, Part 2." *DM Review* 12,6 (June): 16, 18.

Rogers, U. 1989. "Denormalization: Why, What, and How?" *Database Programming & Design* 2,12 (December): 46–53.

Schumacher, R. 1997. "Oracle Performance Strategies." *DBMS* 10,5 (May): 89–93.

Further Reading

Ballinger, C. 1998. "Introducing the Join Index." *Teradata Review* 1,3 (Fall): 18–23. (Note: *Teradata Review* is now *Teradata Magazine*.)

Bieniek, D. 2006. "The Essential Guide to Table Partitioning and Data Lifecycle Management." *Windows IT Pro (March)*, accessed at **www.windowsITpro.com**.

Bontempo, C. J., and C. M. Saracco. 1996. "Accelerating Indexed Searching." *Database Programming & Design* 9,7 (July): 37–43.

DeLoach, A. 1987. "The Path to Writing Efficient Queries in SQL/DS." *Database Programming & Design* 1,1 (January): 26–32.

Elmasri, R., and S. Navathe. 2010. *Fundamentals of Database Systems*, 6th ed. Reading, MA: Addison Wesley.

Loney, K., E. Aronoff, and N. Sonawalla. 1996. "Big Tips for Big Tables." *Database Programming & Design* 9,11 (November): 58–62.

Roti, S. 1996. "Indexing and Access Mechanisms." *DBMS* 9,5 (May): 65–70.

Viehman, P. 1994. "Twenty-four Ways to Improve Database Performance." *Database Programming & Design* 7,2 (February): 32–41.

Web Resources

www.SearchOracle.com and **www.SearchSQLServer.com** *Sites* that contain a wide variety of information about database management and DBMSs. New "tips" are added daily, and you can subscribe to an alert service for new postings to the site. Many tips deal with improving the performance of queries through better database and query design.

www.tdan.com Web site of *The Data Administration Newsletter*, which frequently publishes articles on all aspects of database development and design.

www.teradatamagazine.com A journal for Teradata data warehousing products that includes articles on database design. You can search the site for key terms from this chapter, such as *join index*, and find many articles on these topics.

PART IV

Implementation

AN OVERVIEW OF PART FOUR

This chapter considers topics associated with implementing relational systems, including Web-enabled Internet applications and data warehouses. Database implementation, as indicated in Chapter 1, includes coding and testing database processing programs, completing database documentation and training materials, and installing databases and converting data, as necessary, from prior systems. Here, at last, is the point in the systems development life cycle for which we have been preparing. Our prior activities—enterprise modeling, conceptual data modeling, and logical and physical database design—are necessary previous stages. At the end of implementation, we expect a functioning system that meets users' information requirements. After that, the system will be put into production use, and database maintenance will be necessary for the life of the system. This chapter in Part IV helps develop an initial understanding of the complexities and challenges of implementing a database system.

Chapter 6 describes Structured Query Language (SQL), which has become a standard language (especially on database servers) for creating and processing relational databases. In addition to a brief history of SQL that includes a thorough introduction to SQL:1999, currently used by most DBMSs, along with discussion of the SQL:2008 standard that is implemented by many relational systems, the syntax of SQL is explored. Data definition language (DDL) commands used to create a database are included, as are single-table data manipulation language (DML) commands used to query a database. Dynamic views, which constrain a user's environment to relevant tables necessary to complete the user's work, are also covered.

Chapter 7 continues the explanation of more advanced SQL syntax and constructs. Multiple-table queries, along with subqueries and correlated subqueries, are demonstrated. These capabilities provide SQL with much of its power. Transaction integrity issues and an explanation of data dictionary construction place SQL within a wider context. Additional programming capabilities, including triggers and stored procedures, and embedding SQL in other programming language programs (such as Oracle's PL/SQL) further demonstrate the capabilities of SQL. Online transaction processing (OLTP) is contrasted with online analytical processing (OLAP) features of SQL:1999 and SQL:2008; OLAP queries, necessary for accessing data warehouses, are introduced. Strategies for writing and testing queries, from simple to more complex, are offered.

Chapter 8 provides a discussion of the concepts of client/server architecture, applications, middleware, and database access in contemporary database environments. Technologies that are commonly used in creating two- and three-tier applications are presented, and sample application programs are used to demonstrate how to access databases from popular programming languages such as Java, VB.NET, ASP.NET, and JSP. The impact of cloud computing on database applications is also explored. The chapter also presents expanded coverage of the emerging role of Extensible Markup Language (XML) and related technologies in data storage and retrieval. Topics covered include basics of XML schemas, XQuery, XSLT, Web services, and service-oriented architecture (SOA).

Chapter 9 describes the basic concepts of data warehousing, the reasons data warehousing is regarded as critical to competitive advantage in many organizations, and the database design activities and structures unique to data warehousing. Topics include alternative data warehouse architectures, types of data warehouse data, and the dimensional data model (star schema) for data marts. Database design for data marts, including surrogate keys, fact table grain, modeling dates and time, conformed dimensions, and helper/hierarchy/reference tables, is explained and illustrated. This chapter also introduces two new approaches to data warehouses: columnar databases and NoSQL. A brief introduction to data governance and data quality completes this final chapter of the text.

As indicated by this brief synopses of the chapters, Part IV provides both a conceptual understanding of the issues involved in implementing database applications and a practical initial understanding of the procedures necessary to construct a database prototype. The introduction of common strategies, such as client/server, Web enabled, Web services, and data warehousing, equip you to understand expected future developments in databases.

Introduction to SQL

LEARNING OBJECTIVES

After studying this chapter, you should be able to:

- Concisely define each of the following key terms: **relational DBMS (RDBMS), catalog, schema, data definition language (DDL), data manipulation language (DML), data control language (DCL), scalar aggregate, vector aggregate, base table, virtual table,** and **dynamic view**.
- Interpret the history and role of SQL in database development.
- Define a database using the SQL data definition language.
- Write single-table queries using SQL commands.
- Establish referential integrity using SQL.
- Discuss the SQL:1999 and SQL:2008 standards.

Visit www.pearsonhighered.com/ hoffer to view the accompanying video for this chapter.

INTRODUCTION

Pronounced "S-Q-L" by some and "sequel" by others, SQL has become the de facto standard language for creating and querying relational databases. (Can the next standard be the sequel to SQL?) The primary purpose of this chapter is to introduce SQL, the most common language for relational systems. It has been accepted as a U.S. standard by the American National Standards Institute (ANSI) and is a Federal Information Processing Standard (FIPS). It is also an international standard recognized by the International Organization for Standardization (ISO). ANSI has accredited the International Committee for Information Technology Standards (INCITS) as a standards development organization; INCITS is working on the next version of the SQL standard to be released.

The SQL standard is like afternoon weather in Florida (and maybe where you live, too)—wait a little while, and it will change. The ANSI SQL standards were first published in 1986 and updated in 1989, 1992 (SQL-92), 1999 (SQL:1999), 2003 (SQL:2003), 2006 (SQL:2006), and 2008 (SQL:2008). (See **http://en.wikipedia.org/ wiki/SQL** for a summary of this history.) The standard is now generally referred to as SQL:2008 (they will need SQL:201n any day now!).

At the time of this writing, most database management systems claim SQL:1992 compliance and partial compliance with SQL:1999 and SQL:2008.

Except where noted as a particular vendor's syntax, the examples in this chapter conform to the SQL standard. Concerns have been expressed about SQL:1999 and SQL:2003/SQL:2008 being true standards because conformance with the standard is no longer certified by the U.S. Department of Commerce's

TABLE 6-1 Handling Date and Time Values (Arvin, 2005, based on content currently and previously available at http://troelsarvin.blogspot.com/)

TIMESTAMP data type: A core feature, the standard requires that this data type store year, month, day, hour, minute, and second (with fractional seconds; default is six digits).

TIMESTAMP WITH TIME ZONE data type: Extension to TIMESTAMP also stores the time zone.

		Implementation:
Product	Follows Standard?	Comments
DB2	TIMESTAMP only	Includes validity check and will not accept an entry such as 2010–02–29 00:05:00.
MS-SQL	No	DATETIME stores date and time, with only three digits for fractional seconds; DATETIME2 has a larger date range and greater fractional precision. Validity check similar to DB2's is included.
MySQL	No	TIMESTAMP updates to current date and time when other data in the row are updated and displays the value for the time zone of the user. DATETIME is similar to MS-SQL, but validity checking is less accurate and may result in values of zero being stored.
Oracle	TIMESTAMP and TIMESTAMP WITH TIME ZONE	TIMESTAMP WITH TIME ZONE not allowed as part of a unique key. Includes validity check on dates.

National Institute of Standards and Technology (NIST) (Gorman, 2001). "Standard SQL" may be considered an oxymoron (like safe investment or easy payments)! Vendors' interpretations of the SQL standard differ from one another, and vendors extend their products' capabilities with proprietary features beyond the stated standard. This makes it difficult to port SQL from one vendor's product to another. One must become familiar with the particular version of SQL being used and not expect that SQL code will transfer exactly as written to another vendor's version. Table 6-1 demonstrates differences in handling date and time values to illustrate discrepancies one encounters across SQL vendors (IBM DB2, Microsoft SQL Server, MySQL [an open source DBMS], and Oracle).

SQL has been implemented in both mainframe and personal computer systems, so this chapter is relevant to both computing environments. Although many of the PC-database packages use a query-by-example (QBE) interface, they also include SQL coding as an option. QBE interfaces use graphic presentations and translate the QBE actions into SQL code before query execution occurs. In Microsoft Access, for example, it is possible to switch back and forth between the two interfaces; a query that has been built using a QBE interface can be viewed in SQL by clicking a button. This feature may aid you in learning SQL syntax. In client/server architectures, SQL commands are executed on the server, and the results are returned to the client workstation.

ORIGINS OF THE SQL STANDARD

The concepts of relational database technology were first articulated in 1970, in E. F. Codd's classic paper "A Relational Model of Data for Large Shared Data Banks." Workers at the IBM Research Laboratory in San Jose, California, undertook development of System R, a project whose purpose was to demonstrate the feasibility of implementing the relational model in a database management system. They used a language called Sequel, also developed at the San Jose IBM Research Laboratory. Sequel was renamed SQL during the project, which took place from 1974 to 1979. The knowledge gained was applied in the development of SQL/DS, the first relational database management system available commercially (from IBM). SQL/DS was first available in 1981, running on the DOS/VSE operating system. A VM version followed in 1982, and the MVS version, DB2, was announced in 1983.

When System R was well received at the user sites where it was installed, other vendors began developing relational products that used SQL. One product, Oracle, from Relational Software, was actually on the market before SQL/DS (1979). Other products included INGRES from Relational Technology (1981), IDM from Britton-Lee (1982), DG/SQL from Data General Corporation (1984), and Sybase from Sybase, Inc. (1986). To provide some directions for the development of relational DBMSs, ANSI and the ISO approved a standard for the SQL relational query language (functions and syntax) that was originally proposed by the X3H2 Technical Committee on Database (Technical Committee X3H2—Database, 1986; ISO, 1987), often referred to as SQL/86. For a more detailed history of the SQL standard, see the documents available at **www.wiscorp.com**.

The following were the original purposes of the SQL standard:

1. To specify the syntax and semantics of SQL data definition and manipulation languages
2. To define the data structures and basic operations for designing, accessing, maintaining, controlling, and protecting an SQL database
3. To provide a vehicle for portability of database definition and application modules between conforming DBMSs
4. To specify both minimal (Level 1) and complete (Level 2) standards, which permit different degrees of adoption in products
5. To provide an initial standard, although incomplete, that will be enhanced later to include specifications for handling such topics as referential integrity, transaction management, user-defined functions, join operators beyond the equi-join, and national character sets

In terms of SQL, when is a standard not a standard? As explained earlier, most vendors provide unique, proprietary features and commands for their SQL database management system. So what are the advantages and disadvantages of having an SQL standard, when there are such variations from vendor to vendor? The benefits of such a standardized relational language include the following (although these are not pure benefits because of vendor differences):

- *Reduced training costs* Training in an organization can concentrate on one language. A large labor pool of IS professionals trained in a common language reduces retraining for newly hired employees.
- *Productivity* IS professionals can learn SQL thoroughly and become proficient with it from continued use. An organization can afford to invest in tools to help IS professionals become more productive. And because they are familiar with the language in which programs are written, programmers can more quickly maintain existing programs.
- *Application portability* Applications can be moved from machine to machine when each machine uses SQL. Further, it is economical for the computer software industry to develop off-the-shelf application software when there is a standard language.
- *Application longevity* A standard language tends to remain so for a long time; hence there will be little pressure to rewrite old applications. Rather, applications will simply be updated as the standard language is enhanced or new versions of DBMSs are introduced.
- *Reduced dependence on a single vendor* When a nonproprietary language is used, it is easier to use different vendors for the DBMS, training and educational services, application software, and consulting assistance; further, the market for such vendors will be more competitive, which may lower prices and improve service.
- *Cross-system communication* Different DBMSs and application programs can more easily communicate and cooperate in managing data and processing user programs.

On the other hand, a standard can stifle creativity and innovation; one standard is never enough to meet all needs, and an industry standard can be far from ideal because it may be the offspring of compromises among many parties. A standard may be difficult to change (because so many vendors have a vested interest in it), so fixing deficiencies may take considerable effort. Another disadvantage of standards that can be extended with proprietary features is that using special features added to SQL by a particular vendor may result in the loss of some advantages, such as application portability.

Many products are available that support SQL, and they run on machines of all sizes, from small personal computers to large mainframes. The database market is maturing, and the rate of significant changes in products may slow, but they will continue to be SQL based. The number of relational database vendors with significant market share has continued to consolidate. According to iStockAnalyst.com, Gartner Group reports that Oracle controlled more than 48 percent of the overall database market in 2010, IBM is in second place, and Microsoft comes in a close third. Sybase and Teradata also had significant—albeit much smaller—shares, and open source products, such as MySQL, PostgreSQL, and Ingres, combined for about 10 percent market share. MySQL, an open source version of SQL that runs on Linux, UNIX, Windows, and Mac OS X operating systems, has achieved considerable popularity. (Download MySQL for free from **www.mysql.com**.) The market position of MySQL may change over time now that Oracle has acquired MySQL as part of its purchase of Sun Microsystems. Opportunities still exist for smaller vendors to prosper through industry-specific systems or niche applications. Upcoming product releases may change the relative strengths of the database management systems by the time you read this book. But all of them will continue to use SQL, and they will follow, to a certain extent, the standard described here.

Because of its significant market share, we most often illustrate SQL in this text using Oracle 11g syntax. We illustrate using a specific relational DBMS not to promote or endorse Oracle but rather so we know that the code we use will work with some DBMS. In the vast majority of the cases, the code will, in fact, work with many relational DBMSs because it complies with standard ANSI SQL.

THE SQL ENVIRONMENT

With today's relational DBMSs and application generators, the importance of SQL within the database architecture is not usually apparent to the application users. Many users who access database applications have no knowledge of SQL at all. For example, sites on the Web allow users to browse their catalogs. The information about an item that is presented, such as size, color, description, and availability, is stored in a database. The information has been retrieved using an SQL query, but the user has not issued an SQL command. Rather, the user has used a prewritten program (e.g., written in Java) with embedded SQL commands for database processing.

An SQL-based relational database application involves a user interface, a set of tables in the database, and a relational database management system (RDBMS) with an SQL capability. Within the RDBMS, SQL will be used to create the tables, translate user requests, maintain the data dictionary and system catalog, update and maintain the tables, establish security, and carry out backup and recovery procedures. A **relational DBMS (RDBMS)** is a data management system that implements a relational data model, one where data are stored in a collection of tables, and the data relationships are represented by common values, not links. This view of data was illustrated in Chapter 2 for the Pine Valley Furniture Company database system and will be used throughout this chapter's SQL query examples.

Figure 6-1 is a simplified schematic of an SQL environment, consistent with SQL:2008 standard. As depicted, an SQL environment includes an instance of an SQL database management system along with the databases accessible by that DBMS and the users and programs that may use that DBMS to access the databases. Each database is contained in a **catalog**, which describes any object that is a part of the database, regardless of which user created that object. Figure 6-1 shows two catalogs: DEV_C and

Relational DBMS (RDBMS)
A database management system that manages data as a collection of tables in which all data relationships are represented by common values in related tables.

Catalog
A set of schemas that, when put together, constitute a description of a database.

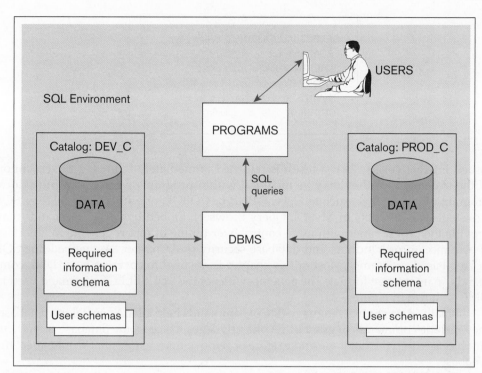

FIGURE 6-1 A simplified schematic of a typical SQL environment, as described by the SQL:2008 standards

PROD_C. Most companies keep at least two versions of any database they are using. The production version, PROD_C here, is the live version, which captures real business data and thus must be very tightly controlled and monitored. The development version, DEV_C here, is used when the database is being built and continues to serve as a development tool where enhancements and maintenance efforts can be thoroughly tested before being applied to the production database. Typically, this database is not as tightly controlled or monitored, because it does not contain live business data. Each database will have a named schema(s) associated with a catalog. A **schema** is a collection of related objects, including but not limited to base tables and views, domains, constraints, character sets, triggers, and roles.

> **Schema**
>
> A structure that contains descriptions of objects created by a user, such as base tables, views, and constraints, as part of a database.

If more than one user has created objects in a database, combining information about all users' schemas will yield information for the entire database. Each catalog must also contain an information schema, which contains descriptions of all schemas in the catalog, tables, views, attributes, privileges, constraints, and domains, along with other information relevant to the database. The information contained in the catalog is maintained by the DBMS as a result of the SQL commands issued by the users and can be rebuilt without conscious action by the user. It is part of the power of the SQL language that the issuance of syntactically simple SQL commands may result in complex data management activities being carried out by the DBMS software. Users can browse the catalog contents by using SQL SELECT statements.

SQL commands can be classified into three types. First, there are **data definition language (DDL)** commands. These commands are used to create, alter, and drop tables, views, and indexes, and they are covered first in this chapter. There may be other objects controlled by the DDL, depending on the DBMS. For example, many DBMSs support defining synonyms (abbreviations) for database objects or a field to hold a specified sequence of numbers (which can be helpful in assigning primary keys to rows in tables). In a production database, the ability to use DDL commands will generally be restricted to one or more database administrators in order to protect the database structure from unexpected and unapproved changes. In development or student databases, DDL privileges will be granted to more users.

> **Data definition language (DDL)**
>
> Commands used to define a database, including those for creating, altering, and dropping tables and establishing constraints.

Next, there are **data manipulation language (DML)** commands. Many consider the DML commands to be the core commands of SQL. These commands are used for updating, inserting, modifying, and querying the data in the database. They may be

> **Data manipulation language (DML)**
>
> Commands used to maintain and query a database, including those for updating, inserting, modifying, and querying data.

FIGURE 6-2 General syntax of the SELECT statement used in DML

```
SELECT [ALL/DISTINCT] column_list
FROM table_list
[WHERE conditional expression]
[GROUP BY group_by_column_list]
[HAVING conditional expression]
[ORDER BY order_by_column_list]
```

issued interactively, so that a result is returned immediately following the execution of the statement, or they may be included within programs written in a procedural programming language, such as C, Java, PHP, or COBOL, or with a GUI tool (e.g., SQL Assistant with Teradata or MySQL Query Browser). Embedding SQL commands may provide the programmer with more control over timing of report generation, interface appearance, error handling, and database security (see Chapter 8 on embedding SQL in Web-based programs). Most of this chapter is devoted to covering basic DML commands, in interactive format. The general syntax of the SQL SELECT command used in DML is shown in Figure 6-2.

Data control language (DCL)

Commands used to control a database, including those for administering privileges and committing (saving) data.

Finally, **data control language (DCL)** commands help a DBA control the database; they include commands to grant or revoke privileges to access the database or particular objects within the database and to store or remove transactions that would affect the database.

Each DBMS has a defined list of data types that it can handle. All contain numeric, string, and date/time-type variables. Some also contain graphic data types, spatial data types, or image data types, which greatly increase the flexibility of data manipulation. When a table is created, the data type for each attribute must be specified. Selection of a particular data type is affected by the data values that need to be stored and the expected uses of the data. A unit price will need to be stored in a numeric format because mathematical manipulations such as multiplying unit price by the number of units ordered are expected. A phone number may be stored as string data, especially if foreign phone numbers are going to be included in the data set. Even though a phone number contains only digits, no mathematical operations, such as adding or multiplying phone numbers, make sense with a phone number. And because character data will process more quickly, numeric data should be stored as character data if no arithmetic calculations are expected. Selecting a date field rather than a string field will allow the developer to take advantage of date/time interval calculation functions that cannot be applied to a character field. See Table 6-2 for a few examples of SQL data types. SQL:2008

TABLE 6-2 Sample SQL Data Types

String	CHARACTER (CHAR)	Stores string values containing any characters in a character set. CHAR is defined to be a fixed length.
	CHARACTER VARYING (VARCHAR or VARCHAR2)	Stores string values containing any characters in a character set but of definable variable length.
	BINARY LARGE OBJECT (BLOB)	Stores binary string values in hexadecimal format. BLOB is defined to be a variable length. (Oracle also has CLOB and NCLOB, as well as BFILE for storing unstructured data outside the database.)
Number	NUMERIC	Stores exact numbers with a defined precision and scale.
	INTEGER (INT)	Stores exact numbers with a predefined precision and scale of zero.
Temporal	TIMESTAMP TIMESTAMP WITH LOCAL TIME ZONE	Stores a moment an event occurs, using a definable fraction-of-a-second precision. Value adjusted to the user's session time zone (available in Oracle and MySQL).
Boolean	BOOLEAN	Stores truth values: TRUE, FALSE, or UNKNOWN.

includes three new data types: BIGINT, MULTISET, and XML. Watch for these new data types to be added to RDBMSs that had not previously introduced them as an enhancement of the existing standard.

Given the wealth of graphic and image data types, it is necessary to consider business needs when deciding how to store data. For example, color may be stored as a descriptive character field, such as "sand drift" or "beige." But such descriptions will vary from vendor to vendor and do not contain the amount of information that could be contained in a spatial data type that includes exact red, green, and blue intensity values. Such data types are now available in universal servers, which handle data warehouses, and can be expected to appear in RDBMSs as well. In addition to the predefined data types included in Table 6-2, SQL:1999 and SQL:2008 support constructed data types and user-defined types. There are many more predefined data types than those shown in Table 6-2. It will be necessary to familiarize yourself with the available data types for each RDBMS with which you work to achieve maximum advantage from its capabilities.

We are almost ready to illustrate sample SQL commands. The sample data that we will be using are shown in Figure 6-3 (which was captured in Microsoft Access). The data model corresponds to that shown in Figure 2-21. The PVFC database files are available for your use on this text Web site; the files are available in several formats, for use with different DBMSs, and the database is also available on Teradata University Network. Instructions for locating them are included inside the front cover of the book. There are two PVFC files. The one used here is named BookPVFC (also called Standard PVFC), and you can use it to work through the SQL queries demonstrated in Chapters 6 and 7. Another file, BigPVFC, contains more data and does not always correspond to

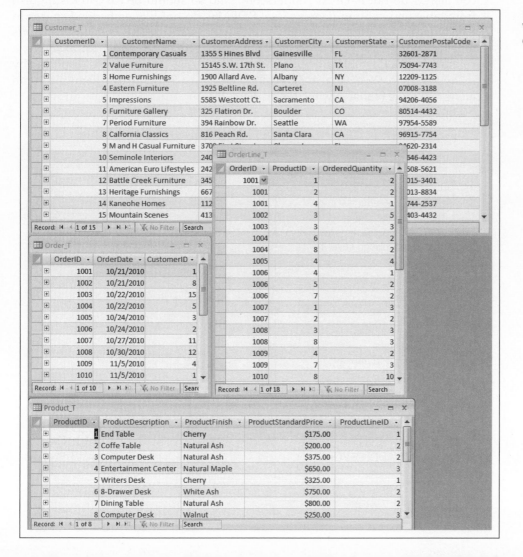

FIGURE 6-3 Sample Pine Valley Furniture Company data

Figure 2-21, nor does it always demonstrate good database design. Big PVFC is used for some of the exercises at the end of the chapter.

Each table name follows a naming standard that places an underscore and the letter T (for table) at the end of each table name, such as Order_T or Product_T. (Most DBMSs do not permit a space in the name of a table nor typically in the name of an attribute.) When looking at these tables, note the following:

1. Each order must have a valid customer ID included in the Order_T table.
2. Each item in an order line must have both a valid product ID and a valid order ID associated with it in the OrderLine_T table.
3. These four tables represent a simplified version of one of the most common sets of relations in business database systems—the customer order for products. SQL commands necessary to create the Customer_T table and the Order_T table were included in Chapter 2 and are expanded here.

The remainder of the chapter will illustrate DDL, DML, and DCL commands. Figure 6-4 gives an overview of where the various types of commands are used throughout the database development process. We will use the following notation in the illustrative SQL commands:

1. All-capitalized words denote commands. Type them exactly as shown, though capitalization may not be required by the RDBMSs. Some RDBMSs will always show data names in output using all capital letters, even if they can be entered in mixed case. (This is the style of Oracle, which is what we follow except where noted.) Tables, columns, named constraints, and so forth are shown in mixed case. Remember that table names follow the "underscore T" convention. SQL commands do not have an "underscore" and so should be easy to distinguish from table and column names. Also, RDBMSs do not like embedded spaces in data names, so multiple-word data names from ERDs are entered with the words together, without spaces between them. A consequence is that, for example, a column named QtyOnHand will become QTYONHAND when it is displayed by many RDBMSs. (You can use the ALIAS clause in a SELECT to rename a column name to a more readable value for display.)

FIGURE 6-4 DDL, DML, DCL, and the database development process

2. Lowercase and mixed-case words denote values that must be supplied by the user.
3. Brackets enclose optional syntax.
4. An ellipsis (. . .) indicates that the accompanying syntactic clause may be repeated as necessary.
5. Each SQL command ends with a semicolon (;). In interactive mode, when the user presses Enter, the SQL command will execute. Be alert for alternate conventions, such as typing GO or having to include a continuation symbol such as a hyphen at the end of each line used in the command. The spacing and indentations shown here are included for readability and are not a required part of standard SQL syntax.

DEFINING A DATABASE IN SQL

Because most systems allocate storage space to contain base tables, views, constraints, indexes, and other database objects when a database is created, you may not be allowed to create a database. Because of this, the privilege of creating databases may be reserved for the database administrator, and you may need to ask to have a database created. Students at a university may be assigned an account that gives access to an existing database, or they may be allowed to create their own database in a limited amount of allocated storage space (sometimes called *perm space* or *table space*). In any case, the basic command for creating a database structure is

> CREATE SCHEMA AUTHORIZATION owner_user_id

The database will be owned by the authorized user, although it is possible for other specified users to work with the database or even to transfer ownership of the database. Physical storage of the database is dependent on both the hardware and software environment and is usually the concern of the system administrator. The amount of control over physical storage that a database administrator is able to exert depends on the RDBMS being used. Little control is possible when using Microsoft Access, but Microsoft SQL Server 2008 and later versions allow for more control of the physical database. A database administrator may exert considerable control over the placement of data, control files, index files, schema ownership, and so forth, thus improving the ability to tune the database to perform more efficiently and to create a secure database environment.

Generating SQL Database Definitions

Several SQL DDL CREATE commands are included in SQL:2008 (and each command is followed by the name of the object being created):

CREATE SCHEMA	Used to define the portion of a database that a particular user owns. Schemas are dependent on a catalog and contain schema objects, including base tables and views, domains, constraints, assertions, character sets, collations, and so forth.
CREATE TABLE	Defines a new table and its columns. The table may be a base table or a derived table. Tables are dependent on a schema. Derived tables are created by executing a query that uses one or more tables or views.
CREATE VIEW	Defines a logical table from one or more tables or views. Views may not be indexed. There are limitations on updating data through a view. Where views can be updated, those changes can be transferred to the underlying base tables originally referenced to create the view.

You don't have to be perfect when you create these objects, and they don't have to last forever. Each of these CREATE commands can be reversed by using a DROP command. Thus, DROP TABLE *tablename* will destroy a table, including its definition, contents, and any constraints, views, or indexes associated with it. Usually, only the table creator may delete the table. DROP SCHEMA or DROP VIEW will also destroy the named schema or view. ALTER TABLE may be used to change the definition of an existing base table by adding, dropping, or changing a column or by dropping a constraint. Some RDBMSs will not allow you to alter a table in a way that the current data in that table will violate the new definitions (e.g., you cannot create a new constraint when current data will violate that constraint, or if you change the precision of a numeric column you may lose the extra precision of more precise existing values).

Creating Tables

Once the data model is designed and normalized, the columns needed for each table can be defined, using the SQL CREATE TABLE command. The general syntax for CREATE TABLE is shown in Figure 6-5. Here is a series of steps to follow when preparing to create a table:

1. Identify the appropriate data type, including length, precision, and scale, if required, for each attribute.
2. Identify the columns that should accept null values, as discussed in Chapter 5. Column controls that indicate a column cannot be null are established when a table is created and are enforced for every update of the table when data are entered.
3. Identify the columns that need to be unique. When a column control of UNIQUE is established for a column, the data in that column must have a different value for each row of data within that table (i.e., no duplicate values). Where a column or set of columns is designated as UNIQUE, that column or set of columns is a candidate key, as discussed in Chapter 4. Although each base table may have multiple candidate keys, only one candidate key may be designated as a PRIMARY KEY. When a column(s) is specified as the PRIMARY KEY, that column(s) is also assumed to be NOT NULL, even if NOT NULL is not explicitly stated. UNIQUE and PRIMARY KEY are both column constraints. Note that a table with a composite primary key, OrderLine_T, is defined in Figure 6-6. The OrderLine_PK constraint includes both OrderID and ProductID in the primary key constraint, thus creating a composite key. Additional attributes may be included within the parentheses as needed to create the composite key.
4. Identify all primary key–foreign key mates, as presented in Chapter 4. Foreign keys can be established immediately, as a table is created, or later by altering the table. The parent table in such a parent–child relationship should be created first so that the child table will reference an existing parent table when it is created. The column constraint REFERENCES can be used to enforce referential integrity (e.g., the Order_FK constraint on the Order_T table).

FIGURE 6-5 General syntax of the CREATE TABLE statement used in data definition language

```
CREATE TABLE tablename
( {column definition      [table constraint] } . , . .
[ON COMMIT {DELETE | P RESERVE} ROWS] );

where column definition ::=
column_name
        {domain name | datatype [(size)] }
        [column_constraint_clause. . .]
        [default value]
        [collate clause]

and table constraint ::=
        [CONSTRAINT constraint_name]
        Constraint_type [constraint_attributes]
```

FIGURE 6-6 SQL database definition commands for Pine Valley Furniture Company (Oracle 11g)

```
CREATE TABLE Customer_T
              (CustomerID                  NUMBER(11,0)       NOT NULL,
               CustomerName                VARCHAR2(25)       NOT NULL,
               CustomerAddress             VARCHAR2(30),
               CustomerCity                VARCHAR2(20),
               CustomerState               CHAR(2),
               CustomerPostalCode          VARCHAR2(9),
CONSTRAINT Customer_PK PRIMARY KEY (CustomerID));

CREATE TABLE Order_T
              (OrderID                     NUMBER(11,0)       NOT NULL,
               OrderDate                   DATE DEFAULT SYSDATE,
               CustomerID                  NUMBER(11,0),
CONSTRAINT Order_PK PRIMARY KEY (OrderID),
CONSTRAINT Order_FK FOREIGN KEY (CustomerID) REFERENCES Customer_T(CustomerID));

CREATE TABLE Product_T
              (ProductID                   NUMBER(11,0)       NOT NULL,
               ProductDescription          VARCHAR2(50),
               ProductFinish               VARCHAR2(20)
                             CHECK (ProductFinish IN ('Cherry', 'Natural Ash', 'White Ash',
                                     'Red Oak', 'Natural Oak', 'Walnut')),
               ProductStandardPrice        DECIMAL(6,2),
               ProductLineID               INTEGER,
CONSTRAINT Product_PK PRIMARY KEY (ProductID));

CREATE TABLE OrderLine_T
              (OrderID                     NUMBER(11,0)       NOT NULL,
               ProductID                   INTEGER            NOT NULL,
               OrderedQuantity             NUMBER(11,0),
CONSTRAINT OrderLine_PK PRIMARY KEY (OrderID, ProductID),
CONSTRAINT OrderLine_FK1 FOREIGN KEY (OrderID) REFERENCES Order_T(OrderID),
CONSTRAINT OrderLine_FK2 FOREIGN KEY (ProductID) REFERENCES Product_T(ProductID));
```

5. Determine values to be inserted in any columns for which a default value is desired. DEFAULT can be used to define a value that is automatically inserted when no value is inserted during data entry. In Figure 6-6, the command that creates the Order_T table has defined a default value of SYSDATE (Oracle's name for the current date) for the OrderDate attribute.

6. Identify any columns for which domain specifications may be stated that are more constrained than those established by data type. Using CHECK as a column constraint, it may be possible to establish validation rules for values to be inserted into the database. In Figure 6-6, creation of the Product_T table includes a check constraint, which lists the possible values for Product_Finish. Thus, even though an entry of 'White Maple' would meet the VARCHAR data type constraints, it would be rejected because 'White Maple' is not in the checklist.

7. Create the table and any desired indexes, using the CREATE TABLE and CREATE INDEX statements. (CREATE INDEX is not a part of the SQL:1999 standard because indexing is used to address performance issues, but it is available in most RDBMSs.)

Figure 6-6 shows database definition commands using Oracle 11g that include additional column constraints, as well as primary and foreign keys given names. For example, the Customer table's primary key is CustomerID. The primary key constraint is named Customer_PK. In Oracle, for example, once a constraint has been given a meaningful name by the user, a database administrator will find it easy to identify the primary key constraint on the customer table because its name, Customer_PK, will be the

PINE
VALLEY
FURNITURE

value of the constraint_name column in the DBA_CONSTRAINTS table. If a meaningful constraint name were not assigned, a 16-byte system identifier would be assigned automatically. These identifiers are difficult to read and even more difficult to match up with user-defined constraints. Documentation about how system identifiers are generated is not available, and the method can be changed without notification. Bottom line: Give all constraints names or be prepared for extra work later.

When a foreign key constraint is defined, referential integrity will be enforced. This is good: We want to enforce business rules in the database. Fortunately, you are still allowed to have a null value for the foreign key (signifying a zero cardinality of the relationship) as long as you do not put the NOT NULL clause on the foreign key column. For example, if you try to add an order with an invalid CustomerID value (every order has to be related to some customer, so the minimum cardinality is one next to Customer for the Submits relationship in Figure 2-21), you will receive an error message. Each DBMS vendor generates its own error messages, and these messages may be difficult to interpret. Microsoft Access, being intended for both personal and professional use, provides simple error messages in dialog boxes. For example, for a referential integrity violation, Access displays the following error message: "You cannot add or change a record because a related record is required in table Customer_T." No record will be added to Order_T until that record references an existing customer in the Customer_T table.

Oracle, MySQL, and some other RDBMSs have an interesting "dummy" table that is automatically defined with each database—the Dual table. The Dual table is used to run an SQL command against a system variable. For example,

```
SELECT Sysdate FROM Dual;
```

displays the current date, and

```
SELECT 8 + 4 FROM Dual;
```

displays the result of this arithmetic.

Creating Data Integrity Controls

We have seen the syntax that establishes foreign keys in Figure 6-6. To establish referential integrity constraint between two tables with a 1:*M* relationship in the relational data model, the primary key of the table on the one side will be referenced by a column in the table on the many side of the relationship. Referential integrity means that a value in the matching column on the many side must correspond to a value in the primary key for some row in the table on the one side or be NULL. The SQL REFERENCES clause prevents a foreign key value from being added if it is not already a valid value in the referenced primary key column, but there are other integrity issues.

Changing Table Definitions

Base table definitions may be changed by using ALTER on the column specifications. The ALTER TABLE command can be used to add new columns to an existing table. Existing columns may also be altered. Table constraints may be added or dropped. The ALTER TABLE command may include keywords such as ADD, DROP, or ALTER and allow the column's names, data type, length, and constraints to be changed. Usually, when adding a new column, its null status will be NULL so that data that have already been entered in the table can be dealt with. When the new column is created, it is added to all of the instances in the table, and a value of NULL would be the most reasonable. The ALTER command cannot be used to change a view.

Syntax:

```
ALTER TABLE table_name alter_table_action;
```

Some of the alter_table_actions available are:

ADD [COLUMN] column_definition
ALTER [COLUMN] column_name **SET DEFAULT** default-value
ALTER [COLUMN] column_name **DROP DEFAULT**
DROP [COLUMN] column_name **[RESTRICT] [CASCADE]**
ADD table_constraint

Command: To add a customer type column named CustomerType to the Customer table.

ALTER TABLE CUSTOMER_T
ADD COLUMN CustomerType VARCHAR2 (2) DEFAULT "Commercial";

The ALTER command is invaluable for adapting a database to inevitable modifications due to changing requirements, prototyping, evolutionary development, and mistakes. It is also useful when performing a bulk data load into a table that contains a foreign key. The constraint may be temporarily dropped. Later, after the bulk data load has finished, the constraint can be enabled. When the constraint is re-enabled, it is possible to generate a log of any records that have referential integrity problems. Rather than have the data load balk each time such a problem occurs during the bulk load, the database administrator can simply review the log and reconcile the few (hopefully few) records that were problematic.

Removing Tables

To remove a table from a database, the owner of the table may use the DROP TABLE command. Views are dropped by using the similar DROP VIEW command.

Command: To drop a table from a database schema.

DROP TABLE Customer_T;

This command will drop the table and save any pending changes to the database. To drop a table, you must either own the table or have been granted the DROP ANY TABLE system privilege. Dropping a table will also cause associated indexes and privileges granted to be dropped. The DROP TABLE command can be qualified by the keywords RESTRICT or CASCADE. If RESTRICT is specified, the command will fail, and the table will not be dropped if there are any dependent objects, such as views or constraints, that currently reference the table. If CASCADE is specified, all dependent objects will also be dropped as the table is dropped. Many RDBMSs allows users to retain the table's structure but remove all of the data that have been entered in the table with its TRUNCATE TABLE command. Commands for updating and deleting part of the data in a table are covered in the next section.

INSERTING, UPDATING, AND DELETING DATA

Once tables have been created, it is necessary to populate them with data and maintain those data before queries can be written. The SQL command that is used to populate tables is the INSERT command. When entering a value for every column in the table, you can use a command such as the following, which was used to add the first row of data to the Customer_T table for Pine Valley Furniture Company. Notice that the data values must be ordered in the same order as the columns in the table.

Command: To insert a row of data into a table where a value will be inserted for every attribute.

INSERT INTO Customer_T VALUES
(001, 'Contemporary Casuals', '1355 S. Himes Blvd.', 'Gainesville', 'FL', 32601);

When data will not be entered into every column in the table, either enter the value NULL for the empty fields or specify those columns to which data are to be added. Here, too, the data values must be in the same order as the columns have been specified in the INSERT command. For example, the following statement was used to insert one row of data into the Product_T table, because there was no product line ID for the end table.

Command: To insert a row of data into a table where some attributes will be left null.

INSERT INTO Product_T (ProductID,
ProductDescription, ProductFinish, ProductStandardPrice)
    VALUES (1, 'End Table', 'Cherry', 175, 8);

In general, the INSERT command places a new row in a table, based on values supplied in the statement, copies one or more rows derived from other database data into a table, or extracts data from one table and inserts them into another. If you want to populate a table, CaCustomer_T, that has the same structure as CUSTOMER_T, with only Pine Valley's California customers, you could use the following INSERT command.

Command: Populating a table by using a subset of another table with the same structure.

INSERT INTO CaCustomer_T
SELECT * FROM Customer_T
    WHERE CustomerState = 'CA';

In many cases, we want to generate a unique primary identifier or primary key every time a row is added to a table. Customer identification numbers are a good example of a situation where this capability would be helpful. SQL:2008 had added a new feature, identity columns, that removes the previous need to create a procedure to generate a sequence and then apply it to the insertion of data. To take advantage of this, the CREATE TABLE Customer_T statement displayed in Figure 6-6 may be modified (emphasized by bold print) as follows:

CREATE TABLE Customer_T
(CustomerID INTEGER GENERATED ALWAYS AS IDENTITY
    (START WITH 1
    INCREMENT BY 1
    MINVALUE 1
    MAXVALUE 10000
    NO CYCLE),
CustomerName   VARCHAR2(25) NOT NULL,
CustomerAddress   VARCHAR2(30),
CustomerCity   VARCHAR2(20),
CustomerState   CHAR(2),
CustomerPostalCode   VARCHAR2(9),
CONSTRAINT Customer_PK PRIMARY KEY (CustomerID);

Only one column can be an identity column in a table. When a new customer is added, the CustomerID value will be assigned implicitly if the vendor has implemented identity columns.

Thus, the command that adds a new customer to Customer_T will change from this:

INSERT INTO Customer_T VALUES
(001, 'Contemporary Casuals', '1355 S. Himes Blvd.', 'Gainesville',
    'FL', 32601);

to this:

INSERT INTO Customer_T VALUES
('Contemporary Casuals', '1355 S. Himes Blvd.', 'Gainesville', 'FL', 32601);

The primary key value, 001, does not need to be entered, and the syntax to accomplish the automatic sequencing has been simplified in SQL:2008.

Deleting Database Contents

Rows can be deleted from a database individually or in groups. Suppose Pine Valley Furniture decides that it will no longer deal with customers located in Hawaii. Customer_T rows for customers with addresses in Hawaii could all be eliminated using the next command.

Command: Deleting rows that meet a certain criterion from the Customer table.

DELETE FROM Customer_T
WHERE CustomerState = 'HI';

The simplest form of DELETE eliminates all rows of a table.

Command: Deleting all rows from the Customer table.

DELETE FROM Customer_T;

This form of the command should be used very carefully!

Deletion must also be done with care when rows from several relations are involved. For example, if we delete a Customer_T row, as in the previous query, before deleting associated Order_T rows, we will have a referential integrity violation, and the DELETE command will not execute. (Note: Including the ON DELETE clause with a field definition can mitigate such a problem. Refer to the "Creating Data Integrity Controls" section in this chapter if you've forgotten about the ON clause.) SQL will actually eliminate the records selected by a DELETE command. Therefore, always execute a SELECT command first to display the records that would be deleted and visually verify that only the desired rows are included.

Updating Database Contents

To update data in SQL, we must inform the DBMS what relation, columns, and rows are involved. If an incorrect price is entered for the dining table in the Product_T table, the following SQL UPDATE statement would establish the correction.

Command: To modify standard price of product 7 in the Product table to 775.

UPDATE Product_T
SET ProductStandardPrice = 775
    WHERE ProductID = 7;

The SET command can also change a value to NULL; the syntax is SET column_name = NULL. As with DELETE, the WHERE clause in an UPDATE command may contain a subquery, but the table being updated may not be referenced in the subquery. Subqueries are discussed in Chapter 7.

INTERNAL SCHEMA DEFINITION IN RDBMSs

The internal schema of a relational database can be controlled for processing and storage efficiency. The following are some techniques used for tuning the operational performance of the relational database internal data model:

1. Choosing to index primary and/or secondary keys to increase the speed of row selection, table joining, and row ordering. You can also drop indexes to increase

speed of table updating. You may want to review the section in Chapter 5 on selecting indexes.

2. Selecting file organizations for base tables that match the type of processing activity on those tables (e.g., keeping a table physically sorted by a frequently used reporting sort key).

3. Selecting file organizations for indexes, which are also tables, appropriate to the way the indexes are used and allocating extra space for an index file so that an index can grow without having to be reorganized.

4. Clustering data so that related rows of frequently joined tables are stored close together in secondary storage to minimize retrieval time.

5. Maintaining statistics about tables and their indexes so that the DBMS can find the most efficient ways to perform various database operations.

Not all of these techniques are available in all SQL systems. Indexing and clustering are typically available, however, so we discuss these in the following sections.

Creating Indexes

Indexes are created in most RDBMSs to provide rapid random and sequential access to base-table data. Because the ISO SQL standards do not generally address performance issues, no standard syntax for creating indexes is included. The examples given here use Oracle syntax and give a feel for how indexes are handled in most RDBMSs. Note that although users do not directly refer to indexes when writing any SQL command, the DBMS recognizes which existing indexes would improve query performance. Indexes can usually be created for both primary and secondary keys and both single and concatenated (multiple-column) keys. In some systems, users can choose between ascending and descending sequences for the keys in an index.

For example, an alphabetical index on CustomerName in the Customer_T table in Oracle is created here.

Command: To create an alphabetical index on customer name in the Customer table.

```
CREATE INDEX Name_IDX ON Customer_T (CustomerName);
```

RDBMSs usually support several different types of indexes, each of which assists in different kinds of keyword searches. For example, in MySQL you can create unique (appropriate for primary keys), nonunique (secondary keys), fulltext (used for full-text searches), spatial (used for spatial data types), and hash (which is used for in-memory tables).

Indexes can be created or dropped at any time. If data already exist in the key column(s), index population will automatically occur for the existing data. If an index is defined as UNIQUE (using the syntax CREATE UNIQUE INDEX . . .) and the existing data violate this condition, the index creation will fail. Once an index is created, it will be updated as data are entered, updated, or deleted.

When we no longer need tables, views, or indexes, we use the associated DROP statements. For example, the NAME_IDX index from the previous example is dropped here.

Command: To remove the index on the customer name in the Customer table.

```
DROP INDEX Name_IDX;
```

Although it is possible to index every column in a table, use caution when deciding to create a new index. Each index consumes extra storage space and also requires overhead maintenance time whenever indexed data change value. Together, these costs may noticeably slow retrieval response times and cause annoying delays for online users. A system may use only one index even if several are available for keys in a complex qualification. A database designer must know exactly how indexes are used by the particular RDBMS in order to make wise choices about indexing. Oracle includes an explain plan tool that can be used to look at the order in which an SQL statement will be processed and at the indexes that will be used. The output also includes a cost estimate that can be compared with estimates from running the statement with different indexes to determine which is most efficient.

PROCESSING SINGLE TABLES

"Processing single tables" may seem like Friday night at the hottest club in town, but we have something else in mind. Sorry, no dating suggestions (and sorry for the pun).

Four data manipulation language commands are used in SQL. We have talked briefly about three of them (UPDATE, INSERT, and DELETE) and have seen several examples of the fourth, SELECT. Although the UPDATE, INSERT, and DELETE commands allow modification of the data in the tables, it is the SELECT command, with its various clauses, that allows users to query the data contained in the tables and ask many different questions or create ad hoc queries. The basic construction of an SQL command is fairly simple and easy to learn. Don't let that fool you; SQL is a powerful tool that enables users to specify complex data analysis processes. However, because the basic syntax is relatively easy to learn, it is also easy to write SELECT queries that are syntactically correct but do not answer the exact question that is intended. Before running queries against a large production database, always test them carefully on a small test set of data to be sure that they are returning the correct results. In addition to checking the query results manually, it is often possible to parse queries into smaller parts, examine the results of these simpler queries, and then recombine them. This will ensure that they act together in the expected way. We begin by exploring SQL queries that affect only a single table. In Chapter 7, we join tables and use queries that require more than one table.

Clauses of the SELECT Statement

Most SQL data retrieval statements include the following three clauses:

SELECT	Lists the columns (including expressions involving columns) from base tables, derived tables, or views to be projected into the table that will be the result of the command. (That's the technical way of saying it lists the data you want to display.)
FROM	Identifies the tables, derived tables, or views from which columns will be chosen to appear in the result table and includes the tables, derived tables, or views needed to join tables to process the query.
WHERE	Includes the conditions for row selection within the items in the FROM clause and the conditions between tables, derived tables, or views for joining. Because SQL is considered a set manipulation language, the WHERE clause is important in defining the set of rows being manipulated.

The first two clauses are required, and the third is necessary when only certain table rows are to be retrieved or multiple tables are to be joined. (Most examples for this section are drawn from the data shown in Figure 6-3.) For example, we can display product name and quantity on hand from the PRODUCT table for all Pine Valley Furniture Company products that have a standard price of less than $275.

PINE VALLEY FURNITURE

Query: Which products have a standard price of less than $275?

```
SELECT ProductDescription, ProductStandardPrice
    FROM Product_T
        WHERE ProductStandardPrice < 275;
```

Result:

PRODUCTDESCRIPTION	PRODUCTSTANDARDPRICE
End Table	175
Computer Desk	250
Coffee Table	200

As stated before, in this text, we show results (except where noted) in the style of Oracle, which means that column headings are in all capital letters. If this is too annoying for users, then the data names should be defined with an underscore between the words rather than run-on words, or you can use an alias (described later in this section) to redefine a column heading for display.

Every SELECT statement returns a result table (a set of rows) when it executes. So, SQL is consistent—tables in, tables out of every query. This becomes important with more complex queries because we can use the result of one query (a table) as part of another query (e.g., we can include a SELECT statement as one of the elements in the FROM clause, creating a derived table, which we illustrate later in this chapter).

Two special keywords can be used along with the list of columns to display: DISTINCT and *. If the user does not wish to see duplicate rows in the result, SELECT DISTINCT may be used. In the preceding example, if the other computer desk carried by Pine Valley Furniture had also cost $250, the results of the query would have had duplicate rows. SELECT DISTINCT ProductDescription would display a result table without the duplicate rows. SELECT *, where * is used as a wildcard to indicate all columns, displays all columns from all the items in the FROM clause.

Also, note that the clauses of a SELECT statement must be kept in order, or syntax error messages will occur and the query will not execute. It may also be necessary to qualify the names of the database objects according to the SQL version being used. If there is any ambiguity in an SQL command, you must indicate exactly from which table, derived table, or view the requested data are to come. For example, in Figure 6-3 CustomerID is a column in both Customer_T and Order_T. When you own the database being used (i.e., the user created the tables) and you want CustomerID to come from Customer_T, specify it by asking for Customer_T. CustomerID. If you want CustomerID to come from Order_T, then ask for Order_T.CustomerID. Even if you don't care which table CustomerID comes from, it must be specified because SQL can't resolve the ambiguity without user direction. When you are allowed to use data created by someone else, you must also specify the owner of the table by adding the owner's user ID. Now a request to SELECT the CustomerID from Customer_T may look like this: OWNER_ID.Customer_T. CustomerID. The examples in this text, assume that the reader owns the tables or views being used, as the SELECT statements will be easier to read without the qualifiers. Qualifiers will be included where necessary and may always be included in statements if desired. Problems may occur when qualifiers are left out, but no problems will occur when they are included.

If typing the qualifiers and column names is wearisome (computer keyboards aren't, yet, built to accommodate the two-thumb cellphone texting technique), or if the column names will not be meaningful to those who are reading the reports, establish aliases for data names that will then be used for the rest of the query. Although SQL:1999 does not include aliases or synonyms, they are widely implemented and aid in readability and simplicity in query construction.

Query: What is the address of the customer named Home Furnishings? Use an alias, Name, for the customer name. (The AS clauses are bolded for emphasis only.)

```
SELECT CUST.CustomerName AS Name, CUST.CustomerAddress
    FROM ownerid.Customer_T AS Cust
        WHERE Name = 'Home Furnishings';
```

This retrieval statement will give the following result in many versions of SQL. In Oracle's SQL*Plus, the alias for the column cannot be used in the rest of the SELECT statement, except in a HAVING clause, so in order for the query to run, CustomerName would have to be used in the last line rather than Name. Notice that the column header prints as Name rather than CustomerName and that the table alias may be used in the SELECT clause even though it is not defined until the FROM clause.

Result:

NAME	CUSTOMERADDRESS
Home Furnishings	1900 Allard Ave.

You've likely concluded that SQL generates pretty plain output. Using an alias is a good way to make column headings more readable. (Aliases also have other uses, which we'll address later.) Many RDBMSs have other proprietary SQL clauses to improve the display of data. For example, Oracle has the COLUMN clause of the SELECT statement, which can be used to change the text for the column heading, change alignment of the column heading, reformat the column value, or control wrapping of data in a column, among other properties. You may want to investigate such capabilities for the RDBMS you are using.

When you use the SELECT clause to pick out the columns for a result table, the columns can be rearranged so that they will be ordered differently in the result table than in the original table. In fact, they will be displayed in the same order as they are included in the SELECT statement. Look back at Product_T in Figure 6-3 to see the different ordering of the base table from the result table for this query.

Query: List the unit price, product name, and product ID for all products in the Product table.

```
SELECT ProductStandardPrice, ProductDescription, ProductID
FROM Product_T;
```

Result:

PRODUCTSTANDARDPRICE	PRODUCTDESCRIPTION	PRODUCTID
175	End Table	1
200	Coffee Table	2
375	Computer Desk	3
650	Entertainment Center	4
325	Writer's Desk	5
750	8-Drawer Desk	6
800	Dining Table	7
250	Computer Desk	8

Using Expressions

The basic SELECT . . . FROM . . . WHERE clauses can be used with a single table in a number of ways. You can create expressions, which are mathematical manipulations of the data in the table, or take advantage of stored functions, such as SUM or AVG, to manipulate the chosen rows of data from the table. Mathematical manipulations can be constructed by using the + for addition, – for subtraction, * for multiplication, and / for division. These operators can be used with any numeric columns. Expressions are computed for each row of the result table, such as displaying the difference between the standard price and unit cost of a product, or they can involve computations of columns and functions, such as standard price of a product multiplied by the amount of that product sold on a particular order (which would require summing OrderedQuantities). Some systems also have an operand called modulo, usually indicated by %. A modulo is the integer remainder that results from dividing two integers. For example, 14 % 4 is 2 because 14/4 is 3, with a remainder of 2. The SQL standard supports year–month and day–time intervals, which makes it possible to perform date and time arithmetic (e.g., to calculate someone's age from today's date and a person's birthday).

Perhaps you would like to know the current standard price of each product and its future price if all prices were increased by 10 percent. Using SQL*Plus, here are the query and the results.

Query: What are the standard price and standard price if increased by 10 percent for every product?

```
SELECT ProductID, ProductStandardPrice, ProductStandardPrice*1.1 AS
Plus10Percent
  FROM Product_T;
```

Result:

PRODUCTID	PRODUCTSTANDARDPRICE	PLUS10PERCENT
2	200.0000	220.00000
3	375.0000	412.50000
1	175.0000	192.50000
8	250.0000	275.00000
7	800.0000	880.00000
5	325.0000	357.50000
4	650.0000	715.00000
6	750.0000	825.00000

The precedence rules for the order in which complex expressions are evaluated are the same as those used in other programming languages and in algebra. Expressions in parentheses will be calculated first. When parentheses do not establish order, multiplication and division will be completed first, from left to right, followed by addition and subtraction, also left to right. To avoid confusion, use parentheses to establish order. Where parentheses are nested, the innermost calculations will be completed first.

Using Functions

Standard SQL identifies a wide variety of mathematical, string and date manipulation, and other functions. We will illustrate some of the mathematical functions in this section. You will want to investigate what functions are available with the DBMS you are using, some of which may be proprietary to that DBMS. The standard functions include the following:

Mathematical	MIN, MAX, COUNT, SUM, ROUND (to round up a number to a specific number of decimal places), TRUNC (to truncate insignificant digits), and MOD (for modular arithmetic)
String	LOWER (to change to all lower case), UPPER (to change to all capital letters), INITCAP (to change to only an initial capital letter), CONCAT (to concatenate), SUBSTR (to isolate certain character positions), and COALESCE (finding the first not NULL values in a list of columns)
Date	NEXT_DAY (to compute the next date in sequence), ADD_MONTHS (to compute a date a given number of months before or after a given date), and MONTHS_BETWEEN (to compute the number of months between specified dates)
Analytical	TOP (find the top n values in a set, e.g., the top 5 customers by total annual sales)

Perhaps you want to know the average standard price of all inventory items. To get the overall average value, use the AVG stored function. We can name the resulting expression with an alias, AveragePrice. Using SQL*Plus, here are the query and the results.

Query: What is the average standard price for all products in inventory?

```
SELECT AVG (ProductStandardPrice) AS AveragePrice
FROM Product_T;
```

Result:

AVERAGEPRICE
     440.625

SQL:1999 stored functions include ANY, AVG, COUNT, EVERY, GROUPING, MAX, MIN, SOME, and SUM. SQL:2008 adds LN, EXP, POWER, SQRT, FLOOR, CEILING, and WIDTH_BUCKET. New functions tend to be added with each new SQL standard, and more functions have been added in SQL:2003 and SQL:2008, many of which are for advanced analytical processing of data (e.g., calculating moving averages and statistical sampling of data). As seen in the above example, functions such as COUNT, MIN, MAX, SUM, and AVG of specified columns in the column list of a SELECT command may be used to specify that the resulting answer table is to contain aggregated data instead of row-level data. Using any of these aggregate functions will give a one-row answer.

Query: How many different items were ordered on order number 1004?

```
SELECT COUNT (*)
  FROM OrderLine_T
    WHERE OrderID = 1004;
```

Result:

COUNT (*)
    2

It seems that it would be simple enough to list order number 1004 by changing the query.

Query: How many different items were ordered on order number 1004, and what are they?

```
SELECT ProductID, COUNT (*)
  FROM OrderLine_T
    WHERE OrderID = 1004;
```

In Oracle, here is the result.

Result:

ERROR at line 1:
ORA-00937: not a single-group group function

And in Microsoft SQL Server, the result is as follows.

Result:

Column 'OrderLine_T.ProductID' is invalid in the select list because
it is not contained in an Aggregate function and there is no
GROUP BY clause.

The problem is that ProductID returns two values, 6 and 8, for the two rows selected, whereas COUNT returns one aggregate value, 2, for the set of rows with ID = 1004. In most implementations, SQL cannot return both a row value and a set value; users must run two separate queries, one that returns row information and one that returns set information.

A similar issue arises if we try to find the difference between the standard price of each product and the overall average standard price (which we calculated above). You might think the query would be

```
SELECT ProductStandardPrice – AVG(ProductStandardPrice)
   FROM Product_T;
```

However, again we have mixed a column value with an aggregate, which will cause an error. Remember that the FROM list can contain tables, derived tables, and views. One approach to developing a correct query is to make the aggregate the result of a derived table, as we do in the following sample query.

Query: Display for each product the difference between its standard price and the overall average standard price of all products.

```
SELECT ProductStandardPrice – PriceAvg AS Difference
   FROM Product_T, (SELECT AVG(ProductStandardPrice) AS PriceAvg
      FROM Product_T);
```

Result:

DIFFERENCE
   −240.63
   −65.63
   −265.63
   −190.63
   359.38
   −115.63
   209.38
   309.38

Also, it is easy to confuse the functions COUNT (*) and COUNT. The function COUNT (*), used in the previous query, counts all rows selected by a query, regardless of whether any of the rows contain null values. COUNT tallies only rows that contain values; it ignores all null values.

SUM and AVG can only be used with numeric columns. COUNT, COUNT (*), MIN, and MAX can be used with any data type. Using MIN on a text column, for example, will find the lowest value in the column, the one whose first column is closest to the beginning of the alphabet. SQL implementations interpret the order of the alphabet differently. For example, some systems may start with A–Z, then a–z, and then 0–9 and special characters. Others treat upper- and lowercase letters as being equivalent. Still others start with some special characters, then proceed to numbers, letters, and other special characters. Here is the query to ask for the first ProductName in Product_T alphabetically, which was done using the AMERICAN character set in Oracle 11g.

Query: Alphabetically, what is the first product name in the Product table?

```
SELECT MIN (ProductDescription)
   FROM Product_T;
```

It gives the following result, which demonstrates that numbers are sorted before letters in this character set. [Note: The following result is from Oracle. Microsoft SQL Server returns the same result but labels the column (No column name) in SQL Query Analyzer, unless the query specifies a name for the result.]

Result:

MIN(PRODUCTDESCRIPTION)
8-Drawer Desk

Using Wildcards

The use of the asterisk (*) as a wildcard in a SELECT statement has been previously shown. Wildcards may also be used in the WHERE clause when an exact match is not possible. Here, the keyword LIKE is paired with wildcard characters and usually a string containing the characters that are known to be desired matches. The wildcard character, %, is used to represent any collection of characters. Thus, using LIKE '%Desk' when searching ProductDescription will find all different types of desks carried by Pine Valley Furniture Company. The underscore (_) is used as a wildcard character to represent exactly one character rather than any collection of characters. Thus, using LIKE '_-drawer' when searching ProductName will find any products with specified drawers, such as 3-, 5-, or 8-drawer dressers.

Using Comparison Operators

With the exception of the very first SQL example in this section, we have used the equality comparison operator in our WHERE clauses. The first example used the greater (less) than operator. The most common comparison operators for SQL implementations are listed in Table 6-3. (Different SQL DBMSs can use different comparison operators.) You are used to thinking about using comparison operators with numeric data, but you can also use them with character data and dates in SQL. The query shown here asks for all orders placed after 10/24/2010.

Query: Which orders have been placed since 10/24/2010?

```
SELECT OrderID, OrderDate
   FROM Order_T
      WHERE OrderDate > '24-OCT-2010';
```

Notice that the date is enclosed in single quotes and that the format of the date is different from that shown in Figure 6-3, which was taken from Microsoft Access. The query was run in SQL*Plus. You should check the reference manual for the SQL language you are using to see how dates are to be formatted in queries and for data input.

TABLE 6-3 Comparison Operators in SQL

Operator	Meaning
=	Equal to
>	Greater than
>=	Greater than or equal to
<	Less than
<=	Less than or equal to
<>	Not equal to
!=	Not equal to

Result:

ORDERID	ORDERDATE
1007	27-OCT-10
1008	30-OCT-10
1009	05-NOV-10
1010	05-NOV-10

Query: What furniture does Pine Valley carry that isn't made of cherry?

```
SELECT ProductDescription, ProductFinish
   FROM Product_T
      WHERE ProductFinish != 'Cherry';
```

Result:

PRODUCTDESCRIPTION	PRODUCTFINISH
Coffee Table	Natural Ash
Computer Desk	Natural Ash
Entertainment Center	Natural Maple
8-Drawer Desk	White Ash
Dining Table	Natural Ash
Computer Desk	Walnut

Using Null Values

Columns that are defined without the NOT NULL clause may be empty, and this may be a significant fact for an organization. You will recall that a null value means that a column is missing a value; the value is not zero or blank or any special code—there simply is no value. We have already seen that functions may produce different results when null values are present than when a column has a value of zero in all qualified rows. It is not uncommon, then, to first explore whether there are null values before deciding how to write other commands, or it may be that you simply want to see data about table rows where there are missing values. For example, before undertaking a postal mail advertising campaign, you might want to pose the following query.

Query: Display all customers for whom we do not know their postal code.

SELECT * FROM Customer_T WHERE CustomerPostalCode IS NULL;

Result:

Fortunately, this query returns 0 rows in the result in our sample database, so we can mail advertisements to all our customers because we know their postal codes. The term IS NOT NULL returns results for rows where the qualified column has a non-null value. This allows us to deal with rows that have values in a critical column, ignoring other rows.

Using Boolean Operators

You probably have taken a course or part of a course on finite or discrete mathematics—logic, Venn diagrams, and set theory, oh my! Remember we said that SQL is a set-oriented language, so there are many opportunities to use what you learned in finite math to write complex SQL queries. Some complex questions can be answered by adjusting the WHERE clause further. The Boolean or logical operators AND, OR, and NOT can be used to good purpose:

AND	Joins two or more conditions and returns results only when all conditions are true.
OR	Joins two or more conditions and returns results when any conditions are true.
NOT	Negates an expression.

If multiple Boolean operators are used in an SQL statement, NOT is evaluated first, then AND, then OR. For example, consider the following query.

Query A: List product name, finish, and standard price for all desks and all tables that cost more than $300 in the Product table.

```
SELECT ProductDescription, ProductFinish, ProductStandardPrice
   FROM Product_T
     WHERE ProductDescription LIKE '%Desk'
       OR ProductDescription LIKE '%Table'
       AND ProductStandardPrice > 300;
```

Result:

PRODUCTDESCRIPTION	PRODUCTFINISH	PRODUCTSTANDARDPRICE
Computer Desk	Natural Ash	375
Writer's Desk	Cherry	325
8-Drawer Desk	White Ash	750
Dining Table	Natural Ash	800
Computer Desk	Walnut	250

All of the desks are listed, even the computer desk that costs less than $300. Only one table is listed; the less expensive ones that cost less than $300 are not included.

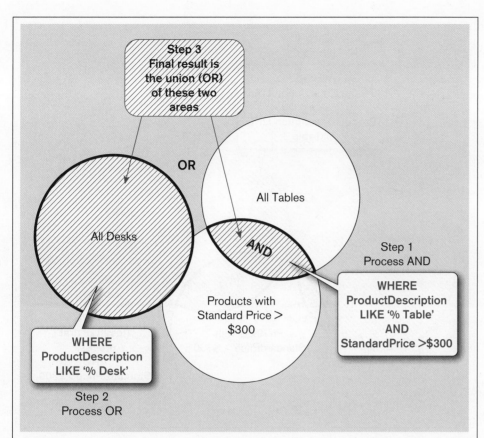

FIGURE 6-7 Boolean query A without the use of parentheses

With this query (illustrated in Figure 6-7), the AND will be processed first, returning all tables with a standard price greater than $300. Then the part of the query before the OR is processed, returning all desks, regardless of cost. Finally, the results of the two parts of the query are combined (OR), with the final result of all desks along with all tables with standard price greater than $300.

If we had wanted to return only desks *and* tables costing more than $300, we should have put parentheses after the WHERE and before the AND, as shown in Query B below. Figure 6-8 shows the difference in processing caused by the judicious use of parentheses in the query. The result is all desks and tables with a standard price of more than $300, indicated by the filled area with the darker horizontal lines. The walnut computer desk has a standard price of $250 and is not included.

Query B: List product name, finish, and standard price for all desks and tables in the PRODUCT table that cost more than $300.

```
SELECT ProductDescription, ProductFinish, ProductStandardPrice
  FROM Product_T;
  WHERE (ProductDescription LIKE '%Desk'
    OR ProductDescription LIKE '%Table')
    AND ProductStandardPrice > 300;
```

The results follow. Only products with unit price greater than $300 are included.

Result:

PRODUCTDESCRIPTION	PRODUCTFINISH	PRODUCTSTANDARDPRICE
Computer Desk	Natural Ash	375
Writer's Desk	Cherry	325
8-Drawer Desk	White Ash	750
Dining Table	Natural Ash	800

**FIGURE 6-8 Boolean query B
with the use of parentheses**

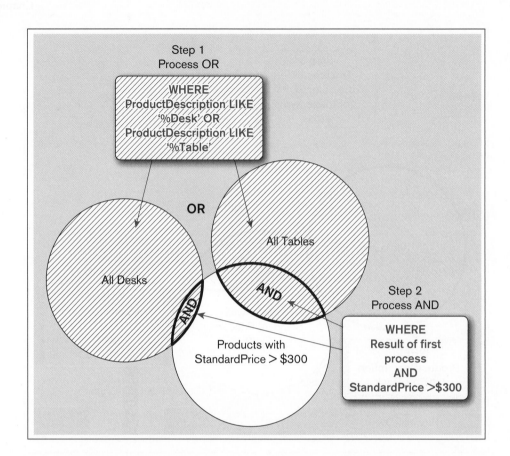

This example illustrates why SQL is considered a set-oriented, not a record-oriented, language. (C, Java, and Cobol are examples of record-oriented languages because they must process one record, or row, of a table at a time.) To answer this query, SQL will find the set of rows that are Desk products, and then it will union (i.e., merge) that set with the set of rows that are Table products. Finally, it will intersect (i.e., find common rows) the resultant set from this union with the set of rows that have a standard price above $300. If indexes can be used, the work is done even faster, because SQL will create sets of index entries that satisfy each qualification and do the set manipulation on those index entry sets, each of which takes up less space and can be manipulated much more quickly. You will see in Chapter 7 even more dramatic ways in which the set-oriented nature of SQL works for more complex queries involving multiple tables.

Using Ranges for Qualification

The comparison operators < and > are used to establish a range of values. The keywords BETWEEN and NOT BETWEEN can also be used. For example, to find products with a standard price between $200 and $300, the following query could be used.

Query: Which products in the Product table have a standard price between $200 and $300?

```
SELECT ProductDescription, ProductStandardPrice
  FROM Product_T
     WHERE ProductStandardPrice > 199 AND ProductStandardPrice < 301;
```

Result:

PRODUCTDESCRIPTION	PRODUCTSTANDARDPRICE
Coffee Table	200
Computer Desk	250

The same result will be returned by the following query.

Query: Which products in the PRODUCT table have a standard price between $200 and $300?

```
SELECT ProductDescription, ProductStandardPrice
    FROM Product_T
        WHERE ProductStandardPrice BETWEEN 200 AND 300;
```

Result: Same as previous query.

Adding NOT before BETWEEN in this query will return all the other products in Product_T because their prices are less than $200 or more than $300.

Using Distinct Values

Sometimes when returning rows that don't include the primary key, duplicate rows will be returned. For example, look at this query and the results that it returns.

Query: What order numbers are included in the OrderLine table?

```
SELECT OrderID
    FROM OrderLine_T;
```

Eighteen rows are returned, and many of them are duplicates because many orders were for multiple items.

Result:

ORDERID
1001
1001
1001
1002
1003
1004
1004
1005
1006
1006
1006
1007
1007
1008
1008
1009
1009
1010

18 rows selected.

Do we really need the redundant OrderIDs in this result? If we add the keyword DISTINCT, then only 1 occurrence of each OrderID will be returned, 1 for each of the 10 orders represented in the table.

Query: What are the distinct order numbers included in the OrderLine table?

```
SELECT DISTINCT OrderID
   FROM OrderLine_T;
```

Result:

ORDERID
1001
1002
1003
1004
1005
1006
1007
1008
1009
1010

10 rows selected.

DISTINCT and its counterpart, ALL, can be used only once in a SELECT statement. It comes after SELECT and before any columns or expressions are listed. If a SELECT statement projects more than one column, only rows that are identical for every column will be eliminated. Thus, if the previous statement also includes OrderedQuantity, 14 rows are returned because there are now only 4 duplicate rows rather than 8. For example, both items ordered on OrderID 1004 were for 2 items, so the second pairing of 1004 and 2 will be eliminated.

Query: What are the unique combinations of order number and order quantity included in the OrderLine table?

```
SELECT DISTINCT OrderID, OrderedQuantity
   FROM OrderLine_T;
```

Result:

ORDERID	ORDEREDQUANTITY
1001	1
1001	2
1002	5
1003	3
1004	2
1005	4
1006	1
1006	2
1007	2
1007	3
1008	3
1009	2
1009	3
1010	10

14 rows selected.

Using IN and NOT IN with Lists

To match a list of values, consider using IN.

Query: List all customers who live in warmer states.

```
SELECT CustomerName, CustomerCity, CustomerState
  FROM Customer_T
    WHERE CustomerState IN ('FL', 'TX', 'CA', 'HI');
```

Result:

CUSTOMERNAME	CUSTOMERCITY	CUSTOMERSTATE
Contemporary Casuals	Gainesville	FL
Value Furniture	Plano	TX
Impressions	Sacramento	CA
California Classics	Santa Clara	CA
M and H Casual Furniture	Clearwater	FL
Seminole Interiors	Seminole	FL
Kaneohe Homes	Kaneohe	HI
7 rows selected.		

IN is particularly useful in SQL statements that use subqueries, which will be covered in Chapter 7. The use of IN is also very consistent with the set nature of SQL. Very simply, the list (set of values) inside the parentheses after IN can be literals, as illustrated here, or can be a SELECT statement with a single result column, the result of which will be plugged in as the set of values for comparison. In fact, some SQL programmers always use IN, even when the set in parentheses after IN includes only one item. Similarly, any "table" of the FROM clause can be itself a derived table defined by including a SELECT statement in parentheses in the FROM clause (as we saw earlier, with the query about the difference between the standard price of each product and the average standard price of all products). The ability to include a SELECT statement anyplace within SQL where a set is involved is a very powerful and useful feature of SQL, and, of course, totally consistent with SQL being a set-oriented language, as illustrated in Figures 6-7 and 6-8.

Sorting Results: The ORDER BY Clause

Looking at the preceding results, it may seem that it would make more sense to list the California customers, followed by the Floridians, Hawaiians, and Texans. That brings us to the other three basic parts of the SQL statement:

ORDER BY	Sorts the final results rows in ascending or descending order.
GROUP BY	Groups rows in an intermediate results table where the values in those rows are the same for one or more columns.
HAVING	Can only be used following a GROUP BY and acts as a secondary WHERE clause, returning only those groups that meet a specified condition.

So, we can order the customers by adding an ORDER BY clause.

Query: List customer, city, and state for all customers in the Customer table whose address is Florida, Texas, California, or Hawaii. List the customers alphabetically by state and alphabetically by customer within each state.

```
SELECT CustomerName, CustomerCity, CustomerState
  FROM Customer_T
    WHERE CustomerState IN ('FL', 'TX', 'CA', 'HI')
      ORDER BY CustomerState, CustomerName;
```

Now the results are easier to read.

Result:

CUSTOMERNAME	CUSTOMERCITY	CUSTOMERSTATE
California Classics	Santa Clara	CA
Impressions	Sacramento	CA
Contemporary Casuals	Gainesville	FL
M and H Casual Furniture	Clearwater	FL
Seminole Interiors	Seminole	FL
Kaneohe Homes	Kaneohe	HI
Value Furniture	Plano	TX
7 rows selected.		

Notice that all customers from each state are listed together, and within each state, customer names are alphabetized. The sorting order is determined by the order in which the columns are listed in the ORDER BY clause; in this case, states were alphabetized first, then customer names. If sorting from high to low, use DESC as a keyword, placed after the column used to sort. Instead of typing the column names in the ORDER BY clause, you can use their column positions in the select list; for example, in the preceding query, we could have written the clause as

```
ORDER BY 3, 1;
```

For cases in which there are many rows in the result table but you need to see only a few of them, many SQL systems (including MySQL) support a LIMIT clause, such as the following, which would show only the first five rows of the result:

```
ORDER BY 3, 1 LIMIT 5;
```

The following would show five rows after skipping the first 30 rows:

```
ORDER BY 3, 1 LIMIT 30, 5;
```

How are NULLs sorted? Null values may be placed first or last, before or after columns that have values. Where the NULLs will be placed will depend upon the SQL implementation.

Categorizing Results: The GROUP BY Clause

Scalar aggregate

A single value returned from an SQL query that includes an aggregate function.

Vector aggregate

Multiple values returned from an SQL query that includes an aggregate function.

GROUP BY is particularly useful when paired with aggregate functions, such as SUM or COUNT. GROUP BY divides a table into subsets (by groups); then an aggregate function can be used to provide summary information for that group. The single value returned by the previous aggregate function examples is called a **scalar aggregate**. When aggregate functions are used in a GROUP BY clause and several values are returned, they are called **vector aggregates**.

Query: Count the number of customers with addresses in each state to which we ship.

```
SELECT CustomerState, COUNT (CustomerState)
    FROM Customer_T
        GROUP BY CustomerState;
```

Result:

CUSTOMERSTATE	COUNT(CUSTOMERSTATE)
CA	2
CO	1
FL	3
HI	1
MI	1
NJ	2
NY	1
PA	1
TX	1
UT	1
WA	1
11 rows selected.	

It is also possible to nest groups within groups; the same logic is used as when sorting multiple items.

Query: Count the number of customers with addresses in each city to which we ship. List the cities by state.

```
SELECT CustomerState, CustomerCity, COUNT (CustomerCity)
    FROM Customer_T
        GROUP BY CustomerState, CustomerCity;
```

Although the GROUP BY clause seems straightforward, it can produce unexpected results if the logic of the clause is forgotten (and this is a common "gotcha" for novice SQL coders). When a GROUP BY is included, the columns allowed to be specified in the SELECT clause are limited. Only a column with a single value for each group can be included. In the previous query, each group is identified by the combination of a city and its state. The SELECT statement includes both the city and state columns. This works because each combination of city and state is one COUNT value. But if the SELECT clause of the first query in this section had also included city, that statement would fail because the GROUP BY is only by state. Because a state can have more than one city, the requirement that each value in the SELECT clause have only one value in the GROUP BY group is not met, and SQL will not be able to present the city information so that it makes sense. *If you write queries using the following rule, your queries will work*: Each column referenced in the SELECT statement must be referenced in the GROUP BY clause, unless the column is an argument for an aggregate function included in the SELECT clause.

Qualifying Results by Categories: The HAVING Clause

The HAVING clause acts like a WHERE clause, but it identifies groups, rather than rows, that meet a criterion. Therefore, you will usually see a HAVING clause following a GROUP BY clause.

Query: Find only states with more than one customer.

```
SELECT CustomerState, COUNT (CustomerState)
  FROM Customer_T
    GROUP BY CustomerState
    HAVING COUNT (CustomerState) > 1;
```

This query returns a result that has removed all states (groups) with one customer. Remember that using WHERE here would not work because WHERE doesn't allow aggregates; further, WHERE qualifies a set of rows, whereas HAVING qualifies a set of groups. As with WHERE, the HAVING qualification can be compared to the result of a SELECT statement, which computes the value for comparison (i.e., a set with only one value is still a set).

Result:

CUSTOMERSTATE	COUNT(CUSTOMERSTATE)
CA	2
FL	3
NJ	2

To include more than one condition in the HAVING clause, use AND, OR, and NOT just as in the WHERE clause. In summary, here is one last command that includes all six clauses; remember that they must be used in this order.

Query: List, in alphabetical order, the product finish and the average standard price for each finish for selected finishes having an average standard price less than 750.

```
SELECT ProductFinish, AVG (ProductStandardPrice)
  FROM Product_T
    WHERE ProductFinish IN ('Cherry', 'Natural Ash', 'Natural Maple',
    'White Ash')
      GROUP BY ProductFinish
        HAVING AVG (ProductStandardPrice) < 750
        ORDER BY ProductFinish;
```

Result:

PRODUCTFINISH	AVG(PRODUCTSTANDARDPRICE)
Cherry	250
Natural Ash	458.333333
Natural Maple	650

Figure 6-9 shows the order in which SQL processes the clauses of a statement. Arrows indicate the paths that may be followed. Remember, only the SELECT and FROM clauses are mandatory. Notice that the processing order is different from the order of the syntax used to create the statement. As each clause is processed, an intermediate results table is produced that will be used for the next clause. Users do not see the intermediate results tables; they see only the final results. A query can be debugged by remembering the order shown in Figure 6-9. Take out the optional clauses and then add them back in one at a time in the order in which they will be processed. In this way, intermediate results can be seen and problems often can be spotted.

FIGURE 6-9 SQL statement processing order (based on van der Lans, 2006, p. 100)

```
FROM
Identifies
involved tables

        WHERE
        Finds all rows
        meeting stated
        condition(s)

            GROUP BY
            Organizes rows
            according to values
            in stated column(s)

                HAVING
                Finds all groups
                meeting stated
                condition(s)

                    SELECT
                    Identifies
                    columns

                        ORDER BY
                        Sorts rows

                            results
```

Using and Defining Views

The SQL syntax shown in Figure 6-6 demonstrates the creation of four **base tables** in a database schema using Oracle 11g SQL. These tables, which are used to store data physically in the database, correspond to relations in the logical database design. By using SQL queries with any RDBMS, it is possible to create **virtual tables**, or **dynamic views**, whose contents materialize when referenced. These views may often be manipulated in the same way as a base table can be manipulated, through SQL SELECT queries.

The often-stated purpose of a view is to simplify query commands, but a view may also improve data security and significantly enhance programming consistency and productivity for a database. To highlight the convenience of using a view, consider Pine Valley's invoice processing. Construction of the company's invoice requires access to the four tables from the Pine Valley database of Figure 6-3: Customer_T, Order_T, OrderLine_T, and Product_T. A novice database user may make mistakes or be unproductive in properly formulating queries involving so many tables. A view allows us to predefine this association into a single virtual table as part of the database. With this view, a user who wants only customer invoice data does not have to reconstruct the joining of tables to produce the report or any subset of it. Table 6-4 summarizes the pros and cons of using views.

A view, Invoice_V, is defined by specifying an SQL query (SELECT . . . FROM . . . WHERE) that has the view as its result. If you decide to try this query as is, without

Base table

A table in the relational data model containing the inserted raw data. Base tables correspond to the relations that are identified in the database's conceptual schema.

Virtual table

A table constructed automatically as needed by a DBMS. Virtual tables are not maintained as real data.

Dynamic view

A virtual table that is created dynamically upon request by a user. A dynamic view is not a temporary table. Rather, its definition is stored in the system catalog, and the contents of the view are materialized as a result of an SQL query that uses the view.

TABLE 6-4 Pros and Cons of Using Dynamic Views	
Positive Aspects	**Negative Aspects**
Simplify query commands	Use processing time re-creating the view each time it is referenced
Help provide data security and confidentiality	May or may not be directly updateable
Improve programmer productivity	
Contain most current base table data	
Use little storage space	
Provide a customized view for a user	
Establish physical data independence	

selecting additional attributes, remove the comma after OrderedQuantity. The example assumes you will elect to include additional attributes in the query.

> *Query:* What are the data elements necessary to create an invoice for a customer? Save this query as a view named Invoice_V.

```
CREATE VIEW Invoice_V AS
  SELECT Customer_T.CustomerID, CustomerAddress, Order_T.OrderID,
  Product_T.ProductID,ProductStandardPrice,
  OrderedQuantity, and other columns as required
    FROM Customer_T, Order_T, OrderLine_T, Product_T
      WHERE Customer_T.CustomerID = Order_T.CustomerID
      AND Order_T.OrderID = OrderLine_T.OrderD
      AND Product_T.ProductID = OrderLine_T.ProductID;
```

The SELECT clause specifies, or projects, what data elements (columns) are to be included in the view table. The FROM clause lists the tables and views involved in the view development. The WHERE clause specifies the names of the common columns used to join Customer_T to Order_T to OrderLine_T to Product_T. (You'll learn about joining in Chapter 7, but for now remember the foreign keys that were defined to reference other tables; these are the columns used for joining.) Because a view is a table, and one of the relational properties of tables is that the order of rows is immaterial, the rows in a view may not be sorted. But queries that refer to this view may display their results in any desired sequence.

We can see the power of such a view when building a query to generate an invoice for order number 1004. Rather than specify the joining of four tables, we can have the query include all relevant data elements from the view table, Invoice_V.

> *Query:* What are the data elements necessary to create an invoice for order number 1004?

```
SELECT CustomerID, CustomerAddress, ProductID,
  OrderedQuantity, and other columns as required
    FROM Invoice_V
      WHERE OrderID = 1004;
```

A dynamic view is a virtual table; it is constructed automatically, as needed, by the DBMS and is not maintained as persistent data. Any SQL SELECT statement may be used to create a view. The persistent data are stored in base tables, those that have been defined by CREATE TABLE commands. A dynamic view always contains the most current derived values and is thus superior in terms of data currency to constructing a temporary real table from several base tables. Also, in comparison to a temporary real table, a view consumes very little storage space. A view is costly, however, because its contents must be calculated each time they are requested (that is, each time the view is used in an SQL statement).

A view may join together multiple tables or views and may contain derived (or virtual) columns. For example, if a user of the Pine Valley Furniture database only wants to know the total value of orders placed for each furniture product, a view for this can be created from Invoice_V. The following example in SQL*Plus illustrates how this is done with Oracle, although this can be done with any RDBMS that supports views.

Query: What is the total value of orders placed for each furniture product?

```
CREATE VIEW OrderTotals_V AS
    SELECT ProductID Product, SUM (ProductStandardPrice*OrderedQuantity)
    Total
        FROM Invoice_V
        GROUP BY ProductID;
```

We can assign a different name (an alias) to a view column rather than use the associated base table or expression column name. Here, Product is a renaming of ProductID, local to only this view. Total is the column name given the expression for total sales of each product. (Total may not be a legal alias with some relational DBMSs because it might be a reserved word for a proprietary function of the DBMS; you always have to be careful when defining columns and aliases not to use a reserved word.) The expression can now be referenced via this view in subsequent queries as if it were a column rather than a derived expression. Defining views based on other views can cause problems. For example, if we redefine Invoice_V so that StandardPrice is not included, then OrderTotals_V will no longer work because it will not be able to locate standard unit prices.

Views can also help establish security. Tables and columns that are not included will not be obvious to the user of the view. Restricting access to a view with GRANT and REVOKE statements adds another layer of security. For example, granting some users access rights to aggregated data, such as averages, in a view but denying them access to detailed base table data will not allow them to display the base table data.

Privacy and confidentiality of data can be achieved by creating views that restrict users to working with only the data they need to perform their assigned duties. If a clerical worker needs to work with employees' addresses but should not be able to access their compensation rates, they may be given access to a view that does not contain compensation information.

Summary

This chapter has introduced the SQL language for relational database definition (DDL), manipulation (DML), and control (DCL) languages, commonly used to define and query relational database management systems (RDBMSs). This standard has been criticized as having many flaws. In reaction to these criticisms and to increase the power of the language, extensions are constantly under review by the ANSI X3H2 committee and International Committee for Information Technology Standards (INCITS). The current generally implemented standard is SQL:1999, but SQL:2008 is being implemented by some RDBMSs.

The establishment of SQL standards and conformance certification tests has contributed to relational systems being the dominant form of new database development. Benefits of the SQL standards include reduced training costs, improved productivity, application portability and longevity, reduced dependence on single vendors, and improved cross-system communication.

The SQL environment includes an instance of an SQL DBMS along with accessible databases and associated users and programs. Each database is included in a catalog and has a schema that describes the database objects. Information contained in the catalog is maintained by the DBMS itself rather than by the users of the DBMS.

The SQL DDL commands are used to define a database, including its creation and the creation of its tables, indexes, and views. Referential integrity is also established through DDL commands. The SQL DML commands are used to load, update, and query the database through use of the SELECT command. DCL commands are used to establish user access to the database.

SQL commands may directly affect the base tables, which contain the raw data, or they may affect a database view that has been created. Changes and updates made to views may or may not be passed on to the base tables. The basic syntax of an SQL SELECT statement contains the following keywords: SELECT, FROM, WHERE,

ORDER BY, GROUP BY, and HAVING. SELECT determines which attributes will be displayed in the query results table. FROM determines which tables or views will be used in the query. WHERE sets the criteria of the query, including any joins of multiple tables that are necessary. ORDER BY determines the order in which the results will be displayed. GROUP BY is used to categorize results and

may return either scalar aggregates or vector aggregates. HAVING qualifies results by categories.

Understanding the basic SQL syntax presented in this chapter should enable the reader to start using SQL effectively and to build a deeper understanding of the possibilities for more complex querying with continued practice. Advanced SQL topics are covered in Chapter 7.

Chapter Review

Key Terms

Base table 223	Data definition language	Dynamic view 223	Schema 195
Catalog 194	(DDL) 195	Relational DBMS	Vector aggregate 220
Data control language	Data manipulation	(RDBMS) 194	Virtual table 223
(DCL) 196	language (DML) 195	Scalar aggregate 220	

Review Questions

1. Define each of the following terms:
   a. base table
   b. data definition language
   c. data manipulation language
   d. dynamic view
   e. referential integrity constraint
   f. relational DBMS (RDBMS)
   g. schema
   h. virtual table
2. Match the following terms to the appropriate definitions:
   _____ view
   _____ referential integrity constraint
   _____ dynamic view
   _____ SQL:2008
   _____ null value
   _____ scalar aggregate
   _____ vector aggregate
   _____ catalog
   _____ schema
   _____ host language

   a. list of values
   b. description of a database
   c. logical table
   d. missing or nonexistent value
   e. descriptions of database objects of a database
   f. programming language in which SQL commands are embedded
   g. established in relational data models by use of foreign keys
   h. view that exists as a table
   i. currently proposed standard relational query and definition language
   j. single value
3. Contrast the following terms:
   a. base table; view
   b. catalog; schema
4. Describe a relational DBMS (RDBMS), its underlying data model, its data storage structures, and how data relationships are established.
5. List six potential benefits of achieving an SQL standard that is widely accepted.
6. Describe the components and structure of a typical SQL environment.
7. Distinguish among data definition commands, data manipulation commands, and data control commands.
8. Explain some possible purposes of creating a view using SQL. In particular, explain how a view can be used to reinforce data security.

9. Explain why it is necessary to limit the kinds of updates performed on data when referencing data through a view.
10. Describe a set of circumstances for which using a view can save reprogramming effort.
11. Drawing on material covered in prior chapters, explain the factors to be considered in deciding whether to create a key index for a table in SQL.
12. Explain and provide at least one example of how to qualify the ownership of a table in SQL. What has to occur for one user to be allowed to use a table in a database owned by another user?
13. How is the order in which attributes appear in a result table changed? How are the column heading labels in a result table changed?
14. What is the difference between COUNT, COUNT DISTINCT, and COUNT(*) in SQL? When will these three commands generate the same and different results?
15. What is the evaluation order for the Boolean operators (AND, OR, NOT) in an SQL command? How can one be sure that the operators will work in the desired order rather than in this prescribed order?
16. If an SQL statement includes a GROUP BY clause, the attributes that can be requested in the SELECT statement will be limited. Explain that limitation.
17. Describe a situation in which you would need to write a query using the HAVING clause.
18. In what clause of a SELECT statement is an IN operator used? What follows the IN operator? What other SQL operator can sometimes be used to perform the same operation as the IN operator? Under what circumstances can this other operator be used?
19. Explain why SQL is called a set-oriented language.
20. When would the use of the LIKE keyword with the CREATE TABLE command be helpful?
21. What is an identity column? Explain the benefits of using the identity column capability in SQL.
22. In what order are the clauses of an SQL statement processed?
23. Within which clauses of an SQL statement can a derived table be defined?

24. In an ORDER BY clause, what are the two ways to refer to the columns to be used for sorting the results of the query?
25. Explain the purpose of the CHECK clause within a CREATE TABLE SQL command. Explain the purpose of the WITH CHECK OPTION in a CREATE VIEW SQL command.
26. What can be changed about a table definition, using the ALTER SQL command? Can you identify anything about a table definition that cannot be changed using the ALTER SQL command?
27. Is it possible to use both a WHERE clause and a HAVING clause in the same SQL SELECT statement? If so, what are the different purposes of these two clauses?

Problems and Exercises

Problems and Exercises 1 through 9 are based on the class scheduling 3NF relations along with some sample data shown in Figure 6-10. Not shown in this figure are data for an ASSIGNMENT relation, which represents a many-to-many relationship between faculty and sections.

1. Write a database description for each of the relations shown, using SQL DDL (shorten, abbreviate, or change any data names, as needed for your SQL version). Assume the following attribute data types:

StudentID (integer, primary key)
StudentName (25 characters)
FacultyID (integer, primary key)
FacultyName (25 characters)

STUDENT (StudentID, StudentName)

StudentID	StudentName
38214	Letersky
54907	Altvater
66324	Aiken
70542	Marra
...	

QUALIFIED (FacultyID, CourseID, DateQualified)

FacultyID	CourseID	DateQualified
2143	ISM 3112	9/1988
2143	ISM 3113	9/1988
3467	ISM 4212	9/1995
3467	ISM 4930	9/1996
4756	ISM 3113	9/1991
4756	ISM 3112	9/1991
...		

FACULTY (FacultyID, FacultyName)

FacultyID	FacultyName
2143	Birkin
3467	Berndt
4756	Collins
...	

SECTION (SectionNo, Semester, CourseID)

SectionNo	Semester	CourseID
2712	I-2008	ISM 3113
2713	I-2008	ISM 3113
2714	I-2008	ISM 4212
2715	I-2008	ISM 4930
...		

COURSE (CourseID, CourseName)

CourseID	CourseName
ISM 3113	Syst Analysis
ISM 3112	Syst Design
ISM 4212	Database
ISM 4930	Networking
...	

REGISTRATION (StudentID, SectionNo, Semester)

StudentID	SectionNo	Semester
38214	2714	I-2008
54907	2714	I-2008
54907	2715	I-2008
66324	2713	I-2008
...		

FIGURE 6-10 Class scheduling relations (missing ASSIGNMENT)

CourseID (8 characters, primary key)
CourseName (15 characters)
DateQualified (date)
SectionNo (integer, primary key)
Semester (7 characters)

2. Use SQL to define the following view:

StudentID	StudentName
38214	Letersky
54907	Altvater
54907	Altvater
66324	Aiken

3. Because of referential integrity, before any row can be entered into the SECTION table, the CourseID to be entered must already exist in the COURSE table. Write an SQL assertion that will enforce this constraint.

4. Write SQL data definition commands for each of the following queries:
   a. How would you add an attribute, Class, to the Student table?
   b. How would you remove the Registration table?
   c. How would you change the FacultyName field from 25 characters to 40 characters?

5. Write SQL commands for the following:
   a. Create two different forms of the INSERT command to add a student with a student ID of 65798 and last name Lopez to the Student table.
   b. Now write a command that will remove Lopez from the Student table.
   c. Create an SQL command that will modify the name of course ISM 4212 from Database to Introduction to Relational Databases.

6. Write SQL queries to answer the following questions:
   a. Which students have an ID number that is less than 50000?
   b. What is the name of the faculty member whose ID is 4756?
   c. What is the smallest section number used in the first semester of 2008?

7. Write SQL queries to answer the following questions:
   a. How many students are enrolled in Section 2714 in the first semester of 2008?
   b. Which faculty members have qualified to teach a course since 1993? List the faculty ID, course, and date of qualification.

8. Write SQL queries to answer the following questions:
   a. Which students are enrolled in Database and Networking? (Hint: Use SectionNo for each class so you can determine the answer from the Registration table by itself.)
   b. Which instructors cannot teach both Syst Analysis and Syst Design?
   c. Which courses were taught in the first semester of 2008 but not in the second semester of 2008?

9. Write SQL queries to answer the following questions:
   a. What are the courses included in the Section table? List each course only once.
   b. List all students in alphabetical order by StudentName.
   c. List the students who are enrolled in each course in Semester I, 2008. Group the students by the sections in which they are enrolled.
   d. List the courses available. Group them by course prefix. (ISM is the only prefix shown, but there are many others throughout the university.)

Problems and Exercises 10 through 15 are based on the relations shown in Figure 6-11. The database tracks an adult literacy program. Tutors complete a certification class offered by the agency. Students complete an assessment interview that results in a report for the tutor and a recorded Read score. When matched with a student, a tutor meets with the student for one to four hours per week. Some students work with the same tutor for years, some for less than a month. Other students change tutors if their learning style does not match the tutor's tutoring style. Many tutors are retired and are available to tutor only part of the year. Tutor status is recorded as Active, Temp Stop, or Dropped.

10. How many tutors have a status of Temp Stop? Which tutors are active?
11. What are the TutorIDs for tutors who have not yet tutored anyone?
12. How many students were matched with someone in the first five months of the year?
13. Which student has the highest Read score?
14. How long had each student studied in the adult literacy program?
15. What is the average length of time a student stayed (or has stayed) in the program?

Problems and Exercises 16 through 43 are based on the entire ("big" version) Pine Valley Furniture Company database. Note: Depending on what DBMS **PINE VALLEY FURNITURE**
you are using, some field names may have changed to avoid using reserved words for the DBMS. When you first use the DBMS, check the table definitions to see what the exact field names are for the DBMS you are using. The data is available at **www.teradatauniversitynetwork.com**.

16. Modify the Product_T table by adding an attribute QtyOnHand that can be used to track the finished goods inventory. The field should be an integer field of five characters and should accept only positive numbers.

17. Enter sample data of your own choosing into QtyOnHand in the Product_T table. Test the modification you made in Problem and Exercise 16 by attempting to update a product by changing the inventory to 10,000 units. Test it again by changing the inventory for the product to –10 units. If you do not receive error messages and are successful in making these changes, then you did not establish appropriate constraints in Problem and Exercise 16.

18. Add an order to the Order_T table and include a sample value for every attribute.
   a. First, look at the data in the Customer_T table and enter an order from any one of those customers.
   b. Enter an order from a new customer. Unless you have also inserted information about the new customer in the Customer_T table, your entry of the order data should be rejected. Referential integrity constraints should prevent you from entering an order if there is no information about the customer.

19. Use the Pine Valley database to answer the following questions:
   a. How many work centers does Pine Valley have?
   b. Where are they located?

20. List the employees whose last names begin with an *L*.

21. Which employees were hired during 1999?

22. List the customers who live in California or Washington. Order them by zip code, from high to low.

23. List all raw materials that are made of cherry and that have dimensions (thickness and width) of 12 by 12.

FIGURE 6-11 Adult literacy program (for Problems and Exercises 10 through 15)

TUTOR (TutorID, CertDate, Status)

TutorID	CertDate	Status
100	1/05/2008	Active
101	1/05/2008	Temp Stop
102	1/05/2008	Dropped
103	5/22/2008	Active
104	5/22/2008	Active
105	5/22/2008	Temp Stop
106	5/22/2008	Active

STUDENT (StudentID, Read)

StudentID	Read
3000	2.3
3001	5.6
3002	1.3
3003	3.3
3004	2.7
3005	4.8
3006	7.8
3007	1.5

MATCH HISTORY (MatchID, TutorID, StudentID, StartDate, EndDate)

MatchID	TutorID	StudentID	StartDate	EndDate
1	100	3000	1/10/2008	
2	101	3001	1/15/2008	5/15/2008
3	102	3002	2/10/2008	3/01/2008
4	106	3003	5/28/2008	
5	103	3004	6/01/2008	6/15/2008
6	104	3005	6/01/2008	6/28/2008
7	104	3006	6/01/2008	

24. List the MaterialID, MaterialName, Material, MaterialStandardPrice, and Thickness for all raw materials made of cherry, pine, or walnut. Order the listing by Material, MaterialStandardPrice, and Thickness.

25. Display the product line ID and the average standard price for all products in each product line.

26. For every product that has been ordered, display the product ID and the total quantity ordered (label this result TotalOrdered). List the most popular product first and the least popular last.

27. For each customer, list the CustomerID and total number of orders placed.

28. For each salesperson, display a list of CustomerIDs.
29. Display the product ID and the number of orders placed for each product. Show the results in decreasing order by the number of times the product has been ordered and label this result column NumOrders.
30. For each customer, list the CustomerID and the total number of orders placed in 2010.
31. For each salesperson, list the total number of orders.
32. For each customer who had more than two orders, list the CustomerID and the total number of orders placed.
33. List all sales territories (TerritoryID) that have more than one salesperson.
34. Which product is ordered most frequently?
35. Display the territory ID and the number of salespersons in the territory for all territories that have more than one salesperson. Label the number of salespersons NumSalesPersons.
36. Display the SalesPersonID and a count of the number of orders for that salesperson for all salespersons except salespersons 3, 5, and 9. Write this query with as few clauses or components as possible, using the capabilities of SQL as much as possible.
37. For each salesperson, list the total number of orders by month for the year 2010. (Hint: If you are using Access, use the Month function. If you are using Oracle, convert the date to a string, using the TO_CHAR function, with the format string 'Mon' [i.e., TO_CHAR(order_date,'MON')]. If you are using another DBMS, you will need to investigate how to deal with months for this query.)
38. List MaterialName, Material, and Width for raw materials that are *not* cherry or oak and whose width is greater than 10 inches. Show how you constructed this query using a Venn diagram.

39. List ProductID, ProductDescription, ProductFinish, and ProductStandardPrice for oak products with a ProductStandardPrice greater than $400 or cherry products with a StandardPrice less than $300. Show how you constructed this query using a Venn diagram.
40. For each order, list the order ID, customer ID, order date, and most recent date among all orders. Show how you constructed this query using a Venn diagram.
41. For each customer, list the customer ID, the number of orders from that customer, and the ratio of the number of orders from that customer to the total number of orders from all customers combined. (This ratio, of course, is the percentage of all orders placed by each customer.)
42. For products 1, 2, and 7, list in one row and three respective columns that product's total unit sales; label the three columns Prod1, Prod2, and Prod7.
43. Not all versions of this database include referential integrity constraints for all foreign keys. Use whatever commands are available for the RDBMS you are using, investigate if any referential integrity constraints are missing. Write any missing constraints and, if possible, add them to the associated table definitions.
44. Tyler Richardson set up a house alarm system when he moved to his new home in Seattle. For security purposes, he has all of his mail, including his alarm system bill, mailed to his local UPS store. Although the alarm system is activated and the company is aware of its physical address, Richardson receives repeated offers mailed to his physical address, imploring him to protect his house with the system he currently uses. What do you think the problem might be with that company's database(s)?

References

Arvin, T. 2005. "Comparison of Different SQL Implementations" this and other information accessed at **http://troelsarvin.blogspot.com**.

Codd, E. F. 1970. "A Relational Model of Data for Large Shared Data Banks." *Communications of the ACM* 13,6 (June): 77–87.

Gorman, M. M. 2001. "Is SQL a Real Standard Anymore?" *The Data Administration Newsletter* (July), available at **www.tdan.com/i016hy01.htm**.

van der Lans, R. F. 2006. *Introduction to SQL; Mastering the Relational Database Language*, 4th ed. Workingham, UK: Addison-Wesley.

Further Reading

Bagui, S., and R. Earp. 2006. *Learning SQL on SQL Server 2005*. Sebastopol, CA: O'Reilly Media, Inc.

Bordoloi, B., and D. Bock. 2004. *Oracle SQL*. Upper Saddle River, NJ: Pearson Prentice Hall.

Celko, J. 2006. *Joe Celko's SQL Puzzles & Answers*, 2nd ed. San Francisco: Morgan Kaufmann.

Eisenberg, A., J. Melton, K. Kulkarni, J. E. Michels, and F. Zemke. 2004. "SQL:2003 Has Been Published." *SIGMOD Record* 33,1 (March):119–26.

Guerrero, F. G., and C. E. Rojas. 2001. *Microsoft SQL Server 2000 Programming by Example*. Indianapolis: QUE Corporation.

Gulutzan, P., and T. Petzer. 1999. *SQL-99 Complete, Really*. Lawrence, KS: R&D Books.

Nielsen, P. 2003. *Microsoft SQL Server 2000 Bible*. New York: Wiley Publishing, Inc.

Web Resources

http://standards.ieee.org The home page of the IEEE Standards Association.

http://troelsarvin.blogspot.com/ Blog that provides a detailed comparison of different SQL implementations, including DB2, Microsoft SQL, MySQL, Oracle, and PostGreSQL.

www.1keydata.com/sql/sql.html Web site that provides tutorials on a subset of ANSI standard SQL commands.

www.ansi.org Information on ANSI and the latest national and international standards.

www.coderecipes.net Web site that explains and shows examples for a wide range of SQL commands.

www.fluffycat.com/SQL/ Web site that defines a sample database and shows examples of SQL queries against this database.

www.incits.org The home page of the International Committee for Information Technology Standards, which used to be the National Committee for Information Technology Standards, which used to be the Accredited Standard Committee X3.

http://www.iso.org/iso/home.html International Organization for Standardization Web site, from which copies of current standards may be purchased.

www.itl.nist.gov/div897/ctg/dm/sql_examples.htm Web site that shows examples of SQL commands for creating tables and views, updating table contents, and performing some SQL database administration commands.

www.java2s.com/Code/SQL/CatalogSQL.htm Web site that provides tutorials on SQL in a MySQL environment.

www.mysql.com The official home page for MySQL, which includes many free downloadable components for working with MySQL.

www.paragoncorporation.com/ArticleDetail.aspx?ArticleID=27 Web site that provides a brief explanation of the power of SQL and a variety of sample SQL queries.

www.sqlcourse.com and **www.sqlcourse2.com** Web sites that provide tutorials for a subset of ANSI SQL, along with a practice database.

www.teradatauniversitynetwork.com Web site where your instructor may have created some course environments for you to use Teradata SQL Assistant, Web Edition, with one or more of the Pine Valley Furniture and Mountain View Community Hospital data sets for this text.

www.tizag.com/sqlTutorial/ A set of tutorials on SQL concepts and commands.

www.wiscorp.com/SQLStandards.html Whitemarsh Information Systems Corp., a good source of information about SQL standards, including SQL:2003 and later standards.

CHAPTER 7

Advanced SQL

Visit www.pearsonhighered.com/
hoffer to view the accompanying
video for this chapter.

LEARNING OBJECTIVES

After studying this chapter, you should be able to:

- Concisely define each of the following key terms: **join, equi-join, natural join, outer join, correlated subquery, transaction, backward recovery (rollback), trigger, function, procedure, embedded SQL,** and **dynamic SQL**.
- Write single- and multiple-table queries using SQL commands.
- Define three types of join commands and use SQL to write these commands.
- Write noncorrelated and correlated subqueries and know when to write each.
- Understand the use of SQL in procedural languages, both standard (e.g., PHP) and proprietary (e.g., PL/SQL).
- Understand common uses of database triggers and stored procedures.

INTRODUCTION

The previous chapter introduced SQL and explored its capabilities for querying one table. The real power of the relational model derives from its storage of data in many related entities. Taking advantage of this approach to data storage requires establishing relationships and constructing queries that use data from multiple tables. This chapter examines multiple-table queries in some detail. Different approaches to getting results from more than one table are demonstrated, including the use of subqueries, inner and outer joins, and union joins.

Once an understanding of basic SQL syntax is gained, it is important to understand how SQL is used in the creation of applications. Triggers, small modules of code that include SQL, execute automatically when a particular condition, defined in the trigger, exists. Procedures are similar modules of code but must be called before they execute. SQL commands are often embedded within modules written in a host language, such as C, PHP, .NET, or Java. Dynamic SQL creates SQL statements on the fly, inserting parameter values as needed, and is essential to Web applications. Brief introductions and examples of each of these methods are included in this chapter. Oracle, a leading relational database management system (RDBMS) vendor, is SQL:1999 compliant.

Completion of this chapter gives the student an overview of SQL and some of the ways in which it may be used. Many additional features, often referred to as "obscure" in more detailed SQL texts, will be needed in particular situations. Practice with the syntax included in this chapter will give you a good start toward mastery of SQL.

232

PROCESSING MULTIPLE TABLES

Now that we have explored some of the possibilities for working with a single table, it's time to bring out the light sabers, jet packs, and tools for heavy lifting: We will work with multiple tables simultaneously. The power of RDBMSs is realized when working with multiple tables. When relationships exist among tables, the tables can be linked together in queries. Remember from Chapter 4 that these relationships are established by including a common column(s) in each table where a relationship is needed. Often this is accomplished by setting up a primary key–foreign key relationship, where the foreign key in one table references the primary key in another, and the values in both come from a common domain. We can use these columns to establish a link between two tables by finding common values in the columns. Figure 7-1 carries forward two relations from Figure 6-3, depicting part of the Pine Valley Furniture Company database. Notice that CustomerID values in Order_T correspond to CustomerID values in Customer_T. Using this correspondence, we can deduce that Contemporary Casuals placed orders 1001 and 1010 because Contemporary Casuals's CustomerID is 1, and Order_T shows that OrderID 1001 and 1010 were placed by customer 1. In a relational system, data from related tables are combined into one result table or view and then displayed or used as input to a form or report definition.

The linking of related tables varies among different types of relational systems. In SQL, the WHERE clause of the SELECT command is also used for multiple-table operations. In fact, SELECT can include references to two, three, or more tables in the same command. As illustrated next, SQL has two ways to use SELECT for combining data from related tables.

The most frequently used relational operation, which brings together data from two or more related tables into one resultant table, is called a **join**. Originally, SQL specified a join implicitly by referring in a WHERE clause to the matching of common columns over which tables were joined. Since SQL-92, joins may also be specified in the FROM clause. In either case, two tables may be joined when each contains a column that shares a common domain with the other. As mentioned previously, a primary key from one table and a foreign key that references the table with the primary key will share a common domain and are frequently used to establish a join. Occasionally, joins will be established using columns that share a common domain but not the primary-foreign key relationship, and that also works (e.g., we might join customers and salespersons based on common postal codes, for which there is no relationship in the data model for the database). The result of a join operation is a single table. Selected columns from all the tables are included. Each row returned contains data from rows in the different input tables where values for the common columns match.

Explicit JOIN . . . ON commands are included in the FROM clause. The following join operations are included in the standard, though each RDBMS product is likely to support only a subset of the keywords: INNER, OUTER, FULL, LEFT, RIGHT, CROSS, and UNION. (We'll explain these in a following section.) NATURAL is an optional keyword. No matter what form of join you are using, *there should be one ON or WHERE specification for each pair of tables being joined.* Thus, if two tables are to be combined, one ON or WHERE condition

Join
A relational operation that causes two tables with a common domain to be combined into a single table or view.

FIGURE 7-1 Pine Valley Furniture Company Customer_T and Order_T tables, with pointers from customers to their orders

would be necessary, but if three tables (A, B, and C) are to be combined, then two ON or WHERE conditions would be necessary because there are 2 pairs of tables (A-B and B-C), and so forth. Most systems support up to 10 pairs of tables within one SQL command.

The various types of joins are described in the following sections.

Equi-join

Equi-join

A join in which the joining condition is based on equality between values in the common columns. Common columns appear (redundantly) in the result table.

With an **equi-join**, the joining condition is based on *equality* between values in the common columns. For example, if we want to know data about customers who have placed orders, that information is kept in two tables, Customer_T and Order_T. It is necessary to match customers with their orders and then collect the information about, for example, customer name and order number in one table in order to answer our question. We call the table created by the query the result or *answer table*.

Query: What are the customer IDs and names of all customers, along with the order IDs for all the orders they have placed?

```
SELECT Customer_T.CustomerID, Order_T.CustomerID,
    CustomerName, OrderID
        FROM Customer_T, Order_T
            WHERE Customer_T.CustomerID = Order_T. CustomerID
            ORDER BY OrderID
```

Result:

CUSTOMERID	CUSTOMERID	CUSTOMERNAME	ORDERID
1	1	Contemporary Casuals	1001
8	8	California Classics	1002
15	15	Mountain Scenes	1003
5	5	Impressions	1004
3	3	Home Furnishings	1005
2	2	Value Furniture	1006
11	11	American Euro Lifestyles	1007
12	12	Battle Creek Furniture	1008
4	4	Eastern Furniture	1009
1	1	Contemporary Casuals	1010

10 rows selected.

The redundant CustomerID columns, one from each table, demonstrate that the customer IDs have been matched and that matching gives one row for each order placed. We prefixed the CustomerID columns with the names of their respective tables so SQL knows which CustomerID column we referenced in each element of the SELECT list; we did not have to prefix CustomerName nor OrderID with their associated table names because each of these columns is found in only one table in the FROM list. We suggest that you study Figure 7-1 to see that the 10 arrows in the figure correspond to the 10 rows in the query result. Also, notice that there are no rows in the query result for those customers with no orders, because there is no match in Order_T for those CustomerIDs.

The importance of achieving the match between tables can be seen if the WHERE clause is omitted. That query will return all combinations of customers and orders, or 150 rows, and includes all possible combinations of the rows from the two tables (i.e., an order will be matched with every customer, not just the customer who placed that order). In this case, this join does not reflect the relationships that exist between the tables and is not a useful or meaningful result. The number of rows is equal to the number of rows in each table, multiplied together (10 orders × 15 customers = 150 rows).

This is called a *Cartesian join*. Cartesian joins with spurious results will occur when any joining component of a WHERE clause with multiple conditions is missing or erroneous. In the rare case that a Cartesian join is desired, omit the pairings in the WHERE clause. (Use this query only if you really mean to because a cross join against a production database can produce hundreds of thousands of rows and can consume significant computer time—plenty of time to receive a pizza delivery!)

The keywords INNER JOIN . . . ON are used to establish an equi-join in the FROM clause. While the syntax demonstrated here is Microsoft Access SQL syntax, note that some systems, such as Oracle and Microsoft SQL Server, treat the keyword JOIN by itself without the word INNER to establish an equi-join:

Query: What are the customer IDs and names of all customers, along with the order IDs for all the orders they have placed?

```
SELECT Customer_T.CustomerID, Order_T.CustomerID,
   CustomerName, OrderID
FROM Customer_T INNER JOIN Order_T ON
   Customer_T.CustomerID = Order_T.CustomerID
ORDER BY OrderID;
```

Result: Same as the previous query.

Simplest of all would be to use the JOIN . . . USING syntax, if this is supported by the RDBMS you are using. If the database designer thought ahead and used identical column names for the primary and foreign keys, as has been done with CustomerID in the Customer_T and Order_T tables, the following query could be used:

```
SELECT Customer_T.CustomerID, Order_T.CustomerID,
   CustomerName, OrderID
FROM Customer_T INNER JOIN Order_T USING CustomerID
ORDER BY OrderID ;
```

Notice that the WHERE clause now functions only in its traditional role as a filter as needed. Since the FROM clause is generally evaluated prior to the WHERE clause, some users prefer using the newer syntax of ON or USING in the FROM clause. A smaller record set that meets the join conditions is all that must be evaluated by the remaining clauses, and performance may improve. All database management system (DBMS) products support the traditional method of defining joins within the WHERE clause. Microsoft SQL Server supports the INNER JOIN . . . ON syntax, Oracle has supported it since 9i, and MySQL has supported it since version 3.23.17.

We again emphasize that SQL is a set-oriented language. Thus, this join example is produced by taking the customer table and the order table as two sets and appending together those rows from Customer_T with rows from Order_T that have equal CustomerID values. This is a set intersection operation, which is followed by appending the selected columns from the matching rows. Figure 7-2 uses set diagrams to display the most common types of two-table joins.

Natural Join

A **natural join** is the same as an equi-join, except that it is performed over matching columns, and one of the duplicate columns is eliminated in the result table. The natural join is the most commonly used form of join operation. (No, a "natural" join is not a more healthy join with more fiber, and there is no unnatural join; but you will find it a natural and essential function with relational databases.) Notice in the command below that CustomerID must still be qualified because there is still ambiguity; CustomerID exists in both Customer_T and Order_T, and therefore it must be specified from which table CustomerID should be displayed. NATURAL is an optional keyword when the join is defined in the FROM clause.

Query: For each customer who has placed an order, what is the customer's ID, name, and order number?

Natural join

A join that is the same as an equi-join except that one of the duplicate columns is eliminated in the result table.

FIGURE 7-2 **Visualization of different join types, with the results returned in the shaded area**

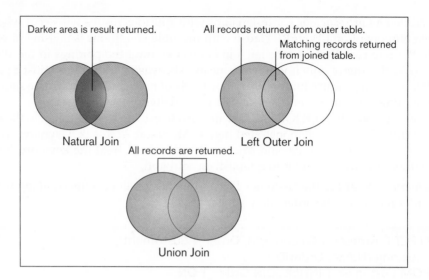

```
SELECT Customer_T.CustomerID, CustomerName, OrderID
FROM Customer_T NATURAL JOIN Order_T ON
Customer_T.CustomerID = Order_T.CustomerID;
```

Note that the order of table names in the FROM clause is immaterial. The query optimizer of the DBMS will decide in which sequence to process each table. Whether indexes exist on common columns will influence the sequence in which tables are processed, as will which table is on the 1 and which is on the M side of 1:*M* relationship. If a query takes significantly different amounts of time depending on the order in which tables are listed in the FROM clause, the DBMS does not have a very good query optimizer.

Outer Join

In joining two tables, we often find that a row in one table does not have a matching row in the other table. For example, several CustomerID numbers do not appear in the Order_T table. In Figure 7-1, pointers have been drawn from customers to their orders. Contemporary Casuals has placed two orders. Furniture Gallery, Period Furniture, M & H Casual Furniture, Seminole Interiors, Heritage Furnishings, and Kaneohe Homes have not placed orders in this small example. We can assume that this is because those customers have not placed orders since 10/21/2010, or their orders are not included in our very short sample Order_T table. As a result, the equi-join and natural join shown previously do not include all the customers shown in Customer_T.

Of course, the organization may be very interested in identifying those customers who have not placed orders. It might want to contact them to encourage new orders, or it might be interested in analyzing these customers to discern why they are not ordering. Using an **outer join** produces this information: Rows that do not have matching values in common columns are also included in the result table. Null values appear in columns where there is not a match between tables.

Outer joins can be handled by the major RDBMS vendors, but the syntax used to accomplish an outer join varies across vendors. The example given here uses ANSI standard syntax. When an outer join is not available explicitly, use UNION and NOT EXISTS (discussed later in this chapter) to carry out an outer join. Here is an outer join.

> *Query:* List customer name, identification number, and order number for all customers listed in the Customer table. Include the customer identification number and name even if there is no order available for that customer.

Outer join

A join in which rows that do not have matching values in common columns are nevertheless included in the result table.

```
SELECT Customer_T.CustomerID, CustomerName, OrderID
  FROM Customer_T LEFT OUTER JOIN Order_T
  WHERE Customer_T.CustomerID = Order_T. CustomerID;
```

The syntax LEFT OUTER JOIN was selected because the Customer_T table was named first, and it is the table from which we want all rows returned, regardless of whether there is a matching order in the Order_T table. Had we reversed the order in which the tables were listed, the same results would be obtained by requesting a RIGHT OUTER JOIN. It is also possible to request a FULL OUTER JOIN. In that case, all rows from both tables would be returned and matched, if possible, including any rows that do not have a match in the other table. INNER JOINs are much more common than OUTER JOINs because outer joins are necessary only when the user needs to see data from all rows, even those that have no matching row in another table.

Also, the result table from an outer join may indicate NULL (or a symbol, such as ??) as the values for columns in the second table where no match was achieved. If those columns could have NULL as a data value, you cannot know whether the row returned is a matched row or an unmatched row unless you run another query that checks for null values in the base table or view. Also, a column that is defined as NOT NULL may be assigned a NULL value in the result table of an OUTER JOIN. In the following result, NULL values are shown by an empty value (i.e., a customer without any orders is listed with no value for OrderID).

Result:

CUSTOMERID	CUSTOMERNAME	ORDERID
1	Contemporary Casuals	1001
1	Contemporary Casuals	1010
2	Value Furniture	1006
3	Home Furnishings	1005
4	Eastern Furniture	1009
5	Impressions	1004
6	Furniture Gallery	
7	Period Furniture	
8	California Classics	1002
9	M & H Casual Furniture	
10	Seminole Interiors	
11	American Euro Lifestyles	1007
12	Battle Creek Furniture	1008
13	Heritage Furnishings	
14	Kaneohe Homes	
15	Mountain Scenes	1003

16 rows selected.

It may help you to glance back at Figures 7-1 and 7-2. In Figure 7-2, customers are represented by the left circle and orders are represented by the right. With a NATURAL JOIN of Customer_T and Order_T, only the 10 rows that have arrows drawn in Figure 7-1 will be returned. The LEFT OUTER JOIN on Customer_T returns all of the customers along with the orders they have placed, and customers are returned even if they have not placed orders. Because Customer 1, Contemporary Casuals, has placed two orders, a total of 16 rows are returned because rows are returned for both orders placed by Contemporary Casuals.

The advantage of an outer join is that information is not lost. Here, all customer names were returned, whether or not they had placed orders. Requesting a RIGHT

OUTER join would return all orders. (Because referential integrity requires that every order be associated with a valid customer ID, this right outer join would ensure that only referential integrity is being enforced.) Customers who had not placed orders would not be included in the result.

> *Query:* List customer name, identification number, and order number for all orders listed in the Order table. Include the order number, even if there is no customer name and identification number available.

```
SELECT Customer_T.CustomerID, CustomerName, OrderID
  FROM Customer_T RIGHT OUTER JOIN Order_T ON
    Customer_T.CustomerID = Order_T.CustomerID;
```

Sample Join Involving Four Tables

Much of the power of the relational model comes from its ability to work with the relationships among the objects in the database. Designing a database so that data about each object are kept in separate tables simplifies maintenance and data integrity. The capability to relate the objects to each other by joining the tables provides critical business information and reports to employees. Although the examples provided in Chapter 6 and this chapter are simple and constructed only to provide a basic understanding of SQL, it is important to realize that these commands can be and often are built into much more complex queries that provide exactly the information needed for a report or process.

Here is a sample join query that involves a four-table join. This query produces a result table that includes the information needed to create an invoice for order number 1006. We want the customer information, the order and order line information, and the product information, so we will need to join four tables. Figure 7-3a shows an annotated ERD of the four tables involved in constructing this query; Figure 7-3b shows an abstract instance diagram of the four tables with order 1006 hypothetically having two line items for products Px and Py, respectively. We encourage you to draw such diagrams to help conceive the data involved in a query and how you might then construct the corresponding SQL command with joins.

> *Query:* Assemble all information necessary to create an invoice for order number 1006.

```
SELECT Customer_T.CustomerID, CustomerName, CustomerAddress,
    CustomerCity, CustomerState, CustomerPostalCode, Order_T.OrderID,
    OrderDate, OrderedQuantity, ProductDescription, StandardPrice,
    (OrderedQuantity * ProductStandardPrice)
  FROM Customer_T, Order_T, OrderLine_T, Product_T
    WHERE Order_T.CustomerID = Customer_T.CustomerID
      AND Order_T.OrderID = OrderLine_T.OrderID
      AND OrderLine_T.ProductID = Product_T.ProductID
      AND Order_T.OrderID = 1006;
```

The results of the query are shown in Figure 7-4. Remember, because the join involves four tables, there are three column join conditions, as follows:

1. Order_T.CustomerID = Customer_T.CustomerID links an order with its associated customer.
2. Order_T.OrderID = OrderLine_T.OrderID links each order with the details of the items ordered.
3. OrderLine_T.ProductID = Product_T.ProductID links each order detail record with the product description for that order line.

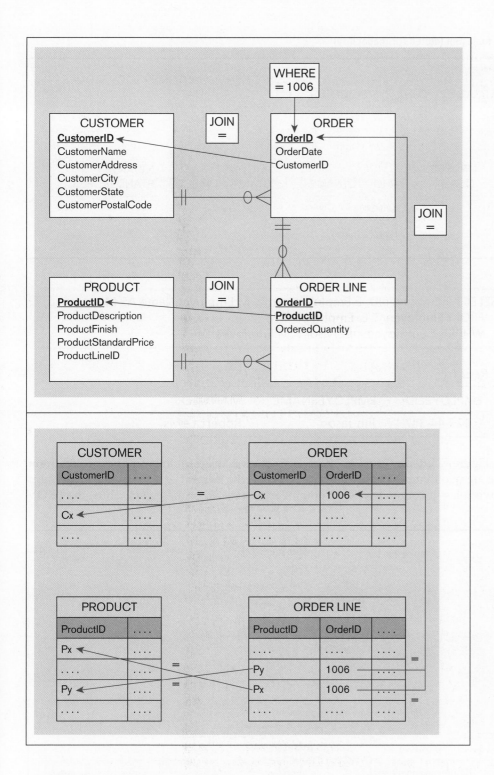

FIGURE 7-3 Diagrams depicting a four-table join (a) Annotated ERD with relations used in a four-table join

(b) Annotated instance diagram of relations used in a four-table join

Self-Join

There are times when a join requires matching rows in a table with other rows in that same table—that is, joining a table with itself. There is no special command in SQL to do this, but people generally call this operation a *self-join*. Self-joins arise for several reasons, the most common of which is a unary relationship. This relationship is implemented, for example, by placing in the EmployeeSupervisor column the EmployeeID (foreign key) of the employee's supervisor, another employee. With this recursive foreign key column, we can ask the following question:

> *Query:* What are the employee ID and name of each employee and the name of his or her supervisor (label the supervisor's name Manager)?

FIGURE 7-4 Results from a four-table join (edited for readability)

CUSTOMERID	CUSTOMERNAME	CUSTOMERADDRESS	CUSTOMER CITY	CUSTOMER STATE	CUSTOMER POSTALCODE
2	Value Furniture	15145 S. W. 17th St.	Plano	TX	75094 7743
2	Value Furniture	15145 S. W. 17th St.	Plano	TX	75094 7743
2	Value Furniture	15145 S. W. 17th St.	Plano	TX	75094 7743

ORDERID	ORDERDATE	ORDERED QUANTITY	PRODUCTNAME	PRODUCT STANDARDPRICE	(QUANTITY* STANDARDPRICE)
1006	24-OCT -10	1	Entertainment Center	650	650
1006	24-OCT -10	2	Writer's Desk	325	650
1006	24-OCT -10	2	Dining Table	800	1600

```
SELECT E.EmployeeID, E.EmployeeName, M.EmployeeName AS Manager
   FROM Employee_T E, Employee_T M
   WHERE E.EmployeeSupervisor = M.EmployeeID;
```

Result:

EMPLOYEEID	EMPLOYEENAME	MANAGER
123-44-347	Jim Jason	Robert Lewis

Figure 7-5 depicts this query in both a Venn diagram and an instance diagram. There are two things to note in this query. First, the Employee table is, in a sense, serving two roles: It contains a list of employees and a list of managers. Thus, the FROM

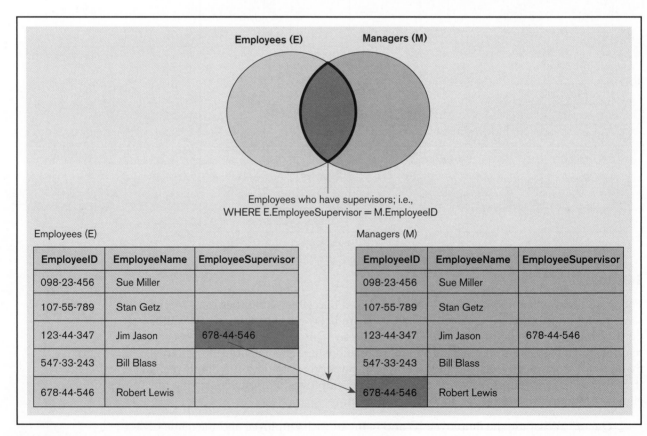

FIGURE 7-5 Example of a self-join

clause refers to the Employee_T table twice, once for each of these roles. However, to distinguish these roles in the rest of the query, we give the Employee_T table an alias for each role (in this case, E for employee and M for manager roles, respectively). Then the columns from the SELECT list are clear: first the ID and name of an employee (with prefix E) and then the name of a manager (with prefix M). Which manager? That then is the second point: The WHERE clause joins the "employee" and "manager" tables based on the foreign key from employee (EmployeeSupervisor) to manager (EmployeeID). As far as SQL is concerned, it considers the E and M tables to be two different tables that have identical column names, so the column names must have a suffix to clarify from which table a column is to be chosen each time it is referenced.

It turns out that there are various interesting queries that can be written using self-joins following unary relationships. For example, which employees have a salary greater than the salary of their manager (not uncommon in professional baseball, but generally frowned on in business or government organizations), or (if we had these data in our database) is anyone married to his or her manager (not uncommon in a family-run business but possibly prohibited in many organizations)? Several of the Problems and Exercises at the end of this chapter require queries with a self-join.

As with any other join, it is not necessary that a self-join be based on a foreign key and a specified unary relationship. For example, when a salesperson is scheduled to visit a particular customer, she might want to know who are all the other customers in the same postal code as the customer she is scheduled to visit. Remember, it is possible to join rows on columns from different (or the same) tables as long as those columns come from the same domain of values and the linkage of values from those columns makes sense. For example, even though ProductFinish and EmployeeCity may have the identical data type, they don't come from the same domain of values, and there is no conceivable business reason to link products and employees on these columns. However, one might conceive of some reason to understand the sales booked by a salesperson by looking at order dates of the person's sales relative to his or her hire date. It is amazing what questions SQL can answer (although we have limited control on how SQL displays the results).

Subqueries

The preceding SQL examples illustrate one of the two basic approaches for joining two tables: the joining technique. SQL also provides the subquery technique, which involves placing an inner query (SELECT . . . FROM . . . WHERE) within a WHERE or HAVING clause of another (outer) query. The inner query provides a set of one or more values for the search condition of the outer query. Such queries are referred to as subqueries or nested subqueries. Subqueries can be nested multiple times. Subqueries are prime examples of why SQL is a set-oriented language.

Sometimes, either the joining or the subquery technique can be used to accomplish the same result, and different people will have different preferences about which technique to use. Other times, only a join or only a subquery will work. The joining technique is useful when data from *several relations* are to be retrieved and displayed, and the relationships are not necessarily nested, whereas the subquery technique allows you to display data from only the tables mentioned in the outer query. Let's compare two queries that return the same result. Both answer the question, what is the name and address of the customer who placed order number 1008? First, we will use a join query, which is graphically depicted in Figure 7-6a.

Query: What are the name and address of the customer who placed order number 1008?

```
SELECT CustomerName, CustomerAddress, CustomerCity,
   CustomerState, CustomerPostalCode
FROM Customer_T, Order_T
WHERE Customer_T.CustomerID = Order_T. CustomerID
   AND OrderID = 1008;
```

FIGURE 7-6   Graphical depiction of two ways to answer a query with different types of joins

(a) Join query approach

(b) Subquery approach

In set-processing terms, this query finds the subset of the Order_T table for OrderID = 1008 and then matches the row(s) in that subset with the rows in the Customer_T table that have the same CustomerID values. In this approach, it is not necessary that only one order have the OrderID value 1008. Now, look at the equivalent query using the subquery technique, which is graphically depicted in Figure 7-6b.

Query: What are the name and address of the customer who placed order number 1008?

```
SELECT CustomerName, CustomerAddress, CustomerCity,
CustomerState, CustomerPostalCode
  FROM Customer_T
    WHERE Customer_T.CustomerID =
      (SELECT Order_T.CustomerID
        FROM Order_T
          WHERE OrderID = 1008);
```

Notice that the subquery, shaded in blue and enclosed in parentheses, follows the form learned for constructing SQL queries and could stand on its own as an independent query. That is, the result of the subquery, as with any other query, is a set of rows—in this case, a set of CustomerID values. We know that only one value will be in the result. (There is only one CustomerID for the order with OrderID 1008.) To be safe, we can, and probably should, use the IN operator rather than = when writing subqueries. *The subquery approach may be used for this query because we need to display data from only the table in the outer query.* The value for OrderID does not appear in the query result; it is used as the selection criterion in the inner query. To include data from the subquery in the result, use the join technique, because data from a subquery cannot be included in the final results.

As noted previously, we know in advance that the preceding subquery will return at most one value, the CustomerID associated with OrderID 1008. The result will be empty if an order with that ID does not exist. (It is advisable to check that your query will work if a subquery returns zero, one, or many values.) A subquery can also return a list (set) of values (with zero, one, or many entries) if it includes the keyword IN. *Because the result of the subquery is used to compare with one attribute (CustomerID, in this query), the select list of a subquery may include only one attribute.* For example, which customers have placed orders? Here is a query that will answer that question.

Query: What are the names of customers who have placed orders?

```
SELECT CustomerName
  FROM Customer_T
    WHERE CustomerID IN
      (SELECT DISTINCT CustomerID
      FROM Order_T);
```

This query produces the following result. As required, the subquery select list contains only the one attribute, CustomerID, needed in the WHERE clause of the outer query. Distinct is used in the subquery because we do not care how many orders a customer has placed, as long as they have placed an order. For each customer identified in the Order_T table, that customer's name has been returned from Customer_T. (You will study this query again in Figure 7-8a.)

Result:

CUSTOMERNAME
Contemporary Casuals
Value Furniture
Home Furnishings
Eastern Furniture
Impressions
California Classics
American Euro Lifestyles
Battle Creek Furniture
Mountain Scenes
9 rows selected.

The qualifiers NOT, ANY, and ALL may be used in front of IN or with logical operators such as = , >, and <. Because IN works with zero, one, or many values from the inner query, many programmers simply use IN instead of = for all queries, even if the equal sign would work. The next example shows the use of NOT, and it also demonstrates that a join can be used in an inner query.

Query: Which customers have not placed any orders for computer desks?

```
SELECT CustomerName
  FROM Customer_T
  WHERE CustomerID NOT IN
  (SELECT CustomerID
    FROM Order_T, OrderLine_T, Product_T
      WHERE Order_T.OrderID = OrderLine_T.OrderID
        AND OrderLine_T.ProductID = Product_T.ProductID
        AND ProductDescription = 'Computer Desk');
```

Result:

CUSTOMERNAME
Value Furniture
Home Furnishings
Eastern Furniture
Furniture Gallery
Period Furniture
M & H Casual Furniture
Seminole Interiors
American Euro Lifestyles
Heritage Furnishings
Kaneohe Homes

10 rows selected.

The result shows that 10 customers have not yet ordered computer desks. The inner query returned a list (set) of all customers who had ordered computer desks. The outer query listed the names of those customers who were not in the list returned by the inner query. Figure 7-7 graphically breaks out the results of the subquery and main query.

Qualifications such as < ANY or >= ALL instead of IN are also useful. For example, the qualification >= ALL can be used to match with the maximum value in a set. But be careful: Some combinations of qualifications may not make sense, such as = ALL (which makes sense only when the all the elements of the set have the same value).

Two other conditions associated with using subqueries are EXISTS and NOT EXISTS. These keywords are included in an SQL query at the same location where IN would be, just prior to the beginning of the subquery. EXISTS will take a value of *true* if the subquery returns an intermediate result table that contains one or more rows (i.e., a nonempty set) and *false* if no rows are returned (i.e., an empty set). NOT EXISTS will take a value of *true* if no rows are returned and *false* if one or more rows are returned.

So, when do you use EXISTS versus IN, and when do you use NOT EXISTS versus NOT IN? You use EXISTS (NOT EXISTS) when your only interest is whether the subquery returns a nonempty (empty) set (i.e., you don't care what is in the set, just whether it is empty), and you use IN (NOT IN) when you need to know what values are (are not) in the set. Remember, IN and NOT IN return a set of values from only one column, which can then be compared to one column in the outer query. EXISTS and NOT EXISTS returns only a true or false value depending on whether there are any rows in the answer table of the inner query or subquery.

Consider the following SQL statement, which includes EXISTS.

Query: What are the order IDs for all orders that have included furniture finished in natural ash?

FIGURE 7-7 Using the NOT IN qualifier

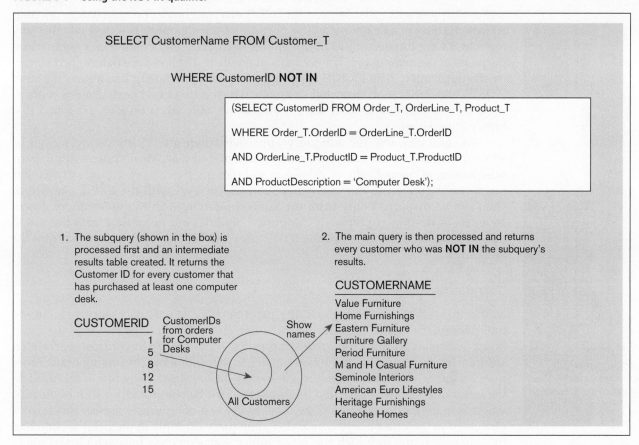

SELECT CustomerName FROM Customer_T

WHERE CustomerID **NOT IN**

(SELECT CustomerID FROM Order_T, OrderLine_T, Product_T

WHERE Order_T.OrderID = OrderLine_T.OrderID

AND OrderLine_T.ProductID = Product_T.ProductID

AND ProductDescription = 'Computer Desk');

1. The subquery (shown in the box) is processed first and an intermediate results table created. It returns the Customer ID for every customer that has purchased at least one computer desk.

CUSTOMERID
1
5
8
12
15

2. The main query is then processed and returns every customer who was **NOT IN** the subquery's results.

CUSTOMERNAME

Value Furniture
Home Furnishings
Eastern Furniture
Furniture Gallery
Period Furniture
M and H Casual Furniture
Seminole Interiors
American Euro Lifestyles
Heritage Furnishings
Kaneohe Homes

```
SELECT DISTINCT OrderID FROM OrderLine_T
WHERE EXISTS
  (SELECT *
    FROM Product_T
      WHERE ProductID = OrderLine_T.ProductID
      AND ProductFinish = 'Natural Ash');
```

The subquery is executed for each order line in the outer query. The subquery checks for each order line to see if the finish for the product on that order line is natural ash (indicated by the arrow added to the query above). If this is true (EXISTS), the outer query displays the order ID for that order. The outer query checks this one row at a time for every row in the set of referenced rows (the OrderLine_T table). There have been seven such orders, as the result shows. (We discuss this query further in Figure 7-8b.)

Result:

ORDERID
1001
1002
1003
1006
1007
1008
1009

7 rows selected.

When EXISTS or NOT EXISTS is used in a subquery, the select list of the subquery will usually just select all columns (SELECT *) as a placeholder because it does not matter which columns are returned. The purpose of the subquery is to test whether any rows fit the conditions, not to return values from particular columns for comparison purposes in the outer query. The columns that will be displayed are determined strictly by the outer query. The EXISTS subquery illustrated previously, like almost all other EXISTS subqueries, is a correlated subquery, which is described next. Queries containing the keyword NOT EXISTS will return a result table when no rows are found that satisfy the subquery.

In summary, use the subquery approach when qualifications are nested or when qualifications are easily understood in a nested way. Most systems allow pairwise joining of *one and only one column* in an inner query with one column in an outer query. An exception to this is when a subquery is used with the EXISTS keyword. Data can be displayed only from the table(s) referenced in the outer query. Up to 16 levels of nesting are typically supported. Queries are processed from the inside out, although another type of subquery, a correlated subquery, is processed from the outside in.

Correlated Subqueries

Correlated subquery

In SQL, a subquery in which processing the inner query depends on data from the outer query.

In the first subquery example in the prior section, it was necessary to examine the inner query before considering the outer query. That is, the result of the inner query was used to limit the processing of the outer query. In contrast, **correlated subqueries** use the result of the outer query to determine the processing of the inner query. That is, the inner query is somewhat different for each row referenced in the outer query. In this case, the inner query must be computed for *each* outer row, whereas in the earlier examples, the inner query was computed *only once* for all rows processed in the outer query. The EXISTS subquery example in the prior section had this characteristic, in which the inner query was executed for each OrderLine_T row, and each time it was executed, the inner query was for a different ProductID value—the one from the OrderLine_T row in the outer query. Figures 7-8a and 7-8b depict the different processing orders for each of the examples from the previous section on subqueries.

Let's consider another example query that requires composing a correlated subquery.

Query: List the details about the product with the highest standard price.

```
SELECT ProductDescription, ProductFinish, ProductStandardPrice
FROM Product_T PA
    WHERE PA.ProductStandardPrice > ALL
    (SELECT ProductStandardPrice FROM Product_T PB
        WHERE PB.ProductID ! = PA.ProductID);
```

As you can see in the following result, the dining table has a higher unit price than any other product.

Result:

PRODUCTDESCRIPTION	PRODUCTFINISH	PRODUCTSTANDARDPRICE
Dining Table	Natural Ash	800

The arrow added to the query above illustrates the cross-reference for a value in the inner query to be taken from a table in the outer query. The logic of this SQL statement is that the subquery will be executed once for each product to be sure that no other product has a higher standard price. Notice that we are comparing rows in a table to themselves and that we are able to do this by giving the table two aliases, PA and PB; you'll recall we identified this earlier as a self-join. First, ProductID 1, the end table, will be considered. When the subquery is executed, it will return a set of values, which are

FIGURE 7-8 Subquery processing

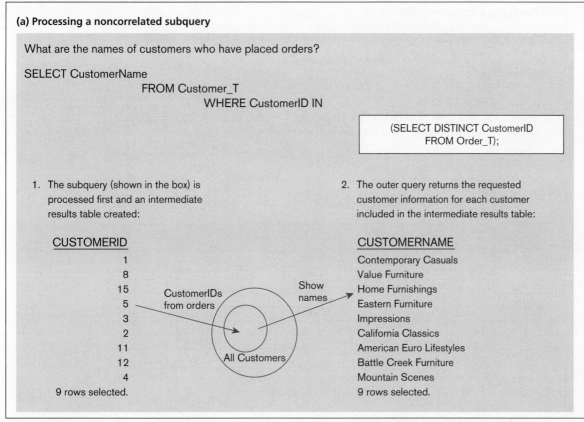

(a) Processing a noncorrelated subquery

What are the names of customers who have placed orders?

SELECT CustomerName
        FROM Customer_T
                WHERE CustomerID IN

> (SELECT DISTINCT CustomerID
> FROM Order_T);

1. The subquery (shown in the box) is processed first and an intermediate results table created:

2. The outer query returns the requested customer information for each customer included in the intermediate results table:

CUSTOMERID
1
8
15
5
3
2
11
12
4
9 rows selected.

CustomerIDs from orders

Show names

All Customers

CUSTOMERNAME
Contemporary Casuals
Value Furniture
Home Furnishings
Eastern Furniture
Impressions
California Classics
American Euro Lifestyles
Battle Creek Furniture
Mountain Scenes
9 rows selected.

(Figure 7-8 continues on the next page)

the standard prices of every product except the one being considered in the outer query (product 1, for the first time it is executed). Then, the outer query will check to see if the standard price for the product being considered is greater than all of the standard prices returned by the subquery. If it is, it will be returned as the result of the query. If not, the next standard price value in the outer query will be considered, and the inner query will return a list of all the standard prices for the other products. The list returned by the inner query changes as each product in the outer query changes; that makes it a correlated subquery. Can you identify a special set of standard prices for which this query will not yield the desired result (see Problem and Exercise 38)?

Using Derived Tables

Subqueries are not limited to inclusion in the WHERE clause. As we saw in Chapter 6, they may also be used in the FROM clause to create a temporary derived table (or set) that is used in the query. Creating a derived table that has an aggregate value in it, such as MAX, AVG, or MIN, allows the aggregate to be used in the WHERE clause. Here, pieces of furniture that exceed the average standard price are listed.

> *Query:* Show the product description, product standard price, and overall average standard price for all products that have a standard price that is higher than the average standard price.

```
SELECT ProductDescription, ProductStandardPrice, AvgPrice
   FROM
      (SELECT AVG(ProductStandardPrice) AvgPrice FROM Product_T),
         Product_T
   WHERE ProductStandardPrice > AvgPrice;
```

FIGURE 7-8 *(continued)*

(b) Processing a correlated subquery

What are the order IDs for all orders that have included furniture finished in natural ash?

SELECT DISTINCT OrderID FROM OrderLine_T
WHERE EXISTS
        (SELECT *
         FROM Product _T
            WHERE ProductID = OrderLine_T.ProductID
            AND Productfinish = 'Natural Ash');

		ProductID	ProductDescription	ProductFinish	ProductStandardPrice	ProductLineID
▶	⊞	1	End Table	Cherry	$175.00	10001
	⊞	**2** → 2 Coffee Table		Natural Ash	$200.00	20001
	⊞	**4** → 3 Computer Desk		Natural Ash	$375.00	20001
	⊞	4	Entertainment Center	Natural Maple	$650.00	30001
	⊞	5	Writer's Desk	Cherry	$325.00	10001
	⊞	6	8-Drawer Dresser	White Ash	$750.00	20001
	⊞	7	Dining Table	Natural Ash	$800.00	20001
	⊞	8	Computer Desk	Walnut	$250.00	30001
✳		(AutoNumber)			$0.00	

1. The first order ID is selected from OrderLine_T: OrderID =1001.

2. The subquery is evaluated to see if any product in that order has a natural ash finish. Product 2 does, and is part of the order. EXISTS is valued as true and the order ID is added to the result table.

3. The next order ID is selected from OrderLine_T: OrderID =1002.

4. The subquery is evaluated to see if the product ordered has a natural ash finish. It does. EXISTS is valued as true and the order ID is added to the result table.

5. Processing continues through each order ID. Orders 1004, 1005, and 1010 are not included in the result table because they do not include any furniture with a natural ash finish. The final result table is shown in the text on page 245.

Result:

PRODUCTDESCRIPTION	PRODUCTSTANDARDPRICE	AVGPRICE
Entertainment Center	650	440.625
8-Drawer Dresser	750	440.625
Dining Table	800	440.625

So, why did this query require a derived table rather than, say, a subquery? The reason is we want to display both the standard price and the average standard price for each of the selected products. The similar query in the prior section on correlated subqueries worked fine to show data from only the table in the outer query, the product table. However, to show both standard price and the average standard price in each displayed row, we have to get both values into the "outer" query, as is done in the query above.

Combining Queries

Sometimes, no matter how clever you are, you can't get all the rows you want into the single answer table using one SELECT statement. Fortunately, you have a lifeline! The

UNION clause is used to combine the output (i.e., union the set of rows) from multiple queries together into a single result table. To use the UNION clause, each query involved must output the same number of columns, and they must be UNION compatible. This means that the output from each query for each column should be of compatible data types. Acceptance as a compatible data type varies among the DBMS products. When performing a union where output for a column will merge two different data types, it is safest to use the CAST command to control the data type conversion yourself. For example, the DATE data type in Order_T might need to be converted into a text data type. The following SQL command would accomplish this:

SELECT **CAST(OrderDate AS CHAR)** FROM Order_T;

The following query determines the customer(s) who has in a given line item purchased the largest quantity of any Pine Valley product and the customer(s) who has in a given line item purchased the smallest quantity and returns the results in one table.

Query:

```
SELECT C1.CustomerID, CustomerName, OrderedQuantity,
'Largest Quantity' AS Quantity
FROM Customer_T C1,Order_T O1, OrderLine_T Q1
    WHERE C1.CustomerID = O1.CustomerID
    AND O1.OrderID = Q1.OrderID
    AND OrderedQuantity =
    (SELECT MAX(OrderedQuantity)
    FROM OrderLine_T)
UNION
SELECT C1.CustomerID, CustomerName, OrderedQuantity,
'Smallest Quantity'
FROM Customer_T C1, Order_T O1, OrderLine_T Q1
    WHERE C1.CustomerID = O1.CustomerID
    AND O1.OrderID = Q1.OrderID
    AND OrderedQuantity =
    (SELECT MIN(OrderedQuantity)
    FROM OrderLine_T)
ORDER BY 3;
```

Notice that an expression Quantity has been created in which the strings 'Smallest Quantity' and 'Largest Quantity' have been inserted for readability. The ORDER BY clause has been used to organize the order in which the rows of output are listed. Figure 7-9 breaks the query into parts to help you understand how it processes.

Result:

CUSTOMERID	CUSTOMERNAME	ORDEREDQUANTITY	QUANTITY
1	Contemporary Casuals	1	Smallest Quantity
2	Value Furniture	1	Smallest Quantity
1	Contemporary Casuals	10	Largest Quantity

Did we have to answer this question by using UNION? Could we instead have answered it using one SELECT and a complex, compound WHERE clause with many ANDs and ORs? In general, the answer is sometimes (another good academic answer, like "it depends"). Often, it is simply easiest to conceive of and write a query using several simply SELECTs and a UNION. Or, if it is a query you frequently run, maybe one

FIGURE 7-9   Combining queries using UNION

```
SELECT C1.CustomerID, CustomerName, OrderedQuantity, 'Largest Quantity' AS Quantity
    FROM Customer_T C1,Order_T O1, OrderLine_T Q1
    WHERE C1.CustomerID = O1.CustomerID
          AND O1.OrderID = Q1.OrderID
          AND OrderedQuantity =
                      (SELECT MAX(OrderedQuantity)
                       FROM OrderLine_T)
```

1. In the above query, the subquery is processed first and an intermediate results table created.
   It contains the maximum quantity ordered from OrderLine_T and has a value of 10.
2. Next the main query selects customer information for the customer or customers who ordered 10
   of any item. Contemporary Casuals has ordered 10 of some unspecified item.

```
SELECT C1.CustomerID, CustomerName, OrderedQuantity, 'Smallest Quantity'
    FROM Customer_T C1, Order_T O1, OrderLine_T Q1
    WHERE C1.CustomerID = O1.CustomerID
          AND O1.OrderID = Q1.OrderID
          AND OrderedQuantity =
                      (SELECT MIN(OrderedQuantity)
                       FROM OrderLine_T)
ORDER BY 3;
```

1. In the second main query, the same process is followed but the result returned is for the minimum order quantity.
2. The results of the two queries are joined together using the UNION command.
3. The results are then ordered according to the value in OrderedQuantity. The default is ascending value,
   so the orders with the smallest quantity, 1, are listed first.

way will process more efficiently than another. You will learn from experience which approach is most natural for you and best for a given situation.

Now that you remember the union set operation from finite mathematics, you may also remember that there are other set operations—intersect (to find the elements in common between two sets) and minus (to find the elements in one set that are not in another set). These operations—INTERSECT and MINUS—are also available in SQL, and they are used just as UNION was above to manipulate the result sets created by two SELECT statements.

TIPS FOR DEVELOPING QUERIES

SQL's simple basic structure results in a query language that is easy for a novice to use to write simple ad hoc queries. At the same time, it has enough flexibility and syntax options to handle complicated queries used in a production system. Both characteristics, however, lead to potential difficulties in query development. As with any other computer programming, you are likely not to write a query correctly the first time. Be sure you have access to an explanation of the error codes generated by the RDBMS. Work initially with a test set of data, usually small, for which you can compute the desired answer by hand as a way to check your coding. This is especially true if you are writing INSERT, UPDATE, or DELETE commands, and it is why organizations have test, development, and production versions of a database, so inevitable development errors do not harm production data.

As a novice query writer, you will find it easy to write a query that runs without error. Congratulations, but the results may not be exactly what you intended. Sometimes it will be obvious to you that there is a problem, especially if you forget to define the links between tables with a WHERE clause and get a Cartesian join of all possible combinations of records. Other times, your query will appear to be correct, but close inspection using a test set of data may reveal that your query returns 24 rows when it should return 25. Sometimes it will return duplicates you don't want or just a few of the records you want, and sometimes it won't run because you are trying to group data that can't be grouped. Watch carefully for these types of errors before you turn in your homework. Working through a well-thought-out set of test data by hand will help you catch your errors. When you are constructing a set of test data, include some examples of common data values. Then think about possible exceptions that could occur. For example, real data might unexpectedly include null data, out-of-range data, or impossible data values.

Certain steps are necessary in writing any query. The graphical interfaces now available make it easier to construct queries and to remember table and attribute names as you work. Here are some suggestions to help you (we assume that you are working with a database that has been defined and created):

- Familiarize yourself with the data model and the entities and relationships that have been established. The data model expresses many of the business rules that may be idiosyncratic for the business or problem you are considering. It is very important to have a good grasp of the data that are available with which to work. As demonstrated in Figures 7-8a and 7-8b, you can draw the segment of the data model you intend to reference in the query and then annotate it to show qualifications and joining criteria. Alternatively you can draw figures such as Figures 7-6 and 7-7 with sample data and Venn diagrams to also help conceive of how to construct subqueries or derived tables that can be used as components in a more complex query.
- Be sure that you understand what results you want from your query. Often, a user will state a need ambiguously, so be alert and address any questions you have after working with users.
- Figure out what attributes you want in your query result. Include each attribute after the SELECT keyword.
- Locate within the data model the attributes you want and identify the entity where the required data are stored. Include these after the FROM keyword.
- Review the ERD and all the entities identified in the previous step. Determine what columns in each table will be used to establish the relationships. Consider what type of join you want between each set of entities.
- Construct a WHERE equality for each link. Count the number of entities involved and the number of links established. Usually there will be one more entity than there are WHERE clauses. When you have established the basic result set, the query may be complete. In any case, run it and inspect your results.
- When you have a basic result set to work with, you can begin to fine-tune your query by adding GROUP BY and HAVING clauses, DISTINCT, NOT IN, and so forth. Test your query as you add keywords to it to be sure you are getting the results you want.
- Until you gain query writing experience, your first draft of a query will tend to work with the data you expect to encounter. Now, try to think of exceptions to the usual data that may be encountered and test your query against a set of test data that includes unusual data, missing data, impossible values, and so forth. If you can handle those, your query is almost complete. Remember that checking by hand will be necessary; just because an SQL query runs doesn't mean it is correct.

As you start to write more complicated queries using additional syntax, debugging queries may be more difficult for you. If you are using subqueries, errors of logic can often be located by running each subquery as a freestanding query. Start with the subquery that is nested most deeply. When its results are correct, use that tested subquery with the outer query that uses its result. You can follow a similar process with derived tables. Follow this procedure until you have tested the entire query. If you are having syntax trouble with a simple query, try taking apart the query to find the problem. You may find it easier to spot a problem if you return just a few crucial attribute values and investigate one manipulation at a time.

As you gain more experience, you will be developing queries for larger databases. As the amount of data that must be processed increases, the time necessary to successfully run a query may vary noticeably, depending on how you write the query. Query optimizers are available in the more powerful database management systems such as Oracle, but there are also some simple strategies for writing queries that may prove helpful for you. The following are some common strategies to consider if you want to write queries that run more efficiently:

- Rather than use the SELECT * option, take the time to include the column names of the attributes you need in a query. If you are working with a wide table and need only a few of the attributes, using SELECT * may generate a significant amount of unnecessary network traffic as unnecessary attributes are fetched over the network. Later, when the query has been incorporated into a production system, changes in the base table may affect the query results. Specifying the attribute names will make it easier to notice and correct for such events.
- Try to build your queries so that your intended result is obtained from one query. Review your logic carefully to reduce the number of subqueries in the query as much as possible. Each subquery you include requires the DBMS to return an interim result set and integrate it with the remaining subqueries, thus increasing processing time.
- Sometimes data that reside in one table will be needed for several separate reports. Rather than obtain those data in several separate queries, create a single query that retrieves all the data that will be needed; you reduce the overhead by having the table accessed once rather than repeatedly. It may help you recognize such a situation by thinking about the data that are typically used by a department and creating a view for the department's use.

Guidelines for Better Query Design

Now you have some strategies for developing queries that will give you the results you want. But will these strategies result in efficient queries, or will they result in the "query from hell," giving you plenty of time for the pizza to be delivered, to watch the *Star Trek* anthology, or to organize your closet? Various database experts, such as DeLoach (1987) and Holmes (1996), provide suggestions for improving query processing in a variety of settings. Also see the Web Resources at the end of this chapter and prior chapters for links to sites where query design suggestions are continually posted. We summarize here some of these suggestions that apply to many situations:

1. *Understand how indexes are used in query processing* Many DBMSs will use only one index per table in a query—often the one that is the most discriminating (i.e., has the most key values). Some will never use an index with only a few values compared to the number of table rows. Others may balk at using an index for which the column has many null values across the table rows. Monitor accesses to indexes and then drop indexes that are infrequently used. This will improve the performance of database update operations. In general, queries that have equality criteria for selecting table rows (e.g., WHERE Finish = "Birch" OR "Walnut") will result in faster processing than queries involving more complex qualifications do (e.g., WHERE Finish NOT = "Walnut") because equality criteria can be evaluated via indexes.
2. *Keep optimizer statistics up-to-date* Some DBMSs do not automatically update the statistics needed by the query optimizer. If performance is degrading, force the running of an update-statistics-like command.
3. *Use compatible data types for fields and literals in queries* Using compatible data types will likely mean that the DBMS can avoid having to convert data during query processing.
4. *Write simple queries* Usually the simplest form of a query will be the easiest for a DBMS to process. For example, because relational DBMSs are based on set theory, write queries that manipulate sets of rows and literals.
5. *Break complex queries into multiple simple parts* Because a DBMS may use only one index per query, it is often good to break a complex query into multiple, simpler parts (which each use an index) and then combine together the results of the smaller queries. For example, because a relational DBMS works with sets, it is very easy for the DBMS to UNION two sets of rows that are the result of two simple, independent queries.

6. ***Don't nest one query inside another query***   Usually, nested queries are less efficient than a query that avoids subqueries to produce the same result. This is another case where using UNION, INTERSECT, or MINUS and multiple queries may produce results more efficiently.
7. ***Don't combine a table with itself***   Avoid, if possible, using self-joins. It is usually better (i.e., more efficient for processing the query) to make a temporary copy of a table and then to relate the original table with the temporary one. Temporary tables, because they quickly get obsolete, should be deleted soon after they have served their purpose.
8. ***Create temporary tables for groups of queries***   When possible, reuse data that are used in a sequence of queries. For example, if a series of queries all refer to the same subset of data from the database, it may be more efficient to first store this subset in one or more temporary tables and then refer to those temporary tables in the series of queries. This will avoid repeatedly combining the same data together or repeatedly scanning the database to find the same database segment for each query. The trade-off is that the temporary tables will not change if the original tables are updated when the queries are running. Using temporary tables is a viable substitute for derived tables, and they are created only once for a series of references.
9. ***Combine update operations***   When possible, combine multiple update commands into one. This will reduce query processing overhead and allow the DBMS to seek ways to process the updates in parallel.
10. ***Retrieve only the data you need***   This will reduce the data accessed and transferred. This may seem obvious, but there are some shortcuts for query writing that violate this guideline. For example, in SQL the command SELECT * from EMP will retrieve all the fields from all the rows of the EMP table. But, if the user needs to see only some of the columns of the table, transferring the extra columns increases the query processing time.
11. ***Don't have the DBMS sort without an index***   If data are to be displayed in sorted order and an index does not exist on the sort key field, then sort the data outside the DBMS after the unsorted results are retrieved. Usually a sort utility will be faster than a sort without the aid of an index by the DBMS.
12. ***Learn!***   Track query processing times, review query plans with the EXPLAIN command, and improve your understanding of the way the DBMS determines how to process queries. Attend specialized training from your DBMS vendor on writing efficient queries, which will better inform you about the query optimizer.
13. ***Consider the total query processing time for ad hoc queries***   The total time includes the time it takes the programmer (or end user) to write the query as well as the time to process the query. Many times, for ad hoc queries, it is better to have the DBMS do extra work to allow the user to more quickly write a query. And isn't that what technology is supposed to accomplish—to allow people to be more productive? So, don't spend too much time, especially for ad hoc queries, trying to write the most efficient query. Write a query that is logically correct (i.e., produces the desired results) and let the DBMS do the work. (Of course, do an EXPLAIN first to be sure you haven't written "the query from hell" so that all other users will see a serious delay in query processing time.) This suggests a corollary: When possible, run your query when there is a light load on the database, because the total query processing time includes delays induced by other load on the DBMS and database.

All options are not available with every DBMS, and each DBMS has unique options due to its underlying design. You should refer to reference manuals for your DBMS to know which specific tuning options are available to you.

ENSURING TRANSACTION INTEGRITY

RDBMSs are no different from other types of database managers in that one of their primary responsibilities is to ensure that data maintenance is properly and completely handled. Even with extensive testing, as suggested in the prior section, bad things can happen to good data managers: A data maintenance program may not work correctly because someone submitted the job twice, some unanticipated anomaly in the data

**FIGURE 7-10 An SQL
transaction sequence
(in pseudocode)**

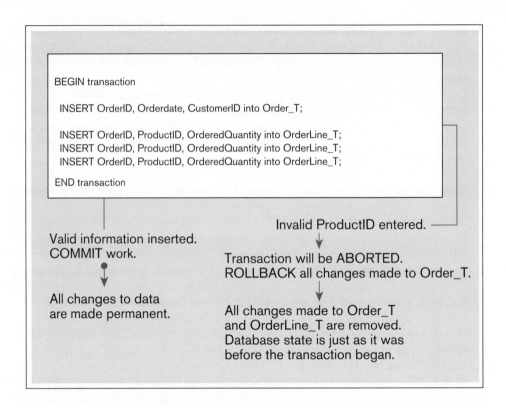

BEGIN transaction

  INSERT OrderID, Orderdate, CustomerID into Order_T;

  INSERT OrderID, ProductID, OrderedQuantity into OrderLine_T;
  INSERT OrderID, ProductID, OrderedQuantity into OrderLine_T;
  INSERT OrderID, ProductID, OrderedQuantity into OrderLine_T;

END transaction

Valid information inserted.
COMMIT work.

All changes to data
are made permanent.

Invalid ProductID entered.

Transaction will be ABORTED.
ROLLBACK all changes made to Order_T.

All changes made to Order_T
and OrderLine_T are removed.
Database state is just as it was
before the transaction began.

Transaction

A discrete unit of work that must
be completely processed or not
processed at all within a computer
system. Entering a customer order
is an example of a transaction.

Backward recovery (rollback)

The backout, or undo, of unwanted
changes to a database. Before
images of the records that have
been changed are applied to
the database, and the database
is returned to an earlier state.
Rollback is used to reverse the
changes made by transactions that
have been aborted or terminated
abnormally.

occurred, or there was a computer hardware, software, or power malfunction during
the transaction. Data maintenance is defined in units of work called **transactions**, which
involve one or more data manipulation commands. A transaction is a complete set of
closely related update commands that must all be done, or none of them done, for the
database to remain valid. Consider Figure 7-10, for example. When an order is entered
into the Pine Valley database, all of the items ordered should be entered at the same
time. Thus, either all OrderLine_T rows from this form are to be entered, along with
all the information in Order_T, or none of them should be entered. Here, the business
transaction is the complete order, not the individual items that are ordered. What we
need are commands to define the boundaries of a transaction, to commit the work of a
transaction as a permanent change to the database, and to abort a transaction on purpose and correctly, if necessary. In addition, we need data recovery services to clean
up after abnormal termination of database processing in the middle of a transaction.
Perhaps the order form is accurate, but in the middle of entering the order, the computer system malfunctions or loses power. In this case, we do not want some of the changes
made and not others. It's all or nothing at all if we want a valid database.

When a single SQL command constitutes a transaction, some RDBMSs will
automatically commit or roll back after the command is run. With a user-defined transaction, however, where multiple SQL commands need to be run and either entirely committed or entirely rolled back, commands are needed to manage the transaction explicitly.
Many systems will have BEGIN TRANSACTION and END TRANSACTION commands,
which are used to mark the boundaries of a logical unit of work. BEGIN TRANSACTION
creates a log file and starts recording all changes (insertions, deletions, and updates) to
the database in this file. END TRANSACTION or COMMIT (WORK) takes the contents
of the log file and applies them to the database, thus making the changes permanent, and
then empties the log file. ROLLBACK (WORK) asks SQL to empty the log file, effectively
cancelling all changes and resulting in rollback or **backward recovery**. Some RDBMSs
also have an AUTOCOMMIT (ON/OFF) command that specifies whether changes are
made permanent after each data modification command (ON) or only when work is explicitly made permanent (OFF) by the COMMIT WORK command.

User-defined transactions can improve system performance because transactions
will be processed as sets rather than as individual transactions, thus reducing system
overhead. When AUTOCOMMIT is set to OFF, changes will not be made automatically

until the end of a transaction is indicated. When AUTOCOMMIT is set to ON, changes will be made automatically at the end of each SQL statement; this would not allow for user-defined transactions to be committed or rolled back only as a whole.

SET AUTOCOMMIT is an interactive command; therefore, a given user session can be dynamically controlled for appropriate integrity measures. Each SQL INSERT, UPDATE, and DELETE command typically works on only one table at a time. Some data maintenance requires updating of multiple tables for the work to be complete. Therefore, these transaction-integrity commands are important in clearly defining whole units of database changes that must be completed in full for the database to retain integrity.

Further, some SQL systems have concurrency controls that handle the updating of a shared database by concurrent users. These can journalize database changes so that a database can be recovered after abnormal terminations in the middle of a transaction. They can also undo erroneous transactions. For example, in a banking application, the update of a bank account balance by two concurrent users should be cumulative. Such controls are transparent to the user in SQL; no user programming is needed to ensure proper control of concurrent access to data. To ensure the integrity of a particular database, be sensitive to transaction integrity and recovery issues and make sure that application programmers are appropriately informed of when these commands are to be used.

DATA DICTIONARY FACILITIES

RDBMSs store database definition information in secure system-created tables; we can consider these system tables as a data dictionary. Becoming familiar with the systems tables for any RDBMS being used will provide valuable information, whether you are a user or a database administrator. Because the information is stored in tables, it can be accessed by using SQL SELECT statements that can generate reports about system usage, user privileges, constraints, and so on. Also, the RDBMS will provide special SQL (proprietary) commands, such as SHOW, HELP, or DESCRIBE, to display predefined contents of the data dictionary, including the DDL that created database objects. Further, a user who understands the systems-table structure can extend existing tables or build other tables to enhance built-in features (e.g., to include data on who is responsible for data integrity). A user is, however, often restricted from modifying the structure or contents of the system tables directly, because the DBMS maintains them and depends on them for its interpretation and parsing of queries.

Each RDBMS keeps various internal tables for these definitions. In Oracle 11g, there are 522 data dictionary views for DBAs to use. Many of these views, or subsets of the DBA view (i.e., information relevant to an individual user), are also available to users who do not possess DBA privileges. Those view names begin with USER (anyone authorized to use the database) or ALL (any user) rather than DBA. Views that begin with V$ provide updated performance statistics about the database. Here is a short list of some of the tables (accessible to DBAs) that keep information about tables, clusters, columns, and security. There are also tables related to storage, objects, indexes, locks, auditing, exports, and distributed environments.

Table	Description
DBA_TABLES	Describes all tables in the database
DBA_TAB_COMMENTS	Comments on all tables in the database
DBA_CLUSTERS	Describes all clusters in the database
DBA_TAB_COLUMNS	Describes columns of all tables, views, and clusters
DBA_COL_PRIVS	Includes all grants on columns in the database
DBA_COL_COMMENTS	Comments on all columns in tables and views
DBA_CONSTRAINTS	Constraint definitions on all tables in the database
DBA_USERS	Information about all users of the database

To give an idea of the type of information found in the system tables, consider DBA_USERS. DBA_USERS contains information about the valid users of the database; its 12 attributes include user name, user ID, encrypted password, default tablespace, temporary tablespace, date created, and profile assigned. DBA_TAB_COLUMNS has 31 attributes, including owner of each table, table name, column name, data type, data length, precision, and scale, among others. An SQL query against DBA_TABLES to find out who owns PRODUCT_T follows. (Note that we have to specify PRODUCT_T, not Product_T, because Oracle stores data names in all capital letters.)

Query: Who is the owner of the PRODUCT_T table?

```
SELECT OWNER, TABLE_NAME
  FROM DBA_TABLES
    WHERE TABLE_NAME = 'PRODUCT_T';
```

Result:

OWNER	TABLE_NAME
MPRESCOTT	PRODUCT_T

TRIGGERS AND ROUTINES

Trigger

A named set of SQL statements that are considered (triggered) when a data modification (i.e., INSERT, UPDATE, DELETE) occurs or if certain data definitions are encountered. If a condition stated within a trigger is met, then a prescribed action is taken.

Triggers and routines are very powerful database objects because they are stored in the database and controlled by the DBMS. Thus, the code required to create them is stored in only one location and is administered centrally. As with table and column constraints, this promotes stronger data integrity and consistency of use within the database; it can be useful in data auditing and security to create logs of information about data updates. Not only can triggers be used to prevent unauthorized changes to the database, they can also be used to evaluate changes and take actions based on the nature of the changes. Because triggers are stored only once, code maintenance is also simplified (Mullins, 1995). Also, because they can contain complex SQL code, they are more powerful than table and column constraints; however, constraints are usually more efficient and should be used instead of the equivalent triggers, if possible. A significant advantage of a trigger over a constraint to accomplish the same control is that the processing logic of a trigger can produce a customized user message about the occurrence of a special event, whereas a constraint will produce a standardized, DBMS error message, which often is not very clear about the specific event that occurred.

Both triggers and routines consist of blocks of procedural code. Routines are stored blocks of code that must be called to operate (see Figure 7-11). They do not run automatically. In contrast, trigger code is stored in the database and runs automatically whenever the triggering event, such as an UPDATE, occurs. Triggers are a special type of stored procedure and may run in response to either DML or DDL commands. Trigger syntax and functionality vary from RDBMS to RDBMS. A trigger written to work with an Oracle database will need to be rewritten if the database is ported to Microsoft SQL Server and vice versa. For example, Oracle triggers can be written to fire once per INSERT, UPDATE, or DELETE command or to fire once per row affected by the command. Microsoft SQL Server triggers can fire only once per DML command, not once per row.

Triggers

Because triggers are stored and executed in the database, they execute against all applications that access the database. Triggers can also cascade, causing other triggers to fire. Thus, a single request from a client can result in a series of integrity or logic checks being performed on the server without causing extensive network traffic between client and server. Triggers can be used to ensure referential integrity, enforce business rules, create audit trails, replicate tables, or activate a procedure (Rennhackkamp, 1996).

Constraints can be thought of as a special case of triggers. They also are applied (triggered) automatically as a result of data modification commands, but their

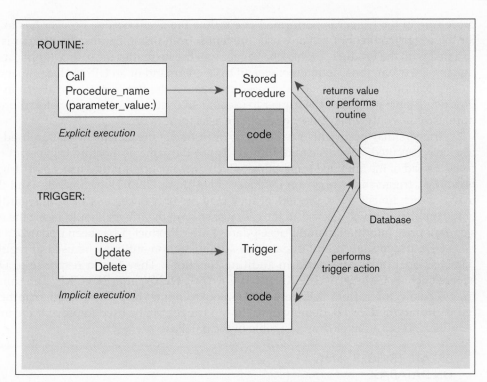

FIGURE 7-11 Triggers contrasted with stored procedures
Source: Based on Mullins (1995).

precise syntax is determined by the DBMS and does not have the flexibility of a trigger.

Triggers are used when you need to perform, under specified conditions, a certain action as the result of some database event (e.g., the execution of a DML statement such as INSERT, UPDATE, or DELETE or the DDL statement ALTER TABLE). Thus, a trigger has three parts—the *event*, the *condition*, and the *action*—and these parts are reflected in the coding structure for triggers. (See Figure 7-12 for a simplified trigger syntax.) Consider the following example from Pine Valley Furniture Company: Perhaps the manager in charge of maintaining inventory needs to know (the action of being informed) when an inventory item's standard price is updated in the Product_T table (the event). After creating a new table, PriceUpdates_T, a trigger can be written that enters each product when it is updated, the date that the change was made, and the new standard price that was entered. The trigger is named StandardPriceUpdate, and the code for this trigger follows:

```
CREATE TRIGGER StandardPriceUpdate
AFTER UPDATE OF ProductStandardPrice ON Product_T
FOR EACH ROW
INSERT INTO PriceUpdates_T VALUES (ProductDescription, SYSDATE,
ProductStandardPrice);
```

In this trigger, the *event* is an update of ProductStandardPrice, the *condition* is FOR EACH ROW (i.e., not just certain rows), and the *action after the event* is to insert the specified values in the PriceUpdates_T table, which stores a log of when (SYSDATE) the change occurred and important information about changes made to the ProductStandardPrice of any row in the table. More complicated conditions are possible, such as taking the action for rows where the new ProductStandardPrice meets some limit or the product is associated with only a certain product line. It is important to remember that the

FIGURE 7-12 Trigger syntax in SQL:2008

```
CREATE TRIGGER trigger_name
    {BEFORE| AFTER | INSTEAD OF} {INSERT | DELETE | UPDATE} ON
    table_name
    [FOR EACH {ROW | STATEMENT}] [WHEN ( search condition)]
    <triggered SQL statement here>;
```

procedure in the trigger is performed every time the event occurs; no user has to ask for the trigger to fire, nor can any user prevent it from firing. Because the trigger is associated with the Product_T table, the trigger will fire no matter the source (application) causing the event; thus, an interactive UPDATE command or an UPDATE command in an application program or stored procedure against the ProductStandardPrice in the Product_T table will cause the trigger to execute. In contrast, a routine (or stored procedure) executes only when a user or program asks for it to run.

Triggers may occur either *before*, *after*, or *instead of* the statement that aroused the trigger is executed. An "instead of" trigger is not the same as a before trigger but executes instead of the intended transaction, which does not occur if the "instead of" trigger fires. DML triggers may occur on INSERT, UPDATE, or DELETE commands. And they may fire each time a *row* is affected, or they may fire only once per *statement*, regardless of the number of rows affected. In the case just shown, the trigger should insert the new standard price information into PriceUpdate_T after Product_T has been updated.

DDL triggers are useful in database administration and may be used to regulate database operations and perform auditing functions. They fire in response to DDL events such as CREATE, ALTER, DROP, GRANT, DENY, and REVOKE. The sample trigger below, taken from SQL Server 2008 Books Online (**http://msdn2.microsoft.com /en-us/library/ms175941),** demonstrates how a trigger can be used to prevent the unintentional modification or drop of a table in the database:

```
CREATE TRIGGER safety
ON DATABASE
FOR DROP_TABLE, ALTER_TABLE
AS
    PRINT 'You must disable Trigger "safety" to drop or alter tables!'
    ROLLBACK;
```

Routines

In contrast to triggers, which are automatically run when a specified event occurs, routines must be explicitly called, just as the MIN built-in function is called. SQL-invoked routines can be either procedures or functions. The terms *procedure* and *function* are used in the same manner as they are in other programming languages. A **function** returns one value and has only input parameters. You have already seen the many built-in functions included in SQL. A **procedure** may have input parameters, output parameters, and parameters that are both input and output parameters. You may declare and name a unit of procedural code using proprietary code of the RDBMS product being used or invoke (via a CALL to an external procedure) a host-language library routine. SQL products had developed their own versions of routines prior to the issuance of SQL:1999, so be sure to become familiar with the syntax and capabilities of any product you use. Some of these proprietary languages, such as Microsoft SQL Server's Transact-SQL and Oracle's PL/SQL, are in wide use and will continue to be available. To give you an idea of how much stored procedure syntax has varied across products, Table 7-1 examines the CREATE PROCEDURE syntax used by three RDBMS vendors; this is the syntax for a procedure stored with the database. This table comes from **www.tdan.com/i023fe03 .htm** by Peter Gulutzan (accessed June 6, 2007, but no longer accessible).

The following are some of the advantages of SQL-invoked routines:

- *Flexibility* Routines may be used in more situations than constraints or triggers, which are limited to data-modification circumstances. Just as triggers have more code options than constraints, routines have more code options than triggers.
- *Efficiency* Routines can be carefully crafted and optimized to run more quickly than slower, generic SQL statements.
- *Sharability* Routines may be cached on the server and made available to all users so that they do not have to be rewritten.
- *Applicability* Routines are stored as part of the database and may apply to the entire database rather than be limited to one application. This advantage is a corollary to sharability.

Function

A stored subroutine that returns one value and has only input parameters.

Procedure

A collection of procedural and SQL statements that are assigned a unique name within the schema and stored in the database.

TABLE 7-1   Comparison of Vendor Syntax Differences in Stored Procedures

The vendors' syntaxes differ in stored procedures more than in ordinary SQL. For an illustration, here is a chart that shows what CREATE PROCEDURE looks like in three dialects. We use one line for each significant part, so you can compare dialects by reading across the line.

SQL:1999/IBM	MICROSOFT/SYBASE	ORACLE (PL/SQL)
CREATE PROCEDURE	CREATE PROCEDURE	CREATE PROCEDURE
Sp_proc1	Sp_proc1	Sp_proc1
(param1 INT)	@param1 INT	(param1 IN OUT INT)
MODIFIES SQL DATA BEGIN DECLARE num1 INT;	AS DECLARE @num1 INT	AS num1 INT; BEGIN
IF param1 <> 0	IF @param1 <> 0	IF param1 <> 0
THEN SET param1 = 1;	SELECT @param1 = 1;	THEN param1 :=1;
END IF		END IF;
UPDATE Table1 SET column1 = param1;	UPDATE Table1 SET column1 = @param1	UPDATE Table1 SET column1 = param1;
END		END

Source: Data from *SQL Performance Tuning* (Gulutzan and Pelzer, Addison-Wesley, 2002). Viewed at **www .tdan.com/i023fe03.htm**, June 6, 2007 (no longer available from this site).

The SQL:2008 syntax for procedure and function creation is shown in Figure 7-13. As you can see, the syntax is complicated, and we will not go into the details about each clause here. However, a simple procedure follows, to give you an idea of how the code works.

A procedure is a collection of procedural and SQL statements that are assigned a unique name within the schema and stored in the database. When it is needed to run the procedure, it is called by name. When it is called, all of the statements in the procedure will be executed. This characteristic of procedures helps reduce network traffic, because all of the statements are transmitted at one time, rather than sent individually. A procedure can access database contents and may have local variables. When the procedure accesses database contents, the procedure will generate an error message if the user/program calling the procedure does not have the necessary rights to access the part of the database used by the procedure.

Example Routine in Oracle's PL/SQL

In this section, we show an example of a procedure using Oracle's PL/SQL. PL/SQL is an extensive programming language for hosting SQL. We have space here to show only this one simple example.

PINE VALLEY FURNITURE

FIGURE 7-13   Syntax for creating a routine, SQL:2008

```
{CREATE PROCEDURE | CREATE FUNCTION} routine_name
([parameter [{,parameter} . . .]])
[RETURNS data_type result_cast]    /* for functions only */
[LANGUAGE {ADA | C | COBOL | FORTRAN | MUMPS | PASCAL | PLI | SQL}]
[PARAMETER STYLE {SQL | GENERAL}]
[SPECIFIC specific_name]
[DETERMINISTIC | NOT DETERMINISTIC]
[NO SQL | CONTAINS SQL | READS SQL DATA | MODIFIES SQL DATA]
[RETURNS NULL ON NULL INPUT | CALLED ON NULL INPUT]
[DYNAMIC RESULT SETS unsigned_integer]     /* for procedures only */
[STATIC DISPATCH]                          /* for functions only */
[NEW SAVEPOINT LEVEL | OLD SAVEPOINT LEVEL]
routine_body
```

To build a simple procedure that will set a sale price, the existing Product_T table in Pine Valley Furniture company is altered by adding a new column, SalePrice, that will hold the sale price for the products:

```
ALTER TABLE Product_T
ADD (SalePrice DECIMAL (6,2));
```

Result:

```
Table altered.
```

This simple PL/SQL procedure will execute two SQL statements, and there are no input or output parameters; if present, parameters are listed and given SQL data types in a parenthetical clause after the name of the procedure, similar to the columns in a CREATE TABLE command. The procedure scans all rows of the Product_T table. Products with a ProductStandardPrice of $400 or higher are discounted 10 percent, and products with a ProductStandardPrice of less than $400 are discounted 15 percent. As with other database objects, there are SQL commands to create, alter, replace, drop, and show the code for procedures. The following is an Oracle code module that will create and store the procedure named ProductLineSale:

```
CREATE OR REPLACE PROCEDURE ProductLineSale
  AS BEGIN
    UPDATE Product_T
      SET SalePrice = .90 * ProductStandardPrice
      WHERE ProductStandardPrice > = 400;
    UPDATE Product_T
      SET SalePrice = .85 * ProductStandardPrice
      WHERE ProductStandardPrice < 400;
END;
```

Oracle returns the comment "Procedure created" if the syntax has been accepted.

To run the procedure in Oracle, use this command (which can be run interactively, as part of an application program, or as part of another stored procedure):

```
SQL > EXEC ProductLineSale
```

Oracle gives this response:

```
PL/SQL procedure successfully completed.
```

Now Product_T contains the following:

PRODUCTLINE	PRODUCTID	PRODUCTDESCRIPTION	PRODUCTFINISH	PRODUCTSTANDARDPRICE	SALEPRICE
10001	1	End Table	Cherry	175	148.75
20001	2	Coffee Table	Natural Ash	200	170
20001	3	Computer Desk	Natural Ash	375	318.75
30001	4	Entertainment Center	Natural Maple	650	585
10001	5	Writer's Desk	Cherry	325	276.25
20001	6	8-Drawer Dresser	White Ash	750	675
20001	7	Dining Table	Natural Ash	800	720
30001	8	Computer Desk	Walnut	250	212.5

We have emphasized numerous times that SQL is a set-oriented language, meaning that, in part, the result of an SQL command is a set of rows. You probably noticed in Figure 7-13 that procedures can be written to work with many different host languages, most of which are record-oriented languages, meaning they are designed to manipulate one record, or row, at a time. This difference is often called an *impedance mismatch* between SQL and the host language that uses SQL commands. When SQL calls an SQL procedure, as in the example above, this is not an issue, but when the procedure is called, for example, by a C program, it can be an issue. In the next section, we consider embedding SQL in host languages and some of the additional capabilities needed to allow SQL to work seamlessly with languages not designed to communicate with programs written in other, set-oriented languages.

EMBEDDED SQL AND DYNAMIC SQL

We have been using the interactive, or direct, form of SQL. With interactive SQL, one SQL command is entered and executed at a time. Each command constitutes a logical unit of work, or a transaction. The commands necessary to maintain a valid database, such as ROLLBACK and COMMIT, are transparent to the user in most interactive SQL situations. SQL was originally created to handle database access alone and did not have flow control or the other structures necessary to create an application. SQL/PSM, introduced in SQL:1999, provides for the types of programmatic extensions needed to develop a database application.

Prior to SQL/PSM, two other forms of SQL were widely used in creating applications on both clients and servers; they are referred to as **embedded SQL** and **dynamic SQL**. SQL commands can be embedded in third-generation languages (3GLs), such as Ada and COBOL, as well as in C, PHP, .NET, and Java if the commands are placed at appropriate locations in a 3GL host program. As we saw in the prior section, Oracle also offers PL/SQL or SQL Procedural Language, a proprietary language that extends SQL by adding some procedural language features such as variables, types, control structures (including IF-THEN-ELSE loops), functions, and procedures. PL/SQL blocks of code can also be embedded within 3GL programs.

Dynamic SQL derives the precise SQL statement at run time. Programmers write to an application programming interface (API) to achieve the interface between languages. Embedded SQL and dynamic SQL will continue to be used. Programmers are used to them, and in many cases they are still an easier approach than attempting to use SQL as an application language in addition to using it for database creation, administration, and querying.

There are several reasons to consider embedding SQL in a 3GL:

Embedded SQL

Hard-coded SQL statements included in a program written in another language, such as C or Java.

Dynamic SQL

Specific SQL code generated on the fly while an application is processing.

1. It is possible to create a more flexible, accessible interface for the user. Using interactive SQL requires a good understanding of both SQL and the database structure—understanding that a typical application user may not have. Although many RDBMSs come with form, report, and application generators (or such capabilities available as add-ons), developers frequently envision capabilities that are not easily accomplished with these tools but that can be easily accomplished using a 3GL. Large, complex programs that require access to a relational database may best be programmed in a 3GL with embedded SQL calls to an SQL database.

2. It may be possible to improve performance by using embedded SQL. Using interactive SQL requires that each query be converted to executable machine code each time the query is processed. Or, the query optimizer, which runs automatically in a direct SQL situation, may not successfully optimize the query, causing it to run slowly. With embedded SQL, the developer has more control over database access and may be able to create significant performance improvements. Knowing when to rely on the SQL translator and optimizer and when to control it through the program depends on the nature of the problem, and making this trade-off is best accomplished through experience and testing.

3. Database security may be improved by using embedded SQL. Restricted access can be achieved by a DBA through the GRANT and REVOKE permissions in SQL and through the use of views. These same restrictions can also be invoked in an embedded SQL application, thus providing another layer of protection. Complex data integrity checks also may be more easily accomplished, including cross-field consistency checks.

A program that uses embedded SQL will consist of the host program written in a 3GL such as C or COBOL, and there will also be sections of SQL code sprinkled throughout. Each section of SQL code will begin with EXEC SQL, keywords used to indicate an embedded SQL command that will be converted to the host source code when run through the precompiler. You will need a separate precompiler for each host language that you plan to use. Be sure to determine that the 3GL compiler is compatible with your RDBMS's precompiler for each language.

When the precompiler encounters an EXEC SQL statement, it will translate that SQL command into the host program language. Some, but not all, precompilers will check for correct SQL syntax and generate any required error messages at this point. Others will not generate an error message until the SQL statement actually attempts to execute. Some products' precompilers (DB2, SQL/DS, Ingres) create a separate file of SQL statements that is then processed by a separate utility called a binder, which determines that the referenced objects exist, that the user possesses sufficient privileges to run the statement, and the processing approach that will be used. Other products (Oracle, Informix) interpret the statements at run time rather than compiling them. In either case, the resulting program will contain calls to DBMS routines, and the link/editor programs will link these routines into the program.

Dynamic SQL is used to generate appropriate SQL code on the fly while an application is processing. Most programmers write to an API, such as ODBC, which can then be passed through to any ODBC-compliant database. Dynamic SQL is central to most Internet applications. The developer is able to create a more flexible application because the exact SQL query is determined at run time, including the number of parameters to be passed, which tables will be accessed, and so forth. Dynamic SQL is very useful when an SQL statement shell will be used repeatedly, with different parameter values being inserted each time it executes.

Embedded and dynamic SQL code is vulnerable to malicious modification. Any procedure that has or especially constructs SQL statements should be reviewed for such vulnerabilities. A common form of such an attack involves insertion of the malicious code into user input variables that are concatenated with SQL commands and then executed. Alternatively, malicious code can be included in text stored in the database. As long as the malicious code is syntactically correct, the SQL database engine will process it. Preventing and detecting such attacks can be complicated, and this is beyond the scope of this text. The reader is encouraged to do an Internet search on the topic of SQL injection for recommendations. At a minimum, user input should be carefully validated, strong typing of columns should be used to limit exposure, and input data can be filtered or modified so that special SQL characters (e.g., ;) or words (e.g., DELETE) are put in quotes so they cannot be executed.

Currently, the Open Database Connectivity (ODBC) standard is the most commonly used API. SQL:1999 includes the SQL Call Level Interface (SQL/CLI). Both are written in C, and both are based on the same earlier standard. Java Database Connectivity (JDBC) is an industry standard used for connecting from Java. It is not yet an ISO standard. No new functionality has been added in SQL:2008.

As SQL:2008 becomes implemented more completely, the use of embedded and dynamic SQL will become more standardized because the standard creates a computationally complete SQL language for the first time. Because most vendors have created these capabilities independently, though, the next few years will be a period in which SQL:2008-compliant products will exist side by side with older, but entrenched, versions. The user will need to be aware of these possibilities and deal with them.

Summary

This chapter continues from Chapter 6, which introduced the SQL language. Equi-joins, natural joins, outer joins, and union joins have been considered. Equi-joins are based on equal values in the common columns of the tables that are being joined and will return all requested results including the values of the common columns from each table included in the join. Natural joins return all requested results, but values of the common columns are included only once. Outer joins return all the values in one of the tables included in the join, regardless of whether or not a match exists in the other table. Union joins return a table that includes all data from each table that was joined.

Nested subqueries, where multiple SELECT statements are nested within a single query, are useful for more complex query situations. A special form of the subquery, a correlated subquery, requires that a value be known from the outer query before the inner query can be processed. Other subqueries process the inner query, return a result to the next outer query, and then process that outer query.

Other advanced SQL topics include the use of embedded SQL and the use of triggers and routines. SQL can be included within the context of many third-generation languages, including COBOL, C, Fortran, and Ada, and more modern languages such as C, PHP, .NET, and Java. The use of embedded SQL allows for the development of more flexible interfaces, improved performance, and improved database security. User-defined functions that run automatically when records are inserted, updated, or deleted are called triggers. Procedures are user-defined code modules that can be called to execute. OLTP and OLAP are used for operational transaction processing and data analysis, respectively.

SQL-invoked routines, including triggers, functions, and procedures, were included in SQL:1999. Users must realize that these capabilities have been included as vendor-specific extensions and will continue to exist for some time.

Dynamic SQL is an integral part of Web-enabling databases and will be demonstrated in more detail in Chapter 8. This chapter has presented some of the more complex capabilities of SQL and has created awareness of the extended and complex capabilities of SQL that must be mastered to build database application programs.

Chapter Review

Key Terms

Backward recovery (rollback) *254*	Dynamic SQL *261*	Join *233*	Trigger *256*
Correlated subquery *246*	Embedded SQL *261*	Natural join *235*	Transaction *254*
	Equi-join *234*	Outer join *236*	
	Function *258*	Procedure *258*	

Review Questions

1. Define each of the following terms:
   a. dynamic SQL
   b. correlated subquery
   c. embedded SQL
   d. procedure
   e. join
   f. equi-join
   g. self join
   h. outer join
   i. function

2. Match the following terms to the appropriate definition:

   _____ equi-join
   _____ natural join
   _____ outer join
   _____ trigger

   _____ procedure
   _____ embedded SQL

   _____ COMMIT

   _____ Dynamic SQL

   _____ ROLLBACK

   a. undoes changes to a table
   b. returns all records of designated table
   c. keeps redundant columns
   d. makes changes to a table permanent
   e. process that includes SQL statements within a host language
   f. process of making an application capable of generating specific SQL code on the fly
   g. does not keep redundant columns
   h. set of SQL statements that execute under stated conditions
   i. stored, named collection of procedural and SQL statements

3. When is an outer join used instead of a natural join?
4. Explain the processing order of a correlated subquery.

5. Explain the following statement regarding SQL: Any query that can be written using the subquery approach can also be written using the joining approach but not vice versa.
6. What is the purpose of the COMMIT command in SQL? How does commit relate to the notion of a business transaction (e.g., entering a customer order or issuing a customer invoice)?
7. Care must be exercised when writing triggers for a database. What are some of the problems that could be encountered?
8. Explain the structure of a module of code that defines a trigger.
9. Under what conditions can a UNION clause be used?
10. Discuss the differences between triggers and stored procedures.
11. List four advantages of SQL-invoked routines.
12. When would you consider using embedded SQL? When would you use dynamic SQL?
13. When do you think that the CASE keyword in SQL would be useful?
14. Explain the use of derived tables.
15. Describe an example in which you would want to use a derived table.
16. What is PL/SQL, and what does it include in addition to SQL?
17. If two queries involved in a UNION operation contained columns that were data type incompatible, how would you recommend fixing this?
18. Can an outer join be easily implemented when joining more than two tables? Why or why not?
19. This chapter discusses the data dictionary views for Oracle 11g. Research another RDBMS, such as Microsoft SQL Server, and report on its data dictionary facility and how it compares with Oracle.

Problems and Exercises

*Problems and Exercises 1 through 5 are based on the class sched-
ule 3NF relations along with some sample data in Figure 7-14. For
Problems and Exercises 1 through 5, draw a Venn or ER diagram and
mark it to show the data you expect your query to use to produce the
results.*

1. Write SQL retrieval commands for each of the following
   queries:
   a. Display the course ID and course name for all courses
      with an ISM prefix.
   b. Display all courses for which Professor Berndt has been
      qualified.
   c. Display the class roster, including student name, for all
      students enrolled in section 2714 of ISM 4212.
2. Write an SQL query to answer the following question:
   Which instructors are qualified to teach ISM 3113?
3. Write an SQL query to answer the following question: Is any
   instructor qualified to teach ISM 3113 and not qualified to
   teach ISM 4930?

4. Write SQL queries to answer the following questions:
   a. How many students were enrolled in section 2714 dur-
      ing semester I-2008?
   b. How many students were enrolled in ISM 3113 during
      semester I-2008?
5. Write an SQL query to answer the following question:
   Which students were not enrolled in any courses during
   semester I-2008?

*Problems and Exercises 6 through 14 are based on Figure 7-15. This
problem set continues from Chapter 6, Problems and Exercises 10
through 15, which were based on Figure 6-11.*

6. Determine the relationships among the four entities in
   Figure 7-15. List primary keys for each entity and any
   foreign keys necessary to establish the relationships and
   maintain referential integrity. Pay particular attention to
   the data contained in TUTOR REPORTS when you set up
   its primary key.

STUDENT (StudentID, StudentName)

StudentID	StudentName
38214	Letersky
54907	Altvater
66324	Aiken
70542	Marra
...	

QUALIFIED (FacultyID, CourseID, DateQualified)

FacultyID	CourseID	DateQualified
2143	ISM 3112	9/1988
2143	ISM 3113	9/1988
3467	ISM 4212	9/1995
3467	ISM 4930	9/1996
4756	ISM 3113	9/1991
4756	ISM 3112	9/1991
...		

FACULTY (FacultyID, FacultyName)

FacultyID	FacultyName
2143	Birkin
3467	Berndt
4756	Collins
...	

SECTION (SectionNo, Semester, CourseID)

SectionNo	Semester	CourseID
2712	I-2008	ISM 3113
2713	I-2008	ISM 3113
2714	I-2008	ISM 4212
2715	I-2008	ISM 4930
...		

COURSE (CourseID, CourseName)

CourseID	CourseName
ISM 3113	Syst Analysis
ISM 3112	Syst Design
ISM 4212	Database
ISM 4930	Networking
...	

REGISTRATION (StudentID, SectionNo, Semester)

StudentID	SectionNo	Semester
38214	2714	I-2008
54907	2714	I-2008
54907	2715	I-2008
66324	2713	I-2008
...		

FIGURE 7-14 Class scheduling relations (for Problems and Exercises 1–5)

FIGURE 7-15 Adult literacy program (for Problems and Exercises 6–14)

TUTOR (TutorID, CertDate, Status)

TutorID	CertDate	Status
100	1/05/2008	Active
101	1/05/2008	Temp Stop
102	1/05/2008	Dropped
103	5/22/2008	Active
104	5/22/2008	Active
105	5/22/2008	Temp Stop
106	5/22/2008	Active

STUDENT (StudentID, Read)

StudentID	Read
3000	2.3
3001	5.6
3002	1.3
3003	3.3
3004	2.7
3005	4.8
3006	7.8
3007	1.5

MATCH HISTORY (MatchID, TutorID, StudentID, StartDate, EndDate)

MatchID	TutorID	StudentID	StartDate	EndDate
1	100	3000	1/10/2008	
2	101	3001	1/15/2008	5/15/2008
3	102	3002	2/10/2008	3/01/2008
4	106	3003	5/28/2008	
5	103	3004	6/01/2008	6/15/2008
6	104	3005	6/01/2008	6/28/2008
7	104	3006	6/01/2008	

TUTOR REPORT (MatchID, Month, Hours, Lessons)

MatchID	Month	Hours	Lessons
1	6/08	8	4
4	6/08	8	6
5	6/08	4	4
4	7/08	10	5
1	7/08	4	2

7. Write the SQL command to add MATH SCORE to the STUDENT table.
8. Write the SQL command to add SUBJECT to TUTOR. The only values allowed for SUBJECT will be Reading, Math, and ESL.
9. What do you need to do if a tutor signs up and wants to tutor in both reading and math? Draw the new ERD and write any SQL statements that would be needed to handle this development.
10. Write the SQL command to find any tutors who have not submitted a report for July.
11. Where do you think student and tutor information such as name, address, phone, and e-mail should be kept? Write the necessary SQL commands to capture this information.
12. List all active students in June by name. (Make up names and other data if you are actually building a prototype database.) Include the number of hours students received tutoring and how many lessons they completed.
13. Which tutors, by name, are available to tutor? Write the SQL command.
14. Which tutor needs to be reminded to turn in reports? Write the SQL command. Show how you constructed this query using a Venn or other type of diagram.

PINE VALLEY FURNITURE

Problems and Exercises 15 through 44 are based on the entire ("big" version) Pine Valley Furniture Company database.

Note: Depending on what DBMS you are using, some field names may have changed to avoid conflicting with reserved words for the DBMS. When you first use the DBMS, check the table definitions to see what the field names are for the DBMS you are using. This database is available at **www.teradatauniversitynetwork.com**.

15. Write an SQL command that will find any customers who have not placed orders.
16. List the names and number of employees supervised (label this value HeadCount) for each supervisor who supervises more than two employees.
17. List the name of each employee, his or her birth date, the name of his or her manager, and the manager's birth date for those employees who were born before their manager was born; label the manager's data Manager and ManagerBirth. Show how you constructed this query using a Venn or other type of diagram.
18. Write an SQL command to display the order number, customer number, order date, and items ordered for some particular customer.
19. Write an SQL command to display each item ordered for order number 1, its standard price, and the total price for each item ordered.
20. Write an SQL command to total the cost of order number 1.
21. Calculate the total raw material cost (label TotCost) for each product compared to its standard product price. Display product ID, product description, standard price, and the total cost in the result.

22. For every order that has been received, display the order ID, the total dollar amount owed on that order (you'll have to calculate this total from attributes in one or more tables; label this result TotalDue), and the amount received in payments on that order (assume that there is only one payment made on each order). To make this query a little simpler, you don't have to include those orders for which no payment has yet been received. List the results in decreasing order of the difference between total due and amount paid.

23. Write an SQL query to list each customer who has bought computer desks and the number of units sold to each customer. Show how you constructed this query using a Venn or other type of diagram.

24. List, in alphabetical order, the names of all employees (managers) who are now managing people with skill ID BS12; list each manager's name only once, even if that manager manages several people with this skill.

25. Display the salesperson name, product finish, and total quantity sold (label as TotSales) for each finish by each salesperson.

26. Write a query to list the number of products produced in each work center (label as TotalProducts). If a work center does not produce any products, display the result with a total of 0.

27. The production manager at PVFC is concerned about support for purchased parts in products owned by customers. A simple analysis he wants done is to determine for each customer how many vendors are in the same state as that customer. Develop a list of *all* the PVFC customers by name with the number of vendors in the same state as that customer. (Label this computed result NumVendors.)

28. Display the order IDs for customers who have not made any payment, yet, on that order. Use the set command UNION, INTERSECT, or MINUS in your query.

29. Display the names of the states in which customers reside but for which there is no salesperson residing in that state. There are several ways to write this query. Try to write it without any WHERE clause. Write this query two ways, using the set command UNION, INTERSECT, or MINUS and not using any of these commands. Which was the most natural approach for you, and why?

30. Write an SQL query to produce a list of all the products (i.e., product description) and the number of times each product has been ordered. Show how you constructed this query using a Venn or other type of diagram.

31. Display the customer ID, name, and order ID for all customer orders. For those customers who do not have any orders, include them in the display once.

32. Display the EmployeeID and EmployeeName for those employees who do not possess the skill Router. Display the results in order by EmployeeName. Show how you constructed this query using a Venn or other type of diagram.

33. Display the name of customer 16 and the names of all the customers that are in the same zip code as customer 16. (Be sure this query will work for any customer.)

34. Rewrite your answer to Problem and Exercise 33 for each customer, not just customer 16.

35. Display the customer ID, name, and order ID for all customer orders. For those customers who do not have any orders, include them in the display once by showing order ID 0.

36. Show the customer ID and name for all the customers who have ordered both products with IDs 3 and 4 on the same order.

37. Display the customer names of all customer who have ordered (on the same or different orders) both products with IDs 3 and 4.

38. Review the first query in the "Correlated Subqueries" section. Can you identify a special set of standard prices for which this query will not yield the desired result? How might you rewrite the query to handle this situation?

39. Write an SQL query to list the order number and order quantity for all customer orders for which the order quantity is greater than the average order quantity of that product. (Hint: This involves using a correlated subquery.)

40. Write an SQL query to list the salesperson who has sold the most computer desks.

41. Display in product ID order the product ID and total amount ordered of that product by the customer who has bought the most of that product; use a derived table in a FROM clause to answer this query.

42. Display employee information for all the employees in each state who were hired before the most recently hired person in that state.

43. The head of marketing is interested in some opportunities for cross-selling of products. She thinks that the way to identify cross-selling opportunities is to know for each product how many other products are sold to the same customer on the same order (e.g., a product that is bought by a customer in the same order with lots of other products is a better candidate for cross-selling than a product bought by itself).

    a. To help the marketing manager, first list the IDs for all the products that have sold in total more than 20 units across all orders. (These are popular products, which are the only products she wants to consider as triggers for potential cross-selling.)

    b. Make a new query that lists all the IDs for the orders that include products that satisfy the first query, along with the number of products on those orders. Only orders with three or more products on them are of interest to the marketing manager. Write this query as general as possible to cover any answer to the first query, which might change over time. To clarify, if product X is one of the products that is in the answer set from part a, then in part b we want to see the desired order information for orders that include product X.

    c. The marketing manager needs to know what other products were sold on the orders that are in the result for part b. (Again, write this query for the general, not specific, result to the query in part b.) These are products that are sold, for example, with product X from part a, and these are the ones that if people buy that product, we'd want to try to cross-sell them product X because history says they are likely to buy it along with what else they are buying. Write a query to identify these other products by ID and description. It is okay to include "product X" in your result (i.e., you don't need to exclude the products in the result of part a.).

44. For each product, display in ascending order, by product ID, the product ID and description, along with the customer ID and name for the customer who has bought the most of that product; also show the total quantity ordered by that customer (who has bought the most of that product). Use a correlated subquery.

References

DeLoach, A. 1987. "The Path to Writing Efficient Queries in SQL/DS." *Database Programming & Design* 1,1 (January): 26–32.

Holmes, J. 1996. "More Paths to Better Performance." *Database Programming & Design* 9, 2 (February):47–48.

Mullins, C. S. 1995. "The Procedural DBA." *Database Programming & Design* 8,12 (December): 40–45.

Rennhackkamp, M. 1996. "Trigger Happy." *DBMS* 9,5 (May): 89–91, 95.

Further Reading

American National Standards Institute. 2000. *ANSI Standards Action* 31,11 (June 2): 20.

Celko, J. 2006. *Analytics and OLAP in SQL*. San Francisco: Morgan Kaufmann.

Codd, E. F. 1970. "A Relational Model of Data for Large Shared Data Banks." *Communications of the ACM* 13,6 (June): 77–87.

Date, C. J., and H. Darwen. 1997. *A Guide to the SQL Standard*. Reading, MA: Addison-Wesley.

Itzik, B., L. Kollar, and D. Sarka. 2006. *Inside Microsoft SQL Server 2005 T-SQL Querying*. Redmond, WA: Microsoft Press.

Eisenberg, A., J. Melton, K. Kulkarni, J. E. Michels, and F. Zemke. 2004. "SQL:2003 Has Been Published." *SIGMOD Record* 33,1 (March):119–26.

Itzik B., D. Sarka, and R. Wolter. 2006. *Inside Microsoft SQL Server 2005: T-SQL Programming*. Redmond, WA: Microsoft Press.

Kulkarni, K. 2004. "Overview of SQL:2003." Accessed at **www .wiscorp.com/SQLStandards.html#keyreadings**.

Melton, J. 1997. "A Case for SQL Conformance Testing." *Database Programming & Design* 10,7 (July): 66–69.

van der Lans, R. F. 1993. *Introduction to SQL*, 2nd ed. Workingham, UK: Addison-Wesley.

Winter, R. 2000. "SQL-99's New OLAP Functions." *Intelligent Enterprise* 3,2 (January 20): 62, 64–65.

Winter, R. 2000. "The Extra Mile." *Intelligent Enterprise* 3,10 (June 26): 62–64.

See also "Further Reading" in Chapter 6.

Web Resources

www.ansi.org Web site of the American National Standards Institute. Contains information on the ANSI federation and the latest national and international standards.

www.coderecipes.net Web site that explains and shows examples for a wide range of SQL commands.

www.fluffycat.com/SQL/ Web site that defines a sample database and shows examples of SQL queries against this database.

www.iso.ch The International Organization for Standardization's (ISO's) Web site, which provides information about the ISO. Copies of current standards may be purchased here.

www.sqlcourse.com and **www.sqlcourse2.com** Web sites that provide tutorials for a subset of ANSI SQL with a practice database.

standards.ieee.org The home page of the IEEE standards organization.

www.tizag.com/sqlTutorial/ Web site that provides a set of tutorials on SQL concepts and commands.

http://troelsarvin.blogspot.com/ Blog that provides a detailed comparison of different SQL implementations, including DB2, Microsoft SQL, MySQL, Oracle, and PostGreSQL

www.teradatauniversitynetwork.com Web site where your instructor may have created some course environments for you to use Teradata SQL Assistant, Web Edition, with one or more of the Pine Valley Furniture and Mountain View Community Hospital data sets for this text.

Database Application Development

LEARNING OBJECTIVES

After studying this chapter, you should be able to:

- Concisely define each of the following key terms: **client/server system, application partitioning, fat client, database server, middleware, application program interface (API), Open Database Connectivity (ODBC), three-tier architecture, thin client, Java servlet, Extensible Markup Language (XML), XML Schema Definition (XSD), XPath, XQuery, Extensible Stylesheet Language Transformation (XSLT), Web services, Universal Description, Discovery, and Integration (UDDI), Web Services Description Language (WSDL), Simple Object Access Protocol (SOAP),** and **Service-Oriented Architecture (SOA)**.

- Explain the three components of client/server systems: data presentation services, processing services, and storage services.

- Distinguish between two-tier and three-tier architectures.

- Describe how to connect to databases in a two-tier application in VB.NET and Java.

- Describe the key components of a Web application and the information flow between the various components.

- Describe how to connect to databases in a three-tier Web application using Java Server Pages (JSP) and ASP.NET.

- Explain the purpose of XML and its uses in standardizing data exchange across the Internet.

- Understand how XQuery can be used to query XML documents.

- Explain how XML has led to the spread of Web services and the emergence of service-oriented architectures.

INTRODUCTION

Client/server system

A networked computing model that distributes processes between clients and servers, which supply the requested services. In a database system, the database generally resides on a server that processes the DBMS. The clients may process the application systems or request services from another server that holds the application programs.

Client/server systems operate in networked environments, splitting the processing of an application between a front-end client and a back-end processor. Generally, the client process requires some resource, which the server provides to the client. Clients and servers can reside in the same computer, or they can be on different computers that are networked together. Both clients and servers are intelligent and programmable, so the computing power of both can be used to devise effective and efficient applications.

It is difficult to overestimate the impact that client/server applications have had in the past 20 years. Advances in personal computer technology and the rapid evolution of graphical user interfaces (GUIs), networking, and communications have changed the way businesses use computing systems to meet ever more demanding business needs.

Electronic commerce requires that client browsers be able to access dynamic Web pages attached to databases that provide real-time information. Personal computers linked through networks that support workgroup computing are the norm. Mainframe applications have been rewritten to run in client/server environments and take advantage of the greater cost-effectiveness of networks of personal computers and workstations. The need for strategies that fit specific business environments is being filled by client/server solutions because they offer flexibility, scalability (the ability to upgrade a system without having to redesign it), and extensibility (the ability to define new data types and operations).

CLIENT/SERVER ARCHITECTURES

Client/server architectures can be distinguished by how application logic components are distributed across clients and servers. There are three components of application logic (see Figure 8-1). The first is the input/output (I/O), or presentation logic, component. This component is responsible for formatting and presenting data on the user's screen or other output device and for managing user input from a keyboard or other input device. Presentation logic often resides on the client and is the mechanism with which the user interacts with the system. The second component is the processing logic. This handles data processing logic, business rules logic, and data management logic. Data processing logic includes such activities as data validation and identification of processing errors. Business rules that have not been coded at the Database Management System (DBMS) level may be coded in the processing component. Data management logic identifies the data necessary for processing the transaction or query. Processing logic resides on both the client and servers. The third component is storage, the component responsible for data storage and retrieval from the physical storage devices associated with the application. Storage logic usually resides on the database server, close to the physical location of the data. Activities of a DBMS occur in the storage logic component. For example, data integrity control activities, such as constraint checking, are typically placed there. Triggers, which will always fire when appropriate conditions are met, are associated with insert, modify, update, and delete commands, are also placed here. Stored procedures that use the data directly are usually also stored on the database server.

Client/server architectures are normally categorized into three types: two-, three-, or *n*-tier architectures, depending on the placement of the three types of application

FIGURE 8-1   Application logic components

logic. There is no one optimal client/server architecture that is the best solution for all business problems. Rather, the flexibility inherent in client/server architectures offers organizations the possibility of tailoring their configurations to fit their particular processing needs. **Application partitioning** helps in this tailoring.

Figure 8-2a depicts three commonly found configurations of two-tier systems based on the placement of the processing logic. In the **fat client**, the application processing occurs entirely on the client, whereas in the thin client, this processing occurs primarily on the server. In the distributed example, application processing is partitioned between the client and the server.

Figure 8-2b presents the typical setup of three-tier and *n*-tier architectures. These types of architectures are most prevalent in Web-based systems. As in two-tier systems, some processing logic could be placed on the client, if desired. But a typical client in a Web-enabled client/server environment will be a thin client, using a browser for its presentation logic. The middle tiers are typically coded in a portable language such as C or Java. The flexibility and easier manageability of the *n*-tier approaches account for its increasing popularity, in spite of the increased complexity of managing the communication among the tiers. The fast-paced, distributed, and heterogeneous environment of the Internet and e-commerce initiatives have also led to the development of many *n*-tier architectures.

FIGURE 8-2   Common logic distributions
(a) Two-tier client/server environments

(b) Three-tier and *n*-tier client/server environments

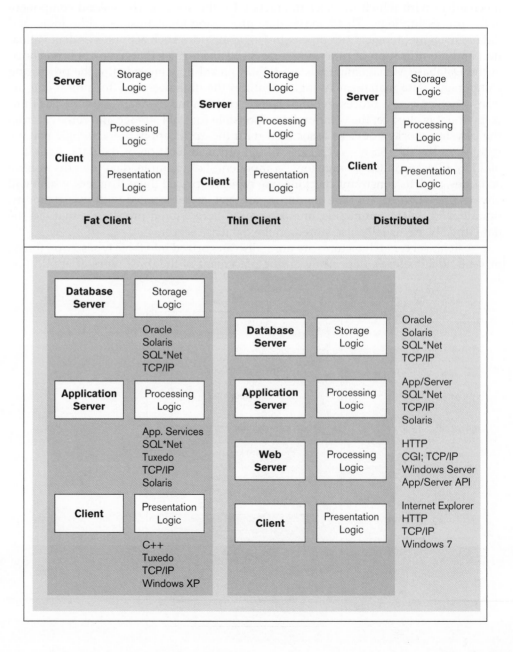

Now that we have examined the different types of client/server architectures and their advantages and disadvantages in general, in the next two sections, we show specific examples of the role of databases in these types of architectures.

DATABASES IN A TWO-TIER ARCHITECTURE

In a two-tier architecture, a client workstation is responsible for managing the user interface, including presentation logic, data processing logic, and business rules logic, and a **database server** is responsible for database storage, access, and processing. Figure 8-3 shows a typical database server architecture. With the DBMS placed on the database server, Local Area Network (LAN) traffic is reduced because only those records that match the requested criteria are transmitted to the client station, rather than entire data files. Some people refer to the central DBMS functions as the *back-end functions*, whereas they call the application programs on the client PCs *front-end programs*.

With this architecture, only the database server requires processing power adequate to handle the database, and the database is stored on the server, not on the clients. Therefore, the database server can be tuned to optimize database-processing performance. Because fewer data are sent across the LAN, the communication load is reduced. User authorization, integrity checking, data dictionary maintenance, and query and update processing are all performed at one location, on the database server.

Client/server projects that use two-tier architectures tend to be departmental applications, supporting a relatively small number of users. Such applications are not mission critical and have been most successful when transaction volumes are low, immediate availability is not critical, and security is not of the highest concern. As companies have sought to gain expected benefits from client/server projects, such as scalability, flexibility, and lowered costs, they have had to develop new approaches to client/server architectures.

Most two-tier applications are written in a programming language such as Java, VB.NET, or C#. Connecting an application written in these common programming languages to a database is achieved through the use of special software called *database-oriented middleware*. Middleware is often referred to as the glue that holds together client/server applications. It is a term that is commonly used to describe any software component between the PC client and the relational database in *n*-tier

Database server

A computer that is responsible for database storage, access, and processing in a client/server environment. Some people also use this term to describe a two-tier client/server application.

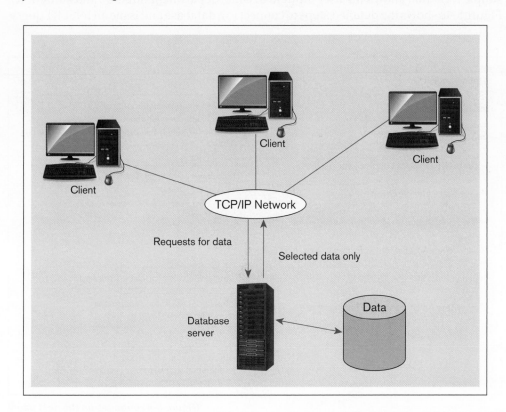

FIGURE 8-3 Database server architecture (two-tier architecture)

Middleware

Software that allows an application to interoperate with other software without requiring the user to understand and code the low-level operations necessary to achieve interoperability.

Application program interface (API)

Sets of routines that an application program uses to direct the performance of procedures by the computer's operating system.

Open database connectivity (ODBC)

An application programming interface that provides a common language for application programs to access and process SQL databases independent of the particular DBMS that is accessed.

architectures. Simply put, **middleware** is any of several classes of software that allows an application to interoperate with other software without requiring the user to understand and code the low-level operations required to achieve interoperability (Hurwitz, 1998). The database-oriented middleware needed to connect an application to a database consists of two parts: an **application programming interface (API)** and a database driver to connect to a specific type database (e.g., SQL Server or Oracle). The most common APIs are **Open Database Connectivity (ODBC)** and ADO.NET for the Microsoft platform (VB.NET and C#) and Java Database Connectivity (JDBC) for use with Java programs.

No matter which API or language is used, the basic steps for accessing a database from an application remain surprisingly similar:

1. Identify and register a database driver.
2. Open a connection to a database.
3. Execute a query against the database.
4. Process the results of the query.
5. Repeat steps 3–4 as necessary.
6. Close the connection to the database.

A VB.NET Example

Let us take a look at these steps in action in the context of a simple VB.NET application. The purpose of the code snippet shown in Figure 8-4 is to insert a new record into a student database. For simplicity, we will not show code related to error handling. Also, while we show the password embedded in the code below, in commercial applications, other mechanisms to retrieve passwords are used.

The VB.NET code shown in Figure 8-4 uses the ADO.NET data access framework and .NET data providers to connect to the database. The .NET Framework has different data providers (or database drivers) that allow you to connect a program written in a .NET programming language to a database. Common data providers available in the framework are for SQL Server and Oracle.

The VB.NET code illustrates how a simple INSERT query can be executed against the Oracle database. Figure 8-4a shows the VB.NET code needed to create a simple form that allows the user input to a name, department number, and student ID. Figure 8-4b shows the detailed steps to connect to a database and issue an INSERT query.

FIGURE 8-4 Sample VB.NET code that demonstrates an INSERT in a database

(a) Setup form for receiving user input

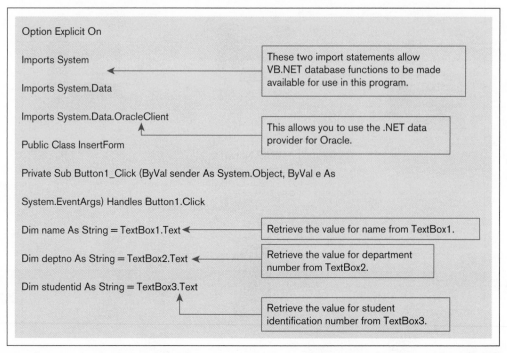

(Figure 8-4 continues on the next page)

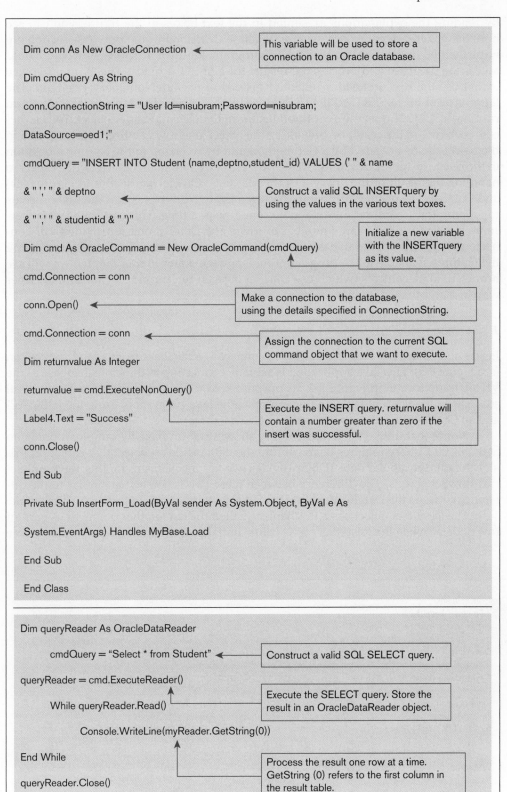

FIGURE 8-4   *(continued)*
**(b) Connecting to a database
and issuing an INSERT query**

```
Dim conn As New OracleConnection         ←  This variable will be used to store a
                                            connection to an Oracle database.

Dim cmdQuery As String

conn.ConnectionString = "User Id=nisubram;Password=nisubram;

DataSource=oed1;"

cmdQuery = "INSERT INTO Student (name,deptno,student_id) VALUES (' " & name

& " ',' " & deptno        ←  Construct a valid SQL INSERTquery by
                             using the values in the various text boxes.

& " ',' " & studentid & " ')"

Dim cmd As OracleCommand = New OracleCommand(cmdQuery)
                                    ↑  Initialize a new variable
                                       with the INSERTquery
cmd.Connection = conn                  as its value.

conn.Open()    ←  Make a connection to the database,
                  using the details specified in ConnectionString.

cmd.Connection = conn    ←  Assign the connection to the current SQL
                            command object that we want to execute.

Dim returnvalue As Integer

returnvalue = cmd.ExecuteNonQuery()

Label4.Text = "Success"    ←  Execute the INSERT query. returnvalue will
                              contain a number greater than zero if the
conn.Close()                  insert was successful.

End Sub

Private Sub InsertForm_Load(ByVal sender As System.Object, ByVal e As

System.EventArgs) Handles MyBase.Load

End Sub

End Class
```

**(c) Sample code snippet for using
a SELECT query**

```
Dim queryReader As OracleDataReader

    cmdQuery = "Select * from Student"    ←  Construct a valid SQL SELECT query.

queryReader = cmd.ExecuteReader()

    While queryReader.Read()    ←  Execute the SELECT query. Store the
                                   result in an OracleDataReader object.

        Console.WriteLine(myReader.GetString(0))

End While    ←  Process the result one row at a time.
                GetString (0) refers to the first column in
queryReader.Close()    the result table.
```

By reading the explanations presented in the text boxes in the figure, you can see how the generic steps for accessing a database described in the previous section are implemented in the context of a VB.NET program. Figure 8-4c shows how you would access the database and process the results for a SELECT query. The main difference is that use the ExecuteReader() method instead of ExecuteNonQuery() method. The latter is used for INSERT, UPDATE, and DELETE queries. The table that results from running a SELECT query are captured inside an OracleDataReader object. You can access each row in the result by traversing the object, one row at a time. Each column in the object can be accessed by a Get method and by referring to the column's position in the query result (or by name). ADO.NET provides two main choices with respect to handling the result of the query: DataReader (e.g., OracleDataReader in Figure 8-4c) and DataSet. The primary difference between the two options is that the first limits us to looping through the result of a query one row at a time. This can be very cumbersome if the result has a large number of rows. The DataSet object provides a disconnected snapshot of the database that we can then manipulate in our program using the features available in the programming language. Later in this chapter, we will see how .NET data controls (which use DataSet objects) can provide a cleaner and easier way to manipulate data in a program.

A Java Example

Let us now look at an example of how to connect to a database from a Java application (see Figure 8-5). This Java application is actually connecting to the same database as the VB.NET application in Figure 8-4. Its purpose is to retrieve and print the names of all students in the Student table. In this example, the Java program is using the JDBC API and an Oracle thin driver to access the Oracle database.

Notice that unlike the INSERT query shown in the VB.NET example, running an SQL SELECT query requires us to capture the data inside an object that can appropriately handle the tabular data. JDBC provides two key mechanisms for this: the ResultSet and RowSet objects. The difference between these two is somewhat similar to the difference between the DataReader and DataSet objects described in the VB.NET example.

The ResultSet object has a mechanism, called the cursor, that points to its current row of data. When the ResultSet object is first initialized, the cursor is positioned before

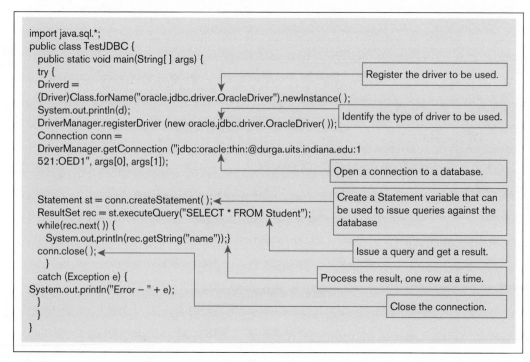

FIGURE 8-5 Database access from a Java program

TABLE 8-1 Common Java-to-SQL Mappings

SQL Type	Java Type	Common Get/Set Methods
INTEGER	int	getInt(), setInt()
CHAR	String	getString, setString()
VARCHAR	String	getString, setString()
DATE	java.util.Date	getDate(), setDate()
TIME	java.sql.Time	getTime(), setTime()
TIMESTAMP	java.sql.Timestamp	getTimestamp(), setTimestamp()

the first row. This is why we need to first call the next() method before retrieving data. The ResultSet object is used to loop through and process each row of data and retrieve the column values that we want to access. In this case, we access the value in the name column using the rec.getString method, which is a part of the JDBC API. For each of the common database types, there is a corresponding *get* and *set* method that allows for retrieval and storage of data in the database. Table 8-1 provides some common examples of SQL-to-Java mappings.

It is important to note that while the ResultSet object maintains an active connection to the database, depending on the size of the table, the entire table (i.e., the result of the query) may or may not actually be in memory on the client machine. How and when data are transferred between the database and client is handled by the Oracle driver. By default, a ResultSet object is read-only and can be traversed only in one direction (forward). However, advanced versions of the ResultSet object allow scrolling in both directions and can be updateable as well.

THREE-TIER ARCHITECTURES

In general, a **three-tier architecture** includes another server layer in addition to the client and database server layers previously mentioned (see Figure 8-6). Such configurations are also referred to as *n*-tier, multitier, or enhanced client/server architectures.

Three-tier architecture

A client/server configuration that includes three layers: a client layer and two server layers. Although the nature of the server layers differs, a common configuration contains an application server and a database server.

FIGURE 8-6 Generic three-tier architecture

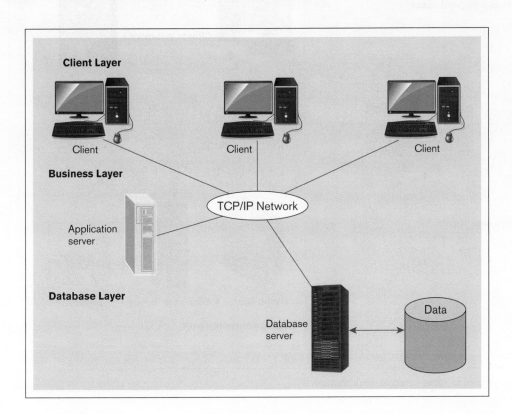

The additional server in a three-tier architecture may be used for different purposes. Often, application programs reside and are run on the additional server, in which case it is referred to as an application server. Or the additional server may hold a local database while another server holds the enterprise database. Each of these configurations is likely to be referred to as a three-tier architecture, but the functionality of each differs, and each is appropriate for a different situation. Advantages of the three-tier compared with the two-tier architecture, such as increased scalability, flexibility, performance, and reusability, have made three-layer architectures a popular choice for Internet applications and net-centric information systems. These advantages are discussed in more detail later.

In some three-tier architectures, most application code is stored on the application server. This case realizes the same benefits as those that come from putting stored procedures on the database server in a two-tier architecture. Using an application server can also improve performance through the use of true machine code, easier portability of the application code to other platforms, and less reliance on proprietary languages. In many situations, most business processing occurs on the application server rather than on the client workstation or database server, resulting in a **thin client**. The use of Internet browsers for accessing the Web is an example of a thin client. Applications that reside on a server and execute on that server without downloading to the client are becoming more common. Thus, upgrading application programs requires loading the new version only on the application server, rather than on client workstations.

The most common type of three-tier application in use in modern organizations is a Web-based application. Such applications can be accessed from either the Internet or an intranet. Figure 8-7 depicts the basic environment needed to set up both intranet and Internet database-enabled connectivity. In the box on the right side of the diagram is a depiction of an intranet. The client/server nature of the architecture is evident from the

Thin client

An application where the client (PC) accessing the application primarily provides the user interfaces and some application processing, usually with no or limited local data storage.

FIGURE 8-7 A database-enabled intranet/Internet environment

labeling. The network that connects the client workstations, Web server, and database server uses TCP/IP. While multitier intranet structures are also used, Figure 8-7 depicts a simpler architecture, where a request from a client browser will be sent through the network to the Web server, which stores pages scripted in HTML to be returned and displayed through the client browser. If the request requires that data be obtained from the database, the Web server constructs a query and sends it to the database server, which processes the query and returns the results set when the query is run against the database. Similarly, data entered at the client station can be passed through and stored in the database by sending it to the Web server, which passes it on to the database server, which commits the data to the database.

The processing flow described here is similar when connecting from outside the company. This is the case whether the connection is available only to a particular customer or supplier or to any workstation connected to the Internet. However, opening up the Web server to the outside world requires that additional data security measures be in place.

Internally, access to data is typically controlled by the database management system, with the database administrator setting the permissions that determine employee access to data. Firewalls limit external access to the company's data and the movement of company data outside the company's boundaries. All communication is routed through a proxy server outside of the organization's network. The proxy server controls the passage of messages or files through to the organization's network. It can also improve a site's performance by caching frequently requested pages that can then be displayed without having to attach to the Web server.

Given that the most common type of three-tier application is a Web application, in the next section we take a closer look at the key components of a Web application. We then present examples of simple Web applications written in two common languages: Java Server Pages (JSP) and ASP.NET.

WEB APPLICATION COMPONENTS

Figure 8-2 shows the various components of a typical Web application. Four key components must be used together to create a Web application site:

1. *A database server* This server hosts the storage logic for the application and hosts the DBMS. You have read about many of them, including Oracle, Microsoft SQL Server, Informix, Sybase, DB2, Microsoft Access, and MySQL. The DBMS may reside either on a separate machine or on the same machine as the Web server.
2. *A Web server* The Web server provides the basic functionality needed to receive and respond to requests from browser clients. These requests use HTTP or HTTPS as a protocol. The most common Web server software in use is Apache, but you are also likely to encounter Microsoft's Internet Information Server (IIS) Web server. Apache can run on different operating systems, such as Windows, UNIX, or Linux. IIS is primarily intended to run on Windows servers.
3. *An application server* This software provides the building blocks for creating dynamic Web sites and Web-based applications. Examples include the .NET Framework from Microsoft; Java Platform, Enterprise Edition (Java EE); and ColdFusion. Also, while technically not considered an application server platform, software that enables you to write applications in languages such as PHP, Python, and Perl also belong to this category.
4. *A Web browser* Microsoft's Internet Explorer, Mozilla's Firefox, Apple's Safari, Google's Chrome, and Opera are examples.

As you can see, a bewildering collection of tools are available to use for Web application development. Although Figure 8-7 gives an overview of the architecture required, there is no one right way to put together the components. Often, Web technologies within the same category can be used interchangeably. One tool may solve the same problem as well as another tool. However, the following are the most common combinations you will encounter:

- IIS Web server, SQL Server/Oracle as the DBMS, and applications written in ASP.NET
- Apache Web server, Oracle/IBM as the DBMS, and applications written using Java
- Apache Web server, Oracle/IBM/SQL Server as the DBMS, and applications written using ColdFusion
- The Linux operating system, Apache Web server, a MySQL database, and applications written in PHP/Python or Perl (also sometimes referred to as the LAMP stack).

Your development environment is likely to be determined by your employer. When you know what environment you will be using, there are many alternatives available for becoming familiar and proficient with the tools. Your employer may send you to training classes or even hire a subject matter expert to work with you. You will find one or more books specific to each tool when you search online or in a bookstore. Figure 8-8 presents a visual depiction of the components necessary to create a dynamic Web site.

DATABASES IN THREE-TIER APPLICATIONS

Figure 8-9a presents a general overview of the information flow in a Web application. A user submitting a Web page request is unaware of whether the request being submitted is returning a static Web page or a Web page whose content is a mixture of static information and dynamic information retrieved from the database. The data returned from the Web server is always in a format that can be rendered by the browser (i.e., HTML or XML).

As shown in Figure 8-9a, if the Web server determines that the request from the client can be satisfied without passing the request on to the application server, it will process the request and then return the appropriately formatted information to the client machine. This decision is most often based on the file suffix. For example, all .html and .htm files can be processed by the Web server itself.

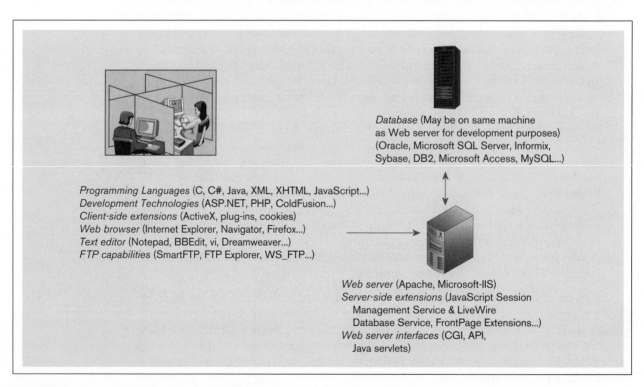

Database (May be on same machine as Web server for development purposes) (Oracle, Microsoft SQL Server, Informix, Sybase, DB2, Microsoft Access, MySQL...)

Programming Languages (C, C#, Java, XML, XHTML, JavaScript...)
Development Technologies (ASP.NET, PHP, ColdFusion...)
Client-side extensions (ActiveX, plug-ins, cookies)
Web browser (Internet Explorer, Navigator, Firefox...)
Text editor (Notepad, BBEdit, vi, Dreamweaver...)
FTP capabilities (SmartFTP, FTP Explorer, WS_FTP...)

Web server (Apache, Microsoft-IIS)
Server-side extensions (JavaScript Session Management Service & LiveWire Database Service, FrontPage Extensions...)
Web server interfaces (CGI, API, Java servlets)

FIGURE 8-8 Dynamic Web development environment

FIGURE 8-9 Information flow in a three-tier architecture

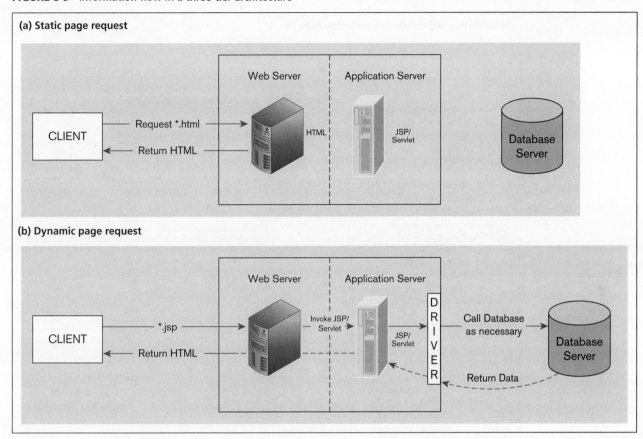

However, if the request has a suffix that requires application server intervention, the information flow show in Figure 8-9b is invoked. The application invokes the database, as necessary, using one of the mechanisms described previously (ADO.NET or JDBC) or a proprietary one. While the internal details of how each of the popular platforms (JSP/Java servlets, ASP.NET, ColdFusion, and PHP) handles the requests are likely very different, the general logic for creating Web applications is very similar to what is shown in Figure 8-9b.

A JSP Web Application

As indicated previously, there are several suitable languages and development tools available with which to create dynamic Web pages. One of the most popular languages in use is Java Server Pages (JSP). JSP pages are a mixture of HTML and Java. The HTML parts are used to display information on the browser. The Java parts are used to process information sent from an HTML form.

The code in Figure 8-10 shows a sample JSP application whose purpose is to capture user registration information and store the data in a database. Let us assume that the name of the page is registration.jsp. This JSP page performs the following functions:

- Displays the registration form
- Processes the user's filled-in form and checks it for common errors, such as missing items and matching password fields
- If there is an error, redisplays the entire form, with an error message in red
- If there is no error, enters the user's information into a database and sends the user to a "success" screen.

Let us examine the various pieces of the code to see how it accomplishes the above functions. All Java code is found between <% and %> and is not displayed in the browser. The only items displayed in the browser are the ones enclosed in HTML tags.

FIGURE 8-10   Sample JSP application

(a) Validation and database connection code

```
<%@ page import="java.sql.*" %>
<%

// Create an empty new variable
String message = null;

// Handle the form
if (request.getParameter("submit") != null)
{
  String firstName = null;
  String lastName = null;
  String email = null;
  String userName = null;
  String password = null;

  // Check for a first name
  if (request.getParameter("first_name")=="") {
    message = "<p>You forgot to enter your first name!</p>";
    firstName = null;
  }
  else {
    firstName = request.getParameter("first_name");
  }

  // Check for a last name
  if (request.getParameter("last_name")=="") {
    message = "<p>You forgot to enter your last name!</p>";
    lastName = null;
  }
  else {
    lastName = request.getParameter("last_name");
  }

  // Check for an email address
  if (request.getParameter("email")=="") {
    message = "<p>You forgot to enter your email address!</p>";
    email = null;
  }
  else {
    email = request.getParameter("email");
  }

  // Check for a username
  if (request.getParameter("username")=="") {
    message = "<p>You forgot to enter your username!</p>";
    userName = null;
  }
  else {
    userName = request.getParameter("username");
  }

  // Check for a password and match against the confirmed password
  if (request.getParameter("password1")=="") {
    message = "<p>You forgot to enter your password!</p>";
    password = null;
  }
```

The <%@ page %>directive applies to the entire JSP page. The import attribute specifies the Java packages that should be included within the JSP file.

Check whether the form needs to be processed.

Validate first name

Validate last name

Validate e-mail address

Validate username

Validate the password

(Figure 8-10 continues on the next page)

When a user accesses the registration.jsp page in a browser by typing in a URL similar to **http://myserver.mydomain.edu/regapp/registration.jsp**, the value of the message Web parameter is NULL. Because the IF condition fails, the HTML form is displayed without an error message. Notice that this form has a submit button and that

FIGURE 8-10 *(continued)*

(a) Validation and database connection code

```
else {
  if(request.getParameter("password1").equals(request.getParameter("password2"))) {
    password = request.getParameter("password1");
  }
  else {
  password = null;
  message = "<p>Your password did not match the confirmed password!</p>";
  }
}

// If everything's OK
PreparedStatement stmt = null;
Connection conn = null;
if (firstName!=null && lastName!=null && email!=null && userName!=null && password!=null) {

// Call method to register student
 try {

// Connect to the db
DriverManager.registerDriver(new oracle.jdbc.driver.OracleDriver( ));
conn=DriverManager.getConnection("jdbc:oracle:thin:@localhost:1521:xe","scott","tiger");

// Make the query
String ins_query="INSERT INTO users VALUES ('"+firstName+"','"+lastName+"','"
+email+"','"+userName+"','"+password+"')";
stmt=conn.prepareStatement(ins_query);

// Run the query
int result = stmt.executeUpdate(ins_query);
conn.commit();
message = "<p><b> You have been registered ! </b></p>";

// Close the database connection
stmt.close();
conn.close();
}
catch (SQLException ex) {

message = "<p><b> You could not be registered due to a system error. We apologize
for any inconvenience. </b></p>"+ex.getMessage()+"</p>";
stmt.close();
conn.close();
}
}
else {
  message = message+"<p>.Please try again</p>";
}
}
%>
```

- If all user information has been validated, the data will be inserted into the database (an Oracle Database in this case)
- Connect to the Database : Connection String : jdbc:oracle:thin:@localhost:1521:xe Username : scott Password : tiger
- Prepare and Execute INSERT query
- If the INSERT was successful print message
- Close Connection and Statement
- If the INSERT was not successful print error message
- End of JSP code

(Figure 8-10 continues on the next page)

the action value in the form indicates that the page that is going to process the data is also registration.jsp.

After the user fills in the details and clicks the submit button, the data are sent to the Web server. The Web server passes on the data (called parameters) to the application server, which in turn invokes the code in the page specified in the actions parameter (i.e., the registration.jsp page). This is the code in the page that is enclosed in the <% and %> and is written in Java. This code has several IF-ELSE statements for error checking purposes as well as a portion that contains the logic to store the user form data in a database.

FIGURE 8-10 *(continued)*

(b) HTML code to create a form in the JSP application

```
HTML code to create a form in the JSP application
<html>                                              ◄────── Beginning of HTML form
<head><title> Register </title></head>
<body>
<% if (message!=null) {%>
<font color ='red'><%=message%></font>
<%}%>
<form method="post">
<fieldset>
<legend>Enter your information in the form below:</legend>
<p><b> First Name:      </b>
        <input type="text"    name="first_name" size="15" maxlength ="15" value=""/></p>
<p><b> Last Name:       </b>
        <input type="text"    name="last_name"  size="30" maxlength ="30" value=""/></p>
<p><b> Email Address:   </b>
        <input type="text"    name="email"      size="40" maxlength ="40" value=""/></p>
<p><b> User Name:       </b>
        <input type="text"    name="username"   size="10" maxlength ="20" value=""/></p>
<p><b> Password:        </b>
        <input type="password" name="password1"  size="20" maxlength ="20" value=""/></p>
<p><b> Confirm Password: </b>
        <input type="password" name="password2"  size="20" maxlength ="20" value=""/></p>
</fieldset>
<div align="center"><input type="submit" name="submit" value="Register"/></div>
</form><!-- End of Form -->
</body>
</html>
```

(c) Sample form output from the JSP application

Enter your information in the form below.

First Name:

Last Name:

Email Address:

User Name:

Password:

Confirm Password:

Register

If any of the user entries are missing or if the passwords don't match, the Java code sets the message value to something other than NULL. At the end of that check, the original form is displayed, but now an error message in red will be displayed at the top of the form because of the very first IF statement.

On the other hand, if the form has been filled correctly, the code segment for inserting the data into the database is executed. Notice that this code segment is very similar to the code we showed in the Java example before. After the user information is inserted into the database, <jsp:forward> causes the application server to execute a new JSP page called success.jsp. Notice that the message that should be displayed by this page is the value that is in the message variable and is passed to it in the form of a Web parameter. It is worthwhile to note that all JSP pages are actually compiled into **Java servlets** on the application server before execution.

Java servlet

A Java program that is stored on the server and contains the business and database logic for a Java-based application.

If you examine the segments of the application from a database access perspective (starting from the try block), you will notice that there is nothing fundamentally different about how the code inside a JSP page looks compared to the code in a the Java application, as described earlier. It still follows the same six steps identified earlier in the chapter. The primary difference is that in this case, the database access code is now part of a Java servlet that runs on the application server instead of the client.

An ASP.NET Example

A final code segment that we will examine (Figure 8-11) shows how the registration page can be written in ASP.NET.

(a) Sample ASP.NET code for user registration

```
<%@ Page Language="C#" AutoEventWireup="true" CodeFile="users.aspx.cs" Inherits="users" %>
<html xmlns="http://www.w3.org/1999/xhtml" >
<head runat="server">
  <title>Register</title>
</head>
<body>
<form id="form1" runat="server">
<div>
<asp:DetailsView ID="manageUsers" runat="server" DataSourceID="usersDataSource">
      <Fields>
            <asp:BoundField DataField="username" HeaderText="User Name" />
            <asp:BoundField DataField="first_name" HeaderText="First Name" />
            <asp:BoundField DataField="last_name" HeaderText="Last Name" />
            <asp:BoundField DataField="email" HeaderText="Email Address" />
            <asp:BoundField DataField="password" HeaderText="Password" />
            <asp:CommandField ShowInsertButton="True" ButtonType="Button" />
      </Fields>
      </asp:DetailsView>
<asp:SqlDataSource ID="usersDataSource" runat="server"
      ConnectionString="<%$ ConnectionStrings:StudentConnectionString %>"
      InsertCommand="INSERT INTO users(username, first_name, last_name, email, password,
      registration_date) VALUES (@username, @first_name, @last_name, @email, @password, GETDATE())"
      SelectCommand="SELECT [username], [first_name], [last_name], [email], [password] FROM [users]">
</asp:SqlDataSource>
</div>
</form>
</body>
</html>
```

(b) Form for the ASP.NET application

FIGURE 8-11   A registration page written in ASP.NET

Notice that the ASP.NET code is considerably shorter than either the PHP or JSP code. This is partially because we have not included all the error checking aspects in this code. Further, we have used some powerful built-in controls available in ASP.NET to perform the majority of the functions that we were writing code for ourselves in the other two languages. The DetailsView control, for example, automatically grabs data from the various text fields in the Web page and assigns the values to the corresponding data field variable in the control (e.g., the User Name form field is stored in the username data field). Further, the SqlDataSource control hides the details of the steps needed to connect to the database, issue SQL queries, and retrieve the results.

KEY CONSIDERATIONS IN THREE-TIER APPLICATIONS

In describing the database component of the applications in the preceding sections, we observed that the basics of connecting, retrieving, and storing data in a database do not change substantially when we move from a two-tier application to a three-tier application. In fact, what changes is where the code for accessing the database is located. However, there are several key considerations that application developers need to keep in mind in order to be able to create a stable high-performance application.

Stored Procedures

Stored procedures (same as procedures; see Chapter 7 for a definition) are modules of code that implement application logic and are included on the database server. As pointed out by Quinlan (1995), stored procedures have the following advantages:

- Performance improves for compiled SQL statements.
- Network traffic decreases as processing moves from the client to the server.
- Security improves if the stored procedure rather than the data is accessed and code is moved to the server, away from direct end-user access.
- Data integrity improves as multiple applications access the same stored procedure.
- Stored procedures result in a thinner client and a fatter database server.

However, writing stored procedures can also take more time than using Visual Basic or Java to create an application. Also, the proprietary nature of stored procedures reduces their portability and may make it difficult to change DBMSs without having to rewrite the stored procedures. However, using stored procedures appropriately, can lead to more efficient processing of database code.

Figure 8-12a shows an example of a stored procedure written in Oracle's PL/SQL that is intended to check whether a user name already exists in the database. Figure 8-12b shows a sample code segment that illustrates that this stored procedure can be called from a Java program.

Transactions

In the examples shown so far, we have only examined code that consists of a single SQL action. However, most business applications require several SQL queries to complete a business transaction. By default, most database connections assume that you would like to commit the results of executing a query to the database immediately. However, it is possible to define the notion of a business transaction in your program. Figure 8-13 shows how a Java program would execute a database transaction.

Given that there might be thousands of users simultaneously trying to access and/or update a database through a Web application at any given point time (think **Amazon.com** or eBay), application developers need to be well versed in the concepts of database transactions and need to use them appropriately when developing applications.

Database Connections

In most three-tier applications, while it is very common to have the Web servers and application servers located on the same physical machine, the database server is often located on a different machine. In this scenario, the act of making a database connection and keeping the connection alive can be very resource intensive. Further, most

FIGURE 8-12 Example Oracle PL/SQL stored procedure

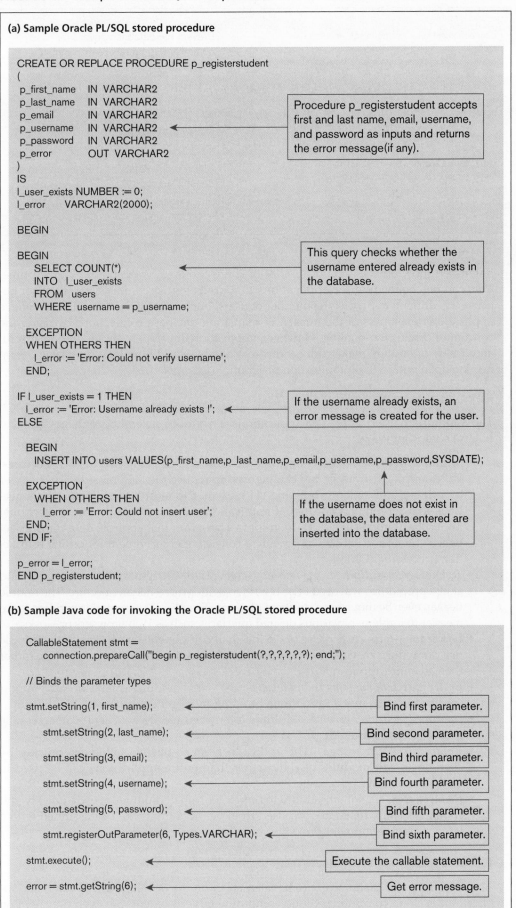

(a) Sample Oracle PL/SQL stored procedure

```
CREATE OR REPLACE PROCEDURE p_registerstudent
(
p_first_name   IN  VARCHAR2
p_last_name    IN  VARCHAR2
p_email        IN  VARCHAR2
p_username     IN  VARCHAR2
p_password     IN  VARCHAR2
p_error           OUT  VARCHAR2
)
IS
l_user_exists NUMBER := 0;
l_error     VARCHAR2(2000);

BEGIN

BEGIN
   SELECT COUNT(*)
   INTO   l_user_exists
   FROM   users
   WHERE  username = p_username;

 EXCEPTION
 WHEN OTHERS THEN
   l_error := 'Error: Could not verify username';
 END;

IF l_user_exists = 1 THEN
   l_error := 'Error: Username already exists !';
ELSE

 BEGIN
   INSERT INTO users VALUES(p_first_name,p_last_name,p_email,p_username,p_password,SYSDATE);

 EXCEPTION
   WHEN OTHERS THEN
     l_error := 'Error: Could not insert user';
 END;
END IF;

p_error = l_error;
END p_registerstudent;
```

Procedure p_registerstudent accepts first and last name, email, username, and password as inputs and returns the error message(if any).

This query checks whether the username entered already exists in the database.

If the username already exists, an error message is created for the user.

If the username does not exist in the database, the data entered are inserted into the database.

(b) Sample Java code for invoking the Oracle PL/SQL stored procedure

```
CallableStatement stmt =
    connection.prepareCall("begin p_registerstudent(?,?,?,?,?,?); end;");

// Binds the parameter types

stmt.setString(1, first_name);

    stmt.setString(2, last_name);

    stmt.setString(3, email);

    stmt.setString(4, username);

    stmt.setString(5, password);

    stmt.registerOutParameter(6, Types.VARCHAR);

stmt.execute();

error = stmt.getString(6);
```

Bind first parameter.

Bind second parameter.

Bind third parameter.

Bind fourth parameter.

Bind fifth parameter.

Bind sixth parameter.

Execute the callable statement.

Get error message.

FIGURE 8-13   Sample Java code snippet for an SQL transaction

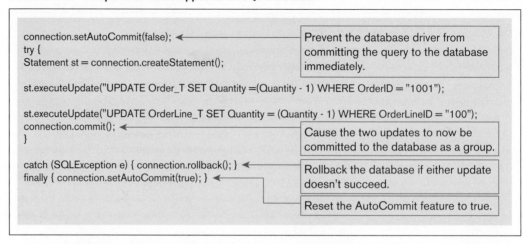

```
connection.setAutoCommit(false);  ◄─────────────    Prevent the database driver from
try {                                                committing the query to the database
Statement st = connection.createStatement();         immediately.

st.executeUpdate("UPDATE Order_T SET Quantity =(Quantity - 1) WHERE OrderID = "1001");

st.executeUpdate("UPDATE OrderLine_T SET Quantity = (Quantity - 1) WHERE OrderLineID = "100");
connection.commit();  ◄─────────────               Cause the two updates to now be
}                                                    committed to the database as a group.

catch (SQLException e) { connection.rollback(); }  ◄────   Rollback the database if either update
finally { connection.setAutoCommit(true); }  ◄──────        doesn't succeed.

                                                    Reset the AutoCommit feature to true.
```

databases allow only a limited number of connections to be open at any given time. This can be challenging for applications that are being accessed via the Internet because it is difficult to predict the number of users. Luckily, most database drivers relieve application developers of the burden of managing database connections by using the concept of connection pooling. However, application developers should still be careful about how often they make connections to a database and how long they keep a connection open within their application program.

Key Benefits of Three-Tier Applications

The appropriate use of three-tier applications can lead to several benefits in organizations (Thompson, 1997):

- *Scalability*   Three-tier architectures are more scalable than two-tier architectures. For example, the middle tier can be used to reduce the load on a database server by using a transaction processing (TP) monitor to reduce the number of connections to a server, and additional application servers can be added to distribute application processing. A TP monitor is a program that controls data transfer between clients and servers to provide a consistent environment for online transaction processing (OLTP).
- *Technological flexibility*   It is easier to change DBMS engines, although triggers and stored procedures will need to be rewritten, with a three-tier architecture. The middle tier can even be moved to a different platform. Simplified presentation services make it easier to implement various desired interfaces such as Web browsers or kiosks.
- *Lower long-term costs*   Use of off-the-shelf components or services in the middle tier can reduce costs, as can substitution of modules within an application rather than an entire application.
- *Better match of systems to business needs*   New modules can be built to support specific business needs rather than building more general, complete applications.
- *Improved customer service*   Multiple interfaces on different clients can access the same business processes.
- *Competitive advantage*   The ability to react to business changes quickly by changing small modules of code rather than entire applications can be used to gain a competitive advantage.
- *Reduced risk*   Again, the ability to implement small modules of code quickly and combine them with code purchased from vendors limits the risk assumed with a large-scale development project.

Cloud Computing and Three-Tier Applications

An emerging trend that is likely to have an effect on the development of three-tier applications is cloud computing. Cloud computing advertisements are even prevalent on primetime TV and in major airports around the world!

So what exactly is cloud computing? According to Mell and Grance (2011), the phrase *cloud computing* refers to a model for providing "ubiquitous, convenient and on-demand network access" to a set of shared computing resources (networks, servers, applications, and services).

All cloud technologies share the following characteristics (Mell and Grance, 2011):

1. On-demand self-service—IT capabilities can be created or released with minimal interaction with the service provider.
2. Broad network access—IT capabilities can be accessed via commonly used network technologies using a wide variety of devices (mobile phones, desktops, etc.).
3. Resource pooling—The service provider is capable of serving multiple consumer organizations and pools their resources (storage, servers, etc.) so as to be able to deal with varying consumer demand for the services.
4. Rapid elasticity—The consumer is able to easily (and often automatically) scale up or down the capabilities needed from the service provider.
5. Measured service—Consumers are able to control how much capability they need to use and pay only for the services they use. To achieve this, the service provider should be able to measure the usage of its services by consumers at an appropriate level.

Mell and Grance (2011) also present a popular categorization of cloud technologies:

1. Infrastructure-as-a Service: This category of cloud computing refers to the use of technologies such as servers, storage, and networks from external service providers. The primary benefit to organizations is that the tasks of buying, running, and maintaining the equipment and software are borne by the service providers. Popular examples of the IaaS model are Microsoft's Azure and Rackspace.
2. Platform-as-a Service: This category of cloud computing refers to the provision of building blocks of key technological solutions on the cloud. Examples include application servers, Web servers, and database technologies. Popular databases such as SQL Server, MySQL, Oracle, and IBM's DB2 are all available through this model and offered by the vendors directly, for example, Microsoft's SQL Azure/Oracle's Public cloud, or through cloud services such as Amazon's EC^2.
3. Software-as-a Service: This refers to an entire application or application suite being run on the cloud via the Internet instead of on an organization's own infrastructure. A popular example of this model is Salesforce.com's CRM system. Companies such as SAP and Oracle have also recently announced "cloud ready" versions of their enterprise applications.

From your perspective as a database applications development professional, the proliferation of cloud computing is likely to affect you in two key ways. First, when developing three (or more) tier applications, it is likely that one or more of the tiers—Web, application and/or database—might be hosted by a cloud service provider. Second, the ubiquitous availability of cloud database/application platforms will make it easier for you to develop and deploy applications using a variety of databases/application platforms because the tasks of buying, installing, configuring, and maintaining the various components of the typical *n*-tier application will now be much simplified. This would be particularly beneficial for those working in organizations with limited IT budgets/resources. It is worthwhile noting that cloud computing does not substantially change the core principles around developing three-tier applications that were discussed earlier in this chapter. However, databases hosted in the cloud will have substantial implications for database administrators.

EXTENSIBLE MARKUP LANGUAGE (XML)

Extensible Markup Language (XML) is a key development that is likely to continue to revolutionize the way data are exchanged over the Internet. XML addresses the issue of representing data in a structure and format that can both be exchanged over the Internet and be interpreted by different components (i.e., browsers, Web servers, application servers). XML does not replace Hypertext Markup Language (HTML), but it works with HTML to facilitate the transfer, exchange, and manipulation of data.

Extensible Markup Language (XML)

A text-based scripting language used to describe data structures hierarchically, using HTML-like tags.

XML uses tags, short descriptions enclosed in angle brackets (< >), to characterize data. The use of angle brackets in XML is similar to their use for HTML tags. But whereas HTML tags are used to describe the appearance of content, XML tags are used to describe the content, or data, itself. Consider the following XML document stored in a file called PVFC.xml that is intended to provide the description of a product in PVFC:

```
<?xml version = "1.0"/>
<furniturecompany>
    <product ID="1">
        <description>End Table</description>
        <finish>Cherry</finish>
        <standard price>175.00</standard price>
        <line>1</line>
    </product>
</furniturecompany>
```

The notations <description>, <finish>, and so on are examples of XML tags; <description>End Table</description> is an example of an element. Hence, an XML document consists of a series of nested elements. There are few restrictions on what can and cannot constitute tags in an XML element. However, an XML document itself must conform to a set of rules in terms of its structure. Three main techniques are used to validate that an XML document is structured correctly (i.e., follows all the rules for what constitutes a valid XML document): document structure declarations (DSDs), **XML Schema Definition (XSD)**, and Relax NG. All of these are alternatives to document type declarations (DTDs). DTDs were included in the first version XML but have some limitations. They cannot specify data types and are written in their own language, not in XML. In addition, DTDs do not support some newer features of XML, such as namespaces.

To overcome these difficulties, the World Wide Web Consortium (W3C) published the XML Schema standard in May 2001. It defines the data model and establishes data types for the document data. The W3C XML Schema Definition (XSD) language uses a custom XML vocabulary to describe XML documents. It represents a step forward from using DTDs because it allows data types to be denoted. The following is very simple XSD schema that describes the structure, data typing, and validation of a salesperson record.

XML Schema Definition (XSD)

Language used for defining XML databases that has been recommended by the W3C.

```
<?xml version="1.0" encoding="utf-8" ?>
<xsd:schema id="salespersonSchema"
xmlns:xsd="http://www.w3.org/2001/XMLSchema">
  <xsd:element name="Salesperson" type="SalespersonType" />
  <xsd:complexType name="SalespersonType">
    <xsd:sequence>
      <xsd:elementname="SalespersonID"
              type="xsd:integer"/>
      <xsd:elementname="SalespersonName"
              type="xsd:string" />
      <xsd:element name="SalespersonTelephone"
              type="PhoneNumberType">
      <xsd:element name="SalespersonFax"
              type="PhoneNumber" minOccurs="0" />
      </xsd:element>
    </xsd:sequence>
  </xsd:complexType>
  <xsd:simpleType name="PhoneNumberType">
    <xsd:restriction base="xsd:string">
      <xsd:length value="12" />
      <xsd:pattern value="\d{3}-\d{3}-\d{4}" />
    </xsd:restriction>
  </xsd:simpleType>
</xsd:schema>
```

The following XML document conforms to the schema listed previously.

```
<?xml version="1.0" encoding="utf-8" ?>
<Salesperson xmlns:xsi=http://www.w3.org/2001/XMLSchema-instance
xsi:noNamespaceSchemaLocation="salespersonSchema.xsd">
    <SalespersonID>1</SalespersonID>
    <SalespersonName>Doug Henny</SalespersonName>
    <SalespersonTelephone>813-444-5555</SalespersonTelephone>
</Salesperson>
```

While it is possible to set up your own XML vocabulary, as we have just done, a wide variety of public XML vocabularies already exist and can be used to mark up your data. Many of them are listed at **http://wdvl.com/Authoring/Languages /XML/Specifications.html** and **www.service-architecture.com/xml/articles/xml _vocabularies.html**. Such vocabularies make it easier for an organization to exchange data with other organizations without having to engage in individual agreements with each business partner. Selecting the best XML vocabulary to use to describe a database is very important. As XML gains popularity, more libraries of external XML schemas should become available, but for now, Web searches and word of mouth are the most likely mechanisms for you to find the appropriate schemas for your application.

New XML-based vocabularies, such as Extensible Business Reporting Language (XBRL) and Structured Product Labeling (SPL), have emerged as open standards that allow meaningful and unambiguous comparisons that could not be made easily previously. Financial organizations that adhere to XBRL may record up to 2,000 financial data points, such as cost, assets, and net income, using standard XBRL tag definitions. These data points may then be combined or compared across institutions' financial reports. As products that enable easier use of XBRL come to market, large financial institutions expect to spend much less time cleansing and normalizing their data and exchanging data with business partners. Smaller institutions can anticipate improved and more affordable access to financial analysis (Henschen, 2005). The FDA is also beginning to require the use of Structured Product Labeling (SPL), to record the information provided on drug labels, for both prescription and over-the-counter drugs.

Now that you have a basic understanding of what constitutes an XML document, we can turn our attention to how XML data can be used in the modern computing environment and the unique challenges they bring to the table.

Storing XML Documents

One of the biggest questions that needs to be answered as XML data becomes more prevalent is "Where do we store these data?" While it is possible to store XML data as a series of files, doing so brings back into play the same disadvantages with file processing systems that we discussed in Chapter 1. Luckily, we have several choices when it comes to storing XML data:

1. *Store XML data in a relational database by shredding the XML document* Shredding an XML document essentially means that we store each element of an XML schema independently in a relational table and use other tables to store the relationships among the elements. Modern databases such as Microsoft SQL Server and Oracle provide capabilities beyond standard SQL to help store and retrieve XML data.
2. *Store an entire XML document in a field capable of storing large objects, such as a binary large object (BLOB) or a character large object (CLOB)* This technique is not very useful if you have to actually search for data within the XML document.
3. *Store the XML document using special XML columns that are made available as part of database* These columns can be associated with an XSD, for example, to ensure that the XML document that is being inserted is a valid document.
4. *Store the XML document using a native XML database* These are non-relational databases designed specifically to store XML documents.

In general, the latter two options are used when the majority of the information being processed is originally in XML format. For example, many academic and practitioner conferences are beginning to require that authors submit their presentations and papers in XML format. On the other hand, the first two options are used primarily if XML is used as a data exchange format between a browser and an application server.

Retrieving XML Documents

XPath

One of a set of XML technologies that supports XQuery development. XPath expressions are used to locate data in XML documents.

XQuery

An XML transformation language that allows applications to query both relational databases and XML data.

Modern databases provide extensive support for retrieving information from databases in XML format. The key technologies behind XML data retrieval are **XPath** and XQuery. Each of the storage options listed above provides specific mechanisms by which you can retrieve data in XML format. For the first three options, these take the form of extensions to the SQL language (based on XPath and XQuery). In the case of a native XML database, the most likely choice is XQuery itself. XQuery helps in locating and extracting elements from XML documents; it can be used to accomplish such activities as transforming XML data to XHTML, providing information for use by Web services, generating summary reports, and searching Web documents.

The XML Query Working Group describes **XQuery** most simply in these words, published at **www.w3c.org/XML/Query**: "XQuery is a standardized language for combining documents, databases, Web pages and almost anything else. It is very widely implemented. It is powerful and easy to learn. XQuery is replacing proprietary middleware languages and Web application development languages. XQuery is replacing complex Java or C++ programs with a few lines of code. XQuery is simpler to work with and easier to maintain than many other alternatives."

Built on XPath expressions, XQuery is now supported by the major relational database engines, including those from IBM, Oracle, and Microsoft.

Take a look at the XML document shown in Figure 8-14a. Now, consider the following XQuery expression that returns all product elements that have a standard price > 300.00:

```
for $p in doc("PVFC.xml")/furniture company/product
where $p/standardprice>300.00
order by $p/description
return $p/description
```

You can see the similarities between XQuery and SQL in this example. It is often said that XQuery is to XML as SQL is to relational databases. This example demonstrates the ease with which you will become fluent in XQuery as your understanding of SQL increases. The XQuery expression shown previously is called a FLWOR expression. FLWOR is an acronym for For, LET, Where, Order by, and Return:

- The FOR clause selects all product elements from furniture company into the variable named $p.
- The WHERE clause selects all product elements with a standard price greater than $300.00.
- The ORDER BY clause sets the sorting order of the results to be by the description element.
- The RETURN clause specifies that the description elements should be returned.

The results of the above XQuery are as follows:

```
<description>8-Drawer Desk</description>
<description>Computer Desk</description>
<description>Dining Table</description>
<description>Entertainment Center</description>
<description>Writer's Desk</description>
```

```
<?xml version = "1.0"?>
<furniture company>
    <product ID="1">
        <description>End Table</description>
        <finish>Cherry</finish>
        <standard price>175.00</standard price>
        <line>1</line>
    </product>
    <product ID="2">
        <description>Coffee Table</description>
        <finish>Natural Ash</finish>
        <standard price>200.00</standard price>
        <line>2</line>
    </product>
    <product ID="3">
        <description>Computer Desk</description>
        <finish>Natural Ash</finish>
        <standard price>375.00</standard price>
        <line>2</line>
    </product>
    <product ID="4">
        <description>Entertainment Center</description>
        <finish>Natural Maple</finish>
        <standard price>650.00</standard price>
        <line>3</line>
    </product>
    <product ID="5">
        <description>Writers Desk</description>
        <finish>Cherry</finish>
        <standard price>325.00</standard price>
        <line>1</line>
    </product>
    <product ID="6">
        <description>8-Drawer Desk</description>
        <finish>White Ash</finish>
        <standard price>750.00</standard price>
        <line>2</line>
    </product>
    <product ID="7">
        <description>Dining Table</description>
        <finish>Natural Ash</finish>
        <standard price>800.00</standard price>
        <line>2</line>
    </product>
    <product ID="8">
        <description>Computer Desk</description>
        <finish>Walnut</finish>
        <standard price>250.00</standard price>
        <line>3</line>
    </product>
</furniture company>
```

(Figure 8-14 continues on the next page)

This example shows how to query data that is in XML format. Given the importance of XML as a data exchange format, many relational databases also provide mechanisms to return data from relational tables in an XML format. In Microsoft SQL Server, this can be achieved by adding the statement FOR XML AUTO or PATH to the end of a typical SELECT query. Essentially, the result table from the SELECT is converted into an XML form and returned to the calling program. Behind the scenes, many of these additional features use XPath as the basis for the queries.

Displaying XML Data

Notice that in the XML examples so far, we have provided little information about what to do with XML data. In fact, the separation of how data are formatted from

FIGURE 8-14 *(continued)*
(b) XSLT code

```
<?xml version = "1.0"?>
<xsl:stylesheet version="1.0" xmlns:xsl="http://www.w3.org/1999/XSL/Transform">
<xsl:template match="/">
    <html>
        <body>
        <h2>Product Listing</h2>
        <table border="1">
        <tr bgcolor="orange">
                <th>Description</th>
                <th>Finish</th>
                <th>Price</th>
        </tr>
        <xsl:for-each select="furniturecompany/product">
        <tr>
            <td><xsl:value-of select="description"/></td>
            <td><xsl:value-of select="finish"/></td>
            <td><xsl:value-of select="price"/></td>
        </tr>
        </xsl:for-each>
        </table>
        </body>
    </html>
</xsl:template>
</xsl:stylesheet>
```

(c) Output of XSLT transformation

Product Listing

Description	Finish	Price
End Table	Cherry	175.00
Coffee Table	Natural Ash	200.00
Computer Desk	Natural Ash	375.00
Entertainment Center	Natural Maple	650.00
Writers Desk	Cherry	325.00
8-Drawer Desk	White Ash	750.00
Dining Table	Natural Ash	800.00
Computer Desk	Walnut	250.00

Extensible Stylesheet Language Transformation (XSLT)

A language used to transform complex XML documents and also used to create HTML pages from XML documents.

how the data are displayed is one of the key reasons XML is gaining popularity over HTML, where the data and formatting are intermingled. The display of XML data on a Web browser is controlled by a stylesheet specified using the **Extensible Stylesheet Language Transformation (XSLT)**. Most modern browsers and programming languages provide support for XSLT. Thus, the transformation of the XML can happen either at the Web server layer or the application server layer. Figure 8-14b shows a sample XSLT specification for displaying the Salesperson data in the form of an HTML table. The resultant output is shown in Figure 8-14c.

One of the advantages of XSLT is that it can be used to handle the myriad devices that now use the Internet. Smartphone devices have built-in browsers that allow a user to access the Internet. Some of the browsers require that content delivered to them use the Wireless Application Protocol (WAP), using the Wireless Markup Language (WML). Others can handle HTML, as long as it has been appropriately transformed for optimal viewing on the screen size of a mobile device. By using XSLT, XML, and other technologies, the same set of data can be rendered onto the different devices without having to write a separate page for each device type.

XML and Web Services

The Internet has served as a powerful driver to encourage the integration of communication between the providers of software applications and the users of those applications. As the Internet evolves as a distributed computing platform, a set of emerging standards is affecting software development and distribution practices. Easing the automatic communication of software programs through the use of XML coding and Internet protocols such as HTTP and e-mail protocols, a new class of applications called **Web services** is improving the ability of computers to communicate over the Internet automatically, thus aiding the development and deployment of applications within a company or across an industry. Existing methods of establishing communication, such as electronic data interchange (EDI), are still being used, but the widespread availability of XML means that the Web services approach promises to make it much easier to create program application modules that execute in a distributed environment.

The promise of Web services is the development of a standardized communication system among different applications, using XML based technologies at their core. Easier integration of applications is possible because developers need not be familiar with the technical details associated with the applications being integrated, nor must they learn the programming language of the application being integrated. Anticipation of increased business agility derived from significant reductions in the time and effort needed to establish enterprise application integration and B2B relationships is driving the interest in the Web services approach. Figure 8-15 is a very simple diagram of an order entry system that includes both internal Web services (Order Entry and Accounting) and Web services that are outsourced to companies that provide authentication and credit validation services over the Web (Newcomer, 2002).

Web services

A set of emerging standards that define protocols for automatic communication between software programs over the Web. Web services are XML based and usually run in the background to establish transparent communication among computers.

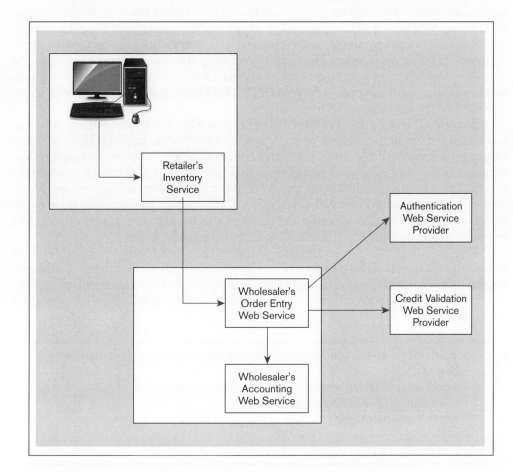

FIGURE 8-15 A typical order entry system that uses Web services

Source: Based on Newcomer (2002).

FIGURE 8-16 **Web services protocol stack**

Publish, Find, Use Services	UDDI	**U**niversal **D**escription, **D**iscovery, **I**ntegration
Describe Services	WSDL	**W**eb **S**ervices **D**escription **L**anguage
Service Interactions	SOAP	**S**imple **O**bject **A**ccess **P**rotocol
Data Format	XML	e**X**tensible **M**arkup **L**anguage
Open Communications	Internet	

Universal Description, Discovery, and Integration (UDDI)

A technical specification for creating a distributed registry of Web services and businesses that are open to communicating through Web services.

Web Services Description Language (WSDL)

An XML-based grammar or language used to describe a Webservice and specify a public interface for that service.

Simple Object Access Protocol (SOAP)

An XML-based communication protocol used for sending messages between applications via the Internet.

There are some key additional terms that are associated with using Web services. Figure 8-16 depicts a common database/Web services protocol stack. The transformation and communication of data into and out of application programs and databases rely on a set of XML-based protocols. **Universal Description, Discovery, and Integration (UDDI)** is a technical specification for creating a distributed registry of Web services and businesses that are open to communicating through Web services. **Web Services Description Language (WSDL)** is an XML-based grammar or language used to describe what a Web service can do and to specify a public interface for how to use that service. WSDL is used to create a file that automatically generates a client interface, allowing a developer to attend to the business logic rather than the communications requirements of an application. The definition of the public interface may indicate data types for XML messages, message format, location information for the specified Web service, the transport protocol to be used (HTTP, HTTPS, or e-mail), and so forth. These descriptions are stored in a UDDI repository.

Simple Object Access Protocol (SOAP) is an XML-based communication protocol used for sending messages between applications via the Internet. Because it is a language-independent platform, it enables communication between diverse applications. As SOAP moves toward becoming a W3C standard, it generalizes a capability that was previously established on an ad hoc basis between specific programs. Many view it as the most important Web service. SOAP structures a message into three parts: an optional header, a required body, and optional attachments. The header can support in-transit processing and can thus deal with firewall security issues.

The following is an example, adapted from an example displayed at **http://en.wikipedia.org/wiki/SOAP**, of how Pine Valley Furniture Company might format a SOAP message requesting product information from one of its suppliers. PVFC needs to know which product corresponds to the supplier's product ID 32879.

```
<soap:Envelope xmlns:soap=http://schemas.xmlsoap.org/soap/envelope/>
  <soap:Body>
    <getProductDetails xmlns=http://supplier.example.com/ws
      <productID>32879</productID>
    </getProductDetails>
  </soap:Body>
</soap:Envelope>
```

The supplier's Web service could format its reply message, which contains the requested information about the product, in this way:

```
<soap:Envelope xmlns:soap=http://schemas.xmlsoap.org/soap/envelope/>
  <soap:Body>
    <getProductDetailsResponse xmlns="suppliers.example.com/ws">
      <getProductDetailsResult>
        <productName>Dining Table</productName>
        <Finish>Natural Ash</Finish>
        <Price>800</Price>
        <inStock>True</inStock>
      </getProductDetailsResult>
    </getProductDetailsResponse>
  </soap:Body>
</soap:Envelope>
```

Figure 8-17 shows the interaction of applications and systems with Web services. Note that as a transaction flows from one business to another or from a customer to a business, a SOAP processor creates a message envelope that allows the exchange of formatted XML data across the Web. Because SOAP messages connect remote sites, appropriate security measures must be implemented in order to maintain data integrity.

Web services, with their promise of automatic communication between businesses and customers, whether they are other businesses or individual retail customers, have generated much discussion and anticipation in the past few years. Concerns about adopting a Web services approach focus on transaction speed, security, and reliability. The open system implied in establishing automatic communication among computers attached to the Web must be further developed before the security and reliability match those of traditional business applications.

However, it is clear that Web services are here to stay. Several organizations have already attracted attention by their use of Web services. Both Amazon.com and Google,

FIGURE 8-17   Web services deployment

Source: Based on Newcomer (2002).

two companies with high-profile Web presence, use Web services extensively. Google began its program in April 2002, allowing developers to access its search database directly for noncommercial uses and to create their own interfaces to the data. Access to Amazon.com's inventory database was made available in July 2002. Combining the service with a blog tool, an API allows bloggers to create a link to a relevant Amazon.com product in one step. Programmers benefit from improved ease of access, customers conduct more efficient searches, and Amazon.com and Google continue to spread and support their brands. Google "Amazon Web services documentation" or "Google Web services" to become more familiar with these free opportunities.

Others charge for using their Web services. Microsoft .NET developers can use Microsoft's MapPoint Web Service to provide location-based services (LBS) from their Web sites. MapPoint Web Service provides both location and mapping capabilities that may be accessed over any HTTPS connection. MapQuest offers similar capabilities. After paying a setup fee, users may elect to pay on an annual or monthly basis. Charges depend on transaction count. Topographic and satellite images are available through MSR Maps (see **http://msrmaps.com**).

The growing popularity and availability of Web services is also leading to a change in the way organizations think about developing their IT applications and capabilities. A new paradigm called **service-oriented architecture (SOA)** is gaining a foothold. An SOA is a collection of services that communicate with each other in some manner, usually passing data or coordinating a business activity. While these services do not have to be Web services, Web services are the predominant mechanism used. SOAs differ from traditional object-oriented approaches in that the services are loosely coupled and very interoperable. The software components are very reusable and operate across different development platforms, such as Java and .NET. Using XML, SOAP, and WSDL eases the establishment of necessary connections.

Using an SOA approach leads to the establishment of a modeling, design, and software development process that supports the efficient development of applications. Organizations that have adopted such an approach have found their development time reduced by at least 40 percent. Not only are the organizations experiencing shorter development time, they also hope to demonstrate more flexibility in responding to the rapidly changing business environment.

Service-oriented architecture (SOA)

A collection of services that communicate with each other in some manner, usually by passing data or coordinating a business activity.

Summary

Client/server architectures have offered businesses opportunities to better fit their computer systems to their business needs. Establishing the appropriate balance between client/server and mainframe DBMSs is a matter of much current discussion. Client/server architectures are prominent in providing Internet applications, including dynamic data access. Application partitioning assigns portions of application code to client or server partitions after it is written in order to achieve better performance and interoperability. Application developer productivity is expected to increase as a result of using application partitioning, but the developer must understand each process intimately to place it correctly.

In a two-tier architecture, the client manages the user interface and business logic, while the database server manages database storage and access. This architecture reduces network traffic, reduces the power required for each client, and centralizes user authorization, integrity checking, data dictionary maintenance, and query and update processing on the database server. We looked at examples of a two-tier application written in VB.NET and Java and examined the six key steps needed to retrieve data from a database.

Three-tier architectures, which include another server in addition to the client and database server layers, allow application code to be stored on the additional server. This approach allows business processing to be performed on the additional server, resulting in a thin client. Advantages of the three-tier architecture can include scalability, technological flexibility, lower long-term costs, better matching of systems to business needs, improved customer service, competitive advantage, and reduced risk. But higher short-term costs, advanced tools and training, shortages of experienced personnel, incompatible standards, and lack of end-user tools are some of the challenges related to using three-tier or *n*-tier architectures.

The most common type of three-tier application is the Internet-based Web application. In its simplest form, a request from a client browser is sent through the network to the Web server. If the request requires that data be obtained from the database, the Web server constructs a query and sends it to the database server, which processes the query and returns the results. Firewalls are used to limit external access to the company's data. Cloud computing is likely to become a popular paradigm for three-tier applications in the coming years.

Common components of Internet architecture are certain programming and markup languages, Web servers, applications servers, database servers, and database drivers and other middleware that can be used to connect the various components together. To aid in our understanding of how to create a Web application, we looked at examples of three-tier applications written in JSP, and ASP.NET and examined some of the key database-related issues in such applications.

Finally, we discussed the role of XML as a data exchange standard on the Internet. We examined issues related to the storage of XML documents in databases, retrieval of XML using languages such as XQuery and XPath, as well transformation of XML data into presentation formats such as HTML. We also examined various XML-based technologies, UDDI, WSDL, and SOAP, which are all fueling the interest in SOA and Web services. These allow disparate applications within a company or around the globe to be able to talk to each other.

Chapter Review

Key Terms

Application partitioning 270
Application program interface (API) 272
Client/server system 268
Database server 271
Extensible Markup Language (XML) 287
Extensible Stylesheet Language Transformation (XSLT) 292
Fat client 270
Java servlet 283
Middleware 272
Open Database Connectivity (ODBC) 272
Service-oriented architecture (SOA) 296
Simple Object Access Protocol (SOAP) 294
Thin client 276
Three-tier architecture 275
Universal Description, Discovery, and Integration (UDDI) 294
Web services 293
Web Services Description Language (WSDL) 294
XML Schema Definition (XSD) 288
XPath 290
XQuery 290

Review Questions

1. Define each of the following terms:
   a. application partitioning
   b. application program interface (API)
   c. client/server system
   d. middleware
   e. stored procedure
   f. three-tier architecture
   g. Java Database Connectivity (JDBC)
   h. XML Schema
   i. Web services
   j. XSLT
   k. SOAP

2. Match each of the following terms with the most appropriate definition:
   _____ client/server system
   _____ application program interface (API)
   _____ fat client
   _____ database server
   _____ middleware
   _____ three-tier architecture
   _____ thin client
   _____ XSD
   _____ SOA

   a. a client that is responsible for processing, including application logic and presentation logic
   b. a PC configured for handling the presentation layer and some business logic processing for an application
   c. a collection of services that communicate with each other in some manner
   d. software that facilitates interoperability, reducing programmer coding effort
   e. device responsible for database storage and access
   f. systems where the application logic components are distributed
   g. software that facilitates communication between front-end programs and back-end database servers
   h. three-layer client/server configuration
   i. language used for defining XML databases

3. List several major advantages of the client/server architecture compared with other computing approaches.

4. Contrast the following terms:
   a. two-tier architecture; three-tier architecture
   b. fat client; thin client
   c. ODBC; JDBC
   d. XHTML; XSLT
   e. SQL; XQuery
   f. Web services; SOA

5. Describe the advantages and disadvantages of two-tier architectures.

6. Describe the advantages and disadvantages of three-tier architectures.

7. Describe the common components needed to create a Web-based application.

8. What database APIs are commonly used to access databases from various programming languages?

9. What are the six common steps needed to access databases from a typical program?

10. If you were charged with developing a client/server application, how would you ensure success?

11. What are the three common types of cloud computing services?

12. What are the four common approaches to storing XML data?

13. Explain why using XML Schema is a step forward from using document type declarations (DTDs).

14. What is XSLT, and how does it differ from XML? What role does it play in the creation of a Web application?

15. Discuss UDDI. Compare and contrast it with the white, yellow, and green pages of the telephone book. (If your telephone book does not have green pages, you will need to research this feature found in some telephone books.)

Problems and Exercises

1. You have been asked to prepare a report that evaluates possible client/server solutions to handle a new customer application system for all branch offices. What business characteristics would you evaluate? What technology characteristics would you evaluate? Why?

2. Explain the difference between a static Web site and a dynamic one. What are the characteristics of a dynamic Web site that enable it to better support the development of e-business?

3. Historically, what types of applications have moved quickly to client/server database systems? What types have moved more slowly, and why? What do you think will happen in the future to the ratio of client/server database systems versus mainframe database systems?

4. Discuss some of the languages that are associated with Internet application development. Classify these languages according to the functionality they provide for each application. It is not necessary that you use the same classification scheme used in the chapter.

5. Find some dynamic Web site code such as that included in Figures 8-10 and 8-11. Annotate the code, as is done in these figures, to explain each section, especially the elements that involve interaction with the database. (Hint: Google "JSP," "ASP.NET," to find a rich set of sample code to explore.)

6. Rewrite the example shown in Figure 8-5 using VB.NET.

7. Rewrite the example show in Figure 8-4 using Java.

8. Consider the example code shown in Figures 8-10 and 8-11. Assume that instead of accessing data from a local server, you are going to access data from a cloud provider that offers the appropriate application server (e.g., ASP.NET) and database technologies. What changes, if any, do you have to make to the example code segment(s)?

9. Visit the Web sites of at least two cloud service providers that offer cloud database services. What are some of the common benefits of using cloud database services listed on these Web sites? If you are not sure where to start, try **aws.amazon.com or cloud.oracle.com**.

10. Construct a simple XML schema that describes a tutor. Include the tutor's last name, first name, phone, e-mail address, and certification date as child elements of the TUTOR element.

11. Using your schema from Question 10, write an FLWOR XQuery expression that lists only the tutors' names and lists them alphabetically by last name.

12. Using your schema from Question 10, write an XSLT program to display the tutor information in the form of an HTML table.

13. Discuss how Web services can be used to effectively integrate business applications and data. Search the Web for resources on current Web services that employ XML, SOAP, UDDI, and WSDL. Find at least three and discuss how each is used, including examples from industry.

References

Henschen, D. 2005. "XBRL Offers a Faster Route to Intelligence." *Intelligent Enterprise 8,8* (August): 12.

Hurwitz, J. 1998. "Sorting Out Middleware." *DBMS* 11,1 (January): 10–12.

Mell, P., and T. Grance. 2011. "The NIST Definition of Cloud Computing" *National Institute of Standards and Technology,* **http://csrc.nist.gov/publications/nistpubs/800-145 /SP800-145.pdf**, accessed 12/18/2011.

Newcomer, E. 2002. *Understanding Web Services, XML, WSDL, SOAP, and UDDI.* Boston: Addison-Wesley.

Quinlan, T. 1995. "The Second Generation of Client/Server." *Database Programming & Design* 8,5 (May): 31–39.

Thompson, C. 1997. "Committing to Three-Tier Architecture." *Database Programming & Design* 10,8 (August): 26–33.

Further Reading

Anderson, G., and B. Armstrong. 1995. "Client/Server: Where Are We Really?" *Health Management Technology* 16,6 (May): 34, 36, 38, 40, 44.

Cerami, E. 2002. *Web Services Essentials*. Sebastopol, CA: O'Reilly & Associates, Inc.

Frazer, W. D. 1998. "Object/Relational Grows Up." *Database Programming & Design* 11,1 (January): 22–28.

Innocenti, C. 2006. "XQuery Levels the Data Integration Playing Field." *DM Review* accessed at *DM Direct*, **http://www.information-management.com/infodirect /20061201/1069184-1.html** (December).

Mason, J. N., and M. Hofacker. 2001. "Gathering Client-Server Data." *Internal Auditor* 58:6 (December): 27–29.

Melton, J., and S. Buxton. 2006. *Querying XML, XQuery, XPath, and SQL/XML in Context*. Morgan Kaufmann Series in Data Management Systems. San Francisco: Morgan Kaufmann.

Morrison, M., and J. Morrison. 2003. *Database-Driven Web Sites*, 2nd ed. Cambridge, MA: Thomson-Course Technologies.

Richardson, L., S. Ruby, and D. H. Hansson. 2007. *RESTful Web Services*. Sebastopol, CA: O'Reilly Media, Inc.

Wamsley, P. 2007. *XQuery*. Sebastopol, CA: O'Reilly Media, Inc.

Web Resources

www.javacoffeebreak.com/articles/jdbc/index.html "Getting Started with JDBC" by David Reilly.

http://www.w3schools.com/ASPNET/default.asp Tutorial on ASP.NET.

www.cs.wisc.edu/arch/www The WWW Computer Architecture site, maintained by the Computer Architecture Group in the Computer Sciences area at the University of Wisconsin.

www.w3.org/html/wg W3C's home page for HTML.

www.w3.org/MarkUp W3C's home page for XHTML.

www.w3.org/XML/Query W3C's home page for XQuery.

www.w3.org/XML/1999/XML-in-10-points The W3C article "XML in 10 points," which presents basic XML concepts.

www.netcraft.com The Netcraft Web Server survey, which tracks the market share of different Web servers and SSL site operating systems.

www.projectliberty.org The home page of the Liberty Alliance. Open standards specifications and drafts of specifications may be downloaded here.

www.w3schools.com/default.asp A Web developers' site that provides Web-building tutorials on topics from basic HTML and XHTML to advanced XML, SQL, databases, multimedia, and WAP.

www.ws-i.org The home page of the Web Services Interoperability Organization (WS-I).

www.oasis-open.org/home/index.php The home page of the Organization for the Advancement of Structured Information Standards (OASIS).

xml.apache.org/cocoon The Cocoon project, a Java Web publishing framework that separates document content, style, and logic, allowing the independent design, creation, and management of each.

CHAPTER 9

Data Warehousing

LEARNING OBJECTIVES

After studying this chapter, you should be able to:

- Concisely define each of the following key terms: **data warehouse, operational system, informational system, data mart, independent data mart, dependent data mart, enterprise data warehouse (EDW), operational data store (ODS), logical data mart, real-time data warehouse, reconciled data, derived data, transient data, periodic data, star schema, grain, conformed dimension, snowflake schema, big data, NoSQL, online analytical processing (OLAP), relational OLAP (ROLAP), multidimensional OLAP (MOLAP), data visualization, data mining, data governance,** and **data steward**.

- Give two important reasons why an "information gap" often exists between an information manager's need and the information generally available.

- List two major reasons most organizations today need data warehousing.

- Name and briefly describe the three levels in a data warehouse architecture.

- Describe the two major components of a star schema.

- Estimate the number of rows and total size, in bytes, of a fact table, given reasonable assumptions concerning the database dimensions.

- Design a data mart using various schemes to normalize and denormalize dimensions and to account for fact history, hierarchical relationships between dimensions, and changing dimension attribute values.

- Develop the requirements for a data mart from questions supporting decision making.

INTRODUCTION

Everyone agrees that readily available high-quality information is vital in business today. Consider the following actual critical situation:

> In September 2004, Hurricane Frances was heading for the Florida Atlantic Coast. Fourteen hundred miles away, in Bentonville, Arkansas, Wal-Mart executives were getting ready. By analyzing 460 terabytes of data in their data warehouse, focusing on sales data from several weeks earlier, when Hurricane Charley hit the Florida Gulf Coast, the executives were able to predict what products people in Miami would want to buy. Sure, they needed flashlights, but Wal-Mart also discovered that people also bought strawberry Pop-Tarts and, yes, beer. Wal-Mart was able to stock its stores with

300

plenty of the in-demand items, providing what people wanted and avoiding stockouts, thus gaining what would otherwise have been lost revenue.

Beyond special circumstances like hurricanes, by studying a market basket of what individuals buy, Wal-Mart can set prices to attract customers who want to buy "loss leader" items because they will also likely put several higher-margin products in the same shopping cart. Detailed sales data also help Wal-Mart determine how many cashiers are needed at different hours in different stores given the time of year, holidays, weather, pricing, and many other factors. Wal-Mart's data warehouse contains general sales data, sufficient to answer the questions for Hurricane Frances, and it also enables Wal-Mart to match sales with many individual customer demographics when people use their credit and debit cards to pay for merchandise. At the company's Sam's Club chain, membership cards provide the same personal identification. With this identifying data, Wal-Mart can associate product sales with location, income, home prices, and other personal demographics. The data warehouse facilitates target marketing of the most appropriate products to individuals. Further, the company uses sales data to improve its supply chain by negotiating better terms with suppliers for delivery, price, and promotions. All this is possible through an integrated, comprehensive, enterprise-wide data warehouse with significant analytical tools to make sense out of this mountain of data. (Adapted from Hays, 2004)

In light of this strong emphasis on information and the recent advances in information technology, you might expect most organizations to have highly developed systems for delivering information to managers and other users. Yet, this is often not the case. In fact, despite having mountains of data (as in petabytes—1000 terabytes or 1000^5 bytes), and often many databases, few organizations have more than a fraction of the information they need. Managers are often frustrated by their inability to access or use the data and information they need. This situation contributes to why some people claim that "business intelligence" is an oxymoron.

Modern organizations are said to be drowning in data but starving for information. Despite the mixed metaphor, this statement seems to portray quite accurately the situation in many organizations. What is the reason for this state of affairs? Let's examine two important (and related) reasons why an information gap has been created in most organizations.

The first reason for the information gap is the fragmented way in which organizations have developed information systems—and their supporting databases—for many years. The emphasis in this text is on a carefully planned, architectural approach to systems development that should produce a compatible set of databases. However, in reality, constraints on time and resources cause most organizations to resort to a "one-thing-at-a-time" approach to developing islands of information systems. This approach inevitably produces a hodgepodge of uncoordinated and often inconsistent databases. Usually, databases are based on a variety of hardware, software platforms, and purchased applications and have resulted from different organizational mergers, acquisitions, and reorganizations. Under these circumstances, it is extremely difficult, if not impossible, for managers to locate and use accurate information, which must be synthesized across these various systems of record.

The second reason for the information gap is that most systems are developed to support operational processing, with little or no thought given to the information or analytical tools needed for decision making. *Operational processing*, also called transaction processing, captures, stores, and manipulates data to support daily operations of the organization. It tends to focus database design on optimizing access to a small set of data related to a transaction (e.g., a customer, order, and associated product data). *Informational processing* is the analysis of data or other forms of information to support decision making. It needs large "swatches" of data from which to derive information (e.g., sales of all products, over several years, from every sales region). Most systems that are developed internally or purchased from outside vendors are designed to support operational processing, with little thought given to informational processing.

Bridging the information gap are *data warehouses* that consolidate and integrate information from many internal and external sources and arrange it in a meaningful format for making accurate and timely business decisions. They support executives, managers, and business analysts in making complex business decisions through applications such as the analysis of trends, target marketing, competitive analysis, customer relationship management, and so on. Data warehousing has evolved to meet these needs without disturbing existing operational processing.

The proliferation of Web-based customer interactions has made the situation much more interesting and more real time. The activities of customers and suppliers on an organization's Web site provide a wealth of new clickstream data to help understand behaviors and preferences and create a unique opportunity to communicate the right message (e.g., product cross-sales message). Extensive details, such as time, IP address, pages visited, context from where the page request was made, links taken, elapsed time on page, and so forth, can be captured unobtrusively. These data, along with customer transaction, payment, product return, inquiry, and other history consolidated into the data warehouse from a variety of transaction systems, can be used to personalize pages. Such reasoned and active interactions can lead to satisfied customers and business partners and more profitable business relationships. A similar proliferation of data for decision making is resulting from the growing use of radio-frequency identification (RFID) and global positioning system (GPS)-generated data to track the movement of packages, inventory, or people.

This chapter provides an overview of data warehousing. This exceptionally broad topic normally requires an entire text, especially when the expansive topic of business intelligence is the focus. This is why most texts on the topic are devoted to just a single aspect, such as data warehouse design or administration, data quality and governance, or business intelligence. We focus on the two areas relevant to a text on database management: data architecture and database design for data warehousing. You will learn first how a data warehouse relates to databases in existing operational systems. Described next is the three-tier data architecture, which characterizes most data warehouse environments. Then, we show special database design elements frequently used in data warehousing. Next, we introduce the latest approaches to a data warehouse, columnar databases—to address what the field is calling "big data" (how about that for a creative term!)—and NoSQL—for searching data warehouses of unstructured or textual data. Finally, you will see how users interact with the data warehouse, including online analytical processing, data mining, and data visualization. This last topic provides the bridge from this text to the broader context in which data warehousing is most often applied—business intelligence.

Data warehousing requires extracting data from existing operational systems, cleansing and transforming data for decision making, and loading them into a data warehouse—what is often called the extract–transform–load (ETL) process. An inherent part of this process are activities to ensure data quality, which is of special concern when data are consolidated across disparate systems. Data quality and data governance are particularly important for data warehousing and related activities; therefore, we will close this chapter with brief introductions to these essential topic areas.

BASIC CONCEPTS OF DATA WAREHOUSING

Data warehouse

A subject-oriented, integrated, time-variant, nonupdateable collection of data used in support of management decision-making processes.

A **data warehouse** is a subject-oriented, integrated, time-variant, nonupdateable collection of data used in support of management decision-making processes and business intelligence (Inmon and Hackathorn, 1994). The meaning of each of the key terms in this definition follows:

- *Subject-oriented* A data warehouse is organized around the key subjects (or high-level entities) of the enterprise. Major subjects may include customers, patients, students, products, and time.

- *Integrated* The data housed in the data warehouse are defined using consistent naming conventions, formats, encoding structures, and related characteristics gathered from several internal systems of record and also often from sources external to the organization. This means that the data warehouse holds the one version of "the truth."
- *Time-variant* Data in the data warehouse contain a time dimension so that they may be used to study trends and changes.
- *Nonupdateable* Data in the data warehouse are loaded and refreshed from operational systems but cannot be updated by end users.

A data warehouse is not just a consolidation of all the operational databases in an organization. Because of its focus on business intelligence, external data, and time-variant data (not just current status), a data warehouse is a unique kind of database. Fortunately, you don't need to learn a different set of database skills to work with a data warehouse. Most data warehouses are relational databases designed in a way optimized for decision support, not operational data processing. Thus, everything you have learned so far in this text still applies. In this chapter, you will learn the additional features, database design structures, and concepts that make a data warehouse unique.

Data warehousing is the process whereby organizations create and maintain data warehouses and extract meaning and inform decision making from their informational assets through these data warehouses. Successful data warehousing requires following proven data warehousing practices, sound project management, strong organizational commitment, as well as making the right technology decisions.

A Brief History of Data Warehousing

Data warehousing emerged as a result of advances in the field of information systems over several decades. The following were some key advances:

- Improvements in database technology, particularly the development of the relational data model and relational database management systems (RDBMSs)
- Advances in computer hardware, particularly the emergence of affordable mass storage and parallel computer architectures
- The emergence of end-user computing, facilitated by powerful, intuitive computer interfaces and tools
- Advances in middleware products that enable enterprise database connectivity across heterogeneous platforms (Hackathorn, 1993)

The key discovery that triggered the development of data warehousing was the recognition (and subsequent definition) of the fundamental differences between operational (or transaction processing) systems (sometimes called *systems of record* because their role is to keep the official, legal record of the organization) and informational (or decision support) systems. Devlin and Murphy (1988) published the first article describing the architecture of a data warehouse, based on this distinction. In 1992, Inmon published the first book describing data warehousing (Inmon, 1992), and he has subsequently become one of the most prolific authors in this field.

The Need for Data Warehousing

Two major factors drive the need for data warehousing in most organizations today:

1. A business requires an integrated, company-wide view of high-quality information.
2. The information systems department must separate informational from operational systems to improve performance dramatically in managing company data.

NEED FOR A COMPANY-WIDE VIEW Data in operational systems are typically fragmented and inconsistent, forming so-called silos, or islands, of data. They are also generally distributed on a variety of incompatible hardware and software platforms. For example, one file containing customer data may be located on a UNIX-based server running an Oracle DBMS, whereas another may be located on an IBM mainframe running the DB2 DBMS. Yet, for decision-making purposes, it is often necessary to provide a single, corporate view of that information.

FIGURE 9-1 Examples of heterogeneous data

STUDENT DATA

StudentNo	LastName	MI	FirstName	Telephone	Status	...
123-45-6789	Enright	T	Mark	483-1967	Soph	
389-21-4062	Smith	R	Elaine	283-4195	Jr	

STUDENT EMPLOYEE

StudentID	Address	Dept	Hours	...
123-45-6789	1218 Elk Drive, Phoenix, AZ 91304	Soc	8	
389-21-4062	134 Mesa Road, Tempe, AZ 90142	Math	10	

STUDENT HEALTH

StudentName	Telephone	Insurance	ID	...
Mark T. Enright	483-1967	Blue Cross	123-45-6789	
Elaine R. Smith	555-7828	?	389-21-4062	

To understand the difficulty of deriving a single corporate view, look at the simple example shown in Figure 9-1. This figure shows three tables from three separate systems of record, each containing similar student data. The STUDENT DATA table is from the class registration system, the STUDENT EMPLOYEE table is from the personnel system, and the STUDENT HEALTH table is from a health center system. Each table contains some unique data concerning students, but even common data (e.g., student names) are stored using different formats.

Suppose you want to develop a profile for each student, consolidating all data into a single file format. Some of the issues that you must resolve are as follows:

- *Inconsistent key structures* The primary key of the first two tables is some version of the student Social Security number, whereas the primary key of STUDENT HEALTH is StudentName.
- *Synonyms* In STUDENT DATA, the primary key is named StudentNo, whereas in STUDENT EMPLOYEE, it is named StudentID. (We discussed how to deal with synonyms in Chapter 4.)
- *Free-form fields versus structured fields* In STUDENT HEALTH, StudentName is a single field. In STUDENT DATA, StudentName (a composite attribute) is broken into its component parts: LastName, MI, and FirstName.
- *Inconsistent data values* Elaine Smith has one telephone number in STUDENT DATA but a different number in STUDENT HEALTH. Is this an error, or does this person have two telephone numbers?
- *Missing data* The value for Insurance is missing (or null) for Elaine Smith in the STUDENT HEALTH table. How will this value be located?

This simple example illustrates the nature of the problem of developing a single corporate view but fails to capture the complexity of that task. A real-life scenario would likely have dozens (if not hundreds) of files and thousands (or millions) of records.

Why do organizations need to bring data together from various systems of record? Ultimately, of course, the reason is to be more profitable, to be more competitive, or to grow by adding value for customers. This can be accomplished by increasing the speed and flexibility of decision making, improving business processes, or gaining a clearer understanding of customer behavior. For the previous student example, university administrators may want to investigate if the health or number of hours students work on campus is related to student academic performance; if taking certain courses is related to the health of students; or whether poor academic performers cost more to support, for example, due to increased health care as well as other costs. In general, certain trends in organizations encourage the need for data warehousing; these trends include the following:

- *No single system of record*   Almost no organization has only one database. Seems odd, doesn't it? Remember our discussion in Chapter 1 about the reasons for using a database compared to using separate file-processing systems? Because of the heterogeneous needs for data in different operational settings, because of corporate mergers and acquisitions, and because of the sheer size of many organizations, multiple operational databases exist.

- *Multiple systems are not synchronized*   It is difficult, if not impossible, to make separate databases consistent. Even if the metadata are controlled and made the same by one data administrator, the data values for the same attributes will not agree. This is because of different update cycles and separate places where the same data are captured for each system. Thus, to get one view of the organization, the data from the separate systems must be periodically consolidated and synchronized into one additional database. We will see that there can be actually two such consolidated databases—an operational data store and an enterprise data warehouse, both of which we include under the topic of data warehousing.

- *Organizations want to analyze the activities in a balanced way*   Many organizations have implemented some form of a balanced scorecard—metrics that show organization results in financial, human, customer satisfaction, product quality, and other terms simultaneously. To ensure that this multidimensional view of the organization shows consistent results, a data warehouse is necessary. When questions arise in the balanced scorecard, analytical software working with the data warehouse can be used to "drill down," "slice and dice," visualize, and in other ways mine business intelligence.

- *Customer relationship management*   Organizations in all sectors are realizing that there is value in having a total picture of their interactions with customers across all touch points. Different touch points (e.g., for a bank, these touch points include ATMs, online banking, tellers, electronic funds transfers, investment portfolio management, and loans) are supported by separate operational systems. Thus, without a data warehouse, a teller may not know to try to cross-sell a customer one of the bank's mutual funds if a large, atypical automatic deposit transaction appears on the teller's screen. Having a total picture of the activity with a given customer requires a consolidation of data from various operational systems.

- *Supplier relationship management*   Managing the supply chain has become a critical element in reducing costs and raising product quality for many organizations. Organizations want to create strategic supplier partnerships based on a total picture of their activities with suppliers, from billing, to meeting delivery dates, to quality control, to pricing, to support. Data about these different activities can be locked inside separate operational systems (e.g., accounts payable, shipping and receiving, production scheduling, and maintenance). ERP systems have improved this situation by bringing many of these data into one database. However, ERP systems tend to be designed to optimize operational, not informational or analytical, processing, which we discuss next.

TABLE 9-1 Comparison of Operational and Informational Systems

Characteristic	Operational Systems	Informational Systems
Primary purpose	Run the business on a current basis	Support managerial decision making
Type of data	Current representation of state of the business	Historical point-in-time (snapshots) and predictions
Primary users	Clerks, salespersons, administrators	Managers, business analysts, customers
Scope of usage	Narrow, planned, and simple updates and queries	Broad, ad hoc, complex queries and analysis
Design goal	Performance: throughput, availability	Ease of flexible access and use
Volume	Many constant updates and queries on one or a few table rows	Periodic batch updates and queries requiring many or all rows

Operational system

A system that is used to run a business in real time, based on current data. Also called a system of record.

Informational system

A system designed to support decision making based on historical point-in-time and prediction data for complex queries or data-mining applications.

NEED TO SEPARATE OPERATIONAL AND INFORMATIONAL SYSTEMS An **operational system** is a system that is used to run a business in real time, based on current data. Examples of operational systems are sales order processing, reservation systems, and patient registration systems. Operational systems must process large volumes of relatively simple read/write transactions and provide fast response. Operational systems are also called *systems of record*.

Informational systems are designed to support decision making based on historical point-in-time and prediction data. They are also designed for complex queries or data-mining applications. Examples of informational systems are systems for sales trend analysis, customer segmentation, and human resources planning.

The key differences between operational and informational systems are shown in Table 9-1. These two types of processing have very different characteristics in nearly every category of comparison. In particular, notice that they have quite different communities of users. Operational systems are used by clerks, administrators, salespersons, and others who must process business transactions. Informational systems are used by managers, executives, business analysts, and (increasingly) by customers who are searching for status information or who are decision makers.

The need to separate operational and informational systems is based on three primary factors:

1. A data warehouse centralizes data that are scattered throughout disparate operational systems and makes them readily available for decision support applications.
2. A properly designed data warehouse adds value to data by improving their quality and consistency.
3. A separate data warehouse eliminates much of the contention for resources that results when informational applications are confounded with operational processing.

DATA WAREHOUSE ARCHITECTURES

The architecture for data warehouses has evolved, and organizations have considerable latitude in creating variations. We will review here two core structures that form the basis for most implementations. The first is a three-level architecture that characterizes a bottom-up, incremental approach to evolving the data warehouse; the second is also a three-level data architecture that appears usually from a more top-down approach that emphasizes more coordination and an enterprise-wide perspective. Even with their differences, there are many common characteristics to these approaches.

Independent Data Mart Data Warehousing Environment

The independent data mart architecture for a data warehouse is shown in Figure 9-2. Building this architecture requires four basic steps (moving left to right in Figure 9-2):

1. Data are extracted from the various internal and external source system files and databases. In a large organization, there may be dozens or even hundreds of such files and databases.

FIGURE 9-2 Independent data mart data warehousing architecture

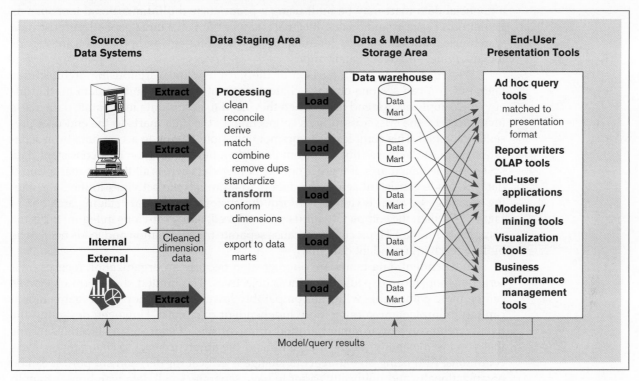

2. The data from the various source systems are transformed and integrated before being loaded into the data marts. Transactions may be sent to the source systems to correct errors discovered in data staging. The data warehouse is considered to be the collection of data marts.
3. The data warehouse is a set of physically distinct databases organized for decision support. It contains both detailed and summary data.
4. Users access the data warehouse by means of a variety of query languages and analytical tools. Results (e.g., predictions, forecasts) may be fed back to data warehouse and operational databases.

Extraction and loading happen periodically—sometimes daily, weekly, or monthly. Thus, the data warehouse often does not have, nor does it need to have, current data. Remember, the data warehouse is not (directly) supporting operational transaction processing, although it may contain transactional data (but more often summaries of transactions and snapshots of status variables, such as account balances and inventory levels). For most data warehousing applications, users are not looking for a reaction to an individual transaction but rather for trends and patterns in the state of the organization across a large subset of the data warehouse. At a minimum, five fiscal quarters of data are kept in a data warehouse so that at least annual trends and patterns can be discerned. Older data may be purged or archived. We will see later that one advanced data warehousing architecture, real-time data warehousing, is based on a different assumption about the need for current data.

Contrary to many of the principles discussed so far in this chapter, the independent data marts approach does not create one data warehouse. Instead, this approach creates many separate data marts, each based on data warehousing, not transaction processing database technologies. A **data mart** is a data warehouse that is limited in scope, customized for the decision-making applications of a particular end-user group. Its contents either are obtained from independent ETL processes, as shown in Figure 9-2 for an **independent data mart**, or are derived from the data warehouse, which we will discuss in the next two sections. A data mart is designed to optimize the performance for well-defined and predicable uses, sometimes as few as a single or a couple of queries. For example, an organization may have a marketing data mart, a finance data mart, a supply chain data mart, and so on to support known analytical

Data mart

A data warehouse that is limited in scope, whose data are obtained by selecting and summarizing data from a data warehouse or from separate extract, transform, and load processes from source data systems.

Independent data mart

A data mart filled with data extracted from the operational environment, without the benefit of a data warehouse.

processing. It is possible that each data mart is built using different tools; for example, a financial data mart may be built using a proprietary multidimensional tool such as Hyperion's Essbase, and a sales data mart may be built on a more general-purpose data warehouse platform, such as Teradata, using MicroStrategy and other tools for reporting, querying, and data visualization.

We will provide a comparison of the various data warehousing architectures later, but you can see one obvious characteristic of the independent data mart strategy: the complexity for end users when they need to access data in separate data marts (evidenced by the crisscrossed lines connecting all the data marts to the end-user presentation tools). This complexity comes not only from having to access data from separate data mart databases but also from possibly a new generation of inconsistent data systems—the data marts. If there is one set of metadata across all the data marts, and if data are made consistent across the data marts through the activities in the data staging area (e.g., by what is called "conform dimensions" in the data staging area box in Figure 9-2), then the complexity for users is reduced. Not so obvious in Figure 9-2 is the complexity for the ETL processes, because separate transformation and loads need to be built for each independent data mart.

Independent data marts are often created because an organization focuses on a series of short-term, expedient business objectives. The limited short-term objectives can be more compatible with the comparably lower cost (money and organizational capital) to implement yet one more independent data mart. However, designing the data warehousing environment around different sets of short-term objectives means that you lose flexibility for the long term and the ability to react to changing business conditions. And being able to react to change is critical for decision support. It can be organizationally and politically easier to have separate, small data warehouses than to get all organizational parties to agree to one view of the organization in a central data warehouse. Also, some data warehousing technologies have technical limitations for the size of the data warehouse they can support—what we will call later a scalability issue. Thus, technology, rather than the business, may dictate a data warehousing architecture if you first lock yourself into a particular data warehousing set of technologies before you understand your data warehousing requirements. We discuss the pros and cons of the independent data mart architecture compared with its prime competing architecture in the next section.

Dependent Data Mart and Operational Data Store Architecture: A Three-Level Approach

The independent data mart architecture in Figure 9-2 has several important limitations (Marco, 2003; Meyer, 1997):

1. A separate ETL process is developed for each data mart, which can yield costly redundant data and processing efforts.
2. Data marts may not be consistent with one another because they are often developed with different technologies, and thus, they may not provide a clear enterprise-wide view of data concerning important subjects such as customers, suppliers, and products.
3. There is no capability to drill down into greater detail or into related facts in other data marts or a shared data repository, so analysis is limited, or at best very difficult (e.g., doing joins across separate platforms for different data marts). Essentially, relating data across data marts is a task performed by users outside the data warehouse.
4. Scaling costs are excessive because every new application that creates a separate data mart repeats all the extract and load steps. Usually, operational systems have limited time windows for batch data extracting, so at some point, the load on the operations systems may mean that new technology is needed, with additional costs.
5. If there is an attempt to make the separate data marts consistent, the cost to do so is quite high.

The value of independent data marts has been hotly debated. Kimball (1997) strongly supports the development of independent data marts as a viable strategy for a phased development of decision support systems. Armstrong (1997), Inmon (1997, 2000), and Marco (2003) point out the five fallacies previously mentioned and many more. There are two debates as to the actual value of independent data marts:

1. One debate deals with the nature of the phased approach to implementing a data warehousing environment. The essence of this debate is whether each data mart should or should not evolve in a bottom-up fashion from a subset of enterprise-wide decision support data.
2. The other debate deals with the suitable database architecture for analytical processing. This debate centers on the extent to which a data mart database should be normalized.

The essences of these two debates are addressed throughout this chapter. We provide an exercise at the end of the chapter for you to explore these debates in more depth.

One of the most popular approaches to addressing the independent data mart limitations raised earlier is to use a three-level approach represented by the dependent data mart and operational data store architecture (see Figure 9-3). Here the new level is the operational data store, and the data and metadata storage level is reconfigured. The first and second limitations are addressed by loading the **dependent data marts** from an **enterprise data warehouse (EDW)**, which is a central, integrated data warehouse that is the control point and single "version of the truth" made available to end users for decision support applications. Dependent data marts still have a purpose to provide a simplified and high-performance environment that is tuned to the decision-making needs of user groups. A data mart may be a separate physical database (and different data marts may be on different platforms) or can be a logical (user view) data mart instantiated on the fly when accessed. We explain logical data marts in the next section.

A user group can access its data mart, and then when other data are needed, users can access the EDW. Redundancy across dependent data marts is planned, and redundant data are consistent because each data mart is loaded in a synchronized way from one common source of data (or is a view of the data warehouse). Integration of data is

Dependent data mart

A data mart filled exclusively from an enterprise data warehouse and its reconciled data.

Enterprise data warehouse (EDW)

A centralized, integrated data warehouse that is the control point and single source of all data made available to end users for decision support applications.

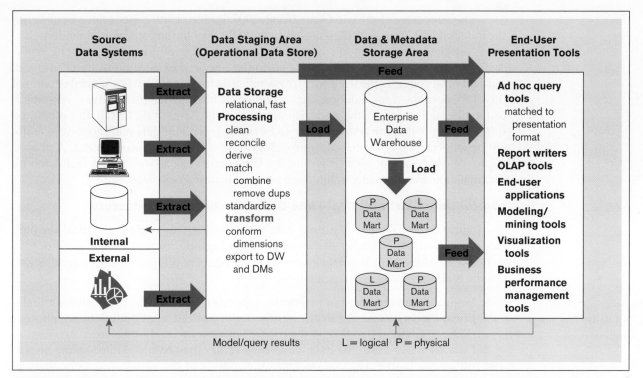

FIGURE 9-3 Dependent data mart and operational data store: A three-level architecture

the responsibility of the IT staff managing the enterprise data warehouse; it is not the end users' responsibility to integrate data across independent data marts for each query or application. The dependent data mart and operational data store architecture is often called a "hub and spoke" approach, in which the EDW is the hub and the source data systems and the data marts are at the ends of input and output spokes.

Operational data store (ODS)

An integrated, subject-oriented, continuously updateable, current-valued (with recent history), enterprise-wide, detailed database designed to serve operational users as they do decision support processing.

The third limitation is addressed by providing an integrated source for all the operational data in an operational data store. An **operational data store (ODS)** is an integrated, subject-oriented, continuously updateable, current-valued (with recent history), organization-wide, detailed database designed to serve operational users as they do decision support processing (Imhoff, 1998; Inmon, 1998). An ODS is typically a relational database and normalized like databases in the systems of record, but it is tuned for decision-making applications. For example, indexes and other relational database design elements are tuned for queries that retrieve broad groups of data, rather than for transaction processing or querying individual and directly related records (e.g., a customer order). Because it has volatile, current, and only recent history data, the same query against an ODS very likely will yield different results at different times. An ODS typically does not contain "deep" history, whereas an EDW typically holds a multiyear history of snapshots of the state of the organization. An ODS may be fed from the database of an ERP application, but because most organizations do not have only one ERP database and do not run all operations against one ERP, an ODS is usually different from an ERP database. The ODS also serves as the staging area for loading data into the EDW. The ODS may receive data immediately or with some delay from the systems of record, whichever is practical and acceptable for the decision-making requirements that it supports.

The dependent data mart and operational data store architecture is also called a *corporate information factory (CIF)* (see Imhoff, 1999). It is considered to be a comprehensive view of organizational data in support of all user data requirements.

Different leaders in the field endorse different approaches to data warehousing. Those who endorse the independent data mart approach argue that this approach has two significant benefits:

1. It allows for the concept of a data warehouse to be demonstrated by working on a series of small projects.
2. The length of time until there is some benefit from data warehousing is reduced because the organization is not delayed until all data are centralized.

The advocates of the CIF (Armstrong, 2000; Inmon, 1999) raise serious issues with the independent approach; these issues include the five limitations of independent data marts outlined earlier. Inmon suggests that an advantage of physically separate *dependent* data marts is that they can be tuned to the needs of each community of users. In particular, he suggests the need for an *exploration warehouse*, which is a special version of the EDW optimized for data mining and business intelligence using advanced statistical, mathematical modeling, and visualization tools. Armstrong (2000) and others go further to argue that the benefits claimed by the independent data mart advocates really are benefits of taking a phased approach to data warehouse development. A phased approach can be accomplished within the CIF framework as well and is facilitated by the final data warehousing architecture we review in the next section.

Logical Data Mart and Real-Time Data Warehouse Architecture

The logical data mart and real-time data warehouse architecture is practical for only moderate-sized data warehouses or when using high-performance data warehousing technology, such as the Teradata system. As can be seen in Figure 9-4, this architecture has the following unique characteristics:

Logical data mart

A data mart created by a relational view of a data warehouse.

1. **Logical data marts** are not physically separate databases but rather different relational views of one physical, slightly denormalized relational data warehouse. (Refer to Chapter 6 to review the concept of views.)
2. Data are moved into the data warehouse rather than to a separate staging area to utilize the high-performance computing power of the warehouse technology to perform the cleansing and transformation steps.

FIGURE 9-4   Logical data mart and real-time data warehouse architecture

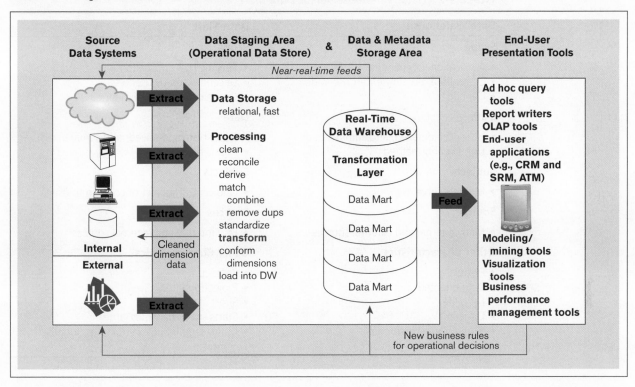

3. New data marts can be created quickly because no physical database or database technology needs to be created or acquired and no loading routines need to be written.
4. Data marts are always up-to-date because data in a view are created when the view is referenced; views can be materialized if a user has a series of queries and analysis that need to work off the same instantiation of the data mart.

Whether logical or physical, data marts and data warehouses play different roles in a data warehousing environment; these different roles are summarized in Table 9-2. Although limited in scope, a data mart may not be small. Thus, scalable technology is often critical. A significant burden and cost are placed on users when they themselves need to integrate the data across separate physical data marts (if this is even possible). As data marts are added, a data warehouse can be built in phases; the easiest way for this to happen is to follow the logical data mart and real-time data warehouse architecture.

The **real-time data warehouse** aspect of the architecture in Figure 9-4 means that the source data systems, decision support services, and the data warehouse *exchange* data and business rules at a *near*-real-time pace because there is a need for rapid response (i.e., action) to a current, comprehensive picture of the organization. The purpose of real-time data warehousing is to know what is happening, when it is happening, and to make desirable things happen through the operational systems. For example, a help desk professional answering questions and logging problem tickets will have a total picture of the customer's most recent sales contacts, billing and payment transactions, maintenance activities, and orders. With this information, the system supporting the help desk can, based on operational decision rules created from a continuous analysis of up-to-date warehouse data, automatically generate a script for the professional to sell what the analysis has shown to be a likely and profitable maintenance contract, an upgraded product, or another product bought by customers with a similar profile. A critical event, such as entry of a new product order, can be considered immediately so that the organization knows at least as much about the relationship with its customer, as does the customer.

Another example of real-time data warehousing (with real-time analytics) would be an express mail and package delivery service using frequent scanning of parcels

Real-time data warehouse

An enterprise data warehouse that accepts near-real-time feeds of transactional data from the systems of record, analyzes warehouse data, and in near-real-time relays business rules to the data warehouse and systems of record so that immediate action can be taken in response to business events.

TABLE 9-2 Data Warehouse versus Data Mart

Data Warehouse	Data Mart
Scope	**Scope**
• Application independent	• Specific DSS application
• Centralized, possibly enterprise-wide	• Decentralized by user area
• Planned	• Organic, possibly not planned
Data	**Data**
• Historical, detailed, and summarized	• Some history, detailed, and summarized
• Lightly denormalized	• Highly denormalized
Subjects	**Subjects**
• Multiple subjects	• One central subject of concern to users
Sources	**Sources**
• Many internal and external sources	• Few internal and external sources
Other Characteristics	**Other Characteristics**
• Flexible	• Restrictive
• Data oriented	• Project oriented
• Long life	• Short life
• Large	• Starts small, becomes large
• Single complex structure	• Multi, semi-complex structures, together complex

to know exactly where a package is in its transportation system. Real-time analytics, based on this package data, as well as pricing, customer service–level agreements, and logistics opportunities, could automatically reroute packages to meet delivery promises for their best customers. RFID technologies are allowing these kinds of opportunities for real-time data warehousing (with massive amounts of data) coupled with real-time analytics to be used to greatly reduce the latency between event data capture and appropriate actions being taken.

The orientation is that each event with, say, a customer, is a potential opportunity for a customized, personalized, and optimized communication based on a strategic decision of how to respond to a customer with a particular profile. Thus, decision making and the data warehouse are actively involved in guiding operational processing, which is why some people call this active data warehousing. The goal is to shorten the cycle to do the following:

- Capture customer data at the time of a business event (what did happen)
- Analyze customer behavior (why did something happen) and predict customer responses to possible actions (what will happen)
- Develop rules for optimizing customer interactions, including the appropriate response and channel that will yield the best results
- Take immediate *action* with customers at touch points based on best responses to customers as determined by decision rules in order to make desirable results happen

The idea is that the potential value of taking the right action decays the longer the delay from event to action. The real-time data warehouse is where all the intelligence comes together to reduce this delay. Thus, real-time data warehousing moves data warehousing from the back office to the front office. For a thorough status report on real-time data warehousing, see Hackathorn (2002). Other authors refer to real-time data warehousing as action-oriented or active (@ctive) data warehousing.

Three-Layer Data Architecture

Figure 9-5 shows a three-layer data architecture for a data warehouse. This architecture is characterized by the following:

1. Operational data are stored in the various operational systems of record throughout the organization (and sometimes in external systems).

2. Reconciled data are the type of data stored in the enterprise data warehouse and an operational data store. **Reconciled data** are detailed, current data intended to be the single, authoritative source for all decision support applications.
3. Derived data are the type of data stored in each of the data marts. **Derived data** are data that have been selected, formatted, and aggregated for end-user decision support applications.

The process for reconciling data across source systems is part of data quality and integration, and it is affected by organizational rules and processes related to data governance. These are topics larger than simply data warehousing; we will give a brief introduction to them in a separate section at the end of this chapter. Pertinent to data warehousing is derived data, which we cover in a subsequent section of the current chapter. Two components shown in Figure 9-5 play critical roles in the data architecture: the enterprise data model and metadata.

ROLE OF THE ENTERPRISE DATA MODEL   In Figure 9-5, we show the reconciled data layer linked to the enterprise data model. Recall from Chapter 1 that the enterprise data model presents a total picture explaining the data required by an organization. If the reconciled data layer is to be the single, authoritative source for all data required for decision support, it must conform to the design specified in the enterprise data model. Thus, the enterprise data model controls the phased evolution of the data warehouse. Usually, the enterprise data model evolves as new problems and decision applications are addressed. It takes too long to develop the enterprise data model in one step, and the dynamic needs for decision making will change before the warehouse is built.

ROLE OF METADATA   Figure 9-5 also shows a layer of metadata linked to each of the three data layers. Recall from Chapter 1 that metadata are technical and business data that describe the properties or characteristics of other data. Following is a brief description of the three types of metadata shown in Figure 9-5.

1. *Operational metadata*   describe the data in the various operational systems (as well as external data) that feed the enterprise data warehouse. Operational metadata typically exist in a number of different formats and unfortunately are often of poor quality.

Reconciled data

Detailed, current data intended to be the single, authoritative source for all decision support applications.

Derived data

Data that have been selected, formatted, and aggregated for end-user decision support applications.

FIGURE 9-5   Three-layer data architecture for a data warehouse

2. *Enterprise data warehouse (EDW) metadata* are derived from (or at least consistent with) the enterprise data model. EDW metadata describe the reconciled data layer as well as the rules for extracting, transforming, and loading operational data into reconciled data.

3. *Data mart metadata* describe the derived data layer and the rules for transforming reconciled data to derived data.

For a thorough review of data warehouse metadata, see Marco (2000).

SOME CHARACTERISTICS OF DATA WAREHOUSE DATA

To understand and model the data in each of the three layers of the data architecture for a data warehouse, you need to learn some basic characteristics of data as they are stored in data warehouse databases. The characteristics of data for a data warehouse are different from those of data for operational databases.

Status Versus Event Data

The difference between status data and event data is shown in Figure 9-6. The figure shows a typical log entry recorded by a DBMS when processing a business transaction for a banking application. This log entry contains both status and event data: The "before image" and "after image" represent the status of the bank account before and then after a withdrawal. Data representing the withdrawal (or update event) are shown in the middle of the figure.

Transactions are business activities that cause one or more business events to occur at a database level. An event results in one or more database actions (create, update, or delete). The withdrawal transaction in Figure 9-6 leads to a single update, which is the reduction in the account balance from 750 to 700. On the other hand, the transfer of money from one account to another would lead to two actions: two updates to handle a withdrawal and a deposit. Sometimes nontransactions, such as an abandoned online shopping cart, busy signal or dropped network connection, or an item put in a shopping cart and then taken out before checkout, can also be important activities that need to be recorded in the data warehouse.

Both status data and event data can be stored in a database. However, in practice, most of the data stored in databases (including data warehouses) are status data. A data warehouse likely contains a history of snapshots of status data or a summary (say,

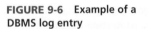

FIGURE 9-6 Example of a DBMS log entry

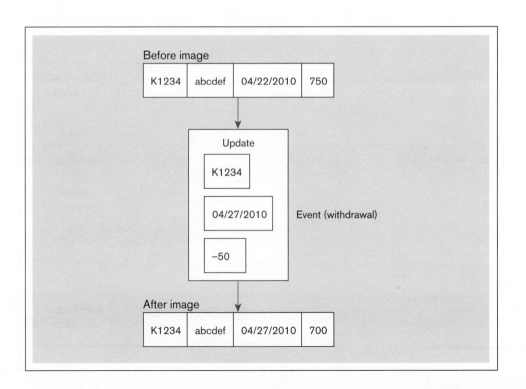

an hourly total) of transaction or event data. Event data, which represent transactions, may be stored for a defined period but are then deleted or archived to save storage space. Both status and event data are typically stored in database logs (as represented in Figure 9-6) for backup and recovery purposes. As will be explained later, the database log plays an important role in filling the data warehouse.

Transient Versus Periodic Data

In data warehouses, it is typical to maintain a record of when events occurred in the past. This is necessary, for example, to compare sales or inventory levels on a particular date or during a particular period with the previous year's sales on the same date or during the same period.

Most operational systems are based on the use of transient data. **Transient data** are data in which changes to existing records are written over previous records, thus destroying the previous data content. Records are deleted without preserving the previous contents of those records.

You can easily visualize transient data by again referring to Figure 9-6. If the after image is written over the before image, the before image (containing the previous balance) is lost. However, because this is a database log, both images are normally preserved.

Periodic data are data that are never physically altered or deleted once added to the store. The before and after images in Figure 9-6 represent periodic data. Notice that each record contains a time stamp that indicates the date (and time, if needed) when the most recent update event occurred. (We introduced the use of time stamps in Chapter 2.)

An Example of Transient and Periodic Data

A more detailed example comparing transient and periodic data is shown in Figures 9-7 and 9-8.

TRANSIENT DATA Figure 9-7 shows a relation (Table X) that initially contains four rows. The table has three attributes: a primary key and two nonkey attributes, A and B. The values for each of these attributes on the date 10/09 are shown in the figure. For example, for record 001, the value of attribute A on this date is a.

Transient data

Data in which changes to existing records are written over previous records, thus destroying the previous data content.

Periodic data

Data that are never physically altered or deleted once they have been added to the store.

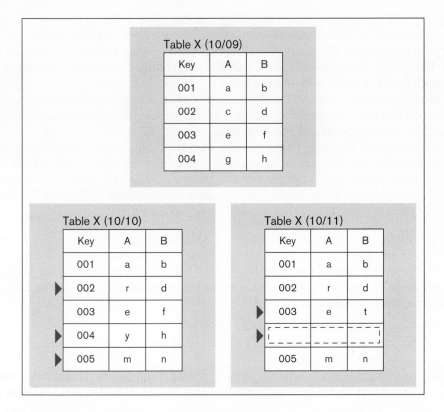

FIGURE 9-7 Transient operational data

FIGURE 9-8   Periodic warehouse data

Table X (10/09)

Key	Date	A	B	Action
001	10/09	a	b	C
002	10/09	c	d	C
003	10/09	e	f	C
004	10/09	g	h	C

Table X (10/10)

Key	Date	A	B	Action
001	10/09	a	b	C
002	10/09	c	d	C
▶ 002	10/10	r	d	U
003	10/09	e	f	C
004	10/09	g	h	C
▶ 004	10/10	y	h	U
▶ 005	10/10	m	n	C

Table X (10/11)

Key	Date	A	B	Action
001	10/09	a	b	C
002	10/09	c	d	C
002	10/10	r	d	U
003	10/09	e	f	C
▶ 003	10/11	e	t	U
004	10/09	g	h	C
004	10/10	y	h	U
▶ 004	10/11	y	h	D
005	10/10	m	n	C

On date 10/10, three changes are made to the table (changes to rows are indicated by arrows to the left of the table). Row 002 is updated, so the value of A is changed from c to r. Row 004 is also updated, so the value of A is changed from g to y. Finally, a new row (with key 005) is inserted into the table.

Notice that when rows 002 and 004 are updated, the new rows replace the previous rows. Therefore, the previous values are lost; there is no historical record of these values. This is characteristic of transient data.

More changes are made to the rows on date 10/11 (to simplify the discussion, we assume that only one change can be made to a given row on a given date). Row 003 is updated, and row 004 is deleted. Notice that there is no record to indicate that row 004 was ever stored in the database. The way the data are processed in Figure 9-7 is characteristic of the transient data typical in operational systems.

PERIODIC DATA   One typical objective for a data warehouse is to maintain a historical record of key events or to create a time series for particular variables such as sales. This often requires storing periodic data, rather than transient data. Figure 9-8 shows the table used in Figure 9-7, now modified to represent periodic data. The following changes have been made in Figure 9-8:

1. Two new columns have been added to Table X:
   a. The column named Date is a time stamp that records the most recent date when a row has been modified.
   b. The column named Action is used to record the type of change that occurred. Possible values for this attribute are C (Create), U (Update), and D (Delete).

2. Once a record has been stored in the table, that record is never changed. When an update operation occurs on a record, both the before image and the after image are stored in the table. Although a record may be *logically* deleted, a historical version of the deleted record is maintained in the database for as much history (at least five quarters) as needed to analyze trends.

Now let's examine the same set of actions that occurred in Figure 9-7. Assume that all four rows were created on the date 10/09, as shown in the first table.

In the second table (for 10/10), rows 002 and 004 have been updated. The table now contains both the old version (for 10/09) and the new version (for 10/10) for these rows. The table also contains the new row (005) that was created on 10/10.

The third table (for 10/11) shows the update to row 003, with both the old and new versions. Also, row 004 is deleted from this table. This table now contains three versions of row 004: the original version (from 10/09), the updated version (from 10/1010), and the deleted version (from 10/11). The D in the last row for record 004 indicates that this row has been logically deleted, so that it is no longer available to users or their applications.

If you examine Figure 9-8, you can see why data warehouses tend to grow very rapidly. Storing periodic data can impose large storage requirements. Therefore, users must choose very carefully the key data that require this form of processing.

OTHER DATA WAREHOUSE CHANGES Besides the periodic changes to data values outlined previously, six other kinds of changes to a warehouse data model must be accommodated by data warehousing:

1. *New descriptive attributes* For example, new characteristics of products or customers that are important to store in the warehouse must be accommodated. Later in the chapter, we call these attributes of dimension tables. This change is fairly easily accommodated by adding columns to tables and allowing null values for existing rows (if historical data exist in source systems, null values do not have to be stored).
2. *New business activity attributes* For example, new characteristics of an event already stored in the warehouse, such as a column C for the table in Figure 9-8, must be accommodated. This can be handled as in item 1, but it is more difficult when the new facts are more refined, such as a data associated with days of the week, not just month and year, as in Figure 9-8.
3. *New classes of descriptive attributes* This is equivalent to adding new tables to the database.
4. *Descriptive attributes become more refined* For example, data about stores must be broken down by individual cash register to understand sales data. This change is in the grain of the data, an extremely important topic, which we discuss later in the chapter. This can be a very difficult change to accommodate.
5. *Descriptive data are related to one another* For example, store data are related to geography data. This causes new relationships, often hierarchical, to be included in the data model.
6. *New source of data* This is a very common change, in which some new business need causes data feeds from an additional source system or some new operational system is installed that must feed the warehouse. This change can cause almost any of the previously mentioned changes, as well as the need for new extract, transform, and load processes.

It is usually not possible to go back and reload a data warehouse to accommodate all of these kinds of changes for the whole data history maintained. But it is critical to accommodate such changes smoothly to enable the data warehouse to meet new business conditions and information and business intelligence needs. Thus, designing the warehouse for change is very important.

THE DERIVED DATA LAYER

We turn now to the derived data layer. This is the data layer associated with logical or physical data marts (see Figure 9-5). It is the layer with which users normally interact for their decision support applications. Ideally, the reconciled data level is designed first and is the basis for the derived layer, whether data marts are dependent, independent, or logical. In order to derive any data mart we might need, it is necessary that the EDW be a fully normalized relational database accommodating transient and periodic data; this gives us the greatest flexibility to combine data into the simplest form for all user needs, even those that are unanticipated when the EDW is designed. In this section, we first discuss the characteristics of the derived data layer. We then introduce the star schema (or dimensional model), which is the data model most commonly used today to implement this data layer. A star schema is a specially designed, denormalized relational data model. We emphasize that the derived data layer can use normalized relations in the enterprise data warehouse; however, most organizations still build many data marts.

Characteristics of Derived Data

Earlier we defined *derived data* as data that have been selected, formatted, and aggregated for end-user decision support applications. In other words, derived data are information instead of raw data. As shown in Figure 9-5, the source of the derived data is the reconciled data, created from what can be a rather complex data process to integrate and make consistent data from many systems of record inside and outside the organization. Derived data in a data mart are generally optimized for the needs of particular user groups, such as departments, workgroups, or even individuals, to measure and analyze business activities and trends. A common mode of operation is to select the relevant data from the enterprise data warehouse on a daily basis, format and aggregate those data as needed, and then load and index those data in the target data marts. A data mart typically is accessed via online analytical processing (OLAP) tools, which we describe and illustrate in a later section of this chapter.

The objectives that are sought with derived data are quite different from the objectives of reconciled data. Typical objectives are the following:

- Provide ease of use for decision support applications
- Provide fast response for predefined user queries or requests for information (information usually in the form of metrics used to gauge the health of the organization in areas such as customer service, profitability, process efficiency, or sales growth)
- Customize data for particular target user groups
- Support ad hoc queries and data mining and other analytical applications

To satisfy these needs, we usually find the following characteristics in derived data:

- Both detailed data and aggregate data are present:
  a. Detailed data are often (but not always) periodic—that is, they provide a historical record.
  b. Aggregate data are formatted to respond quickly to predetermined (or common) queries.
- Data are distributed to separate data marts for different user groups.
- The data model that is most commonly used for a data mart is a dimensional model, usually in the form of a star schema, which is a relational-like model (such models are used by relational online analytical processing [ROLAP] tools). Proprietary models (which often look like hypercubes) are also sometimes used (such models are used by multidimensional online analytical processing [MOLAP] tools); these tools will be illustrated later in this chapter.

The Star Schema

Star schema

A simple database design in which dimensional data are separated from fact or event data. A dimensional model is another name for a star schema.

A **star schema** is a simple database design (particularly suited to ad hoc queries) in which dimensional data (describing how data are commonly aggregated for reporting) are separated from fact or event data (describing business activity). A star schema is one version of a dimensional model (Kimball, 1996a). Although the star schema is suited to ad hoc queries (and other forms of informational processing), it is not suited to online transaction processing, and therefore, it is not generally used in operational systems, operational data stores, or an EDW. It is called a star schema because of its visual appearance, not because it has been recognized on the Hollywood Walk of Fame.

FACT TABLES AND DIMENSION TABLES   A star schema consists of two types of tables: one fact table and one or more dimension tables. *Fact tables* contain factual or quantitative data (measurements that are numerical, continuously valued, and additive) about a business, such as units sold, orders booked, and so on. *Dimension tables* hold descriptive data (context) about the subjects of the business. The dimension tables are usually the source of attributes used to qualify, categorize, or summarize facts in queries, reports, or graphs; thus, dimension data are usually textual and discrete (even if numeric). A data mart might contain several star schemas with similar dimension tables but each with a different fact table. Typical business dimensions (subjects) are Product, Customer, and Period. Period, or time, is always one of the dimensions. This structure is shown in Figure 9-9, which contains four dimension tables. As we will see shortly, there are variations on this basic star structure that provide further abilities to summarize and categorize the facts.

Each dimension table has a one-to-many relationship to the central fact table. Each dimension table generally has a simple primary key, as well as several nonkey attributes. The primary key, in turn, is a foreign key in the fact table (as shown in Figure 9-9). The primary key of the fact table is a composite key that consists of the concatenation of all of the foreign keys (four keys in Figure 9-9), plus possibly other components that do not correspond to dimensions. The relationship between each dimension table and the fact table provides a join path that allows users to query the database easily, using SQL statements for either predefined or ad hoc queries.

By now you have probably recognized that the star schema is not a new data model, but instead a denormalized implementation of the relational data model. The fact table plays the role of a normalized *n*-ary associative entity that links the instances of the various dimensions, which are in second, but possibly not third, normal form. To review associative entities, see Chapter 2, and for an example of the use of an associative entity, see Figures 2-11 and 2-14. The dimension tables are denormalized. Most experts view this denormalization as acceptable because dimensions are not updated and avoid costly joins; thus, the star is optimized around certain facts and business objects to respond to specific information needs. Relationships between dimensions are not allowed; although such a relationship might exist in the organization (e.g., between employees and departments), such relationships are outside the scope of a star schema.

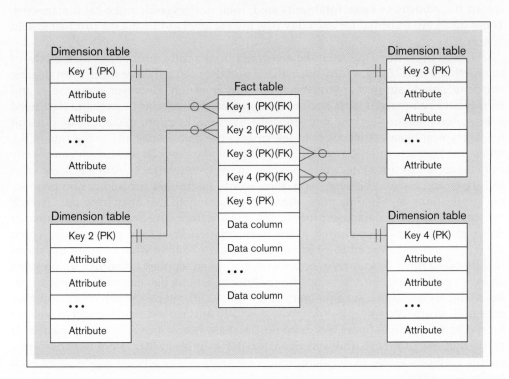

FIGURE 9-9 Components of a star schema

FIGURE 9-10 Star schema example

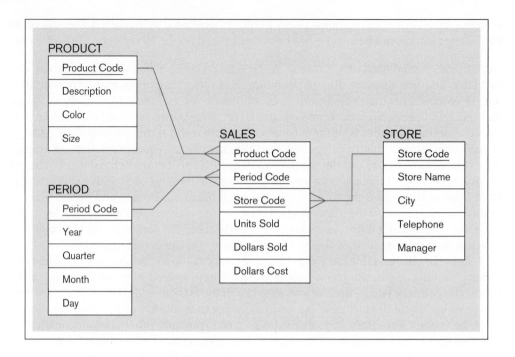

As we will see later, there may be other tables related to dimensions, but these tables are never related directly to the fact table.

EXAMPLE STAR SCHEMA A star schema provides answers to a domain of business questions. For example, consider the following questions:

1. Which cities have the highest sales of large products?
2. What is the average monthly sales for each store manager?
3. In which stores are we losing money on which products? Does this vary by quarter?

A simple example of a star schema that could provide answers to such questions is shown in Figure 9-10. This example has three dimension tables: PRODUCT, PERIOD, and STORE, and one fact table, named SALES. The fact table is used to record three business facts: total units sold, total dollars sold, and total dollars cost. These totals are recorded for each day (the lowest level of PERIOD) a product is sold in a store.

Could these three questions be answered from a fully normalized data model of transactional data? Sure, a fully normalized and detailed database is the most flexible structure, able to support answering almost any question. However, more tables and joins would be involved, data need to be aggregated in standard ways, and data need to be sorted in an understandable sequence. These tasks might make it more difficult for the typical business manager to interrogate the data (especially using raw SQL), unless the business intelligence (OLAP) tool he or she uses can mask such complexity from them (see sections later in this chapter on the user interface). And sufficient sales history would have to be kept, more than would be needed for transaction processing applications. With a data mart, the work of joining and summarizing data (which can cause extensive database processing) into the form needed to directly answer these questions has been shifted to the reconciliation layer, and processes in which the end user does not need to be involved. However, exactly what range of questions will be asked must be known in order to design the data mart for sufficient, optimal, and easy processing. Further, once these three questions become no longer interesting to the organization, the data mart (if it is physical) can be thrown away, and new ones built to answer new questions, whereas fully normalized models tend to be built for the long term to support less dynamic database needs (possibly with logical data marts that exist to meet transient needs). Later in this chapter, we will show some simple methods to use to decide how to determine a star schema model from such business questions.

FIGURE 9-11 **Star schema sample data**

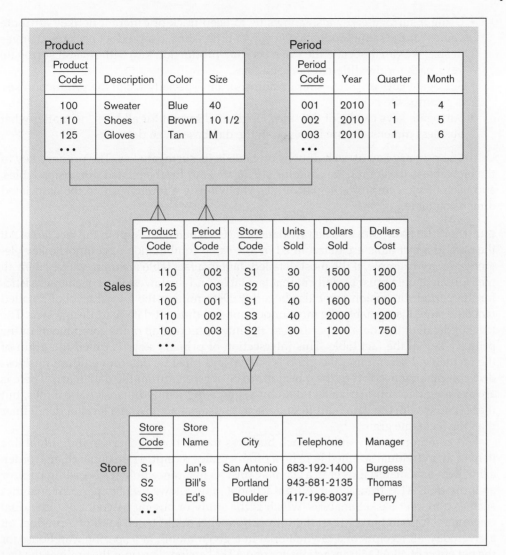

Some sample data for this schema are shown in Figure 9-11. From the fact table, we find (for example) the following facts for product number 110 during period 002:

1. Thirty units were sold in store S1. The total dollar sale was 1500, and total dollar cost was 1200.
2. Forty units were sold in store S3. The total dollar sale was 2000, and total dollar cost was 1200.

Additional detail concerning the dimensions for this example can be obtained from the dimension tables. For example, in the PERIOD table, we find that period 002 corresponds to year 2010, quarter 1, month 5. Try tracing the other dimensions in a similar manner.

SURROGATE KEY Every key used to join the fact table with a dimension table should be a surrogate (nonintelligent or system-assigned) key, not a key that uses a business value (sometimes called a natural, smart, or production key). That is, in Figure 9-10, Product Code, Store Code, and Period Code should all be surrogate keys in both the fact and dimension tables. If, for example, it is necessary to know the product catalog number, engineering number, or inventory item number for a product, these attributes would be stored along with Description, Color, and Size as attributes of the product dimension table. The following are the main reasons for this surrogate-key rule (Kimball, 1998a):

• Business keys change, often slowly, over time, and we need to remember old and new business key values for the same business object. As we will see in a later section on slowly changing dimensions, a surrogate key allows us to handle changing and unknown keys with ease.

- Using a surrogate key also allows us to keep track of different nonkey attribute values for the same production key over time. Thus, if a product package changes in size, we can associate the same product production key with several surrogate keys, each for the different package sizes.
- Surrogate keys are often simpler and shorter, especially when the production key is a composite key.
- Surrogate keys can be of the same length and format for all keys, no matter what business dimensions are involved in the database, even dates.

The primary key of each dimension table is its surrogate key. The primary key of the fact table is the composite of all the surrogate keys for the related dimension tables, and each of the composite key attributes is obviously a foreign key to the associated dimension table.

GRAIN OF THE FACT TABLE The raw data of a star schema are kept in the fact table. All the data in a fact table are determined by the same combination of composite key elements; so, for example, if the most detailed data in a fact table are daily values, then all measurement data must be daily in that fact table, and the lowest level of characteristics for the period dimension must also be a day. Determining the lowest level of detailed fact data stored is arguably the most important and difficult data mart design step. The level of detail of this data is specified by the intersection of all of the components of the primary key of the fact table. This intersection of primary keys is called the **grain** of the fact table. Determining the grain is critical and must be determined from business decision-making needs (i.e., the questions to be answered from the data mart). There is always a way to summarize fact data by aggregating using dimension attributes, but there is no way in the data mart to understand business activity at a level of detail finer than the fact table grain.

A common grain would be each business transaction, such as an individual line item or an individual scanned item on a product sales receipt, a personnel change order, a line item on a material receipt, a claim against an insurance policy, a boarding pass, or an individual ATM transaction. A transactional grain allows users to perform analytics such as a market basket analysis, which is the study of buying behavior of individual customers. A grain higher than the transaction level might be all sales of a product on a given day, all receipts of a raw material in a given month at a specific warehouse, or the net effect of all ATM transactions for one ATM session. The finer the grain of the fact table, the more dimensions exist, the more fact rows exist, and often the closer the data mart model is to a data model for the operational data store.

With the explosion of Web-based commerce, clicks become the possible lowest level of granularity. An analysis of Web site buying habits requires clickstream data (e.g., time spent on page, pages migrated from and to). Such an analysis may be useful to understand Web site usability and to customize messages based on navigational paths taken. However, this very fine level of granularity actually may be too low to be useful. It has been estimated that 90 percent or more of clickstream data are worthless (Inmon, 2006); for example, there is no business value to knowing a user moved a cursor when such movements are due to irrelevant events such as exercising the wrist, bumping a mouse, or moving a mouse to get it out of the way of something on the person's desk.

Kimball (2001) and others recommend using the smallest grain possible, given the limitations of the data mart technology. Even when data mart user information requirements imply a certain level of aggregated grain, often after some use, users ask more detailed questions (drill down) as a way to explain why certain aggregated patterns exist. You cannot "drill down" below the grain of the fact tables (without going to other data sources, such as the EDW, ODS, or the original source systems, which may add considerable effort to the analysis).

DURATION OF THE DATABASE As in the case of the EDW or ODS, another important decision in the design of a data mart is the amount of history to be kept, that is, the duration of the database. The natural duration is about 13 months or 5 calendar quarters, which is sufficient to see annual cycles in the data. Some businesses, such as financial institutions, have a need for longer durations. Older data may be difficult to source and cleanse if additional attributes are required from data sources. Even if sources of

Grain

The level of detail in a fact table, determined by the intersection of all the components of the primary key, including all foreign keys and any other primary key elements.

old data are available, it may be most difficult to find old values of dimension data, which are less likely than fact data to have been retained. Old fact data without associated dimension data at the time of the fact may be worthless.

SIZE OF THE FACT TABLE As you would expect, the grain and duration of the fact table have a direct impact on the size of that table. We can estimate the number of rows in the fact table as follows:

1. Estimate the number of possible values for each dimension associated with the fact table (in other words, the number of possible values for each foreign key in the fact table).
2. Multiply the values obtained in the first step after making any necessary adjustments.

Let's apply this approach to the star schema shown in Figure 9-11. Assume the following values for the dimensions:

Total number of stores = 1000
Total number of products = 10,000
Total number of periods = 24 (2 years' worth of monthly data)

Although there are 10,000 total products, only a fraction of these products are likely to record sales during a given month. Because item totals appear in the fact table only for items that record sales during a given month, we need to adjust this figure. Suppose that on average 50 percent (or 5000) items record sales during a given month. Then an estimate of the number of rows in the fact table is computed as follows:

Total rows = 1000 stores × 5000 active products × 24 months
= 120,000,000 rows (!)

Thus, in our relatively small example, the fact table that contains two years' worth of monthly totals can be expected to have well over 100 million rows. This example clearly illustrates that the size of the fact table is many times larger than the dimension tables. For example, the STORE table has 1000 rows, the PRODUCT table 10,000 rows, and the PERIOD table 24 rows.

If we know the size of each field in the fact table, we can further estimate the size (in bytes) of that table. The fact table (named SALES) in Figure 9-11 has six fields. If each of these fields averages four bytes in length, we can estimate the total size of the fact table as follows:

Total size = 120,000,000 rows × 6 fields × 4 bytes/field
= 2,880,000,000 bytes (or 2.88 gigabytes)

The size of the fact table depends on both the number of dimensions and the grain of the fact table. Suppose that after using the database shown in Figure 9-11 for a short period of time, the marketing department requests that *daily* totals be accumulated in the fact table. (This is a typical evolution of a data mart.) With the grain of the table changed to daily item totals, the number of rows is computed as follows:

Total rows = 1000 stores × 2000 active products × 720 days (2 years)
= 1,440,000,000 rows

In this calculation, we have assumed that 20 percent of all products record sales on a given day. The database can now be expected to contain well over 1 *billion* rows. The database size is calculated as follows:

Total size = 1,440,000,000 rows × 6 fields × 4 bytes/field
= 34,560,000,000 bytes (or 34.56 gigabytes)

FIGURE 9-12 Modeling dates

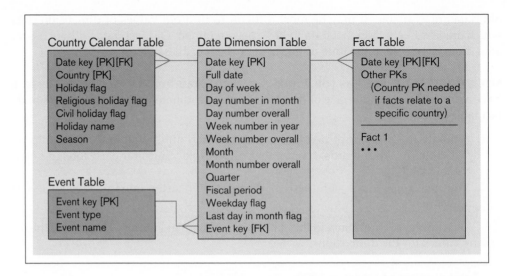

Practically all large retailers (e.g., Wal-Mart, Kmart, Sears) and e-businesses (e.g., Travelocity.com, Amazon.com) now have data warehouses (or data marts). The size of most of these data warehouses is in the multiple-terabyte range and growing rapidly as marketing people continue to press for more dimensions and an ever-finer grain in the fact table.

MODELING DATE AND TIME Because data warehouses and data marts record facts about dimensions over time, date and time (henceforth simply called *date*) is always a dimension table, and a date surrogate key is always one of the components of the primary key of any fact table. Because a user may want to aggregate facts on many different aspects of date or different kinds of dates, a date dimension may have many nonkey attributes. Also, because some characteristics of dates are country or event specific (e.g., whether the date is a holiday or there is some standard event on a given day, such as a festival or football game), modeling the date dimension can be more complex than illustrated so far.

Figure 9-12 shows a typical design for the date dimension. As we have seen before, a date surrogate key appears as part of the primary key of the fact table and is the primary key of the date dimension table. The nonkey attributes of the date dimension table include all of the characteristics of dates that users use to categorize, summarize, and group facts that do not vary by country or event. For an organization doing business in several countries (or several geographical units in which dates have different characteristics), we have added a Country Calendar table to hold the characteristics of each date in *each country*. Thus, the Date key is a foreign key in the Country Calendar table, and each row of the Country Calendar table is unique by the combination of Date key and Country, which form the composite primary key for this table. A special event may occur on a given date. (We assume here, for simplicity, no more than one special event may occur on a given date.) We have normalized the Event data by creating an Event table, so descriptive data on each event (e.g., the "Strawberry Festival" or the "Homecoming Game") are stored only once.

It is possible that there will be several kinds of dates associated with a fact, including the date the fact occurred, the date the fact was reported, the date the fact was recorded in the database, and the date the fact changed values. Each of these may be important in different analyses.

MULTIPLE FACT TABLES It is often desirable for performance or other reasons to define more than one fact table in a given star schema. For example, suppose that various users require different levels of aggregation (in other words, a different table grain). Performance can be improved by defining a different fact table for each level of aggregation. The obvious trade-off is that storage requirements may increase dramatically with each new fact table. More commonly, multiple fact tables are needed to store facts for different combinations of dimensions, possibly for different user groups.

FIGURE 9-13 Conformed dimensions

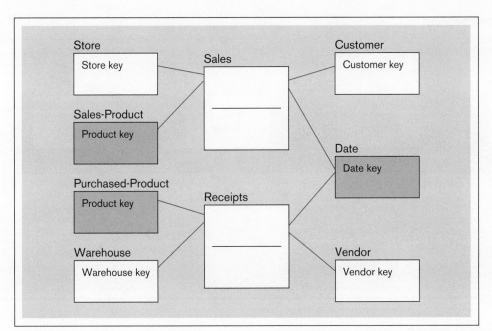

Figure 9-13 illustrates a typical situation of multiple fact tables with two related star schemas. In this example, there are two fact tables, one at the center of each star:

1. Sales—facts about the sale of a product to a customer in a store on a date
2. Receipts—facts about the receipt of a product from a vendor to a warehouse on a date

As is common, data about one or more business subjects (in this case, Product and Date) need to be stored in dimension tables for each fact table, Sales and Receipts. Two approaches have been adopted in this design to handle shared dimension tables. In one case, because the description of product is quite different for sales and receipts, two separate product dimension tables have been created. On the other hand, because users want the same descriptions of dates, one date dimension table is used. In each case, we have created a **conformed dimension**, meaning that the dimension means the same thing with each fact table and, hence, uses the same surrogate primary keys. Even when the two star schemas are stored in separate physical data marts, if dimensions are conformed, there is a potential for asking questions across the data marts (e.g., Do certain vendors recognize sales more quickly, and are they able to supply replenishments with less lead time?). In general, conformed dimensions allow users to do the following:

Conformed dimension
One or more dimension tables associated with two or more fact tables for which the dimension tables have the same business meaning and primary key with each fact table.

- Share nonkey dimension data
- Query across fact tables with consistency
- Work on facts and business subjects for which all users have the same meaning

HIERARCHIES Many times a dimension in a star schema forms a natural, fixed depth hierarchy. For example, there are geographical hierarchies (e.g., markets within a state, states within a region, and regions within a country) and product hierarchies (packages or sizes within a product, products within bundles, and bundles within product groups). When a dimension participates in a hierarchy, a database designer has two basic choices:

1. Include all the information for each level of the hierarchy in a single denormalized dimension table for the most detailed level of the hierarchy, thus creating considerable redundancy and update anomalies. Although it is simple, this is usually not the recommended approach.
2. Normalize the dimension into a nested set of a fixed number of tables with 1:*M* relationships between them. Associate only the lowest level of the hierarchy with the fact table. It will still be possible to aggregate the fact data at any level of the hierarchy, but now the user will have to perform nested joins along the hierarchy or be given a view of the hierarchy that is prejoined.

FIGURE 9-14   Fixed product hierarchy

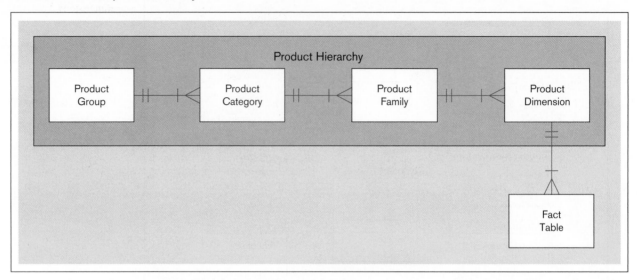

When the depth of the hierarchy can be fixed, each level of the hierarchy is a separate dimensional entity. Some hierarchies can more easily use this scheme than can others. Consider the product hierarchy in Figure 9-14. Here each product is part of a product family (e.g., Crest with Tartar Control is part of Crest), and a product family is part of a product category (e.g., toothpaste), and a category is part of a product group (e.g., health and beauty). This works well if every product follows this same hierarchy. Such hierarchies are very common in data warehouses and data marts.

Now, consider the more general example of a typical consulting company that invoices customers for specified time periods on projects. A revenue fact table in this situation might show how much revenue is billed and for how many hours on each invoice, which is for a particular time period, customer, service, employee, and project. Because consulting work may be done for different divisions of the same organization, if we want to understand the total role of consulting in any level of a customer organization, we need a customer hierarchy. This hierarchy is a recursive relationship between organizational units. As shown in Figure 4-17 for a supervisory hierarchy, the standard way to represent this in a normalized database is to put into the company row a foreign key of the Company key for its parent unit.

Recursive relationships implemented in this way are difficult for the typical end user because specifying how to aggregate at any arbitrary level of the hierarchy requires complex SQL programming. One solution is to transform the recursive relationship into a fixed number of hierarchical levels by combining adjacent levels into general categories; for example, for an organizational hierarchy, the recursive levels above each unit could be grouped into enterprise, division, and department. Each instance of an entity at each hierarchical level gets a surrogate primary key and attributes to describe the characteristics of that level needed for decision making. Work done in the reconciliation layer will form and maintain these instances.

Another simple but more general alternative appears in Figure 9-15. Figure 9-15a shows how this hierarchy is typically modeled in a data warehouse using a helper table (Chisholm, 2000; Kimball, 1998b). Each customer organizational unit the consulting firm serves is assigned a different surrogate customer key and row in the Customer dimension table, and the customer surrogate key is used as a foreign key in the Revenue fact table; this foreign key relates to the Sub customer key in the Helper table because the revenue facts are associated at the lowest possible level of the organizational hierarchy. The problem with joining in a recursive relationship of arbitrary depth is that the user has to write code to join an arbitrary number of times (once for each level of subordination) and these joins in a data warehouse, because of its massive size, can be very time-consuming (except for some high-performance data warehouse technologies that use parallel processing). To avoid this problem, the helper table flattens out the hierarchy

FIGURE 9-15 Representing hierarchical relationships within a dimension

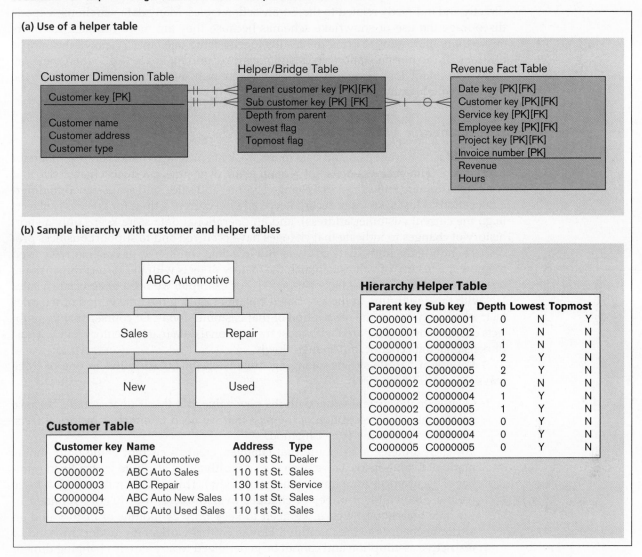

by recording a row for each organizational subunit and each of its parent organizational units (including itself) all the way up to the top unit of the customer organization. Each row of this helper table has three descriptors: the number of levels the subunit is from its parent unit for *that* table row, a flag indicating whether this subunit is the lowest in the hierarchy, and a flag indicating whether this subunit is the highest in the hierarchy. Figure 9-15b depicts an example customer organizational hierarchy and the rows that would be in the helper table to represent that total organization. (There would be other rows in the helper table for the subunit–parent unit relationships within other customer organizations.)

The Revenue fact table in Figure 9-15a includes a primary key attribute of Invoice number. Invoice number is an example of a *degenerative dimension*, which has no interesting dimension attributes. (Thus, no dimension table exists, and Invoice number is not part of the table's primary key.) Invoice number also is not a fact that will be used for aggregation because mathematics on this attribute has no meaning. This attribute may be helpful if there is a need to explore an ODS or source systems to find additional details about the invoice transaction or to group together related fact rows (e.g., all the revenue line items on the same invoice).

When the dimension tables are further normalized by using helper tables (sometimes called *bridge tables* or *reference tables*), the simple star schema turns into a **snowflake schema**. A snowflake schema resembles a segment of an ODS or source database

Snowflake schema

An expanded version of a star schema in which dimension tables are normalized into several related tables.

centered on the transaction tables summarized into the fact table and all of the tables directly and indirectly related to these transaction tables. Many data warehouse experts discourage the use of snowflake schemas because they are more complex for users and require more joins to bring the results together into one table. A snowflake may be desirable if the normalization saves significant redundant space (e.g., when there are many redundant, long textual attributes) or when users may find browsing through the normalized tables themselves useful.

Slowly Changing Dimensions

Recall that data warehouses and data marts track business activities over time, often for many years. The business does not remain static over time; products change size and weight, customers relocate, stores change layouts, and sales staff are assigned to different locations. Most systems of record keep only the current values for business subjects (e.g., the current customer address), and an operational data store keeps only a short history of changes to indicate that changes have occurred and to support business processes handling the immediate changes. But in a data warehouse or data mart, we need to know the history of values to match the history of facts with the correct dimensional descriptions at the time the facts happened. For example, we need to associate a sales fact with the description of the associated customer during the time period of the sales fact, which may not be the description of that customer today. Of course, business subjects change slowly compared with most transactional data (e.g., inventory level). Thus, dimensional data change, but change slowly.

We might handle slowly changing dimension (SCD) attributes in one of three ways (Kimball, 1996b, 1999):

1. Overwrite the current value with the new value, but this is unacceptable because it eliminates the description of the past that we need to interpret historical facts. Kimball calls this the Type 1 method.
2. For each dimension attribute that changes, create a current value field and as many old value fields as we wish (i.e., a multivalued attribute with a fixed number of occurrences for a limited historical view). This schema might work if there were a predictable number of changes over the length of history retained in the data warehouse (e.g., if we need to keep only 24 months of history and an attribute changes value monthly). However, this works only under this kind of restrictive assumption and cannot be generalized to any slowly changing dimension attribute. Further, queries can become quite complex because which column is needed may have to be determined within the query. Kimball calls this the Type 3 method.
3. Create a new dimension table row (with a new surrogate key) each time the dimension object changes; this new row contains all the dimension characteristics at the time of the change; the new surrogate key is the original surrogate key plus the start date for the period when these dimension values are in effect. A fact row is associated with the surrogate key whose attributes apply at the date/time of the fact (i.e., the fact date/time falls between the start and end dates of a dimension row for the same original surrogate key). We likely also want to store in a dimension row the date/time the change ceases being in effect (which will be the maximum possible date or null for the current row for each dimension object) and a reason code for the change. This approach allows us to create as many dimensional object changes as necessary. However, it becomes unwieldy if rows frequently change or if the rows are very long. Kimball calls this the Type 2 method, and it is the one most often used.

Changes in some dimensional attributes may not be important. Hence, the first policy can be used for these attributes. The Type 2 scheme is the most frequently used approach for handling slowly changing dimensions for which changes matter. Under this scheme, we likely also store in a dimension row the surrogate key value for the original object; this way, we can relate all changes to the same object. In fact, the primary key of the dimension table becomes a composite of the original surrogate

FIGURE 9-16 Example of Type 2 SCD Customer dimension table

key plus the date of the change, as depicted in Figure 9-16. In this example, each time an attribute of Customer changes, a new customer row is written to the Customer dimension table; the primary key of that row is the original surrogate key for that customer plus the date of the change. The nonkey elements are the values for all the nonkey attributes at the time of the change (i.e., some attributes will have new values due to the change, but probably most will remain the same as for the most recent row for the same customer).

Determining Dimensions and Facts

Which dimensions and facts are required for a data mart is driven by the context for decision making. Each decision is based on specific metrics to monitor the status of some important factor (e.g., inventory turns) or to predict some critical event (e.g., customer churn). Many decisions are based on a mixture of metrics, balancing financial, process efficiency, customer, and business growth factors. Decisions usually start with questions such as how much did we sell last month, why did we sell what we did, how much do we think we will sell next month, and what can we do to sell the amount we want to sell?

The answers to questions often cause us to ask new questions. Consequently, although for a given domain we can anticipate the initial questions someone might ask of a data mart, we cannot perfectly predict everything the users will want to know. This is why independent data marts are discouraged. With dependent data marts, it is much easier to expand an existing data mart or for the user to be given access to other data marts or to the EDW when their new questions require data in addition to what is in the current data mart.

The starting point for determining what data should be in a data mart is the initial questions the users want answered. Each question can be broken down into discrete items of business information the user wants to know (facts) and the criteria used to access, sort, group, summarize, and present the facts (dimension attributes). An easy way to model the questions is through a matrix, such as that illustrated in Figure 9-17a. In this figure, the rows are the qualifiers (dimension or dimension attributes) and the columns are the metrics (facts) referenced in the questions. The cells of the matrix contain codes to indicate which qualifiers and metrics are included in each question. For example, question 3 uses the fact number of complaints and the dimension attributes of product category, customer territory, year, and month. One or several star schemas may be required for any set of questions. For the example in Figure 9-17a, we have designed two fact tables, shown in Figure 9-17b because the grain of the facts are different (e.g., we determined complaints have nothing to do with stores or salespersons). We also created hierarchical relationships between product and product category and between customer and customer territory; alternatively it would have been possible, for example, to collapse product category into product, with resulting redundancy. We also understood season as a separate concept from month, and to be territory dependent. Product, Customer, and Month are conformed dimensions because they are shared by two fact tables.

FIGURE 9-17 Determining dimensions and facts

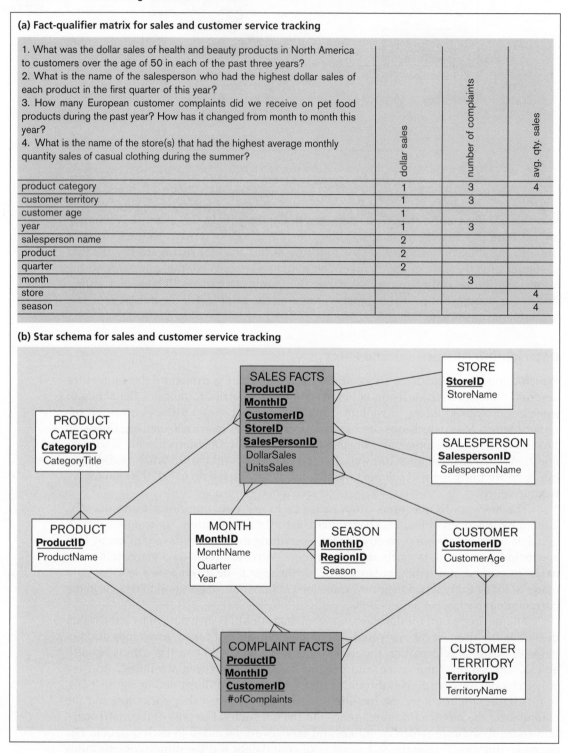

(a) Fact-qualifier matrix for sales and customer service tracking

1. What was the dollar sales of health and beauty products in North America to customers over the age of 50 in each of the past three years?
2. What is the name of the salesperson who had the highest dollar sales of each product in the first quarter of this year?
3. How many European customer complaints did we receive on pet food products during the past year? How has it changed from month to month this year?
4. What is the name of the store(s) that had the highest average monthly quantity sales of casual clothing during the summer?

	dollar sales	number of complaints	avg. qty. sales
product category	1	3	4
customer territory	1	3	
customer age	1		
year	1	3	
salesperson name	2		
product	2		
quarter	2		
month		3	
store			4
season			4

(b) Star schema for sales and customer service tracking

So, if the type of analysis depicted in Figure 9-17 represents the starting point for determining the dimensions and facts of a dimensional model, when do you know you are done? We don't know of a definitive answer to this question (and let's hope you really are never done, but simply need to continue to expand the coverage of the data model). However, Ross (2009) has identified what the consulting practice for Ralph Kimball and Kimball University considers to be the 10 essential rules of dimensional modeling. We summarize these rules in Table 9-3; we think you will find these rules to be a helpful synthesis of many principles outlined in this chapter. When these rules are satisfied, you are done (for the time being).

TABLE 9-3 Ten Essential Rules of Dimensional Modeling

1. **Use atomic facts:** Eventually, users want detailed data, even if their initial requests are for summarized facts.
2. **Create single-process fact tables:** Each fact table should address the important measurements for one business process, such as taking a customer order or placing a material purchase order.
3. **Include a date dimension for every fact table:** A fact should be described by the characteristics of the associated day (or finer) date/time to which that fact is related.
4. **Enforce consistent grain:** Each measurement in a fact table must be atomic for the same combination of keys (the same grain).
5. **Disallow null keys in fact tables:** Facts apply to the combination of key values, and helper tables may be needed to represent some *M:N* relationships.
6. **Honor hierarchies:** Understand the hierarchies of dimensions and carefully choose to snowflake the hierarchy or denormalize into one dimension.
7. **Decode dimension tables:** Store descriptions of surrogate keys and codes used in fact tables in associated dimension tables, which can then be used to report labels and query filters.
8. **Use surrogate keys:** All dimension table rows should be identified by a surrogate key, with descriptive columns showing the associated production and source system keys.
9. **Conform dimensions:** Conformed dimensions should be used across multiple fact tables.
10. **Balance requirements with actual data:** Unfortunately, source data may not precisely support all business requirements, so you must balance what is technically possible with what users want and need.

Source: Based on Ross (2009).

BIG DATA AND COLUMNAR DATABASES

No, big data is not what little data aspire to be. And there is no BDOC (Big Data on Campus). **Big data** is an ill-defined term applied to databases whose volume, velocity, and variety (Dumbill, 2012) strain the ability of commonly used relational DBMSs to capture, manage, and process the data within a tolerable elapsed time. Big data sizes are also ill defined, ranging from a few dozen terabytes to many petabytes of data in a single database. Big data include structured data, but also Weblogs, social network posts, Internet text and documents, call detail records, RFID signal data, research data, military surveillance, and medical records, to name a few. Maybe you remember IBM's Watson beating Ken Jennings and Brad Rutter on the TV game show *Jeopardy* in September 2010. This was the processing of big data in a rather spectacular setting. According to a Bughin, Livingston, and Marwaha (2011), "Large-scale data gathering and analytics are quickly becoming a new frontier of competitive differentiation." For example, AstraZeneca, a major pharmaceutical manufacturer, and WellPoint, one of the largest health insurance and claims processing firms, have teamed up for a big data project to combine medical claims and clinical data to discover ways to improve patient health care.

Data warehousing and business intelligence (BI) queries typically access many rows based on common values for a few columns, such as summarizing sales data to find the top 10 selling products in the Northwest region. This tends to be the opposite of transaction processing tasks, which seek values for many of the columns but for one row and some related rows, such as a particular customer order and its related customer record, line items, and associated product details.

Whereas some RDBMS vendors (e.g., Oracle, IBM) have typically added features to accommodate analytical query processing, others (e.g., Teradata, Netezza) have developed whole new relational database engines to handle data warehousing and business intelligence processing. These vendors originally built their technologies around the standard relational data model of tables of rows and columns and physical structures that store data as files of records for rows, with columns as fields in each record. These technologies originated almost 30 years ago, before the era of big data.

Big data

An ill-defined term applied to databases whose volume, velocity, and variety strain the ability of commonly used relational DBMSs to capture, manage, and process the data within a tolerable elapsed time.

Emerging, but viable, vendors claim that different storage structures are needed for analytical queries involving big data—ones that store data on a column basis rather than a row basis. That is, values are stored in sequence for one column, followed by the values for another column, and so on, thus virtually turning a table of data 90 degrees. Today, most traditional data warehouse technology vendors offer both standard relational table and column-oriented products; adopters can choose which is best for their given situation.

Vendors of column-based products claim to reduce storage space (because data compression techniques are used, for example, to store a value only once) and to speed query processing time because the data are physically organized to support analytical queries. The conceptual and logical data models for the data warehouse do not change. SQL is still the query language, and you do not have to write queries any differently; the DBMS simply stores and accesses the data differently than in traditional row-oriented RDBMSs. Data compression and storage depend on the data and queries. For example, with Vertica (a division of HP), one of the leading column database management system providers, the logical relational database is defined in SQL as with any RDBMS. Then a set of sample queries and data are presented to a database design tool. This tool analyses the predicates (WHERE clauses) of the queries and the redundancy in the sample data to suggest a data compression scheme and storage of columnar data. Different data compression techniques are used depending on the type of predicate data (numeric, textual, limited versus a wide range of values, etc.). The database administrator can override any recommendations made by the design tool.

Column database technologies trade off storage space savings (data compression of more than 70 percent is common) for computing time. For example, a customer ID might be stored only once in the database for all the places it appears, such as the identifier of customer data, but also as foreign keys associated with customer orders, payments, product returns, service visits, and other activities. This would be true for any column of data, such as gender, city names, street names, names of all types of parties, and so on. Internal encoding of data is used to associate the business data value with physical database references to that value throughout the database. A query can then search rapidly through very condensed storage space for the codes associated with the column value used in the query. The claims for the advantage of column databases over row-based relational databases are based on the assumption that disk storage space and the bandwidth to access disk storage are more expensive than CPU time to reconstruct the business data from compressed storage into the relational table result format of SQL. With compressed storage, overall query processing time is reduced.

Details about physical column database technology are beyond the scope of this text because the discussion would address the design of a DBMS and physical data structures rather than the design of a database. However, it is important for you to understand that new DBMS technologies designed from the ground up for analytical queries are emerging and should be considered in the overall architecture design of a data warehousing environment. Major vendors of column-based databases include Sybase and Vertica, and there is an open source option from Infobright that works with MySQL. Teradata provides the option within one data warehouse DBMS for customers to use either columnar or traditional table structures.

IF YOU KNEW SQL LIKE I NoSQL

Oh, Oh, Oh what a query language (with regrets to Eddie Cantor, see **www.youtube.com/watch?v=Boy8QOa4xPA**). Not all data are easily structured into relational tables and then searched, sorted, and aggregated as columns of data using SQL. E-mails, Web site posts, text messages, and other textual elements, which are significant elements of the big data explosion, contain potential insights. For example, unstructured data, such as reactions to a new product, opinions on a political issue, research summaries, diplomatic dispatches (can you say "WikiLeaks"?), and customer complaints, can all be mined to discover trends.

NoSQL, short for "Not only SQL," is a class of database technology used to store and access textual and other unstructured data, using more flexible structures than the rows and columns format of relational databases. NoSQL is for situations when the user is unsure of what structure to use for data. A common physical structure for NoSQL is a string of key-value pairs. A NoSQL technology adds a special application programming interface, or API, to SQL to allow SQL to work with data not stored in the traditional relational table format. The power of NoSQL lies in its ability to handle large volumes of unstructured data faster and more efficiently than can traditional relational database management systems.

Many data warehouse vendors (e.g., Oracle and IBM) have added some form of NoSQL capabilities to their products to support the storage and analysis of the exebytes (i.e., 10^{18}) of textual and graphical data now being collected. The Oracle product is based on Java and Berkeley DB, an open source DBMS developed at the University of California at Berkeley. The IBM NoSQL offering works with the IBM DBMSs DB2 and Informix. In general, extensions to SQL or a special query language such as UnQL (Unstructured Query Language) are required with a NoSQL implementation. XQuery, associated with the XML document labeling and storage scheme (see Chapter 8), is another NoSQL query language. Major products not associated with traditional data warehouse and relational database system vendors include MongoDB, CouchDB, and OrientDB. Lotus Notes, from IBM, is also considered an early NoSQL technology. Some people classify object-oriented database systems and their associated query languages as a form of NoSQL. Many NoSQL systems do not include the full range of DBMS facilities. In fact, some NoSQL technologies are meant for only in-memory databases, which are not stored on disk storage devices.

One widely used NoSQL technology, Apache Cassandra, was initiated by Facebook to store and access the huge number of status updates and content from Facebook users. Cassandra is typical of many NoSQL technologies because it exists in a distributed database environment. See Wayner (2011) for an explanation of Cassandra and an overview of many of the leading NoSQL database systems. Hadoop, from the Apache Software Foundation, and the related MapReduce data filtering algorithm from Google, are used by a variety of search engines and other software to search extremely large, unstructured data warehouses stored on a network of computers. The parallel and distributed nature of these technologies, coupled with the flexible data storage structured used, allow for rapid keyword searches of textual data. Hadoop along with MapReduce support efficient indexing and, hence, searching of extensive amounts of unstructured data. Many data warehouse technologies provide interfaces to Hadoop and MapReduce to add to their more structured data analysis services.

NoSQL

Short for "Not only SQL," NoSQL is a class of database technology used to store and access textual and other unstructured data, using more flexible structures than the rows and columns format of relational databases.

THE USER INTERFACE

Although we have covered most of what you need to know to get started designing a data warehouse, you may still wonder "what can I do with it?" Even a well-designed data mart or enterprise data warehouse, loaded with relevant data, may not be used unless users are provided with a powerful, intuitive interface that allows them to access and analyze those data easily. In this section, we provide a brief introduction to contemporary interfaces for data warehouses and marts.

A variety of tools are available to query and analyze data stored in data warehouses and data marts. These tools may be classified as follows:

- Traditional query and reporting tools
- OLAP, MOLAP, and ROLAP tools
- Data visualization tools
- Business performance management and dashboard tools
- Data-mining tools

Traditional query and reporting tools include spreadsheets, personal computer databases, and report writers and generators. For reasons of space (and because they are covered elsewhere), we do not describe these tools in this chapter. We describe the remaining four categories of tools after discussing the role of metadata.

Role of Metadata

The first requirement for building a user-friendly interface is a set of metadata that describes the data in the data mart in business terms that users can easily understand. We show the association of metadata with data marts in the overall three-level data architecture in Figure 9-5.

The metadata associated with data marts are often referred to as a "data catalog," "data directory," or some similar term. Metadata serve as kind of a "yellow pages" directory to the data in the data marts. The metadata should allow users to easily answer questions such as the following:

1. What subjects are described in the data mart? (Typical subjects are customers, patients, students, products, courses, and so on.)
2. What dimensions and facts are included in the data mart? What is the grain of the fact table?
3. How are the data in the data mart derived from the enterprise data warehouse data? What rules are used in the derivation?
4. How are the data in the enterprise data warehouse derived from operational data? What rules are used in this derivation?
5. What reports and predefined queries are available to view the data?
6. What drill-down and other data analysis techniques are available?
7. Who is responsible for the quality of data in the data marts, and to whom are requests for changes made?

SQL OLAP Querying

The most common database query language, SQL (see Chapters 6 and 7), is being extended to support some types of calculations and querying needed for a data warehousing environment. In general, however, SQL is not an analytical language (Mundy, 2001). At the heart of analytical queries is the ability to perform categorization (e.g., group data by dimension characteristics), aggregation (e.g., create averages per category), and ranking (e.g., find the customer in some category with the highest average monthly sales). Consider the following business question:

Which customer has bought the most of each product we sell? Show the product ID and description, customer ID and name, and the total quantity sold of that product to that customer; show the results in sequence by product ID.

Even with the limitations of standard SQL, this analytical query can be written without the OLAP extensions to SQL. One way to write this query, using the large version of the Pine Valley Furniture database provided with this textbook, is as follows:

```
SELECT P1.ProductId, ProductDescription, C1.CustomerId,
   CustomerName,SUM(OL1.OrderedQuantity) AS TotOrdered
   FROM Customer_T AS C1, Product_T AS P1, OrderLine_T
      AS OL1, Order_T AS O1
   WHERE C1.CustomerId = O1.CustomerId
      AND O1.OrderId = OL1.OrderId
      AND OL1.ProductId = P1.ProductId
   GROUP BY P1.ProductId, ProductDescription,
      C1.CustomerId, CustomerName
   HAVING TotOrdered >= ALL
   (SELECT SUM(OL2.OrderedQuantity)
   FROM OrderLine_T AS OL2, Order_T AS O2
   WHERE OL2.ProductId = P1.ProductId
      AND OL2.OrderId = O2.OrderId
      AND O2.CustomerId <> C1.CustomerId
   GROUP BY O2.CustomerId)
ORDER BY P1.ProductId;
```

This approach uses a correlated subquery to find the set of total quantity ordered across all customers for each product, and then the outer query selects the customer whose total is greater than or equal to all of these (in other words, equal to the maximum of the set). Until you write many of these queries, this can be very challenging to develop and is often beyond the capabilities of even well-trained end users. And even this query is rather simple because it does not have multiple categories, does not ask for changes over time, or does not want to see the results graphically. Finding the second in rank is even more difficult.

Some versions of SQL support special clauses that make ranking questions easier to write. For example, Microsoft SQL Server and some other RDBMSs support clauses of FIRST *n*, TOP *n*, LAST *n*, and BOTTOM *n* rows. Thus, the query shown previously could be greatly simplified by adding TOP 1 in front of the SUM in the outer query and eliminating the HAVING and subquery. TOP 1 was illustrated in Chapter 7, in the section on "More Complicated SQL Queries."

Online Analytical Processing (OLAP) Tools

A specialized class of tools has been developed to provide users with multidimensional views of their data. Such tools also usually offer users a graphical interface so that they can easily analyze their data. In the simplest case, data are viewed as a simple three-dimensional cube.

Online analytical processing (OLAP) is the use of a set of query and reporting tools that provides users with multidimensional views of their data and allows them to analyze the data using simple windowing techniques. The term *online analytical processing* is intended to contrast with the more traditional term *online transaction processing (OLTP)*. The differences between these two types of processing were summarized in Table 9-1. The term *multidimensional analysis* is often used as a synonym for OLAP.

An example of a "data cube" (or multidimensional view) of data that is typical of OLAP is shown in Figure 9-18. This three-dimensional view corresponds quite closely to the star schema introduced in Figure 9-10. Two of the dimensions in Figure 9-18 correspond to the dimension tables (PRODUCT and PERIOD) in Figure 9-10, whereas the third dimension (named measures) corresponds to the data in the fact table (named SALES) in Figure 9-10.

Online analytical processing (OLAP)

The use of a set of graphical tools that provides users with multidimensional views of their data and allows them to analyze the data using simple windowing techniques.

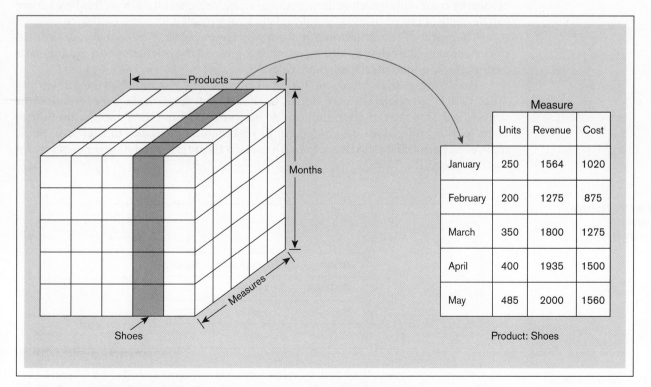

FIGURE 9-18 Slicing a data cube

Relational OLAP (ROLAP)

OLAP tools that view the database as a traditional relational database, in either a star schema or other normalized or denormalized set of tables.

Multidimensional OLAP (MOLAP)

OLAP tools that load data into an intermediate structure, usually a three- or higher-dimensional array.

OLAP is actually a general term for several categories of data warehouse and data mart access tools (Dyché, 2000). **Relational OLAP (ROLAP)** tools use variations of SQL and view the database as a traditional relational database, in either a star schema or another normalized or denormalized set of tables. ROLAP tools access the data warehouse or data mart directly. **Multidimensional OLAP (MOLAP)** tools load data into an intermediate structure, usually a three- or higher-dimensional array (hypercube). We illustrate MOLAP in the next few sections because of its popularity. It is important to note with MOLAP that the data are not simply viewed as a multidimensional hypercube, but rather a MOLAP data mart is created by extracting data from the data warehouse or data mart and then storing the data in a specialized separate data store through which data can be viewed only through a multidimensional structure. Other, less-common categories of OLAP tools are database OLAP (DOLAP), which includes OLAP functionality in the DBMS query language (there are proprietary, non-ANSI standard SQL systems that do this) and hybrid OLAP (HOLAP), which allows access via both multidimensional cubes or relational query languages.

SLICING A CUBE Figure 9-18 shows a typical MOLAP operation: slicing the data cube to produce a simple two-dimensional table or view. In Figure 9-18, this slice is for the product named shoes. The resulting table shows the three measures (units, revenues, and cost) for this product by period (or month). Other views can easily be developed by the user by means of simple "drag and drop" operations. This type of operation is often called *slicing and dicing* the cube.

Another operation closely related to slicing and dicing is data pivoting (similar to the pivoting possible in Microsoft Excel). This term refers to rotating the view for a particular data point to obtain another perspective. For example, Figure 9-18 shows sales of 400 units of shoes for April. The analyst could pivot this view to obtain (for example) the sales of shoes by store for the same month.

DRILL-DOWN Another type of operation often used in multidimensional analysis is *drill-down*—that is, analyzing a given set of data at a finer level of detail. An example of drill-down is shown in Figure 9-19. Figure 9-19a shows a summary report for the total sales of three package sizes for a given brand of paper towels: 2-pack, 3-pack, and 6-pack. However, the towels come in different colors, and the analyst wants a further breakdown of sales by color within each of these package sizes. Using an OLAP tool, this breakdown can be easily obtained using a "point-and-click" approach with a mouse device.

The result of the drill-down is shown in Figure 9-19b. Notice that a drill-down presentation is equivalent to adding another column to the original report. (In this case, a column was added for the attribute color.)

Executing a drill-down (as in this example) may require that the OLAP tool "reach back" to the data warehouse to obtain the detail data necessary for the drill-down. This type of operation can be performed by an OLAP tool (without user participation) only if an integrated set of metadata is available to that tool. Some tools even permit the OLAP tool to reach back to the operational data if necessary for a given query.

FIGURE 9-19 Example of drill-down (a) Summary report

Brand	Package size	Sales
SofTowel	2-pack	$75
SofTowel	3-pack	$100
SofTowel	6-pack	$50

(Figure 9-19 continues on the next page)

FIGURE 9-19 *(Continued)*
(b) Drill-down with color attribute added

Brand	Package size	Color	Sales
SofTowel	2-pack	White	$30
SofTowel	2-pack	Yellow	$25
SofTowel	2-pack	Pink	$20
SofTowel	3-pack	White	$50
SofTowel	3-pack	Green	$25
SofTowel	3-pack	Yellow	$25
SofTowel	6-pack	White	$30
SofTowel	6-pack	Yellow	$20

SUMMARIZING MORE THAN THREE DIMENSIONS It is straightforward to show a three-dimensional hypercube in a spreadsheet-type format using columns, rows, and sheets (pages) as the three dimensions. It is possible, however, to show data in more than three dimensions by cascading rows or columns and using drop-down selections to show different slices. Figure 9-20 shows a portion of a report from a Microsoft Excel pivot table with four dimensions, with travel method and number of days in cascading columns. OLAP query and reporting tools usually allow this way to handle sharing dimensions within the limits of two-dimension printing or display space. Data visualization tools, to be shown in the next section, allow using shapes, colors, and other properties of multiples of graphs to include more than three dimensions on the same display.

Country	(All)														

Average of Price	Travel Method	No. of Days													
	Coach			Coach Total	Plane									Plane Total
Resort Name	4	5	7		6	7	8	10	14	16	21	32	60	
Aviemore			135	135										
Barcelona														
Black Forest	69			69										
Cork							269							269
Grand Canyon													1128	1128
Great Barrier Reef												750		750
Lake Geneva							699							699
London														
Los Angeles						295		375						335
Lyon								399						399
Malaga									234					234
Nerja					198			255						226.5
Nice						289								289
Paris–Euro Disney														
Prague		95		95										
Seville								199						199
Skiathos											429			429
Grand Total	69	95	135	99.66666667	198	292	484	199	343	234	429	750	1128	424.5384615

FIGURE 9-20 **Sample pivot table with four dimensions: Country (pages), Resort Name (rows), Travel Method, and No. of Days (columns)**

Data Visualization

Data visualization

The representation of data in graphical and multimedia formats for human analysis.

Often the human eye can best discern patterns when data are represented graphically. **Data visualization** is the representation of data in graphical and multimedia formats for human analysis. Benefits of data visualization include the ability to better observe trends and patterns and to identify correlations and clusters. Data visualization is often used in conjunction with data mining and other analytical techniques.

In essence, data visualization is a way to show multidimensional data not as numbers and text but as graphs. Thus, precise values are often not shown, but rather the intent is to more readily show relationships between the data. As with OLAP tools, the data for the graphs are computed often from SQL queries against a database (or possibly from data in a spreadsheet). The SQL queries are generated automatically by the OLAP or data visualization software simply from the user indicating what he or she wants to see.

Figure 9-21 shows a simple visualization of sales data using the data visualization tool Tableau. This visualization uses a common technique called small multiples, which places many graphs on one page to support comparison. Each small graph plots metrics of SUM(Total Sales) on the horizontal axis and SUM(Gross Profit) on the vertical axis. There is a separate graph for the dimensions region and year; different market segments are shown via different symbols for the plot points. The user simply drags and drops these metrics and dimensions to a menu and then selects the style of visualization or lets the tool pick what it thinks would be the most illustrative type of graph. The user indicates what he or she wants to see and in what format, not how to retrieve the data from the data mart or data warehouse.

Business Performance Management and Dashboards

A business performance management (BPM) system allows managers to measure, monitor, and manage key activities and processes to achieve organizational goals. Dashboards are often used to provide an information system in support of BPM. Dashboards, just as those in a car or airplane cockpit, include a variety of displays to show different aspects of the organization. Often the top dashboard, an executive dashboard, is based on a balanced scorecard, in which different measures show metrics from different processes and disciplines, such as operations efficiency, financial status, customer service, sales, and human resources. Each display of a dashboard will address different areas in different ways. For example, one display may have alerts about key customers and their purchases. Another display may show key performance indicators for manufacturing, with "stoplight" symbols of red, yellow, and green to indicate if the

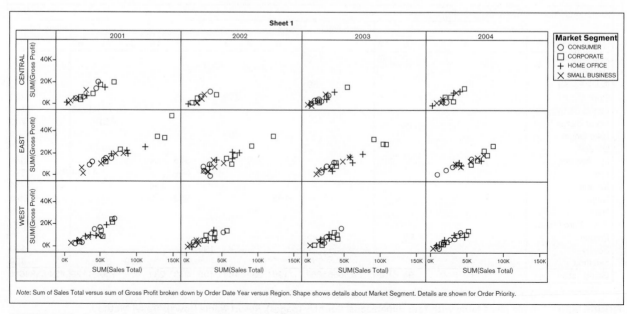

Note: Sum of Sales Total versus sum of Gross Profit broken down by Order Date Year versus Region. Shape shows details about Market Segment. Details are shown for Order Priority.

FIGURE 9-21 Sample data visualization with small multiples

FIGURE 9-22 Sample dashboard

Net Profit Margin Review

Revenue

Gross Profit

2010

2009

2008

$600 — 18%
$460 — 12%
$300 — 8%
$160 — 4%
$0 — 0%
−$160 — −4%
−$300 — −8%

$470 $555 $200 $157 $151

2008 2009 2010 1st Half 2010 Q3 2010 Q4

■ Revenue
○ Net Profit Margin

Last 14-Day Revenue

$7,500
$5,000
$2,500
$0

17-Dec 18-Dec 19-Dec 20-Dec 21-Dec 22-Dec 23-Dec 24-Dec 25-Dec 26-Dec 27-Dec 28-Dec 29-Dec 30-Dec

measures are inside or outside tolerance limits. Each area of the organization may have its own dashboard to determine health of that function. For example, Figure 9-22 is a simple dashboard for one financial measure, revenue. The left panel shows dials about revenue over the past three years, with needles indicating where these measures fall within a desirable range. Other panels show more details to help a manager find the source of out-of-tolerance measures.

Each of the panels is a result of complex queries to a data mart or data warehouse. As a user wants to see more details, there often is a way to click on a graph to get a menu of choices for exploring the details behind the icon or graphic. A panel may be the result of running some predictive model against data in the data warehouse to forecast future conditions (so-called predictive modeling).

Integrative dashboard displays are possible only when data are consistent across each display, which requires a data warehouse and dependent data marts. Stand-alone dashboards for independent data marts can be developed, but then it is difficult to trace problems between areas (e.g., production bottlenecks due to higher sales than forecast).

Data-Mining Tools

With OLAP, users are searching for answers to questions, such as "Are health-care costs greater for single or married persons?" With data mining, users are looking for patterns or trends in a collection of facts or observations. **Data mining** is knowledge discovery using a sophisticated blend of techniques from traditional statistics, artificial intelligence, and computer graphics (Weldon, 1996).

The goals of data mining are threefold:

1. *Explanatory* To explain some observed event or condition, such as why sales of pickup trucks have increased in Colorado
2. *Confirmatory* To confirm a hypothesis, such as whether two-income families are more likely to buy family medical coverage than single-income families
3. *Exploratory* To analyze data for new or unexpected relationships, such as what spending patterns are likely to accompany credit card fraud

Data mining

Knowledge discovery, using a sophisticated blend of techniques from traditional statistics, artificial intelligence, and computer graphics.

TABLE 9-4 Data-Mining Techniques

Technique	Function
Regression	Test or discover relationships from historical data
Decision tree induction	Test or discover if . . . then rules for decision propensity
Clustering and signal processing	Discover subgroups or segments
Affinity	Discover strong mutual relationships
Sequence association	Discover cycles of events and behaviors
Case-based reasoning	Derive rules from real-world case examples
Rule discovery	Search for patterns and correlations in large data sets
Fractals	Compress large databases without losing information
Neural nets	Develop predictive models based on principles modeled after the human brain

DATA-MINING TECHNIQUES Several different techniques are commonly used for data mining. See Table 9-4 for a summary of the most common of these techniques. The choice of an appropriate technique depends on the nature of the data to be analyzed, as well as the size of the data set. Data mining can be performed against either the data marts or the enterprise data warehouse (or both).

DATA-MINING APPLICATIONS Data-mining techniques have been successfully used for a wide range of real-world applications. A summary of some of the typical types of applications, with examples of each type, is presented in Table 9-5. Data-mining applications are growing rapidly, for the following reasons:

- The amount of data in data warehouses and data marts is growing exponentially. Users need the type of automated techniques provided by data-mining tools to mine the knowledge in these data.

TABLE 9-5 Typical Data-Mining Applications

Data-Mining Application	Example
Profiling populations	Developing profiles of high-value customers, credit risks, and credit-card fraud.
Analysis of business trends	Identifying markets with above-average (or below-average) growth.
Target marketing	Identifying customers (or customer segments) for promotional activity.
Usage analysis	Identifying usage patterns for products and services.
Campaign effectiveness	Comparing campaign strategies for effectiveness.
Product affinity	Identifying products that are purchased concurrently or identifying the characteristics of shoppers for certain product groups.
Customer retention and churn	Examining the behavior of customers who have left for competitors to prevent remaining customers from leaving.
Profitability analysis	Determining which customers are profitable, given the total set of activities the customer has with the organization.
Customer value analysis	Determining where valuable customers are at different stages in their life.
Upselling	Identifying new products or services to sell to a customer based upon critical events and life-style changes.

Source: Based on Dyché (2000).

- New data-mining tools with expanded capabilities are continually being introduced.
- Increasing competitive pressures are forcing companies to make better use of the information and knowledge contained in their data.

For thorough coverage of data mining and all analytical aspects of business intelligence from a data warehousing perspective, see Turban et al. (2008).

DATA GOVERNANCE AND DATA QUALITY

Governance and quality of data, while vitally important in all areas of data management, are particularly closely related to the way data warehousing is managed and organized. Therefore, we will finish this chapter with a brief introduction to high-level organizational processes called data governance and the management of data quality in organizations.

Data Governance

Data governance is a set of processes and procedures aimed at managing the data within an organization with an eye toward high-level objectives such as availability, integrity, and compliance with regulations. Data governance oversees data access policies by measuring risk and security exposures (Leon, 2007). Data governance provides a mandate for dealing with data issues. According to a The Data Warehousing Institute (TDWI) 2005 (Russom, 2006) survey, only about 25 to 28 percent of organizations (depending on how the question was asked) have a data governance approach. Certainly, broad-based data governance programs are still emerging. Data governance is a function that has to be jointly owned by IT and the business. Successful data governance will require support from upper management in the firm. A key role in enabling success of data governance in an organization is that of a data steward.

The Sarbanes-Oxley Act of 2002 has made it imperative that organizations undertake actions to ensure data accuracy, timeliness, and consistency (Laurent, 2005). Although not mandated by regulations, many organizations require the CIO as well as the CEO and CFO to sign off on financial statements, recognizing the role of IT in building procedures to ensure data quality. Establishment of a business information advisory committee consisting of representatives from each major business unit who have the authority to make business policy decisions can contribute to the establishment of high data quality (Carlson, 2002; Moriarty, 1996). These committee members act as liaisons between IT and their business unit and consider not only their functional unit's data needs but also enterprise-wide data needs. The members are subject–matter experts for the data they steward and hence need to have a strong interest in managing information as a corporate resource, an in-depth understanding of the business of the organization, and good negotiation skills. Such members (typically high-level managers) are sometimes referred to as **data stewards**, people who have the responsibility to ensure that organizational applications properly support the organization's enterprise goals.

A data governance program needs to include the following:

- Sponsorship from both senior management and business units
- A data steward manager to support, train, and coordinate the data stewards
- Data stewards for different business units, data subjects, source systems, or combinations of these elements
- A governance committee, headed by one person, but composed of data steward managers, executives and senior vice presidents, IT leadership (e.g., data administrators), and other business leaders, to set strategic goals, coordinate activities, and provide guidelines and standards for all enterprise data management activities

The goals of data governance are transparency—within and outside the organization to regulators—and increasing the value of data maintained by the organization.

Data governance

High-level organizational groups and processes that oversee data stewardship across the organization. It usually guides data quality initiatives, data architecture, data integration and master data management, data warehousing and business intelligence, and other data-related matters.

Data steward

A person assigned the responsibility of ensuring that organizational applications properly support the organization's enterprise goals for data quality.

The data governance committee measures data quality and availability, determines targets for quality and availability, directs efforts to overcome risks associated with bad or unsecured data, and reviews the results of data audit processes. Data governance is best chartered by the most senior leadership in the organization.

Managing Data Quality

The importance of high-quality data cannot be overstated. According to Brauer (2002):

> Critical business decisions and allocation of resources are made based on what is found in the data. Prices are changed, marketing campaigns created, customers are communicated with, and daily operations evolve around whatever data points are churned out by an organization's various systems. The data that serves as the foundation of these systems *must be good data*. Otherwise we fail before we ever begin. It doesn't matter how pretty the screens are, how intuitive the interfaces are, how high the performance rockets, how automated the processes are, how innovative the methodology is, and how far-reaching the access to the system is, *if the data are bad—the systems fail*. Period. And if the systems fail, or at the very least provide inaccurate information, every process, decision, resource allocation, communication, or interaction with the system will have a damaging, if not disastrous impact on the business itself.

This quote is, in essence, a restatement of the old IT adage "garbage-in, garbage-out" (GIGO), but with increased emphasis on the dramatically high stakes in today's environment.

High-quality data—that is, data that are accurate, consistent, and available in a timely fashion—are essential to the management of organizations today. Organizations must strive to identify the data that are relevant to their decision making to develop business policies and practices that ensure the accuracy and completeness of the data, and to facilitate enterprise-wide data sharing. Managing the quality of data is an organization-wide responsibility, with data administration often playing a leading role in planning and coordinating the efforts.

What is your data quality ROI? In this case, we don't mean *return on investment*; rather, we mean *risk of incarceration*. According to Yugay and Klimchenko (2004), "The key to achieving SOX [Sarbanes-Oxley] compliance lies within IT, which is ultimately the single resource capable of responding to the charge to create effective reporting mechanisms, provide necessary data integration and management systems, ensure data quality and deliver the required information on time." Poor data quality can put executives in jail. Specifically, SOX requires organizations to measure and improve metadata quality; ensure data security; measure and improve data accessibility and ease of use; measure and improve data availability, timeliness, and relevance; measure and improve accuracy, completeness, and understandability of general ledger data; and identify and eliminate duplicates and data inconsistencies. According to Informatica (2005), a leading provider of technology for data quality and integration, data quality is important to

- *Minimize IT project risk* Dirty data can cause delays and extra work on information systems projects, especially those that involve reusing data from existing systems.
- *Make timely business decisions* The ability to make quick and informed business decisions is compromised when managers do not have high-quality data or when they lack confidence in their data.
- *Ensure regulatory compliance* Not only is quality data essential for SOX and Basel II (Europe) compliance, quality data can also help an organization in justice, intelligence, and antifraud activities.
- *Expand the customer base* Being able to accurately spell a customer's name or to accurately know all aspects of customer activity with your organization will help in up-selling and cross-selling new business.

Characteristics of Quality Data

What, then, are quality data? Redman (2004) summarizes data quality as "fit for their intended uses in operations, decision making, and planning." In other words, this means that data are free of defects and possess desirable features (relevant, comprehensive, proper level of detail, easy to read, and easy to interpret). Loshin (2006) and Russom (2006) further delineate the characteristics of quality data:

- *Uniqueness*   Uniqueness means that each entity exists no more than once within the database, and there is a key that can be used to uniquely access each entity. This characteristic requires identity matching (finding data about the same entity) and resolution to locate and remove duplicate entities.

- *Accuracy*   Accuracy has to do with the degree to which any datum correctly represents the real-life object it models. Often accuracy is measured by agreement with some recognized authority data source (e.g., one source system or even some external data provider). Data must be both accurate and precise enough for their intended use. For example, knowing sales accurately is important, but for many decisions, knowing sales only to the nearest $1000 per month for each product is sufficient. Data can be valid (i.e., satisfy a specified domain or range of values) and not be accurate.

- *Consistency*   Consistency means that values for data in one data set (database) are in agreement with the values for related data in another data set (database). Consistency can be within a table row (e.g., the weight of a product should have some relationship to its size and material type), between table rows (e.g., two products with similar characteristics should have about the same prices, or data that are meant to be redundant should have the same values), between the same attributes over time (e.g., the product price should be the same from one month to the next unless there was a price change event), or within some tolerance (e.g., total sales computed from orders filled and orders billed should be roughly the same values). Consistency also relates to attribute inheritance from super- to subtypes. For example, a subtype instance cannot exist without a corresponding supertype, and overlap or disjoint subtype rules are enforced.

- *Completeness*   Completeness refers to data having assigned values if they need to have values. This characteristic encompasses the NOT NULL and foreign key constraints of SQL, but more complex rules might exist (e.g., male employees do not need a maiden name but female employees may have a maiden name). Completeness also means that all data needed are present (e.g., if we want to know total dollar sales, we may need to know both total quantity sold and unit price, or if an employee record indicates that an employee has retired, we need to have a retirement date recorded). Sometimes completeness has an aspect of precedence. For example, an employee in an employee table who does not exist in an applicant table may indicate a data quality issue.

- *Timeliness*   Timeliness means meeting the expectation for the time between when data are expected and when they are readily available for use. As organizations attempt to decrease the latency between when a business activity occurs and when the organization is able to take action on that activity, timeliness is becoming a more important quality of data characteristic (i.e., if we don't know in time to take action, we don't have quality data). A related aspect of timeliness is retention, which is the span of time for which data represent the real world. Some data need to be time-stamped to indicate from when to when they apply, and missing from or to dates may indicate a data quality issue.

- *Currency*   Currency is the degree to which data are recent enough to be useful. For example, we may require that customers' phone numbers be up-to-date so we can call them at any time, but the number of employees may not need to be refreshed in real time. Varying degrees of currency across data may indicate a quality issue (e.g., if the salaries of different employees have drastically different updated dates).

- *Conformance* Conformance refers to whether data are stored, exchanged, or presented in a format that is as specified by their metadata. The metadata include both domain integrity rules (e.g., attribute values come from a valid set or range of values) and actual format (e.g., specific location of special characters, precise mixture of text, numbers, and special symbols).
- *Referential integrity* Data that refer to other data need to be unique and satisfy requirements to exist (i.e., satisfy any mandatory one or optional one cardinalities).

These are high standards. Quality data requires more than defect correction; it also requires prevention and reporting. Because data are frequently updated, achieving quality data requires constant monitoring and measurement as well as improvement actions. Quality data are also not perfectly achievable nor absolutely necessary in some situations (there are obvious situations of life and death where perfection is the goal); "just enough quality" may be the best business decision to trade off costs versus returns.

Summary

Despite the vast quantities of data collected in organizations today, most managers have difficulty obtaining the information they need for decision making. Two major factors contribute to this "information gap." First, data are often heterogeneous and inconsistent as a result of the piecemeal systems development approaches that have commonly been used. Second, systems are developed (or acquired) primarily to satisfy operational objectives, with little thought given to the information needs of managers.

There are major differences between operational and informational systems and between the data that appear in those systems. Operational systems are used to run the business on a current basis, and the primary design goal is to provide high performance to users who process transactions and update databases. Informational systems are used to support managerial decision making, and the primary design goal is to provide ease of access and use for information workers.

The purpose of a data warehouse is to consolidate and integrate data from a variety of sources and to format those data in a context for making accurate business decisions. A data warehouse is an integrated and consistent store of subject-oriented data obtained from a variety of sources and formatted into a meaningful context to support decision making in an organization.

Most data warehouses today follow a three-layer architecture. The first layer consists of data distributed throughout the various operational systems. The second layer is an enterprise data warehouse, which is a centralized, integrated data warehouse that is the control point and single source of all data made available to end users for decision support applications. The third layer is a series of data marts. A data mart is a data warehouse whose data are limited in scope for the decision-making needs of a particular user group. A data mart can be independent of an enterprise data warehouse (EDW), derived from the EDW, or a logical subset of the EDW.

The data layer in an enterprise data warehouse is called the reconciled data layer. The characteristics of this data layer (ideally) are the following: It is detailed, historical, normalized, comprehensive, and quality controlled. Reconciled data are obtained by filling the enterprise data warehouse or operational data store from the various operational systems. Reconciling the data requires four steps: capturing the data from the source systems, scrubbing the data (to remove inconsistencies), transforming the data (to convert it to the format required in the data warehouse), and loading and indexing the data in the data warehouse. Reconciled data are not normally accessed directly by end users.

The data layer in the data marts is referred to as the derived data layer. These are the data that are accessed by end users for their decision support applications.

Data are most often stored in a data mart using a variation of the relational model called the star schema, or dimensional model. A star schema is a simple database design where dimensional data are separated from fact or event data. A star schema consists of two types of tables: dimension tables and fact tables. The size of a fact table depends, in part, on the grain (or level of detail) in that table. Fact tables with more than 1 billion rows are common in data warehouse applications today. There are several variations of the star schema, including snowflake schemas that arise when one or more dimensions have a hierarchical structure. The emerging technology of column-based databases provide new options for storing and accessing data warehouse and data mart data.

A variety of end-user interfaces are available to access and analyze decision support data. Online analytical processing (OLAP) is the use of a set of graphical tools that provides users with multidimensional views of their data (data are normally viewed as a cube). Increasingly data visualization tools make multidimensional data easier to understand. OLAP facilitates data analysis operations such as slice and dice, data pivoting, and drill-down. Dashboards and business performance monitoring provide high-level views to assist managers in identifying which areas to drill down or where to pivot data. Data mining is a form of knowledge discovery that uses a sophisticated blend of techniques from traditional statistics, artificial intelligence, and computer graphics.

Chapter Review

Key Terms

Big data *331*
Conformed dimension *325*
Data governance *341*
Data mart *307*
Data mining *339*
Data steward *341*
Data visualization *338*
Data warehouse *302*
Dependent data mart *309*
Derived data *313*
Enterprise data warehouse (EDW) *309*
Grain *322*
Independent data mart *307*
Informational system *306*
Logical data mart *310*
Multidimensional OLAP (MOLAP) *336*
NoSQL *333*
Online analytical processing (OLAP) *335*
Operational data store (ODS) *310*
Operational system *306*
Periodic data *315*
Real-time data warehouse *311*
Reconciled data *313*
Relational OLAP (ROLAP) *336*
Snowflake schema *327*
Star schema *318*
Transient data *315*

Review Questions

1. Define each of the following terms:
   a. data warehouse
   b. data mart
   c. reconciled data
   d. derived data
   e. online analytical processing
   f. big data
   g. star schema
   h. snowflake schema
   i. grain
   j. conformed dimension
2. Match the following terms and definitions:
   _____ periodic data
   _____ data mart
   _____ star schema
   _____ data mining
   _____ reconciled data
   _____ dependent data mart
   _____ data visualization
   _____ transient data
   _____ snowflake schema
   a. lost previous data content
   b. detailed historical data
   c. data not altered or deleted
   d. data warehouse of limited scope
   e. dimension and fact tables
   f. form of knowledge discovery
   g. data filled from a data warehouse
   h. structure that results from hierarchical dimensions
   i. data represented in graphical formats
3. Contrast the following terms:
   a. transient data; periodic data
   b. data warehouse; data mart; operational data store
   c. reconciled data; derived data
   d. fact table; dimension table
   e. star schema; snowflake schema
   f. independent data mart; dependent data mart; logical data mart
   g. SQL; NoSQL
4. List the five major trends that necessitate data warehousing in many organizations today.
5. Briefly describe the major components of a data warehouse architecture.
6. List the three types of metadata that appear in a three-layer data warehouse architecture and briefly describe the purpose of each.
7. List four characteristics of a data warehouse.
8. List five claimed limitations of independent data marts.
9. List two claimed benefits of independent data marts.
10. Briefly describe three types of operations that can easily be performed with OLAP tools.
11. List four objectives of derived data.
12. Is a star schema a relational data model? Why or why not?
13. Explain how the volatility of a data warehouse is different from the volatility of a database for an operational information system.
14. Explain the pros and cons of logical data marts.
15. What is a helper table, and why is it often used to help organize derived data?
16. Describe the characteristics of a surrogate key as used in a data warehouse or data mart.
17. Why is time almost always a dimension in a data warehouse or data mart?
18. What is the purpose of conformed dimensions for different star schemas within the same data warehousing environment?
19. What are the added capabilities of NoSQL technologies that extend what SQL can do?
20. In what ways are dimension tables often not normalized?
21. What is a hierarchy as it relates to a dimension table?
22. What is the meaning of the phrase "slowly changing dimension"?
23. Explain the most common approach used to handle slowly changing dimensions.
24. One of the claimed characteristics of a data warehouse is that it is nonupdateable. What does this mean?
25. In what ways are a data staging area and an enterprise data warehouse different?

Problems and Exercises

1. Examine the three tables with student data shown in Figure 9-1. Design a single-table format that will hold all of the data (nonredundantly) that are contained in these three tables. Choose column names that you believe are most appropriate for these data.
2. The following table shows some simple student data as of the date 06/20/2010:

Key	Name	Major
001	Amy	Music
002	Tom	Business
003	Sue	Art
004	Joe	Math
005	Ann	Engineering

The following transactions occur on 06/21/2010:
- Student 004 changes major from Math to Business.
- Student 005 is deleted from the file.
- New student 006 is added to the file: Name is Jim, Major is Phys Ed.

The following transactions occur on 06/22/2010:
- Student 003 changes major from Art to History.
- Student 006 changes major from Phys Ed to Basket Weaving.

Your assignment involves two parts:
a. Construct tables for 06/21/2010 and 06/22/2010, reflecting these transactions; assume that the data are transient (refer to Figure 9-7).
b. Construct tables for 06/21/2010 and 06/22/2010, reflecting these transactions; assume that the data are periodic (refer to Figure 9-8).
3. Millennium College wants you to help design a star schema to record grades for courses completed by students. There are four dimension tables, with attributes as follows:

CourseSection	Attributes: CourseID, SectionNumber, CourseName, Units, RoomID, and RoomCapacity. During a given semester, the college offers an average of 500 course sections.
Professor	Attributes: ProfID, ProfName, Title, DepartmentID, and DepartmentName. There are typically 200 professors at Millennium at any given time.
Student	Attributes: StudentID, StudentName, and Major. Each course section has an average of 40 students, and students typically take five courses per period.
Period	Attributes: SemesterID and Year. The database will contain data for 30 periods (a total of 10 years).

The only fact that is to be recorded in the fact table is CourseGrade.
a. Design a star schema for this problem. See Figure 9-10 for the format you should follow.

b. Estimate the number of rows in the fact table, using the assumptions stated previously.
c. Estimate the total size of the fact table (in bytes), assuming that each field has an average of 5 bytes.
d. If you didn't want to or didn't have to stick with a strict star schema for this data mart, how would you change the design? Why?
e. Various characteristics of sections, professors, and students change over time. How do you propose designing the star schema to allow for these changes? Why?
4. Having mastered the principles of normalization described in Chapter 4, you recognize immediately that the star schema you developed for Millennium College (Problem and Exercise 3) is not in third normal form. Using these principles, convert the star schema to a snowflake schema. What impact (if any) does this have on the size of the fact table for this problem?
5. You are to construct a star schema for Simplified Automobile Insurance Company (see Kimball, 1996b, for a more realistic example). The relevant dimensions, dimension attributes, and dimension sizes are as follows:

InsuredParty	Attributes: InsuredPartyID and Name. There is an average of two insured parties for each policy and covered item.
CoverageItem	Attributes: CoverageKey and Description. There is an average of 10 covered items per policy.
Agent	Attributes: AgentID and AgentName. There is one agent for each policy and covered item.
Policy	Attributes: PolicyID and Type. The company has approximately 1 million policies at the present time.
Period	Attributes: DateKey and FiscalPeriod.

Facts to be recorded for each combination of these dimensions are PolicyPremium, Deductible, and NumberOfTransactions.
a. Design a star schema for this problem. See Figure 9-10 for the format you should follow.
b. Estimate the number of rows in the fact table, using the assumptions stated previously.
c. Estimate the total size of the fact table (in bytes), assuming an average of 5 bytes per field.
6. Simplified Automobile Insurance Company would like to add a Claims dimension to its star schema (see Problem and Exercise 5). Attributes of Claim are ClaimID, ClaimDescription, and ClaimType. Attributes of the fact table are now PolicyPremium, Deductible, and MonthlyClaimTotal.
a. Extend the star schema from Problem and Exercise 5 to include these new data.
b. Calculate the estimated number of rows in the fact table, assuming that the company experiences an average of 2000 claims per month.
7. Millennium College (see Problem and Exercise 3) now wants to include new data about course sections: the department offering the course, the academic unit to which the department reports, and the budget unit to which the department is assigned. Change your answer to Problem and

Exercise 3 to accommodate these new data requirements. Explain why you implemented the changes in the star schema the way you did.

8. As mentioned in the chapter, Kimball (1997), Inmon (1997, 2000), and Armstrong (2000) have debated the merits of independent and dependent data marts and normalized versus denormalized data marts. Obtain copies of these articles from your library or from online sources and summarize the arguments made by each side of this debate.

9. A food manufacturing company needs a data mart to summarize facts about orders to move goods. Some orders transfer goods internally, some are sales to customers, some are purchases from vendors, and some are returns of goods from customers. The company needs to treat customers, vendors, plants, and storage locations as distinct dimensions that can be involved at both ends of a movement event. For each type of destination or origin, the company wants to know the type of location (i.e., customer, vendor, etc.), name, city, and state. Facts about each movement include dollar volume moved, cost of movement, and revenue collected from the move (if any, and this can be negative for a return). Design a star-type schema to represent this data mart. Hint: After you design a typical star schema, think about how you might simplify the design through the use of generalization.

10. Visit **www.kimballgroup.com** and locate Kimball University Design Tip 37. Study this design tip and draw the dimensional model for the recommended design for a "pipeline" application for university admissions.

11. Visit **www.teradatauniversitynetwork.com** and download the dimensional modeling tool located under the downloadable software section. (Your instructor will have to give you the current password to access this site.) Use this tool to draw your answers to Problems and Exercises 3, 5, 6, and 9. Write a report that comments on the usefulness of this modeling tool. What other features would you like the tool to have? Is this tool better or worse than other database diagramming tools you've used (such as Visio, SmartDraw, ERWin, or others)? Why or why not?

 PINE VALLEY FURNITURE

12. Pine Valley Furniture wants you to help design a data mart for analysis of sales. The subjects of the data mart are as follows:

Salesperson	Attributes: SalespersonID, Years with PVFC, SalespersonName, and SupervisorRating.
Product	Attributes: ProductID, Category, Weight, and YearReleasedToMarket.
Customer	Attributes: CustomerID, CustomerName, CustomerSize, and Location. Location is also a hierarchy over which they want to be able to aggregate data. Each Location has attributes LocationID, AverageIncome, PopulationSize, and NumberOfRetailers. For any given customer, there is an arbitrary number of levels in the Location hierarchy.
Period	Attributes: DayID, FullDate, WeekdayFlag, and LastDay of MonthFlag.

Data for this data mart come from an enterprise data warehouse, but there are many systems of record that feed this data to the data warehouse. The only fact that is to be recorded in the fact table is Dollar Sales.

a. Design a typical multidimensional schema to represent this data mart.

b. Among the various dimensions that change is Customer information. In particular, over time, customers may change their location and size. Redesign your answer to part a to accommodate keeping the history of these changes so that the history of DollarSales can be matched with the precise customer characteristics at the time of the sales.

c. As was stated, a characteristic of Product is its category. It turns out that there is a hierarchy of product categories, and management would like to be able to summarize sales at any level of category. Change the design of the data mart to accommodate product hierarchies.

Problems 13 through 18 are based upon the Fitchwood Insurance Company case study, which is described next.

Fitchwood Insurance Company, which is primarily involved in the sale of annuity products, would like to design a data mart for its sales and marketing organization. Presently, the OLTP system is a legacy system residing on a Novell network consisting of approximately 600 different flat files. For the purposes of our case study, we can assume that 30 different flat files are going to be used for the data mart. Some of these flat files are transaction files that change constantly. The OLTP system is shut down overnight on Friday evening beginning at 6 P.M. for backup. During that time, the flat files are copied to another server, an extraction process is run, and the extracts are sent via FTP to a UNIX server. A process is run on the UNIX server to load the extracts into Oracle and rebuild the star schema. For the initial loading of the data mart, all information from the 30 files was extracted and loaded. On a weekly basis, only additions and updates will be included in the extracts.

Although the data contained in the OLTP system are broad, the sales and marketing organization would like to focus on the sales data only. After substantial analysis, the ERD shown in Figure 9-23 was developed to describe the data to be used to populate the data mart.

From this ERD, we get the set of relations shown in Figure 9-24. Sales and marketing is interested in viewing all sales data by territory, effective date, type of policy, and face value. In addition, the data mart should be able to provide reporting by individual agent on sales as well as commissions earned. Occasionally, the sales territories are revised (i.e., zip codes are added or deleted). The Last Redistrict attribute of the Territory table is used to store the date of the last revision. Some sample queries and reports are listed here:

- Total sales per month by territory, by type of policy
- Total sales per quarter by territory, by type of policy
- Total sales per month by agent, by type of policy
- Total sales per month by agent, by zip code
- Total face value of policies by month of effective date
- Total face value of policies by month of effective date, by agent
- Total face value of policies by quarter of effective date

FIGURE 9-23 Fitchwood Insurance Company ERD

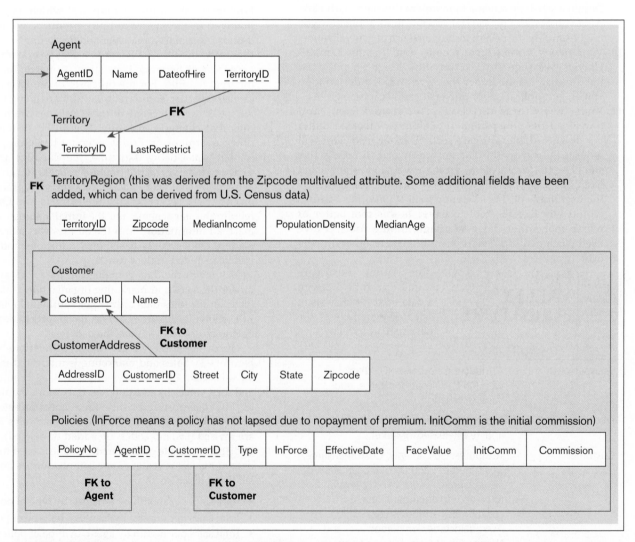

FIGURE 9-24 Relations for Fitchwood Insurance Company

- Total number of policies in force, by agent
- Total number of policies not in force, by agent
- Total face value of all policies sold by an individual agent
- Total initial commission paid on all policies to an agent
- Total initial commission paid on policies sold in a given month by agent
- Total commissions earned by month, by agent
- Top-selling agent by territory, by month

Commissions are paid to an agent upon the initial sale of a policy. The InitComm field of the policy table contains the percentage of the face value paid as an initial commission. The Commission field contains a percentage that is paid each month as long as a policy remains active or in force. Each month, commissions are calculated by computing the sum of the commission on each individual policy that is in force for an agent.

13. Create a star schema for this case study. How did you handle the time dimension?
14. Would you prefer to normalize (snowflake) the star schema of your answer to Problem and Exercise 13? If so, how and why? Redesign the star schema to accommodate your recommended changes.
15. Agents change territories over time. If necessary, redesign your answer to Problem and Exercise 14 to handle this changing dimensional data.
16. Customers may have relationships with one another (e.g., spouses, parents and children). Redesign your answer to Problem and Exercise 15 to accommodate these relationships.
17. Management would like to use the data mart for drill-down online reporting. For example, a sales manager might want to view a report of total sales for an agent by month and then drill down into the individual types of policies to see how sales are broken down by type of policy. What type of tool would you recommend for this? What additional tables, other than those required by the tool for administration, might need to be added to the data mart?
18. Do you see any opportunities for data mining using the Fitchwood data mart? Research data-mining tools and recommend one or two for use with the data mart.

Problems and Exercises 19 through 26 deal with the Sales Analysis Module data mart available on Teradata University Network (**www.teradatauniversitynetwork.com**). *To use Teradata University Network, you will need to obtain the current TUN password from your instructor. Go to the Assignments section of Teradata University Network or to this textbook's Website to find the document "SAM Assignment Instructions" in order to prepare to do the following Problems and Exercises.*

19. Review the metadata file for the db_samwh database and the definitions of the database tables. (You can use SHOW TABLE commands to display the DDL for tables.) Explain the methods used in this database for modeling hierarchies. Are hierarchies modeled as described in this chapter?
20. Review the metadata file for the db_samwh database and the definitions of the database tables. (You can use SHOW TABLE commands to display the DDL for tables.) Explain what dimension data, if any, are maintained to support slowly changing dimensions. If there are slowly changing

dimension data, are they maintained as described in this chapter?
21. Review the metadata file for the db_samwh database and the definitions of the database tables. (You can use SHOW TABLE commands to display the DDL for tables.) Are dimension tables conformed in this data mart? Explain.
22. The database you are using was developed by MicroStrategy, a leading business intelligence software vendor. The MicroStrategy software is also available on TSN. Most business intelligence tools generate SQL to retrieve the data they need to produce the reports and charts and to run the models users want. Go to the Apply & Do area on the Teradata University Network main screen and select MicroStrategy, then select MicroStrategy Application Modules, and then the Sales Force Analysis Module. Then make the following selections: Shared Reports → Sales Performance Analysis → Quarterly Revenue Trend by Sales Region → 2005 → Run Report. Go to the File menu and select the Report Details option. You will then see the SQL statement that was used, along with some MicroStrategy functionality, to produce the chart in the report. Cut and paste this SQL code into SQL Assistant and run this query in SQL Assistant. (You may want to save the code as an intermediate step to a Word file so you don't lose it.) Produce a file with the code and the SQL Assistant query result (answer set) for your instructor. You have now done what is called *screen scrapping* the SQL. This is often necessary to create data for analysis that is beyond the capabilities of a business intelligence package.
23. Take the query you scrapped from Problem and Exercise 22 and modify it to show only the U.S. region grouped by each quarter, not just for 2005 but for all years available, in order by quarter. Label the total orders by quarter with the heading TOTAL and the region ID simply as ID in the result. Produce a file with the revised SQL code and the answer set for your instructor.
24. Using the MDIFF "ordered analytical function" in Teradata SQL (see the Functions and Operators manual), show the differences (label the difference CHANGE) in TOTAL (which you calculated in the previous Problem and Exercise) from quarter to quarter. Hint: You will likely create a derived table based on your query above, similar to what is shown in examples in the Functions and Operators manual; when you do so, you will need to give the derived table an alias name and then use that alias name in the outer select statement when you ask to display the results of the query. Save your query and answer set to a file to give your instructor. (By the way, MDIFF is not standard SQL; this is an analytical SQL function proprietary to Teradata.)
25. Because data warehouses and even data marts can become very large, it may be sufficient to work with a subset of data for some analyses. Create a sample of orders from 2004 using the SAMPLE SQL command (which is standard SQL); put a randomized allocation of 10 percent of the rows into the sample. Include in the sample results the order ID, product ID, sales rep region ID, month description, and order amount. Show the results, in sequence, by month. Run the query two times to check that the sample is actually random. Put your SQL query and a portion of the two

answer sets (enough to show that they are different) into a file for your instructor.

26. GROUP BY by itself creates subtotals by category, and the ROLLUP extension to GROUP BY creates even more categories for subtotals. Using all the orders, do a rollup to get total order amounts by product, sales region, and month and all combinations, including a grand total. Display the results sorted by product, region, and month. Put your query and the first portion of the answer set, including all of product 1 and a few rows for product 2, into a file for your instructor. Also, do a regular GROUP BY and put this query and the similar results from it into the file and then place an explanation in the file of how GROUP BY and GROUP BY with ROLLUP are different.

References

Armstrong, R. 1997. "A Rebuttal to the Dimensional Modeling Manifesto." A white paper produced by NCR Corporation.

Armstrong, R. 2000. "Avoiding Data Mart Traps." *Teradata Review* (Summer): 32–37.

Brauer, B. 2002. "Data Quality—Spinning Straw into Gold," **www2.sas.com/proceedings/sugi26/p117-26.pdf**.

Bughin, J., J. Livingston, and S. Marwaha. 2011. "Seizing the Potential of 'Big Data'." *McKinsey Quarterly* (October).

Carlson, D. 2002. "Data Stewardship Action," *DM Review* 12,5 (May): 37, 62.

Chisholm, M. 2000. "A New Understanding of Reference Data." *DM Review* 10,10 (October): 60, 84–85.

Devlin, B., and P. Murphy. 1988. "An Architecture for a Business Information System." *IBM Systems Journal* 27,1 (March): 60–80.

Dyché, J. 2000. *e-Data: Turning Data into Information with Data Warehousing*. Reading, MA: Addison-Wesley.

Dumbill, E. 2012. "What is Big Data?" *Planning for Big Data*, Sebastopol, CA: O'Reilly, 2012.

Hackathorn, R. 1993. *Enterprise Database Connectivity*. New York: Wiley.

Hackathorn, R. 2002. "Current Practices in Active Data Warehousing," available at **www.teradata.com** under White Papers.

Hays, C. 2004. "What They Know About You." *New York Times*. November 14: section 3, page 1.

Informatica. 2005. "Addressing Data Quality at the Enterprise Level." (October).

Imhoff, C. 1998. "The Operational Data Store: Hammering Away." *DM Review* 8,7 (July) available at **www.dmreview .com/article_sub.cfm?articleID=470**.

Imhoff, C. 1999. "The Corporate Information Factory." *DM Review* 9,12 (December), available at **www.dmreview .com/article_sub.cfm?articleID=1667**.

Inmon, W. 1992. *Building the Data Warehouse*. New York: Wiley.

Inmon, W. 1997. "Iterative Development in the Data Warehouse." *DM Review* 7,11 (November): 16, 17.

Inmon, W. 1998. "The Operational Data Store: Designing the Operational Data Store." *DM Review* 8,7 (July), available at **www.dmreview.com/article_sub.cfm?article ID=469.**

Inmon, W. 1999. "What Happens When You Have Built the Data Mart First?" *TDAN* accessed at **www.tdan.com/i012fe02 .htm** (no longer available as of June, 2009).

Inmon, W. 2000. "The Problem with Dimensional Modeling." *DM Review* 10,5 (May): 68–70.

Inmon, W. 2006. "Granularity of Data: Lowest Level of Usefulness." *B-Eye Network* (December 14) available at **www.b-eye-network.com/view/3276.**

Inmon, W., and R. D. Hackathorn. 1994. *Using the Data Warehouse*. New York: Wiley.

Kimball, R. 1996a. *The Data Warehouse Toolkit*. New York: Wiley.

Kimball, R. 1996b. "Slowly Changing Dimensions." *DBMS* 9,4 (April): 18–20.

Kimball, R. 1997. "A Dimensional Modeling Manifesto." *DBMS* 10,9 (August): 59.

Kimball, R. 1998a. "Pipelining Your Surrogates." *DBMS* 11,6 (June): 18–22.

Kimball, R. 1998b. "Help for Hierarchies." *DBMS* 11,9 (September) 12–16.

Kimball, R. 1999. "When a Slowly Changing Dimension Speeds Up." *Intelligent Enterprise* 2,8 (August 3): 60–62.

Kimball, R. 2001. "Declaring the Grain." from Kimball University, Design Tip 21, available at **www.kimballgroup.com.**

Laurent, W. 2005. "The Case for Data Stewardship." *DM Review* 15,2 (February): 26–28.

Leon, M. 2007. "Escaping Information Anarchy." *DB2 Magazine* 12,1: 23–26.

Loshin, D. 2001. "The Cost of Poor Data Quality." *DM Review* (June 29) available at **www.information-management.com /infodirect/20010629/3605-1.html.**

Marco, D. 2000. *Building and Managing the Meta Data Repository: A Full Life-Cycle Guide*. New York: Wiley.

Marco, D. 2003. "Independent Data Marts: Stranded on Islands of Data, Part 1." *DM Review* 13,4 (April): 30, 32, 63.

Meyer, A. 1997. "The Case for Dependent Data Marts." *DM Review* 7,7 (July–August): 17–24.

Moriarty, T. 1996. "Better Business Practices." *Database Programming & Design* 9,7 (September): 59–61.

Mundy, J. 2001. "Smarter Data Warehouses." *Intelligent Enterprise* 4,2 (February 16): 24–29.

Redman, T. 2004. "Data: An Unfolding Quality Disaster." *DM Review* 14,8 (August): 21–23, 57.

Ross, M. 2009. "Kimball University: The 10 Essential Rules of Dimensional Modeling." (May 29), available at **www.intelligententerprise.com/showArticle .jhtml?articleID=217700810.**

Russom, P. 2006. "Taking Data Quality to the Enterprise through Data Governance." *TDWI Report Series* (March).

Turban, E., R. Sharda, J. Aronson, and D. King 2008. *Business Intelligence*. Upper Saddle River, NJ: Prentice Hall.

Wayner, P. 2011. "NoSQL Standouts: New Databases for New Applications." Available from **www.infoworld.com** (posted July 21, 2011).

Weldon, J. L. 1996. "Data Mining and Visualization." *Database Programming & Design* 9,5 (May): 21–24.

Yugay, I., and V. Klimchenko. 2004. "SOX Mandates Focus on Data Quality & Integration." *DM Review* 14,2 (February): 38–42.

Further Reading

Gallo, J. 2002. "Operations and Maintenance in a Data Warehouse Environment." *DM Review* 12,12 (2003 Resource Guide): 12–16.

Goodhue, D., M. Mybo, and L. Kirsch. 1992. "The Impact of Data Integration on the Costs and Benefits of Information Systems." *MIS Quarterly* 16,3 (September): 293–311.

Jenks, B. 1997. "Tiered Data Warehouse." *DM Review* 7,10 (October): 54–57.

Kimball, R. 2002. "What Changed?" *Intelligent Enterprise* 5,8 (August 12): 22, 24, 52.

Kimball, R. 2006. "Adding a Row Change Reason Attribute." from Kimball University, Design Tip 80, available at **www.kimballgroup.com.**

Mundy, J., W. Thornthwaite, and R. Kimball. 2006. *The Microsoft Data Warehouse Toolkit: With SQL Server 2005 and the Microsoft Business Intelligence Toolset.* Hoboken, NJ: Wiley.

Poe, V. 1996. *Building a Data Warehouse for Decision Support.* Upper Saddle River, NJ: Prentice Hall.

Web Resources

www.teradata.com/tdmo Web site of *Teradata* magazine, which contains articles on the technology and application of the Teradata data warehouse system. (This magazine recently changed its name. Articles under the magazine's new and previous names can be found at **www.teradatamagazine.com**.)

www.information-management.com Web site of *Information Management*, a monthly trade magazine that contains articles and columns about data warehousing.

www.tdan.com An electronic journal on data warehousing.

www.inmoncif.com Web site of Bill Inmon, a leading authority on data management and data warehousing.

www.kimballgroup.com Web site of Ralph Kimball, a leading authority on data warehousing.

www.tdwi.org Web site of The Data Warehousing Institute, an industry group that focuses on data warehousing methods and applications.

www.datawarehousing.org The Data Warehousing Knowledge Center, which contains links to many vendors.

www.information-quality.com Web site for Larry English, one of the leaders in data quality management.

www.teradatauniversitynetwork.com A portal to resources for databases, data warehousing, and business intelligence. Data sets from this textbook are stored on the software site, from which you can use SQL, data mining, dimensional modeling, and other tools. Also, some very large data warehouse databases are available through this site to resources at the University of Arkansas. New articles and Webinars are added to this site all the time, so visit it frequently or subscribe to its RSS feed service to know when new materials are added. You will need to obtain a password to this site from your instructor.

GLOSSARY OF ACRONYMS

ACM	Association for Computing Machinery	FDA	Food and Drug Administration
ANSI	American National Standards Institute	FK	Foreign key
API	Application programming interface	FTC	Federal Trade Commission
ASP	Active Server Pages	FTP	File Transfer Protocol
ATM	Automated teller machine	GPA	Grade point average
BOM	Bill of materials	GUI	Graphical user interface
BPM	Business performance management	HIPAA	Health Insurance Portability and Accountability Act
B2B	Business-to-business		
B2C	Business-to-consumer	HTML	Hypertext Markup Language
CAD/CAM	Computer-aided design/computer-aided manufacturing	HTTP	Hypertext Transfer Protocol
		IBM	International Business Machines
CASE	Computer-aided software engineering	ID	Identifier
CD-ROM	Compact Disc read-only memory	IDE	Integrated development environment
CEO	Chief executive officer	IE	Information engineering
CFO	Chief financial officer	INCITS	International Committee for Information Technology Standards
CGI	Common Gateway Interface		
CIF	Corporate information factory	I/O	Input/output
CIO	Chief information officer	IP	Internet Protocol
COO	Chief operating officer	IS	Information system
CPU	Central processor unit	ISO	International Standards Organization
CRM	Customer relationship management	IT	Information technology
C/S	Client/server	JDBC	Java Database Connectivity
CSF	Critical success factor	JSP	Java Server Pages
DA	Data administrator (or data administration)	LAN	Local area network
		LDB	Logical database
DBA	Database administrator (or database administration)	LDM	Logical data model
		MB	Megabytes (million bytes)
DBD	Database description	MIS	Management information system
DBMS	Database management system	M:N	Many-to-many
DB2	Database 2 (an IBM Relational DBMS)	M:1	Many-to-one
DCL	Data control language	MOLAP	Multidimensional online analytical processing
DDL	Data definition language		
DFD	Data flow diagram	MRP	Material requirements planning
DML	Data manipulation language	MS	Microsoft
DSS	Decision support system	NIST	National Institute of Standards and Technology
DTD	Document type declaration		
DVD	Digital versatile disc	ODBC	Open database connectivity
EAI	Enterprise application integration	ODS	Operational data store
EDI	Electronic data interchange	OLAP	Online analytical processing
EDW	Enterprise data warehouse	OLTP	Online transaction processing
EER	Enhanced entity-relationship	PC	Personal computer
EFT	Electronic funds transfer	PDA	Personal digital assistant
EII	Enterprise information integration	PIN	Personal identification number
E-R	Entity-relationship	PK	Primary key
ERD	Entity-relationship diagram	PL/SQL	Programming Language/SQL
ERP	Enterprise resource planning	PVFC	Pine Valley Furniture Company
ETL	Extract–transform–load		

RAD	Rapid application development
RAID	Redundant array of inexpensive disks
RAM	Random access memory
RDBMS	Relational database management system
ROI	Return on investment
ROLAP	Relational online analytical processing
SCD	Slowly changing dimension
SCM	Supply chain management
SDLC	Systems development life cycle
SOA	Service-oriented architecture
SOAP	Simple Object Access Protocol
SOX	Sarbanes-Oxley Act
SPL	Structured Product Labeling
SQL	Structured Query Language
SQL/CLI	SQL/Call Level Interface
SQL/DS	Structured Query Language/Data System (an IBM relational DBMS)
SQL/PSM	SQL/Persistent Stored Modules
SSL	Secure Sockets Layer
TCP/IP	Transmission Control Protocol/Internet Protocol

TDWI	The Data Warehousing Institute
TQM	Total quality management
UDDI	Universal Description, Discovery, and Integration
UDT	User-defined data type
UML	Unified Modeling Language
URI	Universal resource identifier
URL	Uniform resource locator
WSDL	Web Services Description Language
WWW	World Wide Web
W3C	World Wide Web Consortium
XBRL	Extensible Business Reporting Language
XML	Extensible Markup Language
XSL	Extensible Style Language
XSLT	XML Stylesheet Language Transformation
1:1	One-to-one
1:M	One-to-many
1NF	First normal form
2NF	Second normal form
3GL	Third-generation language
3NF	Third normal form

GLOSSARY OF TERMS

Note: Number in parenthesis corresponds to the chapter in which the term is found.

Agile software development An approach to database and software development that emphasizes "**individuals and interactions** over processes and tools, **working software** over comprehensive documentation, **customer collaboration** over contract negotiation, and **response to change** over following a plan." (1)

Alias An alternative name used for an attribute. (4)

Anomaly An error or inconsistency that may result when a user attempts to update a table that contains redundant data. The three types of anomalies are insertion, deletion, and modification anomalies. (4)

Application partitioning The process of assigning portions of application code to client or server partitions after it is written to achieve better performance and interoperability (ability of a component to function on different platforms). (8)

Application program interface (API) Sets of routines that an application program uses to direct the performance of procedures by the computer's operating system. (8)

Associative entity An entity type that associates the instances of one or more entity types and contains attributes that are peculiar to the relationship between those entity instances. (2)

Attribute A property or characteristic of an entity or relationship type that is of interest to the organization. (2)

Attribute inheritance A property by which subtype entities inherit values of all attributes and instances of all relationships of their supertype. (3)

Backward recovery (rollback) The backout, or undo, of unwanted changes to a database. Before images of the records that have been changed are applied to the database, and the database is returned to an earlier state. Rollback is used to reverse the changes made by transactions that have been aborted, or terminated abnormally. (7)

Base table A table in the relational data model containing the inserted raw data. Base tables correspond to the relations that are identified in the database's conceptual schema. (6)

Big data An ill-defined term applied to databases whose volume, velocity, and variety strains the ability of commonly used relational DBMSs to capture, manage, and process the data within a tolerable elapsed time. (9)

Binary relationship A relationship between the instances of two entity types. (2)

Business rule A statement that defines or constrains some aspect of the business. It is intended to assert business structure or to control or influence the behavior of the business. (2)

Candidate key An attribute, or combination of attributes, that uniquely identifies a row in a relation. (4)

Cardinality constraint A rule that specifies the number of instances of one entity that can (or must) be associated with each instance of another entity. (2)

Catalog A set of schemas that, when put together, constitute a description of a database. (6)

Client/server system A networked computing model that distributes processes between clients and servers, which supply the requested services. In a database system, the database generally resides on a server that processes the DBMS. The clients may process the application systems or request services from another server that holds the application programs. (8)

Completeness constraint A type of constraint that addresses whether an instance of a supertype must also be a member of at least one subtype. (3)

Composite attribute An attribute that has meaningful component parts (attributes). (2)

Composite identifier An identifier that consists of a composite attribute. (2)

Composite key A primary key that consists of more than one attribute. (4)

Computer-aided software engineering (CASE) tools Software tools that provide automated support for some portion of the systems development process. (1)

Conceptual schema A detailed, technology-independent specification of the overall structure of organizational data. (1)

Conformed dimension One or more dimension tables associated with two or more fact tables for which the dimension tables have the same business meaning and primary key with each fact table. (9)

Constraint A rule that cannot be violated by database users. (1)

Correlated subquery In SQL, a subquery in which processing the inner query depends on data from the outer query. (7)

Data Stored representations of objects and events that have meaning and importance in the user's environment. (1)

Data administration A high-level function that is responsible for the overall management of data resources in an organization, including maintaining corporate-wide definitions and standards. (1)

Database An organized collection of logically related data. (1)

Database administration A technical function that is responsible for physical database design and for dealing with technical issues, such as security enforcement, database performance, and backup and recovery. (1)

Database application An application program (or set of related programs) that is used to perform a series of database activities (create, read, update, and delete) on behalf of database users. (1)

Database management system (DBMS) A software system that is used to create, maintain, and provide controlled access to user databases. (1)

Database server A computer that is responsible for database storage, access, and processing in a client/server environment. Some people also use this term to describe a two-tier client/server applications. (8)

Data control language (DCL) Commands used to control a database, including those for administering privileges and committing (saving) data. (6)

Data definition language (DDL) Commands used to define a database, including those for creating, altering, and dropping tables and establishing constraints. (6)

Data governance High-level organizational groups and processes that oversee data stewardship across the organization. It usually guides data quality initiatives, data architecture, data integration and master data management, data warehousing and business intelligence, and other data-related matters. (9)

Data independence The separation of data descriptions from the application programs that use the data. (1)

Data manipulation language (DML) Commands used to maintain and query a database, including those for updating, inserting, modifying, and querying data. (6)

Data mart A data warehouse that is limited in scope, whose data are obtained by selecting and summarizing data from a data warehouse or from separate extract, transform, and load processes from source data systems. (9)

Data mining Knowledge discovery, using a sophisticated blend of techniques from traditional statistics, artificial intelligence, and computer graphics. (9)

Data model Graphical systems used to capture the nature and relationships among data. (1)

Data steward A person assigned the responsibility of ensuring that organizational applications properly support the organization's enterprise goals for data quality. (9)

Data type A detailed coding scheme recognized by system software, such as a DBMS, for representing organizational data. (5)

Data visualization The representation of data in graphical and multimedia formats for human analysis. (9)

Data warehouse A subject-oriented, integrated, time-variant, nonupdateable collection of data used in support of management decision-making processes. (9) An integrated decision support database whose content is derived from the various operational databases. (1)

Degree The number of entity types that participate in a relationship. (2)

Denormalization The process of transforming normalized relations into non-normalized physical record specifications. (5)

Dependent data mart A data mart filled exclusively from an enterprise data warehouse and its reconciled data. (9)

Derived attribute An attribute whose values can be calculated from related attribute values. (2)

Derived data Data that have been selected, formatted, and aggregated for end-user decision support applications. (9)

Determinant The attribute on the left side of the arrow in a functional dependency. (4)

Disjoint rule A rule that specifies that an instance of a supertype may not simultaneously be a member of two (or more) subtypes. (3)

Disjointness constraint A constraint that addresses whether an instance of a supertype may simultaneously be a member of two (or more) subtypes. (3)

Dynamic SQL Specific SQL code generated on the fly while an application is processing. (7)

Dynamic view A virtual table that is created dynamically upon request by a user. A dynamic view is not a temporary table. Rather, its definition is stored in the system catalog, and the contents of the view are materialized as a result of an SQL query that uses the view. It differs from a materialized view, which may be stored on a disk and refreshed at intervals or when used, depending on the RDBMS. (6)

Embedded SQL Hard-coded SQL statements included in a program written in another language, such as C or Java. (7)

Enhanced entity-relationship (EER) model A model that has resulted from extending the original E-R model with new modeling constructs. (3)

Enterprise data modeling The first step in database development, in which the scope and general contents of organizational databases are specified. (1)

Enterprise data warehouse (EDW) A centralized, integrated data warehouse that is the control point and single source of all data made available to end users for decision support applications. (9)

Enterprise resource planning (ERP) A business management system that integrates all functions of the enterprise, such as manufacturing, sales, finance, marketing, inventory, accounting, and human resources. ERP systems are software applications that provide the data necessary for the enterprise to examine and manage its activities. (1)

Entity A person, a place, an object, an event, or a concept in the user environment about which the organization wishes to maintain data. (1)

Entity instance A single occurrence of an entity type. (2)

Entity integrity rule A rule that states that no primary key attribute (or component of a primary key attribute) may be null. (4)

Entity-relationship diagram (E-R diagram, or ERD) A graphical representation of an entity-relationship model. (2)

Entity-relationship model (E-R model) A logical representation of the data for an organization or for a business area, using entities for categories of data and relationships for associations between entities. (2)

Entity type A collection of entities that share common properties or characteristics. (2)

Equi-join A join in which the joining condition is based on equality between values in the common columns. Common columns appear (redundantly) in the result table. (7)

Extensible Markup Language (XML) A text-based scripting language used to describe data structures hierarchically, using HTML-like tags. (8)

Extensible Stylesheet Language Transformation (XSLT) A language used to transform complex XML documents and also used to create HTML pages from XML documents. (8)

Extent A contiguous section of disk storage space. (5)

Fat client A client PC that is responsible for processing presentation logic, extensive application and business rules logic, and many DBMS functions. (8)

Field The smallest unit of application data recognized by system software. (5)

File organization A technique for physically arranging the records of a file on secondary storage devices. (5)

First normal form (1NF) A relation that has a primary key and in which there are no repeating groups. (4)

Foreign key An attribute in a relation that serves as the primary key of another relation in the same database. (4)

Function A stored subroutine that returns one value and has only input parameters. (7)

Functional dependency A constraint between two attributes in which the value of one attribute is determined by the value of another attribute. (4)

Generalization The process of defining a more general entity type from a set of more specialized entity types. (3)

Grain The level of detail in a fact table, determined by the intersection of all the components of the primary key, including all foreign keys and any other primary key elements. (9)

Hash index table A file organization that uses hashing to map a key into a location in an index, where there is a pointer to the actual data record matching the hash key. (5)

Hashed file organization A storage system in which the address for each record is determined using a hashing algorithm. (5)

Hashing algorithm A routine that converts a primary key value into a relative record number or relative file address. (5)

Homonym An attribute that may have more than one meaning. (4)

Identifier An attribute (or combination of attributes) whose value distinguishes instances of an entity type. (2)

Identifying owner The entity type on which the weak entity type depends. (2)

Identifying relationship The relationship between a weak entity type and its owner. (2)

Independent data mart A data mart filled with data extracted from the operational environment, without the benefit of a data warehouse. (9)

Index A table or other data structure used to determine in a file the location of records that satisfy some condition. (5)

Indexed file organization The storage of records either sequentially or nonsequentially with an index that allows software to locate individual records. (5)

Information Data that have been processed in such a way as to increase the knowledge of the person who uses the data. (1)

Informational system A system designed to support decision making based on historical point-in-time and prediction data for complex queries or data-mining applications. (9)

Java servlet A Java program that is stored on the server and contains the business and database logic for a Java-based application. (8)

Join A relational operation that causes two tables with a common domain to be combined into a single table or view. (7)

Join index An index on columns from two or more tables that come from the same domain of values. (5)

Logical data mart A data mart created by a relational view of a data warehouse. (9)

Logical schema The representation of a database for a particular data management technology. (1)

Maximum cardinality The maximum number of instances of one entity that may be associated with each instance of another entity. (2)

Metadata Data that describe the properties or characteristics of end-user data and the context of those data. (1)

Middleware Software that allows an application to interoperate with other software without requiring the user to understand and code the low-level operations necessary to achieve interoperability. (8)

Minimum cardinality The minimum number of instances of one entity that may be associated with each instance of another entity. (2)

Multidimensional OLAP (MOLAP) OLAP tools that load data into an intermediate structure, usually a three- or higher-dimensional array. (9)

Multivalued attribute An attribute that may take on more than one value for a given entity (or relationship) instance. (2)

Natural join A join that is the same as an equi-join except that one of the duplicate columns is eliminated in the result table. (7)

Normal form A state of a relation that requires that certain rules regarding relationships between attributes (or functional dependencies) are satisfied. (4)

Normalization The process of decomposing relations with anomalies to produce smaller, well-structured relations. (4)

NoSQL Short for "Not only SQL," a class of database technology used to store and access textual and other unstructured data, using more flexible structures than the rows and columns format of relational databases. (9)

Null A value that may be assigned to an attribute when no other value applies or when the applicable value is unknown. (4)

Online analytical processing (OLAP) The use of a set of graphical tools that provides users with multidimensional views of their data and allows them to analyze the data using simple windowing techniques. (9)

Open database connectivity (ODBC) An application programming interface that provides a common language for application programs to access and process SQL databases independent of the particular DBMS that is accessed. (8)

Operational data store (ODS) An integrated, subject-oriented, continuously updateable, current-valued (with recent history), enterprise-wide, detailed database designed to serve operational users as they do decision support processing. (9)

Operational system A system that is used to run a business in real-time, based on current data. Also called a system of record. (9)

Optional attribute An attribute that may not have a value for every entity (or relationship) instance with which it is associated. (2)

Outer join A join in which rows that do not have matching values in common columns are nevertheless included in the result table. (7)

Overlap rule A rule that specifies that an instance of a supertype may simultaneously be a member of two (or more) subtypes. (3)

Partial functional dependency A functional dependency in which one or more nonkey attributes are functionally dependent on part (but not all) of the primary key. (4)

Partial specialization rule A rule that specifies that an entity instance of a supertype is allowed not to belong to any subtype. (3)

Periodic data Data that are never physically altered or deleted once they have been added to the store. (9)

Physical file A named portion of secondary memory (such as a hard disk) allocated for the purpose of storing physical records. (5)

Physical schema Specifications for how data from a logical schema are stored in a computer's secondary memory by a database management system. (1)

Pointer A field of data indicating a target address that can be used to locate a related field or record of data. (5)

Primary key An attribute or a combination of attributes that uniquely identifies each row in a relation. (4)

Procedure A collection of procedural and SQL statements that are assigned a unique name within the schema and stored in the database. (7)

Prototyping An iterative process of systems development in which requirements are converted to a working system that is continually revised through close work between analysts and users. (1)

Real-time data warehouse An enterprise data warehouse that accepts near-real-time feeds of transactional data from the systems of record, analyzes warehouse data, and in near-real-time relays business rules to the data warehouse and systems of record so that immediate action can be taken in response to business events. (9)

Reconciled data Detailed, current data intended to be the single, authoritative source for all decision support applications. (9)

Recursive foreign key A foreign key in a relation that references the primary key values of the same relation. (4)

Referential integrity constraint A rule that states that either each foreign key value must match a primary key value in another relation or the foreign key value must be null. (4)

Relation A named two-dimensional table of data. (4)

Relational database A database that represents data as a collection of tables in which all data relationships are represented by common values in related tables. (1)

Relational DBMS (RDBMS) A database management system that manages data as a collection of tables in which all data relationships are represented by common values in related tables. (6)

Relational OLAP (ROLAP) OLAP tools that view the database as a traditional relational database in either a star schema or other normalized or denormalized set of tables. (9)

Relationship instance An association between (or among) entity instances where each relationship instance associates exactly one entity instance from each participating entity type. (2)

Relationship type A meaningful association between (or among) entity types. (2)

Repository A centralized knowledge base of all data definitions, data relationships, screen and report formats, and other system components. (1)

Required attribute An attribute that must have a value for every entity (or relationship) instance with which it is associated. (2)

Scalar aggregate A single value returned from an SQL query that includes an aggregate function. (6)

Schema A structure that contains descriptions of objects created by a user, such as base tables, views, and constraints, as part of a database. (6)

Second normal form (2NF) A relation in first normal form in which every nonkey attribute is fully functionally dependent on the primary key. (4)

Secondary key One field or a combination of fields for which more than one record may have the same combination of values. Also called a nonunique key. (5)

Sequential file organization The storage of records in a file in sequence according to a primary key value. (5)

Service-oriented architecture (SOA) A collection of services that communicate with each other in some manner, usually by passing data or coordinating a business activity. (8)

Simple (or atomic) attribute An attribute that cannot be broken down into smaller components that are meaningful to the organization. (2)

Simple Object Access Protocol (SOAP) An XML-based communication protocol used for sending messages between applications via the Internet. (8)

Snowflake schema An expanded version of a star schema in which dimension tables are normalized into several related tables. (9)

Specialization The process of defining one or more subtypes of the supertype and forming supertype/subtype relationships. (3)

Star schema A simple database design in which dimensional data are separated from fact or event data. A dimensional model is another name for a star schema. (9)

Strong entity type An entity that exists independently of other entity types. (2)

Subtype A subgrouping of the entities in an entity type that is meaningful to the organization and that shares common attributes or relationships distinct from other subgroupings. (3)

Subtype discriminator An attribute of a supertype whose values determine the target subtype or subtypes. (3)

Supertype A generic entity type that has a relationship with one or more subtypes. (3)

Supertype/subtype hierarchy A hierarchical arrangement of supertypes and subtypes in which each subtype has only one supertype. (3)

Surrogate primary key A serial number or other system-assigned primary key for a relation. (4)

Synonyms Two (or more) attributes that have different names but the same meaning. (4)

Systems development life cycle (SDLC) The traditional methodology used to develop, maintain, and replace information systems. (1)

Tablespace A named logical storage unit in which data from one or more database tables, views, or other database objects may be stored. (5)

Ternary relationship A simultaneous relationship among the instances of three entity types. (2)

Thin client An application where the client (PC) accessing the application primarily provides the user interfaces and some application processing, usually with no or limited local data storage. (8)

Third normal form (3NF) A relation that is in second normal form and has no transitive dependencies. (4)

Three-tier architecture A client/server configuration that includes three layers: a client layer and two server layers. Although the nature of the server layers differs, a common configuration contains an application server and a database server. (8)

Time stamp A time value that is associated with a data value, often indicating when some event occurred that affected the data value. (2)

Total specialization rule A rule that specifies that each entity instance of a supertype must be a member of some subtype in the relationship. (3)

Transaction A discrete unit of work that must be completely processed or not processed at all within a computer system. Entering a customer order is an example of a transaction. (7)

Transient data Data in which changes to existing records are written over previous records, thus destroying the previous data content. (9)

Transitive dependency A functional dependency between the primary key and one or more nonkey attributes that are dependent on the primary key via another nonkey attribute. (4)

Trigger A named set of SQL statements that are considered (triggered) when a data modification (i.e., INSERT, UPDATE, DELETE) occurs or if certain data definitions are encountered. If a condition stated within a trigger is met, then a prescribed action is taken. (7)

Unary relationship A relationship between instances of a single entity type. (2)

Universal data model A generic or template data model that can be reused as a starting point for a data modeling project. (3)

Universal Description, Discovery, and Integration (UDDI) A technical specification for creating a distributed registry of Web services and businesses that are open to communicating through Web services. (8)

User view A logical description of some portion of the database that is required by a user to perform some task. (1)

Vector aggregate Multiple values returned from an SQL query that includes an aggregate function. (6)

Virtual table A table constructed automatically as needed by a DBMS. Virtual tables are not maintained as real data. (6)

Weak entity type An entity type whose existence depends on some other entity type. (2)

Web services A set of emerging standards that define protocols for automatic communication between software programs over the Web. Web services are XML based and usually run in the background to establish transparent communication among computers. (8)

Web Services Description Language (WSDL) An XML-based grammar or language used to describe a Web service and specify a public interface for that service. (8)

Well-structured relation A relation that contains minimal redundancy and allows users to insert, modify, and delete the rows in a table without errors or inconsistencies. (4)

XML Schema Definition (XSD) Language used for defining XML databases that has been recommended by the World Wide Web Consortium (W3C). (8)

XPath One of a set of XML technologies that supports XQuery development. XPath expressions are used to locate data in XML documents. (8)

XQuery An XML transformation language that allows applications to query both relational databases and XML data. (8)

INDEX

Note: Boldface entries signify Key Terms.

A

accuracy, data, 14, 343
action (trigger), 257
active data warehousing, 312
addition (+) operator, 209
ADD_MONTHS function, 210
ad hoc queries, 24
    processing time, 253
    star schema, 318, 319
ADO.NET, 272
aggregate data, 318
aggregate functions, 220
agile software development, 21
alerts, defined, 3
aliases, 61, 155
    queries, 208–209
    reserved words, 225
    tables, 246–247
ALL keyword, 218, 243
ALTER command, 202–203
ALTER TABLE command, 200, 202
Amazon.com, 284, 295–296
AMERICAN character set, 212
American National Standards Institute. *See* ANSI (American
    National Standards Institute)
Analysis phase, 18
analytical function, 210
AND Boolean operator, 214–216, 222
anomalies, 130–131, 172
    1NF (first normal form), 150
    removing, 144–145
ANSI (American National Standards Institute), 191
ANSI/SPARC, 21
answer table, 234
ANY function, 211, 243
Apache Cassandra, 24, 333
Apache Web server, 277
APIs (application programming interfaces), 272
    ODBC (Open Database Connectivity)
        standard, 262
application partitioning, 270
application programming interfaces. *See* APIs (application
    programming interfaces)
applications, 15
    accessing databases, 271
    longevity, 193
    portability, 193
    specific functions required for, 12
    transaction-processing, 179
application server and Web applications, 277
Aranow, E. B., 51
"A Relational Model of Data for Large Shared Data
    Banks" (Codd), 192
Armstrong, R., 309, 310
Aronson, J., 341
Arvin, T., 192
ASP.NET, 278, 283–284
associations, 128

B

associative entities, 65, 71, 75, 132, 137–139, 319
    associative relation, 137
    converting relationship to, 69
    full identifiers, 76
    identifiers, 69, 123, 137–139
    surrogate identifiers, 76
associative relation, 137, 139–140
atomic attributes. *See* simple attributes
atomic facts, 331
attributes, 9, 32, 46, 47, 57–62, 125, 132
    aliases, 61, 155
    dimension tables, 317
    relationships, 62, 63–65
authorized user, 199
AUTOCOMMIT (ON/OFF) command, 254–255
average value, 211
AVG function, 211, 212

Babad, Y. M., 171
back-end functions, 271
backups, explicit, 14
Basel Convention, 24
base tables, 223
    null values, 237
    persistent data, 224
    views, 225
B2B (business-to-business) relationships, 28
BEGIN TRANSACTION command, 254
best-practices data models, 110
BETWEEN keyword, 216
big data, 331–332
BIGINT data type, 197
BigPVFC file, 197–198
bill-of-materials structure, 67, 69, 71
binary large object. *See* BLOB (binary large object)
binary relationships, 67
    many-to-many, 135–136, 144
    one-to-many, 135, 144
    one-to-one, 136–137, 144
binder, 262
BLOB (binary large object), 169, 196, 289
BookPVFC file, 197
BOOLEAN data type, 196
Boolean operators, 214–216
BPM (business performance management)
    system, 338–339
Brauer, B., 342
bridge tables, 327–328
Britton-Lee, 193
Bruce, T. A., 60
Bughin, J., 331
business activity, 317
business applications, 28–29
business intelligence processing, 331
business logic, 25, 26
business performance management system. *See* BPM (business
    performance management) system

preventing unauthorized changes, 256
    storage logic, 269
    syntax and functionality, 256
TRUNCATE TABLE command, 203
TRUNC function, 210
Turban, E., 341
two-dimensional tables views, 336
two-tier applications, 271
two-tier architecture
    client/server projects, 271
    client workstation, 271
    database-oriented middleware, 271
    databases, 271–275
    database server, 271
    Java application, 274–275
    VB.NET application, 272–274
two-tier client/server databases, 25–26
two-tier systems configurations, 270

U
**UDDI (Universal Description, Discovery, and
    Integration)**, 294
UDTs (user-defined data types), 197
unary many-to-many relationships, 139–141
unary relationships, 67, 71, 139–141
    bill-of-materials structure, 67
    many-to-many relationships, 67, 144
    1:*M* (one-to-many) relationships, 67, 139, 144
    one-to-one relationships, 67, 144
    representing sequence, cycle, or priority list, 68
    self-joins, 239–241
UNION clause, 249–250
UNION keyword, 233
UNIQUE column control, 200
unique key index, 182–183
uniqueness, data, 343
universal data model, 110
Universal Description, Discovery, and Integration.
    See UDDI (Universal Description, Discovery, and
    Integration)
University of California at Berkeley, 122
unnamed rows, 123
UnQL (Unstructured Query Language), 333
unstructured data, 4, 333
Unstructured Query Language. *See* UnQL (Unstructured Query
    Language)
update anomaly, 150
UPDATE command, 205, 207, 255
UPPER function, 210
U.S. Securities and Exchange Commission (SEC), 168
user-defined constraints, 202
user-defined data types. *See* UDTs (user-defined data types)
user-defined transactions, 254–255
user interface, 15
    BPM (business performance management) system,
        338–339
    dashboards, 338–339
    data marts, 333–341
    data-mining tools, 339
    data visualization, 338
    data warehouses, 333–341
    metadata role, 334
    OLAP (online analytical processing) tools, 335–337
    SQL OLAP querying, 334–335
user views, 12, 148, 306

V
van der Lans, R. F., 223
VARCHAR2 data type, 169, 196
VARCHAR (CHARACTER VARYING) data type, 129, 196
VB.NET application, 272–274
vector aggregates, 220–221
vendor, dependence on, 193
Vertica, 332
views
    aliases, 225
    based on other views, 225
    base tables, 225
    columns, 224, 255
    comments on columns, 255
    data dictionaries, 255
    data elements included, 224
    data security, 223
    defining, 223–225
    destroying, 200
    dynamic, 223–225
    identifying, 207
    joining tables or views, 225
    listing tables and views in, 224
    logical data mart, 311
    manipulating, 223–225
    materialized, 223
    null values, 237
    privacy and confidentiality of data, 225
    productivity, 223
    programming consistency, 223
    pros and cons, 224
    removing, 203
    restricting access to, 225
    security, 225
    simplifying query commands, 223
    storage space, 224
    two-dimensional tables, 336
    usage, 223–225
view table, 224
virtual tables, 223–224
von Halle, B., 122

W
WAP (Wireless Application Protocol), 292
Wayner, P., 333
W3C (World Wide Web Consortium), 288
W3C XSD (XML Schema Definition) language, 288
weak entities, 55, 131, 144
    identifier, 123
    partial identifier, 133–134
    surrogate primary key, 134–135
Web applications
    application server, 277
    ASP.NET, 283–284
    components, 277–278
    database server, 277
    information flow, 278
    JSP (Java Server Pages), 279–283
    Web browsers, 277
    Web server, 277
Web-based applications, 3, 276–277
Web-based customer interactions, 302
Web-based systems and three-tier architectures, 270
Web browsers, 277, 292
Web servers, 277